INTRODUCTION
TO
MORAL PHILOSOPHY

Edited by
Philip E. Davis
California State University, San Jose

Charles E. Merrill Publishing Company
A Bell & Howell Company
Columbus, Ohio

Published by
Charles E. Merrill Publishing Company
A Bell & Howell Company
Columbus, Ohio 43216

ISBN: 0-675-09003-2

Library of Congress Catalog Card Number: 72-92572

2 3 4 5 6 7 — 79 78 77 76 75 74 73

Printed in the United States of America

To my daughters
Kimberly
and
Katherine

Preface

Many persons may wonder why I have entitled this book an *Introduction to Moral Philosophy* rather than an *Introduction to Ethics*. Since both names are used by philosophers to refer to essentially the same study, the choice between them is more or less arbitrary. I must confess, however, that I have a certain preference for "moral philosophy," and although I have no intention of trying to legislate how the terms "moral" and "ethical" should be used, still I do feel obligated at least to explain my preference. Quite simply I think that there is merit in recognizing a difference between a disciplined study and what it is a study of, between *theory* and *subject-matter,* and I think that the name of the discipline or theory should note this distinction. The name of the discipline should at least suggest what it is about. Names such as "Aesthetics," "Metaphysics," and "Ethics," it seems to me, fail to do this. "Philosophy of Art," "Cosmology," and "Moral Philosophy" come closer to achieving this goal. The latter title more clearly suggests a philosophical study of the problems of morality.

As this book amply illustrates, philosophers differ with respect to which problems are properly studied by the moral philosopher. Some think that they are the problems of moral conduct itself, i.e., how we should act; others restrict their attention to problems of moral judgment and belief, namely, how we should think about our actions; still others look upon the problems of moral philosophy as problems about moral language, that is, how we should talk about our moral actions, judgments, and beliefs. Some philosophers restrict the subject to two of these matters; some include all of them. But all philosophers mark off a distinctive subject-matter for their investigation. I have tried to restrict my own use of the term "moral" to topics closely associated with the subject-matter, e.g., I speak of "moral" acts, "moral" judgments, "moral" principles, "moral" language, "moral" reasoning, and I have tried to reserve the adjective "ethical" for theories about these matters, e.g., "ethical" relativism, "ethical" absolutism, "ethical" egoism. In many instances the use of the term "ethical" is unnecessary because the ethical theories themselves have their own distinctive names, such as utilitarianism, emotivism, situationism, and they are not likely to be confused with any nonethical theories.

Although I think that a distinction between theory and subject-matter should always be kept clearly in mind, it does not seem to me to be similarly advisable to separate *theory* altogether from *practice*. It is not that there is no difference between what we think and what we do. Surely there is, but it seems to me that ethical theories must always be formulated with human acts and practices in mind and must in some way or other be applicable to them. An ethical theory which takes little or no account of the human condition and offers no basis for dealing with it is not a very good theory. To say of a moral judgment or belief that "it is true in theory but inapplicable to practice" is, in my view, to make the strongest possible objection to it. A conscious effort has been made, therefore, to include in this book reading materials which are rich in illustrations, practical applications, and ways of testing the theories. Thus the book includes Platonic dialogues, legal case reports, Kant's essay on an alleged right to lie, Hare's discussion of an example adapted from a biblical parable, and James' highly imaginative suggestion of a "moral solitude." Almost every selection contains distinctive examples, applications, and tests by which the theory under discussion can be better understood and related to the ordinary conditions of moral life and practice. Examples by themselves can never teach us all that we need or may want to know about morality, but without them the path to understanding is arid and unnecessarily painful.

The introductions to each of the parts are intended to accomplish three tasks. The first task is to present a preview of the contents of the part so that the reader will have a general idea of the problems there discussed. It is not expected that he will completely comprehend all that is said about the problems and the theories on a first reading. The introductions presuppose that he will eventually read the selections and then may wish to refer to the introduction for a clarification of some of the more technical terms and for alternative expressions of the various theories. I have tried not to repeat what the authors themselves have said in the same way they have said it, unless this type of repetition is deemed especially desirable. In offering alternative ways of saying the same thing, I have undertaken a somewhat hazardous course, since my interpretation may not always accord with the interpretation which others or perhaps even the author himself might conceivably make. But I am only doing what I expect the reader himself to do, and that is to understand and restate what is said in his own terms as best he can. If the reader objects to my interpretation in the light of his own examination of the text, a part at least of my purpose in providing a discussion of the subject will be achieved. He will have begun to think for himself.

The second aim of the introduction is to raise questions about the reading selections and to suggest possible criticisms of them. I have not included a set of study questions at the end of each chapter. Such questions, unless they are very carefully framed and provided with a fully detailed context, have always seemed to me to suffer from one of two defects. They are either apt to be overly simple, almost factual, questions, which can be answered by consulting any dictionary or outline of philosophy, or apt to be too complex to be readily understood. The criticisms and questions I raise in the introduction are to be taken by the reader as questions which he himself might raise and perhaps ought to raise. If he does seriously consider them and attempts to imagine how the authors themselves might respond, I think he will find that he will understand their philosophies better and appreciate them more. A critical attitude in philosophy is essential to understanding. Mere memorization of what a philosopher has said is no substitute. It must not be thought that the questions are to be taken as definitive of my own evaluation of these authors' views. In some cases they are; in others they are not, but that is not important. What is important is whether the proposed criticism is a fair criticism. Is it one that the author must (and perhaps does) answer if his theory is to be believed?

The third objective of the introductions is to provide the reader with some idea of the scope and complexity of the problems involved. What this inevitably leads to is an occasional reference on my part to materials not even included in the selections. But why should the reader be led to suppose that all the answers can be found in one book, even a very large book? He may have to, and is advised to, consult the books listed as recommended reading at the end of this volume. Furthermore, in discussing a particular problem I have not felt constrained to restrict my remarks only to the authors or the selections of a particular part, but have felt free to discuss selections contained in other parts. For example, Plato's *Euthyphro* is discussed in the introductions to parts I, III, and VI; Baier's views are discussed in the introductions to parts II and III; Rawls' views are discussed in the introductions to parts IV and VII. This may prove slightly unnerving to some readers, but I hope that I have said enough in each instance to give the reader a taste of the view under discussion, and to whet his intellectual appetite so that he will want to read more than he is assigned, or more than is contained within the limits of a single part. Philosophical ideas are very difficult to compartmentalize.

To the many students with whom I have discussed the problems of moral philosophy, I wish to express my appreciation for their often surprising and refreshing responses. For many long and stimulating conversations, I am deeply indebted to numerous friends and colleagues. I especially wish to thank Dr. Carolyn Black for reading and voluminously criticizing the entire manuscript, and Dr. Ved Sharma for reading and commenting on a part of it.

Contents

I. MORAL PRINCIPLES   1

INTRODUCTION   3

THE DIVINE WILL PRINCIPLE
Plato: Euthyphro   15

THE PRINCIPLE OF ENLIGHTENED SELF-INTEREST
Thomas Hobbes: Leviathan   31

THE PRINCIPLE OF RATIONAL SELF-REALIZATION
Aristotle: Nicomachean Ethics   43

THE UNIVERSALIZABILITY CRITERION
Immanuel Kant: Fundamental Principles of the
Metaphysic of Morals   62

BENTHAM: THE PRINCIPLE OF UTILITY
Jeremy Bentham: An Introduction to the Principles of
Morals and Legislation   95

MILL: THE PRINCIPLE OF UTILITY
John Stuart Mill: Utilitarianism   103

Contents

II. MORAL POINTS OF VIEW   129

INTRODUCTION   131

ETHICAL SCEPTICISM VERSUS ETHICAL IDEALISM
William James: The Moral Philosopher and the Moral
Life   145

MASTER VERSUS SLAVE MORALITIES
Friedrich Nietzsche: Beyond Good and Evil: The Will
to Power   159

FREEDOM VERSUS FACTICITY
Jean-Paul Sartre: Being and Nothingness   171

SITUATIONS VERSUS SYSTEMS
Joseph Fletcher: Situation Ethics   178

CULTURAL RELATIVISM VERSUS ETHICAL
ABSOLUTISM
W. T. Stace: Ethical Relativity   190

EGOISM VERSUS ABSOLUTE MORALITY
Kurt Baier: The Moral Point of View   205

III. MORAL RULES AND EXCEPTIONS   225

INTRODUCTION   227

UTILITARIANISM AND EXCEPTIONS
Leonard G. Miller: Rules and Exceptions   241

EXCEPTIONLESS RULES
Immanuel Kant: On a Supposed Right to Tell Lies from
Benevolent Motives   254

THE GENERALIZATION ARGUMENT
Marcus G. Singer: Generalization in Ethics   259

Contents

RULE-UTILITARIANISM
John Hospers: Rule-Utilitarianism and Objections To It   282

THE ARISTOTELIAN THEORY OF EXCEPTIONS
Richard A. Wasserstrom: The Aristotelian Theory of
Equity   294

IV.   MORAL RESPONSIBILITY AND EXCUSES   303

INTRODUCTION   305

A DEFENSE OF DETERMINISM
J. M. E. McTaggart: Free Will—Does It Exist?   317

A SPECIAL PROBLEM FOR DETERMINISTS
Richard Taylor: Deliberation and Foreknowledge   334

A DEFENSE OF FREE WILL
C. A. Campbell: Has the Self "Free Will"?   349

A SPECIAL PROBLEM FOR LIBERTARIANS
W. I. Matson: On the Irrelevance of Free-Will to Moral
Responsibility   365

EXCUSABILITY
P. H. Nowell-Smith: Freedom and Responsibility   374

V.   MORAL ACTION   383

INTRODUCTION   385

VOLUNTARY BEHAVIOR
Aristotle: Nicomachean Ethics   392

NEGATIVE ACTS
Frederick A. Siegler: Omissions   399

A CASE OF OMISSION TO SAVE LIFE
Supreme Court of Victoria: Rex Versus Russell   409

Contents

THE LINE BETWEEN ACTS AND CONSEQUENCES
Eric D'Arcy: Human Acts   418

VI.   MORAL REASONING   433

INTRODUCTION   435

KINDS OF MORAL EVIDENCE
G. E. Moore: Principia Ethica   449

PRIMA FACIE EVIDENCE
W. D. Ross: What Makes Right Acts Right?   469

NON-COGNITIVISM
A. J. Ayer: On the Analysis of Moral Judgements   486

A GOLDEN-RULE ARGUMENT
R. M. Hare: A Moral Argument   499

AN ALLEGED MORAL FALLACY
John R. Searle: How to Derive "Ought" from "Is"   514

VII.   MORALITY AND JUSTICE   529

INTRODUCTION   531

THE JUSTIFICATION OF PUNISHMENT
John Rawls: Two Concepts of Rules   544

CLASSICAL DEFINITIONS OF JUSTICE
Plato: The Republic   554

SOCIAL JUSTICE
William K. Frankena: The Concept of Social Justice   576

A CASE OF INJUSTICE
Supreme Court of the United States: Northwestern
Shoshone Indians Versus United States   593

RECOMMENDED READING   607

INDEX   613

I

MORAL PRINCIPLES

Introduction

Moral Justification

At some time or another, we are all confronted by a demand that we explain why we think that certain acts, practices, institutions, or character traits are good or bad, right or wrong. Ordinarily we think it sufficient that we ourselves judge them to be so. But inevitably someone is going to ask us why, and it just will not satisfy the questioner simply to say, "It's right because I say it's right." Something more is demanded. That "something more" has traditionally been thought to be a showing that one's moral judgment ultimately follows from some more general moral belief. "More general" usually means some general proposition or definition which could also be appealed to as a basis for the explanation, justification, or criticism of other, and perhaps quite different, moral judgments.

Thus, when Socrates asks Euthyphro why he judges it "pious" or "holy" to bring an indictment of murder against his own father for the killing of a quarrelsome servant, Euthyphro at first tries to defend his action by saying that "piety is doing as I am doing." Socrates is not satisfied with this answer and requests that Euthyphro broaden his reply by providing a "standard to which I may look, and by which I may measure actions, whether yours or those of any one else." Eventually in the course of the dialogue, Euthyphro formulates the view that piety is doing that which is divinely approved.

Although Socrates presses Euthyphro with numerous objections, Euthyphro is unable and apparently also unwilling to change his basic moral belief. This phenomenon illustrates another feature of a moral principle as it has traditionally been conceived. In addition to being a belief that is sufficiently *general* to account for all our particular moral judgments, it is also an *ultimate* belief in the sense that it is the one that is adopted in preference to all others, even in the face of serious objections.

Hobbes' principle of enlightened self-interest, that one ought to do whatever is necessary to achieve social survival (or peace), supplies another interesting example. Hobbes thought that all questions about what men ought to do could be answered by appealing to this principle. Moreover, he was convinced that men are so motivated by their private and selfish interests that only by "seeking peace and following it" could those interests ever have a chance of being satisfied. The specific means he advises for accomplishing this end is the acceptance of a "social contract," an arrangement whereby every man gives up his natural right to do as he pleases in exchange for the protection of an absolute sovereign who decides all matters of right and wrong. Hobbes was fully aware of the possible disadvantages of such an arrangement. The monarch might become a despot. Would it be reasonable to chance such a disastrous consequence by agreeing to the social contract? Despite these dangers, Hobbes thought that it would be and so upholds his principle.

Classical moral principles are thus all alike insofar as their authors claim both ultimacy and generality for them. The content, as opposed to the form, of each of these principles, however, varies considerably, as an examination of the selections in this section will reveal. Besides the ancient, but also contemporary, principle that moral action consists in doing the will of God, and Hobbes' principle of enlightened self-interest, there is Aristotle's view that those acts are right and those things are good which promote the realization of one's rational self. Kant urges obedience only to those rules which one can freely and rationally will to become universal. Bentham and Mill recommend acts which promote the greatest happiness of the greatest number.

Types of Ethical Theory

As one becomes acquainted with the variety of moral principles, two questions are likely to arise. First, is there really only one moral principle by which moral judgments must ultimately be evaluated? Second, what grounds are there for selecting the best ("truest," "most adequate") one among them? The first question raises not only the issue of *ethical pluralism* (the view that there is more than one moral principle), but also the issue of *moral scepticism* (the view that there are no authoritative moral principles at all). These issues we shall postpone until Part II. The question whether there is only one moral principle rests on a doubt which must be fully explored before we can consider other alternatives. Proponents of the traditional principles make the claim that their principles provide a systematic basis for evaluating all moral judgments. These claims must first be dealt with on their own merits, and this entails an examination of the ethical theories based on those moral principles.

An ethical theory is simply the moral philosopher's attempt to elaborate the insight which he expresses as his supreme moral principle. It is his attempt to show how the principle, in conjunction with a set of fundamental concepts and subordinate rules and principles, will enable us to deal directly and intelligently with moral phenomena. Once the entire theory is understood, we should be in a far better position to determine whether it is capable of performing that task, and so whether the principle on which the theory is based is entitled to exclusive status.

Four questions about any ethical theory need to be answered before one can claim to understand it. (1) What ethical concepts are taken as fundamental? (2) What is asserted by the theory to be the appropriate considerations or factors to be used as a basis for making moral judgments? (3) Is the principle meant to apply directly to individual acts or only to kinds of acts or to rules? (4) What conception of the highest moral ideal or greatest good, if any, is proposed by the theory?

Philosophers have varied considerably in their opinions regarding the basic ethical concepts. Generally speaking, the notions of "good" and "right" are taken as the basic concepts, but even here is a difference in approach. Some take "good" as the most fundamental and define "right" in terms of it, e.g., "right" means whatever promotes the greatest good.

5

Others define "good" in terms of "right," e.g., "good" means whatever is consistent with or results from right actions. Concepts such as "virtue," "happiness," "justice," "piety," "obligation," "satisfaction," and "claim" are then treated as derivative concepts. It sometimes happens, though, that a philosopher will select some notion such as pleasure and define the concept of "good" in terms of it, or will take the notion of "duty" and define "right" in its terms. William James (Part II) takes the notion of "claim" as basic, and explains such terms as "right," "good," and "obligation" by reference to that notion. The selection of *any* key concept is bound to have a profound effect on the way the theory develops and on the type of considerations which the philosopher emphasizes.

Philosophers who choose "empirical" concepts, i.e., those whose meanings can be understood in terms of observable properties by means of the methods of the empirical sciences, are called ethical *naturalists*. Among those who reject this approach are certain philosophers called ethical *intuitionists*. They rely on a kind of intuitive perception as a means of understanding ethical concepts. Unlike *non-cognitivists,* who hold that ethical terms only express feelings and emotions, intuitionists believe that the basic ethical concepts are intelligible, even though indefinable. We shall examine all these views in more detail in Part VI.

Philosophers also differ markedly in their answers to the question regarding the kinds of considerations or factors to be taken into account in making moral judgments. The extreme positions are either that one must take into account *only* the consequences of an act in determining its moral quality, or that one must *never* take consequences into account. By "consequence" philosophers often mean different things: pleasurable or happy results; the purposes or ends of action; or the satisfaction of antecedent demands and claims. Those who stress consequences (of any of these types) as the basis for making moral judgments are called *teleologists*. Those who reject consequences as a basis claim that some non-empirical factor or test is the proper basis of moral evaluation. These tests include an appeal to conscience; natural law; compatibility with God's will; rational consistency; and "good will" or "pure motive." All such philosophers fall within the classification of *deontologists*.

There are, of course, intermediate positions. Hobbes, for example, combines a kind of teleological emphasis on consequences with a deontological emphasis on natural law. Others combine considerations of conscience with considerations of utility. Some intuitionists, while insisting that the ultimate test is a direct perception of some moral quality, nonetheless encourage taking both kinds of considerations into account. Most theories contain a primary emphasis on one kind or the other, and on this basis they are classed as either teleological or deontological. Given the great variety of ethical theories, it should not surprise us that they do not all fit neatly into any one system of classification.

A third aspect of ethical theories which philosophers have fairly recently been concerned with is the applicability of moral principles. In deciding whether a given act is moral, should we apply the principle directly to the case and draw our conclusion immediately, or should we first inquire whether the act falls under a specific rule and then apply the principle, not to the act, but to the rule? Thus a utilitarian (one who holds that we should promote the greatest happiness or good) might judge that a given act of homicide is immoral by reasoning that it would not tend to promote the greatest happiness of the greatest number. If this method of applying the principle is adopted, he is called an *act-utilitarian*. If, however, he judges the act immoral, not because of its particular consequences, but because he sees that the general adoption of a rule permitting that kind of killing would tend to have consequences which would not promote the greatest happiness, then we call him a *rule-utilitarian*. The particular advantages and difficulties of each way of applying the principle of utility are discussed in detail by Hospers in Part III. Since the controversy appears to have developed in connection with the interpretation of Mill's philosophy, it is important that the reader be aware of this distinction and try to decide for himself in connection with the readings in this section whether Mill is an "act" or a "rule" utilitarian, and what difference, if any, it would make as far as the plausibility of his theory is concerned.

Deontological as well as teleological theories may be viewed as either "rule" or "act" theories. Even if the basis of judging morality is some formal principle essentially unconnected with the examination of consequences, one may apply the principle either directly to the act in question or to a rule or maxim of that act. Kant, for example, appears to be a *rule-deontologist*. Ross, whose views appear later (Part VI) appears to be an *act-deontologist*.

This distinction between the ways moral principles are meant to apply clearly formulates a basis for classifying some philosophers as *ethical formalists* (those who stress the application of principles to rules) and *non-formalists* (those who stress the application of principles to particular acts and cases). Since, however, it is common to speak of deontological, as contrasted with teleological, theories as "formalist," it would perhaps be more precise to use Joseph Fletcher's terms, ethical *legalists* and ethical *situationists* (Part II) to mark the distinction, even though these terms are not generally or uniformly employed by philosophers. On this basis, then, we can say with greater accuracy that Kant, a deontologist, is an ethical legalist, whereas Ross, also a deontologist, is an ethical situationist. Incidentally, Fletcher also distinguishes *antinomians* as those who attempt to dispense with rules and principles altogether in arriving at moral decisions.

What conception of the greatest good or highest moral ideal, if any, is proposed by the theory? This is the fourth major question we should ask in order to understand an ethical theory. The classical proponents of a single moral principle, as might be expected, all have such a conception of a "greatest good." In many cases, the moral goal is implicit in the principle itself. For example, for the utilitarians, it is the achievement of a state of affairs in which the greatest possible number of persons is as happy as possible. For Hobbes, it is personal satisfaction within the limitations of a peaceful civil society. For Aristotle, it is the contemplative life, the ultimate in the realization of one's rational self. For Kant, it is the "kingdom of ends," a moral "State" within which all men are conceived both as subject to and authors of the moral law. For proponents of the divine will theory, it is a life in complete harmony with the will of God, or gods, as the case may be.

In addition to understanding just what is involved in each of these conceptions of the highest moral goal for man, two further questions should be entertained. (1) Just exactly how desirable is the goal as set forth? (2) Is it humanly attainable? Suppose, for example, that the utilitarian goal were in fact truly achieved, and that the greatest possible number of persons were made happy. If the cost price of this condition were that a very small minority were made quite miserable, would it be worth it? Or suppose we agree with Hobbes that peace among men is socially the most desirable thing in the world. Is it possible to achieve such a state of affairs by the means he proposes? Such blunt questions must be asked if a full understanding of an ethical theory is to be attained.

Proving a Moral Principle

Once one has examined an ethical theory and knows what its fundamental concepts are, what kinds of factors are to be used in making moral judgments, whether its principles apply directly to acts or to rules, and what conception of the good life is proposed, he is certainly in a better position to judge which of all the competitive principles comes closest to fulfilling the task of giving a complete account of moral phenomena. Unfortunately, this may not be enough to enable him to choose among them. Most of the classical principles do a reasonably good job of supplying a rationale for most if not all of our moral judgments. Yet the principles are often incompatible with one another. Must we then decide among them not simply on the basis of their adequacy to explain and justify moral judgments, but on the basis of simple preference, i.e., because we "like" one better than another?

Various attempts have been made to avoid this seemingly irrational consequence by supplying what often have been referred to as "proofs" of moral principles. The term "proof" as so used has a widely variable meaning, but in general, what is intended is a set of considerations, other than the internal consistency and adequacy of the theory, which are particularly persuasive in making a choice of one theory or principle over another. There have been several different kinds of such proofs. Some are based on appeals to experience, others on the concept of morality itself, some on metaphysical considerations, and still others on special intuitions or revelations. We shall call them, respectively, *empirical, transcendental, metaphysical,* and *religious* proofs.

Empirical proofs. According to Bentham, the greatest happiness principle is not susceptible of what he calls "direct proof." Nonetheless, he does offer two kinds of "indirect" considerations which he thinks fully justify our formal acceptance of it. First, he claims that on most of the occasions of our lives we consciously or unconsciously defer to it anyway. Aside from his general observation that this is so, his specific reason is that any attempt to criticize it, he thinks, presupposes it. One who argues that "it is dangerous to consult the principle" is in effect arguing that "it is not consonant to utility to consult utility." Second, Bentham argues that other principles are worse. Either they lead to "despotical" and "hostile" treatment of human beings, or they are "anarchical," i.e., they lead to the abandonment of all principles and moral argument.

Both considerations involve appeals to experience. With regard to the first, Bentham says, not simply that we ought to, but that as a matter of observable fact we presuppose the principle in all that we do and say. The second consideration amounts to a request that we examine the actual consequences of abandoning the principle. Neither appeal, of course, conclusively establishes the principle as the one, among all others, that we ought to accept. The fact that we frequently *do* employ the principle of utility does not necessarily mean that we *should*. To argue that all other principles lead to bad consequences simply begs the question.

9

John Stuart Mill offers a somewhat different empirical proof (see pp. 122-27), which may be restated as follows:

The only evidence capable of being given that an object is visible is that people actually see it; the only evidence that a sound is audible is that people hear it. By analogy, the sole evidence it is possible to produce that anything is desirable is that people do actually desire it.

Since, as a matter of fact, everyone desires his own happiness, his own happiness is desirable (i.e. good).

The general happiness is nothing but the aggregate of the happiness of everyone. Therefore, the general happiness is the greatest thing desirable (i.e. the greatest good).

Finally, since, as a matter of psychological fact, people never desire anything but happiness except insofar as it is a means to or a part of happiness, it follows that the general happiness is the sole criterion of morality.

Various types of criticism have been made of Mill's proof. It has been claimed that Mill confuses two senses of the term "desirable," namely, "capable of being desired" with "ought to be desired." It is the former sense which parallels the uses of "visible" and "audible," whereas the validity of the argument seems to depend on the latter sense, "ought to be desired."

Most critics have thought that this fallacy destroys Mill's argument, but since Mill's time defenses of this aspect of the argument have been almost periodically advanced and quite similar proofs proposed. Compare, for example, the following one by William James (see p.150):"Take any demand, however slight, which any creature, however weak, may make. Ought it not, for its own sole sake, to be satisfied? If not, prove why not. The only possible kind of proof you could adduce would be the exhibition of another creature who should make a demand that ran the other way. The only possible reason there can be why any phenomenon ought to exist is that such a phenomenon actually is desired."

Other critics have attacked Mill's claim that the only thing we ever desire or that ever ultimately motivates us is happiness (or pleasure). This theory of human motivation is known as *psychological hedonism*. Bentham's view that "nature has placed mankind under the governance of two sovereign masters, pain and pleasure" expresses the same idea. Aside from determining whether it is a true psychological account of human motivation, there is another problem which particularly affects utilitarians: How can I be expected to promote the general happiness if I am motivated, in the first instance at least, always to promote only my own?

A third criticism concerns Mill's claim that the general good or general happiness is nothing but an aggregate of individual goods; in short, that the whole is nothing but the sum or composition of the parts. In opposition to this view it could be argued that it would be good for me not to pay any taxes. I would have money to spend on more pleasant things. Similarly, it would be good for others, individually considered, not to pay taxes. But would it be good for society generally, or good "on the whole" if none of us paid taxes?

A transcendental proof. Immanuel Kant offers an entirely different kind of proof of his moral principle, and one that does not rely on any appeal to experience. He proposes a "transcendental deduction." By this he does not mean a purely logical demonstration. Like other moral philosophers, he is aware that no purely logical demonstration as such can prove a moral principle. "Proof," for Kant, means a kind of "justification" of the principle of morality in terms of purely conceptual considerations, or in other words, in terms of "what it rationally means to be moral." A summary of his proof (see pp. 88-94) is as follows:

> The Categorical Imperative (Kant's moral principle) states that one ought to act only on the basis of those rules which one can will to be obligatory upon all men. But the concept of morality set forth in this principle presupposes freedom of choice ("ought" presupposes "can"). If we are determined by other things to do what we do, we are not free and morality is a fiction. But it is also absurd to suppose that our wills are totally uncaused. The cause of our will, insofar as it is free, can therefore only be a property of the will "to be a law to itself." A free will, then, and a will subject to moral laws are one and the same. Therefore, if we are free, then we are bound by the laws of morality.
>
> This conclusion, however, is based merely on an analysis of the concept of morality, and does not by itself prove that we are in fact free. Nor is it possible to prove empirically that we are free agents. If a proof is to be obtained, it must be non-empirical, and based on a relationship between the idea of freedom and the idea of rationality, for only so can it be shown that *all* rational men are free.
>
> Now it is the case that men make apparently rational moral judgments and perform apparently intelligent and deliberate acts. Yet these judgments and actions would be pointless (i.e., unintelligent and non-deliberate) if they were merely the effects of empirical causes such as outside influences, or our interests and desires. Therefore, since no one can conclusively prove that they are pointless, any more than it can be proved *theoretically* that they are truly rational, we are justified, from a *practical* point of view, in presupposing that all such moral judgments and actions are freely made and done. As Kant says, "We must attribute

to every rational being which has a will that it has also the idea of freedom and acts entirely under this idea."

Unfortunately, the only world we know (the phenomenal world) is deterministic (i.e., governed by natural causes), and the only way we can make sense of the attribution of freedom to the agent is to suppose that we also live in an intelligible world (i.e., a world of pure reason and one in which the same laws of natural causation do not obtain). If such is the case, then it makes sense to presuppose that we are indeed free agents, and the principle of morality is justified.

Kant's argument is a very complicated one which philosophers have had a hard time understanding, much less criticizing. But there is one alleged fallacy in it which even Kant was aware of, and which especially needs to be noted: an apparent "vicious circle." On the one hand, Kant argues that if there is freedom, there is morality. On the other hand, he goes about establishing freedom by assuming that there is morality (i.e., that moral judgments and actions make sense). Has Kant begged the whole question? He thinks not because he feels that he has given enough practical (if not logically demonstrative) reasons to suppose that we cannot simply deny the "moral" fact of freedom. We are "required" to presuppose it, if our speech and action is to make any sense. But even if one finds these practical considerations persuasive, it is at least open to question whether they are as nonempirical or *a priori* as Kant would have us believe. One can, for example, question whether the rationality of our actions is as divorced from a consideration of consequences as he suggests it is.

Metaphysical proofs. Both Hobbes and Aristotle base their respective theories on certain conceptions of man and the world. Hobbes believes that man is essentially selfish, aggressive, and antisocial. Aristotle believes that man by nature is the reverse — a highly social (or political) animal with strong inclinations to live within an organized community of other men with common goals. Hobbes' world is a materialistic one moved by mechanical causes of which the desires of men are simply a subclass. Aristotle's world is purposive, moved not by antecedent causes so much as by final ends or goals toward which all things, including man, aspire. The moral goal of Hobbes, "to seek peace and follow it," is, he thinks, necessitated by the basic nature of man and his world. Unless man agrees to such a goal, his natural tendencies will simply destroy him. Therefore he must (and "ought to") seek peace through a social contract. Aristotle's moral principle that men should seek rational self-realization is likewise a necessity imposed on them by their rational

12

nature. The basic impulse within each of us is to be reasonable and rational.

These kinds of metaphysical "proofs" depend, of course, on the acceptance of the views of man and the world which they presuppose. If for some reason one finds the metaphysics of either unacceptable, the moral principle derived from it is presumably thrown into doubt also. If one does not wish to quarrel with these metaphysical views, he might still question whether the link between the metaphysical and ethical views is as "necessary" as it is described to be. Could not one accept the principles and reject the metaphysics? Is there really a necessary connection between them? For example, might one accept Hobbes' principle but reject his metaphysics and substitute instead Aristotle's view of man and the world? It is not at all clear that this would be inconsistent.

Religious proofs. The principle that moral action consists in doing the will of God has been argued for in a number of different ways. We say "argued for" but of course the notion of proof here, as in the case of the other theories, has a broader meaning than that of logical demonstration. The chief "justification," a more accurate term, for accepting such a principle has been simply a matter of religious conviction, often ultimately based on a special intuition or divine revelation. Sometimes this special intuition is asserted as a purely personal revelation. Sometimes it is based on scriptural revelation, an apparently more public way of ascertaining God's will. Regardless of the kind of intuition or revelation appealed to as a justification for adopting this principle, many difficulties can arise.

If one denies the existence of God, it would be pointless to adopt the principle. If one believes in God's existence, he may still inquire why he should do whatever God wants. The answer, no doubt, would be "because God wants you to." If it is inquired how one knows this is the case, the appeal will ultimately be made to some revelation. The problem then is one of authenticating the revelation. But even if the revelation is accepted, there is a further problem which Socrates poses to Euthyphro and which has dogged this principle throughout the history of its acceptance. Does God want you to follow his will simply because he says so, or does he want you to follow his will because it is the best thing to do? If the former, then the answer to the question, "Why should I obey God's will?" is simply "because he says so," and makes morality an essentially arbitrary and irrational matter. If the latter, and I should obey God's will because it is the best thing to do, then it makes sense to inquire further and ask for the principle which God himself uses as a basis for making His judgments. In that case, the ultimate moral principle would be, not merely that one ought to do God's will, but rather that one ought to act in accordance with that principle by which God's will is also determined.

Perhaps there are ways of avoiding these consequences and retaining the divine will principle. One might argue that the adoption of the first alternative does not make morality arbitrary, because it is God's, not man's, will that is to be obeyed. Since God cannot be wrong or irrational, as man often is, it is the height of rationality to obey such commands simply because they are God's. On the other hand, and in opposition to the claim that the divine will, if rational, is subordinate to an even higher principle, one might argue that there is no further principle beyond God's will except God's own judgment of what is good. In that case, to say that God wills a certain act because it is good means only that in His judgment alone, but for reasons which we may not be able to comprehend, the act is determined as the one that ought to be done. Whether either of these replies fully satisfies the objections is still open to debate.

The Divine Will Principle

Plato

Euthyphro

Persons of the Dialogue: *Socrates, Euthyphro*
Scene: *The Porch of the King Archon*

Euthyphro. Why have you left the Lyceum, Socrates? and what are you doing in the Porch of the King Archon? Surely you cannot be concerned in a suit before the King, like myself?

Socrates. Not in a suit, Euthyphro; impeachment is the word which the Athenians use.

From *Euthyphro* in *The Dialogues of Plato*, trans. by B. Jowett, 3d ed. (1892).

Euth. What! I suppose that some one has been prosecuting you, for I cannot believe that you are the prosecutor of another.

Soc. Certainly not.

Euth. Then some one else has been prosecuting you?

Soc. Yes.

Euth. And who is he?

Soc. A young man who is little known, Euthyphro; and I hardly know him: his name is Meletus, and he is of the deme of Pitthis. Perhaps you may remember his appearance; he has a beak, and long straight hair, and a beard which is ill grown.

Euth. No, I do not remember him, Socrates. But what is the charge which he brings against you?

Soc. What is the charge? Well, a very serious charge, which shows a good deal of character in the young man, and for which he is certainly not to be despised. He says he knows how the youth are corrupted and who are their corruptors. I fancy that he must be a wise man, and seeing that I am the reverse of a wise man, he has found me out, and is going to accuse me of corrupting his young friends. And of this our mother the state is to be the judge. Of all our political men he is the only one who seems to me to begin in the right way, with the cultivation of virtue in youth; like a good husbandman, he makes the young shoots his first care, and clears away us who are the destroyers of them. This is only the first step; he will afterwards attend to the elder branches; and if he goes on as he has begun, he will be a very great benefactor.

Euth. I hope that he may; but I rather fear, Socrates, that the opposite will turn out to be the truth. My opinion is that in attacking you he is simply aiming a blow at the foundation of the state. But in what way does he say that you corrupt the young?

Soc. He brings a wonderful accusation against me, which at first hearing excites surprise: he says that I am a poet or maker of gods, and that I invent new gods and deny the existence of old ones; this is the ground of his indictment.

Euth. I understand, Socrates; he means to attack you about the familiar sign which occasionally, as you say, comes to you. He thinks that you are a neologian, and he is going to have you up before the court for this. He knows that such a charge is readily received by the world, as I myself know too well; for when I speak in the assembly about divine things, and foretell the future to them, they laugh at me and think me a madman. Yet every word that I say is true. But they are jealous of us all; and we must be brave and go at them.

Soc. Their laughter, friend Euthyphro, is not a matter of much consequence. For a man may be thought wise; but the Athenians, I suspect, do not much trouble themselves about him until he begins to impart his wisdom to others; and then for some reason or other, perhaps, as you say, from jealousy, they are angry.

Euth. I am never likely to try their temper in this way.

Soc. I dare say not, for you are reserved in your behaviour, and seldom impart your wisdom. But I have a benevolent habit of pouring out myself to everybody, and would even pay for a listener, and I am afraid that the Athenians may think me too talkative. Now if, as I was saying, they would only laugh at me, as you say that they laugh at you, the time might pass gaily enough in the court; but perhaps they may be in earnest, and then what the end will be you soothsayers only can predict.

Euth. I dare say that the affair will end in nothing, Socrates, and that you will win your cause; and I think that I shall win my own.

Soc. And what is your suit, Euthyphro? are you the pursuer or the defendant?

Euth. I am the pursuer.

Soc. Of whom?

Euth. You will think me mad when I tell you.

Soc. Why, has the fugitive wings?

Euth. Nay, he is not very volatile at his time of life.

Soc. Who is he?

Euth. My father.

Soc. Your father! my good man?

Euth. Yes.

Soc. And of what is he accused?

Euth. Of murder, Socrates.

Soc. By the powers, Euthyphro! how little does the common herd know of the nature of right and truth. A man must be an extraordinary man, and have made great strides in wisdom, before he could have seen his way to bring such an action.

Euth. Indeed, Socrates, he must.

Soc. I suppose that the man whom your father murdered was one of your relatives — clearly he was; for if he had been a stranger you would never have thought of prosecuting him.

Euth. I am amused, Socrates, at your making a distinction between one who is a relation and one who is not a relation; for surely the pollution is the same in either case, if you knowingly associate with the murderer when you ought to clear yourself and him by proceeding against him. The real question is whether the murdered man has been justly slain. If justly, then your duty is to let the matter alone; but if unjustly, then even if the murderer lives under the same roof with you and eats at the same table, proceed against him. Now the man who is dead was a poor dependent of mine who worked for us as a field labourer on our farm in Naxos, and one day in a fit of drunken passion he got into a quarrel with one of our domestic servants and slew him. My father bound him hand and foot and threw him into a ditch, and then sent to Athens to ask of a diviner what he should do with him. Meanwhile he never attended to him and took no care about him, for he regarded him as a murderer; and thought that no great harm would be done even if he did die. Now this was just what happened. For such was the effect of cold and hunger and chains upon him, that before the messenger returned from the diviner, he was dead. And my father and family are angry with me for taking the part of the murderer and prosecuting my father. They say that he did not kill him, and that if he did, the dead man was but a murderer, and I ought not to take any notice, for that a son is impious who prosecutes a father. Which shows, Socrates, how little they know what the gods think about piety and impiety.

Soc. Good heavens, Euthyphro! and is your knowledge of religion and of things pious and impious so very exact, that, supposing the circumstances to be as you state them, you are not afraid lest you too may be doing an impious thing in bringing an action against your father?

Euth. The best of Euthyphro, and that which distinguishes him, Socrates, from other men, is his exact knowledge of all such matters. What should I be good for without it?

Soc. Rare friend! I think that I cannot do better than be your disciple. Then before the trial with Meletus comes on I shall challenge him, and say that I have always had a great interest in religious questions, and now, as he charges me with rash imaginations and innovations in religion, I have become your disciple. You, Meletus, as I shall say to him, acknowledge Euthyphro to be a great theologian, and sound in his opinions; and if you approve of him you ought to approve of me, and not have me into court; but if you disapprove, you should begin by indicting him who is my teacher, and who will be the ruin, not of the young, but of the old; that is to say, of myself whom he instructs, and of his old father whom he admonishes and chastises. And if Meletus refuses to listen to me, but will go on, and will not shift the indictment from me to you, I cannot do better than repeat this challenge in the court.

Euth. Yes, indeed, Socrates; and if he attempts to indict me I am mistaken if I do not find a flaw in him; the court shall have a great deal more to say to him than to me.

Soc. And I, my dear friend, knowing this, am desirous of becoming your discipline. For I observe that no one appears to notice you — not even this Meletus; but his sharp eyes have found me out at once, and he has indicted me for impiety. And therefore, I adjure you to tell me the nature of piety and impiety, which you said that you knew so well, and of murder, and of other offences against the gods. What are they? Is not piety in every action always the same? and impiety, again — is it not always the opposite of piety, and also the same with itself, having, as impiety, one notion which includes whatever is impious?

Euth. To be sure, Socrates.

Soc. And what is piety, and what is impiety?

Euth. Piety is doing as I am doing; that is to say, prosecuting any one who is guilty of murder, sacrilege, or of any similar crime — whether he be your father or mother, or whoever he may be — that makes no difference; and not to prosecute them is impiety. And please to consider, Socrates, what a notable proof I will give you of the truth of my words, a proof which I have already given to others: — of the principle, I mean, that the impious, whoever he may be, ought not to go unpunished. For do not men regard Zeus as the best and most righteous of the gods? — and yet they admit that he bound his father (Cronos) because he wickedly devoured his sons, and that he too had punished his own father (Uranus) for a similar reason, in a nameless manner. And yet when I proceed against my father, they are angry with me. So inconsistent are they in their way of talking when the gods are concerned, and when I am concerned.

Soc. May not this be the reason, Euthyphro, why I am charged with impiety — that I cannot away with these stories about the gods? and therefore I suppose that people think me wrong. But, as you who are well informed about them approve of them, I cannot do better than assent to your superior wisdom. What else can I say, confessing as I do, that I know nothing about them? Tell me, for the love of Zeus, whether you really believe that they are true.

Euth. Yes, Socrates; and things more wonderful still, of which the world is in ignorance.

Soc. And do you really believe that the gods fought with one another, and had dire quarrels, battles, and the like, as the poets say, and as you see represented in the works of great artists? The temples are full of them; and notably the robe of Athene, which is carried up to the Acropolis at the great Panathenaea, is embroidered with them. Are all these tales of the gods true, Euthyphro?

Euth. Yes, Socrates; and as I was saying, I can tell you, if you would like to hear them, many other things about the gods which would quite amaze you.

Soc. I dare say; and you shall tell me them at some other time when I have leisure. But just at present I would rather hear from you a more precise answer, which you have not as yet given, my friend, to the question, What is 'piety'? When asked, you only replied, Doing as you do, charging your father with murder.

Euth. And what I said was true, Socrates.

Soc. No doubt, Euthyphro; but you would admit that there are many other pious acts?

Euth. There are.

Soc. Remember that I did not ask you to give me two or three examples of piety, but to explain the general idea which makes all pious things to be pious. Do you not recollect that there was one idea which made the impious impious, and the pious pious?

Euth. I remember.

Soc. Tell me what is the nature of this idea, and then I shall have a standard to which I may look, and by which I may measure actions, whether yours or those of any one else, and then I shall be able to say that such and such an action is pious, such another impious.

Euth. I will tell you, if you like.

Soc. I should very much like.

Euth. Piety, then, is that which is dear to the gods, and impiety is that which is not dear to them.

Soc. Very good, Euthyphro; you have now given me the sort of answer which I wanted. But whether what you say is true or not I cannot as yet tell, although I make no doubt that you will prove the truth of your words.

Euth. Of course.

Soc. Come, then, and let us examine what we are saying. That thing or person which is dear to the gods is pious, and that thing or person which is hateful to the gods is impious, these two being the extreme opposites of one another. Was not that said?

Euth. It was.

Soc. And well said?

Euth. Yes, Socrates, I thought so; it was certainly said.

Soc. And further, Euthyphro, the gods were admitted to have enmities and hatreds and differences?

Euth. Yes, that was also said.

Soc. And what sort of difference creates enmity and anger? Suppose for example that you and I, my good friend, differ about a number; do differences of this sort make us enemies and set us at variance with one another? Do we not go at once to arithmetic, and put an end to them by a sum?

Euth. True.

Soc. Or suppose that we differ about magnitudes, do we not quickly end the differences by measuring?

Euth. Very true.

Soc. And we end a controversy about heavy and light by resorting to a weighing machine?

Euth. To be sure.

Soc. But what differences are there which cannot be thus decided, and which therefore make us angry and set us at enmity with one another? I dare say the answer does not occur to you at the moment, and therefore I will suggest that these enmities arise when the matters of difference are the just and unjust, good and evil, honourable and dishonourable. Are not these the points about which men differ, and about which when we are unable satisfactorily to decide our differences, you and I and all of us quarrel, when we do quarrel?

Euth. Yes, Socrates, the nature of the differences about which we quarrel is such as you describe.

Soc. And the quarrels of the gods, noble Euthyphro, when they occur, are of a like nature?

Euth. Certainly they are.

Soc. They have differences of opinion, as you say, about good and evil, just and unjust, honourable and dishonourable: there would have been no quarrels among them, if there had been no such differences — would there now?

Euth. You are quite right.

Soc. Does not every man love that which he deems noble and just and good, and hate the opposite of them?

Euth. Very true.

Soc. But, as you say, people regard the same things, some as just and others as unjust, — about these they dispute; and so there arise wars and fightings among them.

Euth. Very true.

Soc. Then the same things are hated by the gods and loved by the gods, and are both hateful and dear to them?

Euth. True.

Soc. And upon this view the same things, Euthyphro, will be pious and also impious?

Euth. So I would suppose.

Soc. Then, my friend, I remark with surprise that you have not answered the question which I asked. For I certainly did not ask you to tell me what action is both pious and impious: but now it would seem that what is loved by the gods is also hated by them. And therefore, Euthyphro, in thus chastising your father you may very likely be doing what is agreeable to Zeus but disagreeable to Cronos or Uranus, and what is acceptable to Hephaestus but unacceptable to Herè, and there may be other gods who have similar differences of opinion.

Euth. But I believe, Socrates, that all the gods would be agreed as to the propriety of punishing a murderer: there would be no difference of opinion about that.

Soc. Well, but speaking of men, Euthyphro, did you ever hear any one arguing that a murderer or any sort of evil-doer ought to be let off?

Euth. I should rather say that these are the questions which they are always arguing, especially in courts of law: they commit all sorts of crimes, and there is nothing which they will not do or say in their own defence.

Soc. But do they admit their guilt, Euthyphro, and yet say that they ought not to be punished?

Euth. No; they do not.

Soc. Then there are some things which they do not venture to say and do: for they do not venture to argue that the guilty are to be unpunished, but they deny their guilt, do they not?

Euth. Yes.

Soc. Then they do not argue that the evil-doer should not be punished, but they argue about the fact of who the evil-doer is, and what he did and when?

Euth. True.

Soc. And the gods are in the same case, if as you assert they quarrel about just and unjust, and some of them say while others deny that injustice is done among them. For surely neither God nor man will ever venture to say that the doer of injustice is not to be punished?

Euth. That is true, Socrates, in the main.

Soc. But they join issue about the particulars — gods and men alike; and, if they dispute at all, they dispute about some act which is called in question, and which by some is affirmed to be just, by others to be unjust. Is not that true?

Euth. Quite true.

Soc. Well then, my dear friend Euthyphro, do tell me, for my better instruction and information, what proof have you that in the opinion of all the gods a servant who is guilty of murder, and is put in chains by the master of the dead man, and dies because he is put in chains before he who bound him can learn from the interpreters of the gods what he ought to do with him, dies unjustly; and that on behalf of such an one a son ought to proceed against his father and accuse him of murder. How would you show that all the gods absolutely agree in approving of his

22

act? Prove to me that they do, and I will applaud your wisdom as long as I live.

Euth. It will be a difficult task; but I could make the matter very clear indeed to you.

Soc. I understand; you mean to say that I am not so quick of apprehension as the judges: for to them you will be sure to prove that the act is unjust, and hateful to the gods.

Euth. Yes indeed, Socrates; at least if they will listen to me.

Soc. But they will be sure to listen if they find that you are a good speaker. There was a notion that came into my mind while you were speaking; I said to myself: 'Well, and what if Euthyphro does prove to me that all the gods regarded the death of the serf as unjust, how do I know anything more of the nature of piety and impiety? For granting that this action may be hateful to the gods, still piety and impiety are not adequately defined by these distinctions, for that which is hateful to the gods has been shown to be also pleasing and dear to them.' And therefore, Euthyphro, I do not ask you to prove this; I will suppose, if you like, that all the gods condemn and abominate such an action. But I will amend the definition so far as to say that what all the gods hate is impious, and what they love pious or holy; and what some of them love and others hate is both or neither. Shall this be our definition of piety and impiety?

Euth. Why not, Socrates?

Soc. Why not! certainly, as far as I am concerned, Euthyphro, there is no reason why not. But whether this admission will greatly assist you in the task of instructing me as you promised, is a matter for you to consider.

Euth. Yes, I should say that what all the gods love is pious and holy, and the opposite which they all hate, impious.

Soc. Ought we to enquire into the truth of this, Euthyphro, or simply to accept the mere statement on our own authority and that of others? What do you say?

Euth. We should enquire; and I believe that the statement will stand the test of enquiry.

Soc. We shall know better, my good friend, in a little while. The point which I should first wish to understand is whether the pious or holy is beloved by the gods because it is holy, or holy because it is beloved of the gods.

Euth. I do not understand your meaning, Socrates.

Soc. I will endeavor to explain: we speak of carrying and we speak of being carried, of leading and being led, seeing and being seen. You know that in all such cases there is a difference, and you know also in what the difference lies?

Euth. I think that I understand.

Soc. And is not that which is beloved distinct from that which loves?

Euth. Certainly.

Soc. Well; and now tell me, is that which is carried in this state of carrying because it is carried, or for some other reason?

Euth. No; that is the reason.

Soc. And the same is true of what is led and of what is seen?

Euth. True.

Soc. And a thing is not seen because it is visible, but conversely, visible because it is seen; nor is a thing led because it is in the state of being led, or carried because it is in the state of being carried, but the converse of this. And now I think Euthyphro, that my meaning will be intelligible; and my meaning is, that any state of action or passion implies previous action or passion. It does not become because it is becoming, but it is in a state of becoming because it becomes; neither does it suffer because it is in a state of suffering, but it is in a state of suffering because it suffers. Do you not agree?

Euth. Yes.

Soc. Is not that which is loved in some state either of becoming or suffering?

Euth. Yes.

Soc. And the same holds as in the previous instances; the state of being loved follows the act of being loved, and not the act the state.

Euth. Certainly.

Soc. And what do you say of piety, Euthyphro: is not piety, according to your definition, loved by all the gods?

Euth. Yes.

Soc. Because it is pious or holy, or for some other reason?

Euth. No, that is the reason.

Soc. It is loved because it is holy, not holy because it is loved?

Euth. Yes.

Soc. And that which is dear to the gods is loved by them, and is in a state to be loved of them because it is loved of them?

Euth. Certainly.

Soc. Then that which is dear to the gods, Euthyphro, is not holy, nor is that which is holy loved of God, as you affirm; but they are two different things.

Euth. How do you mean, Socrates?

Soc. I mean to say that the holy has been acknowledged by us to be loved of God because it is holy, not to be holy because it is loved.

Euth. Yes.

Soc. But that which is dear to the gods is dear to them because it is loved by them, not loved by them because it is dear to them.

Euth. True.

Soc. But, friend Euthyphro, if that which is holy is the same with that which is dear to God, and is loved because it is holy, then that which is dear to God would have been loved as being dear to God; but if that which is dear to God is dear to him because loved by him, then that which is holy would have been holy because loved by him. But now you see that the reverse is the case, and that they are quite different from one another. For one is of a kind to be loved because it is loved, and the other is loved because it is of a kind to be loved. Thus you appear to me, Euthyphro, when I ask you what is the essence of holiness, to offer an attribute only, and not the essence — the attribute of being loved by all the gods. But you still refuse to explain to me the nature of holiness. And therefore, if you please, I will ask you not to hide your treasure, but to tell me once more what holiness or piety really is, whether dear to the gods or not (for that is a matter about which we will not quarrel); and what is impiety?

Euth. I really do not know, Socrates, how to express what I mean. For somehow or other our arguments, on whatever ground we rest them, seem to turn round and walk away from us.

Soc. Your words, Euthyphro, are like the handiwork of my ancestor Daedalus; and if I were the sayer or propounder of them, you might say that my arguments walk away and will not remain fixed where they are placed because I am a descendant of his. But now, since these notions are your own, you must find some other gibe, for they certainly, as you yourself allow, show an inclination to be on the move.

Euth. Nay, Socrates, I shall still say that you are the Daedalus who sets arguments in motion; not I, certainly, but you make them move or go round, for they would never have stirred, as far as I am concerned.

Soc. Then I must be a greater than Daedalus: for whereas he only made his own inventions to move, I move those of other people as well. And the beauty of it is, that I would rather not. For I would give the wisdom of Daedalus, and the wealth of Tantalus, to be able to detain them and keep them fixed. But enough of this. As I perceive that you are lazy, I will myself endeavor to show you how you might instruct me in the nature of piety; and I hope that you will not grudge your labour. Tell me, then, — Is not that which is pious necessarily just?

Euth. Yes.

Soc. And is, then, all which is just pious? or, is that which is pious all just, but that which is just, only in part and not all, pious?

Euth. I do not understand you, Socrates.

Soc. And yet I know that you are as much wiser than I am, as you are younger. But, as I was saying, revered friend, the abundance of your wisdom makes you lazy. Please to exert yourself, for there is no real difficulty in understanding me. What I mean I may explain by an illustration of what I do not mean. The poet (Stasinus) sings —

> 'Of Zeus, the author and creator of all these things,
> You will not tell: for where there is fear there is also
> reverence.'

Now I disagree with this poet. Shall I tell you in what respect?

Euth. By all means.

Soc. I should not say that where there is fear there is also reverence; for I am sure that many persons fear poverty and disease, and the like evils, but I do not perceive that they reverence the objects of their fear.

Euth. Very true.

Soc. But where reverence is, there is fear; for he who has a feeling of reverence and shame about the commission of any action, fears and is afraid of an ill reputation.

Euth. No doubt.

Soc. Then we are wrong in saying that where there is fear there is also reverence; and we should say, where there is reverence there is also fear. But there is not always reverence where there is fear; for fear is a more extended notion, and reverence is a part of fear, just as the odd is a part of number, and number is a more extended notion than the odd. I suppose that you follow me now?

Euth. Quite well.

Soc. That was the sort of question which I meant to raise when I asked whether the just is always the pious, or the pious always the just; and whether there may not be justice where there is not piety; for justice is the more extended notion of which piety is only a part. Do you dissent?

Euth. No, I think that you are quite right.

Soc. Then, if piety is a part of justice, I suppose that we should enquire what part? If you had pursued the enquiry in the previous cases; for instance, if you had asked me what is an even number, and what part of number the even is, I should have had no difficulty in replying, a number which represents a figure having two equal sides. Do you not agree?

Euth. Yes, I quite agree.

Soc. In like manner, I want you to tell me what part of justice is piety or holiness, that I may be able to tell Meletus not to do me injustice, or indict me for impiety, as I am now adequately instructed by you in the nature of piety or holiness, and their opposites.

Euth. Piety or holiness, Socrates, appears to me to be that part of justice which attends to the gods, as there is the other part of justice which attends to men.

Soc. That is good, Euthyphro; yet still there is a little point about which I should like to have further information. What is the meaning of 'attention'? For attention can hardly be used in the same sense when applied to the gods as when applied to other things. For instance, horses are said to require attention, and not every person is able to attend to them, but only a person skilled in horsemanship. Is it not so? *attention = θεραπεια*

Euth. Certainly.

Soc. I should suppose that the art of horsemanship is the art of attending to horses?

Euth. Yes.

Soc. Nor is every one qualified to attend to dogs, but only the huntsman?

Euth. True.

Soc. And I should also conceive that the art of the huntsman is the art of attending to dogs?

Euth. Yes.

Soc. As the art of the oxherd is the art of attending to oxen?

Euth. Very true.

Soc. In like manner holiness or piety is the art of attending to the gods? — that would be your meaning, Euthyphro?

Euth. Yes.

Soc. And is not attention always designed for the good or benefit of that to which the attention is given? As in the case of horses, you may observe that when attended to by the horseman's art they are benefited and improved, are they not?

Euth. True.

Soc. As the dogs are benefited by the huntsman's art, and the oxen by the art of the oxherd, and all other things are tended or attended for their good and not for their hurt?

Euth. Certainly, not for their hurt.

Soc. But for their good?

Euth. Of course.

Soc. And does piety or holiness, which has been defined to be the art of attending to the gods, benefit or improve them? Would you say that when you do a holy act you make any of the gods better?

Euth. No, no; that was certainly not what I meant.

Soc. And I, Euthyphro, never supposed that you did. I asked you the question about the nature of the attention, because I thought that you did not.

Euth. You do me justice, Socrates; that is not the sort of attention which I mean.

Soc. Good: but I must still ask what is this attention to the gods which is called piety?   ὑπηρετικη

Euth. It is such, Socrates, as servants show to their masters.

Soc. I understand — a sort of ministration to the gods.

Euth. Exactly.

Soc. Medicine is also a sort of ministration or service, having in view the attainment of some object — would you not say of health?

Euth. I should.

Soc. Again, there is an art which ministers to the shipbuilder with a view to the attainment of some result?

Euth. Yes, Socrates, with a view to the building of a ship.

Soc. As there is an art which ministers to the housebuilder with a view to the building of a house?

Euth. Yes.

Soc. And now tell me, my good friend, about the art which ministers to the gods: what work does that help to accomplish? For you must surely know if, as you say, you are of all men living the one who is best instructed in religion.

Euth. And I speak the truth, Socrates.

Soc. Tell me then, oh tell me — what is that fair work which the gods do by the help of our ministrations?

Euth. Many and fair, Socrates, are the works which they do.

Soc. Why, my friend, and so are those of a general. But the chief of them is easily told. Would you not say that victory in war is the chief of them?

Euth. Certainly.

Soc. Many and fair, too, are the works of the husbandman, if I am not mistaken; but his chief work is the production of food from the earth?

Euth. Exactly.

Soc. And of the many and fair things done by the gods, which is the chief or principal one?

Euth. I have told you already, Socrates, that to learn all these things accurately will be very tiresome. Let me simply say that piety or holiness is learning how to please the gods in word and deed, by prayers and sacrifices. Such piety is the salvation of families and states, just as the impious, which is unpleasing to the gods, is their ruin and destruction.

Soc. I think that you could have answered in much fewer words the chief question which I asked, Euthyphro, if you had chosen. But I see plainly that you are not disposed to instruct me — clearly not: else why, when we reached the point, did you turn aside? Had you only answered me I should have truly learned of you by this time the nature of piety. Now, as the asker of a question is necessarily dependent on the answerer, whither he leads I must follow; and can only ask again, what is the pious, and what is piety? Do you mean that they are a sort of science of praying and sacrificing?

Euth. Yes, I do.

Soc. And sacrificing is giving to the gods, and prayer is asking of the gods?

Euth. Yes, Socrates.

Soc. Upon this view, then, piety is a science of asking and giving?

Euth. You understand me capitally, Socrates.

Soc. Yes, my friend; the reason is that I am a votary of your science, and give my mind to it, and therefore nothing which you say will be thrown away upon me. Please then to tell me, what is the nature of this service to the gods? Do you mean that we prefer requests and give gifts to them?

Euth. Yes, I do.

Soc. Is not the right way of asking to ask of them what we want?

Euth. Certainly.

Soc. And the right way of giving is to give them in return what they want of us. There would be no meaning in an art which gives to any one that which he does not want.

Euth. Very true, Socrates.

Soc. Then piety, Euthyphro, is an art which gods and men have of doing business with one another?

Euth. That is an expression which you may use, if you like.

Soc. But I have no particular liking for anything but the truth. I wish, however, that you would tell me what benefit accrues to the gods from our gifts. There is no doubt about what they give to us; for there is no good thing which they do not give; but how we can give any good thing to them in return is far from being equally clear. If they give everything and we give nothing, that must be an affair of business in which we have very greatly the advantage of them.

Euth. And do you imagine, Socrates, that any benefit accrues to the gods from our gifts?

Soc. But if not, Euthyphro, what is the meaning of gifts which are conferred by us upon the gods?

Euth. What else, but tributes of honour; and, as I was just now saying, what pleases them?

Soc. Piety, then, is pleasing to the gods, but not beneficial or dear to them?

Euth. I should say that nothing could be dearer.

Soc. Then once more the assertion is repeated that piety is dear to the gods?

Euth. Certainly.

Soc. And when you say this, can you wonder at your words not standing firm, but walking away? Will you accuse me of being the Daedalus who makes them walk away, not perceiving that there is another and far greater artist than Daedalus who makes them go round in a circle, and he is yourself; for the argument, as you will perceive, comes round to the same point. Were we not saying that the holy or pious was not the same with that which is loved of the gods? Have you forgotten?

Euth. I quite remember.

Soc. And are you not saying that what is loved of the gods is holy; and is not this the same as what is dear to them—do you see?

Euth. True.

Soc. Then either we were wrong in our former assertion; or if we were right then, we are wrong now.

Euth. One of the two must be true.

Soc. Then we must begin again and ask, What is piety? That is an enquiry which I shall never be weary of pursuing as far as in me lies; and I entreat you not to scorn me, but to apply your mind to the utmost, and tell me the truth. For, if any man knows, you are he; and therefore I must detain you, like Proteus, until you tell. If you had not certainly known the nature of piety and impiety, I am confident that you would never, on behalf of a serf, have charged your aged father with murder. You would not have run such a risk of doing wrong in the sight of the gods, and you would have had too much respect for the opinions of men. I am sure, therefore, that you know the nature of piety and impiety. Speak out then, my dear Euthyphro, and do not hide your knowledge.

Euth. Another time, Socrates; for I am in a hurry, and must go now.

Soc. Alas! my companion, and will you leave me in despair? I was hoping that you would instruct me in the nature of piety and impiety; and then I might have cleared myself of Meletus and his indictment. I would have told him that I had been enlightened by Euthyphro, and had given up rash innovations and speculations, in which I indulged only through ignorance, and that now I am about to lead a better life.

The Principle of Enlightened Self-Interest

Thomas Hobbes

Leviathan

Chapter XIII
Of the Natural Condition of Mankind
as concerning their Felicity and Misery

Nature hath made men so equal, in the faculties of the body and mind, as that though there be found one man sometimes manifestly stronger in body, or of quicker mind than another, yet when all is reckoned together, the difference between man and man is not so considerable, as that one

From *Leviathan*, Part I, chapters XIII, XIV, XV, Molesworth edition (1841), with some changes in punctuation.

man can thereupon claim to himself any benefit to which another may not pretend as well as he. For as to the strength of body, the weakest has strength enough to kill the strongest, either by secret machination, or by confederacy with others that are in the same danger with himself.

And as to the faculties of the mind, setting aside the arts grounded upon words, and especially that skill of proceeding upon general and infallible rules, call *science*, which very few have and but in few things, as being not a native faculty born with us, nor attained, as prudence, while we look after somewhat else, I find yet a greater equality amongst men, than that of strength. For prudence is but experience, which equal time equally bestows on all men, in those things they equally apply themselves unto. That which may perhaps make such equality incredible is but a vain conceit of one's own wisdom, which almost all men think they have in a greater degree than the vulgar; that is, than all men but themselves, and a few others, whom by fame, or for concurring with themselves, they approve. For such is the nature of men that howsoever they may acknowledge many others to be more witty, or more eloquent, or more learned, yet they will hardly believe there be many so wise as themselves; for they see their own wit at hand, and other men's at a distance. But this proveth rather that men are in that point equal, than unequal. For there is not ordinarily a greater sign of the equal distribution of any thing than that every man is contented with his share.

From this equality of ability ariseth equality of hope in the attaining of our ends. And therefore if any two men desire the same thing, which nevertheless they cannot both enjoy, they become enemies; and in the way to their end (which is principally their own conservation, and sometimes their delectation only) endeavour to destroy or subdue one another. And from hence it comes to pass that where an invader hath no more to fear than another man's single power, if one plant, sow, build, or possess a convenient seat, others may probably be expected to come prepared with forces united to dispossess and deprive him, not only of the fruit of his labour, but also of his life or liberty. And the invader again is in the like danger of another.

And from this diffidence of one another, there is no way for any man to secure himself so reasonable as anticipation; that is, by force, or wiles, to master the persons of all men he can, so long till he see no other power great enough to endanger him; and this is no more than his own conservation requireth, and is generally allowed. Also because there be some that, taking pleasure in contemplating their own power in the acts of conquest, which they pursue farther than their security requires, if others, that otherwise would be glad to be at ease within modest bounds, should not by invasion increase their power, they would not be able, long time, by standing only on their defence, to subsist. And by consequence, such augmentation of dominion over men being necessary to a man's conservation, it ought to be allowed him.

Again, men have no pleasure, but on the contrary a great deal of grief in keeping company where there is no power able to over-awe them all. For every man looketh that his companion should value him at the same rate he sets upon himself, and upon all signs of contempt, or undervaluing, naturally endeavors, as far as he dares (which amongst them that have no common power to keep them in quiet is far enough to make them destroy each other), to extort a greater value from his contemners, by damage; and from others, by the example.

So that in the nature of man, we find three principal causes of quarrel. First, competition; second, diffidence; thirdly, glory.

The first maketh men invade for gain; the second, for safety; and the third, for reputation. The first use violence to make themselves masters of other men's persons, wives, children, and cattle; the second, to defend them; the third, for trifles, as a word, a smile, a different opinion, and any other sign of undervalue, either direct in their persons, or by reflection in their kindred, their friends, their nation, their profession, or their name.

Hereby it is manifest that during the time men live without a common power to keep them all in awe, they are in that condition which is called *war*; and such a war as is of every man against every man. For war consisteth not in battle only, or the act of fighting, but in a tract of time, wherein the will to contend by battle is sufficiently known; and therefore the notion of *time* is to be considered in the nature of war, as it is in the nature of weather. For as the nature of foul weather lieth not in a shower or two of rain, but in an inclination thereto of many days together, so the nature of war consisteth not in actual fighting, but in the known disposition thereto, during all the time there is no assurance to the contrary. All other time is *peace*.

Whatsoever therefore is consequent to a time of war, where every man is enemy to every man, the same is consequent to the time wherein men live without other security than what their own strength and their own invention shall furnish them withal. In such condition, there is no place for industry, because the fruit thereof is uncertain; and consequently no culture of the earth; no navigation, nor use of the commodities that may be imported by sea; no commodious building; no instruments of moving, and removing, such things as require much force; no knowledge of the face of the earth; no account of time; no arts; no letters; no society;

and which is worst of all, continual fear, and danger of violent death; and the life of man, solitary, poor, nasty, brutish, and short.

It may seem strange to some man that has not well weighed these things that Nature should thus dissociate and render men apt to invade and destroy one another; and he may therefore, not trusting to this inference made from the passions, desire perhaps to have the same confirmed by experience. Let him therefore consider with himself: when taking a journey, he arms himself and seeks to go well accompanied; when going to sleep, he locks his doors; when even in his house he locks his chests; and this when he knows there be laws and public officers, armed, to revenge all injuries shall be done him; what opinion he has of his fellow-subjects, when he rides armed; of his fellow citizens, when he locks his doors; and of his children, and servants, when he locks his chests. Does he not there as much accuse mankind by his actions as I do by my words? But neither of us accuse man's nature in it. The desires, and other passions of man, are in themselves no sin. No more are the actions that proceed from those passions, till they know a law that forbids them; which till laws be made they cannot know, nor can any law be made till they have agreed upon the person that shall make it.

It may peradventure be thought there was never such a time nor condition of war as this; and I believe it was never generally so, over all the world; but there are many places where they live so now. For the savage people in many places of America, except the government of small families, the concord whereof dependeth on natural lust, have no government at all, and live at this day in that brutish manner, as I said before. Howsoever, it may be perceived what manner of life there would be, where there were no common power to fear, by the manner of life which men that have formerly lived under a peaceful government use to degenerate into, in a civil war.

But though there had never been any time wherein particular men were in a condition of war one against another, yet in all times, kings and persons of sovereign authority, because of their independency, are in continual jealousies, and in the state and posture of gladiators, having their weapons pointing, and their eyes fixed on one another; that is, their forts, garrisons, and guns upon the frontiers of their kingdoms, and continual spies upon their neighbours, which is a posture of war. But because they uphold thereby the industry of their subjects, there does not follow from it that misery which accompanies the liberty of particular men.

To this war of every man against every man, this also is consequent; that nothing can be unjust. The notions of right and wrong, justice and injustice, have there no place. Where there is no common power, there is no law; where no law, no injustice. Force and fraud are in war the two cardinal virtues. Justice and injustice are none of the faculties neither of the body nor mind. If they were, they might be in a man that were alone in the world, as well as his senses and passions. They are qualities that relate to men in society, not in solitude. It is consequent also to the same condition that there be no propriety, no dominion, no *mine* and *thine* distinct; but only that to be every man's that he can get, and for so long as he can keep it. And thus much for the ill condition which man by mere nature is actually placed in; though with a possibility to come out of it, consisting partly in the passions, partly in his reason.

The passions that incline men to peace are fear of death, desire of such things as are necessary to commodious living, and a hope by their industry to obtain them. And reason suggesteth convenient articles of peace upon which men may be drawn to agreement. These articles are they which otherwise are called the Laws of Nature, whereof I shall speak more particularly in the two following chapters.

Chapter XIV
Of the First and Second Natural Laws, and of Contracts

The *right of nature*, which writers commonly call *jus naturale*, is the liberty each man hath to use his own power, as he will himself, for the preservation of his own nature; that is to say, of his own life; and consequently, of doing anything which, in his own judgment and reason, he shall conceive to be the aptest means thereunto.

By *liberty* is understood, according to the proper signification of the word, the absence of external impediments; which impediments may oft take away part of a man's power to do what he would, but cannot hinder him from using the power left him, according as his judgment and reason shall dictate to him.

A Law of Nature, *lex naturalis*, is a precept or general rule, found out by reason, by which a man is forbidden to do that which is destructive of his life, or taketh away the means of preserving the same, and to omit that by which he thinketh it may be best preserved. For though they that speak of this subject use to confound *jus* and *lex*, *right* and *law*, yet they ought to be distinguished, because *right* consisteth in liberty to do, or to forbear; whereas *law* determineth and bindeth to one of them; so that law and right differ as much as obligation and liberty, which in one and the same matter are inconsistent.

35

And because the condition of man, as hath been declared in the precedent chapter, in a condition of war of every one against every one, in which case every one is governed by his own reason, and there is nothing he can make use of that may not be a help unto him in preserving his life against his enemies; it followeth that in such a condition every man has a right to every thing, even to one another's body. And therefore, as long as this natural right of every man to every thing endureth, there can be no security to any man, how strong or wise soever he be, of living out the time which nature ordinarily alloweth men to live. And consequently it is a precept, or general rule of reason, *that every man ought to endeavour peace, as far as he has hope of obtaining it; and when he cannot obtain it, that he may seek and use all helps and advantages of war.* The first branch of which rule containeth the first and fundamental law of nature, which is, *to seek peace and follow it.* The second, the sum of the right of nature, which is, *by all means we can, to defend ourselves.*

From this fundamental law of nature, by which men are commanded to endeavour peace, is derived this second law: *that a man be willing, when others are so too, as far forth as for peace and defence of himself he shall think it necessary, to lay down this right to all things; and be contented with so much liberty against other men as he would allow other men against himself.* For as long as every man holdeth this right, of doing anything he liketh; so long are all men in the condition of war. But if other men will not lay down their right, as well as he, then there is no reason for anyone to divest himself of his; for that were to expose himself to prey, which no man is bound to, rather than to dispose himself to peace. This is that law of the Gospel: *Whatsoever you require that others should do to you, that do ye to them.* And that law of all men: *Quod tibi fieri non vis, alteri ne feceris.*

To *lay down* a man's *right* to any thing is to *divest* himself of the *liberty* of hindering another of the benefit of his own right to the same. For he that renounceth, or passeth away his right, giveth not to any other man a right which he had not before, because there is nothing to which every man had not right by nature, but only standeth out of his way that he may enjoy his own original right without hindrance from him, not without hindrance from another. So that the effect which redoundeth to one man, by another man's defect of right, is but so much diminution of impediments to the use of his own right original.

Right is laid aside, either by simply renouncing it, or by transferring it to another. By simply *renouncing*, when he cares not to whom the benefit thereof redoundeth. By *transferring*, when he intendeth the benefit thereof to some certain person, or persons. And when a man hath in either manner abandoned, or granted way his right, then is he said to be *obliged*, or *bound*, not to hinder those to whom such right is granted, or abandoned, from the benefit of it; and that he *ought*, and it is his *duty*, not to make void that voluntary act of his own; and that such hindrance is *injustice*, and *injury*, as being *sine jure*; the right being before renounced, or transferred. So that *injury*, or *injustice*, in the controversies of the world, is somewhat like to that which in the disputations of scholars is called *absurdity*. For as it is there called an absurdity to contradict what one maintained in the beginning; so in the world it is called injustice, and injury, voluntarily to undo that which from the beginning he had voluntarily done. The way by which a man either simply renounceth, or transferreth his right, is a declaration, or signification, by some voluntary and sufficient sign, or signs, that he doth so renounce or transfer, or hath so renounced or transferred the same, to him that accepteth it. And these signs are either words only, or actions only; or, as it happeneth most often, both words and actions. And the same are the *bonds* by which men are bound and obliged: bonds that have their strength, not from their own nature, for nothing is more easily broken than a man's word, but from fear of some evil consequence upon the rupture.

Whensoever a man transferreth his right, or renounceth it, it is either in consideration of some right reciprocally transferred to himself, or for some other good he hopeth for thereby. For it is a voluntary act; and of the voluntary acts of every man, the object is some *good to himself*. And therefore there be some rights which no man can be understood by any words, or other signs, to have abandoned or transferred. As first a man cannot lay down the right of resisting them that assault him by force to take away his life, because he cannot be understood to aim thereby at any good to himself. The same may be said of wounds, and chains, and imprisonment; both because there is no benefit consequent to such patience, as there is to the patience of suffering another to be wounded or imprisoned, as also because a man cannot tell, when he seeth men proceed against him by violence, whether they intend his death or not. And lastly the motive and end for which this renouncing and transferring of right is introduced is nothing else but the security of a man's person in his life, and in the means of so preserving life as not to be weary of it. And therefore if a man by words, or other signs, seem to despoil himself of the end for which those signs were intended, he is not to be understood as if he meant it, or that it was his will, but that he was ignorant of how such words and actions were to be interpreted.

The mutual transferring of right is that which men call *contract.* . . .

Chapter XV
Of Other Laws of Nature

From that law of nature by which we are obliged to transfer to another such rights as, being retained, hinder the peace of mankind, there followeth a third; which is this, *that men perform their covenants made*; without which covenants are in vain, and but empty words; and the right of all men to all things remaining, we are still in the condition of war.

And in this law of nature consisteth the fountain and original of *justice*. For where no covenant hath preceded, there hath no right been transferred, and every man has right to every thing; and consequently, no action can be unjust. But when a covenant is made, then to break it is *unjust*; and the definition of *injustice* is no other than *the not performance of covenant*. And whatsoever is not unjust is *just*.

But because covenants of mutual trust, where there is a fear of not performance on either part, as hath been said in the former chapter, are invalid; though the original of justice be the making of covenants; yet injustice actually there can be none, till the cause of such fear be taken away; which, while men are in the natural condition of war, cannot be done. Therefore before the names of *just* and *unjust* can have place, there must be some coercive power to compel men equally to the performance of their covenants, by the terror of some punishment greater than the benefit they expect by the breach of their covenant, and to make good that propriety which by mutual contract men acquire in recompense of the universal right they abandon; and such power there is none before the erection of a commonwealth. And this is also to be gathered out of the ordinary definition of justice in the Schools, for they say that *justice is the constant will of giving every man his own*. And therefore where there is no *own*, that is no propriety, there is no injustice; and where is no coercive power erected, that is, where there is no commonwealth, there is no propriety, all men having right to all things; therefore where there is no commonwealth, there nothing is unjust. So that the nature of justice consisteth in keeping of valid covenants, but the validity of covenants begins not but with the constitution of a civil power sufficient to compel men to keep them; and then it is also that propriety begins. . . .

As justice dependeth on antecedent covenant, so does *gratitude* depend on antecedent grace; that is to say, antecedent free gift; and is the fourth law of nature, which may be conceived in this form: *that a man which receiveth benefit from another of mere grace endeavour that he which giveth it have no reasonable cause to repent him of his good will.* For no man giveth but with intention of good to himself, because gift is voluntary, and of all voluntary acts, the object is to every man his own good; of which if men see they shall be frustrated, there will be no beginning of benevolence or trust; nor consequently of mutual help; nor of reconciliation of one man to another; and therefore they are to remain still in the condition of *war*, which is contrary to the first and fundamental law of nature which commandeth men to *seek peace.* The breach of this law is called *ingratitude*, and hath the same relation to grace that injustice hath to obligation by covenant.

A fifth law of nature is *complaisance*; that is to say, *that every man strive to accommodate himself to the rest.* . . .

A sixth law of nature is this, *that upon caution of the future time, a man ought to pardon the offences past of them that repenting, desire it.* . . .

A seventh is, *that in revenges,* that is, retribution of evil for evil, *men look not at the greatness of the evil past, but the greatness of the good to follow.* . . .

And because all signs of hatred or contempt provoke to fight, insomuch as most men choose rather to hazard their life than not to be revenged, we may in the eighth place, for a law of nature, set down this precept, *that no man by deed, word, countenance, or gesture declare hatred or contempt of another.* . . .

If nature therefore have made men equal, that equality is to be acknowledged; or if nature have made men unequal; yet because men that think themselves equal will not enter into conditions of peace but upon equal terms, such equality must be admitted. And therefore for the ninth law of nature, I put this, *that every man acknowledge another for his equal by nature.* The breach of this precept is *pride.*

On this law dependeth another, *that at the entrance into conditions of peace, no man require to reserve to himself any right which he is not content should be reserved to every one of the rest.* . . .

Also if *a man be trusted to judge between man and man,* it is a precept of the law of nature *that he deal equally between them.* . . .

And from this followeth another law, *that such things as cannot be divided be enjoyed in common, if it can be; and if the quantity of the thing permit, without stint; otherwise proportionably to the number of them that have right.* For otherwise the distribution is unequal and contrary to equity.

But some things there be that can neither be divided nor enjoyed in common. Then, the law of nature which prescribeth equity requireth *that the entire right, or else, making the use alternate, the first possession, be determined by lot.* For equal distribution is of the law of nature, and other means of equal distribution cannot be imagined. . . .

It is also a law of nature *that all men that mediate peace be allowed safe conduct.* For the law that commandeth peace, as the *end,* commandeth intercession, as the *means*; and to intercession the means is safe conduct.

And because, though men be never so willing to observe these laws, there may nevertheless arise questions concerning a man's action: first, whether it were done, or not done; secondly, if done, whether against the law, or not against the law; the former whereof is called a question *of fact,* the latter a question *of right*; therefore unless the parties to the question covenant mutually to stand to the sentence of another, they are as far from peace as ever. This other to whose sentence they submit is called an *arbitrator.* And therefore it is of the law of nature *that they that are at controversy submit their right to the judgment of an arbitrator. . . .*

These are the laws of nature, dictating peace, for a means of the conservation of men in multitudes; and which only concern the doctrine of civil society. There be other things tending to the destruction of particular men; as drunkenness, and all other parts of intemperance, which may therefore also be reckoned amongst those things which the law of nature hath forbidden, but are not necessary to be mentioned, nor are pertinent enough to this place.

And though this may seem too subtle a deduction of the laws of nature to be taken notice of by all men, whereof the most part are too busy in getting food, and the rest too negligent to understand; yet to leave all men inexcusable, they have been contracted into one easy sum, intelligible even to the meanest capacity; and that is, *Do not that to another which thou wouldst not have done to thyself*; which sheweth him that he has no more to do in learning the laws of nature but, when weighing the actions of other men with his own they seem too heavy, to put them into the other part of the balance, and his own into their place, that his own passions and self-love may add nothing to the weight; and then there is none of these laws of nature that will not appear unto him very reasonable.

The laws of nature oblige *in foro interno*; that is to say, they bind to a desire they should take place; but *in foro externo*, that is, to putting them in act, not always. For he that should be modest and tractable, and perform all he promises in such time and place where no man else should do so, should but make himself a prey to others, and procure his own certain ruin, contrary to the ground of all laws of nature, which tend to nature's preservation. And again, he that having sufficient security that others shall observe the same laws towards him, observes them not himself, seeketh not peace, but war, and consequently the destruction of his nature by violence.

And whatsoever laws bind *in foro interno* may be broken, not only by a fact contrary to the law, but also by a fact according to it, in case a man think it contrary. For though his action in this case be according to the law, yet his purpose was against the law; which, where the obligation is *in foro interno*, is a breach.

The laws of nature are immutable and eternal; for injustice, ingratitude, arrogance, pride, iniquity, acceptance of persons, and the rest can never be made lawful. For it can never be that war shall preserve life, and peace destroy it.

The same laws, because they oblige only to a desire and endeavour, I mean an unfeigned and constant endeavour, are easy to be observed. For in that they require nothing but endeavour, he that endeavoureth their performance fulfilleth them, and he that fulfilleth the law is just.

And the science of them is the true and only moral philosophy. For moral philosophy is nothing else but the science of what is *good* and *evil* in the conversation and society of mankind. *Good* and *evil* are names that signify our appetites and aversions, which in different tempers, customs, and doctrines of men are different; and divers men differ not only in their judgment on the senses of what is pleasant and unpleasant to the taste, smell, hearing, touch, and sight; but also of what is conformable or disagreeable to reason in the actions of common life. Nay, the same man, in divers times, differs from himself; and one time praiseth, that is, calleth good, what another time he dispraiseth, and calleth evil: from whence arise disputes, controversies, and at last war. And therefore so long as a man is in the condition of mere nature, which is a condition of war, his private appetite is the measure of good and evil; and consequently all men agree on this, that peace is good, and therefore also the way or means of peace, which, as I have shewed before, are *justice, gratitude, modesty, equity, mercy,* and the rest of the laws of nature, are good; that is to say, *moral virtues;* and their contrary *vices,* evil. Now the science of virtue and vice is moral philosophy; and therefore the true doctrine of the laws of nature is the true moral philosophy. But the writers of moral philosophy, though they acknowledge the same virtues and vices; yet not seeing wherein consisted their goodness, nor that they come to be praised as the means of peaceable, sociable, and comfortable living, place them in a mediocrity of passions; as if not the cause, but the degree of daring, made fortitude; or not the cause, but the quantity of a gift, made liberality.

These dictates of reason men used to call by the name of laws, but improperly; for they are but conclusions or theorems concerning what conduceth to the conservation and defence of themselves; whereas *law*, properly, is the word of him that by right hath command over others. But yet if we consider the same theorem as delivered in the word of God that by right commandeth all things, then are they properly called laws.

The Principle of Rational Self-Realization

Aristotle

Nicomachean Ethics

Book I

1. Every art and every inquiry, and similarly every action and pursuit, is thought to aim at some good; and for this reason the good has rightly been declared to be that at which all things aim. But a certain difference is found among ends; some are activities, others are products apart from the activities that produce them. Where there are ends apart from the actions, it is the nature of the products to be better than the activities.

From *Ethica Nicomachea*, trans. W. D. Ross, in *The Oxford Translation of Aristotle*, ed. W. D. Ross, vol. IX (1925), by permission of The Clarendon Press, Oxford.

Now, as there are many actions, arts, and sciences, their ends also are many; the end of the medical art is health, that of ship-building a vessel, that of strategy victory, that of economics wealth. But where such arts fall under a single capacity — as bridle-making and the other arts concerned with the equipment of horses fall under the art of riding, and this and every military action under strategy, in the same way other arts fall under yet others — in all of these the ends of the master arts are to be preferred to all the subordinate ends; for it is for the sake of the former that the latter are pursued. It makes no difference whether the activities themselves are the ends of the actions, or something else apart from the activities, as in the case of the sciences just mentioned.

2. If, then, there is some end of the things we do, which we desire for its own sake (everything else being desired for the sake of this), and if we do not choose everything for the sake of something else (for at that rate the process would go on to infinity, so that our desire would be empty and vain), clearly this must be the good and the chief good. Will not the knowledge of it, then, have a great influence on life? Shall we not, like archers who have a mark to aim at, be more likely to hit upon what is right? If so, we must try, in outline at least, to determine what it is, and of which of the sciences or capacities it is the object. It would seem to belong to the most authoritative art and that which is most truly the master art. And politics appears to be of this nature; for it is this that ordains which of the sciences should be studied in a state, and which each class of citizens should learn and up to what point they should learn them; and we see even the most highly esteemed of capacities to fall under this, e.g. strategy, economics, rhetoric; now, since politics uses the rest of the sciences, and since, again, it legislates as to what we are to do and what we are to abstain from, the end of this science must include those of the others, so that this end must be the good for man. For even if the end is the same for a single man and for a state, that of the state seems at all events something greater and more complete whether to attain or to preserve; though it is worth while to attain the end merely for one man, it is finer and more godlike to attain it for a nation or for city-states. These, then, are the ends at which our inquiry aims, since it is political science, in one sense of that term.

3. Our discussion will be adequate if it has as much clearness as the subject-matter admits of, for precision is not to be sought for alike in all discussions, any more than in all the products of the crafts. Now fine and just actions, which political science investigates, admit of much variety and fluctuation of opinion, so that they may be thought to exist only by convention, and not by nature. And goods also give rise to a

similar fluctuation because they bring harm to many people; for before now men have been undone by reason of their wealth, and others by reason of their courage. We must be content, then, in speaking of such subjects and with such premises to indicate the truth roughly and in outline, and in speaking about things which are only for the most part true and with premises of the same kind to reach conclusions that are no better. In the same spirit, therefore, should each type of statement be *received;* for it is the mark of an educated man to look for precision in each class of things just so far as the nature of the subject admits; it is evidently equally foolish to accept probable reasoning from a mathematician and to demand from a rhetorician scientific proofs.

Now each man judges well the things he knows, and of these he is a good judge. And so the man who has been educated in a subject is a good judge of that subject, and the man who has received an all-round education is a good judge in general. Hence a young man is not a proper hearer of lectures on political science; for he is inexperienced in the actions that occur in life, but its discussions start from these and are about these; and, further, since he tends to follow his passions, his study will be vain and unprofitable, because the end aimed at is not knowledge but action. And it makes no difference whether he is young in years or youthful in character; the defect does not depend on time, but on his living, and pursuing each successive object, as passion directs. For to such persons, as to the incontinent, knowledge brings no profit; but to those who desire and act in accordance with a rational principle knowledge about such matters will be of great benefit.

These remarks about the student, the sort of treatment to be expected, and the purpose of the inquiry, may be taken as our preface.

4. Let us resume our inquiry and state, in view of the fact that all knowledge and every pursuit aims at some good, what it is that we say political science aims at and what is the highest of all goods achievable by action. Verbally there is very general agreement; for both the general run of men and people of superior refinement say that it is happiness, and identify living well and doing well with being happy; but with regard to what happiness is they differ, and the many do not give the same account as the wise. For the former think it is some plain and obvious thing, like pleasure, wealth, or honour; they differ, however, from one another — and often even the same man identifies it with different things, with health when he is ill, with wealth when he is poor; but, conscious of their ignorance, they admire those who proclaim some great ideal that is above their comprehension. Now some thought that apart from these many goods there is another which is self-subsistent

and causes the goodness of all these as well. To examine all the opinions that have been held were perhaps somewhat fruitless; enough to examine those that are most prevalent or that seem to be arguable. . . .

5. . . . To judge from the lives that men lead, most men, and men of the most vulgar type, seem (not without some ground) to identify the good, or happiness, with pleasure; which is the reason why they love the life of enjoyment. For there are, we may say, three prominent types of life — that just mentioned, the political, and thirdly the contemplative life. Now the mass of mankind are evidently quite slavish in their tastes, preferring a life suitable to beasts, but they get some ground for their view from the fact that many of those in high places share the tastes of Sardanapallus. A consideration of the prominent types of life shows that people of superior refinement and of active disposition identify happiness with honour; for this is, roughly speaking, the end of the political life. But it seems too superficial to be what we are looking for, since it is thought to depend on those who bestow honour rather than on him who receives it, but the good we divine to be something proper to a man and not easily taken from him. Further, men seem to pursue honour in order that they may be assured of their goodness; at least it is by men of practical wisdom that they seek to be honoured, and among those who know them, and on the ground of their virtue; clearly, then, according to them, at any rate, virtue is better. And perhaps one might even suppose this to be, rather than honour, the end of the political life. But even this appears somewhat incomplete; for possession of virtue seems actually compatible with being asleep, or with lifelong inactivity, and, further, with the greatest sufferings and misfortunes; but a man who was living so no one would call happy, unless he were maintaining a thesis at all costs. But enough of this; for the subject has been sufficiently treated even in the current discussions. Third comes the contemplative life, which we shall consider later.

The life of money-making is one undertaken under compulsion, and wealth is evidently not the good we are seeking; for it is merely useful and for the sake of something else. And so one might rather take the aforenamed objects to be ends; for they are loved for themselves. But it is evident that not even these are ends; yet many arguments have been thrown away in support of them. . . .

7. Let us again return to the good we are seeking, and ask what it can be. It seems different in different actions and arts; it is different in medicine, in strategy, and in the other arts likewise. What then is the good of each? Surely that for whose sake everything else is done. In medicine this is health, in strategy victory, in architecture a house, in

any other sphere something else, and in every action and pursuit the end; for it is for the sake of this that all men do whatever else they do. Therefore, if there is an end for all that we do, this will be the good achievable by action, and if there are more than one, these will be the goods achievable by action.

So the argument has by a different course reached the same point; but we must try to state this even more clearly. Since there are evidently more than one end, and we choose some of these (e.g. wealth, flutes, and in general instruments) for the sake of something else, clearly not all ends are final ends; but the chief good is evidently something final. Therefore, if there is only one final end, this will be what we are seeking, and if there are more than one, the most final of these will be what we are seeking. Now we call that which is in itself worthy of pursuit more final than that which is in itself worthy of pursuit for the sake of something else, and that which is never desirable for the sake of something else more final than the things that are desirable both in themselves and for the sake of that other thing, and therefore we call final without qualification that which is always desirable in itself and never for the sake of something else.

Now such a thing happiness, above all else, is held to be; for this we choose always for itself and never for the sake of something else, but honour, pleasure, reason, and every virtue we choose indeed for themselves (for if nothing resulted from them we should still choose each of them), but we choose them also for the sake of happiness, judging that by means of them we shall be happy. Happiness, on the other hand, no one chooses for the sake of these, nor, in general, for anything other than itself.

From the point of view of self-sufficiency the same result seems to follow; for the final good is thought to be self-sufficient. Now by self-sufficient we do not mean that which is sufficient for a man by himself, for one who lives a solitary life, but also for parents, children, wife, and in general for his friends and fellow citizens, since man is born for citizenship. But some limit must be set to this; for if we extend our requirement to ancestors and descendants and friends' friends we are in for an infinite series. Let us examine this question, however, on another occasion; the self-sufficient we now define as that which when isolated makes life desirable and lacking in nothing; and such we think happiness to be; and further we think it most desirable of all things, without being counted as one good thing among others — if it were so counted it would clearly be made more desirable by the addition of even the least of goods; for that which is added becomes an excess of goods, and of goods the greater is always more desirable. Happiness, then, is something final and self-sufficient, and is the end of action.

Presumably, however, to say that happiness is the chief good seems a platitude, and a clearer account of what it is is still desired. This might perhaps be given, if we could first ascertain the function of man. For just as for a flute-player, a sculptor, or any artist, and, in general, for all things that have a function or activity, the good and the 'well' is thought to reside in the function, so would it seem to be for man, if he has a function. Have the carpenter, then, and the tanner certain functions or activities, and has man none? Is he born without a function? Or as eye, hand, foot, and in general each of the parts evidently has a function, may one lay it down that man similarly has a function apart from all these? What then can this be? Life seems to be common even to plants, but we are seeking what is peculiar to man. Let us exclude, therefore, the life of nutrition and growth. Next there would be a life of perception, but *it* also seems to be common even to the horse, the ox, and every animal. There remains, then, an active life of the element that has a rational principle; of this, one part has such a principle in the sense of being obedient to one, the other in the sense of possessing one and exercising thought. And, as 'life of the rational element' also has two meanings, we must state that life in the sense of activity is what we mean; for this seems to be the more proper sense of the term. Now if the function of man is an activity of soul which follows or implies a rational principle, and if we say 'a so-and-so' and 'a good so-and-so' have a function which is the same in kind, e.g. a lyre-player and a good lyre-player, and so without qualification in all cases, eminence in respect of goodness being added to the name of the function (for the function of a lyre-player is to play the lyre, and that of a good lyre-player is to do so well): if this is the case, [and we state the function of man to be a certain kind of life, and this to be an activity or actions of the soul implying a rational principle, and the function of a good man to be the good and noble performance of these, and if any action is well performed when it is performed in accordance with the appropriate excellence: if this is the case,] human good turns out to be activity of soul in accordance with virtue, and if there are more than one virtue, in accordance with the best and most complete.

But we must add 'in a complete life.' For one swallow does not make a summer, nor does one day; and so too one day, or a short time, does not make a man blessed and happy. . . .

13. Since happiness is an activity of soul in accordance with perfect virtue, we must consider the nature of virtue; for perhaps we shall thus see better the nature of happiness. . . . But clearly the virtue we must

study is human virtue; for the good we were seeking was human good and the happiness human happiness. By human virtue we mean not that of the body but that of the soul; and happiness also we call an activity of soul. But if this is so, clearly the student of politics must know somehow the facts about the soul, as the man who is to heal the eyes or the body as a whole must know about the eyes or the body. . . .

Some things are said about it, adequately enough, even in the discussions outside our school, and we must use these; e.g. that one element in the soul is irrational and one has a rational principle. Whether these are separated as the parts of the body or of anything divisible are, or are distinct by definition but by nature inseparable, like convex and concave in the circumference of a circle, does not affect the present question.

Of the irrational element one division seems to be widely distributed, and vegetative in its nature, I mean that which causes nutrition and growth; for it is this kind of power of the soul that one must assign to all nurslings and to embryos, and this same power to full-grown creatures; this is more reasonable than to assign some different power to them. Now the excellence of this seems to be common to all species and not specifically human; for this part or faculty seems to function most in sleep, while goodness and badness are least manifest in sleep (whence comes the saying that the happy are no better off than the wretched for half their lives; and this happens naturally enough, since sleep is an inactivity of the soul in that respect in which it is called good or bad), unless perhaps to a small extent some of the movements actually penetrate to the soul, and in this respect the dreams of good men are better than those of ordinary people. Enough of this subject, however; let us leave the nutritive faculty alone, since it has by its nature no share in human excellence.

There seems to be also another irrational element in the soul — one which in a sense, however, shares in a rational principle. For we praise the rational principle of the continent man and of the incontinent, and the part of their soul that has such a principle, since it urges them aright and towards the best objects; but there is found in them also another element naturally opposed to the rational principle, which fights against and resists that principle. For exactly as paralysed limbs when we intend to move them to the right turn on the contrary to the left, so is it with the soul; the impulses of incontinent people move in contrary directions. But while in the body we see that which moves astray, in the soul we do not. No doubt, however, we must none the less suppose that in the soul too there is something contrary to the rational principle, resisting and opposing it. In what sense it is distinct from the other elements does not concern us. Now even this seems to have a share in a rational principle,

49

as we said; at any rate in the continent man it obeys the rational principle — and presumably in the temperate and brave man it is still more obedient; for in him it speaks, on all matters, with the same voice as the rational principle.

Therefore the irrational element also appears to be twofold. For the vegetative element in no way shares in a rational principle, but the appetitive and in general the desiring element in a sense shares in it, in so far as it listens to and obeys it; this is the sense in which we speak of 'taking account' of one's father or one's friends, not that in which we speak of 'accounting' for a mathematical property. That the irrational element is in some sense persuaded by a rational principle is indicated also by the giving of advice and by all reproof and exhortation. And if this element also must be said to have a rational principle, that which has a rational principle (as well as that which has not) will be twofold, one subdivision having it in the strict sense and in itself, and the other having a tendency to obey as one does one's father.

Virtue too is distinguished into kinds in accordance with this difference; for we say that some of the virtues are intellectual and others moral, philosophic wisdom and understanding and practical wisdom being intellectual, liberality and temperance moral. For in speaking about a man's character we do not say that he is wise or has understanding but that he is good-tempered or temperate; yet we praise the wise man also with respect to his state of mind; and of states of mind we call those which merit praise virtues.

Book II

1. Virtue, then, being of two kinds, intellectual and moral, intellectual virtue in the main owes both its birth and its growth to teaching (for which reason it requires experience and time), while moral virtue comes about as a result of habit, whence also its name *ethike* is one that is formed by a slight variation from the word *ethos* (habit). From this it is also plain that none of the moral virtues arises in us by nature; for nothing that exists by nature can form a habit contrary to its nature. For instance the stone which by nature moves downwards cannot be habituated to move upwards, not even if one tries to train it by throwing it up ten thousand times; nor can fire be habituated to move downwards, nor can anything else that by nature behaves in one way be trained to behave in another. Neither by nature, then, nor contrary to nature do the virtues arise in us; rather we are adapted by nature to receive them, and are made perfect by habit.

Again, of all the things that come to us by nature we first acquire the potentiality and later exhibit the activity (this is plain in the case of the senses; for it was not by often seeing or often hearing that we got these senses, but on the contrary we had them before we used them, and did not come to have them by using them); but the virtues we get by first exercising them, as also happens in the case of the arts as well. For the things we have to learn before we can do them, we learn by doing them, e.g. men become builders by building and lyre-players by playing the lyre; so too we become just by doing just acts, temperate by doing temperate acts, brave by doing brave acts. . . .

Again, it is from the same causes and by the same means that every virtue is both produced and destroyed, and similarly every art; for it is from playing the lyre that both good and bad lyre-players are produced. And the corresponding statement is true of builders and of all the rest; men will be good or bad builders as a result of building well or badly. For if this were not so, there would have been no need of a teacher, but all men would have been born good or bad at their craft. This, then, is the case with the virtues also; by doing the acts that we do in our transactions with other men we became just or unjust, and by doing the acts that we do in the presence of danger, and being habituated to feel fear or confidence, we become brave or cowardly. The same is true of appetites and feelings of anger; some men become temperate and good-tempered, others self-indulgent and irascible, by behaving in one way or the other in the appropriate circumstances. Thus, in one word, states of character arise out of like activities. This is why the activities we exhibit must be of a certain kind; it is because the states of character correspond to the differences between these. It makes no small difference, then, whether we form habits of one kind or of another from our very youth; it makes a very great difference, or rather *all* the difference. . . .

4. The question might be asked, what we mean by saying that we must become just by doing just acts, and temperate by doing temperate acts; for if men do just and temperate acts, they are already just and temperate, exactly as, if they do what is in accordance with the laws of grammar and of music, they are grammarians and musicians.

Or is this not true even of the arts? It is possible to do something that is in accordance with the laws of grammar, either by chance or at the suggestion of another. A man will be a grammarian, then, only when he has both done something grammatical and done it grammatically; and this means doing it in accordance with the grammatical knowledge in himself.

Again, the case of the arts and that of the virtues are not similar; for the products of the arts have their goodness in themselves, so that it is enough that they should have a certain character, but if the acts that are in accordance with the virtues have themselves a certain character it does not follow that they are done justly or temperately. The agent also must be in a certain condition when he does them; in the first place he must have knowledge, secondly he must choose the acts, and choose them for their own sakes, and thirdly his action must proceed from a firm and unchangeable character. These are not reckoned in as conditions of the possession of the arts, except the bare knowledge; but as a condition of the possession of the virtues knowledge has little or no weight, while the other conditions count not for a little but for everything, i.e. the very conditions which result from often doing just and temperate acts.

Actions, then, are called just and temperate when they are such as the just or the temperate man would do; but it is not the man who does these that is just and temperate, but the man who also does them *as* just and temperate men do them. . . .

5. Next we must consider what virtue is. Since things that are found in the soul are of three kinds — passions, faculties, states of character — virtue must be one of these. By passions I mean appetite, anger, fear, confidence, envy, joy, friendly feeling, hatred, longing, emulation, pity, and in general the feelings that are accompanied by pleasure or pain; by faculties the things in virtue of which we are said to be capable of feeling these, e.g. of becoming angry or being pained or feeling pity; by states of character the things in virtue of which we stand well or badly with reference to the passions, e.g. with reference to anger we stand badly if we feel it violently or too weakly, and well if we feel it moderately; and similarly with reference to the other passions.

Now neither the virtues nor the vices are *passions*, because we are not called good or bad on the ground of our passions, but are so called on the ground of our virtues and our vices, and because we are neither praised nor blamed for our passions (for the man who feels fear or anger is not praised, nor is the man who simply feels anger blamed, but the man who feels it in a certain way), but for our virtues and our vices we *are* praised or blamed.

Again, we feel anger and fear without choice, but the virtues are modes of choice or involve choice. Further, in respect of the passions we are said to be moved, but in respect of the virtues and the vices we are said not to be moved but to be disposed in a particular way.

For these reasons also they are not *faculties*; for we are neither called good nor bad, nor praised nor blamed, for the simple capacity of feeling the passions; again, we have the faculties by nature, but we are not made good or bad by nature; we have spoken of this before.

If, then, the virtues are neither passions nor faculties, all that remains is that they should be *states of character*.

Thus we have stated what virtue is in respect of its genus.

6. We must, however, not only describe virtue as a state of character, but also say what sort of state it is. We may remark, then, that every virtue or excellence both brings into good condition the thing of which it is the excellence and makes the work of that thing be done well; e.g. the excellence of the eye makes both the eye and its work good; for it is by the excellence of the eye that we see well. Similarly the excellence of the horse makes a horse both good in itself and good at running and at carrying its rider and at awaiting the attack of the enemy. Therefore, if this is true in every case, the virtue of man also will be the state of character which makes a man good and which makes him do his own work well.

How this is to happen . . . will be made plain . . . by the following consideration of the specific nature of virtue. In everything that is continuous and divisible it is possible to take more, less, or an equal amount, and that either in terms of the thing itself or relatively to us; and the equal is an intermediate between excess and defect. By the intermediate in the object I mean that which is equidistant from each of the extremes, which is one and the same for all men; by the intermediate relatively to us that which is neither too much nor too little — and this is not one, nor the same for all. For instance, if ten is many and two is few, six is the intermediate, taken in terms of the object; for it exceeds and is exceeded by an equal amount; this is intermediate according to arithmetical proportion. But the intermediate relatively to us is not to be taken so; if ten pounds are too much for a particular person to eat and two too little, it does not follow that the trainer will order six pounds; for this also is perhaps too much for the person who is to take it, or too little — too little for Milo[1], too much for the beginner in athletic exercises. The same is true of running and wrestling. Thus a master of any art avoids excess and defect, but seeks the intermediate and chooses this — the intermediate not in the object but relatively to us.

If it is thus, then, that every art does its work well — by looking to the intermediate and judging its works by this standard (so that we often say of good works of art that it is not possible either to take away or to

---

[1]A famous wrestler.—TRANS.

add anything, implying that excess and defect destroy the goodness of works of art, while the mean preserves it; and good artists, as we say, look to this in their work), and if, further, virtue is more exact and better than any art, as nature also is, then virtue must have the quality of aiming at the intermediate. I mean moral virtue; for it is this that is concerned with passions and actions, and in these there is excess, defect, and the intermediate. For instance, both fear and confidence and appetite and anger and pity and in general pleasure and pain may be felt both too much and too little, and in both cases not well; but to feel them at the right times, with reference to the right objects, towards the right people, with the right motive, and in the right way, is what is both intermediate and best, and this is characteristic of virtue. Similarly with regard to actions also there is excess, defect, and the intermediate. Now virtue is concerned with passions and actions, in which excess is a form of failure, and so is defect, while the intermediate is praised and is a form of success; and being praised and being successful are both characteristic of virtue. Therefore virtue is a kind of mean, since, as we have seen, it aims at what is intermediate.

Again, it is possible to fail in many ways (for evil belongs to the class of the unlimited, as the Pythagoreans conjectured, and good to that of the limited), while to succeed is possible only in one way (for which reason also one is easy and the other difficult — to miss the mark easy, to hit it difficult); for these reasons also, then, excess and defect are characteristic of vice, and the mean of virtue;

For men are good in but one way, but bad in many.

Virtue, then, is a state of character concerned with choice, lying in a mean, i.e. the mean relative to us, this being determined by a rational principle, and by that principle by which the man of practical wisdom would determine it. Now it is a mean between two vices, that which depends on excess and that which depends on defect; and again it is a mean because the vices respectively fall short of or exceed what is right in both passions and actions, while virtue both finds and chooses that which is intermediate. Hence in respect of its substance and the definition which states its essence virtue is a mean, with regard to what is best and right an extreme.

But not every action nor every passion admits of a mean; for some have names that already imply badness, e.g. spite, shamelessness, envy, and in the case of actions adultery, theft, murder; for all of these and suchlike things imply by their names that they are themselves bad, and not the excesses or deficiencies of them. It is not possible, then, ever to be right with regard to them: one must always be wrong. Nor does goodness or badness with regard to such things depend on committing adultery with the right woman, at the right time, and in the right way, but simply to do any of them is to go wrong. It would be equally absurd, then, to expect that in unjust, cowardly, and voluptuous action there should be a mean, an excess, and a deficiency; for at that rate there would be a mean of excess and of deficiency, an excess of excess, and a deficiency of deficiency. But as there is no excess and deficiency of temperance and courage because what is intermediate is in a sense an extreme, so too of the actions we have mentioned there is no mean nor any excess and deficiency, but however they are done they are wrong; for in general there is neither a mean of excess and deficiency, nor excess and deficiency of a mean.

7. We must, however, not only make this general statement, but also apply it to the individual facts. For among statements about conduct those which are general apply more widely, but those which are particular are more genuine, since conduct has to do with individual cases, and our statements must harmonize with the facts in these cases. We may take these cases from our table. With regard to feelings of fear and confidence courage is the mean; of the people who exceed, he who exceeds in fearlessness has no name (many of the states have no name), while the man who exceeds in confidence is rash, and he who exceeds in fear and falls short in confidence is a coward. With regard to pleasures and pains — not all of them, and not so much with regard to the pains — the mean is temperance, the excess self-indulgence. Persons deficient with regard to the pleasures are not often found; hence, such persons also have received no name. But let us call them 'insensible.'

With regard to giving and taking of money the mean is liberality, the excess and the defect prodigality and meanness. In these actions people exceed and fall short in contrary ways; the prodigal exceeds in spending and falls short in taking, while the mean man exceeds in taking and falls short in spending. . . . With regard to money there are also other dispositions — a mean, magnificence (for the magnificent man differs from the liberal man; the former deals with large sums, the latter with small ones), an excess, tastelessness and vulgarity, and a deficiency, niggardliness. . . .

With regard to honour and dishonour the mean is proper pride, the excess is known as a sort of 'empty vanity,' and the deficiency is undue humility; and as we said liberality was related to magnificence, differing from it by dealing with small sums, so there is a state similarly related to proper pride, being concerned with small honours while that is concerned with great. For it is possible to desire honour as one ought, and more than one ought, and less, and the man who exceeds in his desires is called ambitious, the man who falls short unambitious, while the intermediate person has no name. The dispositions also are nameless, except that that of the ambitious man is called ambition. Hence the people who are at the extremes lay claim to the middle place; and we ourselves sometimes call the intermediate person ambitious and sometimes unambitious, and sometimes praise the ambitious man and sometimes the unambitious....

There are also means in the passions and concerned with the passions; since shame is not a virtue, and yet praise is extended to the modest man. For even in these matters one man is said to be intermediate, and another to exceed, as for instance the bashful man who is ashamed of everything; while he who falls short or is not ashamed of anything at all is shameless, and the intermediate person is modest. Righteous indignation is a mean between envy and spite, and these states are concerned with the pain and pleasure that are felt at the fortunes of our neighbours; the man who is characterized by righteous indignation is pained at undeserved good fortune, the envious man, going beyond him, is pained at all good fortune, and the spiteful man falls so far short of being pained that he even rejoices....

9. That moral virtue is a mean, then, and in what sense it is so, and that it is a mean between two vices, the one involving excess, the other deficiency, and that it is such because its character is to aim at what is intermediate in passions and in actions, has been sufficiently stated. Hence also it is no easy task to be good. For in everything it is no easy task to find the middle, e.g. to find the middle of a circle is not for every one but for him who knows; so, too, any one can get angry — that is easy — or give or spend money; but to do this to the right person, to the right extent, at the right time, with the right motive, and in the right way, that is not for every one, nor is it easy; wherefore goodness is both rare and laudable and noble....

Book X

6. ... What remains is to discuss in outline the nature of happiness, since this is what we state the end of human nature to be. Our discussion will be more concise if we first sum up what we have said already. We said, then, that it is not a disposition; for if it were it might belong to some one who was asleep throughout his life, living the life of a plant, or, again, to some one who was suffering the greatest misfortunes. If these implica-

tions are unacceptable, and we must rather class happiness as an activity, as we have said before, and if some activities are necessary, and desirable for the sake of something else, while others are so in themselves, evidently happiness must be placed among those desirable in themselves, not among those desirable for the sake of something else; for happiness does not lack anything, but is self-sufficient. Now those activities are desirable in themselves from which nothing is sought beyond the activity. And of this nature virtuous actions are thought to be; for to do noble and good deeds is a thing desirable for its own sake.

Pleasant amusements also are thought to be of this nature; we choose them not for the sake of other things; for we are injured rather than benefited by them, since we are led to neglect our bodies and our property. But most of the people who are deemed happy take refuge in such pastimes, which is the reason why those who are ready-witted at them are highly esteemed at the courts of tyrants; they make themselves pleasant companions in the tyrants' favourite pursuits, and that is the sort of man they want. Now these things are thought to be of the nature of happiness because people in despotic positions spend their leisure in them, but perhaps such people prove nothing; for virtue and reason, from which good activities flow, do not depend on despotic position; nor, if these people, who have never tasted pure and generous pleasure, take refuge in the bodily pleasures, should these for that reason be thought more desirable; for boys, too, think the things that are valued among themselves are the best. It is to be expected, then, that, as different things seem valuable to boys and to men, so they should to bad men and to good. Now . . . those things are both valuable and pleasant which are such to the good man; and to each man the activity in accordance with his own disposition is most desirable, and, therefore, to the good man that which is in accordance with virtue. Happiness, therefore, does not lie in amusement; it would, indeed, be strange if the end were amusement, and one were to take trouble and suffer hardship all one's life in order to amuse oneself. For, in a word, everything that we choose we choose for the sake of something else — except happiness, which is an end. Now to exert oneself and work for the sake of amusement seems silly and utterly childish. But to amuse oneself in order that one may exert oneself, as Anacharsis puts it, seems right; for amusement is a sort of relaxation, and we need relaxation because we cannot work continuously. Relaxation, then, is not an end; for it is taken for the sake of activity.

The happy life is thought to be virtuous; now a virtuous life requires exertion, and does not consist in amusement. And we say that serious things are better than laughable things and those connected with amusement, and that the activity of the better of any two things — whether it be two elements of our being or two men — is the more serious; but the activity of the better is *ipso facto* superior and more of the nature of happiness. And any chance person — even a slave — can enjoy the bodily pleasures no less than the best man; but no one assigns to a slave a share in happiness — unless he assigns to him also a share in human life. For happiness does not lie in such occupations, but, as we have said before, in virtuous activities.

7. If happiness is activity in accordance with virtue, it is reasonable that it should be in accordance with the highest virtue; and this will be that of the best thing in us. Whether it be reason or something else that is this element which is thought to be our natural ruler and guide and to take thought of things noble and divine, whether it be itself also divine or only the most divine element in us, the activity of this in accordance with its proper virtue will be perfect happiness. That this activity is contemplative we have already said.

Now this would seem to be in agreement both with what we said before and with the truth. For, firstly, this activity is the best (since not only is reason the best thing in us, but the objects of reason are the best of knowable objects); and, secondly, it is the most continuous, since we can contemplate truth more continuously than we can *do* anything. And we think happiness has pleasure mingled with it, but the activity of philosophic wisdom is admittedly the pleasantest of virtuous activities; at all events the pursuit of it is thought to offer pleasures marvellous for their purity and their enduringness, and it is to be expected that those who know will pass their time more pleasantly than those who inquire. And the self-sufficiency that is spoken of must belong to the contemplative activity. For while a philosopher, as well as a just man or one possessing any other virtue, needs the necessaries of life, when they are sufficiently equipped with things of that sort the just man needs people towards whom and with whom he shall act justly, and the temperate man, the brave man, and each of the others is in the same case, but the philosopher, even when by himself, can contemplate truth, and the better the wiser he is; he can perhaps do so better if he has fellow-workers, but still he is the most self-sufficient. And this activity alone would seem to be loved for its own sake; for nothing arises from it apart from the contemplating, while from practical activities we gain more or less apart from the action. And happiness is thought to depend on leisure; for we are busy that we may have leisure, and make war that we may live in peace. Now the activity of the practical virtues is exhibited in political or military affairs, but the actions concerned with these seem to be unleisurely. Warlike actions are completely so (for no one chooses to be at war, or provokes war, for the sake of being at war; any one would seem absolutely murderous if he were to make enemies of his friends in order to bring about battle and slaughter); but the action of the statesman is also unleisurely, and — apart from the political action itself — aims at despotic power and honours, or at all events happiness, for him and his fellow citizens — a happiness different from political action, and evidently sought as being different. So if among virtuous actions political and military actions are distinguished by nobility and greatness, and these are unleisurely and aim at an end and are not desirable for their own sake, but the activity of reason, which is contemplative, seems both to be superior in serious worth and to aim at no end beyond itself, and to have its pleasure proper to itself (and this augments the activity), and the self-sufficiency, leisureliness, unweariedness (so far as this is possible for man), and all the other attributes ascribed to the supremely happy man are evidently those connected with this activity, it follows that this will be the complete happiness of man, if it be allowed a complete term of life (for none of the attributes of happiness is *in*complete).

But such a life would be too high for man; for it is not in so far as he is man that he will live so, but in so far as something divine is present in him; and by so much as this is superior to our composite nature is its activity superior to that which is the exercise of the other kind of virtue. If reason is divine, then, in comparison with man, the life according to it is divine in comparison with human life. But we must not follow those who advise us, being men, to think of human things, and being mortal, of mortal things, but must, so far as we can, make ourselves immortal, and strain every nerve to live in accordance with the best thing in us; for even if it be small in bulk, much more does it in power and worth surpass everything. This would seem, too, to be each man himself, since it is the authoritative and better part of him. It would seem strange, then, if he were to choose not the life of his self but that of something else. And what we said before will apply now; that which is proper to each thing is by nature best and most pleasant for each thing; for man, therefore, the life according to reason is best and pleasantest, since reason more than anything else *is* man. This life therefore is also the happiest.

8. But in a secondary degree the life in accordance with the other kind of virtue is happy; for the activities in accordance with this befit our human estate. Just and brave acts, and other virtuous acts, we do in relation to each other, observing our respective duties with regard to contracts and services and all manner of actions and with regard to passions; and all of these seem to be typically human. Some of them seem

even to arise from the body, and virtue of character to be in many ways bound up with the passions. Practical wisdom, too, is linked to virtue of character, and this to practical wisdom, since the principles of practical wisdom are in accordance with the moral virtues and rightness in morals is in accordance with practical wisdom. Being connected with the passions also, the moral virtues must belong to our composite nature; and the virtues of our composite nature are human; so, therefore, are the life and the happiness which correspond to these. The excellence of the reason is a thing apart; we must be content to say this much about it, for to describe it precisely is a task greater than our purpose requires. It would seem, however, also to need external equipment but little, or less than moral virtue does. Grant that both need the necessaries, and do so equally, even if the stateman's work is the more concerned with the body and things of that sort; for there will be little difference there; but in what they need for the exercise of their activities there will be much difference. The liberal man will need money for the doing of his liberal deeds, and the just man too will need it for the returning of services (for wishes are hard to discern, and even people who are not just pretend to wish to act justly); and the brave man will need power if he is to accomplish any of the acts that correspond to his virtue, and the temperate man will need opportunity; for how else is either he or any of the others to be recognized? It is debated, too, whether the will or the deed is more essential to virtue, which is assumed to involve both; it is surely clear that its perfection involves both; but for deeds many things are needed, and more, the greater and nobler the deeds are. But the man who is contemplating the truth needs no such thing, at least with a view to the exercise of his activity; indeed they are, one may say, even hindrances, at all events to his contemplation; but in so far as he is a man and lives with a number of people, he chooses to do virtuous acts; he will therefore need such aids to living a human life.

But that perfect happiness is a contemplative activity will appear from the following considerations as well. We assume the gods to be above all other beings blessed and happy; but what sort of actions must we assign to them? Acts of justice? Will not the gods seem absurd if they make contracts and return deposits, and so on? Acts of a brave man, then, confronting dangers and running risks because it is noble to do so? Or liberal acts? To whom will they give? It will be strange if they are really to have money or anything of the kind. And what would their temperate acts be? Is not such praise tasteless, since they have no bad appetites? If we were to run through them all, the circumstances of action would be found trivial and unworthy of gods. Still, every one supposes that they *live* and therefore that they are active; we cannot suppose them to sleep like Endymion. Now if you take away from a living being action, and still more production, what is left but contemplation? Therefore the activity of God, which surpasses all others in blessedness, must be contemplative; and of human activities, therefore, that which is most akin to this must be most of the nature of happiness.

This is indicated, too, by the fact that the other animals have no share in happiness, being completely deprived of such activity. For while the whole life of the gods is blessed, and that of men too in so far as some likeness of such activity belongs to them, none of the other animals is happy, since they in no way share in contemplation. Happiness extends, then, just so far as contemplation does, and those to whom contemplation more fully belongs are more truly happy, not as a mere concomitant but in virtue of the contemplation; for this is in itself precious. Happiness, therefore, must be some form of contemplation.

But, being a man, one will also need external prosperity; for our nature is not self-sufficient for the purpose of contemplation, but our body also must be healthy and must have food and other attention. Still, we must not think that the man who is to be happy will need many things or great things, merely because he cannot be supremely happy without external goods; for self-sufficiency and action do not involve excess, and we can do noble acts without ruling earth and sea; for even with moderate advantages one can act virtuously (this is manifest enough; for private persons are thought to do worthy acts no less than despots — indeed even more); and it is enough that we should have so much as that; for the life of the man who is active in accordance with virtue will be happy.

The Universalizability Criterion

Immanuel Kant
Fundamental Principles of the Metaphysic of Morals

First Section
Transition From the Common Rational Knowledge
of Morality to the Philosophical

[1. *The Good Will*]

Nothing can possibly be conceived in the world, or even out of it, which can be called good, without qualification, except a Good Will. Intelli-

From *Grundlegung zur Metaphysik der Sitten* (1785), trans. T. K. Abbott as *Fundamental Principles of the Metaphysic of Morals* (1st ed., 1873; 6th ed., 1909).

gence, wit, judgment, and the other *talents* of the mind, however they may be named, or courage, resolution, perseverance, as qualities of temperament, are undoubtedly good and desirable in many respects; but these gifts of nature may also become extremely bad and mischievous if the will which is to make use of them, and which, therefore, constitutes what is called *character*, is not good. It is the same with *gifts of fortune.* Power, riches, honour, even health, and the general well-being and contentment with one's condition which is called *happiness*, inspire pride, and often presumption, if there is not a good will to correct the influence of these on the mind, and with this also to rectify the whole principle of acting, and adapt it to its end. The sight of a being who is not adorned with a single feature of a pure and good will, enjoying unbroken prosperity, can never give pleasure to an impartial rational spectator. Thus a good will appears to constitute the indispensable condition even of being worthy of happiness.

There are even some qualities which are of service to this good will itself, and many facilitate its action, yet which have no intrinsic unconditional value, but always presuppose a good will, and this qualifies the esteem that we justly have for them, and does not permit us to regard them as absolutely good. Moderation in the affections and passions, self-control, and calm deliberation are not only good in many respects, but even seem to constitute part of the intrinsic worth of the person; but they are far from deserving to be called good without qualification, although they have been so unconditionally praised by the ancients. For without the principles of a good will, they may become extremely bad; and the coolness of a villain not only makes him far more dangerous, but also directly makes him more abominable in our eyes than he would have been without it.

A good will is good not because of what it performs or effects, not by its aptness for the attainment of some proposed end, but simply by virtue of the volition, that is, it is good in itself, and considered by itself is to be esteemed much higher than all that can be brought about by it in favour of any inclination, nay, even of the sum-total of all inclinations. Even if it should happen that, owing to special disfavour of fortune, or the niggardly provision of a step-motherly nature, this will should wholly lack power to accomplish its purpose, if with its greatest efforts it should yet achieve nothing, and there should remain only the good will (not, to be sure, a mere wish, but the summoning of all means in our power), then, like a jewel, it would still shine by its own light, as a thing which has its whole value in itself. Its usefulness or fruitlessness can neither add to nor take away anything from this value. It would be, as it were, only the setting to enable us to handle it the more conveniently in common

commerce, or to attract to it the attention of those who are not yet connoisseurs, but not to recommend it to true connoisseurs, or to determine
its value.

[2. *The Practical Purpose of Reason*]

There is, however, something so strange in this idea of the absolute value
of the mere will, in which no account is taken of its utility, that notwithstanding the thorough assent of even common reason to the idea, yet a
suspicion must arise that it may perhaps really be the product of mere
high-flown fancy, and that we may have misunderstood the purpose of
nature in assigning reason as the governor of our will. Therefore we will
examine this idea from this point of view.

In the physical constitution of ·an organized being, that is, a being
adapted suitably to the purposes of life, we assume it as a fundamental
principle that no organ for any purpose will be found but what is also the
fittest and best adapted for that purpose. Now in a being which has reason
and a will, if the proper object of nature were its *conservation*, its *welfare*,
in a word, its *happiness*, then nature would have hit upon a very bad
arrangement in selecting the reason of the creature to carry out this
purpose. For all the actions which the creature has to perform with a view
to this purpose, and the whole rule of its conduct, would be far more
surely prescribed to it by instinct, and that end would have been attained
thereby much more certainly than it ever can be by reason. Should reason
have been communicated to this favoured creature over and above, it
must only have served it to contemplate the happy constitution of its
nature, to admire it, to congratulate itself thereon, and to feel thankful
for it to the beneficent cause, but not that it should subject its desires to
that weak and delusive guidance, and meddle bunglingly with the purpose of nature. In a word, nature would have taken care that reason
should not break forth into *practical exercise*, nor have the presumption,
with its weak insight, to think out for itself the plan of happiness, and of
the means of attaining it. Nature would not only have taken on herself
the choice of the ends, but also of the means, and with wise foresight
would have entrusted both to instinct.

And, in fact, we find that the more a cultivated reason applies itself
with deliberate purpose to the enjoyment of life and happiness, so much
the more does the man fail of true satisfaction. And from this circumstance there arises in many, if they are candid enough to confess it, a

certain degree of *misology*, that is, hatred of reason, especially in the case of those who are most experienced in the use of it, because after calculating all the advantages they derive, I do not say from the invention of all the arts of common luxury, but even from the sciences (which seem to them to be after all only a luxury of the understanding), they find that they have, in fact, only brought more trouble on their shoulders, rather than gained in happiness; and they end by envying, rather than despising, the more common stamp of men who keep closer to the guidance of mere instinct, and do not allow their reason much influence on their conduct. And this we must admit, that the judgment of those who would very much lower the lofty eulogies of the advantages which reason gives us in regard to the happiness and satisfaction of life, or who would even reduce them below zero, is by no means morose or ungrateful to the goodness with which the world is governed, but that there lies at the root of these judgments the idea that our existence has a different and far nobler end, for which, and not for happiness, reason is properly intended, and which must, therefore, be regarded as the supreme condition to which the private ends of man must, for the most part, be postponed.

For as reason is not competent to guide the will with certainty in regard to its objects and the satisfaction of all our wants (which it to some extent even multiplies), this being an end to which an implanted instinct would have led with much greater certainty; and since, nevertheless, reason is imparted to us as a practical faculty, i.e. as one which is to have influence on the *will*, therefore, admitting that nature generally in the distribution of her capacities has adapted the means to the end, its true destination must be to produce a *will*, not merely good as a *means* to something else, but *good in itself*, for which reason was absolutely necessary. This will then, though not indeed the sole and complete good, must be the supreme good and the condition of every other, even of the desire of happiness. Under these circumstances, there is nothing inconsistent with the wisdom of nature in the fact that the cultivation of the reason, which is requisite for the first and unconditional purpose, does in many ways interfere, at least in this life, with the attainment of the second, which is always conditional, namely, happiness. Nay, it may even reduce it to nothing, without nature thereby failing of her purpose. For reason recognizes the establishment of a good will as its highest practical destination, and in attaining this purpose is capable only of a satisfaction of its own proper kind, namely, that from the attainment of an end, which end again is determined by reason only, notwithstanding that this may involve many a disappointment to the ends of inclination.

[3. *The Good Will Clarified in Terms of Duty*]

We have then to develop the notion of a will which deserves to be highly esteemed for itself, and is good without a view to anything further, a notion which exists already in the sound natural understanding, requiring rather to be cleared up than to be taught, and which in estimating the value of our actions always takes the first place, and constitutes the condition of all the rest. In order to do this, we will take the notion of duty, which includes that of a good will, although implying certain subjective restrictions and hindrances. These, however, far from concealing it, or rendering it unrecognizable, rather bring it out by contrast, and make it shine forth so much the brighter.

[4. *Acting From Duty*]

I omit here all actions which are already recognized as inconsistent with duty, although they may be useful for this or that purpose, for with these the question whether they are done *from duty* cannot arise at all, since they even conflict with it. I also set aside those actions which really conform to duty, but to which men have *no* direct *inclination*, performing them because they are impelled thereto by some other inclination. For in this case we can readily distinguish whether the action which agrees with duty is done *from duty*, or from a selfish view. It is much harder to make this distinction when the action accords with duty, and the subject has besides a *direct* inclination to it. For example, it is always a matter of duty that a dealer should not overcharge an inexperienced purchaser; and wherever there is much commerce the prudent tradesman does not overcharge, but keeps a fixed price for everyone, so that a child buys of him as well as any other. Men are thus *honestly* served; but this is not enough to make us believe that the tradesman has so acted from duty and from principles of honesty: his own advantage required it; it is out of the question in this case to suppose that he might besides have a direct inclination in favour of the buyers, so that, as it were, from love he should give no advantage to one over another. Accordingly the action was done neither from duty nor from direct inclination, but merely with a selfish view.

On the other hand, it is a duty to maintain one's life; and, in addition, everyone has also a direct inclination to do so. But on this account the often anxious care which most men take for it has no intrinsic worth, and their maxim has no moral import. They preserve their life *as duty requires*, no doubt, but not *because duty requires*. On the other hand, if adversity and hopeless sorrow have completely taken away the relish for life; if the unfortunate one, strong in mind, indignant at his fate rather than desponding or dejected, wishes for death, and yet preserves his life without loving it—not from inclination or fear, but from duty—then his maxim has a moral worth.

To be beneficent when we can is a duty; and besides this, there are many minds so sympathetically constituted that, without any other motive of vanity or self-interest, they find a pleasure in spreading joy around them, and can take delight in the satisfaction of others so far as it is their own work. But I maintain that in such a case an action of this kind, however proper, however amiable it may be, has nevertheless no true moral worth, but is on a level with other inclinations, *e.g.* the inclination to honour, which, if it is happily directed to that which is in fact of public utility and accordant with duty, and consequently honourable, deserves praise and encouragement, but not esteem. For the maxim lacks the moral import, namely, that such actions be done *from duty,* not from inclination. Put the case that the mind of that philanthropist was clouded by sorrow of his own, extinguishing all sympathy with the lot of others, and that while he still has the power to benefit others in distress, he is not touched by their trouble because he is absorbed with his own; and now suppose that he tears himself out of this dead insensibility, and performs the action without any inclination to it, but simply from duty, then first has his action its genuine moral worth. Further still; if nature has put little sympathy in the heart of this or that man; if he, supposed to be an upright man, is by temperament cold and indifferent to the sufferings of others, perhaps because in respect of his own he is provided with the special gift of patience and fortitude, and supposes, or even requires, that others should have the same — and such a man would certainly not be the meanest product of nature — but if nature had not specially framed him for a philanthropist, would he not still find in himself a source from whence to give himself a far higher worth than that of a good-natured temperament could be? Unquestionably. It is just in this that the moral worth of the character is brought out which is incomparably the highest of all, namely, that he is beneficent, not from inclination, but from duty.

To secure one's own happiness is a duty, at least indirectly; for discontent with one's condition, under a pressure of many anxieties and amidst unsatisfied wants, might easily become a great *temptation to transgression of duty.* But here again, without looking to duty, all men have already the strongest and most intimate inclination to happiness, because it is just in this idea that all inclinations are combined in one total. But the precept of happiness is often of such a sort that it greatly interferes with some inclinations, and yet a man cannot form any definite and certain conception of the sum of satisfaction of all of them which is called happiness. It is not then to be wondered at that a single inclination, definite both as to what it promises and as to the time within which it can be gratified, is often able to overcome such a fluctuating idea, and that a gouty patient, for instance, can choose to enjoy what he likes, and to suffer what he may, since, according to his calculation, on this occasion at least, he has [only] not sacrificed the enjoyment of the present moment to a possibly mistaken expectation of a happiness which is supposed to be found in health. But even in this case, if the general desire for happiness did not influence his will, and supposing that in this particular case health was not a necessary element in this calculation, there yet remains in this, as in all other cases, this law, namely, that he should promote his happiness not from inclination but from duty, and by this would his conduct first acquire true moral worth.

It is in this manner undoubtedly, that we are to understand those passages of Scripture also in which we are commanded to love our neighbor, even our enemy. For love, as an affection, cannot be commanded, but beneficence for duty's sake may; even though we are not impelled to it by any inclination — nay, are even repelled by a natural and unconquerable aversion. This is *practical* love, and not *pathological* — a love which is seated in the will, and not in the propensions of sense — in principles of action and not of tender sympathy; and it is this love alone which can be commanded.

[5. *The Maxims of Action*]

The second[1] proposition is: That an action done from duty derives its moral worth, *not from the purpose* which is to be attained by it, but from the maxim by which it is determined, and therefore does not depend on the realization of the object of the action, but merely on the *principle of volition* by which the action has taken place, without regard to any object of desire. It is clear from what precedes that the purposes which we may have in view in our actions, or their effects regarded as ends and springs of the will, cannot give to actions any unconditional or moral worth. In what, then, can their worth lie, if it is not to consist in the will and in reference to its expected effect? It cannot lie anywhere but in the *principle of the will* without regard to the ends which can be attained by the action.

---

[1]The first proposition was that to have moral worth an action must be done from duty. — TRANS.

For the will stands between its *à priori* principle, which is formal, and its *à posteriori* spring, which is material, as between two roads, and as it must be determined by something, it follows that it must be determined by the formal principle of volition when an action is done from duty, in which case every material principle has been withdrawn from it.

[6. *Respect for Law*]

The third proposition, which is a consequence of the two preceding, I would express thus: *Duty is the necessity of acting from respect for the law.* I may have *inclination* for an object as the effect of my proposed action, but I cannot have *respect* for it, just for this reason, that it is an effect and not an energy of will. Similarly, I cannot have respect for inclination, whether my own or another's; I can at most, if my own, approve it; if another's, sometimes even love it; *i.e.* look on it as favourable to my own interest. It is only what is connected with my will as a principle, by no means as an effect — what does not subserve my inclination, but overpowers it, or at least in case of choice excludes it from its calculation — in other words, simply the law of itself, which can be an object of respect, and hence a command. Now an action done from duty must wholly exclude the influence of inclination, and with it every object of will, so that nothing remains which can determine the will except objectively the *law,* and subjectively *pure respect* for this practical law, and consequently the maxim[2] that I should follow this law even to the thwarting of all my inclinations.

Thus the moral worth of an action does not lie in the effect expected from it, nor in any principle of action which requires to borrow its motive from this expected effect. For all these effects — agreeableness of one's condition, and even the promotion of the happiness of others — could have been also brought about by other causes, so that for this there would have been no need of the will of a rational being; whereas it is in this alone that the supreme and unconditional good can be found. The pre-eminent good which we call moral can therefore consist in nothing else than *the conception of law* in itself, *which certainly is only possible in a rational being,* in so far as this conception, and not the expected effect, determines the will. This is a good which is already present in the person

---

[2]A *maxim* is the subjective principle of volition. The objective principle (*i.e.* that which would also serve subjectively as a practical principle to all rational beings if reason had full power over the faculty of desire) is the practical *law.*

who acts accordingly, and we have not to wait for it to appear first in the result.

[7. *The Categorical Imperative*]

But what sort of law can that be, the conception of which must determine the will, even without paying any regard to the effect expected from it, in order that this will may be called good absolutely and without qualification? As I have deprived the will of every impulse which could arise to it from obedience to any law, there remains nothing but the universal conformity of its actions to law in general, which alone is to serve the will as a principle, *i.e.* I am never to act otherwise than so *that I could also will that my maxim should become a universal law*. Here, now, it is the simple conformity to law in general, without assuming any particular law applicable to certain actions, that serves the will as its principle, and must so serve it, if duty is not to be a vain delusion and a chimerical notion. The common reason of men in its practical judgments perfectly coincides with this, and always has in view the principle here suggested. Let the question be, for example: May I when in distress make a promise with the intention not to keep it? I readily distinguish here between the two significations which the question may have: whether it is prudent, or whether it is right, to make a false promise? The former may undoubtedly often be the case. I see clearly indeed that it is not enough to extricate myself from a present difficulty by means of this subterfuge, but it must be well considered whether there may not hereafter spring from this lie much greater inconvenience than that from which I now free myself, and as, with all my supposed *cunning*, the consequences cannot be so easily foreseen but that credit once lost may be much more injurious to me than any mischief which I seek to avoid at present, it should be considered whether it would not be more *prudent* to act herein according to a universal maxim, and to make it a habit to promise nothing except with the intention of keeping it. But it is soon clear to me that such a maxim will still only be based on the fear of consequences. Now it is a wholly different thing to be truthful from duty, and to be so from apprehension of injurious consequences. In the first case, the very notion of the action already implies a law for me; in the second case, I must first look about elsewhere to see what results may be combined with it which would affect myself. For to deviate from the principle of duty is beyond all doubt wicked; but to be unfaithful to my maxim of prudence may often be very advantageous to me, although to abide by it is certainly safer. The shortest way, however, and an unerring one, to discover the answer to this question whether a lying promise is consistent with duty, is to ask myself,

Should I be content that my maxim (to extricate myself from difficulty by a false promise) should hold good as a universal law, for myself as well as for others? and should I be able to say to myself, "Every one may make a deceitful promise when he finds himself in a difficulty from which he cannot otherwise extricate himself"? Then I presently become aware that while I can will the lie, I can by no means will that lying should be a universal law. For with such a law there would be no promises at all, since it would be in vain to allege my intention in regard to my future actions to those who would not believe this allegation, or if they over-hastily did so, would pay me back in my own coin. Hence my maxim, as soon as it should be made a universal law, would necessarily destroy itself.

I do not, therefore, need any far-reaching penetration to discern what I have to do in order that my will may be morally good. Inexperienced in the course of the world, incapable of being prepared for all its contingencies, I only ask myself: Canst thou also will that thy maxim should be a universal law? If not, then it must be rejected, and that not because of a disadvantage accruing from it to myself or even to others, but because it cannot enter as a principle into a possible universal legislation, and reason extorts from me immediate respect for such legislation. I do not indeed as yet *discern* on what this respect is based (this the philosopher may inquire), but at least I understand this, that it is an estimation of the worth which far outweighs all worth of what is recommended by inclination, and that the necessity of acting from *pure* respect for the practical law is what constitutes duty, to which every other motive must give place, because it is the condition of a will being good *in itself,* and the worth of such a will is above everything.

Thus, then, without quitting the moral knowledge of common human reason, we have arrived at its principle. And although, no doubt, common men do not conceive it in such an abstract and universal form, yet they always have it really before their eyes, and use it as the standard of their decision. . . .

Second Section
Transition From Popular Moral Philosophy
to the Metaphysics of Morals

[1. *Morality Not Derived From Examples*]

If we have hitherto drawn our notion of duty from the common use of our practical reason, it is by no means to be inferred that we have treated it as an empirical notion. On the contrary, if we attend to the experience of men's conduct, we meet frequent and, as we ourselves allow, just complaints that one cannot find a single certain example of the disposition to act from pure duty. Although many things are done in *conformity* with what *duty* prescribes, it is nevertheless always doubtful whether they are done strictly *from duty,* so as to have a moral worth. Hence there have at all times been philosophers who have altogether denied that this disposition actually exists at all in human actions, and have ascribed everything to a more or less refined self-love. Not that they have on that account questioned the soundness of the conception of morality; on the contrary, they spoke with sincere regret of the frailty and corruption of human nature, which though noble enough to take as its rule an idea so worthy of respect, is yet too weak to follow it, and employs reason, which ought to give it the law only for the purpose of providing for the interest of the inclinations, whether singly or at the best in the greatest possible harmony with one another.

In fact, it is absolutely impossible to make out by experience with complete certainty a single case in which the maxim of an action, however right in itself, rested simply on moral grounds and on the conception of duty. Sometimes it happens that with the sharpest self-examination we can find nothing beside the moral principle of duty which could have been powerful enough to move us to this or that action and to so great a sacrifice; yet we cannot from this infer with certainty that it was not really some secret impulse of self-love, under the false appearance of duty, that was the actual determining cause of the will. We like then to flatter ourselves by falsely taking credit for a more noble motive; whereas in fact we can never, even by the strictest examination, get completely behind the secret springs of action; since, when the question is of moral worth, it is not with the actions which we see that we are concerned, but with those inward principles of them which we do not see.

Moreover, we cannot better serve the wishes of those who ridicule all morality as a mere chimera of human imagination overstepping itself from vanity, than by conceding to them that notions of duty must be drawn only from experience (as from indolence, people are ready to think is also the case with all other notions); for this is to prepare for them a certain triumph. I am willing to admit out of love of humanity that even most of our actions are correct, but if we look closer at them we everywhere come upon the dear self which is always prominent, and it is this they have in view, and not the strict command of duty which would often require self-denial. Without being an enemy of virtue, a cool observer, one that does not mistake the wish for good, however lively, for its reality, may sometimes doubt whether true virtue is actually found anywhere in the world, and this especially as years increase and the judgment is partly made wiser by experience, and partly also more acute in observation. This being so, nothing can secure us from falling away altogether from our ideas of duty, or maintain in the soul a well-grounded respect for its law, but the clear conviction that although there should never have been actions which really sprang from such pure sources, yet whether this or that takes place is not at all the question; but that reason of itself, independent on all experience, ordains what ought to take place, that accordingly actions of which perhaps the world has hitherto never given an example, the feasibility even of which might be very much doubted by one who founds everything on experience, are nevertheless inflexibly commanded by reason; that, [e.g.], even though there might never yet have been a sincere friend, yet not a whit the less is pure sincerity in friendship required of every man, because, prior to all experience, this duty is involved as duty in the idea of a reason determining the will by *à priori* principles.

When we add further that, unless we deny that the notion of morality has any truth or reference to any possible object, we must admit that its law must be valid, not merely for men, but for all *rational creatures generally*, not merely under certain contingent conditions or with exceptions, but *with absolute necessity,* then it is clear that no experience could enable us to infer even the possibility of such apodictic laws. For with what right could we bring into unbounded respect as a universal precept for every rational nature that which perhaps holds only under the contingent conditions of humanity? Or how could laws of the determination of *our* will be regarded as laws of the determination of the will of rational beings generally, and for us only as such, if they were merely empirical, and did not take their origin wholly *à priori* from pure but practical reason?

Nor could anything be more fatal to morality than that we should wish to derive it from examples. For every example of it that is set before me must be first itself tested by principles of morality, whether it is worthy to serve as an original example, *i.e.* as a pattern, but by no means can it authoritatively furnish the conception of morality. Even the Holy One of the Gospels must first be compared with our ideal of moral perfection before we can recognize Him as such; and so He says of Himself, "Why call ye Me [whom you see] good; none is good [the model of good] but God only [whom ye do not see]?" But whence have we the conception of

God as the supreme good? Simply from the *idea* of moral perfection, which reason frames *à priori,* and connects inseparably with the notion of a free will. Imitation finds no place at all in morality, and examples serve only for encouragement, *i.e.* they put beyond doubt the feasibility of what the law commands, they make visible that which the practical rule expresses more generally, but they can never authorize us to set aside the true original which lies in reason, and to guide ourselves by examples. . . .

[2. *The Relation of Reason to Will*]

Everything in nature works according to laws. Rational beings alone have the faculty of acting according *to the conception* of laws, that is according to principles, *i.e.* have a *will.* Since the deduction of actions from principles requires *reason,* the will is nothing but practical reason. If reason infallibly determines the will, then the actions of such a being which are recognized as objectively necessary are subjectively necessary also, *i.e.* the will is a faculty to choose *that only* which reason independent on inclination recognizes as practically necessary, *i.e.* as good. But if reason of itself does not sufficiently determine the will, if the latter is subject also to subjective conditions (particular impulses) which do not always coincide with the objective conditions; in a word, if the will does not *in itself* completely accord with reason (which is actually the case with men), then the actions which objectively are recognized as necessary are subjectively contingent, and the determination of such a will according to objective laws is *obligation,* that is to say, the relation of the objective laws to a will that is not thoroughly good is conceived as the determination of the will of a rational being by principles of reason, but which the will from its nature does not of necessity follow.

The conception of an objective principle, in so far as it is obligatory for a will, is called a command (of reason), and the formula of the command is called an Imperative.

All imperatives are expressed by the word *ought* [or *shall*], and thereby indicate the relation of an objective law of reason to a will, which from its subjective constitution is not necessarily determined by it (an obligation). They say that something would be good to do or to forbear, but they say it to a will which does not always do a thing because it is conceived to be good to do it. That is practically *good,* however, which determines the will by means of the conceptions of reason, and consequently not from subjective causes, but objectively, that is on principles which are valid for every rational being as such. It is distinguished from the *pleasant*, as that which influences the will only by means of sensation from merely subjective causes, valid only for the sense of this or that one, and not as a principle of reason, which holds for every one.

A perfectly good will would therefore be equally subject to objective laws (viz. laws of good), but could not be conceived as *obliged* thereby to act lawfully, because of itself from its subjective constitution it can only be determined by the conception of good. Therefore no imperatives hold for the Divine will, or in general for a *holy* will; *ought* is here out of place, because the volition is already of itself necessarily in unison with the law. Therefore imperatives are only formulae to express the relation of objective laws of all volition to the subjective imperfection of the will of this or that rational being, *e.g.* the human will.

[3. *Two Kinds of Imperatives*]

Now all *imperatives* command either *hypothetically* or *categorically*. The former represent the practical necessity of a possible action as means to something else that is willed (or at least which one might possibly will). The categorical imperative would be that which represented an action as necessary of itself without reference to another end, *i.e.,* as objectively necessary.

Since every practical law represents a possible action as good, and on this account, for a subject who is practically determinable by reason, necessary, all imperatives are formulae determining an action which is necessary according to the principle of a will good in some respects. If now the action is good only as a means *to something else*, then the imperative is *hypothetical*; if it is conceived as good *in itself* and consequently as being necessarily the principle of a will which of itself conforms to reason, then it is *categorical*.

Thus the imperative declares what action possible by me would be good, and presents the practical rule in relation to a will which does not forthwith perform an action simply because it is good, whether because the subject does not always know that it is good, or because, even if it knows this, yet its maxims might be opposed to the objective principles of practical reason.

Accordingly the hypothetical imperative only says that the action is good for some purpose, *possible* or *actual*. In the first case it is a Problematical, in the second an Assertorial practical principle. The categorical imperative which declares an action to be objectively necessary in itself without reference to any purpose, *i.e.* without any other end, is valid as an Apodictic (practical) principle.

Whatever is possible only by the power of some rational being may also be conceived as a possible purpose of some will; and therefore the principles of action as regards the means necessary to attain some possible purpose are in fact infinitely numerous. All sciences have a practical part, consisting of problems expressing that some end is possible for us, and of imperatives directing how it may be attained. These may, therefore, be called in general imperatives of Skill. Here there is no question whether the end is rational and good, but only what one must do in order to attain it. The precepts for the physician to make his patient thoroughly healthy, and for a poisoner to ensure certain death, are of equal value in this respect, that each serves to effect its purpose perfectly. Since in early youth it cannot be known what ends are likely to occur to us in the course of life, parents seek to have their children taught a *great many things,* and provide for their *skill* in the use of means for all sorts of arbitrary ends, of none of which can they determine whether it may not perhaps hereafter be an object to their pupil, but which it is at all events *possible* that he might aim at; and this anxiety is so great that they commonly neglect to form and correct their judgment on the value of the things which may be chosen as ends.

There is *one* end, however, which may be assumed to be actually such to all rational beings (so far as imperatives apply to them, viz. as dependent beings), and, therefore, one purpose which they not merely *may* have, but which we may with certainty assume that they all actually *have* by a natural necessity, and this is *happiness.* The hypothetical imperative which expresses the practical necessity of an action as means to the advancement of happiness is Assertorial. We are not to present it as necessary for an uncertain and merely possible purpose, but for a purpose which we may presuppose with certainty and *à priori* in every man, because it belongs to his being. Now skill in the choice of means to his own greatest well-being may be called *prudence*, in the narrowest sense. And thus the imperative which refers to the choice of means to one's own happiness, *i.e.* the precept of prudence, is still always *hypothetical*; the action is not commanded absolutely, but only as means to another purpose.

Finally, there is an imperative which commands a certain conduct immediately, without having as its condition any other purpose to be attained by it. This imperative is Categorical. It concerns not the matter of the action, or its intended result, but its form and the principle of which it is itself a result; and what is essentially good in it consists in the mental disposition, let the consequence be what it may. This imperative may be called that of Morality. . . .

When I conceive a hypothetical imperative, in general I do not know beforehand what it will contain until I am given the condition. But when I conceive a categorical imperative, I know at once what it contains. For as the imperative contains besides the law only the necessity that the maxims[3] shall conform to this law, while the law contains no conditions restricting it, there remains nothing but the general statement that the maxim of the action should conform to a universal law, and it is this conformity alone that the imperative properly represents as necessary.

[4. *The First Formulation of The Categorical Imperative*]

There is therefore but one categorical imperative, namely, this: *Act only on that maxim whereby thou canst at the same time will that it should become a universal law.*

Now if all imperatives of duty can be deduced from this one imperative as from their principle, then, although it should remain undecided whether what is called duty is not merely a vain notion, yet at least we shall be able to show what we understand by it and what this notion means.

Since the universality of the law according to which effects are produced constitutes what is properly called *nature* in the most general sense (as to form), that is the existence of things so far as it is determined by general laws, the imperative of duty may be expressed thus: *Act as if the maxim of thy action were to become by thy will a universal law of nature.*

[5. *Four Sample Applications*]

We will now enumerate a few duties, adopting the usual division of them into duties to ourselves and to others, and into perfect and imperfect duties.[4]

---

[3]A *maxim* is a subjective principle of action, and must be distinguished from the *objective principle,* namely, practical law. The former contains the practical rule set by reason according to the conditions of the subject (often its ignorance or its inclinations), so that it is the principle on which the subject *acts;* but the law is the objective principle valid for every rational being, and is the principle on which it *ought to act* that is an imperative.

[4]It must be noted here that I reserve the division of duties for a future *metaphysic of morals;* so that I give it here only as an arbitrary one (in order to arrange my examples). For the rest, I understand by a perfect duty one that admits no exception in favour of inclination, and then I have not merely external but also internal perfect duties. . . .

1. A man reduced to despair by a series of misfortunes feels wearied of life, but is still so far in possession of his reason that he can ask himself whether it would not be contrary to his duty to himself to take his own life. Now he inquires whether the maxim of his action could become a universal law of nature. His maxim is: From self-love I adopt it as a principle to shorten my life when its longer duration is likely to bring more evil than satisfaction. It is asked then simply whether this principle founded on self-love can become a universal law of nature. Now we see at once that a system of nature of which it should be a law to destroy life by means of the very feeling whose special nature it is to impel to the improvement of life would contradict itself, and therefore could not exist as a system of nature; hence that maxim cannot possibly exist as a universal law of nature, and consequently would be wholly inconsistent with the supreme principle of all duty.

2. Another finds himself forced by necessity to borrow money. He knows that he will not be able to repay it, but sees also that nothing will be lent to him, unless he promies stoutly to repay it in a definite time. He desires to make this promise, but he has still so much conscience as to ask himself: Is it not unlawful and inconsistent with duty to get out of a difficulty in this way? Suppose, however, that he resolves to do so, then the maxim of his action would be expressed thus: When I think myself in want of money, I will borrow money and promise to repay it, although I know that I never can do so. Now this principle of self-love or of one's own advantage may perhaps be consistent with my whole future welfare; but the question now is, Is it right? I change then the suggestion of self-love into a universal law, and state the question thus: How would it be if my maxim were a universal law? Then I see at once that it could never hold as a universal law of nature, but would necessarily contradict itself. For supposing it to be a universal law that everyone when he thinks him-self in a difficulty should be able to promise whatever he pleases, with the purpose of not keeping his promise, the promise itself would become impossible, as well as the end that one might have in view in it, since no one would consider that anything was promised to him, but would ridicule all such statements as vain pretences.

3. A third finds in himself a talent which with the help of some culture might make him a useful man in many respects. But he finds himself in comfortable circumstances, and prefers to indulge in pleasure rather than to take pains in enlarging and improving his happy natural capacities. He asks, however, whether his maxim of neglect of his natural gifts, besides agreeing with his inclination to indulgence, agrees also with

what is called duty. He sees then that a system of nature could indeed subsist with such a universal law although men (like the South Sea islanders) should let their talents rest, and resolve to devote their lives merely to idleness, amusement, and propagation of their species — in a word, to enjoyment; but he cannot possibly *will* that this should be a universal law of nature, or be implanted in us as such by a natural instinct. For, as a rational being, he necessarily wills that his faculties be developed, since they serve him, and have been given him, for all sorts of possible purposes.

4. A fourth, who is in prosperity, while he sees that others have to contend with great wretchedness and that he could help them, thinks: What concern is it of mine? Let everyone be as happy as Heaven pleases, or as he can make himself; I will take nothing from him nor even envy him, only I do not wish to contribute anything to his welfare or to his assistance in distress! Now no doubt if such a mode of thinking were a universal law, the human race might very well subsist, and doubtless even better than in a state in which everyone talks of sympathy and good-will, or even takes care occasionally to put it into practice, but, on the other side, also cheats when he can, betrays the rights of men, or otherwise violates them. But although it is possible that a universal law of nature might exist in accordance with that maxim, it is impossible to *will* that such a principle should have the universal validity of a law of nature. For a will which resolved this would contradict itself, inasmuch as many cases might occur in which one would have need of the love and sympathy of others, and in which, by such a law of nature, sprung from his own will, he would deprive himself of all hope of the aid he desires.

These are a few of the many actual duties, or at least what we regard as such, which obviously fall into two classes on the one principle that we have laid down. We must be *able to will* that a maxim of our action should be a universal law. This is the canon of the moral appreciation of the action generally. Some actions are of such a character that their maxim cannot without contradiction be even *conceived* as a universal law of nature, far from it being possible that we should *will* that it *should* be so. In others this intrinsic impossibility is not found, but still it is impossible to *will* that their maxim should be raised to the universality of a law of nature, since such a will would contradict itself. It is easily seen that the former violate strict or rigorous (inflexible) duty; the latter only laxer (meritorious) duty. Thus it has been completely shown by these examples how all duties depend as regards the nature of the obligation (not the object of the action) on the same principle.

[6. *No Exceptions In One's Favour*]

If now we attend to ourselves on occasion of any transgression of duty, we shall find that we in fact do not will that our maxim should be a universal law, for that is impossible for us; on the contrary, we will that the opposite should remain a universal law, only we assume the liberty of making an *exception* in our own favour or (just for this time only) in favour of our inclination. Consequently if we considered all cases from one and the same point of view, namely, that of reason, we should find a contradiction in our own will, namely, that a certain principle should be objectively necessary as a universal law, and yet subjectively should not be universal, but admit of exceptions. As, however, we at one moment regard our action from the point of view of a will wholly conformed to reason, and then again look at the same action from the point of view of a will affected by inclination, there is not really any contradiction, but an antagonism of inclination to the precept of reason, whereby the universality of the principle is changed into a mere generality, so that the practical principle of reason shall meet the maxim half way. Now, although this cannot be justified in our own impartial judgment, yet it proves that we do really recognize the validity of the categorical imperative and (with all respect for it) only allow ourselves a few exceptions, which we think unimportant and forced from us. . . .

[7. *The Second Formulation of The Categorical Imperative*]

The will is conceived as a faculty of determining oneself to action *in accordance with the conception of certain laws*. And such a faculty can be found only in rational beings. Now that which serves the will as the objective ground of its self-determination is the *end*, and if this is assigned by reason alone, it must hold for all rational beings. On the other hand, that which merely contains the ground of possibility of the action of which the effect is the end, this is called the *means*. The subjective ground of the desire is the *spring*, the objective ground of the volition is the *motive*; hence the distinction between subjective ends which rest on springs, and objective ends which depend on motives valid for every rational being. Practical principles are *formal* when they abstract from all subjective ends; they are *material* when they assume these, and therefore particular springs of action. The ends which a rational being proposes to himself at pleasure as *effects* of his actions (material ends) are all only relative, for it is only their relation to the particular desires of the subject that gives them their worth, which therefore cannot furnish principles universal and necessary for all rational beings and for every volition, that is to say practical laws. Hence all these relative ends can give rise only to hypothetical imperatives.

Supposing, however, that there were something *whose existence* has *in itself* an absolute worth, something which, being *an end in itself*, could be a source of definite laws, then in this and this alone would lie the source of a possible categorical imperative, *i.e.* a practical law.

Now I say: man and generally any rational being *exists* as an end in himself, *not merely as a means* to be arbitrarily used by this or that will, but in all his actions, whether they concern himself or other rational beings, must be always regarded at the same time as an end. All objects of the inclinations have only a conditional worth; for if the inclinations and the wants founded on them did not exist, then their object would be without value. But the inclinations themselves being sources of want are so far from having an absolute worth for which they should be desired, that, on the contrary, it must be the universal wish of every rational being to be wholly free from them. Thus the worth of any object which is *to be acquired* by our action is always conditional. Beings whose existence depends not on our will but on nature's, have nevertheless, if they are rational beings, only a relative value as means, and are therefore called *things*; rational beings, on the contrary, are called *persons*, because their very nature points them out as ends in themselves, that is as something which must not be used merely as means, and so far therefore restricts freedom of action (and is an object of respect). These, therefore, are not merely subjective ends whose existence has a worth *for us* as an effect of our action, but *objective ends*, that is things whose existence is an end in itself: an end moreover for which no other can be substituted, which they should subserve *merely* as means, for otherwise nothing whatever would possess *absolute worth*; but if all worth were conditioned and therefore contingent, then there would be no supreme practical principle of reason whatever.

If then there is a supreme practical principle or, in respect of the human will, a categorical imperative, it must be one which, being drawn from the conception of that which is necessarily an end for everyone because it is *an end in itself*, constitutes an *objective* principle of will, and can therefore serve as a universal practical law. The foundation of this principle is: *rational nature exists as an end in itself*. Man necessarily conceives his own existence as being so: so far then this is a *subjective* principle of human actions. But every other rational being regards its existence similarly, just on the same rational principle that holds for me: so that it is at the same time an objective principle, from which as a supreme practical law all laws of the will must be capable of being deduced. Accordingly the practical imperative will be as follows: *So act as to treat humanity, whether in thine own person or in that of any other, in every case as an end withal, never as means only.* We will now inquire whether this can be practically carried out.

[8. *The Examples Viewed Again*]

To abide by the previous examples:

Firstly, under the head of necessary duty to oneself: He who contemplates suicide should ask himself whether his action can be consistent with the idea of humanity *as an end in itself.* If he destroys himself in order to escape from painful circumstances, he uses a person merely as *a mean* to maintain a tolerable condition up to the end of life. But a man is not a thing, that is to say, something which can be used merely as means, but must in all his actions be always considered as an end in himself. I cannot, therefore, dispose in any way of a man in my own person so as to mutilate him, to damage or kill him. (It belongs to ethics proper to define this principle more precisely, so as to avoid all misunderstanding, *e.g.* as to the amputation of the limbs in order to preserve myself; as to exposing my life to danger with a view to preserve it, &c. This question is therefore omitted here.)

Secondly, as regards necessary duties, or those of strict obligation, towards others; he who is thinking of making a lying promise to others will see at once that he would be using another man *merely as a mean,* without the latter containing at the same time the end in himself. For he whom I propose by such a promise to use for my own purposes cannot possibly assent to my mode of acting towards him, and therefore cannot himself contain the end of this action. This violation of the principle of humanity in other men is more obvious if we take in examples of attacks on the freedom and property of others. For then it is clear that he who transgresses the rights of men intends to use the person of others merely as means, without considering that as rational beings they ought always to be esteemed also as ends, that is, as beings who must be capable of containing in themselves the end of the very same action.[5]

---

[5]Let it not be thought that the common: *quod tibi non vis fieri, &c.* ["Don't do unto others what you would not want them to do unto you."] could serve here as the rule or principle. For it is only a deduction from the former, though with several limitations; it cannot be a universal law, for it does not contain the principle of duties to oneself, nor of the duties of benevolence to others (for many a one would gladly consent that others should not benefit him, provided only that he might be excused from showing benevolence to them), nor finally that of duties of strict obligation to one another, for on this principle the criminal might argue against the judge who punishes him, and so on.

Thirdly, as regards contingent (meritorious) duties to oneself; it is not enough that the action does not violate humanity in our own person as an end in itself, it must also *harmonize with it*. Now there are in humanity capacities of greater perfection which belong to the end that nature has in view in regard to humanity in ourselves as the subject: to neglect these might perhaps be consistent with the *maintenance* of humanity as an end in itself, but not with the *advancement* of this end.

Fourthly, as regards meritorious duties towards others: the natural end which all men have is their own happiness. Now humanity might indeed subsist, although no one should contribute anything to the happiness of others, provided he did not intentionally withdraw anything from it; but after all, this would only harmonize negatively, not positively, with *humanity as an end in itself*, if everyone does not also endeavour, as far as in him lies, to forward the ends of others. For the ends of any subject which is an end in himself, ought as far as possible to be *my* ends also, if that conception is to have its *full* effect with me.

[9. The Third Formulation of The Categorical Imperative]

This principle, that humanity and generally every rational nature is *an end in itself* (which is the supreme limiting condition of every man's freedom of action), is not borrowed from experience, *firstly*, because it is universal, applying as it does to all rational beings whatever, and experience is not capable of determining anything about them; *secondly*, because it does not present humanity as an end to men (subjectively), that is as an object which men do of themselves actually adopt as an end; but as an objective end, which must as a law constitute the supreme limiting condition of all our subjective ends, let them be what we will; it must therefore spring from pure reason. In fact the objective principle of all practical legislation lies (according to the first principle) in *the rule* and its form of universality which makes it capable of being a law (say, *e.g.*, a law of nature); but the *subjective* principle is in the *end*; now by the second principle the subject of all ends is each rational being inasmuch as it is an end in itself. Hence follows the third practical principle of the will which is the ultimate condition of its harmony with the universal practical reason, viz.: the idea of *the will of every rational being as a universally legislative will*.

On this principle all maxims are rejected which are inconsistent with the will being itself universal legislator. Thus the will is not subject simply to the law, but so subject that it must be regarded *as itself giving the law*, and on this ground only, subject to the law (of which it can regard itself as the author).

In the previous imperatives, namely, that based on the conception of the conformity of actions to general laws, as in a *physical system of nature*, and that based on the universal *prerogative* of rational beings as *ends* in themselves — these imperatives just because they were conceived as categorical, excluded from any share in their authority all admixture of any interest as a spring of action; they were, however, only *assumed* to be categorical, because such an assumption was necessary to explain the conception of duty. But we could not prove independently that there are practical propositions which command categorically, nor can it be proved in this section; one thing, however, could be done, namely, to indicate in the imperative itself by some determinate expression, that in the case of volition from duty all interest is renounced, which is the specific criterion of categorical as distinguished from hypothetical imperatives. This is done in the present (third) formula of the principle, namely, in the idea of the will of every rational being as a *universally legislating will.*

For although a will *which is subject to laws* may be attached to this law by means of an interest, yet a will which is itself a supreme lawgiver so far as it is such cannot possibly depend on any interest, since a will so dependent would itself still need another law restricting the interest of its self-love by the condition that it should be valid as universal law.

Thus the *principle* that every human will is *a will which in all its maxims gives universal laws*, provided it be otherwise justified, would be very *well adapted* to be the categorical imperative, in this respect, namely, that just because of the idea of universal legislation it is *not based on any interest*, and therefore it alone among all possible imperatives can be *unconditional.* . . .

Looking back now on all previous attempts to discover the principle of morality, we need not wonder why they all failed. It was seen that man was bound to laws by duty, but it was not observed that the laws to which he is subject are *only those of his own giving*, though at the same time they are *universal*, and that he is only bound to act in conformity with his own will; a will, however, which is designed by nature to give universal laws. For when one has conceived man only as subject to a law (no matter what), then this law required some interest, either by way of attraction or constraint, since it did not originate as a law from *his own* will, but this will was according to a law obliged by *something else* to act in a certain manner. Now by this necessary consequence all the labour spent in finding a supreme principle of *duty* was irrevocably lost. For men never elicited duty, but only a necessity of acting from a certain interest. Whether this interest was private or otherwise, in any case the imperative must be conditional, and could not by any means be capable of being a moral command. I will therefore call this the principle of *Autonomy* of the will, in contrast with every other which I accordingly reckon as *Heteronomy.*

[10. *A Kingdom of Ends*]

The conception of every rational being as one which must consider itself as giving in all the maxims of its will universal laws, so as to judge itself and its actions from this point of view — this conception leads to another which depends on it and is very fruitful, namely, that of a *kingdom of ends.*

By a *kingdom* I understand the union of different rational beings in a system by common laws. Now since it is by laws that ends are determined as regards their universal validity, hence, if we abstract from the personal differences of rational beings, and likewise from all the content of their private ends, we shall be able to conceive all ends combined in a systematic whole (including both rational beings as ends in themselves, and also the special ends which each may propose to himself), that is to say, we can conceive a kingdom of ends, which on the preceding principles is possible.

For all rational beings come under the *law* that each of them must treat itself and all others *never merely as means*, but in every case *at the same time as ends in themselves.* Hence results a systematic union of rational beings by common objective laws, *i.e.*, a kingdom which may be called a kingdom of ends, since what these laws have in view is just the relation of these beings to one another as ends and means. It is certainly only an ideal.

A rational being belongs as a *member* to the kingdom of ends when, although giving universal laws in it, he is also himself subject to these laws. He belongs to it as *sovereign* when, while giving laws, he is not subject to the will of any other.

A rational being must always regard himself as giving laws either as member or as sovereign in a kingdom of ends which is rendered possible by the freedom of will. He cannot, however, maintain the latter position merely by the maxims of his will, but only in case he is a completely independent being without wants and with unrestricted power adequate to his will.

Morality consists then in the reference of all action to the legislation which alone can render a kingdom of ends possible. This legislation must be capable of existing in every rational being, and of emanating from

85

his will, so that the principle of this will is, never to act on any maxim which could not without contradiction be also a universal law, and accordingly always so to act *that the will could at the same time regard itself as giving in its maxims universal laws.* If now the maxims of rational beings are not by their own nature coincident with this objective principle, then the necessity of acting on it is called practical necessitation, i.e. *duty.* Duty does not apply to the sovereign in the kingdom of ends, but it does to every member of it and to all in the same degree.

The practical necessity of acting on this principle, *i.e.* duty, does not rest at all on feelings, impulses, or inclinations, but solely on the relation of rational beings to one another, a relation in which the will of a rational being must always be regarded as *legislative*, since otherwise it could not be conceived as *an end in itself.* Reason then refers every maxim of the will, regarding it as legislating universally, to every other will and also to every action towards oneself; and this not on account of any other practical motive or any future advantage, but from the idea of the *dignity* of a rational being, obeying no law but that which he himself also gives.

In the kingdom of ends everything has either Value or Dignity. Whatever has a value can be replaced by something else which is *equivalent*; whatever, on the other hand, is above all value, and therefore admits of no equivalent, has a dignity.

Whatever has reference to the general inclinations and wants of mankind has a *market value*; whatever, without presupposing a want corresponds to a certain taste, that is to a satisfaction in the mere purposeless play of our faculties, has a *fancy value*; but that which constitutes the condition under which alone anything can be an end in itself, this has not merely a relative worth, *i.e.* value, but an intrinsic worth, that is *dignity.*

Now morality is the condition under which alone a rational being can be an end in himself, since by this alone it is possible that he should be a legislating member in the kingdom of ends. Thus morality, and humanity as capable of it, is that which alone has dignity. Skill and diligence in labour have a market value; wit, lively imagination, and humour, have fancy value; on the other hand, fidelity to promises, benevolence from principle (not from instinct), have an intrinsic worth. Neither nature nor art contains anything which in default of these it could put in their place, for their worth consists not in the effects which spring from them, not in the use and advantage which they secure, but in the disposition of mind, that is, the maxims of the will which are ready to manifest themselves in such actions, even though they should not have the desired effect. . . .

What then is it which justifies virtue or the morally good disposition, in making such lofty claims? It is nothing less than the privilege it secures to the rational being of participating in the giving of universal laws, by which it qualifies him to be a member of a possible kingdom of ends, a privilege to which he was already destined by his own nature as being an end in himself, and on that account legislating in the kingdom of ends; free as regards all laws of physical nature, and obeying those only which he himself gives, and by which his maxims can belong to a system of universal law, to which at the same time he submits himself. For nothing has any worth except what the law assigns it. Now the legislation itself which assigns the worth of everything must for that very reason possess dignity, that is an unconditional incomparable worth; and the word *respect* alone supplies a becoming expression for the esteem which a rational being must have for it. *Autonomy* then is the basis of the dignity of human and of every rational nature. . . .

[11.] *The Autonomy of the Will as the Supreme Principle of Morality*

Autonomy of the will is that property of it by which it is a law to itself (independently on any property of the objects of volition). The principle of autonomy then is: Always so to choose that the same volition shall comprehend the maxims of our choice as a universal law. We cannot prove that this practical rule is an imperative, *i.e.*, that the will of every rational being is necessarily bound to it as a condition, by a mere analysis of the conceptions which occur in it, since it is a synthetical proposition; we must advance beyond the cognition of the objects to a critical examination of the subject, that is of the pure practical reason, for this synthetic proposition which commands apodictically must be capable of being cognized wholly *à priori*. This matter, however, does not belong to the present section. But that the principle of autonomy in question is the sole principle of morals can be readily shown by mere analysis of the conceptions of morality. For by this analysis we find that its principle must be a categorical imperative, and that what this commands is neither more nor less than this very autonomy.

[12.] *Heteronomy of the Will as the Source of all*
Spurious Principles of Morality

If the will seeks the law which is to determine it *anywhere else* than in the fitness of its maxims to be universal laws of its own dictation, consequently if it goes out of itself and seeks this law in the character of any of its objects, there always results *heteronomy*. The will in that case does not give itself the law, but it is given by the object through its relation to the will. This relation, whether it rests on inclination or on conceptions of reason, only admits of hypothetical imperatives: I ought to do something *because I wish for something else*. On the contrary, the moral, and therefore categorical, imperative says: I ought to do so and so, even though I should not wish for anything else. [*E.g.*], the former says: I ought not to lie if I would retain my reputation; the latter says: I ought not to lie although it should not bring me the least discredit. The latter therefore must so far abstract from all objects that they shall have no *influence* on the will, in order that practical reason (will) may not be restricted to administering an interest not belonging to it, but may simply show its own commanding authority as the supreme legislation. Thus, [e.g.], I ought to endeavour to promote the happiness of others, not as if its realization involved any concern of mine (whether by immediate inclination or by any satisfaction indirectly gained through reason), but simply because a maxim which excludes it cannot be comprehended as a universal law in one and the same volition. . . .

Third Section
Transition From the Metaphysic of Morals to the Critique of Pure Practical Reason

[1.] *The Concept of Freedom is the Key that Explains the Autonomy of the Will*

The *will* is a kind of causality belonging to living beings in so far as they are rational, and *freedom* would be this property of such causality that it can be efficient, independently on foreign causes *determining* it; just as *physical necessity* is the property that the causality of all irrational beings has of being determined to activity by the influence of foreign causes.

The preceding definition of freedom is *negative*, and therefore unfruitful for the discovery of its essence; but it leads to a *positive* conception which is so much the more full and fruitful. Since the conception of causality involves that of laws, according to which, by something that we call cause, something else, namely the effect, must be produced [laid down], hence, although freedom is not a property of the will depending on physical laws, yet it is not for that reason lawless; on the contrary, it must be a causality acting according to immutable laws, but of a peculiar kind; otherwise a free will would be an absurdity. Physical necessity is a heteronomy of the efficient causes, for every effect is possible only according to this law, that something else determines the efficient cause to exert its causality. What else then can freedom of the will be but autonomy, that is the property of the will to be a law to itself? But the proposition: The will is in every action a law to itself, only expresses the principle, to act on no other maxim than that which can also have as an object itself as a universal law. Now this is precisely the formula of the categorical imperative and is the principle of morality, so that a free will and a will subject to moral laws are one and the same.

On the hypothesis, then, of freedom of the will, morality together with its principle follows from it by mere analysis of the conception. However, the latter is a synthetic proposition; viz., an absolutely good will is that whose maxim can always include itself regarded as a universal law; for this property of its maxim can never be discovered by analysing the conception of an absolutely good will. Now such synthetic propositions are only possible in this way: that the two cognitions are connected together by their union with a third in which they are both to be found. The *positive* concept of freedom furnishes this third cognition, which cannot, as with physical causes, be the nature of the sensible world (in the concept of which we find conjoined the concept of something in relation as cause to *something else* as effect). We cannot now at once show what this third is to which freedom points us, and of which we have an idea *à priori*, nor can we make intelligible how the concept of freedom is shown to be legitimate from principles of pure practical reason, and with it the possibility of a categorical imperative; but some further preparation is required.

[2.] *Freedom Must Be Presupposed as a Property of the Will of All Rational Beings*

It is not enough to predicate freedom of our own will, from whatever reason, if we have not sufficient grounds for predicating the same of all rational beings. For as morality serves as a law for us only because we are *rational beings*, it must also hold for all rational beings; and as it must be deduced simply from the property of freedom, it must be shown that freedom also is a property of all rational beings. It is not enough, then, to prove it from certain supposed experiences of human nature (which indeed is quite impossible, and it can only be shown *à priori*), but we must show that it belongs to the activity of all rational beings endowed with a will. Now I say every being that cannot act except *under the idea of freedom* is just for that reason in a practical point of view really free, that is to say, all laws which are inseparably connected with freedom have the same force for him as if his will had been shown to be free in itself by a proof theoretically conclusive.[6] Now I affirm that we must attribute to every rational being which has a will that it has also the idea of freedom and acts entirely under this idea. For in such a being we conceive a reason that is practical, that is, has causality in reference to its objects. Now we cannot possibly conceive a reason consciously receiving a bias from any other quarter with respect to its judgments, for then the subject would ascribe the determination of its judgment not to its own reason, but to an impulse. It must regard itself as the author of its principles independent on foreign influences. Consequently as practical reason or as the will of a rational being it must regard itself as free, that is to say, the will of such a being cannot be a will of its own except under the idea of freedom. This idea must therefore in a practical point of view be ascribed to every rational being.

[3. *Does the Argument Contain a "Vicious Circle"?*]

We have finally reduced the definite conception of morality to the idea of freedom. This latter, however, we could not prove to be actually a property of ourselves or of human nature; only we saw that it must be presupposed if we would conceive a being as rational and conscious of its causality in respect of its actions, *i.e.*, as endowed with a will; and so we find that on just the same grounds we must ascribe to every being endowed with reason and will this attitude of determining itself to action under the idea of its freedom.

Now it resulted also from the presupposition of this idea that we became aware of a law that the subjective principles of action, *i.e.*

---

[6]I adopt this method of assuming freedom merely *as an idea* which rational beings suppose in their actions, in order to avoid the necessity of proving it in its theoretical aspect also. The former is sufficient for my purpose; for even though the speculative proof should not be made out, yet a being that cannot act except with the idea of freedom is bound by the same laws that would oblige a being who was actually free. Thus we can escape here from the onus which presses on the theory.

maxims, must also be so assumed that they can also hold as objective, that is, universal principles, and so serve as universal laws of our own dictation. . . .

It must be freely admitted that there is a sort of circle here from which it seems impossible to escape. In the order of efficient causes we assume ourselves free, in order that in the order of ends we may conceive ourselves as subject to moral laws: and we afterwards conceive ourselves as subject to these laws, because we have attributed to ourselves freedom of will: for freedom and self-legislation of will are both autonomy, and therefore are reciprocal conceptions, and for this very reason one must not be used to explain the other or give the reason of it, but at most only for logical purposes to reduce apparently different notions of the same object to one single concept (as we reduce different fractions of the same value to the lowest terms).

[4. *A Way of Escape: Two Perspectives*]

One resource remains to us, namely, to inquire whether we do not occupy different points of view when by means of freedom we think ourselves as causes efficient *à priori*, and when we form our conception of ourselves from our actions as effects which we see before our eyes.

It is a remark which needs no subtle reflection to make, but which we may assume that even the commonest understanding can make, although it be after its fashion by an obscure discernment of judgment which it calls feeling, that all the "ideas" that come to us involuntarily (as those of the senses) do not enable us to know objects otherwise than as they affect us; so that what they may be in themselves remains unknown to us, and consequently that as regards "ideas" of this kind even with the closest attention and clearness that the understanding can apply to them, we can by them only attain to the knowledge of *appearances*, never to that of *things in themselves*. As soon as this distinction has once been made (perhaps merely in consequence of the difference observed between the ideas given us from without, and in which we are passive, and those that we produce simply from ourselves, and in which we show our own activity), then it follows of itself that we must admit and assume behind the appearance something else that is not an appearance, namely, the things in themselves; although we must admit that as they can never be known to us except as they affect us, we can come no nearer to them, nor can we ever know what they are in themselves. This must furnish a distinction, however crude, between a *world of sense* and the *world of understanding*, of which the former may be different according to the difference of the sensuous impressions in various observers, while the second which is its basis always remains the same. . . .

For this reason a rational being must regard himself *qua* intelligence (not from the side of his lower faculties) as belonging not to the world of sense, but to that of understanding; hence he has two points of view from which he can regard himself, and recognize laws of the exercise of his faculties, and consequently of all his actions: *first*, so far as he belongs to the world of sense, he finds himself subject to laws of nature (heteronomy); *secondly*, as belonging to the intelligible world, under laws which, being independent on nature, have their foundation not in experience but in reason alone.

As a reasonable being, and consequently belonging to the intelligible world, man can never conceive the causality of his own will otherwise than on condition of the idea of freedom, for independence on the determining causes of the sensible world (an independence which Reason must always ascribe to itself) is freedom. Now the idea of freedom is inseparably connected with the conception of *autonomy*, and this again with the universal principle of morality which is ideally the foundation of all actions of *rational* beings, just as the law of nature is of all phenomena.

Now the suspicion is removed which we raised above, that there was a latent circle involved in our reasoning from freedom to autonomy, and from this to the moral law, viz.: that we laid down the idea of freedom because of the moral law only that we might afterwards in turn infer the latter from freedom, and that consequently we could assign no reason at all for this law, but could only [present] it as a *petitio principii* which well-disposed minds would gladly concede to us, but which we could never put forward as a provable proposition. For now we see that when we conceive ourselves as free we transfer ourselves into the world of understanding as members of it, and recognize the autonomy of the will with its consequence, morality; whereas, if we conceive ourselves as under obligation, we consider ourselves as belonging to the world of sense, and at the same time to the world of understanding.

[5.] *How Is a Categorical Imperative Possible?*

Every rational being reckons himself *qua* intelligence as belonging to the world of understanding, and it is simply as an efficient cause belonging to that world that he calls his causality a *will*. On the other side he is also conscious of himself as a part of the world of sense in which his actions, which are mere appearances [phenomena] of that causality, are displayed; we cannot, however, discern how they are possible from this causality which we do not know; but instead of that, these actions as belonging to the sensible world must be viewed as determined by other phenomena, namely, desires and inclinations. If therefore I were only a member of the world of understanding, then all my actions would perfectly conform to the principle of autonomy of the pure will; if I were only a part of the world of sense, they would necessarily be assumed to conform wholly to the natural law of desires and inclinations, in other words, to the heteronomy of nature. (The former would rest on morality as the supreme principle, the latter on happiness.) Since, however, *the world of understanding contains the foundation of the world of sense, and consequently of its laws also,* and accordingly gives the law to my will (which belongs wholly to the world of understanding) directly, and must be conceived as doing so, it follows that, although on the one side I must regard myself as a being belonging to the world of sense, yet on the other side I must recognize myself as subject as an intelligence to the law of the world of understanding, *i.e.* to reason, which contains this law in the idea of freedom, and therefore as subject to the autonomy of the will: consequently I must regard the laws of the world of understanding as imperative for me, and the actions which conform to them as duties.

And thus what makes categorical imperatives possible is this, that the idea of freedom makes me a member of an intelligible world, in consequence of which, if I were nothing else, all my actions *would* always conform to the autonomy of the will; but as I at the same time intuite myself as a member of the world of sense, they *ought* so to conform, and this *categorical* "ought" implies a synthetic *à priori* proposition, inasmuch as besides my will as affected by sensible desires there is added further the idea of the same will, but as belonging to the world of the understanding, pure and practical of itself, which contains the supreme condition according to Reason of the former will; precisely as to the intuitions of sense there are added concepts of the understanding which of themselves signify nothing but regular form in general, and in this way synthetic *à priori* propositions become possible, on which all knowledge of physical nature rests.

[6. *Even Bad Men Accept the Validity of the Moral Point of View*]

The practical use of common human reason confirms this reasoning. There is no one, not even the most consummate villain, provided only that he is otherwise accustomed to the use of reason, who, when we set before him examples of honesty of purpose, of steadfastness in following good maxims, of sympathy and general benevolence (even combined with great sacrifices of advantages and comfort), does not wish that he might also possess these qualities. Only on account of his inclinations and impulses he cannot attain this in himself, but at the same time he wishes to be free from such inclinations which are burdensome to himself. He proves by this that he transfers himself in thought with a will free from the impulses of the sensibility into an order of things wholly different from that of his desires in the field of the sensibility; since he cannot expect to obtain by that wish any gratification of his desires, nor any position which would satisfy any of his actual or supposable inclinations (for this would destroy the pre-eminence of the very idea which wrests that wish from him): he can only expect a greater intrinsic worth of his own person. This better person, however, he imagines himself to be when he transfers himself to the point of view of a member of the world of the understanding, to which he is involuntarily forced by the idea of freedom, *i.e.*, of independence on *determining* causes of the world of sense; and from this point of view he is conscious of a good will, which by his own confession constitutes the law for the bad will that he possesses as a member of the world of sense— a law whose authority he recognizes while transgressing it. What he morally "ought" is then what he necessarily "would" as a member of the world of the understanding, and is conceived by him as an "ought" only inasmuch as he likewise considers himself as a member of the world of sense.

Bentham: The Principle of Utility

Jeremy Bentham

An Introduction to the Principles of Morals and Legislation

Chapter I
Of the Principle of Utility

I. Nature has placed mankind under the governance of two sovereign masters, *pain* and *pleasure*. It is for them alone to point out what we ought to do, as well as to determine what we shall do. On the one hand the standard of right and wrong, on the other the chain of causes and effects, are fastened to their throne. They govern us in all we do, in all

From *An Introduction to the Principles of Morals and Legislation,* chapters I, IV (1789).

we say, in all we think: every effort we can make to throw off our subjection, will serve but to demonstrate and confirm it. In words a man may pretend to abjure their empire: but in reality he will remain subject to it all the while. The *principle of utility*[1] recognises this subjection, and assumes it for the foundation of that system, the object of which is to rear the fabric of felicity by the hands of reason and of law. Systems which attempt to question it, deal in sounds instead of sense, in caprice instead of reason, in darkness instead of light.

But enough of metaphor and declamation: it is not by such means that moral science is to be improved.

II. The principle of utility is the foundation of the present work: it will be proper therefore at the outset to give an explicit and determinate account of what is meant by it. By the principle of utility is meant that principle which approves or disapproves of every action whatsoever, according to the tendency which it appears to have to augment or diminish the happiness of the party whose interest is in question: or, what is the same thing in other words, to promote or to oppose that happiness. I say of every action whatsoever; and therefore not only of every action of a private individual, but of every measure of government.

III. By utility is meant that property in any object, whereby it tends to produce benefit, advantage, pleasure, good, or happiness, (all this in the present case comes to the same thing) or (what comes again to the same thing) to prevent the happening of mischief, pain, evil, or unhappiness to the party whose interest is considered: if that party be the community in general, then the happiness of the community: if a particular individual, then the happiness of that individual.

IV. The interest of the community is one of the most general expressions that can occur in the phraseology of morals: no wonder that the meaning of it is often lost. When it has a meaning, it is this. The community is a fictitious *body*, composed of the individual persons who are considered as constituting as it were its *members*. The interest of the community then is, what? — the sum of the interests of the several members who compose it.

V. It is in vain to talk of the interest of the community, without understanding what is the interest of the individual.[2] A thing is said to

---

[1]To this denomination has of late been added, or substituted, the *greatest happiness* or *greatest felicity* principle: this for shortness, instead of saying at length *that principle* which states the greatest happiness of all those whose interest is in question, as being the right and proper, and only right and proper and universally desirable, end of human action. . . .

[2]Interest is one of those words, which not having any superior *genus,* cannot in the ordinary way be defined.

promote the interest, or to be *for* the interest, of an individual, when it tends to add to the sum total of his pleasures: or, what comes to the same thing, to diminish the sum total of his pains.

VI. An action then may be said to be conformable to the principle of utility, or, for shortness sake, to utility, (meaning with respect to the community at large) when the tendency it has to augment the happiness of the community is greater than any it has to diminish it.

VII. A measure of government (which is but a particular kind of action, performed by a particular person or persons) may be said to be conformable to or dictated by the principle of utility, when in like manner the tendency which it has to augment the happiness of the community is greater than any which it has to diminish it.

VIII. When an action, or in particular a measure of government, is supposed by a man to be conformable to the principle of utility, it may be convenient, for the purposes of discourse, to imagine a kind of law or dictate, called a law or dictate of utility: and to speak of the action in question, as being conformable to such law or dictate.

IX. A man may be said to be a partizan of the principle of utility, when the approbation or disapprobation he annexes to any action, or to any measure, is determined by and proportioned to the tendency which he conceives it to have to augment or to diminish the happiness of the community: or in other words, to its conformity or unconformity to the laws or dictates of utility.

X. Of an action that is conformable to the principle of utility one may always say either that it is one that ought to be done, or at least that it is not one that ought not to be done. One may say also, that it is right it should be done; at least that it is not wrong it should be done; that it is a right action; at least that it is not a wrong action. When thus interpreted, the words *ought*, and *right* and *wrong*, and others of that stamp, have a meaning: when otherwise, they have done.

XI. Has the rectitude of this principle been ever formally contested? It should seem that it had, by those who have not known what they have been meaning. Is it susceptible of any direct proof? it should seem not: for that which is used to prove every thing else, cannot itself be proved: a chain of proofs must have their commencement somewhere. To give such proof is as impossible as it is needless.

XII. Not that there is or ever has been that human creature breathing, however stupid or perverse, who has not on many, perhaps on most occasions of his life, deferred to it. By the natural constitution of the human frame, on most occasions of their lives men in general embrace this principle, without thinking of it: if not for the ordering of their own actions, yet for the trying of their own actions, as well as of those of other men. There have been, at the same time, not many, perhaps, even of the most intelligent, who have been disposed to embrace it purely and without reserve. There are even few who have not taken some occasion or other to quarrel with it, either on account of their not understanding always how to apply it, or on account of some prejudice or other which they were afraid to examine into, or could not bear to part with. For such is the stuff that man is made of: in principle and in practice, in a right track and in a wrong one, the rarest of all human qualities is consistency.

XIII. When a man attempts to combat the principle of utility, it is with reason drawn, without his being aware of it, from that very principle itself.[3] His arguments, if they prove anything, prove not that the principle is *wrong,* but that, according to the applications he supposes to be made of it, it is *misapplied.* Is it possible for a man to move the earth? Yes; but he must first find out another earth to stand upon.

XIV. To disprove the propriety of it by arguments is impossible; but, from the causes that have been mentioned, or from some confused or partial view of it, a man may happen to be disposed not to relish it. Where this is the case, if he thinks the settling of his opinions on such a subject worth the trouble, let him take the following steps, and at length, perhaps, he may come to reconcile himself to it.

1. Let him settle with himself, whether he would wish to discard this principle altogether; if so, let him consider what it is that all his reasonings (in matters of politics especially) can amount to?

2. If he would, let him settle with himself, whether he would judge and act without any principle, or whether there is any other he would judge and act by?

3. If there be, let him examine and satisfy himself whether the principle he thinks he has found is really any separate intelligible principle; or whether it be not a mere principle in words, a kind of phrase, which at bottom expresses neither more nor less than the mere averment of his own unfounded sentiments; that is, what in another person he might be apt to call caprice?

4. If he is inclined to think that his own approbation or disapprobation, annexed to the idea of an act, without any regard to its consequences, is a sufficient foundation for him to judge and act upon, let him ask himself whether his sentiment is to be a standard of right and wrong, with

---

[3]'The principle of utility, (I have heard it said) is a dangerous principle: it is dangerous on certain occasions to consult it.' This is as much as to say, what? that it is not consonant to utility, to consult utility: in short, that it is *not* consulting it, to consult it.

respect to every other man, or whether every man's sentiment has the same privilege of being a standard to itself?

5. In the first case, let him ask himself whether his principle is not despotical, and hostile to all the rest of the human race?

6. In the second case, whether it is not anarchical, and whether at this rate there are not as many different standards of right and wrong as there are men? and whether even to the same man, the same thing, which is right today, may not (without the least change in its nature) be wrong tomorrow? and whether the same thing is not right and wrong in the same place at the same time? and in either case, whether all argument is not at an end? and whether, when two men have said, 'I like this,' and 'I don't like it,' they can (upon such a principle) have any thing more to say?

7. If he should have said to himself, No: for that the sentiment which he proposes as a standard must be grounded on reflection, let him say on what particulars the reflection is to turn? if on particulars having relation to the utility of the act, then let him say whether this is not deserting his own principle, and borrowing assistance from that very one in opposition to which he sets it up: or if not on those particulars, on what other particulars?

8. If he should be for compounding the matter, and adopting his own principle in part, and the principle of utility in part, let him say how far he will adopt it?

9. When he has settled with himself where he will stop, then let him ask himself how he justifies to himself the adopting it so far? and why he will not adopt it any farther?

10. Admitting any other principle than the principle of utility to be a right principle, a principle that it is right for a man to pursue; admitting (what is not true) that the word *right* can have a meaning without reference to utility, let him say whether there is any such thing as a *motive* that a man can have to pursue the dictates of it: if there is, let him say what that motive is, and how it is to be distinguished from those which enforce the dictates of utility: if not, then lastly let him say what it is this other principle can be good for?

Chapter IV
Value of a Lot of Pleasure or Pain, How to be Measured

I. Pleasures then, and the avoidance of pains, are the *ends* which the legislator has in view: it behoves him therefore to understand their *value*.

Pleasures and pains are the *instruments* he has to work with: it behoves him therefore to understand their force, which is again, in other words, their value.

II. To a person considered *by himself,* the value of a pleasure or pain considered *by itself,* will be greater or less, according to the four following circumstances:[4]

    1. Its *intensity.*   3. Its *certainty* or *uncertainty.*

    2. Its *duration.*   4. Its *propinquity* or *remoteness.*

III. These are the circumstances which are to be considered in estimating a pleasure or a pain considered each of them by itself. But when the value of any pleasure or pain is considered for the purpose of estimating the tendency of any *act* by which it is produced, there are two other circumstances to be taken into account; these are,

5. Its *fecundity*, or the chance it has of being followed by sensations of the *same* kind: that is, pleasures, if it be a pleasure: pains, if it be a pain.

6. Its *purity*, or the chance it has of *not* being followed by sensations of the *opposite* kind: that is, pains, if it be a pleasure: pleasures, if it be a pain.

These two last, however, are in strictness scarcely to be deemed properties of the pleasure or the pain itself; they are not, therefore, in strictness to be taken into the account of the value of that pleasure or that pain. They are in strictness to be deemed properties only of the act, or other event, by which such pleasure or pain has been produced; and accordingly are only to be taken into the account of the tendency of such act or such event.

IV. To a *number* of persons, with reference to each of whom the value of a pleasure or a pain is considered, it will be greater or less, according to seven circumstances: to wit, the six preceding ones; *viz.*

---

[4]These circumstances have since been denominated *elements* or *dimensions* of *value* in a pleasure or a pain.

Not long after the publication of the first edition, the following memoriter verses were framed, in the view of lodging more effectually, in the memory, these points, on which the whole fabric of morals and legislation may be seen to rest.

    Intense, long, certain, speedy, fruitful, pure —
    Such marks in *pleasures* and in *pains* endure.
    Such pleasures seek if *private* be thy end:
    If it be *public,* wide let them *extend.*
    Such *pains* avoid, whichever be thy view:
    If pains *must* come, let them *extend* to few.

1. Its *intensity*.   4. Its *propinquity* or *remoteness*.

2. Its *duration*.   5. Its *fecundity*.

3. Its *certainty* or *uncertainty*.   6. Its *purity*.

And one other; to wit:

7. Its *extent;* that is, the number of persons to whom it *extends*; or (in other words) who are affected by it.

V. To take an exact account then of the general tendency of any act, by which the interests of a community are affected, proceed as follows. Begin with any one person of those whose interests seem most immediately to be affected by it: and take an account,

1. Of the value of each distinguishable *pleasure* which appears to be produced by it in the *first* instance.

2. Of the value of each *pain* which appears to be produced by it in the *first* instance.

3. Of the value of each pleasure which appears to be produced by it *after* the first. This constitutes the *fecundity* of the first *pleasure* and the *impurity* of the first *pain*.

4. Of the value of each *pain* which appears to be produced by it after the first. This constitutes the *fecundity* of the first *pain,* and the *impurity* of the first pleasure.

5. Sum up all the values of all the *pleasures* on the one side, and those of all the pains on the other. The balance, if it be on the side of pleasure, will give the *good* tendency of the act upon the whole, with respect to the interests of that *individual* person; if on the side of pain, the *bad* tendency of it upon the whole.

6. Take an account of the *number* of persons whose interests appear to be concerned; and repeat the above process with respect to each. *Sum up* the numbers expressive of the degrees of *good* tendency, which the act has, with respect to each individual, in regard to whom the tendency of it is *good* upon the whole: do this again with respect to each individual, in regard to whom the tendency of it is *bad* upon the whole. Take the balance; which, if on the side of *pleasure,* will give the general *good tendency* of the act, with respect to the total number or community of individuals concerned; if on the side of pain, the general *evil tendency,* with respect to the same community.

VI. It is not to be expected that this process should be strictly pursued previously to every moral judgment, or to every legislative or judicial operation. It may, however, be always kept in view: and as near as the process actually pursued on these occasions approaches to it, so near will such process approach to the character of an exact one.

VII. The same process is alike applicable to pleasure and pain, in whatever shape they appear: and by whatever denomination they are distinguished: to pleasure, whether it be called *good* (which is properly the cause or instrument of pleasure) or *profit* (which is distant pleasure, or the cause or instrument of distant pleasure), or *convenience*, or *advantage, benefit, emolument, happiness,* and so forth: to pain, whether it be called *evil* (which corresponds to *good*), or *mischief,* or *inconvenience*, or *disadvantage*, or *loss*, or *unhappiness*, and so forth.

VIII. Nor is this a novel and unwarranted, any more than it is a useless theory. In all this there is nothing but what the practice of mankind, wheresoever they have a clear view of their own interest, is perfectly conformable to. An article of property, an estate in land, for instance, is valuable, on what account? On account of the pleasures of all kinds which it enables a man to produce, and what comes to the same thing the pains of all kinds which it enables him to avert. But the value of such an article of property is universally understood to rise or fall according to the length or shortness of the time which a man has in it: the certainty or uncertainty of its coming into possession: and the nearness or remoteness of the time at which, if at all, it is to come into possession. As to the *intensity* of the pleasures which a man may derive from it, this is never thought of, because it depends upon the use which each particular person may come to make of it; which cannot be estimated till the particular pleasures he may come to derive from it, or the particular pains he may come to exclude by means of it, are brought to view. For the same reason, neither does he think of the *fecundity* or *purity* of those pleasures.

Mill: The Principle of Utility

John Stuart Mill

Utilitarianism

Chapter 1   General Remarks

There are few circumstances among those which make up the present condition of human knowledge, more unlike what might have been expected, or more significant of the backward state in which speculation on the most important subjects still lingers, than the little progress which has been made in the decision of the controversy respecting the criterion of right and wrong. From the dawn of philosophy, the question concern-

From *Utilitarianism,* chapters I, II, IV (1863).

ing the *summum bonum*, or, what is the same thing, concerning the foundation of morality, has been accounted the main problem in speculative thought, has occupied the most gifted intellects, and divided them into sects and schools, carrying on a vigorous warfare against one another. And after more than two thousand years the same discussions continue, philosophers are still ranged under the same contending banners, and neither thinkers nor mankind at large seem nearer to being unanimous on the subject, than when the youth Socrates listened to the old Protagoras, and asserted (if Plato's dialogue be grounded on a real conversation) the theory of utilitarianism against the popular morality of the so-called sophist.

It is true that similar confusion and uncertainty, and in some cases similar discordance, exist respecting the first principles of all the sciences, not excepting that which is deemed the most certain of them, mathematics; without much impairing, generally indeed without impairing at all, the trustworthiness of the conclusions of those sciences. An apparent anomaly, the explanation of which is, that the detailed doctrines of a science are not usually deduced from, nor depend for their evidence upon, what are called its first principles. Were it not so, there would be no science more precarious, or whose conclusions were more insufficiently made out, than algebra; which derives none of its certainty from what are commonly taught to learners as its elements, since these, as laid down by some of its most eminent teachers, are as full of fictions as English law, and of mysteries as theology. The truths which are ultimately accepted as the first principles of a science, are really the last results of metaphysical analysis, practised on the elementary notions with which the science is conversant; and their relation to the science is not that of foundations to an edifice, but of roots to a tree, which may perform their office equally well though they be never dug down to and exposed to light. But though in science the particular truths precede the general theory, the contrary might be expected to be the case with a practical art, such as morals or legislation. All action is for the sake of some end, and rules of action, it seems natural to suppose, must take their whole character and colour from the end to which they are subservient. When we engage in a pursuit, a clear and precise conception of what we are pursuing would seem to be the first thing we need, instead of the last we are to look forward to. A test of right and wrong must be the means, one would think, of ascertaining what is right or wrong, and not a consequence of having already ascertained it.

The difficulty is not avoided by having recourse to the popular theory of a natural faculty, a sense or instinct, informing us of right and wrong.

For — besides that the existence of such a moral instinct is itself one of the matters in dispute — those believers in it who have any pretensions to philosophy, have been obliged to abandon the idea that it discerns what is right or wrong in the particular case in hand, as our other senses discern the sight or sound actually present. Our moral faculty, according to all those of its interpreters who are entitled to the name of thinkers, supplies us only with the general principles of moral judgments; it is a branch of our reason, not of our sensitive faculty; and must be looked to for the abstract doctrines of morality, not for perception of it in the concrete. The intuitive, no less than what may be termed the inductive, school of ethics, insists on the necessity of general laws. They both agree that the morality of an individual action is not a question of direct perception, but of the application of a law to an individual case. They recognize also, to a great extent, the same moral laws; but differ as to their evidence, and the source from which they derive their authority. According to the one opinion, the principles of morals are evident *à priori*, requiring nothing to command assent, except that the meaning of the terms be understood. According to the other doctrine, right and wrong, as well as truth and falsehood, are questions of observation and experience. But both hold equally that morality must be deduced from principles; and the intuitive school affirm as strongly as the inductive, that there is a science of morals. Yet they seldom attempt to make out a list of the *à priori* principles which are to serve as the premises of the science; still more rarely do they make any effort to reduce those various principles to one first principle, or common ground of obligation. They either assume the ordinary precepts of morals as of *à priori* authority, or they lay down as the common groundwork of those maxims, some generality much less obviously authoritative than the maxims themselves, and which has never succeeded in gaining popular acceptance. Yet to support their pretensions there ought either to be some one fundamental principle or law, at the root of all morality, or if there be several, there should be a determinate order of precedence among them; and the one principle, or the rule for deciding between the various principles when they conflict, ought to be self-evident.

To inquire how are the bad effects of this deficiency have been mitigated in practice, or to what extent the moral beliefs of mankind have been vitiated or made uncertain by the absence of any distinct recognition of an ultimate standard, would imply a complete survey and criticism of past and present ethical doctrine. It would, however, be easy to show that whatever steadiness or consistency these moral beliefs have attained, has been mainly due to the tacit influence of a standard not recognised. Although the non-existence of an acknowledged first principle has made ethics not so much a guide as a consecration of men's actual sentiments, still, as men's sentiments, both of favour and of aversion, are greatly influenced by what they suppose to be the effects of things upon their happiness, the principle of utility, or as Bentham latterly called it, the greatest happiness principle, has had a large share in forming the moral doctrines even of those who most scornfully reject its authority. Nor is there any school of thought which refuses to admit that the influence of actions on happiness is a most material and even predominant consideration in many of the details of morals, however unwilling to acknowledge it as the fundamental principle of morality, and the source of moral obligation. I might go much further, and say that to all those *à priori* moralists who deem it necessary to argue at all, utilitarian arguments are indispensable. It is not my present purpose to criticise these thinkers; but I cannot help referring, for illustration, to a systematic treatise by one of the most illustrious of them, the *Metaphysics of Ethics*, by Kant. This remarkable man, whose system of thought will long remain one of the landmarks in the history of philosophical speculation, does, in the treatise in question, lay down a universal first principle as the origin and ground of moral obligation; it is this: — "So act, that the rule on which thou actest would admit of being adopted as a law by all rational beings." But when he begins to deduce from this precept any of the actual duties of morality, he fails, almost grotesquely, to show that there would be any contradiction, any logical (not to say physical) impossibility, in the adoption by all rational beings of the most outrageously immoral rules of conduct. All he shows is that the *consequences* of their universal adoption would be such as no one would choose to incur.

On the present occasion, I shall, without further discussion of the other theories, attempt to contribute something towards the understanding and appreciation of the Utilitarian or Happiness theory, and towards such proof as it is susceptible of. . . .

Chapter 2   What Utilitarianism Is

A passing remark is all that needs be given to the ignorant blunder of supposing that those who stand up for utility as the test of right and wrong, use the term in that restricted and merely colloquial sense in which utility is opposed to pleasure. An apology is due to the philosophical opponents of utilitarianism, for even the momentary appearance of confounding them with any one capable of so absurd a misconception; which is the more extraordinary, inasmuch as the contrary accusation, of referring everything to pleasure, and that too in its grossest form, is another of the common charges against utilitarianism: and, as has been pointedly remarked by an able writer, the same sort of persons, and often the very same persons, denounce the theory "as impracticably dry when the word utility precedes the word pleasure, and as too practically voluptuous when the word pleasure precedes the word utility." Those who know anything about the matter are aware that every writer, from Epicurus to Bentham, who maintained the theory of utility, meant by it, not something to be contradistinguished from pleasure, but pleasure itself, together with exemption from pain; and instead of opposing the useful to the agreeable or the ornamental, have always declared that the useful means these, among other things. Yet the common herd, including the herd of writers, not only in newspapers and periodicals, but in books of weight and pretension, are perpetually falling into this shallow mistake. Having caught up the word utilitarian, while knowing nothing whatever about it but its sound, they habitually express by it the rejection, or the neglect, of pleasure in some of its forms; of beauty, of ornament, or of amusement. Nor is the term thus ignorantly misapplied solely in disparagement, but occasionally in compliment; as though it implied superiority to frivolity and the mere pleasures of the moment. And this perverted use is the only one in which the word is popularly known, and the one from which the new generation are acquiring their sole notion of its meaning. Those who introduced the word, but who had for many years discontinued it as a distinctive appellation, may well feel themselves called upon to resume it, if by doing so they can hope to contribute anything towards rescuing it from this utter degradation.

The creed which accepts as the foundation of morals, Utility, or the Greatest Happiness Principle, holds that actions are right in proportion as they tend to promote happiness, wrong as they tend to produce the reverse of happiness. By happiness is intended pleasure, and the absence of pain; by unhappiness, pain, and the privation of pleasure. To give a clear view of the moral standard set up by the theory, much more requires to be said; in particular, what things it includes in the ideas of pain and pleasure; and to what extent this is left an open question. But these supplementary explanations do not affect the theory of life on which this theory of morality is grounded — namely, that pleasure, and freedom from pain, are the only things desirable as ends; and that all desirable things (which are as numerous in the utilitarian as in any other scheme) are desirable either for the pleasure inherent in themselves, or as means to the promotion of pleasure and the prevention of pain.

Now, such a theory of life excites in many minds, and among them in some of the most estimable in feeling and purpose, inveterate dislike. To suppose that life has (as they express it) no higher end than pleasure — no better and nobler object of desire and pursuit — they designate as utterly mean and grovelling; as a doctrine worthy only of swine, to whom the followers of Epicurus were, at a very early period, contemptuously likened; and modern holders of the doctrine are occasionally made the subject of equally polite comparisons by its German, French, and English assailants.

When thus attacked, the Epicureans have always answered, that it is not they, but their accusers, who represent human nature in a degrading light; since the accusation supposes human beings to be capable of no pleasures except those of which swine are capable. If this supposition were true, the charge could not be gainsaid, but would then be no longer an imputation; for if the sources of pleasure were precisely the same to human beings and to swine, the rule of life which is good enough for the one would be good enough for the other. The comparison of the Epicurean life to that of beasts is felt as degrading, precisely because a beast's pleasures do not satisfy a human being's conceptions of happiness. Human beings have faculties more elevated than the animal appetites, and when once made conscious of them, do not regard anything as happiness which does not include their gratification. I do not, indeed, consider the Epicureans to have been by any means faultless in drawing out their scheme of consequences from the utilitarian principle. To do this in any sufficient manner, many Stoic, as well as Christian elements require to be included. But there is no known Epicurean theory of life which does not assign to the pleasures of the intellect, of the feelings and imagination, and of the moral sentiments, a much higher value as pleasures than to those of mere sensation. It must be admitted, however, that utilitarian writers in general have placed the superiority of mental over bodily pleasures chiefly in the greater permanency, safety, uncostliness, etc., of the former — that is, in their circumstantial advantages rather than in their intrinsic nature. And on all these points utilitarians have fully proved their case; but they might have taken the other, and, as it may be called, higher ground, with entire consistency. It is quite compatible with the principle of utility to recognise the fact, that some *kinds* of pleasure are more desirable and more valuable than others. It would be absurd that while, in estimating all other things, quality is considered as well as quantity, the estimation of pleasures should be supposed to depend on quantity alone.

If I am asked, what I mean by difference of quality in pleasures, or what makes one pleasure more valuable than another, merely as a pleasure, except its being greater in amount, there is but one possible answer. Of two pleasures, if there be one to which all or almost all who have experience of both give a decided preference, irrespective of any feeling of moral obligation to prefer it, that is the more desirable pleasure. If one of the two is, by those who are competently acquainted with both, placed so far above the other that they prefer it, even though knowing it to be attended with a greater amount of discontent, and would not resign it for any quantity of the other pleasure which their nature is capable of, we are justified in ascribing to the preferred enjoyment a superiority in quality, so far outweighing quantity as to render it, in comparison, of small account.

Now it is an unquestionable fact that those who are equally acquainted with, and equally capable of appreciating and enjoying, both, do give a most marked preference to the manner of existence which employs their higher faculties. Few human creatures would consent to be changed into any of the lower animals, for a promise of the fullest allowance of a beast's pleasures; no intelligent human being would consent to be a fool, no instructed person would be an ignoramus, no person of feeling and conscience would be selfish and base, even though they should be persuaded that the fool, the dunce, or the rascal is better satisfied with his lot than they are with theirs. They would not resign what they possess more than he for the most complete satisfaction of all the desires which they have in common with him. If they ever fancy they would, it is only in cases of unhappiness so extreme, that to escape from it they would exchange their lot for almost any other, however undesirable in their own eyes. A being of higher faculties requires more to make him happy, is capable probably of more acute suffering, and certainly accessible to it at more points, than one of an inferior type; but in spite of these liabilities, he can never really wish to sink into what he feels to be a lower grade of existence. We may give what explanation we please of this unwillingness; we may attribute it to pride, a name which is given indiscriminately to some of the most and to some of the least estimable feelings of which mankind are capable: we may refer it to the love of liberty and personal independence, an appeal to which was with the Stoics one of the most effective means for the inculcation of it; to the love of power, or to the love of excitement, both of which do really enter into and contribute to it: but its most appropriate appellation is a sense of dignity, which all human beings possess in one form or other, and in some, though by no means in exact proportion to their higher faculties, and which is so essential a part of the happiness of those in whom it is strong, that nothing which conflicts with it could be, otherwise than momentarily, an object of desire to them. Whoever supposes that this preference takes place at a sacrifice of happiness — that the superior being, in anything like equal circumstances, is not happier than the inferior — confounds the two very different ideas, of happiness, and content. It is indisputable that the being whose capacities of enjoyment are low, has the greatest chance of having them fully satisfied; and a highly endowed being will always feel that any happiness which he can look for, as the world is constituted, is imperfect. But he can learn to bear its imperfections, if they are at all bearable; and they will not make him envy the being who is indeed unconscious of the imperfections, but only because he feels not at all the good which those imperfections qualify. It is better to be a human being dissatisfied than a pig satisfied; better to be Socrates dissatisfied than a fool satisfied. And if the fool, or the pig, are of a different opinion, it is because they only know their own side of the question. The other party to the comparison knows both sides.

It may be objected, that many who are capable of the higher pleasures, occasionally, under the influence of temptation, postpone them to the lower. But this is quite compatible with a full appreciation of the intrinsic superiority of the higher. Men often, from infirmity of character, make their election for the nearer good, though they know it to be the less valuable; and this no less when the choice is between two bodily pleasures, than when it is between bodily and mental. They pursue sensual indulgences to the injury of health, though perfectly aware that health is the greater good. It may be further objected, that many who begin with youthful enthusiasm for everything noble, as they advance in years sink into indolence and selfishness. But I do not believe that those who undergo this very common change, voluntarily choose the lower description of pleasure in preference to the higher. I believe that before they devote themselves exclusively to the one, they have already become incapable of the other. Capacity for the nobler feelings is in most natures a very tender plant, easily killed, not only by hostile influences, but by mere want of sustenance; and in the majority of young persons it speedily dies away if the occupation to which their position in life has devoted them, and the society into which it has thrown them, are not favourable to keeping that higher capacity in exercise. Men lose their high aspirations as they lose their intellectual tastes, because they have not the time or opportunity for indulging them; and they addict themselves to inferior pleasures, not because they deliberately prefer them, but because they are either the only ones to which they have access, or the only ones which they are any longer capable of enjoying. It may be questioned whether any one who has remained equally susceptible to both classes of pleasures, ever knowingly and calmly preferred the lower; though many, in all ages, have broken down in an ineffectual attempt to combine both.

From this verdict of the only competent judges, I apprehend there can be no appeal. On a question which is the best worth having of two pleasures, or which of two modes of existence is the most grateful to the feelings, apart from its moral attributes and from its consequences, the judgment of those who are qualified by knowledge of both, or, if they differ, that of the majority among them, must be admitted as final. And there needs be the less hesitation to accept this judgment respecting the quality of pleasures, since there is no other tribunal to be referred to even on the question of quantity. What means are there of determining which is the acutest of two pains, or the intensest of two pleasurable sensations, except the general suffrage of those who are familiar with both? Neither pains nor pleasures are homogeneous, and pain is always heterogeneous with pleasure. What is there to decide whether a particular pleasure is worth purchasing at the cost of a particular pain, except the feelings and judgment of the experienced? When, therefore, those feelings and judgment declare the pleasures derived from the higher faculties to be preferable *in kind*, apart from the question of intensity, to those of which the animal nature, disjoined from the higher faculties, is susceptible, they are entitled on this subject to the same regard.

I have dwelt on this point, as being a necessary part of a perfectly just conception of Utility or Happiness, considered as the directive rule of human conduct. But it is by no means an indispensable condition to the acceptance of the utilitarian standard; for that standard is not the agent's own greatest happiness, but the greatest amount of happiness altogether; and if it may possibly be doubted whether a noble character is always the happier for its nobleness, there can be no doubt that it makes other people happier, and that the world in general is immensely a gainer by it. Utilitarianism, therefore, could only attain its end by the general cultivation of nobleness of character, even if each individual were only benefited by the nobleness of others, and his own, so far as happiness is concerned, were a sheer deduction from the benefit. But the bare enunciation of such an absurdity as this last, renders refutation superfluous.

According to the Greatest Happiness Principle, as above explained, the ultimate end, with reference to and for the sake of which all other things are desirable (whether we are considering our own good or that of other people), is an existence exempt as far as possible from pain, and as rich as possible in enjoyments, both in point of quantity and quality; the test of quality, and the rule for measuring it against quantity, being the preference felt by those who in their opportunities of experience, to which must be added their habits of self-consciousness and self-observation, are best furnished with the means of comparison. This, being, according to the utilitarian opinion, the end of human action, is necessarily also the standard of morality; which may accordingly be defined, the rules and precepts for human conduct, by the observance of which an existence such as has been described might be, to the greatest extent possible, secured to all mankind; and not to them only, but, so far as the nature of things admits, to the whole sentient creation.

Against this doctrine, however, arises another class of objectors, who say that happiness, in any form, cannot be the rational purpose of human life and action; because, in the first place, it is unattainable: and they contemptuously ask, what right hast thou to be happy? a question which Mr. Carlyle clenches by the addition, What right, a short time ago, hadst thou even *to be*? Next, they say, that men can do *without* happiness; that all noble human beings have felt this, and could not have become noble but by learning the lesson of Entsagen, or renunciation; which lesson, thoroughly learnt and submitted to, they affirm to be the beginning and necessary condition of all virtue.

The first of these objections would go to the root of the matter were it well founded; for if no happiness is to be had at all by human beings, the attainment of it cannot be the end of morality, or of any rational conduct. Though, even in that case, something might still be said for the utilitarian theory; since utility includes not solely the pursuit of happiness, but the prevention or mitigation of unhappiness; and if the former aim be chimerical, there will be all the greater scope and more imperative need for the latter, so long at least as mankind think fit to live, and not take refuge in the simultaneous act of suicide recommended under certain conditions by Novalis. When, however, it is thus positively asserted to be impossible that human life should be happy, the assertion, if not something like a verbal quibble, is at least an exaggeration. If by happiness be meant a continuity of highly pleasurable excitement, it is evident enough that this is impossible. A state of exalted pleasure lasts only moments, or in some cases, and with some intermissions, hours or days, and is the occasional brilliant flash of enjoyment, not its permanent and steady flame. Of this the philosophers who have taught that happiness is the end of life were as fully aware as those who taunt them. The happiness which they meant was not a life of rapture; but moments of such, in an existence made up of few and transitory pains, many and various pleasures, with a decided predominance of the active over the passive, and having as the foundation of the whole, not to expect more from life than it is capable of bestowing. A life thus composed, to those who have been fortunate enough to obtain it, has always appeared worthy of the name of happiness. And such an existence is even now the lot of many, during some considerable portion of their lives. The present wretched education, and wretched social arrangements, are the only real hindrance to its being attainable by almost all.

The objectors perhaps may doubt whether human beings, if taught to consider happiness as the end of life, would be satisfied with such a moderate share of it. But great numbers of mankind have been satisfied with much less. The main constituents of a satisfied life appear to be two, either of which by itself is often found sufficient for the purpose: tranquillity, and excitement. With much tranquillity, many find that they can be content with very little pleasure: with much excitement, many can reconcile themselves to a considerable quantity of pain. There is assuredly no inherent impossibility in enabling even the mass of mankind to unite both; since the two are so far from being incompatible that they are in natural alliance, the prolongation of either being a preparation for, and exciting a wish for, the other. It is only those in whom indolence amounts to a vice, that do not desire excitement after an interval of repose: it is only those in whom the need of excitement is a disease, that feel the tranquillity which follows excitement dull and insipid, instead of pleasurable in direct proportion to the excitement which preceded it. When people who are tolerably fortunate in their outward lot do not find in life sufficient enjoyment to make it valuable to them, the cause generally is, caring for nobody but themselves. To those who have neither public nor private affections, the excitements of life are much curtailed, and in any case dwindle in value as the time approaches when all selfish interests must be terminated by death: while those who leave after them objects of personal affection, and especially those who have also cultivated a fellow-feeling with the collective interests of mankind, retain as lively an interest in life on the eve of death as in the vigour of youth and health. Next to selfishness, the principal cause which makes life unsatisfactory is want of mental cultivation. A cultivated mind — I do not mean that of a philosopher, but any mind to which the fountains of knowledge have been opened, and which has been taught, in any tolerable degree, to exercise its faculties — finds sources of inexhaustible interest in all that surrounds it; in the objects of nature, the achievements of art, the imaginations of poetry, the incidents of history, the ways of mankind, past and present, and their prospects in the future. It is possible, indeed, to become indifferent to all this, and that too without having exhausted a thousandth part of it; but only when one has had from the beginning no moral or human interest in these things, and has sought in them only the gratification of curiosity. . . .

And this leads to the true estimation of what is said by the objectors concerning the possibility, and the obligation, of learning to do without happiness. Unquestionably it is possible to do without happiness; it is done involuntarily by nineteen-twentieths of mankind, even in those parts of our present world which are least deep in barbarism; and it often has to be done voluntarily by the hero or the martyr, for the sake of something which he prizes more than his individual happiness. But this something, what is it, unless the happiness of others, or some of the requisites of happiness? It is noble to be capable of resigning entirely one's own portion of happiness, or chances of it: but, after all, this self-sacrifice must be for some end; it is not its own end; and if we are told that its end is not happiness, but virtue, which is better than happiness, I ask, would the sacrifice be made if the hero or martyr did not believe that it would earn for others immunity from similar sacrifices? Would it be made if he thought that his renunciation of happiness for himself would produce no fruit for any of his fellow creatures, but to make their lot like his, and place them also in the condition of persons who have renounced happiness? All honour to those who can abnegate for themselves the personal enjoyment of life, when by such renunciation they contribute worthily to increase the amount of happiness in the world; but he who does it, or professes to do it, for any other purpose, is no more deserving of admiration than the ascetic mounted on his pillar. He may be an inspiriting proof of what men *can* do, but assuredly not an example of what they *should*.

Though it is only in a very imperfect state of the world's arrangements that any one can best serve the happiness of others by the absolute sacrifice of his own, yet so long as the world is in that imperfect state, I fully acknowledge that the readiness to make such a sacrifice is the highest virtue which can be found in man. I will add that in this condition of the world, paradoxical as the assertion may be, the conscious ability to do without happiness gives the best prospect of realising such happiness as is attainable. For nothing except that consciousness can raise a person above the chances of life, by making him feel that, let fate and fortune do their worst, they have not power to subdue him: which, once felt, frees him from excess of anxiety concerning the evils of life, and enables him, like many a Stoic in the worst times of the Roman Empire, to cultivate in tranquillity the sources of satisfaction accessible to him, without concerning himself about the uncertainty of their duration, any more than about their inevitable end.

Meanwhile, let utilitarians never cease to claim the morality of self devotion as a possession which belongs by as good a right to them, as either to the Stoic or to the Transcendentalist. The utilitarian morality does recognise in human beings the power of sacrificing their own greatest good for the good of others. It only refuses to admit that the sacrifice is itself a good. A sacrifice which does not increase, or tend to increase, the sum total of happiness, it considers as wasted. The only self-renunciation which it applauds, is devotion to the happiness, or to some of the means of happiness, of others; either of mankind collectively, or of individuals within the limits imposed by the collective interests of mankind.

I must again repeat, what the assailants of utilitarianism seldom have the justice to acknowledge, that the happiness which forms the utilitarian standard of what is right in conduct, is not the agent's own happiness, but that of all concerned. As between his own happiness and that of others, utilitarianism requires him to be as strictly impartial as a disinterested and benevolent spectator. In the golden rule of Jesus of Nazareth, we read the complete spirit of the ethics of utility. To do as you would be done by, and to love your neighbour as yourself, constitute the ideal perfection of utilitarian morality. As the means of making the nearest approach to this ideal, utility would enjoin, first, that laws and social arrangements should place the happiness, or (as speaking practically it may be called) the interest, of every individual, as nearly as possible in harmony with the interests of the whole; and secondly, that education and opinion, which have so vast a power over human character, should so use that power as to establish in the mind of every individual an indissoluble association between his own happiness and the good of the whole; especially between his own happiness and the practice of such modes of conduct, negative and positive, as regard for the universal happiness prescribes; so that not only he may be unable to conceive the possibility of happiness to himself, consistently with conduct opposed to the general good, but also that a direct impulse to promote the general good may be in every individual one of the habitual motives of action, and the sentiments connected therewith may fill a large and prominent place in every human being's sentient existence. If the impugners of the utilitarian morality represented it to their own minds in this its true character, I know not what recommendations possessed by any other morality they could possibly affirm to be wanting to it; what more beautiful or more exalted developments of human nature any other ethical system can be supposed to foster, or what springs of action, not accessible to the utilitarian, such systems rely on for giving effect to their mandates.

The objectors to utilitarianism cannot always be charged with representing it in a discreditable light. On the contrary, those among them who entertain anything like a just idea of its disinterested character, sometimes find fault with its standard as being too high for humanity. They say it is exacting too much to require that people shall always act from the inducement of promoting the general interests of society. But this is to mistake the very meaning of a standard of morals, and confound the rule of action with the motive of it. It is the business of ethics to tell us what are our duties, or by what test we may know them; but no system of ethics requires that the sole motive of all we do shall be a feeling of duty; on the contrary, ninety-nine hundredths of all our actions are done from other motives, and rightly so done, if the rule of duty does not condemn them. It is the more unjust to utilitarianism that this particular misapprehension should be made a ground of objection to it, inasmuch as utilitarian moralists have gone beyond almost all others in affirming that the motive has nothing to do with the morality of the action, though much with the worth of the agent. He who saves a fellow creature from drowning does what is morally right, whether his motive be duty, or the hope of being paid for his trouble; he who betrays the friend that trusts him, is guilty of a crime, even if his object be to serve another friend to whom he is under greater obligations. But to speak only of actions done from the motive of duty, and in direct obedience to principle: it is a misapprehension of the utilitarian mode of thought, to conceive it as implying that people should fix their minds upon so wide a generality as the world, or society at large. The great majority of good actions are intended not for the benefit of the world, but for that of individuals, of which the good of the world is made up; and the thoughts of the most virtuous man need not on these occasions travel beyond the particular persons concerned, except so far as is necessary to assure himself that in benefitting them he is not violating the rights, that is, the legitimate and authorised expectations, of any one else. The multiplication of happiness is, according to the utilitarian ethics, the object of virtue: the occasions on which any person (except one in a thousand) has it in his power to do this on an extended scale, in other words to be a public benefactor, are but exceptional; and on these occasions alone is he called on to consider public utility; in every other case, private utility, the interest or happiness of some few persons, is all he has to attend to. Those alone the influence of whose actions extends to society in general, need concern themselves habitually about so large an object. In the case of abstinences indeed —

116

of things which people forbear to do from moral considerations, though the consequences in the particular case might be beneficial — it would be unworthy of an intelligent agent not to be consciously aware that the action is of a class which, if practised generally, would be generally injurious, and that this is the ground of the obligation to abstain from it. The amount of regard for the public interest implied in this recognition, is no greater than is demanded by every system of morals, for they all enjoin to abstain from whatever is manifestly pernicious to society.

The same considerations dispose of another reproach against the doctrine of utility, founded on a still grosser misconception of the purpose of a standard of morality, and of the very meaning of the words right and wrong. It is often affirmed that utilitarianism renders men cold and unsympathising; that it chills their moral feelings towards individuals; that it makes them regard only the dry and hard consideration of the consequences of actions, not taking into their moral estimate the qualities from which those actions emanate. If the assertion means that they do not allow their judgment respecting the rightness or wrongness of an action to be influenced by their opinion of the qualities of the person who does it, this is a complaint not against utilitarianism, but against having any standard of morality at all; for certainly no known ethical standard decides an action to be good or bad because it is done by a good or a bad man, still less because done by an amiable, a brave, or a benevolent man, or the contrary. These considerations are relevant, not to the estimation of actions, but of persons; and there is nothing in the utilitarian theory inconsistent with the fact that there are other things which interest us in persons besides the rightness and wrongness of their actions. The Stoics, indeed, with the paradoxical misuse of language which was part of their system, and by which they strove to raise themselves above all concern about anything but virtue, were fond of saying that he who has that has everything; that he, and only he, is rich, is beautiful, is a king. But no claim of this description is made for the virtuous man by the utilitarian doctrine. Utilitarians are quite aware that there are other desirable possessions and qualities besides virtue, and are perfectly willing to allow to all of them their full worth. They are also aware that a right action does not necessarily indicate a virtuous character, and that actions which are blamable, often proceed from qualities entitled to praise. When this is apparent in any particular case, it modifies their estimation, not certainly of the act, but of the agent. I grant that they are, notwithstanding, of opinion, that in the long run the best proof of a good character is good actions; and resolutely refuse to consider any mental disposition as good, of which the predominant tendency is to produce bad conduct. This makes them unpopular with many people; but it is an unpopularity which they must share with every one who regards the distinction between right and wrong in a serious light; and the reproach is not one which a conscientious utilitarian need be anxious to repel. . . .

We not uncommonly hear the doctrine of utility inveighed against as a *godless* doctrine. If it be necessary to say anything at all against so mere an assumption, we may say that the question depends upon what idea we have formed of the moral character of the Deity. If it be a true belief that God desires, above all things, the happiness of his creatures, and that this was his purpose in their creation, utility is not only not a godless doctrine, but more profoundly religious than any other. If it be meant that utilitarianism does not recognize the revealed will of God as the supreme law of morals, I answer, that a utilitarian who believes in the perfect goodness and wisdom of God, necessarily believes that whatever God has thought fit to reveal on the subject of morals, must fulfil the requirements of utility in a supreme degree. But others besides utilitarians have been of opinion that the Christian revelation was intended, and is fitted, to inform the hearts and minds of mankind with a spirit which should enable them to find for themselves what is right, and incline them to do it when found, rather than to tell them, except in a very general way, what it is; and that we need a doctrine of ethics, carefully followed out, to *interpret* to us the will of God. Whether this opinion is correct or not, it is superfluous here to discuss; since whatever aid religion, either natural or revealed, can afford to ethical investigation, is as open to the utilitarian moralist as to any other. He can use it as the testimony of God to the usefulness or hurtfulness of any given course of action, by as good a right as others can use it for the indication of a transcendental law, having no connection with usefulness or with happiness.

Again, Utility is often summarily stigmatised as an immoral doctrine by giving it the name of Expediency, and taking advantage of the popular use of that term to contrast it with Principle. But the Expedient, in the sense in which it is opposed to the Right, generally means that which is expedient for the particular interest of the agent himself; as when a minister sacrifices the interests of his country to keep himself in place. When it means anything better than this, it means that which is expedient for some immediate object, some temporary purpose, but which violates a rule whose observance is expedient in a much higher degree. The Expedient, in this sense, instead of being the same thing with the useful, is a branch of the hurtful. Thus, it would often be expedient, for the purpose of getting over some momentary embarrassment, or attaining some object immediately useful to ourselves or others, to tell a lie. But inasmuch as the cultivation in ourselves of a sensitive feeling on the subject of veracity, is one of the most useful, and the enfeeblement of that feeling one of the most hurtful, things to which our conduct can be instrumental; and inasmuch as any, even unintentional deviation from truth, does that much towards weakening the trustworthiness of human assertion, which is not only the principal support of all present social well-being, but the insufficiency of which does more than any one thing that can be named to keep back civilization, virtue, everything on which human happiness on the largest scale depends; we feel that the violation, for a present advantage, of a rule of such transcendant expediency, is not expedient, and that he who, for the sake of a convenience to himself or to some other individual, does what depends on him to deprive mankind of the good, and inflict upon them the evil, involved in the greater or less reliance which they can place in each other's word, acts the part of one of their worst enemies. Yet that even this rule, sacred as it is, admits of possible exceptions, is acknowledged by all moralists; the chief of which is when the withholding of some fact (as of information from a malefactor, or of bad news from a person dangerously ill) would save an individual (especially an individual other than oneself) from great and unmerited evil and when the withholding can only be effected by denial. But in order that the exception may not extend itself beyond the need, and may have the least possible effect in weakening reliance on veracity, it ought to be recognized, and, if possible, its limits defined; and if the principle of utility is good for anything, it must be good for weighing these conflicting utilities against one another, and marking out the region within which one or the other preponderates.

Again, defenders of utility often find themselves called upon to reply to such objections as this — that there is not time, previous to action, for calculating and weighing the effects of any line of conduct on the general happiness. This is exactly as if any one were to say that it is impossible to guide our conduct by Christianity, because there is not time, on every occasion on which anything has to be done, to read through the Old and New Testaments. The answer to the objection is, that there has been ample time, namely, the whole past duration of the human species. During all that time, mankind have been learning by experience the tendencies of actions; on which experience all the prudence, as well as all the morality of life, are dependent. People talk as if the commencement of this course of experience had hitherto been put off, and as if at the moment when some man feels tempted to meddle with the property or life of another, he had to begin considering for the first time whether murder and theft are injurious to human happiness. Even then I do not think that he would find the question very puzzling; but, at all events, the matter is now done to his hand. It is truly a whimsical supposition that, if mankind were agreed in considering utility to be the test of morality, they would remain without any agreement as to what *is* useful, and would take no measures for having their notions on the subject taught to the young, and enforced by law and opinion. There is no difficulty in proving any ethical standard whatever to work ill, if we suppose universal idiocy to be conjoined with it; but on any hypothesis short of that, mankind must by this time have acquired positive beliefs as to the effects of some actions on their happiness; and the beliefs which have thus come down are the rules of morality for the multitude, and for the philosopher until he has succeeded in finding better. That philosophers might easily do this, even now, on many subjects; that the received code of ethics is by no means of divine right; and that mankind have still much to learn as to the effects of actions on the general happiness, I admit, or rather, earnestly maintain. The corollaries from the principle of utility, like the precepts of every practical art, admit of indefinite improvement, and, in a progressive state of the human mind, their improvement is perpetually going on. But to consider the rules of morality as improvable, is one thing; to pass over the intermediate generalisations entirely, and endeavour to test each individual action directly by the principle, is another. It is a strange notion that the acknowledgment of a first principle is inconsistent with the admission of secondary ones. To inform a traveller respecting the place of his ultimate destination, is not to forbid the use of landmarks and direction-posts on the way. The proposition that happiness is the end and aim of morality, does not mean that no road ought to be laid down to that goal, or that persons going thither should not be advised to take one direction rather than another. Men really ought to leave off talking a kind of nonsense on this subject, which they would neither talk nor listen to on other matters of practical concernment. Nobody argues that the art of navigation is not founded on astronomy, because sailors cannot wait to calculate the Nautical Almanack. Being rational creatures, they go to sea with it already calculated; and all rational creatures go out upon the sea of life with their minds made up on the common questions of right and wrong, as well as on many of the far more difficult questions of wise and foolish. And this, as long as foresight is a human quality, it is to be presumed they will continue to do. Whatever we adopt as the fundamental principle of morality, we require subordinate principles to apply it by; the impossibility of doing without them, being common to all systems, can afford no argument against any one in particular; but gravely to argue as if no such secondary principles could be had, and as if mankind had remained till now, and always must remain, without drawing any general conclusions from the experience of human life, is as high a pitch, I think, as absurdity has ever reached in philosophical controversy.

The remainder of the stock arguments against utilitarianism mostly consist in laying to its charge the common infirmities of human nature, and the general difficulties which embarrass conscientious persons in shaping their course through life. We are told that a utilitarian will be apt to make his own particular case an exception to moral rules, and, when under temptation, will see a utility in the breach of a rule, greater than he will see in its observance. But is utility the only creed which is able to furnish us with excuses for evil doing, and means of cheating our own conscience? They are afforded in abundance by all doctrines which recognise as a fact in morals the existence of conflicting considerations; which all doctrines do, that have been believed by sane persons. It is not the fault of any creed, but of the complicated nature of human affairs, that rules of conduct cannot be so framed as to require no exceptions, and that hardly any kind of action can safely be laid down as either always obligatory or always condemnable. There is no ethical creed which does not temper the rigidity of its laws, by giving a certain latitude, under the moral responsibility of the agent, for accommodation to peculiarities of circumstances; and under every creed, at the opening thus made, self-deception and dishonest casuistry get in. There exists no moral system under which there do not arise unequivocal cases of conflicting obligation. These are the real difficulties, the knotty points both in the theory of ethics, and in the conscientious guidance of personal conduct. They are overcome practically, with greater or with less success, according to the intellect and virtue of the individual; but it can hardly be pretended that any one will be the less qualified for dealing with them, from possessing an ultimate standard to which conflicting rights and duties can be referred. If utility is the ultimate source of moral obligations, utility may be invoked to decide between them when their demands are incompatible. Though the application of the standard may be difficult, it is better than none at all: while in other systems, the moral laws all claiming independent authority, there is no common umpire entitled to interfere between them; their claims to precedence one over another rest on little better than sophistry, and unless determined, as they generally are, by the unacknowledged influence of considerations of utility, afford a free scope for the action of personal desires and partialities. We must remember that only in these cases of conflict between secondary principles is it requisite that first principles should be appealed to. There is no case of moral obligation in which some secondary principle is not involved; and if only one, there can seldom be any real doubt which one it is, in the mind of any person by whom the principle itself is recognised.

Chapter 4   Of What Sort of Proof the Principle of Utility Is Susceptible

. . . Questions of ultimate ends do not admit of proof, in the ordinary acceptation of the term. To be incapable of proof by reasoning is common to all first principles; to the first premises of our knowledge, as well as to those of our conduct. But the former, being matters of fact, may be the subject of a direct appeal to the faculties which judge of fact — namely, our senses, and our internal consciousness. Can an appeal be made to the same faculties on questions of practical ends? Or by what other faculty is cognisance taken of them?

Questions about ends, in other words, questions what things are desirable. The utilitarian doctrine is, that happiness is desirable, and the only thing desirable, as an end; all other things being only desirable as means to that end. What ought to be required of this doctrine — what conditions is it requisite that the doctrine should fulfil — to make good its claim to be believed?

The only proof capable of being given that an object is visible, is that people actually see it. The only proof that a sound is audible, is that people hear it: and so of the other sources of our experiences. In like manner, I apprehend, the sole evidence it is possible to produce that anything is desirable, is that people do actually desire it. If the end which the utilitarian doctrine proposes to itself were not, in theory and in practice, acknowledged to be an end, nothing could ever convince any person that it was so. No reason can be given why the general happiness is desirable, except that each person, so far as he believes it to be attainable, desires his own happiness. This, however, being a fact, we have not only all the proof which the case admits of, but all which it is possible to require, that happiness is a good: that each person's happiness is a good to that person, and the general happiness, therefore, a good to the aggregate of all persons. Happiness has made out its title as *one* of the ends of conduct; and consequently one of the criteria of morality.

But it has not, by this alone, proved itself to be the sole criterion. To do that, it would seem, by the same rule, necessary to show, not only that people desire happiness, but that they never desire anything else. Now it is palpable that they do desire things which, in common language, are decidedly distinguished from happiness. They desire, for example, virtue, and the absence of vice, no less really than pleasure and the absence of pain. The desire of virtue is not as universal, but it is as authentic a fact, as the desire of happiness. And hence the opponents of the utilitarian standard deem that they have a right to infer that there are other ends of human action besides happiness, and that happiness is not the standard of approbation and disapprobation.

But does the utilitarian doctrine deny that people desire virtue, or maintain that virtue is not a thing to be desired? The very reverse. It maintains not only that virtue is to be desired, but that it is to be desired disinterestedly, for itself. Whatever may be the opinion of utilitarian moralists as to the original conditions by which virtue is made virtue; however they may believe (as they do) that actions and dispositions are only virtuous because they promote another end than virtue; yet this being granted, and it having been decided, from considerations of this description, what *is* virtuous, they not only place virtue at the very head of the things which are good as means to the ultimate end, but they also recognise as a psychological fact the possibility of its being to the individual, a good in itself, without looking to any end beyond it; and hold, that the mind is not in a right state, not in a state conformable to Utility, not in the state most conducive to the general happiness, unless it does love virtue in this manner — as a thing desirable in itself, even although, in the individual instance, it should not produce those other desirable consequences which it tends to produce, and on account of which it is held to be virtue. This opinion is not, in the smallest degree, a departure from the Happiness principle. The ingredients of happiness are very various, and each of them is desirable in itself, and not merely when considered as swelling an aggregate. The principle of utility does not mean that any given pleasure, as music, for instance, or any given exemption from pain, as for example health, is to be looked upon as means to a collective something termed happiness, and to be desired on that account. They are desired and desirable in and for themselves; besides being means, they are a part of the end. Virtue, according to the utilitarian doctrine, is not naturally and originally part of the end, but it is capable of becoming so; and in those who love it disinterestedly it has become so, and is desired and cherished, not as a means to happiness, but as a part of their happiness.

To illustrate this farther, we may remember that virtue is not the only thing, originally a means, and which if it were not a means to anything else, would be and remain indifferent, but which by association with what it is a means to, comes to be desired for itself, and that too with the utmost intensity. What, for example, shall we say of the love of money? There is nothing originally more desirable about money than about any heap of glittering pebbles. Its worth is solely that of the things which it will buy; the desires for other things than itself, which it is a means of gratifying. Yet the love of money is not only one of the strongest moving forces of human life, but money is, in many cases, desired in and for itself; the desire to possess it is often stronger than the desire to use it, and goes on increasing when all the desires which point to ends beyond it, to be compassed by it, are falling off. It may, then, be said truly, that money is desired not for the sake of an end, but as part of the end. From being a means to happiness, it has come to be itself a principal ingredient of the individual's conception of happiness. The same may be said of the majority of the great objects of human life — power, for example, or fame; except that to each of these there is a certain amount of immediate pleasure annexed, which has at least the semblance of being naturally inherent in them; a thing which cannot be said of money. Still, however, the strongest natural attraction, both of power and of fame, is the immense aid they give to the attainment of our other wishes; and it is the strong association thus generated between them and all our objects of desire, which gives to the direct desire of them the intensity it often assumes, so as in some characters to surpass in strength all other desires. In these cases the means have become a part of the end, and a more important part of it than any of the things which they are means to. What was once desired as an instrument for the attainment of happiness, has come to be desired for its own sake. In being desired for its own sake it is, however, desired as *part* of happiness. The person is made, or thinks he would be made, happy by its mere possession; and is made unhappy by failure to obtain it. The desire of it is not a different thing from the desire of happiness, any more than the love of music, or the desire of health. They are included in happiness. They are some of the elements of which the desire of happiness is made up. Happiness is not an abstract idea, but a concrete whole; and these are some of its parts. And the utilitarian standard sanctions and approves their being so. Life would be a poor thing, very ill provided with the sources of happiness, if there were not this provision of nature, by which things originally indifferent, but conducive to, or otherwise associated with, the satisfaction of our primitive desires, become in themselves sources of pleasure more valuable than the primitive pleasures, both in permanency, in the space of human existence that they are capable of covering, and even in intensity.

Virtue, according to the utilitarian conception, is a good of this description. There was no original desire of it, or motive to it, save its conduciveness to pleasure, and especially to protection from pain. But through the association thus formed, it may be felt a good in itself, and desired as such with as great intensity as any other good; and with this difference between it and the love of money, of power, or of fame, that all of these may, and often do, render the individual noxious to the other members of the society to which he belongs, whereas there is nothing which makes him so much a blessing to them as the cultivation of the disinterested love of virtue. And consequently, the utilitarian standard, while it tolerates and approves those other acquired desires, up to the point beyond which they would be more injurious to the general happiness than promotive of it, enjoins and requires the cultivation of the love of virtue up to the greatest strength possible, as being above all things important to the general happiness.

It results from the preceding considerations, that there is in reality nothing desired except happiness. Whatever is desired otherwise than as a means to some end beyond itself, and ultimately to happiness, is desired as itself a part of happiness, and is not desired for itself until it has become so. Those who desire virtue for its own sake, desire it either because the consciousness of it is a pleasure, or because the consciousness of being without it is a pain, or for both reasons united; as in truth the pleasure and pain seldom exist separately, but almost always together, the same person feeling pleasure in the degree of virtue attained, and pain in not having attained more. If one of these gave him no pleasure, and the other no pain, he would not love or desire virtue, or would desire it only for the other benefits which it might produce to himself or to persons whom he cared for.

We have now, then, an answer to the question, of what sort of proof the principle of utility is susceptible. If the option which I have now stated is psychologically true — if human nature is so constituted as to desire nothing which is not either a part of happiness or a means of happiness, we can have no other proof, and we require no other, that these are the only things desirable. If so, happiness is the sole end of human action, and the promotion of it the test by which to judge of all human conduct; from whence it necessarily follows that it must be the criterion of morality, since a part is included in the whole.

And now to decide whether this is really so; whether mankind do desire nothing for itself but that which is a pleasure to them, or of which the absence is a pain; we have evidently arrived at a question of fact and experience, dependent, like all similar questions, upon evidence. It can only be determined by practised self-consciousness and self-observation, assisted by observation of others. I believe that these sources of evidence, impartially consulted, will declare that desiring a thing and finding it pleasant, aversion to it and thinking of it as painful, are phenomena entirely inseparable, or rather two parts of the same phenomenon; in strictness of language, two different modes of naming the same psychological fact: that to think of an object as desirable (unless for the sake of its consequences), and to think of it as pleasant, are one and the same thing; and that to desire anything, except in proportion as the idea of it is pleasant, is a physical and metaphysical impossibility.

So obvious does this appear to me, that I expect it will hardly be disputed: and the objection made will be, not that desire can possibly be directed to anything ultimately except pleasure and exemption from pain, but that the will is a different thing from desire; that a person of confirmed virtue, or any other person whose purposes are fixed, carries out his purposes without any thought of the pleasure he has in contemplating them, or expects to derive from their fulfilment; and persists in acting on them, even though these pleasures are much diminished, by changes in his character or decay of his passive sensibilities, or are outweighed by the pains which the pursuit of the purposes may bring upon him. All this I fully admit, and have stated it elsewhere, as positively and emphatically as any one. Will, the active phenomenon, is a different thing from desire, the state of passive sensibility, and though originally an offshoot from it, may in time take root and detach itself from the parent stock; so much so, that in the case of an habitual purpose, instead of willing the thing because we desire it, we often desire it only because we will it. This however, is but an instance of that familiar fact, the power of habit, and is nowise confined to the case of virtuous actions. Many indifferent things, which men originally did from a motive of some sort, they continue to do from habit. Sometimes this is done unconsciously, the consciousness coming only after the action: at other times with conscious volition, but volition which has become habitual, and is put in operation by the force of habit, in opposition perhaps to the deliberate preference, as often happens with those who have contracted habits of vicious or hurtful indulgence. Third and last comes the case in which the habitual act of will in the individual instance is not in contradiction to the general intention prevailing at other times, but in fulfilment of it; as in the case of the person of confirmed virtue, and of all who pursue deliberately and consistently any determinate end. The distinction between will and desire thus understood is an authentic and highly important psychological fact; but the fact consists solely in this — that will, like all other parts of our constitution, is amenable to habit, and that we may will from habit what we no longer desire for itself, or desire only because we will it. It is not the less true that will, in the beginning, is entirely produced by desire; including in that term the repelling influence of pain as well as the attractive one of pleasure. Let us take into consideration, no longer the person who has a confirmed will to do right, but him in whom that virtuous will is still feeble, conquerable by temptation, and not to be fully relied on; by what means can it be strengthened? How can the will be virtuous, where it does not exist in sufficient force, be implanted or awakened? Only by making the person *desire* virtue — by making him think of it in a pleasurable light, or of its absence in a painful one. It is by associating the doing right with pleasure, or the doing wrong with pain, or by eliciting and impressing and bringing home to the person's experience the pleasure naturally involved in the one or the pain in the other, that it is possible to call forth that will to be virtuous, which when confirmed, acts without any thought of either pleasure or pain. Will is the child of desire, and passes out of the dominion of its parent only to come under that of habit. That which is the result of habit affords no presumption of being intrinsically good; and there would be no reason for wishing that the purpose of virtue should become independent of pleasure and pain, were it not that the influence of the pleasurable and painful associations which prompt to virtue is not sufficiently to be depended on for unerring constancy of action until it has acquired the support of habit. Both in feeling and in conduct, habit is the only thing which imparts certainty; and it is because of the importance to others of being able to rely absolutely on one's feelings and conduct, and to oneself of being able to rely on one's own, that the will to do right ought to be cultivated into this habitual independence. In other words, this state of the will is a means to good, not intrinsically a good; and does not contradict the doctrine that nothing is a good to human beings but in so far as it is either itself pleasurable, or a means of attaining pleasure or averting pain.

But if this doctrine be true, the principle of utility is proved. Whether it is so or not, must now be left to the consideration of the thoughtful reader.

II

MORAL POINTS OF VIEW

Introduction

Ethical Scepticism

We commonly speak of looking at the same thing from different perspectives, and different things from the same perspective. Thus a coroner, a policeman, a relative, a sociologist, and a clergyman might all interpret an act of murder quite differently. Conversely, quite diverse acts such as attempted suicide and sexual intercourse might both be viewed from either physical, psychological, social, religious, or legal perspectives. Indeed it is difficult to understand how anyone could look at anything except from some perspective or other. Thus, if we should be asked whether there is a moral point of view, the answer might seem obvious. Of course there is a moral point of view, just as there are legal, psychological, or religious points of view.

The question, however, is not quite so easily answered as all that. Despite the almost universal claim that there is a distinctively moral point of view from which human acts may be examined and evaluated, there are those who dispute that claim. There have always been persons who have denied that moral expressions such as "right" and "wrong" have any meaning at all. They deny that there are any valid moral principles, and most emphatically deny that there are any moral "experts" upon whose knowledge, background, or experience such a perspective could be based. Let us call those who deny the existence of morality altogether *ethical nihilists*.

Most persons think that nihilism goes too far. Surely there is such a thing as moral language, we commonly employ moral principles of one kind or another to justify our actions, and most of us think of ourselves, if not as moral experts, at least as moral persons whose views on morality are worth defending. But even granting that there is such a thing as a moral perspective, it is possible nonetheless to deny that it is a legitimate way of viewing things. One might adopt the position of the *ethical sceptic* who denies that anyone can ever know that any moral claims are valid, or that there are any authoritative moral principles in terms of which we can confidently and truthfully explain and criticize moral phenomena. "Who is to say what is right and what is wrong?" is his favorite response to anyone's pronouncement or inquiry about morals. His own answer to the question, it is understood, is "No one." His position is, of course, perfectly consistent with there *being* a right answer to the questions of morality, even if no one is in a position to know what it is. The intent of the sceptic, however, is not simply to deny that anyone presently has such knowledge, but moreover that anyone can ever have it.

There are many varieties of ethical scepticism depending on the kinds of reasons advanced for the position. There are what we may call *semantic sceptics*. They argue that morality is not a matter of "knowing" anything. It is not a cognitive enterprise. Moral words such as "good," "bad," "right," and "wrong" are simply verbal ways of expressing our emotions, feelings, and attitudes. Sentences which incorporate such words cannot, therefore, be either true or false. This view is more generally known as *non-cognitivism* and will be examined in more detail in Part VI. It might be thought that this interpretation of moral language supports ethical nihilism rather than ethical scepticism, but, as we shall see, non-cognitivists do not deny that there is such a thing as morality, or that there is a legitimate philosophical study called ethics or moral philosophy.

They only deny that we can say that moral claims are matters of knowledge.

Other philosophers have suggested that man is but a pawn in the scheme of things. His decisions are totally without effect. No matter what we choose to do, certain events will happen anyway. If this view of the *fatalist* is adopted, then it may not be meaningless to talk about morality, or a moral point of view, but it is certainly pointless. Like non-cognitivism, this view, which we may call *metaphysical scepticism*, does not supply grounds for ethical nihilism since it may be the case that some things are good and others bad even if we cannot do anything to bring one or the other of them about. But if our judgments about good and evil are as determined as our actions, and this also the metaphysical sceptic means to assert, then what basis do we have for saying that we know anything? We might just as well attribute moral knowledge to a talking doll who says, "That's right!" This view and others related to the free will problem will be discussed in Part IV.

Still other philosophers have doubted whether general rules and principles can be of any use in making moral decisions. The main reason for their concern is their recognition that attempts to formulate such general moral propositions always seem to encounter difficult cases which just do not fit the rule. An example is the rule "Always tell the truth." How do we handle a case where by telling a lie we can save someone's life? The *norm sceptic*, as we shall call him, does not see how we can and still retain the rule. Whether the norm sceptic finally adopts the thesis of ethical scepticism depends on the extent to which he thinks that morality depends on rules and principles. If he thinks that without rules of some kind there can be no determination of morality, and that all rules have exceptions, then he may be led to assert that we can never know with certainty which acts are moral and which are not. If he thinks that rules are not that important, he may find other ways of making valid moral decisions and so avoid scepticism. The general topic of rules and exceptions will be dealt with in Part III.

Moral Perspectivism

Much more needs to be said, and will be said in the course of this book, regarding ethical scepticism before the thoughtful reader can make up his mind about it. But let us now consider other types of answers to the question of whether there is a distinctively moral point of view. Some philosophers assert that there is not just one moral perspective but many moral perspectives. At first glance, one might wonder just whose view is being opposed by such an assertion. Can there be only *one* perspective? Doesn't the very concept of a perspective entail a plurality of perspectives? Logically this seems to follow, so these philosophers must really be objecting to the claim of certain traditional philosophers that some one perspective is exclusively the correct perspective. As we saw in Part I, Kant made this claim for his theory, as did the utilitarians and the others for theirs.

As it happens, some of those who object to the traditional philosopher's claim of exclusive status for his moral principle also object to his claim that there is only one ultimate moral principle from which all other valid principles are derived. But exclusivity and ultimacy are not to be confused. Some philosophers who reject the privileged status claimed for certain principles do not object to the idea that we must understand all moral phenomena in terms of one principle. What they do object to is another claim made on the part of the traditional moral philosopher, and that is his claim that there is only one kind of thing that is intrinsically valuable (e.g., happiness, for the utilitarians; good will, for Kant). Thus we must be careful to distinguish *methodological pluralists* (those who deny that there is only one moral principle and assert that there are many) from *value pluralists* (those who deny that there is only one kind of moral value and assert that there are many kinds). As we shall see, it is possible to be both a methodological monist and a value pluralist. It is also possible to be a pluralist with respect to both the number of moral principles and the kinds of moral value.

Nietzsche and James are value pluralists. They believe that there are whole systems of values which for one reason or another human beings subscribe to, and that each set of values is as entitled to be called "moral" as any other. Nietzsche expresses the idea very succinctly when he speaks of many "moralities" as contrasted with the traditional concept of (a single) "Morality." James speaks of the many ideals we find existing in the world, and in his criticism of the various attempts to reduce all such values to one type, he says:

> No one of the measures that have been actually proposed has, however, given general satisfaction. Some are obviously not universally present in all cases — *e.g.*, the character of harming no one, or that of following a universal law; for the best course is often cruel; and many acts are reckoned good on the sole condition that they be exceptions, and serve not as examples of a universal law. Other characters, such as following the will of God, are unascertainable and vague. Others again, like survival, are quite indeterminate in their consequences, and leave

us in the lurch where we most need their help: a philosopher of the Sioux Nation, for example, will be certain to use the survival-criterion in a very different way from ourselves.

Coupled with this assertion of a plurality of human values is the denial on the part of both Nietzsche and James of *ethical absolutism*, the view that values exist independently of human interests and desires. James speaks of what he calls the "superstitious" view that an abstract moral order ("an overarching system of moral relations, true 'in themselves' ") pre-exists any actual order of moral ideals. Nietzsche laments the fact that "the natural origin of morality is denied everywhere." To a remarkable extent, James and Nietzsche's moral philosophies are alike. But let us briefly examine their views to see exactly where they lead, and to point out where they differ.

Having adopted the common assumption that there are many "moralities" or "systems of moral ideals," both Nietzsche and James appear to be interested in answering these three questions:

1. What is the origin of our moral ideas?
2. What is the criterion of a morality or moral point of view?
3. Are some moralities or moral points of view better than others?

According to Nietzsche, moral values are "created," not "discovered." In every society, both ancient and modern, there are to be found two kinds of persons: creative individuals or "noblemen" and uncreative individuals who are by nature followers or "slaves." What the nobleman determines to be valuable, i.e., beneficial to himself, he calls "good"; whatever is injurious to him is judged "injurious in itself" or "bad." The nobleman is a born aristocrat, a man of superior talents, superior in intellect, strength, artistic ability, self-control — in short, to use Nietzsche's all-inclusive term, superior in *power*. He exudes a super-abundance of power. By contrast the "slave" is a weakling, inferior in intellect, strength, self-control, and artistry. His chief distinguishing mark is that he is by nature resentful. Because he is unable to compete, he resents whatever the nobleman does. As a consequence, what the nobleman calls "good," he calls "evil," and what the nobleman calls "bad," he calls "good." Because the creative faction within any society is bound to be the numerical minority, it is eventually overwhelmed and suppressed by the inferior majority. Thus an inversion of values takes place.

Nietzsche defines morality as "a system of valuations which is in relation with the conditions of a creature's life." It is a product of certain natural self-preservative instincts. The criterion of a moral point of view (whether of an individual, a community, a race, a state, a church, a belief, or a culture) is the extent to which it promotes its own preservation. A point of view is immoral to the extent that it "brings about ruin." Thus, if a belief or a community upholds "life-denying" values, as the Christian Church does, according to Nietzsche, then it promotes a self-destructive point of view, and so is immoral. Another way he expresses this is by calling Christianity a "slave morality."

It follows that for Nietzsche a "master morality" is better than a "slave morality." What is required, however, since the value systems of most cultures are of the latter type, is what he calls a "transvaluation" of values, an overthrowing of the values of the masses and a reinstatement of the values of the true aristocrat and the point of view of the "strong man."

James, too, argues that values are "made," not discovered, and that the origin of our ideas of "good," "bad," and "obligation" is traceable to "demands" or "claims." But James is more democratic than Nietzsche. Anyone's claim is productive of good. Also, since claim and obligation are correlative terms, wherever there is a claim there is an obligation.

There can be no meaning to morality or to moral terms, says James, in a world in which no sentient life exists. There must be at least one such being (a "moral solitude") in order for there to be an "ethical universe." Given a universe of more than one thinker, however, the notion of obligation emerges as a new moral relation, and the possibility of conflicting demands, opinions, and views arises. In such a situation, the search for a criterion for determining which judgments, viewpoints, or demands are the better ones arises. James dismisses the traditional ethical principles of Bentham, Mill, Kant, and others, largely because he feels that they exclude too much of what different men have actually regarded as good or morally binding. He proposes, instead, as the criterion of morality the following: That view of things is moral which allows for the satisfaction of as many demands as possible, and those ideals are highest which prevail at the least cost.

Though there are no "absolute evils," according to James, and every man's interests (even those of the criminal) count for something, still not everyone's point of view is as preferable as others. The special ideal and task of the philosopher, he says, "is to find an account of the moral relations that obtain among things, which will weave them into a stable system, and make of the world what one may call a genuine universe from the ethical point of view." Such a system cannot be set down in advance of experience (it must await the outcome of human and social experiments), but James thinks that he has provided its guiding principle.

It should be clear from this brief restatement and comparison of the views of Nietzsche and James that their departure from the traditional view is far less than it might at first appear to be. Their main concern is to reject the claims of the moral absolutist who holds that values are discovered, that they pre-exist mankind, and that they are unchanging. They wish to emphasize the diversity of human values, their relativity to human interests and social conditions. But in the end they do not give up the idea that some ways of viewing moral relations are better than others. Nor do they refrain from formulating "guiding principles" or criteria or definitions of morality. This is particularly evident in James' case. Nietzsche, who says that "there are no moral phenomena, but only a moral interpretation of phenomena," nonetheless urges an interpretation of the interpretations by means of a single principle, a procedure which he elsewhere speaks of as a "commandment of method" (See *Beyond Good and Evil*, sections 13 & 36). In short, although Nietzsche and James are unquestionably pluralists in one sense of that term, they are also methodological monists.

Norm Scepticism and Situationism

Among contemporary philosophers who attempt to eliminate rules and principles as definitions of the moral perspective are Jean-Paul Sartre and Joseph Fletcher. Sartre rebels not only against the use of principles as determinants of morality, but also against everything else which might be said to influence or determine man's nature and his action. Man seems, he says, "to be made by climate and earth, race and class, language, the history of the collectivity of which he is a part, heredity, the individual circumstances of his childhood, acquired habits, the great and small events of his life." It is not necessarily so, says Sartre. Man is capable of "absolute freedom." He can "make himself" whatever he chooses. If a particular crag presents a difficulty to a mountain climber, whether it becomes an obstacle or an opportunity depends on how he chooses to look at it.

Man is "abandoned." By this Sartre means that he cannot escape responsibility for his actions by appealing to some principle or ideal. A war breaks out and he joins the war effort. He cannot complain that it is not his war, or that he was forced into it. He could always have chosen not to join it, even if that meant suicide or desertion. If he joins because of the pressure of public opinion, or because of what others might think, or because of the honor of his family, it still remains true that he chose these values rather than others as the basis of his action. Given other values or principles, he could have refused to join. The point is that man chooses (or creates) his values, his ideals, his principles, and then uses them to rationalize his actions. But the values, ideals, principles, even the circumstances cannot be used as excuses for the choice he made. He alone is responsible. Sartre puts it this way: "the peculiar character of human reality is that it is without excuse."

Two questions naturally arise with respect to Sartre's views. First, if there are no grounds or principles for any choice in the sense that they are reasons which independently justify the action, how can one action be regarded as "better" than any other? Second, if man is totally undetermined even by his own character, then what sense is there in holding him responsible in the sense of praising, blaming, or punishing him?

Sartre suggests only the barest answers to these questions. In connection with the first, Sartre suggests that one who allows (or rather, chooses to allow) himself to be governed in his actions by outside factors acts in "bad faith." Those who are consciously aware of their total responsibility and strive to express their absolutely uncontrollable freedom are "authentic" persons. From this it does not follow that one man's actions are better than another's or more "right." It simply means that "one who realizes in anguish his condition as being thrown into a responsibility which extends to his very abandonment has no longer either remorse or regret or excuse." He also suggests (here and elsewhere, cf. *Existentialism and Humanism*) that one condition which a choice must meet is that it be a choice "for all mankind as well as a choice for myself." This does seem to follow from his claim that "I am responsible for everything" and that presumably includes the well-being of other persons. If, however, this is what Sartre intends, such a Kantian-like condition does tend to negate his denial of all reliance on principle as a basis for choice and as a basis for evaluating actions.

In regard to the second question regarding holding persons responsible, it is important to realize just what Sartre means by "responsibility." He says that he is taking it "in its ordinary sense as 'consciousness of being the incontestable author of an event or of an object'." This is analogous to the sense of the term which we might use in speaking of an earthquake as being responsible for the damage to a building. It is only analogous because earthquakes are not conscious as men are, but insofar as both uses of the term "responsible" express causal notions they share an essential similarity. In any case, this causal sense of responsibility does not necessarily entail praising or blaming a person for his act. I may be "responsible" for someone's death in the sense that I am the one who killed him, but if I acted in self-defense, or it was an accident, I may not be blamed for it. Furthermore, in Sartre's view, since my character is self-made, and essentially undetermined by external influences such as punishment, what point would there be in blaming me for my action anyway? It is therefore at least questionable whether Sartre's view can accommodate a theory of blame. We shall return to this particular topic in Part IV.

Fletcher's views differ from Sartre's in at least two important respects. Fletcher is much more impressed with the ability of circumstances to determine right moral decisions, and he accepts one principle as universally applicable, namely, that one should love God and one's neighbor. Fletcher, however, agrees with Sartre's disdain for legalistic ethics which, as Fletcher conceives it, relies mechanically on a system of principles and rules which blind people to the "headaches and heartbreaks of life." He also rejects, as Sartre, Nietzsche, and James also do, "the notion that the good is 'given' in the nature of things objectively." He also denies that "there are any unwritten immutable laws of heaven" and asserts that "all such notions are idolatrous and a demonic pretension."

Every situation that calls for a moral decision, according to Fletcher, requires that we consider all the relevant circumstances in order to find out what is the "fitting" or appropriate thing to do. Fletcher goes so far as to say that "situation ethics aims at a contextual appropriateness — not the 'good' or the 'right' but the *fitting*." Insofar as customary moral rules (for example, the rule against lying) are seen to fit, they are to be relied upon as guides but abandoned or rejected if they do not fit. Thus he says, "If a murderer asks us his victim's whereabouts, our duty might be to lie."

If, of course, one asks how he can tell whether the rule fits, i.e., whether it can be applied or not, Fletcher does not then refer him to a manual of rules or to a general principle such as Kant's or Mill's. Nor does he merely suggest that one rely on one's intuition. His advice in such a case would be to "love God and your neighbor" and do whatever is consistent with that principle of love. If we are still uncertain regarding what love dictates in such a situation, presumably we must consult the Christian religious tradition, though even here Fletcher says of situation ethics: "It goes part of the way with Scriptural law by accepting revelation as the source of the norm while rejecting all 'revealed' norms or laws but the one command — to love God in the neighbor."

We may question whether Fletcher can have it both ways. On the one hand, he argues for the individual treatment of cases on their own merits irrespective of principles and rules while taking into account only the circumstances of the situation; on the other hand, he wishes to say that whatever the circumstances the principle of love must dictate the moral decision. Of course he wishes to insist that the circumstances and the love principle together are enough to settle the matter. But if the circumstances alone cannot decide the issue (what is right in one set of circumstances at one time may not be right in those same circumstances at another), and if the love principle precludes further definition and elaboration (otherwise we end up with a kind of legalism), it seems we are left with no guidance whatever with respect to moral decisions and actions. We are left only with a moral point of view, or as he calls it, a "strategy of love." But it is apparently a strategy without rules.

Relativism and Egoism

According to W. T. Stace, "Any ethical position which denies that there is a single standard which is equally applicable to all men at all times may fairly be called a species of ethical relativity." Taken as it stands, this statement needs considerable clarification and qualification. The denial that there is a single moral standard or principle is compatible with (1) the view that there are no moral standards whatever (ethical nihilism); (2) the view that no moral standards are knowable (ethical scepticism); (3) the view that there are many moral standards in terms of which to explain moral phenomena (methodological pluralism); and (4) the view that there are many different but equally valid moralities or systems of moral value (value pluralism). We can, if we like, call each of these different positions "species" of ethical relativism, but it would perhaps promote greater clarity and understanding to restrict the meaning of that term.

As it turns out, Stace's main concern is with what we have called value pluralism and its opposite ethical absolutism. While not embracing ethical absolutism, he does mean to argue for the idea of a single morality by rejecting methodological pluralism. His aim is to show that the latter leads to ethical scepticism and ultimately to ethical nihilism. Thus he says, "The case against [ethical relativity] consists, to a very large extent, in urging that, if taken seriously and pressed to its logical conclusion, ethical relativity can only end in destroying the conception of morality altogether." Stace's discussion should be useful to the reader in helping him understand all these various positions and their implications with respect to each other. He should be careful, however, to keep in mind their differences in assessing Stace's criticisms.

If, therefore, we take what Stace means by ethical relativism to be a combination of methodological pluralism and value pluralism (we have seen that James and Nietzsche adopt the second but not the first), we can define ethical relativism somewhat more positively as follows: It is the view that the standard for deciding questions of right conduct or for defining moral goals is the predominant moral belief of a given society, culture, or social group. Since there are many such groups, there are many different moralities and moral standards. On this view, what is right in Communist China may not be what is right in the U.S.A., but the standards of both are equally valid. Of course each is restricted in the validity of its application to members of the respective groups.

It is important not to confuse ethical relativism with what is often called *cultural* or *anthropological relativism*. The latter is the view that moral practices, beliefs, and values vary from country to country, time to time, group to group. It is a purely *factual* or descriptive theory about what people in different societies think is right or valuable. Ethical relativism, on the other hand, is a *normative* doctrine which asserts that the correctness of moral practices *ought* to be determined by a society's dominant moral code. Ethical relativism presupposes anthropological relativism, but it is quite possible to accept the latter without accepting the former. As Stace points out, even an ethical absolutist can accept, and may even wish to emphasize, what the anthropological relativist asserts, "since he is well aware that different people have different sets of moral ideas, and his whole point is that some of these sets of ideas are false."

One of Stace's criticisms of ethical relativism is that when once the whole of humanity is abandoned as the area to be covered by a single moral standard, the procedure whereby we specify any smaller locus of application for a moral standard is bound to be arbitrary. Do we select the unit of a race, a nation, a tribe, a family, or must we end up finally with the unit of a single individual? It is his view that finally the relativist, if he is to follow out the implications of his view, must assert that "every individual is bound by no standard save his own." To put it differently, "anybody's moral opinion is as good as anybody else's and every man is entitled to be judged by his own standards."

The reader must evaluate this particular argument for himself, but it brings to our attention another ethical position called *egoism*. If Stace is correct, then it is simply a variety of relativism, in fact, the final refutation of relativism since he equates "having no standards but one's own" with "having no standards at all." If the egoistic position he has in mind, namely the view that "whatever I think is right is right," is combined with a theory of motivation which states that no one is ever motivated to promote anyone's benefit except his own, a view known as *psychological egoism*, the resultant theory is known as *individual ethical egoism*. Its principle is "Whatever I think is right *for me* is right," or alternatively, "I *should* always act to promote my own interest." Many philosophers have agreed that it does not represent a truly moral point of view. Baier refers to essentially the same view (he calls it "shortsighted" egoism) as "immoral egoism." But another version of egoism has been argued for somewhat more persuasively and is called *universal ethical egoism*.

Instead of the principle, "*I* should always act to promote my own interests," the universal egoist asserts the principle, "*Everyone* should always act so as to promote his own interest." The question is whether this position can consistently be maintained as an independent philosophical theory, or whether it finally reduces to individual egoism. Certainly it is a view which has often been held. Most of the ancient Greek philosophers held it in one form or another. Hobbes' theory is a good example of universal or *enlightened egoism*, as it has sometimes also been called. Sidgwick regards universal ethical egoism as a legitimate "method of ethics" on the ground that everyone could consistently adopt the egoistic point of view, although he himself rejects it on the basis of an intuition that it is false. Others, however, have doubted whether it is even consistent. Can I, if I am an egoist, consistently and rationally will that others look out only for themselves and not for me?

Baier rejects egoism for a variety of reasons, and in so doing provides his own conception of the moral point of view. He argues, first of all, that self-interest cannot be the final determiner of morality because it is incapable of resolving conflicts of interest. But by the moral point of view we mean, he says, "a point of view which is a court of appeal for conflicts of interest." He offers an argument to show that moral talk is impossible for a consistent egoist. He also rejects the implied tenet of ethical egoism that all moral rules are "rules of thumb" to be abandoned whenever they do not advance the egoist's aim. The mark of a truly moral rule, according to Baier, is that it does not allow exceptions in one's favor, but this is precisely what egoism is required by his theory to allow. Baier also criticizes egoism on the ground that although it appears to allow for universalization of rules, nevertheless it cannot. The egoist's rules perhaps cannot be shown to be self-contradictory when universalized, but they are nonetheless "unteachable," for they are, or can be shown to be, either "self-frustrating," "self-defeating," or "morally impossible." An example of a self-frustrating rule would be "When you are in need, ask for help, but never help another man when he is in need." An example of a self-defeating rule would be "Give a promise even when you know or think that you can never keep it, or when you don't intend to keep it."

142

An example of a morally impossible rule would be "Always assert what you think not to be the case." Finally, Baier argues that moral rules must be for the good or at least in the interest of everyone alike. This denies the egoist's basic belief that the ultimate object of any choice must be one's own benefit or interest.

It should be noted that in attempting to spell out the defining features of the moral point of view, Baier is not simply reasserting the position of the traditional ethical absolutist who claims that there is only one true morality. Baier's view is that there are indeed many moralities, some of which are true and some of which are false. He insists that the very idea of "a morality" (as opposed to a system of conventions, customs or laws) depends on the assumption that moral convictions can be either true or false. What he means by saying that a moral conviction or a morality is true is simply that it is "required or acceptable from the moral point of view."

On the other hand, Baier does think that there is such a thing as "absolute morality." By this he means that if we abstract from all true moralities that set of convictions which are true irrespective of any particular social conditions and are true whether anyone holds them or not, then that set of true convictions constitutes "absolute morality." Every true morality will have at its core certain tenets of absolute morality, but it will also contain many convictions whose truth is dependent upon particular social circumstances and so are not components in every other morality. Thus, according to Baier, "Killing is wrong" is a part of absolute morality but "It is wrong to take more than one wife" is not because the latter depends for its truth on the institution of monogamous marriage which exists in some societies but not in others.

Baier's conception of the moral point of view and his criticisms of the self-interest perspective in morality deserve close attention. Specifically the reader might inquire how an egoist might defend his own perspective as a moral one. There would seem to be two ways in which he might attempt to do so. He might simply reassert his own way of viewing morality. Baier himself admits that it is "plausible to hold that a person could not have a reason for doing anything whatsoever unless his behavior was designed to promote his own good." He even agrees that egoism's guiding principle satisfies one formulation of Kant's Categorical Imperative; that is to say, the egoist could in fact will without inconsistency that everyone act on his principle.

The other approach would be to challenge Baier's own conception of the moral point of view. With respect to Baier's claim that self-interest does not provide a "court of appeal" for resolving conflicts, he might argue that it does insofar as your interests can be shown to be mine also, and beyond that perhaps the conflicts are irresolvable anyway. In response to the claim that the moral point of view excludes "exceptions in one's favor," the egoist might reply that this depends on one's conception of rules, and that his allows for just such exceptions. In response to the claim that his rules are not universalizable, he might inquire whether rules can ever attain that status and still be useful and applicable. In response to Baier's claim that moral rules must be for the good of everyone alike, he might inquire whether the observance of rules for *everyone's* good or in *everyone's* interest (if there are such rules) would in fact be as beneficial as more restricted rules which take more account of the particular circumstances and interests of the agent.

The reader may find it interesting to develop these and other kinds of arguments which the egoist might advance against Baier's conception of morality. In any case, it is clear that many of the specific issues involved in this debate concern the status of rules, the consequences of their general application, and the possibility·of exceptions to them. Such questions will be dealt with in Part III.

Ethical Scepticism Versus Ethical Idealism

William James

The Moral Philosopher and the Moral Life

. . . What is the position of him who seeks an ethical philosophy? To begin with, he must be distinguished from all those who are satisfied to be ethical sceptics. He *will* not be a sceptic; therefore so far from ethical scepticism being one possible fruit of ethical philosophizing, it can only be regarded as that residual alternative to all philosophy which from the outset menaces every would-be philosopher who may give up the quest discouraged, and renounce his original aim. That aim is to find an account of the moral relations that obtain among things, which will weave them

From "The Moral Philosopher and the Moral Life," *International Journal of Ethics* I (1891).

into the unity of a stable system, and make of the world what one may call a genuine universe from the ethical point of view. So far as the world resists reduction to the form of unity, so far as ethical propositions seem unstable, so far does the philosopher fail of his ideal. The subject-matter of his study is the ideals he finds existing in the world; the purpose which guides him is this ideal of his own, of getting them into a certain form. This ideal is thus a factor in ethical philosophy whose legitimate presence must never be overlooked; it is a positive contribution which the philosopher himself necessarily makes to the problem. But it is his only positive contribution. At the outset of his inquiry he ought to have no other ideals. Were he interested peculiarly in the triumph of any one kind of good, he would *pro tanto* cease to be a judicial investigator, and become an advocate for some limited element of the case. . . .

[T]he Benthams, the Mills, and the Bains have done a lasting service in taking so many of our human ideals and showing how they must have arisen from the association with acts of simple bodily pleasures and reliefs from pain. Association with many remote pleasures will unquestionably make a thing significant of goodness in our minds; and the more vaguely the goodness is conceived of, the more mysterious will its source appear to be. But it is surely impossible to explain all our sentiments and preferences in this simple way. . . . Take the love of drunkenness; take bashfulness, the terror of high places, the tendency to seasickness, to faint at the sight of blood, the susceptibility to musical sounds; take the emotion of the comical, the passion for poetry, for mathematics, or for metaphysics — no one of these things can be wholly explained by either association or utility. They *go with* other things that can be so explained, no doubt; and some of them are prophetic of future utilities, since there is nothing in us for which some use may not be found. But their origin is in incidental complications to our cerebral structure, a structure whose original features arose with no reference to the perception of such discords and harmonies as these.

Well, a vast number of our moral perceptions also are certainly of this secondary and brain-born kind. They deal with directly felt fitnesses between things, and often fly in the teeth of all the prepossessions of habit and presumptions of utility. . . . The sense for abstract justice which some persons have is as eccentric a variation, from the natural-history point of view, as is the passion for music or for the higher philosophical consistencies which consumes the soul of others. The feeling of the inward dignity of certain spiritual attitudes, as peace, serenity, simplicity, veracity; and of the essential vulgarity of others, as querulousness, anxiety, egoistic fussiness, etc. — are quite inexplicable except by an innate preference of the more ideal attitude for its own sake. The nobler thing *tastes* better, and that is all that we can say. "Experience" of consequences may truly teach us what things are *wicked*, but what have consequences to do with what is *mean* and *vulgar?* . . .

Our ideals have certainly many sources. They are not all explicable as signifying corporeal pleasures to be gained, and pains to be escaped. And for having so constantly perceived this psychological fact, we must applaud the intuitionist school. Whether or not such applause must be extended to that school's other characteristics will appear as we take up the following questions.

The next one in order is the . . . question, of what we mean by the words "obligation," "good," and "ill."

First of all, it appears that such words can have no application or relevancy in a world in which no sentient life exists. Imagine an absolutely material world, containing only physical and chemical facts, and existing from eternity without a God, without even an interested spectator: would there be any sense in saying of that world that one of its states is better than another? Of if there were two such worlds possible, would there be any rhyme or reason in calling one good and the other bad — good or bad positively, I mean, and apart from the fact that one might relate itself better than the other to the philosopher's private interests? But we must leave these private interests out of the account, for the philosopher is a mental fact, and we are asking whether goods and evils and obligations exist in physical facts *per se*. Surely there is no *status* for good and evil to exist in, in a purely insentient world. How can one physical fact, considered simply as a physical fact, be "better" than another? Betterness is not a physical relation. In its mere material capacity, a thing can no more be good or bad than it can be pleasant or painful. Good for what? Good for the production of another physical fact, do you say? But what in a purely physical universe demands the production of that other fact? Physical facts simply *are* or are *not*; and neither when present or absent, can they be supposed to make demands. If they do, they can only do so by having desires; and then they have ceased to be purely physical facts, and have become facts of conscious sensibility. Goodness, badness, and obligation must be *realized* somewhere in order really to exist; and the first step in ethical philosophy is to see that no merely inorganic "nature of things" can realize them. Neither moral relations nor the moral law can swing *in vacuo*. Their only habitat can be a mind which feels them; and no world composed of merely physical facts can possibly be a world to which ethical propositions apply.

The moment one sentient being, however, is made a part of the universe, there is a chance for goods and evils really to exist. Moral relations now have their *status*, in that being's consciousness. So far as he feels anything to be good, he *makes* it good. It *is* good, for him; and being good for him, is absolutely good, for he is the sole creator of values in that universe, and outside of his opinion things have no moral character at all.

In such a universe as that it would of course be absurd to raise the question of whether the solitary thinker's judgments of good and ill are true or not. Truth supposes a standard outside of the thinker to which he must conform; but here the thinker is a sort of divinity, subject to no higher judge. Let us call the supposed universe which he inhabits a *moral solitude*. In such a moral solitude it is clear that there can be no outward obligation, and that the only trouble the god-like thinker is liable to have will be over the consistency of his own several ideals with one another. Some of these will no doubt be more pungent and appealing than the rest, their goodness will have a profounder, more penetrating taste; they will return to haunt him with more obstinate regrets if violated. So the thinker will have to order his life with them as its chief determinants, or else remain inwardly discordant and unhappy. Into whatever equilibrium he may settle, though, and however he may straighten out his system, it will be a right system; for beyond the facts of his own subjectivity there is nothing moral in the world.

If we now introduce a second thinker with his likes and dislikes into the universe, the ethical situation becomes much more complex, and several possibilities are immediately seen to obtain.

One of these is that the thinkers may ignore each other's attitude about good and evil altogether, and each continue to indulge his own preferences, indifferent to what the other may feel or do. In such a case we have a world with twice as much of the ethical quality in it as our moral solitude, only it is without ethical unity. The same object is good or bad there, according as you measure it by the view which this one or that one of the thinkers takes. Nor can you find any possible ground in such a world for saying that one thinker's opinion is more correct than the other's, or that either has the truer moral sense. Such a world, in short, is not a moral universe but a moral dualism. Not only is there no single point of view within it from which the value of things can be unequivocally judged, but there is not even a demand for such a point of view, since the two thinkers are supposed to be indifferent to each other's thoughts and acts. Multiply the thinkers into a pluralism, and we find realized for us in the ethical sphere something like that world which the antique sceptics conceived of—in which individual minds are the measures of all things, and in which no one "objective" truth, but only a multitude of "subjective" opinions, can be found.

But this is the kind of world with which the philosopher, so long as he holds to the hope of philosophy, will not put up. Among the various ideals represented, there must be, he thinks, some which have the more truth or authority; and to these the others *ought* to yield, so that system and subordination may reign. Here in the word "ought" the notion of *obligation* comes emphatically into view, and the next thing in order must be to make its meaning clear.

Since the outcome of the discussion so far has been to show us that nothing can be good or right except so far as some consciousness feels it to be good or thinks it to be right, we perceive on the very threshold that the real superiority and authority which are postulated by the philosopher to reside in some of the opinions, and the really inferior character which he supposes must belong to others, cannot be explained by any abstract moral "nature of things" existing antecedently to the concrete thinkers themselves with their ideals. Like the positive attributes good and bad, the comparative ones better and worse must be *realized* in order to be real. If one ideal judgment be objectively better than another, that betterness must be made flesh by being lodged concretely in some one's actual perception. It cannot float in the atmosphere, for it is not a sort of meteorological phenomenon, like the aurora borealis or the zodiacal light. Its *esse* is *percipi*, the *esse* of the ideals themselves between which it obtains. The philosopher, therefore, who seeks to know which ideal ought to have supreme weight and which one ought to be subordinated, must trace the *ought* itself to the *de facto* constitution of some existing consciousness, behind which, as one of the data of the universe, he as a purely ethical philosopher is unable to go. This consciousness must make the one ideal right by feeling it to be right, the other wrong by feeling it to be wrong. But now what particular consciousness in the universe *can* enjoy this prerogative of obliging others to conform to a rule which it lays down?

If one of the thinkers were obviously divine, while all the rest were human, there would probably be no practical dispute about the matter. The divine thought would be the model, to which the others should conform. But still the theoretical question would remain, What is the ground of the obligation, even here?

In our first essays at answering this question, there is an inevitable tendency to slip into an assumption which ordinary men follow when they are disputing with one another about questions of good and bad. They imagine an abstract moral order in which the objective truth resides; and each tries to prove that this pre-existing order is more accurately reflected in his own ideas than in those of his adversary. It is because one disputant is backed by this overarching abstract order that we think the other should submit. Even so, when it is a question no longer of two finite thinkers, but of God and ourselves—we follow our usual habit, and imagine a sort of *de jure* relation, which antedates and overarches the mere facts, and would make it right that we should conform our thoughts to God's thoughts, even though he made no claim to that effect, and though we preferred *de facto* to go on thinking for ourselves.

But the moment we take a steady look at the question, *we see not only that without a claim actually made by some concrete person there can be no obligation, but that there is some obligation wherever there is a claim.* Claim and obligation are, in fact, coextensive terms; they cover each other exactly. Our ordinary attitude of regarding ourselves as subject to an overarching system of moral relations, true "in themselves," is therefore either an out-and-out superstition, or else it must be treated as a merely provisional abstraction from that real Thinker in whose actual demand upon us to think as he does our obligation must be ultimately based. In a theistic-ethical philosophy that thinker in question is, of course, the Deity to whom the existence of the universe is due.

I know well how hard it is for those who are accustomed to what I have called the superstitious view, to realize that every *de facto* claim creates in so far forth an obligation. We inveterately think that something which we call the "validity" of the claim is what gives to it its obligatory character, and that this validity is something outside of the claim's mere existence as a matter of fact. It rains down upon the claim, we think, from some sublime dimension of being, which the moral law inhabits, much as upon the steel of the compass-needle the influence of the Pole rains down from out of the starry heavens. But again, how can such an inorganic abstract character of imperativeness, additional to the imperativeness which is in the concrete claim itself, *exist?* Take any demand, however slight, which any creature, however weak, may make. Ought it not, for its own sole sake, to be satisfied? If not, prove why not. The only possible kind of proof you could adduce would be the exhibition of another creature who should make a demand that ran the other way. The only possible reason there can be why any phenomenon ought to exist is that such a phenomenon actually is desired. Any desire is imperative to the extent of its amount; it *makes* itself valid by the fact that it exists at all. Some desires, truly enough, are small desires; they are put forward by insignificant persons, and we customarily make light of the obligations which they bring. But the fact that such personal demands as these impose small obligations does not keep the largest obligations from being personal demands.

150

If we must talk impersonally, to be sure we can say that "the universe" requires, exacts, or makes obligatory such or such an action, whenever it expresses itself through the desires of such or such a creature. But it is better not to talk about the universe in this personified way, unless we believe in a universal or divine consciousness which actually exists. If there be such a consciousness, then its demands carry the most of obligation simply because they are the greatest in amount. But it is even then not *abstractly* right that we should respect them. It is only *concretely* right—or right after the fact, and by virtue of the fact, that they are actually made. Suppose we do not respect them, as seems largely to be the case in this queer world. That ought not to be, we say; that is wrong. But in what way is this fact of wrongness made more acceptable or intelligible when we imagine it to consist rather in the laceration of an *a priori* ideal order than in the disappointment of a living personal God? Do we, perhaps, think that we cover God and protect him and make his impotence over us less ultimate, when we back him up with this *a priori* blanket from which he may draw some warmth of further appeal? But the only force of appeal to *us*, which either a living God or an abstract ideal order can wield, is found in the "everlasting ruby vaults" of our own human hearts, as they happen to beat responsive and not irresponsive to the claim. So far as they do feel it when made by a living consciousness, it is life answering to life. A claim thus livingly acknowledged is acknowledged with a solidity and fulness which no thought of an "ideal" backing can render more complete; while if, on the other hand, the heart's response is withheld, the stubborn phenomenon is there of an impotence in the claims which the universe embodies, which no talk about an eternal nature of things can gloze over or dispel. An ineffective *a priori* is as impotent a thing as an ineffective God; and in the eye of philosophy, it is as hard a thing to explain.

We may now consider that . . . we have learned what the words "good," "bad," and "obligation" severally mean. They mean no absolute natures, independent of personal support. They are objects of feeling and desire, which have no foothold or anchorage in Being, apart from the existence of actually living minds.

Wherever such minds exist, with judgments of good and ill, and demands upon one another, there is an ethical world in its essential feature. Were all other things, gods and men and starry heavens, blotted out from this universe, and were there left but one rock with two loving souls upon it, that rock would have as thoroughly moral a constitution as any possible world which the eternities and immensities could harbor. It would be a tragic constitution, because the rock's inhabitants would die.

But while they lived, there would be real good things and real bad things in the universe; there would be obligations, claims, and expectations; obediences, refusals, and disappointments; compunctions and longings for harmony to come again, and inward peace of conscience when it was restored; there would, in short, be a moral life, whose active energy would have no limit but the intensity of interest in each other with which the hero and heroine might be endowed.

We, on this terrestrial globe, so far as the visible facts go, are just like the inhabitants of such a rock. Whether a God exist, or whether no God exist, in yon blue heaven above us bent, we form at any rate an ethical republic here below. And the first reflection which this leads to is that ethics have as genuine and real a foothold in a universe where the highest consciousness is human, as in a universe where there is a God as well. "The religion of humanity" affords a basis for ethics as well as theism does. . . .

Here we are, in a world where the existence of a divine thinker has been and perhaps always will be doubted by some of the lookers-on, and where, in spite of the presence of a large number of ideals in which human beings agree, there are a mass of others about which no general consensus obtains. It is hardly necessary to present a literary picture of this, for the facts are too well known. The wars of the flesh and the spirit in each man, the concupiscences of different individuals pursuing the same un-shareable material or social prizes, the ideals which contrast so according to races, circumstances, temperaments, philosophical beliefs, etc. — all form a maze of apparently inextricable confusion with no obvious Ariadne's thread to lead one out. Yet the philosopher, just because he is a philosopher, adds his own peculiar ideal to the confusion (with which if he were willing to be a sceptic he would be passably content), and insists that over all these individual opinions there is a *system of truth* which he can discover if he only takes sufficient pains.

We stand ourselves at present in the place of that philosopher, and must not fail to realize all the features that the situation comports. In the first place we will not be sceptics; we hold to it that there is a truth to be ascertained. But in the second place we have just gained the insight that that truth cannot be a self-proclaiming set of laws, or an abstract "moral reason," but can only exist in act, or in the shape of an opinion held by some thinker really to be found. There is, however, no visible thinker invested with authority. Shall we then simply proclaim our own ideals as the lawgiving ones? No; for if we are true philosophers we must throw our own spontaneous ideals, even the dearest, impartially in with that total mass of ideals which are fairly to be judged. But how then can we as philosophers ever find a test; how avoid complete moral scepticism on the one hand, and on the other escape bringing a wayward personal standard of our own along with us, on which we simply pin our faith?

The dilemma is a hard one, nor does it grow a bit more easy as we revolve it in our minds. The entire undertaking of the philosopher obliges him to seek an impartial test. That test, however, must be incarnated in the demand of some actually existent person; and how can he pick out the person save by an act in which his own sympathies and prepossessions are implied?

One method indeed presents itself, and has as a matter of history been taken by the more serious ethical schools. If the heap of things demanded proved on inspection less chaotic than at first they seemed, if they furnished their own relative test and measure, then the casuistic problem would be solved. If it were found that all goods *quâ* goods contained a common essence, then the amount of this essence involved in any one good would show its rank in the scale of goodness, and order could be quickly made; for this essence would be *the* good upon which all thinkers were agreed, and the relatively objective and universal good that the philosopher seeks. Even his own private ideals would be measured by their share of it, and find their rightful place among the rest.

Various essences of good have thus been found and proposed as bases of the ethical system. Thus, to be a mean between two extremes; to be recognized by a special intuitive faculty; to make the agent happy for the moment; to make others as well as him happy in the long run; to add to his perfection or dignity; to harm no one; to follow from reason or flow from universal law; to be in accordance with the will of God; to promote the survival of the human species on this planet—are so many tests, each of which has been maintained by somebody to constitute the essence of all good things or actions so far as they are good.

No one of the measures that have been actually proposed has, however, given general satisfaction. Some are obviously not universally present in all cases—*e.g.,* the character of harming no one, or that of following a universal law; for the best course is often cruel; and many acts are reckoned good on the sole condition that they be exceptions, and serve not as examples of a universal law. Other characters, such as following the will of God, are unascertainable and vague. Others again, like survival, are quite indeterminate in their consequences, and leave us in the lurch where we most need their help; a philosopher of the Sioux Nation, for example, will be certain to use the survival-criterion in a very different way from ourselves. The best, on the whole, of these marks and measures of goodness seems to be the capacity to bring happiness. But in order not to break down fatally, this test must be taken to cover innumerable acts and impulses that never *aim* at happiness; so that, after all, in seeking for a universal principle we inevitably are carried onward to the *most* universal principle—that *the essence of good is simply to satisfy demand*. The demand may be for anything under the sun. There is really no more ground for supposing that all our demands can be accounted for by one universal underlying kind of motive than there is ground for supposing that all physical phenomena are cases of a single law. The elementary forces in ethics are probably as plural as those of physics are. The various ideals have no common character apart from the fact that they are ideals. No single abstract principle can be so used as to yield to the philosopher anything like a scientifically accurate and genuinely useful casuistic scale.

A look at another peculiarity of the ethical universe, as we find it, will still further show us the philosopher's perplexities. As a purely theoretic problem, namely, the casuistic question would hardly ever come up at all. If the ethical philosopher were only asking after the best *imaginable* system of goods he would indeed have an easy task; for all demands as such are *prima facie* respectable, and the best simply imaginary world would be one in which every demand was gratified as soon as made. Such a world would, however, have to have a physical constitution entirely different from that of the one which we inhabit. It would need not only a space, but a time, of *n*-dimensions, to include all the acts and experiences incompatible with one another here below, which would then go on in conjunction—such as spending our money, yet growing rich; taking our holiday, yet getting ahead with our work; shooting and fishing, yet doing no hurt to the beasts; gaining no end of experience, yet keeping our youthful freshness of heart; and the like. There can be no question that such a system of things, however brought about, would be the absolutely ideal system; and that if a philosopher could create universes *a priori*, and provide all the mechanical conditions, that is the sort of universe which he should unhesitatingly create.

But this world of ours is made on an entirely different pattern, and the casuistic question here is most tragically practical. The actually possible in this world is vastly narrower than all that is demanded; and there is always a *pinch* between the ideal and the actual which can only be got through by leaving part of the ideal behind. There is hardly a good which we can imagine except as competing for the possession of the same bit of space and time with some other imagined good. Every end of desire that presents itself appears exclusive of some other end of desire. Shall a man drink and smoke, *or* keep his nerves in condition?—he cannot do both. Shall he follow his fancy for Amelia, *or* for Henrietta?—both cannot be the choice of his heart. Shall he have the dear old Republican party, *or* a spirit of unsophistication in public affairs?—he cannot have both, etc. So that the ethical philosopher's demand for the right scale of subordination in ideals is the fruit of an altogether practical need. Some part of the ideal must be butchered, and he needs to know which part. It is a tragic situation, and no mere speculative conundrum, with which he has to deal.

Now *we* are blinded to the real difficulty of the philosopher's task by the fact that we are born into a society whose ideals are largely ordered already. If we follow the ideal which is conventionally highest, the others which we butcher either die and do not return to haunt us; or if they come back and accuse us of murder, every one applauds us for turning to them a deaf ear. In other words, our environment encourages us not to be philosophers but partisans. . . .

What can he do, then, it will now be asked, except to fall back on scepticism and give up the notion of being a philosopher at all?

But do we not already see a perfectly definite path of escape which is open to him just because he is a philosopher, and not the champion of one particular ideal? Since everything which is demanded is by that fact a good, must not the guiding principle for ethical philosophy (since all demands conjointly cannot be satisfied in this poor world) be simply to satisfy at all times *as many demands as we can?* That act must be the best act, accordingly, which makes for the *best whole,* in the sense of awakening the least sum of dissatisfactions. In the casuistic scale, therefore, those ideals must be written highest which *prevail at the least cost,* or by whose realization the least possible number of other ideals are destroyed. Since victory and defeat there must be, the victory to be philosophically prayed for is that of the more inclusive side—of the side which even in the hour of triumph will to some degree do justice to the ideals in which the vanquished party's interests lay. The course of history is nothing but the story of men's struggles from generation to generation to find the more and more inclusive order. *Invent some manner* of realizing your own ideals which will also satisfy the alien demands—that and that only is the path of peace! Following this path, society has shaken itself into one sort of relative equilibrium after another by a series of social discoveries quite analogous to those of science. Polyandry and polygamy and slavery, private warfare and liberty to kill, judicial torture and arbitrary royal power have slowly succumbed to actually aroused complaints; and though some one's ideals are unquestionably the worse off for each improvement, yet a vastly greater total number of them find shelter in our civilized society than in the older savage ways. So far then, and up to date, the casuistic scale is made for the philosopher already far better than he can ever make it for himself. An experiment of the most searching kind has proved that the laws and usages of the land are what yield the maximum of satisfaction to the thinkers taken all together. The presumption in cases of conflict must always be in favor of the conventionally recognized good. The philosopher must be a conservative, and in the construction of his casuistic scale must put the things most in accordance with the customs of the community on top.

And yet if he is to be a true philosopher he must see that there is nothing final in any actually given equilibrium of human ideals, but that, as our present laws and customs have fought and conquered other past ones, so they will in their turn be overthrown by any newly discovered order which will hush up the complaints that they still give rise to, without producing others louder still. "Rules are made for man, not man for rules"—that one sentence is enough to immortalize Green's *Prolegomena to Ethics.* And although a man always risks much when he breaks away from established rules and strives to realize a larger ideal whole than they permit, yet the philosopher must allow that it is at all times open to any one to make the experiment, provided he fear not to stake his life and character upon the throw. The pinch is always here. Pent in under every system of moral rules are innumerable persons whom it weighs upon, and goods which it represses; and these are always rumbling and grumbling in the background, and ready for any issue by which they may get free. See the abuses which the institution of private property covers, so that even today it is shamelessly asserted among us that one of the prime functions of the national government is to help the adroiter citizens to grow rich. See the unnamed and unnamable sorrows which the tyranny, on the whole so beneficial, of the marriage-institution brings to so many, both of the married and the unwed. See the wholesale loss of opportunity under our *régime* of so-called equality and industrialism, with the drummer and the counter-jumper in the saddle, for so many faculties and graces which could flourish in the feudal world. See our kindliness for the humble and the outcast, how it wars with that stern weeding-out which until now has been the condition of every perfection in the breed. See everywhere the struggle and the squeeze; and everlastingly the problem how to make them less. The anarchists, nihilists, and free-lovers; the free-silverites, socialists, and single-tax men; the free-traders and the civil-service reformers; the prohibitionists and anti-vivisectionists; the radical Darwinians with their idea of the suppression of the weak—these and all the conservative sentiments of society arrayed against them, are simply deciding through actual experiment by what sort of conduct the maximum amount of good can be gained and kept in this world. These experiments are to be judged, not *a priori*, but by actual finding, after the fact of their making, how much more outcry or how much appeasement comes about. What closet-solutions can possibly anticipate the result of trials made on such a scale? Or what can any superficial theorist's judgment be worth, in a world where every one of hundreds of ideals has its special champion already provided in the shape of some genius expressly born to feel it, and to fight to death in its behalf? The pure philosopher can only follow the windings of the spectacle, confident that the line of least resistance will always be towards the richer and the more inclusive arrangement, and that by one tack after another some approach to the kingdom of heaven is incessantly made. . . .

On the whole, then we must conclude that no philosophy of ethics is possible in the old-fashioned absolute sense of the term. Everywhere the ethical philosopher must wait on facts. The thinkers who create the ideals come he knows not whence, their sensibilities are evolved he knows not how; and the question as to which of two conflicting ideals will give the best universe then and there, can be answered by him only through the aid of the experience of other men. . . . In point of fact, there are no absolute evils, and there are no non-moral goods; and the *highest* ethical life—however few may be called to bear its burdens—consists at all times in the breaking of rules which have grown too narrow for the actual case. There is but one unconditional commandment, which is that we should seek incessantly, with fear and trembling, so to vote and to act as to bring about the very largest total universe of good which we can see. Abstract rules indeed can help; but they help the less in proportion as our intuitions are more piercing, and our vocation is the stronger for the moral life. For every real dilemma is in literal strictness a unique situation; and the exact combination of ideals realized and ideals disappointed which each decision creates is always a universe without a precedent, and for which no adequate previous rule exists. The philosopher, then, *quâ* philosopher, is no better able to determine the best universe in the concrete emergency than other men. He sees, indeed, somewhat better than most men what the question always is—not a questioon of this good or that good simply taken, but of the two total universes with which these goods respectively belong. He knows that he must vote always for the richer universe, for the good which seems most organizable, most fit to enter into complex combinations, most apt to be a member of a more inclusive whole. But which particular universe this is he cannot know for certain in advance; he only knows that if he makes a bad mistake the cries of the wounded will soon inform him of the fact. In all this the philosopher is just like the rest of us non-philosophers, so far as we are just and sympathetic instinctively, and so far as we are open to the voice of complaint. His function is in fact indistinguishable from that of the best kind of statesman at the present day. His books upon ethics, therefore, so far as they truly touch the moral life, must more and more ally themselves with a literature which is confessedly tentative and suggestive rather than dogmatic—I mean with novels and dramas of the deeper sort, with sermons, with books on statecraft and philanthropy and social and economical reform. Treated in this way ethical treatises may be voluminous and luminous as well; but they never can be *final*, except in their abstractest and vaguest features; and they must more and more abandon the old-fashioned, clear-cut, and would-be "scientific" form.

Master Versus Slave Moralities

Friedrich Nietzsche

Beyond Good and Evil: The Will to Power

[How Moralities Should Be Viewed[1]]

Under "Morality" I understand a system of valuations which is in relation with the conditions of a creature's life.

Formerly it was said of every form of morality, "Ye shall know them by their fruits." I say of every form of morality: "It is a fruit, and from it I learn the *Soil* out of which it grew."

From Friedrich Nietzsche, *The Complete Works of Friedrich Nietzsche,* translated under the editorship of Oscar Levy (1909–1911). By permission of the publishers, George Allen & Unwin Ltd., London; Russell & Russell, New York (reissued 1964).

[1]From *The Will to Power,* trans. by Anthony M. Ludovici, Sections 256-259, 261, 265; *Beyond Good and Evil,* trans. by Helen Zimmern, Sec. 260.

I have tried to understand all moral judgments as symptoms and a language of signs in which the processes of physiological prosperity or the reverse, as also the consciousness of the conditions of preservation and growth, are betrayed—a mode of interpretation equal in worth to astrology, prejudices, created by instincts (peculiar to races, communities, and different stages of existence, as, for instance, youth or decay, etc.)

Applying this principle to the morality of Christian Europe more particularly, we find that our moral values are signs of decline, of a disbelief in *Life*, and of a preparation for pessimism.

My leading doctrine is this: *there are no moral phenomena, but only a moral interpretation of phenomena. The origin of this interpretation itself lies beyond the pale of morality.* What is the meaning of the fact that we have imagined a *contradiction* in existence? This is of paramount importance: behind all other valuations those moral valuations stand commandingly. Supposing they disappear, according to what standard shall we then measure? And then of what value would knowledge be, etc. etc.???

A point of view: in all valuations there is a definite purpose: the *preservation* of an individual, a community, a race, a state, a church, a belief, or a culture. — Thanks to the fact that people *forget* that all valuing has a purpose, one and the same man may swarm with a host of contradictory valuations, and *therefore with a host of contradictory impulses.* This is the *expression of disease in man* as opposed to the health of animals, in which all the instincts answer certain definite purposes.

This creature full of contradictions, however, has in his being a grand method of acquiring knowledge: he feels the pros and cons, he elevates himself *to Justice* — that is to say, to the ascertaining of principles *beyond the valuations good and evil.*

The wisest man would thus be the *richest in contradictions,* he would also be gifted with mental antennae wherewith he could understand all kinds of men; and with it all he would have his great moments, when all the chords in his being would ring in *splendid unison* — the rarest of *accidents* even in us! A sort of planetary movement.

What is the *criterion* of a moral action? (1) Its disinterestedness, (2) its universal acceptance, etc. But this is parlour-morality. Races must be studied and observed, and, in each case, the criterion must be discovered, as also the thing it expresses: a belief such as: "This particular attitude or behaviour belongs to the principal condition of our existence." Immoral means "that which brings about ruin." Now all societies in which these principles were discovered have met with their ruin: a few of these principles have been used and used again, because every newly established community required them; this was the case, for instance, with "Thou shalt not steal." In ages when people could not be expected to show any marked social instinct (as, for instance, in the age of the Roman Empire) the latter was, religiously speaking, directed towards the idea of "spiritual salvation," or, in philosophical parlance, towards "the greatest happiness." For even the philosophers of Greece did not feel any more for their *polis* [city-state].

There seems to be no knowledge or consciousness of the many *revolutions* that have taken place in moral judgments, and of the number of times that "evil" has really and seriously been christened "good" and *vice versa. . . .*

In a tour through the many finer and coarser moralities which have hitherto prevailed or still prevail on the earth, I found certain traits recurring regularly together, and connected with one another, until finally two primary types revealed themselves to me, and a radical distinction was brought to light. There is *master-morality* and *slave-morality; —* I would at once add, however, that in all higher and mixed civilisations, there are also attempts at the reconciliation of the two moralities; but one finds still oftener the confusion and mutual misunderstanding of them, indeed, sometimes their close juxtaposition — even in the same man, within one soul. The distinctions of moral values have either originated in a ruling caste, pleasantly conscious of being different from the ruled — or among the ruled class, the slaves and dependents of all sorts. In the first case, when it is the rulers who determine the conception "good," it is the exalted, proud disposition which is regarded as the distinguishing feature and that which determines the order of rank. The noble type of man separates from himself the beings in whom the opposite of this exalted, proud disposition displays itself: he despises them. Let it at once be noted that in this first kind of morality the antithesis "good" and "bad" means practically the same as "noble" and "despicable"; — the antithesis "good" and "*evil*" is of a different origin. The cowardly, the timid, the insignificant, and those thinking merely of narrow utility are despised; moreover, also, the distrustful, with their constrained glances, the self-abasing, the dog-like kind of men who let themselves be abused, the mendicant flatterers, and above all the liars: — it is a fundamental belief of all aristocrats that the common people are untruthful. "We truthful ones" — the nobility in ancient Greece called themselves. It is obvious that everywhere the designations of moral value were at first applied to *men,* and were only derivatively and at a later period applied to *actions;*

it is a gross mistake, therefore, when historians of morals start with questions like, "Why have sympathetic actions been praised?" The noble type of man regards *himself* as a determiner of values; he does not require to be approved of; he passes the judgment: "What is injurious to me is injurious in itself"; he knows that it is he himself only who confers honour on things; he is a *creator of values*. He honours whatever he recognises in himself: such morality is self-glorification. In the foreground there is the feeling of plenitude, of power, which seeks to overflow, the happiness of high tension, the consciousness of a wealth which would fain give and bestow: — the noble man also helps the unfortunate, but not — or scarcely — out of pity, but rather from an impulse generated by the super-abundance of power. The noble man honours in himself the powerful one, him also who has power over himself, who knows how to speak and how to keep silence, who takes pleasure in subjecting himself to severity and hardness, and has reverence for all that is severe and hard. "Wotan placed a hard heart in my breast," says an old Scandinavian Saga: it is thus rightly expressed from the soul of a proud Viking. Such a type of man is even proud of *not* being made for sympathy; the hero of the Saga therefore adds warningly: "He who has not a hard heart when young, will never have one." The noble and brave who think thus are the furthest removed from the morality which sees precisely in sympathy, or in acting for the good of others, or in *désintéressement*, the characteristic of the moral; faith in oneself, pride in oneself, a radical enmity and irony towards "selflessness," belong as definitely to noble morality, as do a careless scorn and precaution in presence of sympathy and the "warm heart." — It is the powerful who *know* how to honour, it is their art, their domain for invention. The profound reverence for age and for tradition — all law rests on this double reverence, — the belief and prejudice in favour of ancestors and unfavourable to newcomers, is typical in the morality of the powerful; and if, reversely, men of "modern ideas" believe almost instinctively in "progress" and the "future," and are more and more lacking in respect for old age, the ignoble origin of these "ideas" has complacently betrayed itself thereby. A morality of the ruling class, however, is more especially foreign and irritating to present-day taste in the sternness of its principle that one has duties only to one's equals; that one may act towards beings of a lower rank, towards all that is foreign, just as seems good to one, or "as the heart desires," and in any case "beyond good and evil": it is here that sympathy and similar sentiments can have a place. The ability and obligation to exercise prolonged gratitude and prolonged revenge — both only within the circle of equals, —

artfulness in retaliation, *raffinement* of the idea in friendship, a certain necessity to have enemies (as outlets for the emotions of envy, quarrelsomeness, arrogance — in fact, in order to be a good friend) : all these are typical characteristics of the noble morality, which, as has been pointed out, is not the morality of "modern ideas," and is therefore at present difficult to realise, and also to unearth and disclose. — It is otherwise with the second type of morality, *slave-morality*. Supposing that the abused, the oppressed, the suffering, the unemancipated, the weary, and those uncertain of themselves, should moralise, what will be the common element in their moral estimates? Probably a pessimistic suspicion with regard to the entire situation of man will find expression, perhaps a condemnation of man, together with his situation. The slave has an unfavourable eye for the virtues of the powerful; he has a scepticism and distrust, a *refinement* of distrust of everything "good" that is there honoured — he would fain persuade himself that the very happiness there is not genuine. On the other hand, *those* qualities which serve to alleviate the existence of sufferers are brought into prominence and flooded with light; it is here that sympathy, the kind, helping hand, the warm heart, patience, diligence, humility, and friendliness attain to honour; for here these are the most useful qualities, and almost the only means of supporting the burden of existence. Slave-morality is essentially the morality of utility. Here is the seat of the origin of the famous antithesis "good" and "*evil*": — power and dangerousness are assumed to reside in the evil, a certain dreadfulness, subtlety, and strength, which do not admit of being despised. According to slave-morality, therefore, the "evil" man arouses fear; according to the master-morality, it is precisely the "good" man who arouses fear and seeks to arouse it, while the bad man is regarded as the despicable being. The contrast attains its maximum when, in accordance with the logical consequences of slave-morality, a shade of depreciation — it may be slight and well-intentioned — at last attaches itself even to the "good" man of this morality; because, according to the servile mode of thought, the good man must in any case be the *safe* man: he is good-natured, easily deceived, perhaps a little stupid, *un bonhomme*. Everywhere that slave-morality gains the ascendency, language shows a tendency to approximate the significations of the words "good" and "stupid."—A last fundamental difference: the desire for *freedom,* the instinct for happiness and the refinements of the feeling of liberty belong as necessarily to slave-morals and morality, as artifice and enthusiasm in reverence and devotion are the regular symptoms of an aristocratic mode of thinking and estimating. . . .

[Criticism of Customary Moral Values[2]]

The preponderance of an altruistic way of valuing is the result of a consciousness of the fact that one is botched and bungled. Upon examination, this point of view turns out to be: "I am not worth much," simply a psychological valuation; more plainly still: it is the feeling of impotence, of the lack of the great self-asserting impulses of power (in muscles, nerves, and ganglia). This valuation gets translated, according to the particular culture of these classes, into a moral or religious principle (the pre-eminence of religious or moral precepts is always a sign of low culture): it tries to justify itself in spheres whence, as far as it is concerned, the notion "value" hails. The interpretation by means of which the Christian sinner tries to understand himself, is an attempt at justifying his lack of power and of self-confidence: he prefers to feel himself a sinner rather than feel bad for nothing: it is in itself a symptom of decay when interpretations of this sort are used at all. In some cases the bungled and the botched do not look for the reason of their unfortunate condition in their own guilt (as the Christian does), but in society: when, however, the Socialist, the Anarchist, and the Nihilist are conscious that their existence is something for which some one must be *guilty*, they are very closely related to the Christian, who also believes that he can more easily endure his ill ease and his wretched constitution when he has found some one whom he can hold *responsible* for it. The instinct of *revenge* and *resentment* appears in both cases here as a means of enduring life, as a self-preservative measure, as is also the favour shown to *altruistic* theory and practice. The *hatred of egoism*, whether it be one's own (as in the case of the Christian), or another's (as in the case of the Socialists), thus appears as a valuation reached under the predominance of revenge; and also as an act of prudence on the part of the preservative instinct of the suffering, in the form of an increase in their feelings of co-operation and unity. . . . At bottom, as I have already suggested, the discharge of resentment which takes place in the act of judging, rejecting, and punishing egoism (one's own or that of others) is yet another self-preservative instinct on the part of the bungled and the botched. In short: the cult of altruism is merely a particular form of egoism, which regularly appears under certain definite physiological circumstances.

When the Socialist, with righteous indignation, cries for "justice," "rights," "equal rights," it only shows that he is oppressed by his inade-

---

[2]From *The Will to Power*, sections 373, 200, 204; from *Beyond Good and Evil*, section 62.

quate culture, and is unable to understand why he suffers: he also finds pleasure in crying; — if he were more at ease he would take jolly good care not to cry in that way: in that case he would seek his pleasure elsewhere. The same holds good of the Christian: he curses, condemns, and slanders the "world" — and does not even except himself. But that is no reason for taking him seriously. In both cases we are in the presence of invalids who feel better for crying, and who find relief in slander.

I find Christianity as the most fatal and seductive lie that has ever yet existed — as the greatest and most *impious lie*: I can discern the last sprouts and branches of its ideal beneath every form of disguise, I decline to enter into any compromise or false position in reference to it — I urge people to declare open war with it.

The *morality of paltry people* as the measure of all things: this is the most repugnant kind of degeneracy that civilisation has ever yet brought into existence. And this *kind of ideal* is hanging still, under the name of "God," over men's heads! !

The *law,* which is the fundamentally realistic formula of certain self-preservative measures of a community, forbids certain actions that have a definite tendency to jeopardise the welfare of that community: it does *not* forbid the attitude of mind which gives rise to these actions — for in the pursuit of other ends the community requires these forbidden actions, namely, when it is a matter of opposing its *enemies*. The moral idealist now steps forward and says: "God sees into men's hearts: the action itself counts for nothing; the reprehensible attitude of mind from which it proceeds must be extirpated. . . ." In normal conditions men laugh at such things; it is only in exceptional cases, when a community lives *quite* beyond the need of waging war in order to maintain itself, that an ear is lent to such things. Any attitude of mind is abandoned, the utility of which cannot be conceived.

This was the case, for example, when Buddha appeared among a people that was both peaceable and afflicted with great intellectual weariness.

This was also the case in regard to the first Christian community (as also the Jewish), the primary condition of which was the absolutely *unpolitical* Jewish society. Christianity could grow only upon the soil of Judaism — that is to say, among a people that had already renounced the political life, and which led a sort of parasitic existence within the Roman sphere of government. Christianity goes a step *farther*: it allows men to "emasculate" themselves even more; the circumstances actually favour their doing so. — *Nature* is *expelled* from morality when it is said, "Love ye your enemies": for *Nature's* injunction, "Ye shall *love*

165

your neighbour and *hate* your enemy," has now become senseless in the law (in instinct); now, even *the love a man feels for his neighbour* must first be based upon something (*a sort of love of God*). *God* is introduced everywhere, and *utility* is withdrawn; the natural *origin* of morality is denied everywhere: the *veneration of Nature*, which lies in *acknowledging a natural morality,* is *destroyed* to the roots....

Among men, as among all other animals, there is a surplus of defective, diseased, degenerating, infirm, and necessarily suffering individuals; the successful cases, among men also, are always the exception; and in view of the fact that man is *the animal not yet properly adapted to his environment,* the rare exception. But worse still. The higher the type a man represents, the greater is the improbability that he will *succeed;* the accidental, the law of irrationality in the general constitution of mankind, manifests itself most terribly in its destructive effect on the higher orders of men, the conditions of whose lives are delicate, diverse, and difficult to determine. What, then, is the attitude of the two greatest religions above-mentioned to the *surplus* of failures in life? They endeavour to preserve and keep alive whatever can be preserved; in fact, as the religions *for sufferers,* they take the part of these upon principle; they are always in favour of those who suffer from life as from a disease, and they would fain treat every other experience of life as false and impossible. However highly we may esteem this indulgent and preservative care (inasmuch as in applying to others, it has applied, and applies also to the highest and usually the most suffering type of man), the hitherto *paramount* religions — to give a general appreciation of them — are among the principal causes which have kept the type of "man" upon a lower level — they have preserved too much *that which should have perished.* One has to thank them for invaluable services; and who is sufficiently rich in gratitude not to feel poor at the contemplation of all that the "spiritual men" of Christianity have done for Europe hitherto! But when they had given comfort to the sufferers, courage to the oppressed and despairing, a staff and support to the helpless, and when they had allured from society into convents and spiritual penitentiaries the broken-hearted and distracted: what else had they to do in order to work systematically in that fashion, and with a good conscience, for the preservation of all the sick and suffering, which means, in deed and in truth, to work for *the deterioration of the European race?* To *reverse* all estimates of value — *that* is what they had to do! And to shatter the strong, to spoil great hopes, to cast suspicion on the delight in beauty, to break down everything autonomous, manly, conquering, and imperious — all instincts which are natural to the highest and most successful type of "man" — into uncertainty, distress of conscience, and self-destruction; forsooth, to invert all love of the earthly and of supremacy over the earth, into hatred of the earth and earthly things — *that* is the task the Church imposed on itself. . . .

[The Noble Point of View[3]]

Every elevation of the type "man," has hitherto been the work of an aristocratic society — and so will it always be — a society believing in a long scale of gradations of rank and differences of worth among human beings and requiring slavery in some form or other. Without the *pathos of distance*, such as grows out of the incarnated difference of classes, out of the constant outlooking and downlooking of the ruling caste on subordinates and instruments, and out of their equally constant practice of obeying and commanding, of keeping down and keeping at a distance — that other more mysterious pathos could never have arisen, the longing for an ever new widening of distance within the soul itself, the formation of ever higher, rarer, further, more extended, more comprehensive states, in short, just the elevation of the type "man," the continued "self-surmounting of man," to use a moral formula in a supermoral sense. To be sure, one must not resign oneself to any humanitarian illusions about the history of the origin of an aristocratic society (that is to say, of the preliminary condition for the elevation of the type "man"): the truth is hard. Let us acknowledge unprejudicedly how every higher civilisation hitherto has *originated*! Men with a still natural nature, barbarians in every terrible sense of the word, men of prey, still in possession of unbroken strength of will and desire for power, threw themselves upon weaker, more moral, more peaceful races (perhaps trading or cattle-rearing communities), or upon old mellow civilisations in which the final vital force was flickering out in brilliant fireworks of wit and depravity. At the commencement, the noble caste was always the barbarian caste: their superiority did not consist first of all in their physical, but in their psychical power — they were more *complete* men (which at every point also implies the same as "more complete beasts").

To refrain mutually from injury, from violence, from exploitation, and put one's will on a par with that of others: this may result in a certain rough sense in good conduct among individuals when the necessary conditions are given (namely, the actual similarity of the individuals in

---

[3]From *Beyond Good and Evil*, sections 257, 259.

amount of force and degree of worth, and their co-relation within one organisation). As soon, however, as one wished to take this principle more generally, and if possible even as *the fundamental principle of society*, it would immediately disclose what it really is — namely, a Will to the *denial* of life, a principle of dissolution and decay. Here one must think profoundly to the very basis and resist all sentimental weakness: life itself is *essentially* appropriation, injury, conquest of the strange and weak, suppression, severity, obtrusion of peculiar forms, incorporation, and at the least, putting it mildest, exploitation; — but why should one for ever use precisely these words on which for ages a disparaging purpose has been stamped? Even the organisation within which, as was previously supposed, the individuals treat each other as equal — it takes place in every healthy aristocracy — must itself, if it be a living and not a dying organization, do all that towards other bodies, which the individuals within it refrain from doing to each other: it will have to be the incarnated Will to Power, it will endeavour to grow, to gain ground, attract to itself and acquire ascendency — not owing to any morality or immorality, but because it *lives*, and because life *is* precisely Will to Power. On no point, however, is the ordinary consciousness of Europeans more unwilling to be corrected than on this matter; people now rave everywhere, even under the guise of science, about coming conditions of society in which "the exploiting character" is to be absent: — that sounds to my ears as if they promised to invent a mode of life which should refrain from all organic functions. "Exploitation" does not belong to a depraved, or imperfect and primitive society: it belongs to the *nature* of the living being as a primary organic function; it is a consequence of the intrinsic Will to Power, which is precisely the Will to Life. — Granting that as a theory this is a novelty — as a reality it is the *fundamental fact* of all history: let us be so far honest towards ourselves!

[The Task: To Transvalue Values[4]]

Transvalue values — what does this mean? It implies that all spontaneous motives, all new, future and stronger motives, are still extant; but that they now appear under false names and false valuations, and have not yet become conscious of themselves.

We ought to have the courage to become conscious, and to affirm all that which has been *attained* — to get rid of the humdrum character

---

[4]From *The Will to Power*, sections 1007-1009, 1012-1014.

of old valuations, which makes us unworthy of the best and strongest things that we have achieved.

Any doctrine would be superfluous for which everything is not already prepared in the way of accumulated forces and explosive material. A transvaluation of values can only be accomplished when there is a tension of new needs, and a new set of needy people who feel all old values as painful, — although they are not conscious of what is wrong.

The standpoint from which my values are determined: Is abundance or desire active? . . . Is one a mere spectator, or is one's own shoulder at the wheel — is one looking away or is one turning aside? . . . Is one acting spontaneously, as the result of accumulated strength, or is one merely reacting to a goad or to a stimulus? . . . Is one simply acting as the result of a paucity of elements, or of such an overwhelming dominion over a host of elements that this power enlists the latter into its service if it requires them? . . . Is one a *problem* one's self or is one a *solution* already? . . . Is one *perfect* through the smallness of the task, or *imperfect* owing to the extraordinary character of the aim? . . . Is one genuine or only an *actor*; is one genuine as an actor, or only the bad copy of an actor? is one a representative or the creature represented? Is one a personality or merely a rendezvous of personalities? . . . Is one ill from a disease or from surplus health? Does one lead as a shepherd, or as an "exception" (third alternative: as a fugitive)? Is one in need of dignity, or can one play the clown? Is one in search of resistance, or is one evading it? Is one imperfect owing to one's precocity or to one's tardiness? Is it one's nature to say yea, or no, or is one a peacock's tail of garnish parts? Is one proud enough not to feel ashamed even of one's vanity? Is one still able to feel a bite of conscience (this species is becoming rare; formerly conscience had to bite too often: it is as if it now no longer had enough teeth to do so)? Is one still capable of a "duty"? (there are some people who would lose the whole joy of their lives if they were *deprived* of their duty — this holds good especially of feminine creatures, who are born subjects).

He who urges rational thought forward, thereby also drives its antagonistic power — mysticism and foolery of every kind — to new feats of strength.

We should recognise that every movement is (1) *partly* the manifestation of fatigue resulting from a previous movement (satiety after it, the malice of weakness towards it, and disease); and (2) *partly* a newly awakened accumulation of long slumbering forces, and therefore wanton, violent, healthy.

Health and morbidness: let us be careful! The standard is the bloom of the body, the agility, courage, and cheerfulness of the mind — but also, of course, how much *morbidness a man can bear and overcome,* — and convert into health. That which would send more delicate natures to the dogs, belongs to the stimulating means of *great* health.

It is only a question of power: to have all the morbid traits of the century, but to balance them by means of overflowing, plastic, and rejuvenating power. The *strong* man.

Freedom Versus Facticity

Jean-Paul Sartre

Being and Nothingness

Freedom and Facticity: The Situation. The decisive argument which is
employed by common sense against freedom consists in reminding us
of our impotence. Far from being able to modify our situation at our
whim, we seem to be unable to change ourselves. I am not "free" either
to escape the lot of my class, of my nation, of my family, or even to build
up my own power or my fortune or to conquer my most insignificant
appetites or habits. I am born a worker, a Frenchman, an hereditary

syphilitic, or a tubercular. The history of a life, whatever it may be, is the history of a failure. The coefficient of adversity of things is such that years of patience are necessary to obtain the feeblest result. Again it is necessary "to obey nature in order to command it"; that is, to insert my action into the network of determinism. Much more than he appears "to make himself," man seems "to be made" by climate and the earth, race and class, language, the history of the collectivity of which he is a part, heredity, the individual circumstances of his childhood, acquired habits, the great and small events of his life.

This argument has never greatly troubled the partisans of human freedom. Descartes, first of all, recognized both that the will is infinite and that it is necessary "to try to conquer ourselves rather than fortune." Here certain distinctions ought to be made. Many of the facts set forth by the determinists do not actually deserve to enter into our considerations. In particular the coefficient of adversity in things can not be an argument against our freedom, for it is by us — i.e., by the preliminary positing of an end — that this coefficient of adversity arises. A particular crag, which manifests a profound resistance if I wish to displace it, will be on the contrary a valuable aid if I want to climb upon it in order to look over the countryside. In itself — if one can even imagine what the crag can be in itself — it is neutral; that is, it waits to be illuminated by an end in order to manifest itself as adverse or helpful. Again it can manifest itself in one or the other way only within an instrumental-complex which is already established. Without picks and piolets, paths already worn, and a technique of climbing, the crag would be neither easy nor difficult to climb; the question would not be posited, it would not support any relation of any kind with the technique of mountain climbing. Thus although brute things (what Heidegger calls "brute existents") can from the start limit our freedom of action, it is our freedom itself which must first constitute the framework, the technique, and the ends in relation to which they will manifest themselves as limits. Even if the crag is revealed as "too difficult to climb," and we must give up the ascent, let us note that the crag is revealed as such only because it was originally grasped as "climbable"; it is therefore our freedom which constitutes the limits which it will subsequently encounter.

Of course, even after all these observations, there remains an unnamable and unthinkable *residuum which belongs to the in-itself considered* and which is responsible for the fact that in a world illuminated by our freedom, this particular crag will be more favorable for scaling and that one not. But this *residue* is far from being originally a limit for freedom; in fact, it is thanks to this residue — that is, to the brute in-itself as such — that freedom arises as freedom. Indeed common sense will agree with us that the being who is said to be *free* is the one who can *realize* his projects. But in order for the act to be able to allow a *realization*, the simple projection of a possible end must be distinguished *à priori* from the realization of this end. If conceiving is enough for realizing, then I am plunged in a world like that of a dream in which the possible is no longer in any way distinguished from the real. I am condemned henceforth to see the world modified at the whim of the changes of my consciousness; I can not practice in relation to my conception the "putting into brackets" and the suspension of judgment which will distinguish a simple fiction from a real choice. If the object appears as soon as it is simply conceived, it will no longer be chosen or merely wished for. Once the distinction between the simple *wish*, the *representation* which I could choose, and the *choice* is abolished, freedom disappears too. We are free when the final term by which we make known to ourselves what we are is an end; that is, not a real existent like that which in the supposition which we have made could fulfill our wish, but an object which does not yet exist. But consequently this *end* can be transcendent only if it is separated from us at the same time that it is accessible. Only an ensemble of real existents can separate us from this end — in the same way that this end can be conceived only as a state to-come of the real existents which separate me from it. It is nothing but the outline of an order of existents — that is, a series of dispositions to be assumed by existents on the foundation of their actual relations. By the internal negation, in fact, the for-itself illuminates the existents in their mutual relations by means of the end which it posits, and it projects this end in terms of the determinations which it apprehends in the existent. There is no circle, as we have seen, for the upsurge of the for-itself is effected at one stroke. But if this is the case, then the very order of the existents is indispensable to freedom itself. It is by means of them that freedom is separated from and reunited to the end which it pursues and which makes known to it what it is. Consequently the resistance which freedom reveals in the existent, far from being a danger to freedom, results only in enabling it to arise as freedom. There can be a free for-itself only as engaged in a resisting world. Outside of this engagement the notions of freedom, of determinism, of necessity lose all meaning.

In addition it is necessary to point out to "common sense" that the formula "to be free" does not mean "to obtain what one has wished" but rather "by oneself to determine oneself to wish" (in the broad sense of choosing). In other words success is not important to freedom. The discussion which opposes common sense to philosophers stems here from a misunderstanding: the empirical and popular concept of "freedom" which has been produced by historical, political, and moral circumstances is equivalent to "the ability to obtain the ends chosen." The technical and philosophical concept of freedom, the only one which we are considering here, means only the autonomy of choice. It is necessary, however, to note that the choice, being identical with acting, supposes a commencement of realization in order that the choice may be distinguished from the dream and the wish. Thus we shall not say that a prisoner is always free to go out of prison, which would be absurd, nor that he is always free to long for release, which would be an irrelevant truism, but that he is always free to try to escape (or get himself liberated); that is, that whatever his condition may be, he can project his escape and learn the value of his project by undertaking some action. Our description of freedom, since it does not distinguish between choosing and doing, compels us to abandon at once the distinction between the intention and the act. The intention can no more be separated from the act than thought can be separated from the language which expresses it; and as it happens that our speech informs us of our thought, so our acts will inform us of our intentions. . . .

Freedom and Responsibility. . . . The essential consequence of our earlier remarks is that man being condemned to be free carries the weight of the whole world on his shoulders; he is responsible for the world and for himself as a way of being. We are taking the word "responsibility" in its ordinary sense as "consciousness (of) being the incontestable author of an event or of an object." In this sense the responsibility of the for-itself is overwhelming since he is the one by whom it happens that *there is* a world; since he is also the one who makes himself be, then whatever may be the situation in which he finds himself, the for-itself must wholly assume this situation with its peculiar coefficient of adversity, even though it be insupportable. He must assume the situation with the proud consciousness of being the author of it, for the very worst disadvantages or the worst threats which can endanger my person have meaning only in and through my project; and it is on the ground of the engagement which I am that they appear. It is therefore senseless to think of complaining since nothing foreign has decided what we feel, what we live, or what we are.

Furthermore this absolute responsibility is not resignation; it is simply the logical requirement of the consequences of our freedom. What happens to me happens through me, and I can neither affect myself with it nor revolt against it nor resign myself to it. Moreover everything which happens to me is *mine*. By this we must understand first of all that I am always equal to what happens to me *qua* man, for what happens to a man through other men and through himself can be only human. The most terrible situations of war, the worst tortures do not create a non-human state of things; there is no non-human situation. It is only through fear, flight, and recourse to magical types of conduct that I shall decide on the non-human, but this decision is human, and I shall carry the entire responsibility for it. But in addition the situation is *mine* because it is the image of my free choice of myself, and everything which it presents to me is *mine* in that this represents me and symbolizes me. Is it not I who decide the coefficient of adversity in things and even their unpredictability by deciding myself?

Thus there are no *accidents* in a life; a community event which suddenly bursts forth and involves me in it does not come from the outside. If I am mobilized in a war, this war is *my* war; it is in my image and I deserve it. I deserve it first because I could always get out of it by suicide or by desertion; these ultimate possibles are those which must always be present for us when there is a question of envisaging a situation. For lack of getting out of it, I have *chosen* it. This can be due to inertia, to cowardice in the face of public opinion, or because I prefer certain other values to the value of the refusal to join the war (the good opinion of my relatives, the honor of my family, etc.). Anyway you look at it, it is a matter of a choice. This choice will be repeated later on again and again without a break until the end of the war. Therefore we must agree with the statement by J. Romains, "In war there are no innocent victims."[1] If therefore I have preferred war to death or to dishonor, everything takes place as if I bore the entire responsibility for this war. Of course others have declared it, and one might be tempted perhaps to consider me as a simple accomplice. But this notion of complicity has only a juridical sense, and it does not hold here. For it depended on me that for me and by me this war should not exist, and I have decided that it does exist. There was no compulsion here, for the compulsion could have got no hold on a freedom. I did not have any excuse; for as we have said repeatedly in this book, the peculiar character of human-reality is that it is without excuse. Therefore it remains for me only to lay claim to this war.

But in addition the war is *mine* because by the sole fact that it arises in a situation which I cause to be and that I can discover it there only by engaging myself for or against it, I can no longer distinguish at present the choice which I make of myself from the choice which I make of the war. To live this war is to choose myself through it and to choose it

---

[1] J. Romains: *Les hommes de bonne volonté*; "Prélude à Verdun."

through my choice of myself. There can be no question of considering it as "four years of vacation" or as a "reprieve," as a "recess," the essential part of my responsibilities being elsewhere in my married, family, or professional life. In this war which I have chosen I choose myself from day to day, and I make it mine by making myself. If it is going to be four empty years, then it is I who bear the responsibility for this.

Finally, as we pointed out earlier, each person is an absolute choice of self from the standpoint of a world of knowledges and of techniques which this choice both assumes and illumines; each person is an absolute upsurge at an absolute date and is perfectly unthinkable at another date. It is therefore a waste of time to ask what I should have been if this war had not broken out, for I have chosen myself as one of the possible meanings of the epoch which imperceptibly led to war. I am not distinct from this same epoch; I could not be transported to another epoch without contradiction. Thus *I am* this war which restricts and limits and makes comprehensible the period which preceded it. In this sense we may define more precisely the responsibility of the for-itself if to the earlier quoted statement, "There are no innocent victims," we add the words, "We have the war we deserve." Thus, totally free, undistinguishable from the period for which I have chosen to be the meaning, as profoundly responsible for the war as if I had myself declared it, unable to live without integrating it in *my* situation, engaging myself in it wholly and stamping it with my seal, I must be without remorse or regrets as I am without excuse; for from the instant of my upsurge into being, I carry the weight of the world by myself alone without anything or any person being able to lighten it.

Yet this responsibility is of a very particular type. Someone will say, "I did not ask to be born." This is a naive way of throwing greater emphasis on our facticity. I am responsible for everything, in fact, except for my very responsibility, for I am not the foundation of my being. Therefore everything takes place as if I were compelled to be responsible. I am *abandoned* in the world, not in the sense that I might remain abandoned and passive in a hostile universe like a board floating on the water, but rather in the sense that I find myself suddenly alone and without help, engaged in a world for which I bear the whole responsibility without being able, whatever I do, to tear myself away from this responsibility for an instant. For I am responsible for my very desire of fleeing responsibilities. To make myself passive in the world, to refuse to act upon things and upon Others is still to choose myself, and suicide is one mode among others of being-in-the-world. Yet I find an absolute responsibility for the fact that my facticity (here the fact of my birth) is directly inapprehensible and even inconceivable, for this fact of my birth never appears as a brute fact but always across a projective reconstruction of my for-itself. I am ashamed of being born or I am astonished at it or I rejoice over it, or in attempting to get rid of my life I affirm that I live and I assume this life as bad. Thus in a certain sense I *choose* being born. This choice itself is integrally affected with facticity since I am not able not to choose, but this facticity in turn will appear only in so far as I surpass it toward my ends. Thus facticity is everywhere but inapprehensible; I never encounter anything except my responsibility. That is why I can not ask, "Why was I born?" or curse the day of my birth or declare that I did not ask to be born, for these various attitudes toward by birth — i.e., toward the *fact* that I realize a presence in the world — are absolutely nothing else but ways of assuming this birth in full responsibility and of making it *mine*. Here again I encounter only myself and my projects so that finally my abandonment — i.e., my facticity — consists simply in the fact that I am condemned to be wholly responsible for myself. I am the being which *is* in such a way that in its being its being is in question. And this "is" of my being *is* as present and inapprehensible.

Under these conditions since every event in the world can be revealed to me only as an *opportunity* (an opportunity made use of, lacked, neglected, etc.), or better yet since everything which happens to us can be considered as a *chance* (i.e., can appear to us only as a way of realizing this being which is in question in our being) and since others as transcendences-transcended are themselves only *opportunities* and *chances*, the responsibility of the for-itself extends to the entire world as a peopled-world. It is precisely thus that the for-itself apprehends itself in anguish; that is, as a being which is neither the foundation of its own being nor of the Other's being nor of the in-itselfs which form the world, but a being which is compelled to decide the meaning of being — within it and everywhere outside of it. The one who realizes in anguish his condition as *being* thrown into a responsibility which extends to his very abandonment has no longer either remorse or regret or excuse; he is no longer anything but a freedom which perfectly reveals itself and whose being resides in this very revelation. But as we pointed out at the beginning of this work, most of the time we flee anguish in bad faith.

Situations Versus Systems

Joseph Fletcher

Situation Ethics

There are at bottom only three alternative routes or approaches to
follow in making moral decisions. They are: (1) the legalistic; (2) the
antinomian, the opposite extreme — i.e., a lawless or unprincipled approach; and (3) the situational. All three have played their part in the
history of Western morals, legalism being by far the most common and
persistent. Just as legalism triumphed among the Jews after the exile, so,
in spite of Jesus' and Paul's revolt against it, it has managed to dominate

Christianity constantly from very early days. As we shall be seeing, in many real-life situations legalism demonstrates what Henry Miller, in a shrewd phrase, calls "the immorality of morality."[1]

There is an old joke which serves our purposes. A rich man asked a lovely young woman if she would sleep the night with him. She said, "No." He then asked if she would do it for $100,000? She said, "Yes!" He then asked, $10,000?" She replied, "Well, yes, I would." His next question was, "How about $500?" Her indignant "What do you think I am?" was met by the answer, "We have already established *that*. Now we are haggling over the price." Does any girl who has "relations" (what a funny way to use the word) outside marriage automatically become a prostitute? Is it always, regardless of what she accomplishes for herself or others — is it *always* wrong? Is extramarital sex inherently evil, or can it be a good thing in some situations? Does everybody have his price, and if so, does that mean we are immoral and ethically weak? Let's see if we can find some help in answering these questions.

Approaches to Decision-Making

1. *Legalism*

With this approach one enters into every decision-making situation encumbered with a whole apparatus of prefabricated rules and regulations. Not just the spirit but the letter of the law reigns. Its principles, codified in rules, are not merely guidelines or maxims to illuminate the situation; they are *directives* to be followed. Solutions are preset, and you can "look them up" in a book — a Bible or a confessor's manual.

Judaism, Catholicism, Protestantism — all major Western religious traditions have been legalistic. In morals as in doctrine they have kept to a spelled-out, "systematic" orthodoxy. The ancient Jews, especially under the post-exilic Maccabean and Pharisaic leadership, lived by the law or Torah, and its oral tradition (halakah).[2] It was a code of 613 (or 621) precepts, amplified by an increasingly complicated mass of Mishnaic interpretations and applications.

Statutory and code law inevitably piles up, ruling upon ruling, because the complications of life and the claims of mercy and compassion

---

[1]*Stand Still Like the Hummingbird* (New Directions, 1962), pp. 92-96.

[2]The prophetic J tradition gave way to the E-D tradition, with its precepts and laws.

combine — even with code legalists — to accumulate an elaborate system of exceptions and compromise, in the form of rules for breaking the rules! It leads to that tricky and tortuous now-you-see-it, now-you-don't business of interpretation that the rabbis called pilpul — a hairsplitting and logic-chopping study of the letter of the law, pyramiding from codes (e.g., the Covenant and Holiness) to Pentateuch to Midrash and Mishna to Talmud. It was a tragic death to the prophets' "pathos" (sharing God's loving concern) and "ethos" (living by love as *norm*, not program). With the prophets it had been a question of sensitively seeking "an understanding of *the situation.*"[3]

Any web thus woven sooner or later chokes its weavers. Reformed and even Conservative Jews have been driven to disentangle themselves from it. Only Orthodoxy is still in its coils. Something of the same pilpul and formalistic complication may be seen in Christian history. With Catholics it has taken the form of a fairly ingenious moral theology that, as its twists and involutions have increased, resorts more and more to a casuistry that appears (as, to its credit, it does) to evade the very "laws" of right and wrong laid down in its textbooks and manuals. Love, even with the most stiff-necked of system builders, continues to plead mercy's cause and to win at least partial release from law's cold abstractions. Casuistry is the homage paid by legalism to the love of persons, and to realism about life's relativities.

Protestantism has rarely constructed such intricate codes and systems of law, but what it has gained by its simplicity it has lost through its rigidity, its puritanical insistence on moral rules.[4] In fact, the very lack of a casuistry and its complexity, once people are committed to *even the bare principle* of legalistic morality or law ethics, is itself evidence of their blindness to the factors of doubt and perplexity. They have lost touch with the headaches and heartbreaks of life.

What can be worse, no casuistry at all may reveal a punishing and sadistic use of law to hurt people instead of helping them. How else explain burning at the stake in the Middle Ages for homosexuals (death, in the Old Testament)? Even today imprisonment up to sixty years is the penalty in one state for those who were actually consenting adults, without seduction or public disorder! This is really unavoidable whenever law instead of love is put first. The "puritan" type is a well-known

---

[3] Abraham J. Heschel, *The Prophets* (Harper & Row, Publishers, Inc., 1962), pp. 225, 307-315.

[4] There are, however, atypical works such as Richard Baxter, *Christian Directory* (1673), and William Ames (Amesius), *De Conscientia, eius jure et Casibus* (1632).

example of it. But even if the legalist is truly *sorry* that the law requires unloving or disastrous decisions, he still cries, "Fiat justitia, ruat caelum!" (Do the "right" even if the sky falls down). He is the man Mark Twain called "a good man in the worst sense of the word."

The Christian situation ethicist agrees with Bertrand Russell and his implied judgment, "To this day Christians think an adulterer more wicked than a politician who takes bribes, although the latter probably does a thousand times as much harm."[5] And he thoroughly rejects Cardinal Newman's view: "The Church holds that it were better for sun and moon to drop from heaven, for the earth to fail, and for all the many millions who are upon it to die of starvation in extremest agony . . . than that one soul, I will not say should be lost, but should commit one single venial sin."[6]

A Mrs. X was convicted (later cleared in appellate court) of impairing the morals of her minor daughter. She had tried to teach the child chastity but at thirteen the girl bore the first of three unwanted, neglected babies. Her mother then had said, "If you persist in acting this way, at least be sure the boy wears something!" On this evidence she was convicted and sentenced. The combined forces of "secular" law and legalistic puritanism had tried to prevent loving help to the girl, her bastard victims, and the social agencies trying to help her. Situation ethics would have praised that woman; it would not have pilloried her.

In the language of classical ethics and jurisprudence, the more statutory the law, the greater the need of equity. For, as statutes are applied to actual situations, something has to give; some latitude is necessary for doubtful or perplexed consciences. Inexorably questions arise as to whether in a particular case the law truly applies (doubt), or as to which of several more or less conflicting laws is to be followed (perplexity). The effort to deal with these questions helpfully, even though hamstrung and corseted by rules and "sacred" principles, is what casuistry is. When a law ethic listens to love at all, it tries to rise above its legalism; paradoxically enough, the development of Catholic casuistry is powerful evidence of less legalism in the Catholic fold than the Protestant.

Legalism in the Christian tradition has taken two forms. In the Catholic line it has been a matter of legalistic *reason*, based on nature or natural law. These moralists have tended to adumbrate their ethical rules of applying human reason to the facts of nature, both human and

---

[5] *Why I Am Not a Christian* (Simon and Schuster, Inc., 1957), p. 33.

[6] J. H. Newman, *Certain Difficulties Felt by Anglicans in Catholic Teaching* (Longmans, Green & Co., Inc., 1918), p. 190.

subhuman, and to the lessons of historical experience. By this procedure they claim to have adduced universally agreed and therefore valid "natural" moral laws. Protestant moralists have followed the same adductive and deductive tactics. They have taken Scripture and done with it what the Catholics do with nature. Their Scriptural moral law is, they argue, based on the words and sayings of the Law and the Prophets, the evangelists and apostles of the Bible. It is a matter of legalistic *revelation*. One is rationalistic, the other Biblicistic; one natural, the other Scriptural. But both are legalistic.

Even though Catholic moralists deal also with "revealed law" (e.g., "the divine positive law of the Ten Commandments") and Protestants have tried to use reason in interpreting the sayings of the Bible (hermeneutics), still both by and large have been committed to the doctrines of law ethics.

2. *Antinomianism*

Over against legalism, as a sort of polar opposite, we can put antinomianism. This is the approach with which one enters into the decision-making situation armed with no principles or maxims whatsoever, to say nothing of *rules*. In every "existential moment" or "unique" situation, it declares, one must rely upon the situation of itself, *there and then*, to provide its ethical solution.

The term "antinomianism" (literally, "against law") was used first by Luther to describe Johannes Agricola's views. The ethical concept has cropped up here and there, as among some Anabaptists, some sects of English Puritanism, and some of Wesley's followers. The concept is certainly at issue in I Corinthians (e.g., ch. 6: 12-20). Paul had to struggle with two primitive forms of it among the Hellenistic Jew-Christians whom he visited. They took his attacks on law morality too naively and too literally.

One form was libertinism — the belief that by grace, by the new life in Christ and salvation by faith, law or rules no longer applied to Christians. Their ultimate happy fate was now assured, and it mattered no more *what* they did. (Whoring, incest, drunkenness, and the like are what they did, therefore! This explains the warning in I Peter 2:16, "Live as free men, yet without using your freedom as a pretext for evil; but live as servants of God." This license led by inevitable reaction to an increase of legalism, especially in sex ethics, under which Christians still suffer today.) The other form, less pretentious and more enduring, was a Gnostic claim to special knowledge, so that neither principles nor rules were needed any longer even as guidelines and direction pointers. They would just *know* what was right when they needed to know. They had, they claimed, a superconscience. It is this second "gnostic" form of the approach which is under examination here.

While legalists are preoccupied with law and its stipulations, the Gnostics are so flatly opposed to law — even in principle — that their moral decisions are random, unpredictable, erratic, quite anomalous. Making moral decisions is a matter of spontaneity; it is literally unprincipled, purely *ad hoc* and casual. They follow no forecastable course from one situation to another. They are, exactly, anarchic — i.e., without a rule. They are not only "unbound by the chains of law" but actually sheer extemporizers, impromptu and intellectually irresponsible. They not only cast the old Torah aside; they even cease to think seriously and *care-fully* about the demands of love as it has been shown in Christ, the love norm itself. The baby goes out with the bath water!

This was the issue Paul fought over with the antinomians at Corinth and Ephesus. They were repudiating all law, as such, and all principles, relying in all moral action choices solely upon guidance in the situation. Some were what he called *pneumatikoi*, spirit-possessed. They claimed that *their* guidance came from outside themselves, by the Holy Spirit. Of what use are principles and laws when you can depend on the Holy Spirit? It was a kind of special-providence idea; a version of the inspiration theory of conscience.[7] Other antinomians claimed, and still do, that their guidance comes from within themselves, as a sort of built-in radarlike "faculty," a translegal or clairvoyant conscience as promised in Jer. 31:31-34, written "upon their hearts." This second and more common form of Gnostic antinomianism, found among both Christians and non-Christians, is close to the intuition theory or faculty theory of conscience.[8]

Perhaps a good example of the guidance idea in today's scene is Moral Re-Armament. It has a doctrine of special providence and daily guidance by "spiritual power" to right and wrong actions and causes. Its basic doctrines were first worked out under the leadership of Frank Buchman in the twenties, when it was called "The First Century Christian Fellowship." It has won to itself, not so surprisingly, even the French Catholic existentialist philosopher, Gabriel Marcel.[9]

---

[7]See warnings in Eph. 6:12; I Tim. 4:1.

[8]See note 22, Chapter II.

[9]Cf. Gabriel Marcel, *Fresh Hope for the World* (Longmans, Green & Co., Inc., 1960); see also Tom Driberg, *The Mystery of Moral Re-Armament* (Alfred A. Knopf, Inc., 1965).

In its present form, with its wealthy clientele, it is a "sawdust trail in a dinner jacket." Part of its ideology, understandably, is the perfectionist notion that "members of the fellowship" can achieve and should live by *absolute* purity (sexual!), *absolute* truth, *absolute* unselfishness, and *absolute* love. Its separation of love from unselfishness is as puzzling as its call for "absolute" virtue and perfectionism and is as pretentious. But after all, if we have the power of the Spirit to tell us daily in a special way *what* the good is, surely we can expect to *do* it "absolutely"! Curiously, the Moral Re-Armament ethic is of the kind one would logically expect to find in the Holiness and Pentecostal movements, and yet, in spite of their self-styled pneumatic character, they are for the most part quite legalistic morally — not antinomian about their ethics at all.

Another version of antinomianism, on the whole much subtler philosophically and perhaps more admirable, is the ethics of existentialism. Sartre speaks of "nausea," which is our anxious experience of the *incoherence* of reality. For him any belief in coherence (such as the Christian doctrine of the unity of God's creation and his Lordship over history) is "bad faith." In every moment of moral choice or decision "we have no excuses behind us and no justification before us." Sartre refuses to admit to any *generally* valid principles at all, nothing even ordinarily valid, to say nothing of universal *laws*.[10] Simone de Beauvoir in *The Ethics of Ambiguity* cannot quite bring herself to accept either "the contingent absurdity of the discontinuous" or "the rationalistic necessity of the continuous," proving herself to be less sturdily existential than Sartre, but she admits that the real world is after all "bare and incoherent."[11] She shrinks from a candid antinomianism. But the plain fact is that her ontology — her idea of basic reality — is, like Sartre's, one of radical discontinuity, so that there can be no connective tissue between one situation or moment of experience and another. There is no fabric or web of life, hence no basis for generalizing moral principles *or* laws. Every situation has only its particularity!

On this view, of course, the existentialists rightly reject even all principles, all "generally valid" ethical norms or axioms, as well as all rules or laws or precepts that legalistically absolutize (idolize) such general principles. Radical discontinuity in one's theory of being forces the "absolute particularity" of *tout comprendre, tout pardonner*. Sartre is at least honest and tough-minded. In the absence of any faith in love as

---

[10]Jean-Paul Sartre, *Existentialism*, tr. by B. Frechtman (Philosophical Library, Inc., 1947), p. 27.

[11](Philosophical Library, Inc., 1948), pp. 44, 122.

the norm and in any God as the norm-giver, he says resolutely: "Ontology itself cannot formulate ethical precepts. It is concerned solely with what is, and we cannot possibly derive imperatives from ontology's indicatives."[12] He is, on this score at least, entirely correct!

3. Situationism

A third approach, in between legalism and antinomian unprincipledness, is situation ethics. (To jump from one polarity to the other would be only to go from the frying pan to the fire.) The situationist enters into every decision-making situation fully armed with the ethical maxims of his community and its heritage, and he treats them with respect as illuminators of his problems. Just the same he is prepared in any situation to compromise them or set them aside *in the situation* if love seems better served by doing so.

Situation ethics goes part of the way with natural law, by accepting reason as the instrument of moral judgment, while rejecting the notion that the good is "given" in the nature of things, objectively. It goes part of the way with Scriptural law by accepting revelation as the source of the norm while rejecting all "revealed" norms or laws but the one command — to love God in the neighbor. The situationist follows a moral law or violates it according to love's need. For example, "Alms-giving is a good thing if. . . ." The situationist never says, "Almsgiving is a good thing. Period!" His decisions are hypothetical, not categorical. Only the commandment to love is categorically good. "Owe no one anything, except to love one another." (Rom. 13:8.) If help to an indigent only pauperizes and degrades him, the situationist refuses a handout and finds some other way. He makes no law out of Jesus' "Give to every one who begs from you." It is only one step from that kind of Biblicist literalism to the kind that causes women in certain sects to refuse blood transfusions even if death results — even if they are carrying a quickened fetus that will be lost too. The legalist says that even if he tells a man escaped from an asylum where his intended victim is, if he finds and murders him, at least only one sin has been committed (murder), not two (lying as well)!

As Brunner puts it, "The basis of the Divine Command is always the same, but its content varies with varying circumstances." Therefore, the "error of casuistry does not lie in the fact that it indicates the infinite

---

[12]*Being and Nothingness,* tr. by Hazel Barnes (Philosophical Library, Inc., 1956), p. 625.

variety of forms which the Command of love may assume; its error consists in deducing particular laws from a universal law . . . as though all could be arranged beforehand. . . . Love, however, is free from all this predefinition."[13] We might say, from the situationist's perspective, that it is possible to derive general "principles" from whatever is the one and only universal law (*agapé* for Christians, something else for others), but not laws or rules. We cannot milk universals from a universal!

William Temple put it this way: "Universal obligation attaches not to particular judgments of conscience but to conscientiousness. What acts are right may depend on circumstances . . . but there is an absolute obligation to will whatever may on each occasion be right."[14] Our obligation is relative *to* the situation, but obligation *in* the situation is absolute. We are only "obliged" to tell the truth, for example, if the situation calls for it; if a murderer asks us his victim's whereabouts, our duty might be to lie. There is in situation ethics an absolute element and an element of calculation, as Alexander Miller once pointed out.[15] But it would be better to say it has an absolute *norm* and a calculating method. There is weight in the old saying that what is needed is "faith, hope, and clarity." We have to find out what is "fitting" to be truly ethical, to use H. R. Niebuhr's word for it in his *The Responsible Self*.[16] Situation ethics aims at a contextual appropriateness — not the "good" or the "right" but the *fitting*.

A cartoon in a fundamentalist magazine once showed Moses scowling, holding his stone tablet with its graven laws, all ten, and an eager stonecutter saying to him, "Aaron said perhaps you'd let us reduce them to 'Act responsibly in love.' " This was meant as a dig at the situationists and the new morality, but the legalist humor in it merely states exactly what situation ethics calls for! With Dietrich Bonhoeffer we say, "Principles are only tools in God's hands, soon to be thrown away as unserviceable."[17]

One competent situationist, speaking to students, explained the position this way. Rules are "like 'Punt on fourth down,' or 'Take a pitch

---

[13]*The Divine Imperative*, tr. by Olive Wyon (The Westminster Press, 1947), pp. 132 ff.

[14]*Nature, Man and God* (The Macmillan Company, 1934), p. 405.

[15]*The Renewal of Man* (Doubleday & Company, Inc., 1955), p. 44.

[16](Harper & Row, Publishers, Inc., 1963), pp. 60-61. Precedents are Samuel Clarke, *Unchangeable Obligations of Natural Religion* (London, 1706), and A. C. Ewing, *The Definition of the Good* (The Macmillan Company, 1947).

[17]*Ethics*, tr. by N. H. Smith (The Macmillan Company, 1955), p. 8.

when the count is three balls.' These rules are part of the wise player's know-how, and distinguish him from the novice. But they are not unbreakable. The best players are those who know when to ignore them. In the game of bridge, for example, there is a useful rule which says 'Second hand low.' But have you ever played with anyone who followed the rule slavishly? You say to him (in exasperation), 'Partner, why didn't you play your ace? We could have set the hand.' And he replies, unperturbed, 'Second hand low!' What is wrong? The same thing that was wrong when Kant gave information to the murderer. He forgot the purpose of the game. . . . He no longer thought of winning the hand, but of being able to justify himself by invoking the rule."[18]

This practical temper of the activist or *verb*-minded decision maker, versus contemplative *noun*-mindedness, is a major Biblical rather than Hellenistic trait. In Abraham Heschel's view, "The insistence upon generalization at the price of a total disregard of the particular and concrete is something which would be alien to prophetic thinking. Prophetic words are never detached from the concrete, historic situation. Theirs is not a timeless, abstract message; it always refers to an actual situation. The general is given in the particular and the verification of the abstract is in the concrete."[19] A "leap of faith" is an action decision rather than a leap of thought, for a man's faith is a hypothesis that he takes seriously enough to act on and live by.

There are various names for this approach: situationism, contextualism, occasionalism, circumstantialism, even actualism. These labels indicate, of course, that the core of the ethic they describe is a healthy and primary awareness that "circumstances alter cases" — i.e., that in actual problems of conscience the situational variables are to be weighed as heavily as the normative or "general" constants.

The situational factors are so primary that we may even say "circumstances alter rules and principles." It is said that when Gertrude Stein lay dying she declared, "It is better to ask questions that to give answers, even good answers." This is the temper of situation ethics. It is empirical, fact-minded, data conscious, inquiring. It is antimoralistic as well as antilegalistic, for it is sensitive to variety and complexity. It is neither simplistic nor perfectionist. It is "casuistry" (case-based) in a constructive and nonpejorative sense of the word. We should perhaps call it "neocasuistry." Like classical casuistry, it is case-focused and concrete, concerned to

---

[18]E. LaB. Cherbonnier, unpublished address, Trinity College, December 14, 1964.
[19]*God in Search of Man: A Philosophy of Judaism* (Farrar, Straus & Cudahy, Inc., 1956), p. 204.

bring Christian imperatives into practical operation. But unlike classical casuistry, this neocasuistry repudiates any attempt to anticipate or prescribe real-life decisions in their existential particularity. It works with two guidelines from Paul: "The written code kills, but the Spirit gives life" (II Cor. 3:6), and "For the whole law is fulfilled in one word, 'You shall love your neighbor as yourself' " (Gal. 5:14).

In the words of Millar Burrows' finding in Biblical theology: "He who makes the law his standard is obligated to perform all its precepts, for to break one commandment is to break the law. He who lives by faith and love is not judged on that basis, but by a standard infinitely higher and at the same time more attainable."[20] This is why Msgr. Pietro Palazzini (Secretary of the Sacred Congregation of the Council) freely acknowledges that situation ethics "must not be understood as an escape from the heavy burden of moral integrity. For, though its advocates truly deny the absolute value of universal norms, some are motivated by the belief that in this manner they are better safeguarding the eminent sovereignty of God."[21]

As we shall see, *Christian* situation ethics has only one norm or principle or law (call it what you will) that is binding and unexceptionable, always good and right regardless of the circumstances. That is "love" — the *agapē* of the summary commandment to love God and the neighbor.[22] Everything else without exception, all laws and rules and principles and ideals and norms, are only *contingent*, only valid *if they happen* to serve love in any situation. Christian situation ethics is not a system or program of living according to a code, but an effort to relate love to a world of relativities through a casuistry obedient to love. It is the strategy of love. This strategy denies that there are, as Sophocles thought, any unwritten immutable laws of heaven, agreeing with Bultmann that all such notions are idolatrous and a demonic pretension.[23]

In non-Christian situation ethics some other highest good or *summum bonum* will, of course, take love's place as the one and only standard — such as self-realization in the ethics of Aristotle. But the *Christian* is neighbor-centered first and last. Love is for people, not for principles; i.e., it is personal — and therefore when the impersonal universal con-

---

[20]*An Outline of Biblical Theology* (The Westminster Press, 1946), pp. 163-164.
[21]Article, "Morality, Situation," in *Dictionary of Moral Theology*, ed. by Francesco Cardinal Roberti and Msgr. Pietro Palazzini (The Newman Press, 1962), pp. 800-802.
[22]Matt. 5:43:43-48 and ch. 22:34-40; Luke 6:27-28; 10:25-28 and vs. 29-37; Mark 12:28-34; Gal. 5:14; Rom. 13:8-10; etc.
[23]Rudolf Bultmann, *Essays Philosophical and Theological* (The Macmillan Company, 1955), pp. 22, 154.

flicts with the personal particular, the latter prevails in situation ethics. Because of its mediating position, prepared to act on moral laws or in spite of them, the antinomians will call situationists soft legalists, and legalists will call them cryptoantinomians.

Cultural Relativism Versus Ethical Absolutism

W. T. Stace

Ethical Relativity

I

Any ethical position which denies that there is a single moral standard which is equally applicable to all men at all times may fairly be called a species of ethical relatively. There is not, the relativist asserts, merely one moral law, one code, one standard. There are many moral laws, codes, standards. What morality ordains in one place or age may be quite different from what morality ordains in another place or age. The moral code of Chinamen is quite different from that of Europeans, that of African savages quite different from both. Any morality, therefore, is relative to the age, the place, and the circumstances in which it is found. It is in no sense absolute.

This does not mean merely—as one might at first sight be inclined to suppose—that the very same kind of action which is *thought* right in one country and period may be *thought* wrong in another. This would be a mere platitude, the truth of which everyone would have to admit. Even the absolutist would admit this—would even wish to emphasize it—since he is well aware that different peoples have different sets of moral ideas, and his whole point is that some of these sets of ideas are false. What the relativist means to assert is, not this platitude, but that the very same kind of action which *is* right in one country and period may *be* wrong in another. And this, far from being a platitude, is a very startling assertion.

It is very important to grasp thoroughly the difference between the two ideas. For there is reason to think that many minds tend to find ethical relativity attractive because they fail to keep them clearly apart. It is so very obvious that moral ideas differ from country to country and from age to age. And it is so very easy, if you are mentally lazy, to suppose that to say this means the same as to say that no universal moral standard exists,—or in other words that it implies ethical relativity. We fail to see that the word "standard" is used in two different senses. It is perfectly true that, in one sense, there are many variable moral standards. We speak of judging a man by the standard of his time. And this implies that different times have different standards. And this, of course, is quite true. But when the word "standard" is used in this sense it means simply the set of moral ideas current during the period in question. It means what people *think* right, whether as a matter of fact it *is* right or not. On the other hand when the absolutist asserts that there exists a single universal moral "standard," he is not using the word in this sense at all. He means by "standard" what *is* right as distinct from what people merely think right. His point is that although what people think right varies in different countries and periods, yet what actually is right is everywhere and always the same. And it follows that when the ethical relativist disputes the position of the absolutist and denies that any universal moral standard exists he too means by "standard" what actually is right. But it is exceedingly easy, if we are not careful, to slip loosely from using the word in the first sense to using it in the second sense; and to suppose that the variability of moral beliefs is the same thing as the variability of what really is moral. And unless we keep the two senses of the word "standard" distinct, we are likely to think the creed of ethical relativity much more plausible than it actually is.

The genuine relativist, then, does not merely mean that Chinamen may think right what Frenchmen think wrong. He means that what *is* wrong for the Frenchmen may *be* right for the Chinaman. And if one enquires how, in those circumstances, one is to know what actually is right in China or in France, the answer comes quite glibly. What is right in China is the same as what people think right in China; and what is right in France is the same as what people think right in France. So that, if you want to know what is moral in any particular country or age all you have to do is to ascertain what are the moral ideas current in that age or country. Those ideas are, *for that age or country*, right. Thus what is morally right is identified with what is thought to be morally right, and the distinction which we made above between these two is simply denied. To put the same thing in another way, it is denied that there can be or ought to be any distinction between the two senses of the word "standard." There is only one kind of standard of right and wrong, namely, the moral ideas current in any particular age or country.

Moral right *means* what people think morally right. It has no other meaning. What Frenchmen think right is, therefore, right *for Frenchmen*. And evidently one must conclude—though I am not aware that relativists are anxious to draw one's attention to such unsavory but yet absolutely necessary conclusions from their creed—that cannibalism is right for people who believe in it, that human sacrifice is right for those races which practice it, and that burning widows alive was right for Hindus until the British stepped in and compelled the Hindus to behave immorally by allowing their widows to remain alive.

When it is said that, according to the ethical relativist, what is thought right in any social group is right for that group, one must be careful not to misinterpret this. The relativist does not, of course, mean that there actually is an objective moral standard in France and a different objective standard in England, and that French and British opinions respectively give us correct information about these different standards. His point is rather that there are no objectively true moral standards at all. There is no single universal objective standard. Nor are there a variety of local objective standards. All standards are subjective. People's subjective feelings about morality are the only standards which exist.

To sum up. The ethical relativist consistently denies, it would seem, whatever the ethical absolutist asserts. For the absolutist there is a single universal moral standard. For the relativist there is no such standard. There are only local, ephemeral, and variable standards. For the absolutist there are two senses of the word "standard." Standards in the sense of sets of current moral ideas are relative and changeable. But the standard in the sense of what is actually morally right is absolute and unchanging. For the relativist no such distinction can be made. There is only one meaning of the word standard, namely, that which refers to local and variable sets of moral ideas. Or if it is insisted that the word must be allowed two meanings, then the relativist will say that there is at any rate no actual example of a standard in the absolute sense, and that the word as thus used is an empty name to which nothing in reality corresponds; so that the distinction between the two meanings becomes empty and useless. Finally—though this is merely saying the same thing in another way—the absolutist makes a distinction between what actually is right and what is thought right. The relativist rejects this distinction and identifies what is moral with what is thought moral by certain human beings or groups of human beings. . . .

It was easy enough to believe in a single absolute morality in older times when there was no anthropology, when all humanity was divided clearly into two groups, Christian peoples and the "heathen." Christian peoples knew and possessed the one true morality. The rest were savages whose moral ideas could be ignored. But all this is changed. Greater knowledge has brought greater tolerance. We can no longer exalt our own morality as alone true, while dismissing all other moralities as false or inferior. The investigations of anthropologists have shown that there exist side by side in the world a bewildering variety of moral codes. On this topic endless volumes have been written, masses of evidence piled up. Anthropologists have ransacked the Melanesian Islands, the jungles of New Guinea, the steppes of Siberia, the deserts of Australia, the forests of central Africa, and have brought back with them countless examples of weird, extravagant, and fantastic "moral" customs with which to confound us. We learn that all kinds of horrible practices are, in this, that, or the other place, regarded as essential to virtue. We find that there is nothing, or next to nothing, which has always and everywhere been regarded as morally good by all men. Where then is our universal morality? Can we, in face of all this evidence, deny that it is nothing but an empty dream?

This argument, taken by itself, is a very weak one. It relies upon a single set of facts—the variable moral customs of the world. But this variability of moral ideas is admitted by both parties to the dispute, and is capable of ready explanation upon the hypothesis of either party. The relativist says that the facts are to be explained by the non-existence of any absolute moral standard. The absolutist says that they are to be explained by human ignorance of what the absolute moral standard is. And he can truly point out that men have differed widely in their opinions about all manner of topics including the subject-matters of the physical sciences—just as much as they differ about morals. And if the various different opinions which men have held about the shape of the earth do not prove that it has no one real shape, neither do the various opinions which they have held about morality prove that there is no one true morality.

Thus the facts can be explained equally plausibly on either hypothesis. There is nothing in the facts themselves which compels us to prefer the relativistic hypothesis to that of the absolutist. And therefore the argument fails to prove the relativist conclusion. If that conclusion is to be established, it must be by means of other considerations.

This is the essential point. But I will add some supplementary remarks. The work of the anthropologists, upon which ethical relativists seem to rely so heavily, has as a matter of fact added absolutely nothing *in principle* to what has always been known about the variability of moral ideas. Educated people have known all along that the Greeks tolerated sodomy, which in modern times has been regarded in some countries as an abominable crime; that the Hindus thought it a sacred duty to burn their widows; that trickery, now thought despicable, was once believed to be a virtue; that terrible torture was thought by our own ancestors only a few centuries ago to be a justifiable weapon of justice; that it was only yesterday that western peoples came to believe that slavery is immoral. Even the ancients knew very well that moral customs and ideas vary—witness the writings of Herodotus. Thus the principle of the variability of moral ideas was well understood long before modern anthropology was ever heard of. Anthropology has added nothing to the knowledge of this principle except a mass of new and extreme examples of it drawn from very remote sources. But to multiply examples of a principle already well known and universally admitted adds nothing to the argument which is built upon that principle. The discoveries of the anthropologists have no doubt been of the highest importance in their own sphere. But in my considered opinion they have thrown no new light upon the special problems of the moral philosopher.

Although the multiplication of examples has no logical bearing on the argument, it does have an immense *psychological* effect upon people's minds. These masses of anthropological learning are impressive. They are propounded in the sacred name of "science." If they are quoted in support of ethical relativity—as they often are—people *think* that they must prove something important. They bewilder and over-awe the simpleminded, batter down their resistance, make them ready to receive humbly the doctrine of ethical relativity from those who have acquired a reputation by their immense learning and their claims to be "scientific." Perhaps this is why so much ado is made by ethical relativists regarding the anthropological evidence. But we must refuse to be impressed. We must discount all this mass of evidence about the extraordinary moral customs of remote peoples. Once we have admitted—as everyone who is instructed must have admitted these last two thousand years without any anthropology at all—the principle that moral ideas vary, all this new evidence adds nothing to the argument. And the argument itself proves nothing for the reasons already given. . . .

II

. . . [T]he case against . . . [ethical relativity] consists, to a very large extent, in urging that, if taken seriously and pressed to its logical conclusion, ethical relativity can only end in destroying the conception of morality altogether, in undermining its practical efficacy, in rendering meaningless many almost universally accepted truths about human affairs, in robbing human beings of any incentive to strive for a better world, in taking the life-blood out of every ideal and every aspiration which has ever ennobled the life of man. . . .

First of all, then, ethical relativity, in asserting that the moral standards of particular social groups are the only standards which exist, renders meaningless all propositions which attempt to compare these standards with one another in respect of their moral worth. And this is a very serious matter indeed. We are accustomed to think that the moral ideas of one nation or social group may be "higher" or "lower" than those of another. We believe, for example, that Christian ethical ideals are nobler than those of the savage races of central Africa. Probably most of us would think that the Chinese moral standards are higher than those of the inhabitants of New Guinea. In short we habitually compare one civilization with another and judge the sets of ethical ideas to be found in them to be some better, some worse. The fact that such judgments are very difficult to make with any justice, and that they are frequently made on very superficial and prejudiced grounds, has no bearing on the question now at issue. The question is whether such judgments have any *meaning*. We habitually assume that they have.

But on the basis of ethical relativity they can have none whatever. For the relativist must hold that there is no *common* standard which can be applied to the various civilizations judged. Any such comparison of moral standards implies the existence of some superior standard which is applicable to both. And the existence of any such standard is precisely what the relativist denies. According to him the Christian standard is applicable only to Christians, the Chinese standard only to Chinese, the New Guinea standard only to the inhabitants of New Guinea.

What is true of comparisons between the moral standards of different races will also be true of comparisons between those of different ages. It is not unusual to ask such questions as whether the standard of our own day is superior to that which existed among our ancestors five hundred years ago. And when we remember that our ancestors employed slaves, practiced barbaric physical tortures, and burnt people alive, we may be inclined to think that it is. At any rate we assume that the question is one which has meaning and is capable of rational discussion. But if the ethical relativist is right, whatever we assert on this subject must be totally meaningless. For here again there is no common standard which could form the basis of any such judgments.

This in its turn implies that the whole notion of moral *progress* is a sheer delusion. Progress means an advance from lower to higher, from worse to better. But on the basis of ethical relativity it has no meaning to say that the standards of this age are better (or worse) than those of a previous age. For there is no common standard by which both can be measured. Thus it is nonsense to say that the morality of the New Testament is higher than that of the Old. And Jesus Christ, if he imagined that he was introducing into the world a higher ethical standard than existed before his time, was merely deluded.

There is indeed one way in which the ethical relativist can give some sort of meaning to judgments of higher or lower as applied to the moral ideas of different races or ages. What he will have to say is that we assume *our* standards to be the best simply because they are ours. And we judge other standards by our own. If we say that Chinese moral codes are better than those of African cannibals, what we *mean* by this is that they are better *according to our standards*. We mean, that is to say, that Chinese standards are *more like our own* than African standards are. "Better" accordingly *means* "more like us." "Worse" means "less like us." It thus becomes clear that judgments of better and worse in such cases do not express anything that is really true at all. They merely give expression to our perfectly groundless satisfaction with our own ideas. In short, they give expression to nothing but our egotism and self-conceit. Our moral ideals are not really better than those of the savage. We are simply deluded by our egotism into thinking they are. The African savage has just as good a right to think his morality the best as we have to think ours the best. His opinion is just as well grounded as ours, or rather both opinions are equally groundless. And on this view Jesus Christ can only have been led to the quite absurd belief that his ethical precepts were better than those of Moses by his personal vanity. If only he had read Westermarck and Dewey he would have understood that, so long as people continued to believe in the doctrine of an eye for an eye and a tooth for a tooth, that doctrine was morally *right*; and that there could not be any point whatever in trying to make them believe in his new-fangled theory of loving one's enemies. True, the new morality would *become* right as soon as people came to believe in it, for it would then be the accepted standard. And what people think right is right. But then, if only Jesus Christ and persons with similar ideas had kept these ideas to themselves, people might have gone on believing that the old morality was right. And in that case it would have *been* right, and would have remained so till this day. And that would have saved a lot of useless trouble. For the change which Jesus Christ actually brought about was merely a change from one set of moral ideas to another. And as the new set of ideas was in no way better than the set it displaced—to say that it was better would be meaningless for the reasons already given—the change was really a sheer waste of time. And of course it likewise follows that anyone who in the future tries to improve the moral ideas of humanity will also be wasting his time.

Thus the ethical relativist must treat all judgments comparing the different moralities as either entirely meaningless; or, if this course appears too drastic, he has the alternative of declaring that they have for their meaning-content nothing except the vanity and egotism of those who pass them. We are asked to believe that the highest moral ideals of humanity are not really any better than those of an Australian bushman. But if this is so, why strive for higher ideals? Thus the heart is taken out of all effort, and the meaning out of all human ideals and aspirations.

The ethical relativist may perhaps say that he is being misjudged. It is not true that, on the basis of his doctrine, all effort for moral improvement is vain. For if we take such a civilization as our own, and if we assume that the standard of morals theoretically accepted by it is that of Christian ethics, then there is surely plenty of room for improvement and "progress" in the way of making our practice accord with our theory. Effort may legitimately be directed towards getting people to live up to whatever standards they profess to honour. Such effort will be, on the relativistic basis, perfectly meaningful; for it does not imply a comparison of standards by reference to a common standard, but only a comparison of actual achievements with an admitted and accepted standard within a social group.

Now I do not believe that even this plea can be accepted. For as soon as it comes to be effectively realized that our moral standard is no better than that of barbarians, why should anyone trouble to live up to it? It would be much easier to adopt some lower standard, to preach it assiduously until everyone believes it, when it would automatically become right. But even if we waive this point, and admit that the exhortation to practice what we preach may be meaningful, this does not touch the issue which was raised above. It will still be true that efforts to improve moral *beliefs*, as distinguished from moral *practice*, will be futile. It will still be true that Jesus Christ would have done better had he tried only to persuade humanity to live up to the old barbaric standards than he did in trying to propagate among them a new and more enlightened moral code. It will still be true that any reformer in the future who attempts to make men see even more noble ideals than those which we have inherited from the reformers of the past will be wasting his time.

I come now to a second point. Up to the present I have allowed it to be taken tacitly for granted that, though judgments comparing different races and ages in respect of the worth of their moral codes are impossible for the ethical relativist, yet judgments of comparison between individuals living within the same social group would be quite possible. For individuals living within the same social group would presumably be subject to the same moral code, that of their group, and this would therefore constitute, as between these individuals, a common standard by which they could both be measured. We have not here, as we had in the other case, the difficulty of the absence of any common standard of comparison. It should therefore be possible for the ethical relativist to say quite meaningfully that President Lincoln was a better man than some criminal or moral imbecile of his own time and country, or that Jesus was a better man than Judas Iscariot.

But is even this minimum of moral judgment really possible on relativist grounds? It seems to me that it is not. For when once the whole of humanity is abandoned as the area covered by a single moral standard, what smaller areas are to be adopted as the *loci* of different standards? Where are we to draw the lines of demarcation? We can split up humanity, perhaps,—though the procedure will be very arbitrary—into races, races into nations, nations into tribes, tribes into families, families into individuals. Where are we going to draw the *moral* boundaries? Does the *locus* of a particular moral standard reside in a race, a nation, a tribe, a family, or an individual? Perhaps the blessed phrase "social group" will be dragged in to save the situation. Each such group, we shall be told, has its own moral code which is, for it, right. But what *is* a "group"? Can anyone define it or give its boundaries? . . .

The difficulty is not, as might be thought, merely an academic difficulty of logical definition. If that were all, I should not press the point. But the ambiguity has practical consequences which are disastrous for morality. No one is likely to say that moral codes are confined within the arbitrary limits of the geographical divisions of countries. Nor are the notions of race, nation, or political state likely to help us. To bring out the essentially practical character of the difficulty let us put it in the form of concrete questions. Does the American nation constitute a "group" having a single moral standard? Or does the standard of what I ought to do change continuously as I cross the continent in a railway train? Do different States of the Union have different moral codes? Perhaps every town and village has its own peculiar standard. This may at first sight seem reasonable enough. "In Rome do as Rome does" may seem as good a rule in morals as it is in etiquette. But can we stop there? Within the village are numerous cliques each having its own set of ideas. Why should not each of these claim to be bound only by its own special and peculiar moral standards? And if it comes to that, why should not the gangsters of Chicago claim to constitute a group having its own morality, so that its murders and debaucheries must be viewed as "right" by the only standard which can legitimately be applied to it? And if it be answered that the nation will not tolerate this, that may be so. But this is to put the foundation of right simply in the superior force of the majority. In that case whoever is stronger will be right, however monstrous his ideas and actions. And if we cannot deny to any set of people the right to have its own morality, is it not clear that, in the end, we cannot even deny this right to the individual? Every individual man and woman can put up, on this view, an irrefutable claim to be judged by no standard except his or her own.

If these arguments are valid, the ethical relativist cannot really maintain that there is anywhere to be found a moral standard binding upon anybody against his will. And he cannot maintain that, even within the social group, there is a common standard as between individuals. And if that is so, then even judgments to the effect that one man is morally better than another become meaningless. All moral valuation thus vanishes. There is nothing to prevent each man from being a rule unto himself. The result will be moral chaos and the collapse of all effective standards.

Perhaps, in regard to the difficulty of defining the social group, the relativist may make the following suggestion. If we admit, he may say, that it is impossible or very difficult to define a group territorially or nationally or geographically, it is still possible to define it logically. We will simply define an ethical group as any set of persons (whether they live together in one place or are scattered about in many places over the earth) who recognize one and the same moral standard. As a matter of fact such groups will as a rule be found occupying each something like a single locality. The people in one country, or at least in one village, tend to think much alike. But theoretically at least the members of an ethical group so defined might be scattered all over the face of the globe. However that may be, it will now be possible to make meaningful statements to the effect that one individual is morally better or worse than another, so long as we keep within the ethical group so defined. For the individuals of the ethical group will have as their common standard the ethical belief or beliefs the acknowledgment of which constitutes the defining characteristic of the group. By this common standard they can be judged and compared with one another. Therefore it is not true that ethical relativity necessarily makes all such judgments of moral comparison between individuals meaningless.

I admit the logic of this. Theoretically judgments of comparison can be given meaning in this way. Nevertheless there are fatal objections to the suggestion. In the first place, this is certainly not what the relativist ordinarily understands his doctrine to mean. He never talks in terms of ethical groups defined in this purely logical way. He talks in terms of actual social groups, nations, tribes, or historically existing communities of some kind. We are told that the moral customs of the Athenians of the fifth century B.C. were the only effective standards for the Athenians of the fifth century B.C.; that the moral customs of present day Hottentots are the only effective standards for present day Hottentots; and so on. The suggestion which we are now considering gives to the usual doctrine of relativism a twist which renders it unrecognizable. And if it be said that the logical ethical group is *in fact* usually at least roughly identical with some actual territorial or social group—since people living together tend to share the same moral ideas—I can only reply by denying the truth of this. In the same social group all sorts of different moral ideas may thrive. This is the point of the second objection to the relativist's present suggestion.

The second objection is that the suggested criterion will be useless in practice. For how can I ever know whether two persons whom I wish to compare belong to the same ethical group or not? I wish to say that Jesus was a morally nobler man than Judas Iscariot. If the relativist cannot admit this, then surely his creed revolts our moral sense. But I cannot make this statement unless I have first made certain that Jesus and Judas had the same moral ideals. But had they? Personally I should think it almost certain that they had not. Judas may have paid homage, in some sort, to the moral teachings of his master. He may even have been quite sincere. But it seems to me incredible that he could ever really have made them parts of his mental and moral outlook, or even that he could have effectively understood them. Consequently the judgment that Jesus was better than Judas is meaningless after all. . . . I think it would be in general true to say that wherever there is between people a very wide discrepancy of moral practice, there is almost sure to be also a wide discrepancy of moral belief. And in no such case could we, on the relativistic basis suggested, make meaningful moral comparisons. It can hardly be said, therefore, that this suggestion at all helps the case of the ethical relativist.

But even if we assume that the difficulty about defining moral groups has been surmounted, a further difficulty presents itself. Suppose that we have now definitely decided what are the exact boundaries of the social group within which a moral standard is to be operative. And we will assume—as is invariably done by relativists themselves—that this group is to be some actually existing social community such as a tribe or nation. How are we to know, even then, what actually *is* the moral standard within that group? How is anyone to know? How is even a member of the group to know? For there are certain to be within the group—at least this will be true among advanced peoples—wide differences of opinion as to what is right, what wrong. Whose opinion, then, is to be taken as representing *the* moral standard of the group? Either we must take the opinion of the majority within the group, or the opinion of some minority. If we rely upon the ideas of the majority, the results will be disastrous. Wherever there is found among a people a small band of select spirits, or perhaps one man, working for the establishment of higher and nobler ideals than those commonly accepted by the group, we shall be compelled to hold that, for that people at that time, the majority are right, and that the reformers are wrong and are preaching what is immoral. We shall have to maintain, for example, that Jesus was preaching immoral doctrines to the Jews. Moral goodness will have to be equated always with the mediocre and sometimes with the definitely base and ignoble. If on the other hand we say that the moral standard of the group is to be identified with the moral opinions of some minority, then what minority is this to be? We cannot answer that it is to be the minority composed of the best and most enlightened individuals of the group. This would involve us in a palpably vicious circle. For by what standard are these individuals to be judged the best and the most enlightened? There is no principle by which we could select the right minority. And therefore we should have to consider every minority as good as every other. And this means that we should have no logical right whatever to resist the claim of the gangsters of Chicago — if such a claim were made — that their practices represent the highest standards of American morality. It means in the end that every individual is to be bound by no standard save his own.

The ethical relativists are great empiricists. *What* is the actual moral standard of any group can only be discovered, they tell us, by an examination on the ground of the moral opinions and customs of that group. But will they tell us how they propose to decide, when they get to the ground, which of the many moral opinions they are sure to find there is *the* right one in that group? To some extent they will be able to do this for the Melanesian Islanders — from whom apparently all lessons in the nature of morality are in future to be taken. But it is certain that they cannot do it for advanced peoples whose members have learnt to think for themselves and to entertain among themselves a wide variety of opinions. They cannot do it unless they accept the calamitous view that the ethical opinion of the majority is always right. We are left therefore once more with the conclusion that, even within a particular social group, anybody's moral opinion is as good as anybody else's, and that every man is entitled to be judged by his own standards.

Finally, not only is ethical relativity disastrous in its consequences for moral theory. It cannot be doubted that it must tend to be equally disastrous in its impact upon practical conduct. If men come really to believe that one moral standard is as good as another, they will conclude that their own moral standard has nothing special to recommend it. They might as well then slip down to some lower and easier standard. It is true that, for a time, it may be possible to hold one view in theory and to act practically upon another. But ideas, even philosophical ideas, are not so ineffectual that they can remain forever idle in the upper chambers of the intellect. In the end they seep down to the level of practice. They get themselves acted on.

Speaking of the supposedly dangerous character of ethical relativity Westermarck says "Ethical subjectivism instead of being a danger is more likely to be an advantage to morality. Could it be brought home to people that there is no absolute standard in morality, they would perhaps be on the one hand more tolerant, and on the other hand more critical in their judgments."[1] Certainly, if we believe that any one moral standard is as good as any other we *are* likely to be more tolerant. We shall tolerate widow-burning, human sacrifice, cannibalism, slavery, the infliction of physical torture, or any other of the thousand and one abominations which are, or have been, from time to time approved by one moral code or another. But this is not the kind of toleration that we want, and I do not think its cultivation will prove "an advantage to morality."

These, then, are the main arguments which the anti-relativist will urge against ethical relativity. And perhaps finally he will attempt a diagnosis of the social, intellectual, and psychological conditions of our time to which the emergence of ethical relativism is to be attributed. His diagnosis will be somewhat as follows.

We have abandoned, perhaps with good reason, the oracles of the past. Every age, of course, does this. But in our case it seems that none of us knows any more whither to turn. We do not know what to put in the place of that which has gone. What ought we, supposedly civilized peoples, to aim at? What are to be our ideals? What is right? What is wrong? What is beautiful? What is ugly? No man knows. We drift helplessly in this direction and that. We know not where we stand nor whither we are going.

There are, of course, thousands of voices frantically shouting directions. But they shout one another down, they contradict one another, and the upshot is mere uproar. And because of this confusion there creeps upon us an insidious scepticism and despair. Since no one knows what the truth is, we will deny that there is any truth. Since no one knows what right is, we will deny that there is any right. Since no one knows what the beautiful is, we will deny that there is any beauty. Or at least we will say — what comes to the same thing — that what people (the people of any particular age, region, society) — think to be true is true *for them*; that what people think morally right is morally right *for them*; that what people think beautiful is beautiful *for them*. There is no common and objective standard in any of these matters. Since all the voices contradict

---

[1]*Ethical Relativity*, page 59.

one another, they must be all equally right (or equally wrong, for it makes no difference which we say). It is from the practical confusion of our time that these doctrines issue. When all the despair and defeatism of our distracted age are expressed in abstract concepts, are erected into a philosophy, it is then called relativism — ethical relativism, esthetic relativism, relativity of truth. Ethical relativity is simply defeatism in morals.

And the diagnosis will proceed. Perhaps, it will say, the current pessimism as to our future is unjustified. But there is undoubtedly a wide spread feeling that our civilization is rushing downwards to the abyss. If this should be true, and if nothing should check the headlong descent, . then perhaps some historian of the future will seek to disentangle the causes. The causes will, of course, be found to be multitudinous and enormously complicated. And one must not exaggerate the relative importance of any of them. But it can hardly be doubted that our future historian will include somewhere in his list the failure of the men of our generation to hold steadfastly before themselves the notion of an (even comparatively) unchanging moral idea. He will cite that feebleness of intellectual and moral grasp which has led them weakly to harbour the belief that no one moral aim is really any better than any other, that each is good and true for those who entertain it. This meant, he will surely say, that men had given up in despair the struggle to attain moral truth. Civilization lives in and through its upward struggle. Whoever despairs and gives up the struggle, whether it be an individual or a whole civilization, is already inwardly dead.

Egoism Versus Absolute Morality

Kurt Baier

The Moral Point of View

1. *Moral Convictions Can Be True or False*

It is often argued that our moral convictions are merely expressions of our feelings, emotions, or attitudes, or that they are commands or pseudo commands, and that, therefore, they cannot be true or false. It might be added that they must have some kind of imperatival force, for it must be possible to act in accordance with or contrary to them. But one cannot act in accordance with or contrary to truths or facts. Truths or facts are compatible with any sort of behavior. Truths are, therefore, useless in morality. There we need something in the nature of precepts.

This argument is unsound. Moral convictions can be true or false and also imperatival. To say 'Killing is wrong' is to say that killing constitutes the contravention of a certain sort of rule or commandment, 'Don't kill,' 'Thou shalt not kill.' Hence, 'Killing is wrong' may be true or false, for it may or may not be the contravention of such a rule. On the other hand, it also makes this remark imperatival, for killing is thereby declared to be the contravention of a rule or commandment. If, in a train, I say to my neighbor, 'No smoking in here,' I say something which can be true or false (for it may or may not be a nonsmokers') and also imperatival (for if it is a nonsmokers', then there is a rule forbidding smoking in the compartment). Thus, what makes 'No smoking in here' and 'Killing is wrong' capable of being true or false is the fact that the rules alluded to by these remarks are capable of passing a certain test. 'No smoking in here' can be true (or false), because the rule 'No smoking in this compartment' is (or is not) properly laid down by the Railway Company which is (or is not) entitled to do so. Our main task will, of course, be to show what are the appropriate tests which a moral rule must pass in order that remarks alluding to it should be said to be true. We have to answer questions such as what are the tests which the rule 'Thou shalt not kill' must pass if it is to be true that killing is wrong.

The proof that moral convictions could be true or false and also imperatival seems to me to constitute quite a strong argument in favor of saying that they actually are true or false, for this is what we all naturally think. The only reason why we have doubts is that philosophers have various reasons for saying that propositions cannot be both imperatival and true or false. However, in view of the great popularity of the emotive and imperativalist theories, it is perhaps not out of place to devote some additional space to establishing this conclusion.

My main contention is that we could not properly speak of *a morality*, as opposed to a system of conventions, customs, or laws, until the question of the correctness or incorrectness, truth or falsity, of the rules prevalent in a community is asked, until, in other words, the prevalent rules are subjected to certain tests. It is only when the current rules are no longer regarded as sacrosanct, as incapable of alteration or improvement, only when the current rules are contrasted with other possible, improved, ideal rules, that a group can be said to have a morality as opposed to a mere set of taboos.

We distinguish a great many different moralities — Greek, Roman, Arapesh, Christian, Mohammedan, Communist, feudal, bourgeois, proletarian, and so on. Moralities are always someone's, whether an individual's or a group's. In these respects, moralities are like customs and legal systems.[1] But in another respect, moralities on the one hand and legal systems and customs on the other differ radically. When we have settled whether a line of action is in accordance with or contrary to the law or the customs of the group in question, we have settled conclusively whether this line of action is lawful or unlawful, customary or not customary. We cannot go on to ask, 'Well, perhaps it is legal here or customary there, but is it *really* legal, is it *really* customary?' Nor does it make sense to say, 'There is no law or custom against this sort of thing anywhere, but perhaps this sort of thing is *really* illegal or *really* contrary to custom.' By contrast, this kind of distinction can be and is drawn in moral matters. When we hear that in certain countries virginity above a certain age is regarded as selfish and immoral, or that not having scalped anyone by a certain age is regarded as effeminate or lazy, or that it is "wrong" for women to pass a certain stone without veiling their faces, we do not think that the question whether these sorts of conduct are *really* wrong has been decisively settled. Even whether these things are *wrong in that country* has not been answered. It has only been established that these types of conduct are *believed wrong in that country*.

When we have settled that something is against the customs or laws of a certain group, we cannot go on to ask whether it is merely believed or actually known to be illegal or contrary to custom. A person who goes on to ask that question must be said not to know what he is talking about. On the other hand, a person likewise does not know what he is talking about if he believes that finding out whether some course of action is contrary to the morality of a certain group settles the question whether this course of action is morally wrong. For he ignores the crucial question 'Is what the morality of that group forbids *really* wrong?' or, put differently, 'Are the moral convictions of that group true?' I take it for granted, then, that ordinary usage draws just that distinction between morality on the one hand and custom and law on the other.

But, it might be asked, what does that prove? Our language might be confused. Perhaps we allow that question without having provided a method of answering it. Our moral locutions may be the embodiment of wishful thinking. It is not enough to point out that we *ask*, 'But are the

---

[1]For a slight modification, see above, Chapter Five, section 3, p. 134.

moral convictions of this group really true?' If that question is to make sense, a procedure for answering it has to exist and it must be a sensible one.

I agree with the principle behind this objection. It is not enough to show, for instance, that we frequently do ask the question 'But is this religion true?' If it were enough, certain modern analyses of religious language would be obviously false. Certain philosophers who say that religious language is purely evocative could then be refuted simply by the reminder "But we do ask the question 'Is his religion true?' and your analysis does not permit it to be asked." Or when other philosophers say that the claim 'God exists' is a complex empirical assertion implying that things will not go from bad to worse in the future, but will in the end be all right, they could be refuted simply by saying that this is not implied in the religious assertion that God exists. I do not think that such philosophers can be so easily refuted. A refutation would have to show not only that we all *think* that this is not implied in such remarks or that we all wish to ask whether such remarks are true, but also that what we imply or what we wish to ask is sensible, that there is room for this question, that we can sensibly imply what we intend to, that we can ask this question and imply what we intend without making nonsense of our religious assertions. It is just because this is so difficult that some philosophers have been driven into these alternative analyses of religious assertions.

This is true of moral claims also. It is not enough to say, 'But we *do* ask whether our moral convictions are true.' We must also show what exactly is the sense of this question and how exactly it can be answered. When this is shown, as I shall do presently, our original claim has been made good. Since we want to ask whether our moral convictions are true and since it can be explained what this question means and how it is answered and since it can be shown that it is an eminently sensible question, there can no longer be any objection to allowing it. . . .

2. *True Moralities and Absolute Morality*

Our discussion has brought to light an essential characteristic of a morality: that it should make sense to ask, 'But are these moral convictions true?' or 'Is this moral code correct?' or words to that effect. The question implies that the moral rules and convictions of any group can and should be subjected to certain tests. It implies a distinction between this and that morality on the one hand and true morality on the other.

Let us be quite clear, however, what this distinction amounts to. It is not, in the first place, that between 'a morality' and 'morality as such,' which is analogous to the distinction between a legal system and law as such or between a disease and disease as such. Talking about a morality, say Greek or Tikopia or *fin de siècle* morality, is like talking about Roman, canonic, or Napoleonic law, or about Bright's disease, cancer, or leprosy. But talking about morality as such or the nature of morality is like talking about law as such or the nature of law, disease as such or the nature of disease. When talking in this way, we are drawing attention to the essentials of the concept. We are thinking of the conditions which something must satisfy in order to be properly called 'a morality,' 'a legal system,' 'a disease.' We are asked to neglect all those additional features in virtue of which a given morality, legal system, or disease is always more than just that, is always a particular one, Christian morality, or Napoleonic law, or hepatitis. Morality as such is not a supermorality, any more than law as such is a superlaw, or disease as such a superdisease. Morality as such is not even a morality, but a set of conditions. Morality as such cannot, therefore, be either true or false.

And this brings out an important point. There is no a priori reason to assume that there is only one true morality. There are many moralities, and of these a large number may happen to pass the test which moralities must pass in order to be called true. It would, therefore, be better to speak of 'a true morality' or of 'true moralities' than of 'true morality.'

However, there is one point that makes it desirable to speak of 'true morality' in addition to speaking of 'true moralities.' It is this. True moralities are particular moralities which pass certain tests. We may abstract from all the particular existential conditions of given moralities and think of true morality as a system of true moral convictions not embodied in, but completely independent of, the particular conditions of this or that way of life. There may therefore be true moral convictions which, though possibly no one actually holds them, are true in and for all possible social conditions. But there could be such true convictions only if their content had nothing to do with social conditions. It may, of course, be argued that there are no such convictions, but I think there are.

'True morality' in this sense cannot, of course, be just *one* moral code, the same for any morality which can be said to be true. For there will be many different moralities all of which are true, although each may contain moral convictions which would be out of place in one of the others. Thus, 'Lending money for interest is wrong,' 'A man ought not to marry his brother's widow,' 'It is wrong to take more than one wife,' and so on may be true moral convictions in one set of social conditions, but false in another. However, moral convictions, such as 'Killing is wrong,' 'Harming others is wrong,' 'Lying is wrong,' 'Misusing the institutions of one's society is wrong,' are true quite irrespective of the particular setup of given societies. If these are true moral convictions at all, then they must be absolutely true, for they are based solely on human nature. They are, from their very nature, independent of particular variations of the social pattern. However, they are not true for "all rational beings," as Kant thought, but only for human beings, and they would not necessarily remain true for human beings if there were radical changes in human nature. Thus, if being killed became generally desired and were a pleasurable experience and if one were reborn soon afterwards with a new body but with all memories intact, it would no longer be true that killing was wrong.

I shall, then, distinguish between true moralities and absolute morality. True moralities are actually embodied moralities, those forming part of a given way of life of a society or an individual, which would pass a certain test, if they were subjected to it. Absolute morality, on the other hand, is that set of moral convictions, whether held by anyone or not, which is true quite irrespective of any particular social conditions in which they might be embodied. Every true morality must contain as its core the convictions belonging to absolute morality, but it may also contain a lot more that could not be contained in every other true morality.

It is clear, furthermore, that true moralities are the applications of the most general true moral convictions to the specific conditions of a particular social order. 'It is wrong to misuse social institutions' is part of absolute morality, for it is neutral to the particular form the social institutions take. But even very general precepts, such as 'Stealing is wrong,' 'Adultery is wrong,' 'Promise breaking is wrong,' 'Neglecting your duties is wrong,' 'Failing to discharge your obligations is wrong,' cannot be part of absolute morality, for these refer to specific ways of misusing specific social institutions, which a given society may not have. It is conceivable that in a given society there might be no institution of property or marriage, no such thing as promising or having duties or obligations, and still the group might have a morality, for it might believe that killing is wrong or that hurting others is wrong.

3. *Points of View*

What, then, is the test (if any) which a moral conviction must pass in order to be called true? Many philosophers have held that there is not and cannot be such a test. They would perhaps admit that we may reduce our moral convictions to a few basic moral principles, or perhaps even only one, from which all others can be derived, but they would hold that at least one such principle must simply be selected as we please. Such basic principles are matters for deciding, not for finding out.

I shall argue, on the contrary, that our moral convictions are true if they can be seen to be required or acceptable *from the moral point of view*. It is indeed true that a person must adopt the moral point of view if he is to be moral. But it is not true that this is an arbitrary decision. On the contrary, I shall show that there are the very best reasons for adopting this point of view.

Answers to practical questions can be arrived at by reference to a point of view, which may be defined by a principle. When we adopt a certain point of view, we adopt its defining principle. To look at practical problems from that point of view is to be prepared to answer practical questions of the form 'What shall I do?' 'What should be done?' by reference to its defining principle.

Suppose the problem under discussion is whether or not a certain traffic roundabout should be erected at a certain intersection. I can look at this from various points of view, that of a pedestrian or a motorist, a local politician or a manufacturer of roundabouts, and so on. In cases such as these, we have in mind the point of view of self-interest as applied to certain special positions or jobs or functions in a society. To look at our problem from the point of view of a motorist is to ask whether the erection of a roundabout at this intersection is in the interest of a motorist. For different points of view there may, of course, be different, even opposing, answers to the same practical questions. The roundabout may be in the interest of a motorist but not of a pedestrian, in the interest of a manufacturer of roundabouts but not of a local politician who depends for his votes on the poorer section (the pedestrians) of the population.

However, a point of view is not necessarily defined by the principle of self-interest or its more specific application to a particular position in society. We can, for instance, look at this problem from the point of view of town planners or traffic experts, who may favor the roundabout because their special task is to solve traffic problems. Their point of view is defined by the principle 'Favor anything that keeps the traffic flowing; oppose anything that is likely to cause traffic holdups.' But the erection of the roundabout can hardly be said to be *in their interest*. They do not derive any personal advantage or benefit from the scheme. There are many such disinterested points of view, for example, the point of view of a social worker, a social reformer, an advocate of public health schemes, a missionary.

A person is of good will if he adopts the moral point of view as supreme, that is, as overriding all other points of view. When asking the question 'What shall I do?' or 'What is to be done?' such a person will always engage in moral deliberation, survey and weigh the moral considerations, and give them greater weight than any others. A person has adopted the moral point of view when he reviews the facts in the light of *his* moral convictions. We do not require him to test his moral convictions every time, but only because we presume that he already has true moral convictions. This presumption may be false. He may simply have accepted without much questioning the moral convictions of his group, or he may have departed from them without getting any nearer the truth. In such a case, he merely *means* to adopt the moral point of view, but has not succeeded. He has adopted something which he wrongly believes to be the moral point of view. He must still be called a person of good will because of his intentions, but he cannot arrive at true answers to his question.

Clearly, our central problem is to define the moral point of view.

The Moral Point of View

Throughout the history of philosophy, by far the most popular candidate for the position of the moral point of view has been self-interest. There are obvious parallels between these two standpoints. Both aim at the good. Both are rational. Both involve deliberation, the surveying and weighing of reasons. The adoption of either yields statements containing the word 'ought.' Both involve the notion of self-mastery and control over the desires. It is, moreover, plausible to hold that a person could not have a reason for doing anything whatsoever unless his behavior was designed to promote his own good. Hence, if morality is to have the support of reason, moral reasons must be self-interested, hence the point of view of morality and self-interest must be the same. On the other hand, it seems equally obvious that morality and self-interest are very frequently opposed. Morality often requires us to refrain from doing what self-interest recommends or to do what self-interest forbids. Hence morality and self-interest cannot be the same points of view.

1. *Self-Interest and Morality*

Can we save the doctrine that the moral point of view is that of self-interest? One way of circumventing the difficulty just mentioned is to draw a distinction between two senses of 'self-interest,' shortsighted and enlightened. The shortsighted egoist always follows his short-range interest without taking into consideration how this will affect others and how their reactions will affect him. The enlightened egoist, on the other hand, knows that he cannot get the most out of life unless he pays attention to the needs of others on whose good will he depends. On this view, the standpoint of (immoral) egoism differs from that of morality in that it fails to consider the interests of others even when this costs little or nothing or when the long-range benefits to oneself are likely to be greater than the short-range sacrifices.

This view can be made more plausible still if we distinguish between those egoists who consider each course of action on its own merits and those who, for convenience, adopt certain rules of thumb which they have found will promote their long-range interest. Slogans such as 'Honesty is the best policy,' 'Give to charity rather than to the Department of Internal Revenue,' 'Always give a penny to a beggar when you are likely to be watched by your acquaintances,' 'Treat your servants kindly and they will work for you like slaves,' 'Never be arrogant to anyone — you may need his services one day,' are maxims of this sort. They embody the "wisdom" of a given society. The enlightened long-range egoist may adopt these as rules of thumb, that is, as *prima-facie* maxims, as rules which he will observe unless he has good evidence that departing from them will pay him better than abiding by them. It is obvious that the rules of behavior adopted by the enlightened egoist will be very similar to those of a man who rigidly follows our own moral code.

Sidgwick appears to believe that egoism is one of the legitimate "methods of ethics," although he himself rejects it on the basis of an "intuition" that it is false. He supports the legitimacy of egoism by the argument that everyone could consistently adopt the egoistic point of view. "I quite admit that when the painful necessity comes for another man to choose between his own happiness and the general happiness, he must as a reasonable being prefer his own, i.e. it is right for him to do this on my principle."[2] The consistent enlightened egoist satisfies the categorical imperative, or at least one version of it, 'Act only on that maxim whereby thou canst at the same time will that it should become a universal law.'

However, no "intuition" is required to see that this is not the point of view of morality, even though it can be universally adopted without self-contradiction. In the first place, a consistent egoist adopts for all

---

[2]Henry Sidgwick, *The Methods of Ethics*, 7th ed. (London: Macmillan and Co., 1907), pref. to the 6th ed., p. xvii.

occasions the principle 'everyone for himself' which we allow (at most) only in conditions of chaos, when the normal moral order breaks down. Its adoption marks the return to the law of the jungle, the state of nature, in which the "softer," "more chivalrous" ways of morality have no place.[3]

This point can be made more strictly. It can be shown that those who adopt consistent egoism cannot make moral judgments. Moral talk is impossible for consistent egoists. But this amounts to a *reductio ad absurdum* of consistent egoism.

Let B and K be candidates for the presidency of a certain country and let it be granted that it is in the interest of either to be elected, but that only one can succeed. It would then be in the interest of B but against the interest of K if B were elected, and vice versa, and therefore in the interest of B but against the interest of K if K were liquidated, and vice versa. But from this it would follow that B ought to liquidate K, that it is wrong for B not to do so, that B has not "done his duty" until he has liquidated K; and vice versa. Similarly K, knowing that his own liquidation is in the interest of B and therefore anticipating B's attempts to secure it, ought to take steps to foil B's endeavors. It would be wrong for him not to do so. He would "not have done his duty" until he had made sure of stopping B. It follows that if K prevents B from liquidating him, his act must be said to be both wrong and not wrong — wrong because it is the prevention of what B ought to do, his duty, and wrong for B not to do it; not wrong because it is what K ought to do, his duty, and wrong for K not to do it. But one and the same act (logically) cannot be both morally wrong and not morally wrong. Hence in cases like these morality does not apply.

This is obviously absurd. For morality is designed to apply in just such cases, namely, those where interests conflict. But if the point of view of morality were that of self-interest, then there could *never* be moral solutions of conflicts of interest. However, when there are conflicts of interest, we always look for a "higher" point of view, one from which such conflicts can be settled. Consistent egoism makes everyone's private interest the "highest court of appeal." But by 'the moral point of view' we *mean* a point of view which is a court of appeal for conflicts of interest. Hence it cannot (logically) be identical with the point of view of self-interest. Sidgwick is, therefore, wrong in thinking that consistent egoism is one of the "legitimate methods of ethics." He is wrong in thinking that an "intuition" is required to see that it is not the correct moral point of view. That it is not can be seen in the same way in which we can "see" that the Court of Petty Sessions is not the Supreme Court.

---

[3]See below, Chapter Twelve, section 3.

2. *Morality Involves Doing Things On Principle*

Another feature of consistent egoism is that the rules by which a consistent egoist abides are merely rules of thumb. A consistent egoist has only one supreme principle, to do whatever is necessary for the realization of his one aim, the promotion of his interest. He does not have *principles*, he has only an aim. If one has adopted the moral point of view, then one acts on principle and not merely on rules of thumb designed to promote one's aim. This involves conforming to the rules whether or not doing so favors one's own or anyone else's aim.

Kant grasped this point even if only obscurely. He saw that adopting the moral point of view involves acting on principle. It involves conforming to rules even when doing so is unpleasant, painful, costly, or ruinous to oneself. Kant, furthermore, argued rightly that, since moral action is action on principle (and not merely in accordance with rules of thumb), a moral agent ought not to make exceptions in his own favor, and he interpreted this to mean that moral rules are absolutely inflexible and without exceptions. Accordingly he concluded that if 'Thou shalt not kill' states a moral rule, then any and every act correctly describable as an act of killing someone must be said to be morally wrong.

Kant also saw that this view required him to reject some of our deepest moral convictions; we certainly think that the killing of a man in self-defense or by the hangman is not morally wrong. Kant was prepared to say that our moral convictions are wrong on this point. Can we salvage these moral convictions? The only alternative, to say that acting on principle does not require us not to make exceptions in our own favor, seems to be equally untenable.

It is therefore not surprising that many philosophers have abandoned Kant's (and the commonsense) view that the moral rightness of an act is its property of being in accordance with a moral rule or principle. Thus, the deontologists claim that rightness is a simple property which we can "see" or "intuit" in an act, and the utilitarians, that rightness is a complex property, namely, the tendency of an act to promote the greatest happiness of the greatest number. But, as is well known, these accounts are not plausible and lead to considerable difficulties.

However, this whole problem arises only because of a confusion, the confusion of the expression 'making an exception to a rule' with the expression 'a rule has an exception.' As soon as this muddle is cleared away, it can be seen that Kant is right in saying that acting on principle implies making no exception in anyone's favor, but wrong in thinking that therefore all moral rules must be absolutely without exception.

'No parking in the city' has a number of recognized exceptions which are part of the rule itself, for example, 'except in the official parking areas,' 'except in front of a parking meter,' 'except on Saturday mornings and after 8 P.M. every day.' A person who does not know the recognized exceptions does not completely know the rule, for these exceptions more precisely define its range of application. A policeman who is not booking a motorist parking in front of a parking meter is not granting exemption to (making an exception in favor of) this motorist. On the contrary, he is administering the rule correctly. If he did apply the no-parking rule to the motorist, *he* would be applying it where *it* does not apply, because this is one of the recognized exceptions which are *part* of the rule. On the other hand, a policeman who does not book a motorist parking his vehicle in a prohibited area at peak hour on a busy day is making an exception in the motorist's favor. If he does so because the man is his friend, he illegitimately grants an exemption. If he does so because the motorist is a doctor who has been called to attend to a man lying unconscious on the pavement, this is a "deserving case" and he grants the exemption legitimately.

Apply this distinction to the rules of a given morality. Notice first that moral rules differ from laws and regulations in that they are not administered by special administrative organs such as policemen and magistrates. Everyone "administers" them himself. Nevertheless, it makes sense to speak of making exceptions in one's own favor. For one may refuse to apply the rule to oneself when one knows that it does apply, that is to say, one may refuse to observe it even when one knows one should. And what is true of making exceptions in one's own favor is true also of making them in favor of someone else. It is almost as immoral to make exceptions in favor of one's wife, son, or nephew as in favor of oneself.

When we say, therefore, that a person who has killed a burglar in self-defense has not done anything wrong, we are not making an exception in the houseowner's favor. It is much nearer the truth to say that, in our morality, the rule 'Thou shalt not kill' *has several recognized exceptions*, among them 'in self-defense.' We can say that a man does not know fully our moral rule 'Thou shalt not kill' if he does not know that it has, among others, this exception.

Like other rules of reason, our moral convictions are so only *presumptively.*[4] Killing is wrong *unless* it is killing in self-defense, killing by the hangman, killing of an enemy in wartime, accidental killing, and

---

[4]See above, Chapter Two, sections 5 and 6.

216

possibly mercy killing. If it is one of these types of killing, then it is *not* wrong.

Even if it is one of the wrongful acts of killing, it is so only *prima facie*, other things being equal. For there may have been an overriding moral reason in favor of killing the man, for example, that he is about to blow up a train and that this is the only way of stopping him.

One further point should be made to avoid misunderstanding. Unlike laws and regulations, moral rules have not been laid down by anyone. Knowing moral rules cannot, therefore, involve knowing exactly what a certain person has enjoined and forbidden and what exceptions he has allowed, because there is no such person. In the case of regulations and laws, it was precisely this knowledge which enabled us to draw the distinction between saying that someone was granting an exception and saying that he was merely applying the rule which, for cases of this sort, provided for an exception. Our distinction seems to collapse for moral rules.

However, the answer to this is simple. When a magistrate is empowered to make exceptions or grant exemptions in "deserving cases," the question of what is a "deserving case" is not of course answered in the regulation itself. If it were, the magistrate would not be exercising his power to grant exemption, but would simply apply the regulation as provided in it. How, then, does the magistrate or policeman know what is a deserving case? The doctor who parks his car in a prohibited spot in order to attend to an injured man is such a case, namely, a *morally deserving* case. The principles in accordance with which policemen or magistrates grant exemptions to existing regulations are moral principles. In the case of moral rules, there cannot be any distinction between exceptions which are part of the rule and deserving cases. *Only* deserving cases can be part of the moral rule, and *every* deserving case is properly part of it. Hence while in the case of laws and regulations there is a reason for going beyond the exceptions allowed in the regulation itself (when there is a morally deserving instance), in the case of moral rules there is no such reason. For all deserving cases are, from the nature of the case, part of the moral rule itself. Hence it is never right to make an exception to a moral rule in anyone's favor. Kant is therefore quite right in saying that it is always wrong to make exceptions to moral rules in one's own favor (and for that matter in anyone else's), but he is wrong in thinking that this makes moral rules inflexible.

All this follows from the very nature of moral principles. They are binding on everyone alike quite irrespective of what are the goals or purposes of the person in question. Hence self-interest cannot be the moral point of view, for it sets every individual one supreme goal, his own interest, which overrules all his other maxims.

3. *Moral Rules Are Meant For Everybody*

The point of view of morality is inadequately characterized by saying that *I* have adopted it if *I* act on principles, that is, on rules to which I do not make exceptions whenever acting on them would frustrate one or the other of my purposes or desires. It is characterized by greater universality than that. It must be thought of as a standpoint from which principles are considered as being acted on by *everyone*. Moral principles are not merely principles on which a person must always act without making exceptions, but they are principles *meant for everybody*.

It follows from this that the teaching of morality must be completely universal and open. Morality is meant to be taught to all members of the group in such a way that everyone can and ought always to act in accordance with these rules. It is not the preserve of an oppressed or privileged class or individual. People are neglecting their duties if they do not teach the moral rules to their children. Children are removed from the homes of criminals because they are not likely to be taught the moral rules there. Furthermore, moral rules must be taught quite openly and to everybody without discrimination. An esoteric code, a set of precepts known only to the initiated and perhaps jealously concealed from outsiders, can at best be a religion, not a morality. 'Thou shalt not eat beans and this is a secret' or 'Always leave the third button of your waistcoat undone, but don't tell anyone except the initiated members' may be part of an esoteric religion, but not of a morality. 'Thou shalt not kill, but it is a strict secret' is absurd. 'Esoteric morality' is a contradiction in terms. It is no accident that the so-called higher religions were imbued with the missionary spirit, for they combine the beliefs of daemons and gods and spirits characteristic of primitive religions with *a system of morality*. Primitive religions are not usually concerned to proselytize. On the contrary, they are imbued with the spirit of the exclusive trade secret. If one thinks of one's religion as concentrated wisdom of life revealed solely to the *chosen* people, one will regard it as the exclusive property of the club, to be confined to the elect. If, on the other hand, the rules are thought to be for everyone, one must in consistency want to spread the message.

The condition of universal teachability yields three other criteria of moral rules. They must not, in the first place, be "self-frustrating." They are so if their purpose is frustrated as soon as everybody acts on them, if they have a point only when a good many people act on the opposite principle. Someone might, for instance, act on the maxim 'When you are in need, ask for help, but never help another man when he is in need.' If everybody adopted this principle, then their adoption of the second half would frustrate what obviously is the point of the adoption of the first half, namely, to get help when one is in need. Although such a principle is not self-contradictory — for anybody could consistently adopt it — it is nevertheless objectionable from the moral point of view, for it could not be taught openly to everyone. It would then lose its point. It is a parasitic principle, useful to anyone only if many people act on its opposite.

The same is true of "self-defeating" and "morally impossible" rules. A principle is self-defeating if its point is defeated as soon as a person lets it be known that he has adopted it, for example, the principle 'Give a promise even when you know or think that you can never keep it, or when you don't intend to keep it.' The very point of giving promises is to reassure and furnish a guarantee to the promisee. Hence any remark that throws doubt on the sincerity of the promiser will defeat the purpose of making a promise. And clearly to *let it be known* that one gives promises even when one knows or thinks one cannot, or when one does not intend to keep them, is to raise such doubts. And to say that one acts on the above principle is to imply that one may well give promises in these cases. Hence to reveal that one acts on this principle will tend to defeat one's own purpose.

It has already been said that moral rules must be capable of being taught openly, but this rule is self-defeating when taught openly, for then everyone would be known to act on it. Hence it cannot belong to the morality of any group.

Lastly, there are some rules which it is literally impossible to teach in the way the moral rules of a group must be capable of being taught, for example, the rule 'Always assert what you think not to be the case.' Such *morally impossible* rules differ from self-frustrating and self-defeating rules in that the latter could have been taught in this way, although it would have been quite senseless to do so, whereas the former literally cannot be so taught. The reason why the above rule cannot be taught in this way is that the only possible case of acting on it, doing so secretly, is ruled out by the conditions of *moral teaching*.

(1) Consider first someone secretly adopting this rule. His remarks will almost always mislead people, for *he will be taken to be saying what he thinks true*, whereas he *is* saying the opposite. Moreover, in most

cases what he thinks (and not what he says) will be true. Thus, it will usually be the case that *p* is true when he says 'not-*p*,' and not-*p* when he says '*p*,' whereas people will take it that *p* is true when he says '*p*,' and not-*p* when he says 'not-*p*.' Thus communication between him and other people breaks down, since they will almost always be misled by him whether he wishes to mislead them or not. The possibility of communication depends on a speaker's ability *at will* to say either what he thinks to be the case or what he thinks not to be the case. Our speaker cannot communicate because by his principle he is forced to mislead his hearers.

Thus, anyone secretly adopting the principle 'Always assert what you think not to be the case' cannot communicate with others since he is bound to mislead them whether he wants to or not. Hence he cannot possibly teach the principle to anybody. And if he were to teach the principle without having adopted it himself, then, although he would be understood, those who adopted it would not. At any rate, since moral teaching involves teaching rules such as the taught may openly avow to be observing, this case is ruled out. A principle which is taught for secret acceptance only cannot be embodied in a *moral* rule of the group.

(2) Of course, people might soon come to realize what is the matter with our man. They may discover that in order not to be misled by what he says they have only to substitute '*p*' for 'not-*p*' and vice versa. But if they do this, then they have interpreted his way of speaking, not as a reversal of the general presumption that one says what one thinks is the case (and not the opposite), but as a change of the use of 'not.' In his language, it will be said, 'not' has become an affirmation sign, negation being effected by omitting it. Thus, if communication is to be possible, we must interpret as a change in usage what is intended as the reversal of the presumption that every assertion conveys what the assertor believes to be the case.

If everyone were, by accident, to adopt simultaneously and secretly our principle 'Always assert what you think is not the case,' then, for some time at least communication would be impossible. If, on the other hand, it were adopted openly, then communication would be possible, but only if the adoption of this principle were to be accompanied by a change in the use of "not" which would completely cancel the effect of the adoption of the principle. In that case, however, it can hardly be said that the principle has been adopted.

(3) The case we are considering is neither (1) nor (2). We are considering the open teaching of the principle 'Always assert what you think is not the case,' for open acceptance by everybody, an acceptance which is not to be interpreted as a change in the use of 'not.' But this is

nonsense. We cannot all *openly* tell one another that we are always going to mislead one another in a certain way and insist that we must continue to be mislead, though we know how we could avoid being misled. I conclude that this principle could not be embodied in a rule belonging to the morality of any group.

These points are of general interest in that they clarify some valuable remarks contained in Kant's doctrine of the categorical imperative. In particular they clarify the expression "can will" contained in the formulation 'Act so that thou *canst will* thy maxim to become a universal law of nature.' "Canst will" in one sense means what I have called "morally possible." Your maxim must be a formula which is morally possible, that is, which is logically capable of being a rule belonging to the morality of some group, as the maxim "Always lie" is not. No one *can* wish that maxim to be a rule *of some morality*. To say that one is wishing it is to contradict oneself. One cannot wish it any more than one can wish that time should move backwards.

The second sense of "can will" is that in which no rational person can will certain things. Self-frustrating and self-defeating moral rules are not morally impossible, they are merely senseless. No rational person could wish such rules to become part of any morality. That is to say, anyone wishing that they should, would thereby expose himself to the charge of irrationality, like the person who wishes that he should never attain his ends or that he should (for no reason at all) be plagued by rheumatic pains throughout his life.

The points just made also show the weakness of Kant's doctrine. For while it is true that someone who acts on the maxim 'Always lie' acts on a morally impossible one, it is not true that every liar necessarily acts on that maxim. If he acts on a principle at all, it may, for instance, be 'Lie when it is the only way to avoid harming someone,' or 'Lie when it is helpful to you and harmful to no one else,' or 'Lie when it is entertaining and harmless.' Maxims such as these can, of course, be willed in either of the senses explained.

4. *Moral Rules Must Be For The Good Of Everyone Alike*

The conditions so far mentioned are merely formal. They exclude certain sorts of rule as not coming up to the formal requirements. But moral rules should also have a certain sort of content. Observation of these rules should be *for the good of everyone alike*. Thrasymachus' view that justice is the advantage of the stronger, if true of the societies of his day, is an indictment of their legal systems from the moral point of view. It shows that what goes by the name of morality in these societies is no more than a set of rules and laws which enrich the ruling class at the expense of the masses. But this is wrong because unjust, however much the rules satisfy the formal criteria. For given certain initial social conditions, formal equality before the law may favor certain groups and exploit others.

There is one obvious way in which a rule may be for the good of everyone alike, namely, if it furthers the common good. When I am promoted and my salary is raised, this is to my advantage. It will also be to the advantage of my wife and my family and possibly of a few other people — it will not be to the advantage of my colleague who had hoped for promotion but is now excluded. It may even be to his detriment if his reputation suffers as a result. If the coal miners obtain an increase in their wages, then this is to the advantage of coal miners. It is for their common good. But it may not be to the advantage of anyone else. On the other hand, if production is raised and with it everyone's living standard, that is literally to everyone's advantage. The rule 'Work harder,' if it has these consequences, is for the common good of all.

Very few rules, if any, will be for the common good of everyone. But a rule may be in the interest of everyone alike, even though the results of the observation of the rule are not for the common good in the sense explained. Rules such as 'Thou shalt not kill,' 'Thou shalt not be cruel,' 'Thou shalt not lie' are obviously, in some other sense, for the good of everyone alike. What is this sense? It becomes clear if we look at these rules from the moral point of view, that is, that of an independent, unbiased, impartial, objective, dispassionate, disinterested observer. Taking such a God's-eye point of view, we can see that it is in the interest of everyone alike that everyone should abide by the rules 'Thou shalt not kill.' From the moral point of view, it is clear that it is in the interest of everyone alike if everyone alike should be allowed to pursue his own interest provided this does not adversely affect someone else's interests. Killing someone in the pursuit of my interests would interfere with his.

There can be no doubt that such a God's-eye point of view is involved in the moral standpoint. The most elementary teaching is based on it. The negative version of the so-called Golden Rule sums it up: 'Don't do unto others as you would not have them do unto you.' When we teach children the moral point of view, we try to explain it to them by getting them to put themselves in another person's place: 'How would you like to have that done to you!' 'Don't do evil,' the most readily accepted moral rule of all, is simply the most general form of stating this prohibition. For doing evil is the opposite of doing good. Doing good is doing for another person what, if he were following (self-interested) reason, he would do for himself. Doing evil is doing to another person what it would be contrary to reason for him to do to himself. Harming another, hurting another, doing to another what he dislikes having done to him are the specific forms this takes. Killing, cruelty, inflicting pain, maiming, torturing, deceiving, cheating, rape, adultery are instances of this sort of behavior. They all violate the condition of "reversibility," that is, that the behavior in question must be acceptable to a person whether he is at the "giving" or "receiving" end of it.

It is important to see just what is established by this condition of being for the good of everyone alike. In the first place, anyone is doing wrong who engages in nonreversible behavior. It is irrelevant whether he knows that it is wrong or not, whether the morality of his group recognizes it or not. Such behavior is "wrong in itself," irrespective of individual or social recognition, irrespective of the consequences it has. Moreover, every single act of such behavior is wrong. We need not consider the whole group or the whole of humanity engaging in this sort of behavior, but only a single case. Hence we can say that all nonreversible behavior is morally wrong; hence that anyone engaging in it is doing what, prima facie, he ought not to do. We need not consider whether this sort of behavior has harmful consequences, whether it is forbidden by the morality of the man's group, or whether he himself thinks it wrong.

The principle of reversibility does not merely impose certain prohibitions on a moral agent, but also certain positive injunctions. It is, for instance, wrong — an omission — not to help another person when he is in need and when we are in a position to help him. The story of the Good Samaritan makes this point. The positive version of the Golden Rule makes the same point more generally: 'Do unto others as you would have them do unto you.' Note that it is wrong — not merely not meritorious — to omit to help others when they are in need and when you are in a position to help them. It does not follow from this, however, that it is wrong not to promote the greatest good of the greatest number, or not to promote the greatest amount of good in the world. Deontologists and utilitarians alike make the mistake of thinking that it is one, or the only one, of our moral duties to "do the optimific act." Nothing could be further from the truth. We do not have a duty to do good to others or to ourselves, or to others and/or ourselves in a judicious mixture such that it produces the greatest possible amount of good in the world. We are morally required to do good only to those who are actually in need of our assistance. The view that we always ought to do the optimific act, or whenever we have no more stringent duty to perform, would have the absurd result that we are doing wrong whenever we are relaxing, since on those occasions there will always be opportunities to produce greater good than we can by relaxing. For the relief of suffering is always a greater good than mere enjoyment. Yet it is quite plain that the worker who, after a tiring day, puts on his slippers and listens to the wireless is not doing anything he ought not to, is not neglecting any of his duties, even though it may be perfectly true that there are things he might do which produce more good in the world, even for himself, than, merely relaxing by the fireside.

III

MORAL RULES AND EXCEPTIONS

Introduction

The Problem of Exceptions

One of the factors which have undoubtedly led many philosophers to adopt a more or less sceptical attitude in moral philosophy has been the recognition that most rules have exceptions. This has commonly been regarded as a threat to the entire moral enterprise. How can a philosopher even attempt "to find an account of the moral relations that obtain among things which will weave them into the unity of a stable system" (to quote James' conception of the moral philosopher's task) if every principle, every rule, every judgment has to be qualified by who knows how many exceptions?

Plato was acutely aware of how devastating the admission of an exception might be. In the *Republic* (see the selection in Part VII), Socrates completely invalidates Cephalus' thesis that justice is simply a matter of returning to others what is due them by pointing out that if a friend deposited a weapon with us for safekeeping and then asked for it when he was not in his right mind, there would be justice in *not* returning it to him. Ordinarily we should return what does not belong to us, but this case would seem to be a legitimate exception. Socrates mentions another. It would be right in such circumstances, he says, to lie to a person who was out of his mind. On the other hand, Plato also realized that by no means all alleged exceptions are justified. In the *Euthyphro* (see Part I), Socrates, upon being informed that Euthyphro intends to prosecute his own father for murder, suggests that perhaps it would be right to prosecute his father if he killed a relative, but not if he murdered a stranger. Euthyphro rebukes Socrates for suggesting such an exception. Socrates offers no defense except to express amazement at the certainty with which Euthyphro claims to know what is right.

There are several ways to resolve the problem of uncertainty which the existence of exceptions seems to introduce. One way is that of the extreme sceptic: simply deny the validity of morality altogether. There can hardly be a problem of exceptions if there is no such thing as morality. To most philosophers this solution to the problem seems too drastic and unnecessarily defeatist.

Another method of disposing of the problem is to dispense with rules and principles in determining what is moral. We have seen this approach taken by Sartre and to a considerable extent by Fletcher. Certainly if the problem is reconciling in a consistent fashion the existence of exceptions with the existence of rules, then one solution is to deny the latter (just as one classic solution of the problem of evil is to deny the existence of God!). We have already examined in the previous section some of the difficulties associated with the approach of "rule-sceptics."

A third approach is the converse of the one just mentioned. Instead of denying that there are rules, one simply denies that genuine moral rules and principles ever have exceptions. Perhaps the only explicit philosophical exposition of this view that moral rules are exceptionless is Kant's discussion in his essay, "On a Supposed Right to Tell Lies from Benevolent Motives," although, as we shall see, this essay may not provide us with a complete or altogether accurate statement of Kant's position on exceptions. It is nonetheless the interpretation which is made of Kant's views by most ethical commentators. But as we shall also see, a version, or covert form, of this general theory of exceptions is also held by some so-called rule-utilitarians.

Still a fourth approach to the problem is to assert that while all, or at least most, *rules* have exceptions, *principles* do not. We need only appeal to them, or to some ultimate principle among them, in order to determine which exceptions to rules are admissible and which are not. Miller attributes this view to classical utilitarians such as Bentham and Mill, but also and more generally to "any theory in which it is maintained that some one rule always takes precedence over all others." Miller finds reasons for rejecting all such attempts. The reader is invited to evaluate his criticisms.

A fifth theory is suggested by Sidgwick and developed hypothetically by Miller. This theory attempts to resolve the problem of exceptions by appending to any given rule a list of all the exempting conditions; that is to say, all the cases to which the rule is related but to which it does not apply. Miller finds that this approach too is objectionable.

A final position regarding exceptions is what we shall call the "Aristotelian" theory of exceptions, although very similar views are also held by Roscoe Pound and W. D. Ross (see Part VI). Briefly, it is the view that rules do not, and in fact because of their general nature cannot, apply to all the cases of a certain class, thereby leaving some cases (the exceptions) to be decided by an appeal to intuition rather than by an appeal to rules or principles.

Kant on Exceptions

According to the usual interpretation of Kant's views, he is said to believe that "moral rules are absolutely inflexible and without exceptions." (See K. Baier, p. 215 above). Certainly much in Kant's essay, "On a Supposed Right to Tell Lies from Benevolent Motives," would justify such an interpretation. He speaks of the "unconditioned principle of veracity" as a "command of reason not to be limited by any expediency," and of rules "which in their nature do not admit exceptions." He offers at least two reasons for asserting the existence of exceptionless rules, namely, that rules or principles which have exceptions are self-contradictory, and that "exceptions destroy the universality on account of which they are called principles."

Nonetheless in his *Fundamental Principles* and elsewhere, Kant makes an important distinction between what he variously calls "perfect" or "strict" duties, on the one hand, and "imperfect" or "broad" duties, on the other. A perfect duty he says is "one that admits of no exceptions in favor of inclination." (See footnote, p. 77, of this volume).

He is less explicit regarding broad or imperfect duties, although he does say the following about them in a later work, *The Metaphysical Principles ₁of Virtue* (p. 48):

> For if the law can command only the maxim of actions and not the actions themselves, then this is a sign that the law leaves in its ... observance a latitude ... for free choice, i.e., it cannot definitely assign in what way and to what extent something should be brought about by an action directed to an end which is at the same time a duty. But by a broad duty is not understood a permission to make exceptions to the maxim of actions, but only the permission to limit one maxim of duty by another (e.g., the general love of one's neighbor by the love of one's parents).

The distinction between these two types of duties permits several possible interpretations of Kant's view. One is simply that whereas strict or perfect duties allow no exceptions whatever, broad or imperfect duties do. However, this appears to be an oversimplification of Kant's view and excluded by his statement that broad duties do not grant "permission to make exceptions to the maxim of actions."

Another interpretation is the one W. D. Ross gives of Kant's view, namely, "that there are certain duties of perfect obligation, such as those of fulfilling promises, of paying debts, of telling the truth, which admit of no exception whatever in favour of duties of imperfect obligation, such as that of relieving distress." (See Ross, p. 474 below). This suggests that in cases of conflict between, say, a duty to tell the truth and a duty to save a life, the former rule always takes precedence. But of course, if this is Kant's way of thinking, then in fact he does allow an exception to the duty to save life, which might be expressed: "Always promote human life *except* when this conflicts with a higher duty to tell the truth." Or with respect to another duty: "Be charitable always *except* when this duty conflicts with a duty to pay one's debts."

Unfortunately, this interpretation seems to be ruled out by Kant's further view that a genuine conflict of duties is impossible. As he says, "Since two opposite rules cannot be necessary at the same time, then if it is a duty to act in accordance with one of them, it is not only not a duty, but contrary to duty, to act in accordance with the other. It therefore follows that a conflict of duties and obligations is inconceivable." (*Principles of Virtue*, p. 24.) Thus if there cannot be a conflict of duties in any given situation, then one cannot say that the rule which takes precedence provides the basis for an exception to the other.

230

Yet it is clear that Kant is determined to make a rather sharp distinction between duties of perfect and imperfect obligation, and that this has to do primarily with the fact that perfect duties do not have exceptions. Let's take a closer look at what he's saying. An exception is a "limitation" of some kind which can involve either of two things: a limitation on the maxim of an action or a limitation on the action itself. Apparently perfect or strict duties are unlimited in both ways. If I have made a promise, I am obligated not only by the universalized maxim, "Always keep promises," and by no other, but also by the "terms" of the promise. That is, if I have promised to meet you at three o'clock, then I have no latitude to meet you at two or four o'clock. Apparently it is different with respect to imperfect or broad duties. There can be no limitation on the maxim of my act (no exception in this sense), but there is no such requirement with respect to the action itself. Thus if I am obligated to be charitable to those in need, the maxim itself is quite unexceptionable, but whether I apply it by helping my next door neighbor or my parents is another matter. I do have a latitude to give preferential treatment to my parents. Or, as Kant says with respect to another imperfect duty: "To sacrifice one's own happiness, one's true needs, in order to promote the happiness of others would be a self-contradictory maxim if made a universal law. Therefore, this duty is only a broad one; it has a latitude within which we may do more or less without being able to assign definite limits to it. The law holds only for maxims, not for definite actions." (*Principles of Virtue*, p. 52.)

If this latter interpretation is correct, then Kant's final position on exceptions would seem to be as follows: No moral rules, whether of perfect or imperfect duty, can incorporate in their statements any mention of an exception. This apparently stems from Kant's conviction that an exceptively stated rule would be self-contradictory and non-universal. Thus there can be no formally expressed exceptions to moral rules. Yet there may be another kind of exception, i.e., a limitation with respect to the application of the rules. Kant denies that duties of perfect obligation have even this kind of exception, but apparently allows it with respect to duties of imperfect obligation. Thus one might say, although Kant would undoubtedly resist *expressing* it this way, "I have an obligation to assist others in need *except* when I am more obligated to help my parents." Or, "I have an obligation to promote the happiness of others *except* when it would mean a total cancellation of my own."

The reader is entitled, of course, to reject the above interpretation of Kant's view and to make his own. Yet even if he accepts it, it is still possible for him to take issue with Kant's claim that certain moral rules (e.g., the truth telling and promise keeping rules) are totally without exceptions. One way to do so is to appeal to the almost universal belief that such rules do have exception, or possibly to one's own insight that this is so. Some have thought that Kant's own illustration of the pursuer bent on murder who asks, "Where did he go?" is dramatic proof in itself that Kant's view that we should always tell the truth is simply dead wrong. Benjamin Constant, the critic to whom Kant is responding in his essay, suggests as much, but he also argues the point that Kant's view, if generally adopted, would make all society impossible. Kurt Baier (see Part II) argues that Kant's main error with respect to exceptions lies in a confusion of two expressions, namely, "making an exception to a rule" and "a rule has exceptions." Once this confusion is removed, and the distinction noted, he thinks that it can be seen that Kant was right in saying that we should make no exceptions in anyone's favor, but wrong in saying that moral rules are absolutely without exceptions. Marcus Singer argues that an exception to the truth telling rule in the case Kant cites would not be a violation of the Categorical Imperative. Kant has not shown, he says, that lying in such a situation would involve a self-contradiction or that it would deprive the truth telling rule of the only kind of universality which moral rules can have. His biggest complaint is that Kant does not even attempt to apply the Categorical Imperative to the case of the homicidal pursuer as he did to the case of the deceitful promiser, mentioned as an illustration in Kant's *Fundamental Principles* (p. 78 of this volume). The reader should note the vast differences between these various types of criticism.

Exceptions "to" Rules and Exceptions "of" Rules

Assuming that moral rules can and do have exceptions, the problem becomes one of understanding the nature of the logical relation between exceptions and rules. One way to conceive this relation is to think of exceptions as cases which fall outside and restrict the scope of a rule. We may speak of exceptions conceived in this way as exceptions "to" a rule. Thus if killing in self-defense is an exception to the rule "Killing is wrong," we think of the rule as applying only to cases of nondefensive killing. Another way of conceiving the relation is to think of exceptions as built-in negative specifications of the rule. In this sense an exception is a part "of" the rule, not a case that limits it, so to speak, from the outside. Thus, if killing in self-defense is an exception, we no longer think of the rule as being "Killing is wrong," but as "Killing except in self-defense is wrong." Singer appears to adopt the first way of construing exceptions. Baier appears to adopt the second.

According to Singer, there is a considerable difference between moral principles and moral rules. Moral principles, he says, hold in all circumstances, allow no exceptions and are always relevant, whereas rules hold only generally, do allow exceptions and are not always relevant. Furthermore, principles are apt to be more abstract than moral rules, though, he says, they are not necessarily less definite.

It is by appealing to principles that moral rules, as well as exceptions to them, are justified and established. Ultimately such a justification procedure must involve an application of what Singer calls the Generalization Argument, which, he says, may be thought of indifferently as either an argument or as a moral principle. It may be expressed as follows: "If everyone were to do that, the consequences would be disastrous (or undesirable); therefore no one ought to do that." Actually he finds that this principle (or argument) includes two subordinate principles. The first he calls the Generalization Principle (otherwise known as the principle of fairness, justice, or impartiality): "What is right (or wrong) for one person must be right (or wrong) for any similar person in similar circumstances." The second he calls the Principle of Consequences: "If the consequences of A's doing x would be undesirable, then A ought not to do x." Other principles are derivable from these and from the generalization argument as a whole.

In many respects, Singer's Generalization Argument and Kant's Categorical Imperative are similar. Both involve generalization and both provide a criterion for the application of the principle. Both are supreme principles. The differences include the fact that Kant's principle involves a reference to "willing" and to the maxim of an action, whereas Singer's does not. On the other hand, Singer's incorporates an appeal to undesirable consequences, and this is completely absent from the Categorical Imperative.

Singer's basic task is to show (1) that not every application of the generalization argument is a valid one, and so determine the conditions under which it is valid, and (2) to show that the generalization argument, while capable of establishing and justifying certain moral rules, does not establish them as holding always or in all possible circumstances, and so explain the conditions under which exceptions to rules may be justified.

One of the conditions which Singer mentions in connection with his first task—that of establishing moral rules—has to do with what he calls the "invertibility" of the generalization argument. He means that in order for a given application of the generalization argument to be valid it must not be "invertible" in the sense that the consequences of *everyone's* acting in a certain way would be undesirable and the consequences of *no one's* acting in that way would also be undesirable. Thus, the argument that no one should grow food because if everyone did the consequences would be undesirable (no one would provide other basic necessities) is an invalid argument because it also follows that if no one grew food the consequences would also be undesirable (we would all starve).

Another condition of the validity of an application of the generalization argument is that it not be "reiterable." A generalization argument fails to meet this condition if it is made to apply to some arbitrarily specified aspect of an action. Thus the argument that no one has a right to eat at six o'clock because if everyone did then there would be no one to perform certain essential functions—is reiterable and invalid, because the same reasoning could just as well be applied to other arbitrarily selected times, e.g., eating at five or seven o'clock. It is this last condition of validity, namely, non-reiterability, which is particularly involved in Singer's second task—that of accounting for exceptions.

The problem of exceptions, in terms of Singer's theory, may be stated as follows: "By what procedure can one justify acting in a way in which it would be undesirable for everyone to act?" Singer's answer is that exceptions to moral rules are justified if one can show either (1) that the individual involved is a member of a class of persons such that if every member of that class were to act in that way the consequences would not be undesirable, or (2) that the circumstances of one's action are such that the consequences of everyone's acting in that way in those circumstances would not be undesirable. For example, if it could be shown that it would not be undesirable if everyone having below a certain minimum income did not pay taxes, then that class of persons would constitute a justified exception to a rule that everyone pays taxes. The only restriction Singer places on this application of the generalization argument is that it not be "reiterable" with respect to the class of persons or circumstances selected. That is to say, the class cannot be so defined that everyone may regard himself as a member of the class, or as being in those circumstances. On the other hand, if a person reasons that he should not pay his share of the tax burden because society will not miss his small contribution, he will find, if he tries to apply the generalization argument to his case, that everyone else can equally argue in the same way (i.e., claim to belong to the same class.) The argument is therefore reiterable, making everyone an "exception." Singer regards this as self-contradictory.

There are several points to notice with respect to Singer's theory. First, if moral rules do not always hold, i.e., if the generalization argument with respect to them is not always valid, then moral rules are always of "restricted universality." Second, the notion of a rule without exceptions is self-contradictory, because the reasons which would be sufficient to establish the rule can be the same ones which in certain circumstances would override it. For instance, a rule against killing might be established by showing that if everyone acted in accordance with it the consequences would not be undesirable, but killing in certain circumstances (such as in self-defense) could also be established by means of the same reason. Third, Singer denies that an exception to a rule can ever be singular in nature (i.e., a "unit class," one having just one member) and asserts that in justifying a *class* of exceptions one is, in effect, "modifying the understanding of the original rule by restricting its scope." From this it would seem to follow that the exception, conceived of as a limitation on the scope of the "original rule," is not a part of the expected rule but external to it.

No doubt many philosophers, including Kant, would challenge the claim that the notion of an exceptionless rule is self-contradictory, even those who are perhaps not convinced that any of the usual moral rules are *in fact* exceptionless. If this thesis is challenged then certainly one could also challenge Singer's claim that moral rules are never truly universal. As we shall see, the Aristotelian theory of exceptions stands opposed to Singer's denial that exceptions can ever be singular. The problem with conceiving of an exception as a wholly external limitation on a rule consists in understanding how it can intelligibly be regarded as an *exception to* rather than a *violation of* the rule. For if a case is not governed by the rule, then it is either totally unrelated to the rule or it is a violation of the rule. But normally we would not say that an exception to the rule against lying (to which a lie would be obviously related) is a violation of it. Singer attempts to avoid this problem by saying that no one has a right to violate a moral rule "without a reason," thereby implying that exceptions are indeed violations of rules but not necessarily "wrongful" violations. This way of putting it may or may not satisfy some critics.

Baier's view (see Part II) makes an interesting contrast with Singer's. It is Baier's contention that in making exceptions to laws and legal regulations, magistrates must decide what are the "deserving cases" (i.e., justified exceptions) by appealing to principles, and specifically to *moral* principles. But this is not so with respect to the justification of exceptions in the case of moral rules. There simply is no higher set or kind of rules or principles to which to make such an appeal. It is his view, therefore, that every genuinely moral rule (i.e. one that is consistent with the moral point of view) already contains all of the deserving cases as *parts* of the rule. Thus, for Baier, a rule against homicide, if it is genuinely a moral rule, includes as a part of itself the legitimate case of killing in self-defense. As he says, "When we say, therefore, that a person who has killed a burglar in self-defense has not done anything wrong, we are not making an exception in the houseowner's favor. It is much nearer the truth to say that, in our morality, the rule 'Thou shalt not kill' *has several recognized exceptions*, among them 'in self-defense.' We can say that a man does not know fully our moral rule 'Thou shalt not kill' if he does not know that it has, among others, this exception."

It is clear that Baier cannot be charged with treating an exception as a "violation" of a rule in any sense of that term. If the exception is literally a part of the rule and is governed by it, and if the rule says, "No killing except in self-defense," the exception to killing (self-defense) is perfectly consistent with and is in no way opposed to the rule. The problem here though is whether in conceiving of an exception as a part of the rule, it makes any more sense to call the "excepted cases," e.g. killing in self-defense, exceptions to a rule against killing than to call the "non-excepted cases," e.g. refraining from killing someone, exceptions to a rule permitting self-defense. The point is that though we can distinguish types of cases (i.e. non-killing in certain circumstances from killing in certain other circumstances), are we really making a logical distinction or merely a verbal one in calling one set of cases exceptions and not the others? Furthermore, since one set of cases is as related to and unopposed to the rule as the other, why call either of them "exceptions"? Perhaps (and the reader should judge for himself) we have here another but more covert way of expressing the view that genuine moral rules are exceptionless.

Rule-Utilitarianism

The two views we have just considered, those of Singer and Baier, are in many respects similar to a contemporary development of traditional utilitarianism, now generally referred to as *rule-utilitarianism*. It is the view that the rightness of an action is determined by applying the principle of utility to the rule under which it falls, not directly to the act. Both Baier and Singer agree that an appeal to consequences plays an essential role in determining morality. They also both approve of the generalization (or universalization) criterion as called for by the question, "What would happen if everybody did that?" or "What would be the consequences of a general practice of that kind?" Insofar as objections such as those Hospers mentions against rule-utilitarianism pertain to these matters, they may also be regarded as objections to these other related viewpoints.[1]

The chief difference between rule-utilitarianism and the kinds of views held by Baier and Singer is that both authors reject the utilitarian thesis that the rightness of an act is determined solely by whether our acts (or the rules governing our acts) are "optimific," i.e., productive of the most good possible. As Baier says, "Deontologists and utilitarians alike make the mistake of thinking that it is one, or the only one, of our moral duties to 'do the optimific act.' Nothing could be further from the truth." Singer clearly distinguishes his Principle of Consequences: "If the consequences of A's doing x would be undesirable, then A ought not to do x," from the utilitarian (or as he also calls it, the *obverse*) principle of consequences: "If the consequences of A's doing x would be desirable, then A has a duty to do x." He regards the latter as an unsound moral principle. The specific reasons which Baier and Singer give for holding these views can be found in the selections. It is sufficient here to note that on this rather important point their positions differ from most versions of rule-utilitarianism.

The view of rule-utilitarianism, as presented by Hospers, however, does bring out a further point of similarity that has to do specifically with the problems of exceptions. Like Kant, Singer, and Baier, the rule-utilitarian rejects the idea that there can be any legitimate "exceptions in one's favor." He also rejects the interpretation of the status of rules subscribed to by act-utilitarians, ethical egoists, and situationists, namely, that rules are but provisional guides to be abandoned whenever the consequences of a given act would be more beneficial than harmful. Instead he insists on the view that only those rules whose consequences

---

[1] In an article entitled, "Toward a Credible Form of Utilitarianism," Richard B. Brandt in a footnote lists the following philosophers as among those advocating "types of rule-utilitarianism": J. O. Urmson, Kurt Baier, J. D. Mabbott, Stephen Toulmin, R. F. Harrod, Kai Neilsen, A. MacBeath, C. A. Campbell, Jonathan Harrison, Marcus Singer, and to some extent John Rawls and P. H. Nowell-Smith. It is doubtful that all of these authors would appreciate the title, "rule-utilitarian," but Brandt seems to be nonetheless correct in associating their views because of certain basic points of agreement. Like many recent philosophical developments, however, it has become increasingly difficult to isolate a "pure view" or to point to a given philosopher and say, "He's a rule-utilitarian." The position has become idealized, and that is how Hospers presents it in the selection in this section. For Brandt's article, consult the Recommended Readings, III, at the end of this volume.

would be on the whole beneficial are to count as morally acceptable. Does he then deny that there are exceptions, such as self-defense in the case of the rule against killing? Not at all. Rules are to be "relevantly specified." This means that insofar as self-defense is a relevant consideration which favorably affects the total consequences of the observance of a rule against killing, it is to be made a part of the rule. The original rule is thus transformed from "Killing is wrong" to "Killing is wrong except in cases of self-defense." Thus, insofar as this view argues for the incorporation of exceptions into rules, it bears a considerable resemblance to Baier's view. Insofar as it speaks of "restricting" or "transforming" the original rule, it certainly resembles the way Singer discusses exceptions. The reader will want to estimate the extent of these resemblances.

In any case, as Hospers points out, in the rule-utilitarian view, the rule, once fully stated with all its qualifications and restrictions, admits of no exceptions. They are all built into the rule which then becomes a more complex rule, but at the same time one that is more restricted in its original scope. It also follows from this view that when the rules in question are fully spelled out, there cannot be a conflict of rules. That is to say, there cannot be a conflict between a truth telling rule and a life saving rule, for if the truth telling rule fully meets the utilitarian test of beneficial consequences, i.e., is a truly acceptable moral rule, then it would have built into it already an exception which would have to do with lying in order to save a life. The reader may wish to compare these implications of rule-utilitarianism with Kant's views on the subject.

Aside from the difficulty pointed out in connection with Baier's view as to whether the notion of an exception as a part of a rule is an adequate one or not, it should also be noted that the view proposed by the rule-utilitarian also encounters all of the difficulties which Miller mentions in connection with the type of theory which attempts to append to every rule a list of exempting conditions. Can this in fact always be done? Can we ever be in a position to know that we have incorporated all the conditions? Would not a rule encumbered by so many qualifications, restrictions, limitations, exemptions, and exceptions be totally useless for moral purposes?

The rule-utilitarian, however, appears not to be bothered by these considerations. "Killing is wrong except in self-defense" is still a better rule than "Killing is wrong," even if self-defense is but one of the many possible excepted cases. Leave the rules open-ended. If a problem arises or a new type of case appears, review the rule and modify it if necessary. One does have at hand a criterion for doing so, the utilitarian one. Use it as the occasion demands. Whether the rule-utilitarian can succeed in resolving the difficulty in this way without, in the end, reducing his view to a position very similar to that of act-utilitarianism is another question. As might be expected, act-utilitarians have not been reluctant to raise this doubt.

The Aristotelian Theory

The final theory to be considered is, in a sense, a modified version of rule-scepticism. It does not seek to do away with rules altogether but to restrict them to the cases to which they may properly be applied. It insists that rules are for the most part absolutely essential guides to conduct. It questions only the value of rules to determine which cases and situations are exceptions.

According to Aristotle, in every class of human actions are some cases to which rules cannot be properly applied. Rules must of necessity be formulated as universal statements, but about some things, particularly human actions, it is not always possible to speak both universally and correctly. That is to say, rules inevitably fail to take account of all the relevant peculiarities of some cases and situations. But in saying that rules (or laws, or principles) are "deficient by virtue of their universality," Aristotle does not mean to suggest that all rules are bad or useless. On the contrary, many are perfectly good rules. It is just that rules are rules. Therefore, unless we are to become "rule-worshippers" (which incidentally is a favorite theme of act-utilitarians), and so fail to do the right thing in individual cases just to preserve the integrity and universal application of rules, we must appeal, in certain cases, to another method in order to decide those cases. Fortunately there is such a method: the appeal to intuition.

Wasserstrom finds several things wrong with this approach. Aristotle's contention is that we shall always encounter some cases which are clearly members of a class covered by a rule which are nonetheless ones to which it would be wrong to apply the rule. Wasserstrom cannot think of any such case, i.e., one for which, at least theoretically, a rule could not be formulated which would cover both it and all the other relevant cases. He accuses Aristotle of confusing a law's *universality* with its *generality*. If we insist that rules be "absolutely universal," this would eliminate the possibility of exceptions altogether, at least as something that could be encompassed by the rules themselves. But if we treat universality simply as a formal property of rules and look upon rules from a material point of view, we see that they are only general, i.e., they cover only the particular cases named and controlled by the rule. The claim of an exception then makes sense in relation to the rule, i.e., it is a case which is not covered by the rule but ought to be, or is covered but ought not to be. This problem can be solved practically, according to Wasserstrom, simply by composing the rule so as to include the cases which ought to be covered and exclude the cases which ought not to be covered.

Wasserstrom's solution of the problem of exceptions employs the method advanced by rule-utilitarianism, namely, the incorporation of exceptions, the consequence and aim of which is the elimination of exceptions. As Wasserstrom says, "As more conditions are placed upon membership in the class controlled by the rule, it becomes increasingly unlikely that an 'exceptional' case will arise." As a resolution of the problem it is of course subject to the kinds of objections mentioned earlier against the rule-utilitarian view. There is, however, also a question whether Wasserstrom, or for that matter Singer and Baier too, have made a convincing case against the notion of an exception which Aristotle advocates, namely, the notion of an individual case or situation which is described by the rule but to which the rule ought not to apply. In short, are there not *singular* exceptions as contrasted with *classes* of exceptions? Although this conception is not without its difficulties, as Wasserstrom and the others have pointed out, still it has seemed to many philosophers to make sense nonetheless.

Utilitarianism and Exceptions

Leonard G. Miller

Rules and Exceptions

The fact that there are exceptions to at least some moral rules raises some interesting questions about the status of rules and about the nature of moral behavior and deliberation. Some philosophers may be inclined to think that the occurrence of exceptions introduces or threatens to introduce uncertainty into morality, and as a result they may be tempted to construe rules in such a way as to avoid or remove this uncertainty. In this paper I want to discuss several such attempts.

From Leonard G. Miller, "Rules and Exceptions," *Ethics* LXVI (July 1956): 262-70. Copyright 1956 by The University of Chicago. Reprinted by permission of the author and The University of Chicago Press.

But before I do this, I must attend to several preliminary matters. First, I must note the distinction between questions about the application of rules and questions about exceptions to them. We do not speak of an action as an exception to a rule, of course, unless we believe or assume that the rule applies to the action. If the rule does not apply, there can be no question of an exception; if the rule applies, there could be a question about an exception; and if the rule applies but we are justified in not following it, an exception is allowed. In this paper I am confining my attention to justifiable exceptions and the issues raised by their occurrence.

Secondly, when I speak of "rules" I have in mind statements such as "It is wrong to lie," "It is wrong to inflict pain on animals," "It is wrong to break promises," and similar statements used to prescribe or prohibit some particular kind of behavior and cited as reasons supporting moral judgments. I am not thinking of statements, such as Kant's "Categorical Imperative," which stipulate how we should arrive at or test decisions; nor am I thinking of statements whose primary function is to tell us something about the nature of moral phenomena or reasoning — statements such as "Ought implies can" and "Similar actions are justified in similar circumstances." In restricting myself thus, I am not implying that there is a neat list of rules, that we would or need agree completely about any offered list, or that the way in which such statements function is transparent. These are questions for further inquiry. Nor have I given exact criteria for distinguishing between what I call rules and another sort of general moral statement exemplified by the utilitarian "principle." I cannot here, for the distinction is bound up with the very thing I want to investigate: exceptions and the difficulties they raise in both theory and practice.

I

There are several reasons why it may be thought that exceptions introduce uncertainty into morality. In the first place, a critic may think the rule itself is weakened. Supposing, he may argue, that there are very few exceptions to one rule and a considerable number to another; isn't it the case that the second rule is not so infallible and therefore not so reliable as the first? Or supposing we have discovered that there is a high probability that any instance falling under a rule will be an exception; wouldn't we be inclined to distrust the rule or to reject it altogether? These facts indicate that the reliability of a rule varies inversely as the proportion of exceptions and therefore that the occurrence of any exceptions introduces some degree of uncertainty into morality. The critic may go on to raise the related objection that to admit any exceptions at all to a rule is to open up the possibility of an ever increasing proportion of exceptions. For instance, have not politicians argued against such things as old age pensions on the grounds that, once we admit some exceptions to the principle that the individual is responsible for his own welfare, we cannot tell where to draw the line? If we admit any exceptions to the rule, we open up the way to its ultimate destruction. If exceptions did not occur or could be avoided or if there were some way of restricting their occurrence, these objections would be countered.

So far attention has been focused on the effect of exceptions on a rule, but if that attention is turned to the effect on judgments made in situations falling under the rule, an even more serious question may arise. In so far as a rule admits exceptions, a critic may argue, it will be more difficult to determine whether any given instance of the sort of action forbidden by it is really wrong. This difficulty is not obviated by looking to see whether there are circumstances justifying an exception; for while it may be easy to determine that some such circumstances are not present, it may be very difficult or even impossible to be sure that none is. At best, the occurrence of exceptions increases the difficulty of making and checking judgments; and, at worst, it may be contended, it means we can never be sure the judgment is correct — for neither the rule nor the rule plus any list of exceptions we can provide will function as a conclusive reason.

In addition to the problems it raises about the status of individual rules or judgments, the occurrence of exceptions also raises some questions about the relations between rules and about the status of the moral enterprise as such. When rules clash, how do we know which we are to follow? Does one always take precedence over the others? Can rules be ranked in a hierarchy? If there is no hierarchy, how do we determine when one rule takes precedence over another and when it does not? If it is the case that each rule is usually to be followed but not always and that there is no way of telling when questions about exceptions will arise and how they are to be resolved, then morality itself is left in a rather disorganized and confused state. Worse still, a critic may observe, it seems that the moral enterprise has no sound foundation at all; for if a rule has exceptions, it cannot be regarded as an ultimate court of appeal; and if all rules have exceptions, we cannot find security anywhere in the realm of morality. The whole rambling edifice is unsupported.

I have now indicated a number of reasons why a person interested in moral phenomena would be concerned about exceptions and, most especially, about the uncertainties they seem to, threaten to, or do introduce. In the following pages I shall discuss two quite different ways in which philosophers have treated exceptions in order to discount, eliminate, or control these real or fancied uncertainties. According to the first view, rules having exceptions cannot function as ultimate courts of appeal simply because they are sometimes overruled. Consequently, there must be some criterion which does not have exceptions and which does function as the fundamental moral principle in terms of which all clashes between rules are resolved. According to the second view, the difficulties arise because rules are not ordinarily stated fully or clearly. If we define the area in which the rule operates by listing the conditions under which exceptions are justified or if we formulate the rule in such a way that exceptions will not occur, the source of the difficulties will be removed. In the following pages I shall argue that both views are mistaken.

II

The proponent of the first view starts from the fact that we allow an exception to a rule only if we have a sound reason for doing so and goes on to contend that, since this reason takes precedence over the rule, it must be more ultimate than the rule. If this criterion in turn admits exceptions, the same point will be made with respect to it. This line of thought suggests the view that rules can be ranked in terms of the way in which they take precedence over others and that the resultant hierarchy will be crowned by a rule which takes precedence over all others, which does not admit exceptions, and which is the ultimate criterion of what is right and wrong. In this manner the uncertainty introduced by exceptions will be bypassed and eliminated. This view is embodied in utilitarianism. For instance, Mill recommends his own theory on the ground that it alone eliminates the chaos and confusion which would otherwise follow from the occurrence of exceptions. In a system in which moral laws are not subordinate to some all-embracing principle,

> ... there is no common umpire entitled to interfere between them; their claims to precedence one over another rest on little better than sophistry, and unless determined, as they generally are, by the unacknowledged influence of considerations of utility, afford a free scope for the action of personal desires and partialities.[1]

[1] John Stuart Mill, *Utilitarianism, Liberty, and Representative Government* ("Everyman's Library" [New York: E.P. Dutton & Co., Inc., 1931]), p. 24.

It is true that some rules always do take precedence over certain others and consequently that there is an important sense in which they can be said to be more basic or fundamental. For instance, one would never be justified in killing another person just to obey a traffic rule, even if this was the only way in which the rule could be obeyed. However, instances like this do not prove that it is always the case that the rule in terms of which the exception is justified always takes precedence over the rule to which the exception is allowed. One can imagine quite easily a situation in which it would be obligatory to break a promise in order to prevent the inflicting of pain on an animal, but one can also imagine instances where one would be justified in inflicting pain in order to keep a promise. There are many such two-way relations between rules. One can imagine situations in which it would be impossible to keep a promise to A without interfering with B's welfare, to keep a promise to A without interfering with B's interests, to keep a promise to A and prevent B's suffering, to avoid interfering with A's happiness without inflicting pain on B, or to avoid interfering with A's welfare without interfering with B's privacy. With respect to each of these sorts of situation one would sometimes be obliged to take the first alternative and sometimes the second. Exceptions are allowed even to the rule about killing other people, and these are sometimes justified in terms of rules that are usually over-ruled by it. A hierarchy of rules cannot be generated in the way the present view requires, for it just is not the case that, of any two given rules, one always takes precedence over the other. We may be able to arrange rules in some sort of hierarchy on some other basis, but even if this is possible, it will not help us here. Furthermore, the foregoing examples suggest that if there is some sort of hierarchy, its highest level may be occupied by a number of rules admitting exceptions, and not by one exceptionless rule.

"But," a critic may reply, "you have not shown that there is not an ultimate exceptionless rule. Indeed, your own analysis indicates that there must be one, for if Rule A is sometimes used to justify exceptions to Rule B and Rule B is sometimes used to justify exceptions to Rule A, there must be some criterion in terms of which we decide in any given case which of them takes precedence over the other. In order to fulfil its function, this criterion must be exceptionless." The leading contender for this position has been the principle of utility or some variation of it: "An act is right if it produces as much pleasure as any alternate act." However, this principle will not do if "pleasure" refers to a specific sort of condition, for it will then be susceptible to exceptions. If, for instance, an act would increase the net amount of pleasure by some trifling amount, at the expense of interfering with the interests of a sizable proportion of the populace, an exception would be justified. This rule drags in its train the very problem it was invoked to solve.

A utilitarian may try to avoid this criticism by expanding his list of intrinsic goods to include more than pleasure and generalizing his principle to read "An act is right if it produces as much good as any other." Thus he might expand it, as Mill did implicitly, to include intellectual activity. But such a criterion may still be subject to exceptions, for the cost of maximizing either, or a combination, of these two goods may be too high under certain conditions. Obviously, if the new rule is to be exceptionless, the list of things that are valuable must be expanded to include any conditions which, if excluded, could be grounds for an exception. My main criticism of this procedure is not that it has been carried out only in a very vague way or that it would give us an exceedingly cumbersome rule but rather that it will not give us a rule at all. The utilitarian criterion would take the form "An act is right if it produces as much pleasure and/or intellectual growth and/or spiritual development and/or . . . and/or . . ."; but this is not so much a rule as it is a conjunction of rules — "You ought to maximize pleasure," "You ought to encourage intellectual growth," etc. This procedure provides no answer to the questions raised by exceptions, for the joint assertion of a number of rules will not be a rule that can be used to resolve conflicts between the component rules. In this paragraph I have considered the utilitarian principle as it is formulated in terms of "good." If it is formulated in terms of "happiness" and this concept is meant to embrace many kinds of things, then exactly the same difficulty occurs.

"However," it might be protested, "you have misinterpreted the utilitarian criterion when you insist that it is the joint assertion of a number of rules. Really it is not, for the term 'good' does not refer to a thing or a number of things; it is an adjective standing for a property of certain things. 'Always act so as to maximize goodness' is, then, the fundamental exceptionless rule which can be used to resolve conflicts between subordinate rules." However, this approach will not work either, for though we have been told to maximize goodness, we have not been told whether the reliability of rules is affected by exceptions or whether we can be sure in any given case falling under a rule that we do not have a justified exception. This objection cannot be minimized by arguing that the difficulty in any given case can be resolved by a direct appeal to the ultimate principle; for, as both Sidgwick and Moore realized, the difficulties inherent in the detection and calculation of goodness often make it hard to determine or be sure of what is obligatory. The persistent critic will still want to know, for instance, how he can be sure in any given case that keeping his promise will maximize goodness, and so he is still confronted by the very difficulties the utilitarian principle is here being evoked to avoid.

If "good" is used adjectivally, the principle will not function as a rule simply because freedom from exceptions is sought at the expense of ceasing to refer to any specific sort of activity or behavior. Supposing that right acts have some property in common, it is not the case that we will obtain a rule by asserting that we ought to perform acts that have that property. All right acts have the property of being right, but "Act rightly" is not a rule. In this case we will have rules only if we are told what specific sorts of acts are right or wrong. Similarly, even if all right acts have the property of being acts which produce or maximize goodness, it does not follow that "Maximize goodness" is a moral rule. Here too we will obtain a rule or rules only if we can specify what sorts of things are good. However, if this is done, we will have once more either a rule admitting exceptions, a number of rules, or the joint assertion of a number of rules, and so the perplexing questions will emerge again.

There is yet another reason why the utilitarian principle cannot be an exceptionless criterion which can be used to settle questions about exceptions. As others have frequently pointed out, it does not take into account the fact that the manner in which goods are distributed among men is of moral significance. Since a pattern of distribution may be wrong even though it maximizes the amount of goodness, the principle is susceptible to exceptions. This objection cannot be avoided by assimilating some qualification about distribution into the principle on the grounds that certain distributions would be intrinsically bad; for if the assimilation could be carried out, the result would be either the joint assertion of several rules or a statement in which "good" was used in an adjectival sense. In either case the resultant "principle" would be subject to one or another of the criticisms discussed earlier. And in the second case the projected assimilation encounters an additional difficulty, for the goodness of a distribution would be of a logically different order from the goodness of the things distributed. The utilitarian may assert that it is good that things should be distributed in certain ways, but the good distribution would not be a member of the class of goods that are distributable. The goodness or goods referred to in the utilitarian principle belong to the latter class; the matter of distribution is something else again.

Lest it appear that I have raised objections against only one specific theory, I must emphasize that the term "utilitarianism" has been used in a broad sense. The objections I have raised hold against any teleological theory or more generally against any theory in which it is maintained that some one rule always takes precedence over all others.

Any such theory will fail to remove the difficulties surrounding exceptions, since it will give us either a specific rule which does in fact admit exceptions, a formula cloaking the joint assertion of a number of rules, or a generalization which not only does not function as a rule but also does not resolve our difficulties.

If it be objected that another possible type of exceptionless rule was eliminated at the outset when directives such as Kant's Categorical Imperative were set aside, then several things must be noted. First, because such a directive will function quite differently from the utilitarian principle, an appeal to it will not lead to the sort of theory discussed here. Secondly, such a directive will not be a sufficient criterion of the validity of exceptions or judgments.

III

I turn now to the second sort of theory. According to this view, the uncertainty that may be introduced by exceptions can be prevented if we list the exempting conditions exhaustively. If we do this, the rule will become reliable and judgments certain, for we can now tell exactly when the rule is to be followed or not followed. And if the exempting conditions for all rules are listed exhaustively, no chaos will be introduced into morality by the clash of rules. To my knowledge no one has tried to work out such a system in detail, but it is an ideal suggested by some people. Sidgwick, for instance, suggests this in the case of the rule about promises when he says:

> To sum up: we seem able to state it as a generally accepted principle that a promise, express or tacit, is binding, if made by an individual, if the promiser has a clear belief as to the sense in which it was understood by the promisee, and if the latter is still in a position to grant release from it, but unwilling to do so, if it was not obtained by force or fraud, if it does not conflict with definite prior obligations, if we do not believe that its fulfilment will be harmful to the promisee, or will inflict a disproportionate sacrifice on the promiser, and if circumstances have not materially changed since it was made.[2]

Such a principle is far too cumbersome to be used as a substitute for the corresponding rule, but the proponent of our theory need not advocate

---

[2]Henry Sidgwick, *The Methods of Ethics* (3rd ed., London: Macmillan & Co., 1884), p. 311.

that we do this. It will be sufficient for his purposes, he will maintain, if we are able to produce an exhaustive check list to be used whenever we encounter difficult situations.

He is, however, overly optimistic. His list, exhaustive or not, will not streamline moral deliberation or introduce a higher degree of certainty unless the circumstances under which the exempting conditions take effect are stated clearly and precisely. If he does not do this, questions involving exceptions will break out on another level. Sidgwick says correctly that a promise is not binding if it was obtained by fraud or force; but, as he himself points out, the concept of "fraud and force" is quite vague. We do not agree with each other as to what constitutes fraud, we may find it difficult to make up our own minds about what shall be called "fraud," and we may disagree among ourselves or be unsure ourselves as to what degree of fraud is permissible. In short, it is possible for all sorts of situations to occur where it would be extremely difficult to say whether or not this exempting condition was satisfied and therefore whether or not the rule should be followed. Unfortunately for the proponent of our theory, these are the sorts of situations where most of our difficulties about promises arise. So long as this sort of vagueness occurs, running through a list of exempting conditions will not help us. To do justice to Sidgwick, it is only fair to say that he does not claim his exhaustive list will eliminate any difficulties.

The second major difficulty in such a theory resides in the claim I have granted so far, the claim that the sorts of exceptions can be listed exhaustively. But this claim cannot be supported. How, for instance, can we be sure that Sidgwick has given an exhaustive list? Checking his list against one of our own will not do, for the same question will arise with respect to our list. If we do not have a list, shall we reduplicate his research to check his results? Is it the case that all we must do is set ourselves to the task of examining the various situations in which promises are made, kept, and broken? Suppose that we have done so, that we have thought hard and long about very many different sorts of circumstances under which promises could be given, and that we have supplemented our own efforts by consulting others engaged in similar research. Now, if we discover some instances that are not covered by Sidgwick's statement, we will have shown that his list is incomplete; but can we be sure that our own is complete? How can we tell? What is the criterion? Surely it is not that we cannot think of any more exempting conditions, for Sidgwick could have used that criterion with respect to his list too. And it cannot be that the list will never be supplemented because, in the first place, even if it never were supplemented, this would not show that it was complete and, in the second place, this is not a test we can apply. At least, it is not a test we can apply unless we have some way of determining that our list is exhaustive — but this just brings us back to our starting point. If we could show somehow that we can never encounter moral situations that are not similar to those we have already encountered and considered, we would have a criterion, but this has not been shown. Furthermore, if the way in which we have continually encountered novel situations in the past is any indication of what may occur in the future, this suggestion is based upon a very implausible assumption. Again, if we had some way of discovering or revealing now all those situations which will differ significantly from those we have already encountered, we would have a suitable criterion of completeness, but no such criterion has been suggested. I know of no way in which we can here and now determine what sorts of clashes will occur in the future or what sorts of borderline instances will arise or how rules will be modified or extended. Indeed, there cannot be a way to do this, for some of those future difficulties will arise as a result of our increasing knowledge of the world; and, of course, we cannot know now what we now do not know. Yet the proponent of the present view must be able to determine these things if he is to set up his exhaustive lists.

He can, of course, stipulate what the list of exceptions will be, but this will not help him. In the first place it would be rather odd to say that a list closed in this fashion was a complete list, for it could be an incomplete list too if he chose to say so. In the second place, the problems will continue to arise. When a novel situation is presented to him, either he can open up his list for re-evaluation and re-stipulation, in which case his stipulation has gained him nothing so far as the justification of judgments is concerned; or he can refuse to re-evaluate his list, in which case he runs the risk of moral obtuseness or downright irresponsibility.

I conclude that this way of accounting for exceptions must fail, for it is impossible to determine whether or not any given list of sorts of exceptions is exhaustive. Perhaps, in view of the fact that we have no criterion of completeness and hence cannot say that a list is either complete or incomplete, I should conclude that no clear sense has been given to the phrase "complete list."

IV

At the beginning of this paper I listed three possible sources of the fear that exceptions introduce uncertainty and disorder into morality, a fear which may lead to the elaboration of one or the other of the two theories I have just discussed and rejected. I return now to those three sources.

The first source was the belief that a rule is unreliable in so far as it admits exceptions. But this is not so, for allowing an exception to a rule is not like making a breach in a dike. The fact that I am obliged to beat my horses severely in order to rush a child to the hospital does not support the belief that henceforth it will not be quite so wrong to inflict pain on animals or the belief that it will now be easier to justify exceptions to this rule. The force of the rule has not been affected; it is still to be taken just as seriously as it ever was. The phrase "exception to a rule" is misleading in so far as it suggests that something unfortunate is happening to the rule. But when I argue for an exception, I am objecting to a judgment someone has supported by citing the rule; I am not criticizing or objecting to the rule itself. If anything is defeated in the debate, it will be the judgment or my counterjudgment — not the rule. Indeed, far from weakening rules, exceptions help preserve them, for an exception is a device which enables us to resolve conflicts between rules without defeating the rules themselves.

The second source of the apprehension is the belief that even if exceptions do not weaken the rule itself, they certainly do make it difficult to determine when we are obliged to follow it. How can we ever be sure that the case in point is not an exception? I can point out that we do recognize major exempting conditions and that, because we do, we can resolve many cases readily and eliminate certain possible extenuating circumstances in others and that, as a consequence, the environment in which decisions must be made is not so chaotic as the objector suggests. But this sort of answer will not satisfy him. He may allow that, by accounting for the obvious exceptions, we can tighten up the usage of the rule so that it becomes more and more probable that we should follow it in certain sorts of cases; but he will maintain that the element of uncertainty cannot be removed completely. In any particular case we may be sure that certain extenuating circumstances are not present, but we cannot be sure that no such circumstance is present.

The objection is not well founded, however, because at the very time we admit exceptions to rules we imply that there are cases which are not exceptions. For instance, when we admit exceptions to the rule "It is wrong to break promises," we imply that there are some instances in which a promise can be broken — namely, those instances and only those instances in which there is a good reason for doing so. In order to make this point explicit, we can, for our philosophic purposes only, rephrase the rule to read: "You may break your promise if and only if you have a good reason for doing so." If in any particular instance we can find no reason why we can or should break our promise, then we are obliged to keep it. For instance, if you and I are chatting idly over coffee and I look at my watch and say, "I must go now; I promised to meet my wife at the library at four o'clock and there is just enough time to get there," there will be no questions asked. You may glance at the clock to check the time, thus eliminating a possible exempting condition, but you are not likely to question my decision. You certainly will not argue with me that perhaps I am not obliged to go because there may very well be some reason why I need not, some reason which neither you nor I have been able to think of. If a critic did argue in this fashion, we would ask him to present his reasons or stop his nonsense. It is a feature of moral reasoning that the criteria for reaching decisions do not require that we withhold judgment after we have considered the case carefully. Once the defendant has exercised reasonable precaution in testing his statement, the burden of proof in bringing further objections to light rests upon the persistent critic. If the rule is recognized, if its application to the case in point is unquestioned, and if after careful examination no mitigating circumstances have been revealed — then the judgment has been justified. It is not probably justified; it *is* justified. In such a case, to cite the rule is to give a conclusive reason.

The third source of apprehension about the effect of exceptions is the belief that morality rests upon an insecure foundation if the ultimate courts of appeal are rules having exceptions. In so far as this belief is grounded in the beliefs that rules are weakened and made unreliable or that no particular decision can be justified with certainty, it has been dealt with in the preceding paragraphs. In so far as it is based on the fear that moral deliberations are carried on in the face of a potential threat of an indefinite regress of rules having exceptions, it has been dealt with in my criticism of the utilitarian account of exceptions. As I argued there, the fact that rules admit exceptions shows neither that each must be justified in terms of some other rule nor that rules must be arranged in a hierarchy capped by some fundamental exceptionless rule. In so far as this apprehension rests on the belief that morality cannot be systematized and must therefore be left in a rather unorganized state, there are several things that must be said. If the objection is that we will have no way of predicting beforehand just what sorts of moral problems will arise and how they are to be resolved, then the objection must be admitted unless we can list beforehand all possible sorts of exception to all rules, and this, I have argued, is impossible. Our moral theory must accommodate itself to morality and thus must be understood as being associated primarily with particular concrete situations that arise in a universe that is not a block universe. It would be nice if we lived in a universe where moral dilemmas did not arise or were all of a predictable sort, but this state of affairs would be accomplished only by a modification of the universe, not by the elaboration of a theory of morality. Finally, if the objection that morality is left in an unorganized state is simply the expression of a desire for an elegant account, it must be pointed out again that the complexity of our moral universe must be recognized. And furthermore, even if a simple over-all framework could be established, no practical advantage would be obtained. So far as elegance is concerned, the utilitarian theories have not been surpassed, but their best-known modern proponents, Sidgwick and Moore, knew full well and said quite explicitly that the bearing of the utilitarian principle on the cases that bother us is not obvious or clear.

Exceptionless Rules

Immanuel Kant

On a Supposed Right to Tell Lies
from Benevolent Motives

In the work called *France*, for the year 1797, Part VI, No. 1, on Political Reactions, by *Benjamin Constant*, the following passage occurs, p. 123:

"The moral principle that it is one's duty to speak the truth, if it were taken singly and unconditionally, would make all society impossible. We have the proof of this in the very direct consequences which have been drawn from this principle by a German philosopher, who goes so far as to affirm that to tell a falsehood to a murderer who asked us whether our

From *Kant's Critique of Practical Reason and Other Works on the Theory of Ethics*, trans. T. K. Abbott (London: Longmans, Green & Co., 1873).

friend, of whom he was in pursuit, had not taken refuge in our house, would be a crime."[1]

The French philosopher opposes this principle in the following manner, page 124: "It is a duty to tell the truth. The notion of duty is inseparable from the notion of right. A duty is what in one being corresponds to the right of another. Where there are no rights there are no duties. To tell the truth then is a duty, but only toward him who has a right to the truth. But no man has a right to a truth that injures others." The πρῶτον ψεῦδος [chief fallacy] here lies in the statement that "*To tell the truth is a duty, but only towards him who has a right to the truth.*"

It is to be remarked, first, that the expression "to have a right to the truth" is unmeaning. We should rather say, a man has a right to his own *truthfulness* (*veracitas*), that is, to subjective truth in his own person. For to have a right objectively to truth would mean that, as in *meum* and *tuum* generally, it depends on his will whether a given statement shall be true or false, which would produce a singular logic.

Now, the *first* question in whether a man — in cases where he cannot avoid answering Yes or No — has the *right* to be untruthful. The *second* question is whether, in order to prevent a misdeed that threatens him or some one else, he is not actually bound to be untruthful in a certain statement to which an unjust compulsion forces him.

Truth in utterances that cannot be avoided in the formal duty of a man to everyone[2] however great the disadvantage that may arise from it to him or any other; and although by making a false statement I do no wrong to him who unjustly compels me to speak, yet I do wrong to men in general in the most essential point of duty, so that it may be called a lie (though not in the jurist's sense), that is, so far as in me lies I cause that declarations in general find no credit, and hence that all rights founded on contract should lose their force; and this is a wrong which is done to mankind.

If, then, we define a lie merely as an intentionally false declaration towards another man, we need not add that it must injure another; as

---

[1]"J. D. Michaelis, in Göttingen, propounded the same strange opinion even before Kant. That Kant is the philosopher here referred to, I have been informed by the author of this work himself."—K. F. Cramer.*

[2]I do not wish here to press this principle so far as to say that "falsehood is a violation of duty to oneself." For this principle belongs to Ethics, and here we are speaking only of a duty of justice. Ethics look in this transgression only to the *worthlessness*, the reproach of which the liar draws on himself.

---

*I hereby admit that I have really said this in some place which I cannot now recollect.—I. Kant.

the jurists think proper to put in their definition (*mendacium est falsiloquium in praejudicium alterius*).[3] For it always injures another; if not another individual, yet mankind generally, since it vitiates the source of justice. This benevolent lie *may*, however, by *accident* (*casus*) become punishable even by civil laws; and that which escapes liability to punishment only by accident may be condemned as wrong even by external laws. For instance, if you have *by a lie* hindered a man who is even now planning a murder, you are legally responsible for all the consequences. But if you have strictly adhered to the truth, public justice can find no fault with you, be the unforeseen consequence what it may. It is possible that whilst you have honestly answered Yes to the murderer's question, whether his intended victim is in the house, the latter may have gone out unobserved, and so not have come in the way of the murderer, and the deed therefore have not been done; whereas, if you lied and said he was not in the house, and he had really gone out (though unknown to you), so that the murderer met him as he went, and executed his purpose on him, then you might with justice be accused as the cause of his death. For, if you had spoken the truth as well as you knew it, perhaps the murderer while seeking for his enemy in the house might have been caught by neighbours coming up and the deed been prevented. Whoever then *tells a lie*, however good his intentions may be, must answer for the consequences of it, even before the civil tribunal, and must pay the penalty for them, however unforeseen they may have been; because truthfulness is a duty that must be regarded as the basis of all duties founded on contract, the laws of which would be rendered uncertain and useless if even the least exception to them were admitted.

To be *truthful* (honest) in all declarations is therefore a sacred unconditional command of reason, and not to be limited by any expediency.

M. Constant makes a thoughtful and sound remark on the decrying of such strict principles, which it is alleged lose themselves in impracticable ideas, and are therefore to be rejected (p. 123): — "In every case in which a principle proved to be true seems to be inapplicable, it is because we do not know the *middle principle* which contains the medium of its application." He adduces (p. 121) the doctrine of *equality* as the first link forming the social chain (p. 121): "namely, that no man can be bound by any laws except those to the formation of which he has contributed. In a very contracted society this principle may be directly

---

[3]Literally: "A lie is a deceptively false statement made to the injury (prejudice) of another"; or translating "praejudicium" in a more legal sense: "made with the purpose of depriving another of his rights."—ED.

applied and become the ordinary rule without requiring any middle principle. But in a very numerous society we must add a new principle to that which we here state. This middle principle is, that the individuals may contribute to the formation of the laws either in their own person or by *representatives*. Whoever would try to apply the first principle to a numerous society without taking in the middle principle would infallibly bring about its destruction. But this circumstance, which would only show the ignorance or incompetence of the lawgiver, would prove nothing against the principle itself." He concludes (p. 125) thus: "A principle recognized as truth must, therefore, never be abandoned, however obviously danger may seem to be involved in it." (And yet the good man himself abandoned the unconditional principle of veracity on account of the danger to society, because he could not discover any middle principle which would serve to prevent this danger; and, in fact, no such principle is to be interpolated here.)

Retaining the names of the persons as they have been here brought forward, "the French philosopher" confounds the action by which one does harm (*nocet*) to another by telling the truth, the admission of which he cannot avoid, with the action by which he does him *wrong* (*laedit*). It was merely an *accident* (*casus*) that the truth of the statement did harm to the inhabitant of the house; it was not a free *deed* (in the juridical sense). For to admit his right to require another to tell a lie for his benefit would be to admit a claim opposed to all law. Every man has not only a right, but the strictest duty to truthfulness in statements which he cannot avoid, whether they do harm to himself or others. He himself, properly speaking, does not *do* harm to him who suffers thereby; but this harm is *caused* by accident. For the man is not free to choose, since (if he must speak at all) veracity is an unconditional duty. The "German philosopher" will therefore not adopt as his principle the proposition (p. 124): "It is a duty to speak the truth, but only to him who has *a right to the truth*," first on account of the obscurity of the expression, for truth is not a possession the right to which can be granted to one, and refused to another; and next and chiefly, because the duty of veracity (of which alone we are speaking here) makes no distinction between persons towards whom we have this duty, and towards whom we may be free from it; but is an *unconditional duty* which holds in all circumstances.

Now, in order to proceed from a *metaphysic* of Right (which abstracts from all conditions of experience), to a principle of *politics* (which applies these notions to cases of experience), and by means of this to the solution of a problem of the latter in accordance with the general principle of right, the philosopher will enunciate: (1) An *Axiom*, that is, an apodictically certain proposition, which follows directly from the definition of external right (harmony of the *freedom* of each with the freedom of all by a universal law). (2) A *Postulate* of external public *law* as the united will of all on the principle of *equality*, without which there could not exist the freedom of all. (3) A *Problem*; how it is to be arranged that harmony may be maintained in a society, however large, on principles of freedom and equality (namely, by means of a representative system); and this will then become a principle of the *political system*, the establishment and arrangement of which will contain enactments which, drawn from practical knowledge of men, have in view only the mechanism of administration of justice, and how this is to be suitably carried out. Justice must never be accommodated to the political system, but always the political system to justice.

"A principle recognized as true (I add, recognized *à priori*, and therefore apodictic) must never be abandoned, however obviously danger may seem to be involved in it," says the author. Only here we must not understand the danger of *doing harm* (accidentally), but of *doing wrong*; and this would happen if the duty of veracity, which is quite unconditional, and constitutes the supreme condition of justice in utterances, were made conditional and subordinate to other considerations; and, although by a certain lie I in fact do no wrong to any person, yet I infringe the principle of justice in regard to all indispensably necessary statements *generally* (I do wrong formally, though not materially); and this is much worse than to commit an injustice to any individual, because such a deed does not presuppose any principle leading to it in the subject. The man who, when asked whether in the statement he is about to make he intends to speak truth or not, does not receive the question with indignation at the suspicion thus expressed towards him that he might be a liar, but who asks permission first to consider possible exceptions, is already a liar (*in potentia*), since he shows that he does not recognize veracity as a duty in itself, but reserves exceptions from a rule which in its nature does not admit of exceptions, since to do so would be self-contradictory.

All practical principles of justice must contain strict truths, and the principles here called middle principles can only contain the closer definition of their application to actual cases (according to the rules of politics), and never exceptions from them, since exceptions destroy the universality, on account of which alone they bear the name of principles.

The Generalization Argument

Marcus G. Singer

Generalization in Ethics

Chapter I: Introductory

Section 1. The question "What would happen if everyone did that?" is one with which we are all familiar. We have heard it asked, and perhaps have asked it ourselves. We have some familiarity with the sort of context in which it would be appropriate to ask it. Thus we understand that it is either elliptical for or a prelude to saying, "If everyone did that, the consequences would be disastrous," and that this is often considered a good reason for concluding that one ought not to do that. The situations

From *Generalization in Ethics* (New York: Alfred A. Knopf, 1961). Copyright 1961 by Marcus G. Singer. Excerpted from chapters I, IV, V, and VIII of *Generalization in Ethics*, pp. 3-5, 62-68, 71-75, 80-83, 86-90, 96, 103, 119-24, 228-33, by permission of the author.

in which this sort of consideration might be advanced are of course exceedingly diverse. One who announces his intention of not voting in some election might be met by the question, "What would happen if no one voted?" If no one voted, the government would collapse, or the democratic system would be repudiated, and this is deemed by many to indicate decisively that everyone should vote. Again, one who disapproves of another's attempts to avoid military service might point out: "If everyone refused to serve, we would lose the war." The members of a discussion group, which meets to discuss papers presented by members, presumably all realize that each should take a turn in reading a paper, even one who may not want to and prefers to take part in the discussions only, because if everyone refused the club would dissolve, and there would be no discussions. This sort of consideration would not be decisive to one who did not care whether the club dissolved. But it undoubtedly would be decisive to one who enjoys the meetings and wishes them to continue.

Each of these cases provides an example of the use or application of a type of argument which I propose to call *the generalization argument*: "If everyone were to do that, the consequences would be disastrous (or undesirable); therefore, no one ought to do that." Any argument of the form "The consequences of no one's doing that would be undesirable; therefore everyone ought to do that" is also, obviously, an instance of the generalization argument. It is this line of argument, and considerations resembling it, that will be at the very center of this inquiry.

The basic problem about the generalization argument (which can be thought of indifferently as either an argument or a moral principle) is to determine the conditions under which it is a good or valid one, that is to say, the conditions under which the fact that the consequences of *everyone's* acting in a certain way would be undesirable, provides a good reason for concluding that it is wrong for *anyone* to act in that way. For there are conditions under which the generalization argument is obviously not applicable, and it is necessary to determine just what they are. The instances presented above are ones in which the consideration of the consequences of everyone's acting in a certain way seems clearly relevant to a moral judgment about that way of acting. But there are others in which this sort of consideration is just as clearly irrelevant. For instance, while "humanity would probably perish from cold if everyone produced food, and would certainly starve if everyone made clothes or built houses,"[1] it would be absurd to infer from this that no one ought to produce food or to build houses.

---

[1] Morris R. Cohen, *The Faith of a Liberal* (New York: Henry Holt and Company, 1946), p. 86.

It might be thought that this is a counterexample, which proves the generalization argument to be invalid or fallacious generally. To argue that you ought not to do something because of what would happen if *everyone* did, though it is somewhat like arguing that you ought not to do something because of what would happen if *you* do, is also quite different. On the pattern of, "If you were to do that the consequences would be disastrous, therefore you ought not to do that," we can argue, "If everyone were to do that the consequences would be disastrous, therefore not everyone ought to do that." But the transition from "not everyone ought to do that" to "no one ought to do that," from "not everyone has the right" to "no one has the right," seems surely fallacious. It is like saying that no one has red hair because everyone does. Yet this transition, or something very much like it, is essential to the generalization argument.

But there is actually no fallacy involved in the generalization argument, though there may be in particular applications of it. For it is not always a fallacy to argue from "some" to "all," and the belief that it is always fallacious is merely a prejudice arising out of a preoccupation with certain types of statements. It is a fact of logic that if any one argument of a certain form is invalid then all arguments of that form are invalid, and this is the principle underlying the use of counter-examples. Yet it involves an inference from "some" to "all." It is true that the generalization argument involves an inference from "not everyone has the right" to "no one has the right," from "it would not be right for everyone" to "it would not be right for anyone." This inference, however, is mediated, and therefore qualified, by the principle that *what is right (or wrong) for one person must be right (or wrong) for any similar person in similar circumstances.* For obvious reasons I shall refer to this principle as "the generalization *principle*," even though it has traditionally been known as the principle of fairness or justice or impartiality.

The generalization principle is not likely to be regarded as fallacious. Yet it has frequently been regarded as vacuous and hence devoid of significant application. This also is not so, and the best way of showing this is by showing how it can be significantly and usefully applied. . . .

Chapter IV: The Generalization Argument

. . . That the generalization principle is involved in the generalization argument is no doubt obscured by the fact that in applications of the argument the qualification "all similar persons in similar circumstances" is left inexplicit. But in valid applications of the argument this restriction is either implicitly understood from the context or is indicated by various linguistic devices. For example, the argument "everyone ought to vote because if no one voted the government would collapse" is evidently meant to apply only to those legally permitted to vote. This condition on the argument I shall call that of *restricted universality*, and I shall go on 'to discuss it presently. Before doing so, however, it will be useful to set forth with some precision the various steps involved in the generalization argument, in order to illustrate more clearly its logical structure. For the generalization principle is not the only principle involved in it. Let us consider, then, the anatomy of the generalization argument.

Section 1. The argument involves, in the first place, the principle, "If the consequences of A's doing x would be disastrous, then A ought not to do x." The term "disastrous" is a stronger term than is actually necessary for the statement of this principle, as are such roughly synonymous terms as "terrible" and "catastrophic." It can be replaced by the somewhat weaker and more general term "undesirable." The consequences of an act can be undesirable without being disastrous. But if they are disastrous then they are undesirable. Thus this principle, which I shall call the *principle of consequences*, can be stated as follows: (1) If the consequences of A's doing x would be undesirable, then A ought not to do x. This is, obviously, equivalent to "If the consequences of A's *not* doing x would be undesirable, then A ought to do x." It is not, however, equivalent to "If the consequences of A's doing x would be desirable, then A ought to do x." I doubt very much whether the latter proposition is true. . . . At any rate, it is no part of the generalization argument.

The principle of consequences is a necessary ethical or moral principle. It is necessary not only in the sense that its denial involves self-contradiction. It is necessary also in the sense that like the generalization principle, it is a necessary presupposition or precondition of moral reasoning. There can be sensible and fruitful disagreement about matters within the field delimited by it, but there can be no sensible or fruitful disagreement about the principle itself. We might say that, like the generalization principle, it is both necessary and fundamental.

I do not wish to imply that anyone ever has seriously questioned or denied this principle. It may be that no one has done so, at least explicitly, though there are probably many instances in which it has been denied by implication, just as there are unquestionably many cases in which it has been violated or disregarded. Yet the principle can be misunderstood, especially if the term "undesirable" is not properly understood. This term may be interpreted in either of two senses, with the consequence that there are two ways of interpreting the principle. Though these two ways are consistent with each other, they should be kept distinct.

One sense of "undesirable" is that of "undesirable on the whole." On this interpretation, the principle does not mean that if *some* of the consequences of A's doing x would be undesirable then A ought not to do x. It is perfectly consistent with it for some of the consequences of an act to be desirable and others to be undesirable, or for them to be undesirable in some respects but not in others. And it may well be that while some of the consequences of an act are undesirable, it is not undesirable, on the whole, for the act to be done. For the desirable consequences may *outweigh* the undesirable ones. Or it may be that the consequences of A's not doing x would be worse (more undesirable) than the consequences of his doing it.

In the second sense of "undesirable" it does not have this proviso of "on the whole." On this interpretation, the fact that some of the consequences of A's doing x would be undesirable is a reason for asserting that A ought not to do x, but it is not a conclusive reason. On the basis of this fact one could reasonably presume that it would be wrong for A to do x.[2] This presumption can be rebutted by showing that not all the consequences are undesirable, and that the undesirable consequences are outweighed by (are less important than) the desirable ones; in other words, by showing that the consequences of A's doing x would not be undesirable on the whole. Thus a more adequate, because less elliptical, statement of the principle, on this interpretation, would be: If the consequences of A's doing x would be undesirable, then A ought not to do x *without a reason or justification*. Such statements as "A ought to do x" are usually elliptical in this way.

These brief remarks should make it clear that this principle assumes a good deal less than might at first glance be supposed. It does not by itself determine the meaning of the term "undesirable," or what is desirable or undesirable, or how the various consequences of an action are to be weighed against each other in order to determine whether they are undesirable on the whole. Agreement on the principle is quite consistent with disagreement on these latter questions. Indeed, without agreement on the principle, disagreement on these other matters would have no point.

Now this first step in the generalization argument is the basis for the second, which is a generalization from it: (2) If the consequences of

---

[2] I am using the expressions "A ought not to do x," "It would be wrong for A to do x," and "A has no right to do x," synonymously, and I should say that this is in general conformity with their ordinary use. Thus I am treating "A ought to do x" as equivalent to "It would be wrong for A not to do x" and "A has no right not to do x." Note that the contradictory of "A ought to do x" is not "A ought not to do x," which is rather its contrary (for neither may hold), but "A has the right not to do x" (or "A need not do x").

everyone's doing x would be undesirable, then not everyone ought to do x.[3]

It is in the third step of the argument that the generalization principle comes into play: (3) If not everyone ought to do x, then no one ought to do x. This can of course be stated in the alternative form: If it is wrong for everyone to do x, then it is wrong for anyone to do x. Note that I have left unstated the necessary qualifications.

All of these steps are actually telescoped in the generalization argument itself, which is obviously deducible from (2) and (3): If the consequences of everyone's doing x would be undesirable, then no one ought to do x.

It may be useful to display in one place, in slightly different language, this deduction of the generalization argument from the generalization principle and the principle of consequences. The principle of consequences (C) states that: If the consequences of A's doing x would be undesirable, then A does not have the right to do x. The following principle (GC) is what I called a generalization from C: If the consequences of everyone's doing x would be undesirable, then not everyone has the right to do x. Now the generalization principle (GP) may be stated as follows: If not everyone has the right to do x, then not anyone (no one) has the right to do x. The generalization argument (if the consequences of everyone's doing x would be undesirable, then no one has the right to do x) clearly follows from GP and GC.

Some remarks on this deduction are now in order. In the above generalization from the principle of consequences, (GC), "everyone" is treated collectively, not distributively. The hypothesis "If the consequences of everyone's acting in a certain way would be undesirable" differs from "If the consequences of *each and every act* of that kind would be undesirable." The latter implies that each and every act of that kind would be wrong. This is the true logical generalization of the principle of consequences, but it is not the one intended, nor is it particularly important.

Thus GC has as its consequent "not everyone ought to do x," instead of "everyone ought not to do x," because supposedly if not everyone does x the undesirable consequences that would result from everyone's doing it would be avoided. Hence the generalization argument does not imply

---

[3]Since expressions like "not everyone ought" and "no one ought" can be deceptive, perhaps it should be said here that I definitely do not mean by "not everyone ought" the same as "not everyone is *required*," but rather "not everyone has the right" or "it would not be right for everyone." Similarly, by "no one ought" I do not mean "no one is required, or has the duty," but rather "no one has the right," or "it would not be right for *anyone*." (If one prefers to translate "not everyone ought to do x" by "it ought not to be the case that everyone does x," I can see no objection to it, except that it is not very idiomatic, and I cannot see that it is helpful.)

that the consequences of each and every act of the kind mentioned would be undesirable. By reason of the generalization principle it implies that each and every act of that kind may be presumed to be wrong. Yet from the fact that an act is wrong it does not follow that its consequences would be undesirable.

The generalization argument is to be distinguished from what may be called the *generalized principle of consequences:* If the consequences of doing x would be undesirable (in general, or usually), then it is wrong (in general) to do x. Here "x" refers, not to a specific action, but to a kind of action. The consequences of lying are usually undesirable; hence lying is usually wrong. The generalized principle of consequences refers to the *individual consequences* of actions of a certain kind. The generalization argument refers to the collective consequences of everyone's acting in a certain way. These are not always the same.

From the fact that the generalization principle is involved in the generalization argument, in the way shown, it follows that all the qualifications required by the former are required by the latter. They are therefore necessary for any application of the argument to be valid. The first is that of restricted universality, the restriction to "every similar person in similar circumstances." The second is the elliptical nature of the conclusion that no one has the right to do x. As I mentioned once before, the form of the generalization principle especially appropriate for the proper understanding of the generalization argument is: If not everyone ought to act or be treated in a certain way, then no one ought to act or be treated in that way *without a reason or justification.* A more adequate statement of the generalization argument, therefore, is: If the consequences of everyone's acting or being treated in a certain way would be undesirable, then no one ought to act or be treated in that way *without a reason.* In other words, whoever acts in a way in which it would be undesirable for everyone to act must justify his conduct. The fact that it would be undesirable for everyone to act in that way provides a presumptive reason, and not a conclusive one, for the judgment that his conduct is wrong. One can justify oneself, or show that one is an exception, by showing that one's circumstances are relevantly different from those in which the act is wrong.

But the discussion of the procedures by which one can justify his (or someone else's) acting in a way in which it would be undesirable for everyone to act, or in which it would be generally wrong to act, may be left for later on. What I propose to do now is to consider in somewhat greater detail the condition of restricted universality. . . .

Section 3. "When people begin to admonish me that if everyone did as I did, etc., I answer that humanity would probably perish from cold if everyone produced food, and would certainly starve if everyone made clothes or built houses."[4]

This certainly has the appearance of a genuine counter-example to the generalization argument. Since the consequences of everyone's producing food would be undesirable, on the pattern of the generalization argument it would seem to follow that it is wrong for anyone to do so, and this, of course, is absurd.

But this actually does not follow, and the generalization argument does not at all have this consequence. For consider what would happen if no one produced food. If no one produced food, everyone would starve. Hence on the same line of reasoning it might be argued that everyone ought to produce food. The argument that no one ought to produce food because of what would happen if everyone did can thus be met by the counterargument that everyone ought to produce food because of what would happen if no one did. A valid application of the generalization argument, however, cannot be met by such a counterargument. The argument that everyone ought to vote because of what would happen if no one did cannot be rebutted in this way.

In a case in which the consequences of everyone's acting in a certain way would be undesirable, while the consequences of no one's acting in that way would also be undesirable, I shall say that the argument can be *inverted*. Thus the argument is invertible with respect to producing food, building houses, and making clothes. Now in order for the generalization argument to have a valid application with respect to some action it is necessary that it not be invertible with respect to that action. In other words, an argument of the form, "Since the consequences of everyone's doing x would be undesirable, no one ought to do x," is valid only if it is not the case that the consequences of no one's doing x would also be undesirable.

This condition on the validity of the generalization argument is not something *ad hoc*, devised just to meet this kind of case, though even if it were, this would be no objection to it. It is another of those

---

[4]Morris R. Cohen, *The Faith of a Liberal* (New York: Henry Holt and Company, 1946), p. 86. Part of the sentence just prior to the one quoted in the text is: "It would be a poor world if there were no diversity of function to suit the diversity of natural aptitudes." This is true; it does not follow that we have here a valid counter-example to the generalization argument. Cf. Cohen's *Reason and Nature* (New Work: Harcourt, Brace and Company, 1931), p. 433: "Nor is there any force in the argument that lying is morally bad because it cannot be made universal. The familiar argument, 'If everybody did so and so . . .' applies just as well to baking bread, building houses, and the like. It is just as impossible for everyone to tell lies all the time as to bake bread all the time or to build houses all the time."

conditions implicitly understood but not explicitly stated, and can readily be incorporated into the statement of the argument: "If the consequences of everyone's doing x would be undesirable, while the consequences of no one's doing x would not be undesirable, then no one has the right to do x." This of course also holds in the form: "If the consequences of no one's doing x would be undesirable, while the consequences of everyone's doing x would not be undesirable, then everyone ought to do x." It is important to remember that the restrictions already discussed apply here also. The conclusion that no one has the right to do x is elliptical for "no one has the right to do x *without a reason.*" Furthermore, the terms "everyone" and "no one" involved here are restricted in their scope. Thus, fully stated, incorporating all the restrictions so far discussed, the generalization argument may be stated: "If the consequences of every member of K's doing x in certain circumstances would be undesirable, while the consequence of no member of K's doing x (in those circumstances) would not be undesirable, then no member of K has the right to do x (in such circumstances) without a special reason."

The condition of restricted universality deserves special mention in this context. The terms "everyone" and "no one" must have the same restrictions on their scope in any one application of the argument. For an application of the argument may be invertible, or may seem to be so, if the term "no one" is used in a wider extension than "everyone," or if "everyone" is used with a wider extension than "no one." Such a situation can arise in the following manner. Suppose (1) that if everyone were to act in a certain way the consequences would be undesirable, and (2) that if no one were to act in that way the consequences would be undesirable. Such a case so far conforms to the condition under which the argument is invertible, and hence invalid. However, it may be that in (1) "everyone" is restricted to the members of a certain class K, while in (2) "no one" is not restricted to the members of this class but has a wider range, so that it means, say, "no one at all." In such a case the argument is not really invertible. In order for it to be invertible it is necessary for the consequences of every member of K's acting in that way and the consequences of no member of K's acting in that way both to be undesirable. It may very well be true of some kind of action that the consequences of no one *at all* acting in that way would be undesirable while the consequences of no member of a certain class acting in that way would not be.

Consider a concrete case. Suppose an attempt is made to invert the argument, "Everyone ought to vote, since the consequences would be disastrous if no one voted." To attempt to invert this argument is to raise the question of what would happen if everyone voted. "If everyone were to vote, this would mean that idiots, imbeciles, infants, illiterates, incompetents, lunatics, and public enemies would vote. And it would be just as bad if all these people were to vote as it would be if no one were to vote at all." But this has not the slightest tendency to show that the original argument is invalid. One who claims that everyone ought to vote, because of what would happen if no one did, does not mean that everyone in the universe, including idiots, illiterates, lunatics, and Martians, ought to vote. The conclusion that everyone ought to vote is restricted to the same class or classes of persons to which the term "no one," in the premise, is restricted. This is obviously, or is obviously meant to be, the class of persons of which it is true that if none of them voted the consequences would be disastrous, and does not include imbeciles, infants, or lunatics. For of these people it is not true that if none of them voted the consequences would be disastrous; on the contrary, it would be disastrous if all such people did vote or attempt to vote. (It may be noted that this is normally the consideration invoked in order to justify legal restrictions on the right to vote.) Such people furthermore are not usually among those legally permitted to vote. Yet the argument is certainly restricted to those who are legally permitted to vote in the election in question, though it is hardly necessary for this condition to be made explicit in concrete applications. No one can justly be held responsible for not voting in an election in which he has no legal right to vote, even if there are good grounds for holding that he ought to have this right. (The question whether a law is just, is distinct from the question whether it ought to be broken; though the two are related, an answer to the one is not an automatic answer to the other.) This restriction would be even more obvious if the original premise were phrased "If everyone *refused* to vote . . ." instead of "If no one voted. . . ." For one who is not permitted or has no opportunity to do something cannot sensibly be said to have refused to do so. This argument is therefore not invertible.

It follows that not every application of the generalization argument is invertible, and therefore that this condition is not a trivial one. . . .

Section 5. The generalization argument is invertible with respect to certain actions because there is something wrong in the way they are described. In the cases just considered the actions were described in too general a way. An opposite inadequacy is at the root of another class of invalid applications of the argument.

"If everyone ate at six o'clock there would be no one to perform certain essential functions, things that must be attended to at all times, and so on, with the net result that no one would be able to eat at six or any other time, and with various other undesirable consequences." Does it follow that no one has the right to eat at six o'clock? If it did, we should have a genuine counterexample to the generalization argument.

The important point to notice here is that this argument in no way depends on the exact time specified. If we could argue that no one has the right to eat at six, we could argue that no one has the right to eat at five, or at seven, or at three minutes past two, and so on. We could therefore argue that no one has the right to eat at any time, and this would mean that no one has the right to eat.

In such a case as this the argument may be said to be *reiterable*. Thus the argument is reiterable whenever it is applied to some action arbitrarily specified, as part of its description, as taking place at some particular time, or at some particular place, or by some particular person, or in relation to some particular person or thing. To take another example: "If everyone were to eat in this restaurant it would get so crowded that no one would be able to do so . . . ; therefore no one ought to eat in this restaurant." The reference to *this* restaurant is not essential here; the same argument would apply to *that* one, and to any other one. The argument can obviously be reiterated for every restaurant, and its consequence would be not just that no one ought to eat at this or that restaurant but that no one ought to eat at any restaurant. And the same argument would apply not only to restaurants but to any place or location whatsoever. Hence in this case also the implication would be that no one ought to eat. Furthermore, note that there is no need to restrict ourselves to eating in order to obtain examples of reiterable arguments. Any action, such as walking, talking, sleeping, or drinking — even doing nothing at all — when particularized in this way, will do as well.

This last point should have indicated that such examples as these can have no rational force as counterexamples. Any instance of the generalization argument that is reiterable is invalid. For any instance of the generalization argument that is reiterable is also invertible. Note that the instances just given, which are clearly representative ones, are just as clearly invertible. The argument from "not everyone has the right to eat at six o'clock" to "no one has the right to eat at six o'clock," since it can be reiterated for any time, implies "no one has the right to eat." But what would happen if no one ate? If no one were to eat the consequences would be just as undesirable, presumably, as if everyone were to eat at the same time.

Still there is a clear-cut difference between those instances of the argument that are reiterable, and therefore invertible, and those that are invertible without being reiterable. In the latter instances the actions are described in too general a way. In the former instances the descriptions of the actions are not general enough — the actions are described in too particularized a way. In these cases particular details of the action that are really arbitrary and inessential are treated as though they were essential. These specified details — in the cases considered, the specification of the exact time and place of an action — are shown to be arbitrary, and hence not essential, by the fact that the argument can be reiterated with respect to them. There may be cases in which the exact time or place of an action are morally relevant. In these cases the argument would not be reiterable with respect to time or place, and this is the test of whether such details are essential. In the instances presented above, these details are inessential (arbitrary, irrelevant) because the argument does not depend on them, and this is shown by the fact that it can be reiterated with respect to them. The same argument applies for any given selection of time or place, and hence for every time or place.

It should be evident that the instances of reiterable arguments just given are in all important respects representative of an indefinitely large class of similar instances that might be advanced as counterexamples to the generalization argument. A few further candidates would be the following: "What would happen if everyone tried to sit in the front row?" "What would happen if everyone went to the circus today?" "What would happen if everybody tried to crowd into Times Square on New year's Eve?" and so on. Since these are all reiterable, in one way or another, they are all invalid applications of the generalization argument, and thus provide no reason to suppose that the actions referred to are wrong. Of course, though all of these instances are invertible, not all of them are invertible directly. Yet, since the reference to a particular type of action is no more essential in these instances than the reference to the particular time or place of the action, on the same line of reasoning we could argue with equal cogency that no one ought ever to do anything at all, and this is clearly invertible. This is further evidence that every application of the generalization argument that is reiterable is invertible and hence invalid.

Section 6. This last condition, that the argument not be reiterable, is closely tied up with the procedure by which one can justify acting in a way in which it would be undesirable for everyone to act. One can justify acting in such a way by showing that one is a member of a certain class of persons (has certain characteristics) such that if every member of that class (everyone with those characteristics) were to act in that way the consequences would not be undesirable, or by showing that the circumstances of one's action are such that the consequences of everyone's acting in that way in those circumstances would not be undesirable. This would be to show either that there is a relevant difference in the characteristics of the agents involved, or that there is a relevant difference in the circumstances. But the argument must not be reiterable with respect to the class of persons or circumstances selected. Otherwise, the class in question would be "distinguished" by a characteristic in terms of which everyone would be an exception, and hence not really distinguished at all. . . .

The following example, in which the generalization argument is applied to the question whether one has the duty to pay taxes, should be useful in making this point clear.

> Suppose a man to urge that he will miss the sum he has to pay much more than it would be missed by society. The absence of the few pounds which he has to pay will not, he may urge, make any perceptible difference whatever to the public funds, but it will make a very perceptible difference to himself, therefore to force him to pay it will do more harm than good; and it will be difficult to answer him if we consider the particular act by itself. But the real answer surely is that he still ought to pay it, because this argument, if admitted at all, would apply to practically everybody, and it would therefore be unfair of him to benefit by other people's taxes while not paying his own share. (The unfairness would not arise if he has strong special grounds for exemption which did not apply to everybody.) [5]

This is certainly a valid application of the generalization argument, and though it is not stated very elegantly, it is presented in a way that is most effective for making clear not only the rational force of the argument but also the conditions that must be met to justify the claim that a certain case is a legitimate exception. It is clear that although, considered by themselves, the consequences of A's not paying his taxes may not, on balance, be undesirable, for he may miss the money more than the government would, yet this cannot justify A in not paying his taxes. For exactly the same sort of consideration would apply to everyone. Thus this sort of consideration could not show anyone to be an exception to the rule, simply because it would apply to everyone and hence would imply that everyone is an exception, which is, as I have already mentioned, self-contradictory.

It follows that the class of persons alleged to be an exception to the rule cannot be a unit class (a class of just one member) determined

---

[5] A. C. Ewing, *The Definition of Good* (New York: The Macmillan Company, 1947), pp. 88-9. Ewing adds that it "would be inconsistent . . . for me to try to justify my action by any argument which, if valid at all, would apply to everybody."

simply by the fact that if no member of this class paid his taxes the consequences would not be undesirable. Ignatz McGillicuddy cannot claim that he has the right not to pay his taxes merely on the ground that if no one named Ignatz McGillicuddy paid his taxes the consequences would not be undesirable. If Ignatz McGillicuddy can argue in this way, then so can John Smith, and so can our old friend, Stan Spatz III. The same argument is reiterable with respect to everyone, or with respect to every such unit class. It would apply also to people without a name.

Of course, the class of persons named Ignatz McGillicuddy may not be a unit class. There may be more than one person named Ignatz McGillicuddy. And, though there may be only one Stan Spatz III, there is certainly more than one John Smith. Thus it may well be false that if no one named Ignatz McGillicuddy (or John Smith) were to pay his taxes the consequences would not be undesirable. So let us suppose that Ignatz McGillicuddy refers to himself not simply by name, but as the possessor of certain characteristics that make him unique. In the abstract it is not easy to see what these could be. So let us imagine that Ignatz McGillicuddy is unique in having twelve toes on each foot. Given that if everyone with twelve toes on each foot fails to pay his taxes the consequences would not be undesirable, this is still not a justification. If Ignatz McGillicuddy can claim that he is unique in having twelve toes on each foot and is therefore entitled not to pay taxes, John Smith can claim that he is unique in being the only person named John Smith employed as a bookkeeper by the underwater Pencil Company of Roaring Hide, South Dakota, that if every such person failed to pay taxes the consequences would not be undesirable, and that he is therefore entitled not to pay taxes. And everyone else can make a similar claim. For everyone is unique in some respect; everyone has some characteristics that no one else has. The argument is thus reiterable with respect to any characteristic selected as unique, and therefore applies to everyone.

Consider a somewhat more complicated case. Suppose someone claims, "If everyone who lives in this house were not to pay taxes, the consequences would not be undesirable. I live in this house, and therefore have the right not to pay taxes." This also will not do. For what distinguishes this house from any other house? Everyone, at least everyone who lives in a house, can argue in the same way. So this same argument is reiterable with respect to (may be applied to) every house, and the consequences would be that everyone has the right not to pay taxes. The test for whether the subclass L of persons claimed to be exceptions to the rule has been legitimately defined is not simply that the consequences of every such person's not conforming to the rule would not be undesirable. It must also be the case that the argument is not reiterable with respect to every such subclass. That is, the distinction must not be based on a consideration that implies that everyone to whom the rule applies is an exception to the rule, for this is simply a contradiction. Thus "this house" cannot be distinguished from others (in such a context as this) on the ground that it is painted red or is located on a hill or has fourteen windows, or has any combination of such features in virtue of which it is unique. For every house has features that distinguish it from every other, even if it is only its specific location or history, and it is true of a house with any other topographical or architectural features that if every one in such a house were exempt from paying taxes the consequences would not be undesirable. Such a characteristic as being thirty years old is also not a reasonable ground for exemption. For with respect to age the argument is also reiterable.

As I mentioned previously in dealing with this topic, in connection with the generalization principle, what is important in these cases is not so much the actual specification of the details of one's situation, as the principle on which the specification is made. Just as the argument from "not everyone has the right to eat at six o'clock" to "no one has the right to eat at six o'clock" does not depend on the exact time specified, such arguments as the ones we have just been considering do not depend on the specified respects in which one is different from others. Just as the former argument is reiterable with respect to any time, the latter arguments are reiterable with respect to any feature that differentiates one person's situation from that of others.

But now what would justify the claim to be an exception? It follows from what has been said that the test here is the nonreiterability of the argument with respect to the characteristic selected. One can justify the claim to be an exception only on the basis of some characteristic that would not show everyone to be an exception. In the case of paying taxes one such characteristic, presumably, is earning less than a certain amount of money. For if everyone earning less than a certain amount of money were allowed not to pay taxes the consequences would not be undesirable, but might be quite the contrary. And the distinction between those who earn more money than is necessary for existence and those who do not is, in this context, a relevant and justifiable one. (If there were no one earning an amount barely necessary for existence there would be no question about paying taxes.) Such a distinction is not arbitrary because the principle on which it is based does not imply that everyone is an exception. It is not the case that if everyone earning *more* than a certain amount of money failed to pay taxes the consequences would not be undesirable. This, incidentally, indicates how to answer the "Where do you draw the line?" argument. Ideally, the line is to be drawn at the point at which it is false that if everyone who earns less than this amount were not to pay taxes the consequences would not be undesirable. Of course, the actual tax laws of any one time or place, on even the most charitable estimate, only approximate to this. The fact that this line is a shifting one, varying with the needs of time and with people's varying estimates of these needs, only makes it more difficult to determine. Who can deny that the tax laws actually in force at any one time are almost always inequitable? . . .

Chapter V: Moral Rules and Principles

It has generally been recognized that there is a distinction, of some importance, between moral rules and moral principles. Yet it has not generally received explicit formulation, and there is no general agreement on just what it is. These terms tend to be used in different ways, and consequently the distinction between them has been drawn at different places. I shall make no attempt, however, to take account of all uses of these terms. Different purposes require different classifications and hence different distinctions. I shall use these terms in such a way that moral principles are more general, pervasive, and fundamental than moral rules, and serve as their sources or grounds. It is in accordance with this usage that we sometimes speak of the principle underlying a certain rule, determining its scope and justifying exceptions to it. . . .

Section 2. . . . A moral rule states that a certain kind of action is generally wrong (or obligatory), and leaves open the possibility that an act (or omission) of that kind may be justifiable. Thus moral rules do not hold in all circumstances; they are not invariant; in a useful legal phrase, they are "defeasible." Moral principles, however, hold in all circumstances and allow of no exceptions; they are invariant with respect to every moral judgment and every moral situation. They are thus "indefeasible." A further point of difference between rules and principles is that principles are always *relevant*, whereas rules are not. For example, the rule against lying is not relevant to a situation in which lying is not involved, and the rule against killing is not relevant where killing is not involved. Moral principles, however, are relevant in every moral situation, in every situation in which a moral question arises. It is evident that such principles, at least in most instances, are bound to be somewhat more abstract than moral rules, though they are not necessarily less definite. . . .

Section 5. Let us turn to the question of justifying fundamental moral rules. The procedure, as already indicated, is the same in every case. Moral rules are established by means of the generalization argument. A rule that cannot be derived from an application of the generalization argument cannot be justified.

Since the procedure in every case is the same, it does not matter which rule we select to exemplify it. Let us take the rule that lying is wrong. What is the proof of this? Since to justify a moral rule is equivalent to explaining why a certain kind of action is generally right or wrong, to justify the rule against lying is equivalent to explaining why lying is wrong. Thus it will be sufficient to answer the question "Why is it wrong to lie?"

I cannot refrain from pointing out how utterly fantastic it would be to answer the question "Why is it wrong to lie?" or any question of this kind, by saying, "Lying is wrong because I disapprove of it," or "Lying is wrong because most people disapprove of it." This would not be an answer at all. Lying is not wrong *because* it is disapproved of, that is, *regarded as wrong*. It would be more plausible to say that lying is regarded as wrong because it is wrong, for to explain why lying is wrong is to justify regarding it as wrong. But the fact that lying is disapproved of is as irrelevant to explaining why it is wrong as is the fact that one who lies is likely to be punished for it. It is no answer to say, "Lying is wrong because I'll hit you if you lie." This goes no way to show that, or why, lying is *wrong*. If someone should ask for a reason why he ought not to lie, the assertion that he will be hit or otherwise punished if he does might be a relevant consideration. The fact that someone will be punished if he does something may be a good prudential reason for not doing it. If what he can gain from the lying will not compensate for the punishment then he would be well advised not to lie. But this has no tendency to show that lying is morally wrong, that he has the duty not to lie. The child will be hurt if he touches the fire, but this is a good reason why he should not touch the fire. But this has no tendency to show that it would be morally wrong to do so. Similar considerations apply to the answer in terms of what is disapproved. This might serve as a device to keep someone from lying. We often have to use such devices. But it is irrelevant to the question why it is wrong to lie. For an act that is right might be punished or disapproved of. And it is wrong to lie even in those situations in which one can get away with it, without being punished or disapproved of. The perfect crime is one that goes undetected or unpunished. It is not one that is justified.

In some instances, to be sure, the fact that an act is generally disapproved of can create a presumption against it. But this fact, by itself, could not *make* it wrong, or constitute its wrongness. For this presumption, like others, can be rebutted, and to rebut it would be to show that the act is not wrong even though it is widely and strongly disapproved of. Morality is not the same as public opinion, nor is it always in accordance with it. The existence of a widespread disapproval of some practice is a major source of moral problems, and can be no automatic answer to them. The fact of social disapproval, furthermore, as the source (and sometimes the consequence) of customs and traditions, can establish only local rules, not fundamental ones.

The reason lying is wrong should be obvious from what has already been said. Lying is wrong because of what would happen if everyone lied. It would be nothing short of disastrous if everyone were to lie whenever he wished to, if lying became the rule and truth-telling the exception, which is, however it may seem, actually not the prevailing practice.[6] It follows that lying is generally wrong, or that no one has the right to lie without a reason, and that the mere wish or desire to lie is never a sufficient justification.

This last point, that the mere wish or desire to lie is never a sufficient justification, is shown by the further application of the generalization argument. For suppose that it were, and that I claimed the right to lie on the ground that I wanted to. Then every similar person, and that is, in this context, everyone who wants to lie, would thereby have the right to lie; that is to say, everyone would have the right to lie whenever he wanted to. The consequences of everyone's doing this, as I have already pointed out, would be nothing short of disastrous, and hence not everyone could have this right. But if not everyone can have this right, then no one can have it, without a special reason, and no special reason can here be given, for the desire to lie is not a distinguishing feature. To "reason" or try to justify oneself in this way really involves a contradiction, for it is to claim to be an exception to a rule on grounds that would make everyone an exception. Moreover, if everyone had the right to lie whenever he wanted to, then everyone would have the right to do whatever he pleases under any circumstances whatsoever, and this also is self-contradictory. . . .

---

[6]The fundamental character of such rules is brought out quite vividly by Mill in the following passage: "The moral rules which forbid mankind to hurt one another (in which we must never forget to include wrongful interference with each other's freedom) are more vital to human well-being than any maxims, however important, which only point out the best mode of managing some department of human affairs. . . . It is their observance which alone preserves peace among human beings: if obedience to them were not the rule, and disobedience the exception, everyone would see in everyone else an enemy, against whom he must be perpetually guarding himself" (*Utilitarianism*, chap. V, par. 33, p. 55).

Section 6. It should be clear that the generalization argument does not establish moral rules as holding always or in all possible circumstances. This is a consequence of the generalization principle: If not everyone has the right to act in a certain way then no one has the right to act in that way without a reason. Hence, if it would be undesirable for everyone to lie, no one has the right to lie without a reason. This obviously implies that it is possible for the rule to have exceptions, for it implies that it is possible to have a justification for going against it. Whether a particular case is an exception to the rule is determined by specifying in a more detailed way the circumstances of the act in question. If the circumstances of the act are such that in those or similar circumstances it would not be undesirable for everyone to act in that way, then in those circumstances the act would not be wrong. (But this requires the qualifications elaborated in the last chapter. What is important is the principle on which the circumstances are specified, which must not imply that everyone's circumstances are exceptional.) Hence in justifying an exception one is actually justifying a *class* of exceptions, and is thus, in effect, modifying the understanding of the original rule by restricting its scope. As already mentioned, that moral rules can have exceptions, and thus do not always hold, is also required by the fact that they can come into conflict in particular instances. If moral rules are derivable from the generalization argument, as I have been maintaining, then to maintain of any moral rule that it holds without exception would be self-contradictory. It would, for instance, be self-contradictory to maintain that lying is always, and not just generally, wrong, because the reasons that establish the rule are the very same reasons that, in certain circumstances, would suffice to override it. And I should say, for the reasons already given, that one who maintains that lying is always wrong, without giving any reasons in support of the assertion, is merely saying or indicating something about his attitudes or feelings towards lying.

I would not imply by this, however, that it is impossible for such reasons to be given. That such reasons can be given is clear from the fact that they have been, and it may be useful to examine . . . such reasons. . . .

Chapter VIII: The Categorical Imperative

Section 3. [*The Rule Against Lying*] . . . Let us consider . . . Kant's positive remarks on what he calls "the unconditional principle of veracity" [cf. above p. 257].[7] Along these lines he claims:

---

[7][All references in this section, unless otherwise specified, are to Abbott's translation of Kant's "On a Supposed Right to Tell Lies from Benevolent Motives," as reprinted in this volume.]—ED.

Truth in utterances that cannot be avoided is the formal duty of a man to everyone, however great the disadvantage that may arise from it to him or any other; and although by making a false statement I do no wrong to him who unjustly compels me to speak, yet I do wrong to men in general in the most essential point of duty . . . that is, so far as in me lies I cause that declarations in general find no credit, and hence that all rights founded on contract should lose their force; and this is a wrong which is done to mankind. . . .

A lie . . . always injures another; if not another individual, yet mankind generally, since it vitiates the source of justice . . . [pp. 255-56].

It is to be noted that Kant is really begging the question here. It seems as if he is maintaining that lying in this case would be wrong because, even if it does not injure another individual, it would injure mankind generally. But he is really doing nothing of the sort. What he is really maintaining is that to tell a lie, even in a situation of the sort described, *must* injure mankind generally, because it would be wrong. But whether it would be wrong is precisely the point in question. The claim that a lie must be wrong because it vitiates the source of justice, or would help destroy the foundations of the law of contract, is similarly question-begging. It can be met by the reply that failing to lie in such a situation would be wrong because it would help destroy the bonds of human trust, in terms of which one person may be relied on to shield another against an oppressor.

But all this is really beside the point. What is most important here is that this argument is certainly not an application of the categorical imperative. In fact, Kant does not apply the categorical imperative at all in this essay. A fallacious inference as to what the results of applying it would be can hardly be construed as an application. If Kant were applying his first moral principle to this case he would be arguing that it would be wrong to lie in such a situation because it could not be willed to be a universal law that everyone do so. Instead of doing this, he contents himself with such assertions as the following: "To be *truthful* (honest) in all declarations is therefore a sacred unconditional command of reason, and not to be limited by any expediency . . ." [p. 256].[8] "The duty

---

[8]The use of the word "therefore" in this sentence may be taken as a sign that Kant is arguing rather than baldly asserting. And so, in a way, he is: "Whoever . . . tells a lie, however good his intentions may be, must answer for the consequences of it, even before the civil tribunal, and must pay the penalty for them, however unforeseen they may have been; because truthfulness is a duty that must be regarded as the basis of all duties founded on contract, the laws of which would be rendered uncertain and useless if even the least exception to them were admitted." Though this may be an argument, it is certainly not an application of the categorical imperative.

of veracity . . . is an *unconditional duty* which holds in all circumstances" [p. 257]. The rule of veracity, he continues, "in its nature does not admit of exceptions, since to do so would be self-contradictory" [p. 258].

Now none of these assertions is in any degree warranted by the principle of universality. What Kant is apparently assuming here is that since the rule of veracity is a categorical or unconditional imperative, in the sense of not being a hypothetical imperative, it would be self-contradictory to speak of a justifiable exception to it. And he is assuming that this rule has been established to be a categorical imperative, in the sense of a rule admitting of no exceptions, by some previous application of *the* categorical imperative. But these assumptions are simply false. Nothing of the sort has been established.

Consider the famous illustration in the *Grundlegung* in which Kant applied the categorical imperative to the case of lying (or making a lying promise). What was established by this application of the principle? What was established was that the maxim in this case ("whenever I believe myself short of money, I will borrow money and promise to pay it back, though I know that this will never be done")

> can never rank as a universal law and be self-consistent, but must necessarily contradict itself. For the universality of a law that every one believing himself to be in need may make any promise he pleases with the intention not to keep it would make promising, and the very purpose of promising, itself impossible, since no one would believe that he was being promised anything, but would laugh at utterances of this kind as empty shams.[9]

Kant's point here is that if such a rule were universally followed there could be no promises at all. It would be self-contradictory to say that everyone has the right to make a lying promise whenever he feels like it. It is essential to the nature of a promise that when one promises to do something he can generally be presumed to intend to do it. If one intended to carry out his "promises" no one could be said to have promised; the phrase "I promise" would lose its meaning — it could not be used to make a promise. And since the act therefore could not be right for everyone, it would not be right for anyone, at least without a special reason. But it

---

[9]*Grundlegung*, Paton 54-5, Abbott 48-9. Cf. 19 (Abbott 24): "I can indeed will to lie, but I can by no means will a universal law of lying; for by such a law there could properly be no promises at all, since it would be futile to profess a will for future action to others who would not believe my profession or who, if they did so over-hastily, would pay me back in like coin; and consequently my maxim, as soon as it was made a universal law, would be bound to annul itself."

does not at all follow that it is *always* wrong to lie or make a false promise. All that Kant has shown is that it is generally wrong (and surely this is enough). He has not shown that *no matter what the circumstances*, the supposition that everyone could make a lying promise in those circumstances would have this consequence. But this is what would have to be shown in order to show that lying, or false promising, is always wrong, no matter what the circumstances. And the fact is that this cannot be shown. For it is possible to imagine circumstances such that everyone may make a false promise in those circumstances without thereby making "promising, and the very purpose of promising, itself impossible," either in those circumstances or in general. Indeed, it would be self-contradictory to maintain that lying is always, and not just generally, wrong, *because*, as I have already argued, *the reasons in terms of which the rule is established are the very same reasons which, in certain circumstances, would suffice to override it.*

Now the case in which it is proposed to tell a lie in order to save an innocent person from harm is precisely of this type. The circumstances of the case have already been sufficiently described. . . . But to make it more precise, so that it cannot be said that one has the alternative of refusing to speak at all, let us imagine that the situation is the following. A is hiding in B's house. The murderer arrives and asks B, who happens at the moment to have C for company, whether A is in the house, and says that if B does not answer he and C will be killed. B can do one of three things. He can tell the truth, in which event A will be murdered; he can refuse to answer, in which event he and C, who is just as innocent as A, will be murdered; or he can tell a lie calculated to save the life of A, as well as his own and C's. Now the question Kant should have raised in his treatment of this question is, "Could it be willed to be a universal law that everyone should lie in this sort of situation?" But he did not in fact do this. Instead of raising such a question, he simply assumed that his previous applications of the categorical imperative established the duty of veracity as "an *unconditional duty* which holds in all circumstances." Instead of applying the categorical imperative to these particular circumstances, he applied this hard and fast rule. There is no process of reasoning by which it can be deduced from this that the categorical imperative is somehow defective. What is defective is the way Kant used it. What is more, the result of applying the categorical imperative to this sort of situation would be quite different from what both Kant and his critics so uncritically assumed. For it would not be self-contradictory or self-defeating for everyone to lie in the specified circumstances. And the question is about lying *in the specified circum-*

stances, not about lying in general. Since this is the case, supposing everyone to lie in a similar situation, the lie would be self-defeating— the murderer would fail to believe it—only if the murderer knew what the circumstances were, that is to say, only if he knew that his victim was in the house. But if he knew this the whole question would not arise in the first place. In addition, it should be noted that what it is proposed be done in this situation is to save an innocent man from harm by telling a lie to a murderer. The question "Could it be willed to be a universal law that everyone should lie in order to save an innocent man from harm?" practically answers itself. There is more ground for saying that it is impossible to will the opposite.

.

Rule-Utilitarianism

John Hospers

Rule-Utilitarianism and Objections To It

The batter swings, the ball flies past, the umpire yells "Strike three!" The disappointed batter pleads with the umpire, "Can't I have four strikes just this once?" We all recognize the absurdity of this example. Even if the batter could prove to the umpire's satisfaction that he would be happier for having four strikes this time, that the spectators would be happier for it (since most of the spectators are on his side), that there would be little dissatisfaction on the side of the opposition (who might have the

From *Human Conduct: An Introduction to the Problems of Ethics*, pp. 315-23, 326-28, by John Hospers, © 1961 by Harcourt Brace Jovanovich, Inc. and reprinted by permission of Harcourt Brace Jovanovich, Inc. and Rupert Hart-Davis Ltd.

game clinched anyway), and that there would be no effect on future base-ball games, we would still consider his plea absurd. We might think, "Per-haps baseball would be a better game—i.e., contribute to the greatest total enjoyment of all concerned—if four strikes were permitted. If so, we should change the rules of the game. But until that time, we must play baseball according to the rules which are now the accepted rules of the game."

This example, though only an analogy, gives us a clue to the kind of view we are about to consider—let us call it *rule-utilitarianism*. Briefly stated (we shall amplify it gradually), rule-utilitarianism comes to this: Each act, in the moral life, falls under a *rule*; and we are to judge the rightness or wrongness of the act, not by *its* consequences, but by the consequences of its universalization—that is, by the consequences of the adoption of the *rule* under which this act falls. This is the interpretation of Kant's categorical imperative which we promised . . . to discuss later—an interpretation which differs from Kant in being concerned with conse-quences, but retains the main feature which Kant introduced, that of universalizability.

Thus: The district attorney may do more good in a particular case [one in which he knows that a crime-prone person is innocent of the crime charged] by sitting on the evidence, but even if this case has no consequences for future cases because nobody ever finds out, still, the general policy or *practice* of doing this kind of thing is a very bad one; it uproots one of the basic premises of our legal system, namely that an innocent person should not be condemned. Our persistent conviction that it would be wrong for him to conceal the evidence in this case comes *not* from the conviction that concealing the evidence will produce less good—we may be satisfied that it will produce more good in this case—but from the conviction that the *practice* of doing this kind of thing will have very bad consequences. In other words, "Conceal the evidence when you think that it will produce more happiness" would be a bad rule to follow, and it is because this *rule* (if adopted) would have bad consequences, not because *this act* itself has bad consequences, that we condemn the act.

The same applies in other situations: . . . Perhaps I can achieve more good, . . . [in the case of a student who requests a higher grade than he deserves in order to get into medical school], by changing the student's grade, but the consequences of the general practice of changing students' grades for such reasons as these would be very bad indeed; a graduate school or a future employer would no longer have reason to believe that the grade-transcript of the student had any reference to his real achieve-ment in his courses; he would wonder how many of the high grades resulted from personal factors like pity, need, and irrelevant appeals by the student to the teacher. . . .

There are many other examples of the same kind of thing. If during a water shortage there is a regulation that water should not be used to take baths every day or to water gardens, there will be virtually no bad consequences if only *I* violate the rule. Since there will be no discernible difference to the city water supply and since my plants will remain green and fresh and pleasant to look at, why shouldn't I water my plants? But if everyone watered his plants, there would not be enough water left to drink. My act is judged wrong, not because of *its* consequences, but because the consequences of everyone doing so would be bad. If I walk on the grass where the sign says, "Do not walk on the grass," there will be no ill effects; but if everyone did so it would destroy the grass. There are some kinds of act which have little or no effect if any one person (or two, or three) does them but which have very considerable effects if everyone (or even just a large number) does them. Rule-utilitarianism is designed to take care of just such situations.

Rule-utilitarianism also takes care of situations which are puzzling in traditional utilitariansm, situations which we have already commented on, namely, the secrecy with which an act is performed. "But no one will ever know, so my act won't have any consequences for future acts of the same kind," the utilitarian argued; and we felt that he was being somehow irrelevant, even immoral: that if something is wrong when people know about it, it is just as wrong when done in secret. Yet this condition *is* relevant according to traditional utilitarianism, for if some act with bad consequences is never known to anyone, this ignorance does mitigate the bad consequences, for it undeniably keeps the act from setting an example (except, of course, that it may start a habit in the agent himself). Rule-utilitarianism solves this difficulty. If I change the student's grade in secret, my act is wrong, in spite of its having almost no consequences (and never being known to anyone else), because if I change the grade and don't tell anyone, how do I know how many other teachers are changing their students' grades without telling anybody? It is the result of the *practice* which is bad, not the result of my single action. The result of the practice is bad whether the act is done in secret or not: the result of the practice of changing grades in secret is just as bad as the results of the practice done in full knowledge of everyone; it would be equally deleterious to the grading system, equally a bad index of a student's actual achievement. In fact, if changing grades is done in secret, this in one way is worse; for prospective employers will not know, as they surely ought to know in evaluating their prospective employees, that their grades are not based on achievement but on other factors such as poverty, extra-curricular work load, and persuasive appeal.

Rule-utilitarianism is a distinctively twentieth century amendment of the utilitarianism of Bentham and Mill, often called *act-utilitarianism*. ... Since this pair of labels is brief and indicates clearly the contents of the theories referred to, we prefer these terms to a second pair of labels, which are sometimes used for the same theories: *restricted utilitarianism*, as opposed to *unrestricted* (or *extreme*, or *traditional*) *utilitarianism*. (Whether or not Mill's theory is strictly act-utilitarianism is a matter of dispute. Mill never made the distinction between act-utilitarianism and rule-utilitarianism, and his doctrine has always been interpreted as being act-utilitarianism. This is the interpretation taken by G. E. Moore in his very precise account of act-utilitarianism in Chapters 1 and 2 of his *Ethics*. Some of Mill's examples, however, have to do not with individual acts but with general principles and rules of conduct. Mill and Bentham were both legislators, interested in amending the laws of England into greater conformity to the utilitarian principle; and to the extent that Mill was interested in providing a criterion of judging rules of conduct rather than individual acts, he may be said to have been a rule-utilitarian.)

Much more must be said before the full nature of the rule-utilitarian theory becomes clear. To understand it better, we shall consider some possible questions, comments, and objections that can be put to the theory as thus far stated.

1. Doesn't the same problem arise here that we discussed in connection with Kant, the problem of *what* precisely we are to universalize? Every act can be put into a vast variety of classes of acts; or, in our present terminology, every act can be made to fall under many different general rules. Which rule among this vast variety are we to select? We can pose our problem by means of an imaginary dialogue referring back to Kant's ethics and connecting it with rule-utilitarianism:

A: Whatever may be said for Kant's ethics in general, there is one principle of fundamental importance which must be an indispensable part of every ethics—the principle of universalizability. If some act is right for me to do, it would be right for all rational beings to do it; and if it is wrong for them to do it, it would be wrong for me too.

B: If this principle simply means that nobody should make an exception in his own favor, the principle is undoubtedly true and is psychologically important in view of the fact that people constantly do make exceptions in their own favor. But as it stands I can't follow you in agreeing with Kant's principle. Do you mean that if it is wrong for Smith to get a divorce, it is also wrong for Jones to do so? But this isn't so. Smith may be hopelessly incompatible with his wife, and they may be far better off apart, whereas Jones may be reconcilable with his wife (with some mutual effort) and a divorce in his case would be a mistake. Each case must be judged on its own merits.

A: The principle doesn't mean that if it's right for one person, A, to do it, it is therefore right for B and C and D to do it. It means that if it's right for one person to do it, it is right for anyone *in those circumstances* to do it. And Jones isn't in the same circumstances as Smith. Smith and his wife would be better off apart, and Jones and his wife would be better off together.

B: I see. Do you mean *exactly* the same circumstances or *roughly* the same (similar) circumstances?

A: I think I would have to mean exactly the same circumstances; for if the circumstances were not quite alike, that little difference might make the difference between a right act (done by Smith) and a wrong act (done by Jones). For instance, if in Smith's case there are no children and in Jones's case there are, this fact may make a difference.

B: Right. But I must urge you to go even further. Two men might be in exactly the same *external* circumstances, but owing to their *internal constitution* what would be right for one of them wouldn't be for the other. Jones may have the ability to be patient, impartial, and approach problems rationally, and Smith may not have this ability; here again is a relevant difference between them, although not a difference in their external circumstances. Or: Smith, after he reaches a certain point of fatigue, would do well to go fishing for a few days—this would refresh and relax him as nothing else could. But Jones dislikes fishing; it tries and irritates and bores him; so even if he were equally tired and had an equally responsible position, he would not be well advised to go fishing. Or again: handling explosives might be all right for a trained intelligent person, but not for an ignorant blunderbuss. In the light of such examples as these, you see that under the "same circumstances" you'll have to include not only the external circumstances in which they find themselves but their own internal character.

A: I grant this. So what?

B: But now your universalizability principle becomes useless. For two people never *are* in exactly the same circumstances. Nor can they be: if Smith were in exactly the same circumstances as Jones, including all his traits of character, his idiosyncracies, and his brain cells, he would *be* Jones. You see, your universalizability principle is inapplicable. It would become applicable only under conditions (two people being the same person) which are self-contradictory,—and even if not self-contradictory, you'll have to admit that two exactly identical situations never occur; so once again the rule is inapplicable.

A: I see your point; but I don't think I need go along with your conclusion. Smith and Jones should do the same thing only if their situation or circumstances are the same in certain *relevant respects*. The fact that Jones is wearing a white shirt and Smith a blue one, is a difference of circumstances, but, surely, an *irrelevant* difference, a difference that for moral purposes can be ignored. But the fact that Smith and his wife are emotionally irreconcilable while Jones and his wife could work things out, would be a morally relevant circumstance.

B: Possibly. But how are you going to determine which differences are relevant and which are not?

Kant . . . never solved this problem. He assumed that "telling a lie" was morally relevant but that "telling a lie to save a life" was not; but he gave no reason for making this distinction. The rule-utilitarian has an answer.

Suppose that a red-headed man with one eye and a wart on his right cheek tells a lie on a Tuesday. What rule are we to derive from this event? Red-headed men should not tell lies? People shouldn't lie on Tuesdays? Men with warts on their cheeks shouldn't tell lies on Tuesdays? These rules seem absurd, for it seems so obvious that whether it's Tuesday or not, whether the man has a wart on his cheek or not, has nothing whatever to do with the rightness of his action—these circumstances are just *irrelevant*. But this is the problem: how are we going to establish this irrelevance? What is to be our criterion?

The criterion we tried to apply in discussing Kant was to make the rule more *specific:* instead of saying, "This is a lie and is therefore wrong," as Kant did, we made it more specific and said, "This is a lie told to save a life and is therefore right." We could make the rule more specific still, involving the precise circumstances in which this lie is told, other than the fact that it is told to save a life. But, now it seems, the use of greater specificity will not always work: instead of "Don't tell lies," suppose we say, "Don't tell lies on Tuesdays." The second is certainly more specific than the first, but is it a better rule? It seems plain that it is not—that its being a Tuesday, is, in fact, wholly irrelevant. Why?

"Because," says the rule-utilitarian, "there is no difference between the effects of lies told on Tuesdays and the effects of lies told on any other day. This is simply an empirical fact, and because of this empirical fact, bringing in Tuesday is irrelevant. If lies told on Tuesdays always had good consequences and lies told on other days were disastrous, then a lie's being told on a Tuesday would be relevant to the moral estimation of the act; but in fact this is not true. Thus there is no advantage in specifying the subclass of lies, 'lies told on Tuesdays.' The same is true of 'lies told by redheads' and 'lies told by persons with warts on their cheeks.' The class of lies can be made more specific—that is no problem—but not more *relevantly* specific, at least not in the direction of Tuesdays and redheads. (However, the class can be made more relevantly specific considering certain other aspects of the situation, such as whether the lie was told to produce a good result that could not have been brought about otherwise.)"

Consider by contrast a situation in which the class of acts can easily be made relevantly more specific. A pacifist might argue as follows: "I should never use physical violence in any form against another human being, since if everyone refrained from violence, we would have a warless world." There are aspects of this example that we cannot discuss now, but our present concern with it is as follows. We can break down violence into more specific types such as violence which is unprovoked, violence in defense of one's life against attack by another, violence by a policeman in catching a lawbreaker, violence by a drunkard in response to an imaginary affront. The effects of these subclasses of violence do differ greatly in their effects upon society. Violence used by a policeman in apprehending a lawbreaker (at least under some circumstances, which could be spelled out) and violence used in preventing a would-be murderer from killing you, do on the whole have good effects; but the unprovoked violence of an aggressor or a drunkard does not. Since these subclasses do have different effects, therefore, it *is* relevant to consider them. Indeed, it is imperative to do so: the pacifist who condemns *all* violence would probably, if he thought about it, not wish to condemn the policeman who uses violent means to prevent an armed madman from killing a dozen people. In any event, the effects of the two subclasses of acts are vastly different; and, the rule-utilitarian would say, it is accordingly very important for us to consider them—to break down the general class of violent acts into more specific classes and consider separately the effects of each one until we have arrived at subclasses which cannot *relevantly* be made more specific.

How specific shall we be? Won't we get down to "acts of violence to prevent aggression, performed on Tuesdays at 11:30 P.M. in hot weather" and subclasses of that sort? And aren't these again plainly irrelevant? Of course they are, and the reason has already been given: acts of violence performed on Tuesdays, or at 11:30 P.M., or by people with blue suits, are no different in their effects from acts-of-violence-to-prevent-aggression done in circumstances other than these; and therefore these circumstances, though more specific, are not relevantly more specific. When the consequences of these more specific classes of acts differ from the consequences of the more general class, it is this specific class which should be considered; but when the consequences of the specific classes are not different from those of the more general class, the greater specificity is irrelevant and can be ignored.

The rule, then, is this: we should consider the consequences of the general performance of certain classes of actions only if that class contains within itself no subclasses, the consequences of the general practice of which would be either better or worse than the consequences of the class itself.

Let us take an actual example of how this rule applies. Many people, including Kant, have taken the principle "Thou shalt not kill" as admitting of no exceptions. But as we have just seen, such principles can be relevantly made more specific. Killing for fun is one thing, killing in self-defense another. Suppose, then, that we try to arrive at a general rule on which to base our actions in this regard. We shall try to arrive at that rule the general following of which will have the best results. Not to kill an armed bandit who is about to shoot you if you don't shoot first, would appear to be a bad rule by utilitarian standards; for it would tend to eliminate the good people and preserve the bad ones; moreover, if nobody resisted aggressors, the aggressor, knowing this, would go hog-wild and commit indiscriminate murder, rape, and plunder. Therefore, "Don't kill except in self-defense" (though we might improve this rule too) would be a better rule than "Never kill." But "Don't kill unless you feel angry at the victim" would be a bad rule, because the adoption of this rule would lead to no end of indiscriminate killing for no good reason. The trick is to arrive at the rule which, if adopted, would have the very best possible consequences (which includes, of course, the absolute minimum of bad consequences). Usually no simple or easily statable rule will do this, the world being as complex as it is. There will usually be subclasses of classes-of-acts which are relevantly more specific than the simple, general class with which we began. And even when we think we have arrived at a satisfactory rule, there always remains the possibility that it can relevantly be made more specific, and thus amended, with an increase in accuracy but a consequent decrease in simplicity.

To a considerable extent most people recognize this complexity. Very few people would accept the rule against killing without some qualifications. However much they may preach and invoke the rule "Thou shalt not kill" in situations where it happens to suit them, they would never recommend its adoption in all circumstances: when one is defending himsef against an armed killer, almost everyone would agree that killing is permissible, although he may not have formulated any theory from which this exception follows as a logical consequence. Our practical rule against killing contains within itself (often not explicitly stated) certain *classes of exceptions:* "Don't kill *except* in self-defense, in war against an aggressor nation, in carrying out the verdict of a jury recommending capital punishment." This would be a far better rule—judged by its consequences—than any simple one-line rule on the subject. Each of the classes of exceptions could be argued pro and con, of course. But such arguments would be empirical ones, hinging on whether or not the adoption of such classes of exceptions into the rule would have the maximum results in intrinsic good. (Many would argue, for example, that capital punishment achieves no good effects; on the other hand, few would contend that the man who pulls the switch at Sing Sing is committing a crime in carrying out the orders of the legal representatives of the state.) And there may always be other kinds of situations that we have not previously thought of, situations which, if incorporated into the rule, would improve the rule—that is, make it have better consequences; and thus the rule remains always open, always subject to further qualification if the addition of such qualification would improve the rule.

These qualifications of the rule are not, strictly speaking, *exceptions to* the rule. According to rule-utilitarianism, the rule, once fully stated, admits of no exceptions; but there may be, and indeed there usually are, numerous classes of exceptions *built into the* rule; a simple rule becomes through qualification a more complex rule. Thus, if a man kills someone in self-defense and we do not consider his act wrong, we are not making him an exception to the rule. Rather, his act *falls under* the rule — the rule that includes killing in self-defense as one of the classes of acts which is permissible (or, if you prefer, the rule that includes self-defense as one of the circumstances in which the rule against killing does not apply). Similarly, if a man parks in a prohibited area and the judge does not fine him because he is a physician making a professional call, the judge is not extending any favoritism to the physician; he is not making the physician an exception to the rule; rather, the rule (though it may not always be written out in black and white) includes within itself this recognized class of exceptions—or, more accurately still, the rule includes within itself a reference to just this kind of situation, so that the action of the judge in exonerating the physician is just as much an application of the rule (not an exception to it) as another act of the same judge in imposing a fine on someone else for the same offense.

We can now see how our previous remarks about acts committed in secret fit into the rule-utilitarian scheme. On the one hand, the rule "Don't break a promise except (1) under extreme duress and (2) to promote some very great good" is admittedly somewhat vague, and perhaps it could be improved by still further qualification; but at least it is much better than the simple rule "Never break promises." On the other hand, the rule "Don't break a promise except when nobody will know about it" is a bad rule: there are many situations in which keeping promises is important . . . , situations in which promises could not be relied on if this rule were adopted. That is why, among the circumstances which excuse you from keeping your word, the fact that it was broken in secret is not one of them—and for a very good reason: if this class of exceptions were incorporated into the rule, the rule's adoption would have far worse effects than if it did not contain such a clause. . . .

4. Can't there be, in rule-utilitarianism, a conflict of rules? Suppose you have to choose between breaking a promise and allowing a human life to be lost. . . . What would the rule-utilitarian say? Which rule are we to go by?

No rule-utilitarian would hold such a rule as "Never break a promise" or "Never take a human life." Following such rigid, unqualified rules would certainly not lead to the best consequences—for example, taking Hitler's life would have had better consequences than sparing him. Since such simple rules would never be incorporated into rule-utilitarian ethics to begin with, there would be no conflict between these rules. The rule-utilitarian's rule on taking human life would be of the form, "Do not take human life except in circumstances of types A, B, C . . ." and these circumstances would be those in which taking human life *would* have the best consequences. And the same with breaking promises. Thus, when the rules in question are fully spelled out, there would be no conflict.

In any event, if there were a conflict between rules, there would have to be a second-order rule to tell us which first-order rule to adopt in cases of conflict. Only with such a rule would our rule-utilitarian ethics be *complete,* i.e., made to cover every situation that might arise. But again such a second-order rule would seldom be simple. It would not say, "In cases of conflict between preserving a life and keeping a promise, always preserve the life." For there might always be kinds of cases in which this policy would not produce the best consequences: a president who has promised something to a whole nation or who has signed a treaty with other nations which depend on that treaty being kept and base their own national policies upon it, would not be well advised to say simply, "In cases of conflict, always break your word rather than lose one human life." In cases of this kind, keeping the promise would probably produce the best results, though the particular instance would have to be decided empirically. We would have to go through a detailed empirical examination to discover which rule, among all the rules we might adopt on the matter would have the best consequences if adopted.

5. Well then, why not just make the whole thing simple and say, "Always keep your promises except when breaking them will produce the most good," "Always conserve human life except when taking it will produce the most good"? In other words, "In every case do what will have the best consequences"—why not make this the Rule of Rules? To do so is to have act-utilitarianism with us once again; but why not? Is there anything more obvious in ethics than that we should always try to produce the most good possible?

"No," says the rule-utilitarian, "not if this rule means that we should always do the individual *act* that produces the most good possible. We must clearly distinguish rules from acts. 'Adopt the rule which will have the best consequences' is different from 'Do the act which will have the best consequences.' (When you say, 'Always do the most good,' this is ambiguous—it could mean either one.)" The rule-utilitarian, of course, recommends the former in preference to the latter; for if everyone were to do acts which (taken individually) had the best consequences, the result would *not* in every case be a policy having the best consequences. For example, my not voting but doing something else instead may produce better consequences than my voting (my voting may have no effect at all); your not voting will do the same; and so on for every individual, as long as most *other* people vote. But the results would be very bad, for if each individual adopted the policy of not voting, nobody would vote. In other words, the rule "Vote, except in situations where not voting will do more good" is a rule which, if followed, would *not* produce the best consequences.

Another example: The rule "Don't kill except where killing will do the most good"—which the act-utilitarian would accept—is not, the rule-utilitarian would say, as good a rule to follow as "Don't kill except in self-defense. . . ." (and other classes of acts which we discussed earlier). That is, the rule to prohibit killing except under special kinds of conditions specified in advance would do more good, if followed, than the rule simply to refrain except when not refraining will do more good. The former is better, not just because people will rationalize themselves into believing that what they want to do will produce the most good in a particular situation (though this is very important), but also because when there are certain standard classes of exceptions built into the rule, there will be a greater *predictability* of the results of such actions; the criminal will know what will happen if he is caught. If the law said, "Killing is prohibited except when it will do the most good," what could you expect? Every would-be killer would think it would do the most good in his specific situation. And would you, a potential victim, feel more secure or less secure if such a law were enacted? Every criminal would think that he would be exonerated even if he were caught, and every victim (or would-be victim) would fear that this would be so. The effects of having such a rule, then, would be far worse than the effects of having a general rule prohibiting killing, with certain classes of qualifications built into the rule.

There is, then, it would seem, a considerable difference between act-utilitarianism and rule-utilitarianism.

The Aristotelian Theory of Exceptions

Richard A. Wasserstrom

The Aristotelian Theory of Equity

That all decisions ought to be fully justified solely by an intuition of the justice of the decision is admittedly an extreme position. It is perhaps inaccurate even to attribute its advocacy to any particular legal philosopher. But there are two restricted or modified versions of the theory of particular justice which have been quite explicitly formulated and widely accepted. On the one hand, the *bifurcation theory of justice*, urged most

Reprinted from *The Judicial Decision: Toward a Theory of Legal Justification,* pp. 97-98, 105-13, 184-85, by Richard A. Wasserstrom with the permission of the publishers, Stanford: Stanford University Press; London: Oxford University Press. © 1961 by the Board of Trustees of the Leland Stanford Junior University.

consistently by Roscoe Pound, insists that there is a fundamental distinction between two kinds of cases, namely those which relate to matters of property and contract, and those which involve conflicts of human conduct and enterprises. The former class of cases should, Pound insists, be decided by appeal to rule; the latter class by appeal to intuition. The *Aristotelian theory of equity*, on the other hand, holds that legal rules ought to be used to decide cases of all kinds, but that within every class of cases there are some particular cases to which legal rules are *necessarily* inapplicable. . . .

The acceptance of an argument like Pound's is not uncommon. Far more usual, however, is the recourse to an argument based upon the thesis that rules cannot properly be employed to decide *all* cases of any *class*. There will always be, it is insisted, *some* members of any class for which the application of the desirable legal rule is inappropriate. Legal rules simply cannot take an adequate account of all cases of any kind; some cases must be decided by a direct appeal to considerations of justice.

Such a view has been accepted quite uncritically by almost all commentators upon and philosophers of the law as well as by many courts.[1] The *locus classicus* of this position is Chapter 10, Book v of the *Nicomachean Ethics*; in more recent sources, Aristotle's language is repeated with only a minimum of alteration. As stated by Aristotle and reiterated

---

[1]Cf., for instance, Frank, [*Law and the Modern Mind*], pp. 118-19, and Patterson, *Jurisprudence*, p. 582. Cf. also Salmond, *Jurisprudence*, p. 83: "For the law lays down general principles, taking of necessity no account of the special circumstances of individual cases in which such generality may work injustice. . . . In all such cases, in order to avoid injustice, it may be considered needful to go beyond the law, or even contrary to the law, and to administer justice in accordance with the dictates of natural reason."

For a judicial expression of the same view see *Berkel v. Berwind-White Coal Mining Co.*, 220 Pa. 65 (1908): "The whole system of equity jurisprudence is founded on the theory that the law, by reason of its universality, is unable to do justice between the parties, and equity, not being bound by common-law forms and pleadings, has more elasticity and can better reach this end" (p. 75).

Ehrlich seems to make a still stronger assertion along the same lines: "It is certain that one need not expect better or juster results from such technical decisions than from free ones. Generally speaking, it is undoubtedly much easier to decide a definite case correctly than to establish an abstract rule universally applicable for all imaginable cases; and surely it can hardly be maintained seriously that such a rule will invariably result in the fairest decision, even in those cases which nobody had thought of when the rule was made." (Ehrlich, "Judicial Freedom of Decision," in *Science of Legal Method*, p. 63.)

The dichotomy, as set up by Ehrlich, appears convincing. The difficult problem, however, concerns the ways, if any, in which knowing that a definite case has been decided correctly differs from formulating and applying a rule for that kind of case. If a case cannot be decided correctly without laying down a rule, then the argument advanced by Ehrlich seems less attractive. . . .

by subsequent philosophers, the justification for this hypothesis is, I submit, without substantial foundation. But deference to both its author and its widespread acceptance requires that the proposal be given careful consideration.

Aristotle begins by distinguishing between two kinds of justice: legal justice and some other form of justice with which equity is perhaps to be equated. This distinction is necessary because, says Aristotle, there is something about the generality of rules which makes it incorrect to identify completely justice with rules. The reason this is so

> is that all law is universal but about some things it is not possible to make a universal statement which shall be correct. In those cases, then, in which it is necessary to speak universally, but not possible to do so correctly, the law takes the usual case, though it is not ignorant of the possibility of error. And it is none the less correct; for the error is not in the law nor in the legislator but in the nature of the thing, since the matter of practical affairs is of this kind from the start . . . Hence the equitable is the just, and better than one kind of justice — not better than absolute justice but better than the error that arises from the absoluteness of the statement. And this is the nature of the equitable, a correction of law where it is defective owing to its universality. In fact this is the reason why all things are not determined by law, viz. that about some things it is impossible to lay down a law, so that a decree is needed.[2]

. . . There appear to be two possible interpretations of what Aristotle has in mind. On the one hand, the passage might be construed to be merely putting forth the view that there will always be some cases that will not have been envisioned ahead of time by a legislator. This might be what Aristotle means when he says: "When the law speaks universally, then, and a case arises on it which is not covered by the universal statement, then it is right, where the legislator fails us and has erred by oversimplicity, to correct the omission—to say what the legislator himself would have said had he been present, and would have put into his law if he had known."[3] The Swiss Civil Code appears to follow Aristotle's advice here. "The law must be applied in all cases which come within the letter or the spirit of any of its provisions. Where no provision is applicable, the judge shall decide according to existing Customary Law and, in default thereof, according to the rules which he would lay down

---

[2]Aristotle, *Nichomachean Ethics*, 1137b, 12-29.
[3]*Ibid.*, 20.

if he had himself to act as legislator."[4] If, in other words, a case arises for which there is no relevant legal rule, then the judge clearly must look to something other than the set of positive rules for the justification of his decision.

For example, there is not at present any relevant law on the subject of drivers' licenses for interspace vehicles. The legislator—and here it is immaterial whether he be the legislator *qua* legislator or the judge *qua* legislator—would quite understandably not have enacted such a law simply because there does not, at present, appear to be any need to regulate such a class of occurrences. And there doubtless is a limitless number of classes of cases which at any given time cannot be foreseen and therefore legislated about simply because the existence of any of their members has not yet been envisioned.

On the other hand, it is also apparent that this is not the real import of Aristotle's point. On the contrary, the first passage quoted above rests on quite a different supposition. It seems to depend upon the premise . . . that there are at least some situations that are *simply not amenable to general rules of any* kind. In at least three different places Aristotle comments on this point: "about some things it is not possible to make a universal statement which shall be correct"; "the error is not in the law nor in the legislator but in the nature of the thing"; "about some things it is impossible to lay down a law."

These passages, in turn, would once again appear to support two different interpretations. (1) Aristotle might mean that there are certain classes of acts or situations about which rules ought not to be laid down at all. The characteristics of some kinds of cases do not justifiably permit of that abstraction and classification necessary for the adjudication of particular cases by means of ordinary legal rules. Aristotle might, that is, be suggesting a theory very much like Pound's: There are fundamentally two different kinds of classes of cases.

(2) There is, however, another more plausible interpretation of these same statements. The passages appear to imply that for any given general rule which prescribes how any member of a class of cases is to be treated, there will always be some particular fact situation which is indisputably a member of that class of situations, but which nevertheless ought not to be treated in accordance with that law. This interpretation has been accepted by modern theorists as the explanation for the so-called hardship case.

---

[4]Swiss Civil Code, Article I. See also Cardozo, *The Nature of the Judicial Process*, pp. 142-43.

In many of the hardship cases some characteristic of the individual claimant's situation which indicates weakness (but which is legally irrelevant in private law under the principle of "equality before the law") arouses sympathy for him or her: The widow who bought from the banker her deceased husband's worthless note, giving her valuable promise; the poor city youth who found his precarious recreation on the springboard projecting over the river from the wealthy railroad's right-of-way; the poor manual worker who loyally crippled himself for life in order to save his employer from injury; a veteran of a recent war, seeking a desperately needed home for his family and himself, [who] made a contract on Sunday for the purchase of a house.[5]

It is this second interpretation of Aristotle which calls for careful analysis.

The most troublesome feature of the theory centers about the claim that the fault lies not in the general laws. Aristotle does not appear to argue that the law was improperly or incorrectly formulated, that, in other words, the legislator failed to take into account certain factors which should have been considered. Nor does he rest his claim upon the premise that there are certain borderline cases in which classification is extremely difficult and in which, therefore, there is always the possibility that an unjust result will be reached because the case was not in fact properly a member of the class controlled by the rule. The problem, in short, is neither one of insufficient legislative competence nor one of incorrect judicial application. Rather, the claim appears to be that regardless of the care with which any law may be drafted, it is not possible that it can adequately take into account all relevant cases.

If the latter interpretation is correct, the theory is bewildering simply because it is so difficult to envision a substantiating example. While one can think, for example, of hundreds of cases in which an "unjust" result might be reached by applying a given rule to a case, one cannot think of a single instance in which a rule could not be formulated that would cover the instant case and all other cases of the same kind in such a way as to produce a just result in all cases. If Aristotle is saying merely that *for any given set of rules*, it will probably happen that some unjust results will occur when these rules are applied in all relevant instances, then the thesis is unobjectionable. But if something more is meant, if it is insisted that the continual revision of the rules would still not alleviate the problem, then the theory is less intelligible. For it seems always theoretically possible to formulate a rule whose

---

[5]Patterson, p. 582.

classification would be sufficiently restrictive to exclude all cases in which an "unjust" result might be produced. Another way to make the same point is to observe that in theory to make an exception to a rule is simply to introduce two more restrictive rules in place of the original.

Reference to one of the "hardship cases" may help to clarify the issue. The case of Webb, the devoted employee, is typical.[6] Webb was at work on one of the upper floors of the Smith Company Lumber Mill. He was clearing the floor of scrap wood. The usual and accepted way of doing this was by dropping the wood down to the floor below. As he was just about to drop a 75-pound block of pine, Webb saw that his employer, J. Greely McGowin, was standing directly on the spot that would be hit by the block if it were to fall straight down. The only way by which Webb could prevent McGowin from being seriously injured was for him, Webb, to divert the block from its course of fall; and the only way he could reasonably do this was by falling to the ground with the block. This is precisely what he did. He saved McGowin from harm but only at the cost of inflicting serious injury upon himself. He was, in fact, badly crippled for the remainder of his life.

McGowin, understandably grateful, soon entered into an agreement with Webb whereby he promised to pay Webb $15 every two weeks for the remainder of Webb's life in gratitude for Webb's courageous act. McGowin did this up until the time of his death. His estate continued the payments for another three years and then stopped them even though Webb was still alive. The problem confronting the court when Webb brought suit to compel the estate to continue payment was this: "There was a rule of long standing which held that a promise is binding upon the promisor if and only if it is given in exchange for services which have yet to be performed or for a promise to perform some act in the future. In other words, the fact that Webb acted with no prior request from McGowin, coupled with McGowin's subsequent promise to pay Webb for his past injuries, amounted to a mere "past" or "moral" consideration, the kind of consideration which could not support a legal action to enforce performance of that promise.

Let it be assumed that Webb ought to be able to enforce McGowin's agreement and that an unjust result would be reached if he were not allowed to do so. Let it also be agreed that to apply the extant rule to this case would produce an unjust result. To grant these two premises is still not to grant Aristotle's point. Why, if it is unjust not to give legal effect to this agreement, is this not a *kind* of case for which a rule

---

[6]*Webb v. McGowin*, 27 Ala. App. 82 (1935).

could be formulated that would be capable of producing a just result if applied to all cases of this class? For example, a rule such as the following might be introduced: "Whenever an employee engaged in a proper course of conduct finds that the only way he can reasonably prevent serious injury to his employer is by injuring himself, and whenever a promise is made thereafter by the person saved from injury to pay that person for his injury, this promise is enforcible." It is difficult to find anything which *in theory* requires the inference that if this rule were to be applied to all members of the specified class, some unjust results would necessarily be produced. As will become evident in a moment, there may be weaknesses inherent in rules of this specificity; but the difficulties are practical rather than theoretical. The issue here is simply that there is nothing which *in principle* prevents a situation such as the one Webb found himself in from being treated as one of a definite class of situations. And if it can be treated as a member of one or more classes, then, again, there is nothing in principle that precludes the formulation of a rule which could produce just results when applied to every member of that class.

The plausibility of a view such as Aristotle's derives in part perhaps from a confusion between two different concepts — from the failure to distinguish what I shall call a law's *universality* from its *generality*. To say that a law is or should be *universal* is simply to assert that the law applies without exception to all the members of the class included within the scope of the law. To speak of the universality of law is to refer to that feature which renders the law applicable to every member of the specified class. A strong case can be made for the analytic truth of the proposition that all laws are universal in this sense.

The generality of a law is something quite different. To speak of a law's generality is to observe the degree to which the class which is governed by the law is discriminated from all other possible classes. The generality of a law is concerned, therefore, with the particular class which is named and controlled by the law; universality, on the other hand, is concerned with the way in which the law is to be applied to the members of the class. Universality is a formal characteristic; generality is a material one.

An adherence to this distinction permits more meaningful discussion of the Aristotelian thesis and its implications. For it becomes obvious that the most important problems it raises center about the generality rather than the universality of rules. That all laws should be universal seems evident; that all laws should be of *any particular* generality is far less certain. Two competing considerations are relevant to the question of what constitutes the desirable generality of ordinary rules of law.

First, if all rules of law were absolutely general, i.e., if they dictated the same result for every member of the class consisting of all persons, the number of substantively unjust results would undoubtedly be very great. For as was observed above, it is only as the generality of the rule is "contracted" that the chance of just results in every case increases. As more conditions are placed upon membership in the class controlled by the rule, it becomes increasingly unlikely that an "exceptional" case will arise.

Second, and serving to support the contrary hypothesis that legal rules should "expand" their generality, is the consideration that as rules become too specific their utility *qua* rules diminishes. That is, although the proposed rule for the Webb type of situation may be sufficiently "narrow" so that injustices will not result, it is also so specific that it enables prediction of very few cases. The issue here is wholly analogous to one raised earlier. Rules are useful because they enable one to predict a legal result in advance. But if the rule applies only to a very limited class, if its generality is minimal, then knowledge of the rule does not permit the accurate prediction of many cases. Concomitantly, a minimal generality requires — if prediction is to be possible — a proliferation of rules. Because each rule controls only a small class, many rules are needed to take account of all cases. A mastery of the content of a great number of rules becomes a precondition of successful prediction.

Thus in a different context, Aristotle's position is not without significance. Theoretically, the thesis is untenable. Given an indefinitely large number of rules there is no reason why all cases could not be decided justly by means of an appeal to rules. But as a practical matter, rules cannot become too specific and still fulfill their most important function as rules. The number of rules cannot be multiplied indefinitely without creating a comparable impairment of function. Thus if the rules of a legal system are to be general enough to function properly as rules, there is good reason to suppose that they might not be able to take an adequate account of all cases controlled by the rules. . . .

Before we leave the question of minimal generality one point deserves some mention. It has been argued by Patterson, among others, that the principle of "equality before the law" is at issue here; but it is difficult to see how the introduction of this principle clarifies or solves anything. For this principle, although doubtless commendable in the abstract, proves to have amazingly little content in concrete situations. What does it mean to say that people ought to be treated equally before the law? Does it mean that the only rules of law which are justifiable are those which apply indiscriminately to all persons? If so, then such a law is sufficiently rare as to be a curiosity. For almost every law, either explicitly or implicitly, makes exceptions for children, incompetents, sleep-walkers, and the like. In addition, almost all laws further circumscribe the class of persons who are to be treated in "equal" fashion by specifying the conditions that must be present before the law is to be applied. And here, too, very often these conditions include certain characteristics of possible litigants. For instance, there is generally one property law for good-faith purchasers and another for purchasers with notice; there may be one set of constitutional protections for aliens and another for citizens.

If, on the other hand, the principle of equality before the law imposes a weaker requirement upon justifiable laws — the requirement alluded to earlier that there be some reason for making the distinction made by the law — then appeal to the principle is simply not very helpful in any a priori fashion. Perhaps, for example, there is no good reason for making a rule which expressly recognizes that class of employees who have aided their employer, been injured, and subsequently received a promise of compensation from their grateful employer. Perhaps on balance such a "specialized" classification would be undesirable. But saying this is something quite different from asserting simply that the principle of "equality before the law" is necessarily violated whenever such a classification is made. Unless one is prepared to assert that all classifications, except those which include all human beings without exception, are inherently undesirable, an appeal to the principle of "equality before the law" is not by itself a forceful or convincing criticism of some "less inclusive" law. What must be shown is not the presence of a more selective classification, but rather the undesirability of making this kind of classification in this kind of case.

This does not mean that laws which make distinctions between persons on the basis of race, religion, place of origin, and the like cannot in most circumstances be condemned. This does not mean that laws which treat "equals unequally" are less abhorrent now than before. But it does mean that there may always be good reasons for making certain kinds of distinctions among persons. And it does not mean that it is more appropriate to criticize the reasons offered than just to appeal to the principle of "equality before the law." The fact that a law discriminates among persons does not make the law bad; the fact that the law discriminates badly does. A "bad" law should be shown to be "bad" on this latter ground.

IV

MORAL RESPONSIBILITY AND EXCUSES

Introduction

The Problems of Responsibility

A story is frequently told about the little boy who, having done some mischief, is threatened with punishment by his father. The boy cleverly seeks to avoid responsibility for his act by arguing that, given his naturally mischievous tendencies, he could not help doing what he did, and that therefore it would be unfair to punish him. The father, impressed but unconvinced by his son's argument, replies in turn that, given his own naturally righteous tendencies, he cannot help but spank him!

Undoubtedly the story could be embellished and prolonged. Did the conversation end at this point? Did the boy receive his punishment? Or did he raise other objections such as the following: "But is it ever just or right to hold a person responsible for something that he couldn't help doing?" "Do the words 'right' and 'wrong,' 'good' and 'bad,' 'just' and 'unjust' have any meaning in such a context?" "What good would punishment do anyway?" "What do you mean by saying that I'm 'responsible'?" "Can't I be 'excused' just this once?" These and a host of other questions suggest any number of ways in which the dialogue between father and son might go on if the patience of the one or the ingenuity of the other did not wear out.

Philosophers have persisted in raising just such questions long beyond the point where others have said, "Let's punish the rascal and be done with it!" Philosophical debates on these issues can, and have, extended over centuries. Without attempting to catalogue all the various issues which have ever been raised, or even all those contained in the selections in this chapter, let us try to put some of them in perspective. We shall organize the discussion by asking the following questions:

1. What is the connection, if any, between wrongdoing and responsibility?

2. What is the connection, if any, between responsibility and freedom?

3. What is the connection, if any, between freedom and excusability?

Wrongdoing and Responsibility

We have already considered in previous chapters many of the various ways one might determine whether an action is wrong, so it is unnecessary here to explain what might be meant by, or how one might go about, deciding that question. In any case, everyone is accustomed to making moral judgments regarding wrongdoing whether he carries around with him the baggage of an ethical theory or not. Also it can be taken for granted that everyone knows (or feels) that at least one condition for holding persons responsible is that they have done something wrong. The meaning of the term "responsibility" and whether wrongdoing is always a condition for assigning responsibility must now be discussed.

For our purposes, basically two meanings of the term "responsibility" need to be distinguished. One is the causal sense in which we might speak of an agent's being responsible for an injury. In this sense all we mean to assert by saying "he is responsible" is that "he did it," i.e., he *caused* the injury. We have seen previously (Part II) that Sartre often appears to employ this sense when speaking of a man as "the incontestable author of an event or of an object." The second main sense of "responsibility" is the sense in which we say that a person is liable for or deserving of some sort of penalty for his actions, whether it be punishment, blame, or economic loss. When we "hold a person responsible," we mean that we have judged him to be a proper subject of such treatment.

When an injury or wrongdoing occurs it is natural to make two inquiries: "Who did it?" and "Who, if anyone, is deserving of negative treatment as a result of it?" These questions, of course, correlate with the two notions of responsibility just defined. It is appropriate now to ask whether it follows that if a person is responsible in the first sense he is also responsible in the second sense and vice versa. It appears that neither inference follows. That is to say, it does not necessarily follow that if I cause an injury then I should be made to pay for it. I may have acted in self-defense or had some other perfectly good excuse. Nor if I am thought to be deserving of punishment or blame does it necessarily follow that I caused the injury. I may be held responsible for the misbehavior of my child or of an employee, although he, and not I, caused the injury. Persons have been punished "as examples" to others, and crime-prone persons have been "preventively detained." The point here is not that these are all assignments of responsibility of which we would approve. The point is simply that there is nothing *logically inconsistent* in the notion of holding a person responsible for an injury he himself did not cause, any more than there is anything *logically inconsistent* in the idea of starving oneself to death, although we might have good reasons, and moral ones too, for condemning those particular kinds of behavior.

But if this is so, we must inquire whether wrongdoing is always a moral, if not a logical, condition for responsibility. It is clear that I might be held or judged responsible in the first sense whether or not I commit a wrong or even an injury. If all that "responsible" means is "cause of," then whatever I do, whether it turns out to be injurious or beneficial, right or wrong, good or bad, I may be judged responsible. Thus wrongfulness is neither a necessary nor a sufficient condition of responsibility in this sense. But suppose I am held responsible in the second sense, i.e., I am judged to be deserving of some penalty. Must I not have done something wrong to merit this treatment, and would it be morally justifiable to punish, fine, or blame me if I were totally innocent?

Regarding this latter question there has been considerable dispute, and various theories have provided different answers to it. There is, first of all, what we may call the *retributivist* theory of responsibility, which insists that wrongdoing is a necessary condition for the infliction of any kind of penalty, whether it be a legal sanction for a legal wrong, or a moral sanction (blame in some form) for a moral wrong. It does not, of course, insist that it is a necessary *and* sufficient condition (one which states that if one has done wrong, then in all cases it would be a mistake not to penalize him) for there is always the possibility that despite the wrongfulness of his act, he is excusable, i.e., exempt from responsibility. Second, the classical *utilitarian* theory implies that the wrongfulness of a past act is not even a necessary condition for punishment or blame. What justifies the imposition of a sanction, according to the utilitarian, is not the wrongfulness of the act but whether the sanction, if applied, will serve to bring about more beneficial than harmful social consequences.

The debate between these two opposing theories, insofar as they concern the justification of punishment, is discussed by John Rawls in his article, "Two Concepts of Rules," a portion of which is reproduced in Part VII of this book. As he points out, a frequent criticism of utilitarianism is that theoretically it allows for the punishment of innocent persons. Rawls discusses in this context a practice or social institution which he calls "telishment," an arrangement whereby innocent persons are punished in order to promote the best interests of society. He then suggests why such a practice would be unjustified on rule-utilitarian grounds, however well or badly it fares with traditional utilitarianism.

In addition to these theories, which may be looked upon as general theories of responsibility rather than simply or more narrowly as theories of punishment in the manner in which Rawls considers them, two other accounts at least deserve mention here. One is simply the view that no judgments of responsibility at all are justified. As Rawls points out, probably only a very few persons have ever maintained this view with respect to punishment. Fewer still have probably maintained it with respect to responsibility generally. However, as we shall shortly see, it is a consequence of certain theories of human freedom. Briefly the argument is that if man has no freedom, then the terms "right" and "wrong" have no meaning, nor can he be responsible for his acts. Some fatalists have in fact alleged that man is no more than a robot.

Finally there is a theory which is something of a compromise. It insists that we distinguish sharply between punishment (and other legally or socially applied sanctions) and personal (or moral) blame. We have been speaking so far of responsibility in the sense of liability to punishment, economic loss, or blame, and referring to these forms of treatment more or less indifferently. But according to this theory, which dates as far back as Plato, but which also has modern supporters among psychoanalytically minded philosophers, the moral wrongfulness of an act (if it even makes sense to speak of right or wrong, good or bad, in this connection) in no way justifies blaming a person for his act, nor does a consideration of its beneficial or detrimental social consequences justify personal blame or responsibility. Plato argued that since no one voluntarily does what he knows to be wrong, then if he does wrong, it must be because of ignorance, and ignorance excuses. The psychoanalytic philosophers argue somewhat differently, but to the same end. They argue that we are controlled by certain unconscious motives which determine our personalities in such a way that we never could have helped doing what we did. Personal blame and personal responsibility are thus regarded by them as insidious.

Neither Plato nor the others, however, reject punishment, understood as the non-personal imposition of unwanted treatment. Society has a right to protect itself against wrongdoers (or more neutrally, producers of injurious consequences). As might be expected, they regard remedial or corrective treatment rather than vindictive or retributive punishment as the only justifiable social sanction. On this theory, then, from the standpoint of human personality we are all innocent and non-responsible. From the standpoint of society, however, the wrong we do, or the injury we cause, though personally innocent, *is* relevant to a judgment of responsibility.

Both of these latter theories, let us call them the theory of non-responsibility and the theory of non-personal responsibility, are based on a definite position regarding whether a man is free to will his actions. Our critical discussion of them must await our next question concerning the connection, if any, between responsibility and freedom.

Responsibility and Freedom

Most philosophers would agree, quite independently of the question whether wrongdoing is a necessary condition of responsibility, that an act must have been freely done in order for someone to be held responsible for it. It just does not make sense to hold a person responsible for something he "couldn't help doing." However, philosophers have differed greatly regarding the kind of "freedom" that constitutes a necessary condition for responsibility. Some argue that only a "freedom of action" is required; that is to say, I must be able to do what I choose or will to do. If there are no obstacles to my action then I am free; otherwise not. In this sense, if I choose to walk, and cannot because I am chained to a wall or crippled in both legs, then I am "unfree" or "constrained." One who lacks such disabilities is "free" to walk if he chooses to do so. This notion of freedom is to be contrasted with the "freedom of will." It is not enough, some say, that I am not prevented from acting by either external or internal hindrances, I must also be able to freely will or choose. In this sense, if something (either present or past circumstances, physical or psychological conditions, or anything else) determines my choices, or how I exercise my will, then I am unfree even if nothing otherwise prevents my performing the action.

The so-called free-will problem, insofar as it relates to the assignment of reponsibility, may be stated in terms of this distinction. "Must I be able to freely will my actions in order to be held responsible for them, or is it only necessary that I be free to do them?" Those who maintain that I must be said to have "free will" are generally called "indeterminists." Those who reject the notion of "free will," at least insofar as it entails the idea of an uncaused volition, are generally known as "determinists." Among both groups, however, are shades of opinion. Among indeterminists we can and should distinguish "extreme indeterminists" from "libertarians," and among determinists we can and should distinguish "fatalists" from what we shall call "modified determinists."

Briefly the differences between these four positions are as follows. An extreme indeterminist (e.g. Sartre) holds that man is "absolutely" free, i.e., at any time and under any circumstances a person can always choose to oppose his hereditary, circumstantial, and other influences. A libertarian (e.g. Campbell) holds a more modified position. He holds that choices of action are not completely or always determined by antecedent factors. That is to say, a man may often be determined by heredity, for instance, but not always. He may at crucial moments of decision (he calls them "situations of moral temptation") choose contrarily. He claims that an act is free only if (1) the person is the sole cause or author of it, and (2) his will is capable of being exercised in alternative ways (i.e., he "could have done otherwise" in a categorical sense, not merely in the hypothetical sense that if he had been someone else, or if he had wanted to, he could have done otherwise).

The extreme determinist, or fatalist, is one who not only denies that wills are ever uninfluenced, but specifically asserts that our choices are ineffectual in determining what will in fact occur anyway. Thus a person's death is looked on as a "fixed event." Nothing one does or chooses to do will prevent or alter the manner of its occurrence. If a fatalist is thoroughly consistent, he regards *all* events in the same way, as being immune to change by human choice. For him even the freedom of action, i.e., the freedom to act as one chooses, is incompatible with determinism and is in fact nothing but an illusion.

Historically there have been many types of fatalism. Many are theological in character: the view that God has "pre-ordained," "pre-determined," or "pre-destined" the whole course of events. Others are metaphysical: the world just happens to be the kind it is, namely, one allowing for no independent human interference. Freudian psychology, with its claim that our future behavior is almost completely molded by infantile experiences, and behaviorism, with its claim that human conduct is nothing but the product of external stimuli, suggest kinds of psychological fatalism.

Modified determinists, such as McTaggart, are not fatalists. True, they reject the idea that our wills are ever uninfluenced, but they insist that our choices do make a difference in what occurs and what we do. Our choices are causes as much as our heredity, environment, or characters are causes. They make a difference in what happens, but they do not make the whole difference by any means. Furthermore, although modified determinists cannot accept the notion of "free will" insofar as that notion entails the idea of an uncaused volition, they nonetheless accept the view that freedom of action is compatible with the idea of universal causal determination. Our acts are free, according to this way of thinking, insofar as they are determined primarily by one's own wants and rationally deliberate choices. That is to say, we are free when we are able to do what we want and choose to do. We are unfree when we are compelled either by external forces or by internal psychological states or dispositions to do what we do not want to do or ordinarily would not choose to do.

Fatalism and extreme indeterminism are the most difficult positions to defend against common sense which insists against fatalism that our decisions do have something to do with the course of our lives, and against extreme indeterminism that other factors besides our wills do seem to have a determining influence on what we do. Both libertarianism and modified determinism take account of both these objections, but each has to deal with others.

Against modified determinism the following kinds of argument are made. (1) If determinism is true, value judgments and judgments of obligation (i.e., judgments concerning what one ought to do) become meaningless. (2) If I could not have willed otherwise than in fact I did (i.e., if I had only freedom of action and not freedom of will), it makes no sense to praise, blame, or punish me for the act I performed. (3) If my act was determined by something other than my own self, then there is no place for feelings of shame or remorse.

Against libertarianism, the following kinds of argument are brought. (1) If no reasons (i.e., causal explanations) can be given to explain why a man wills one act rather than another, then the whole notion of a free "act of a self" is unintelligible. (2) If a man's formed character is not the cause of his behavior, then there is no point in praising, blaming, or punishing him. (3) If a man's behavior is undetermined, then it must be impossible to predict his behavior.

The selections by McTaggart and Campbell amplify these types of argument and offer definite answers to them. The reader should correlate the questions with the answers and attempt to evaluate them.

The articles by Taylor and Matson present two special problems, one which confronts the determinist and one which is bound to trouble any would-be libertarian. The problem raised by Taylor is whether a determinist can consistently claim to deliberate about what to do. Matson asks whether any doctrine of causality, including that presupposed by the libertarian, entails any consequences with regard to moral responsibility that differ from those of any other view.

It is best for the reader to examine the respective arguments themselves, but perhaps a few comments are in order here so that certain misunderstandings might be avoided. It should be noted that neither Taylor nor Matson are arguing for or against determinism or libertarianism. They are both attempting to raise issues which, while not resolving the entire problem, are intended to throw a new and different light on it. Taylor, for instance, challenges a rather common practice of confusing deliberation with inference, speculation, and prediction. Once these are properly distinguished, he claims, it becomes clear that if one believes that acts are wholly determined, then it is also impossible to deliberate about what one is going to do. From this conclusion, he does not draw the consequence that determinism is false because most people think that at times they deliberate. Nor does he claim that in fact it is impossible to believe in determinism and also to believe that one deliberates (many a philosopher holds inconsistent beliefs). All he claims is that the two beliefs are logically inconsistent. From this claim, two further consequences follow which affect the reformulation of the problem: (1) Either deliberation is an illusion and determinism is true, or (2) deliberation is not an illusion and determinism is false. Taylor does not here attempt to decide which is the case. He does, however, claim to have eliminated one common objection to the possibility of free choice, and that is the argument from foreknowledge. If men do perform deliberate acts, then, he argues, no one, not even God, could have foreknowledge of what that future act will be.

Matson, similarly, does not undertake a frontal assault on either determinism or indeterminism or attempt a defense of either. Instead he inquires whether any theory of the causal relation (or "difference-making relation") between an agent and his act can ever be said to validate an assignment of moral responsibility. He rejects the "necessitarian" claim that because our acts are wholly determined by antecedent causes, it makes sense to punish a person for their good effects. ("Calling a man morally responsible" and "saying that probably punishing him will have a good effect" are not the same.) He also rejects what he calls the positivist claim that moral responsibility for moral wrongdoing is justified just so long as the agent was not constrained. This simply does not follow, he says. And he rejects the libertarian view that moral responsibility is justified insofar as it can be shown that the act emanated from a non-empirical Self with a power or ability to choose otherwise in total independence of the circumstances. For either this power is acquired or innate. If innate, then one cannot be held responsible for what one was born with. If acquired, then the power to acquire the ability is innate or acquired. If this is innate then the person is not responsible; if acquired, then we are committed to a vicious regress, and so are left with no basis for justifying assignments of moral responsibility.

From these conclusions Matson does not claim that libertarianism or any of the other views are necessarily false. He does think, however, that he has shown that any attempt, including that of the libertarian, to base moral responsibility on a general theory of causality is irrelevant to the problem of ascribing moral responsibility. Does this mean that the whole notion of moral responsibility is "vacuous," "a mere fiction," "a pernicious mode of thought"? Matson suggests that it is, but he also suggests that he favors what we previously called the "theory of non-personal responsibility," which finds a place for punishment in the scheme of things, but none for blame. The reader should try to determine for himself whether this is what Matson means by saying that "the concept of 'moral responsibility' is vacuous, at any rate when taken in its usual sense."

Freedom and Excusability

Let us look at Matson's thesis from another point of view. He has suggested that so long as some kind of causal or "difference-making" relationship must be assumed as a necessary condition for human actions, the consequence is that the notion of free will is irrelevant to the assignment of moral reponsibility. Instead of looking at free will as a necessary condition of responsibility, let us ask whether its absence or negation is a ground of excuse.

Certainly the extreme determinist (or fatalist) would agree that it is. Since he holds that man is never the sole determining cause of his actions and that his decisions never make any real difference in what occurs, he concludes that there is no such thing as moral responsibility, or to put it in terms of excusability, that he is totally "excusable."

The extreme indeterminist would also agree that the absence of freedom (free will) would negate responsibility and provide a ground of excuse. The only difference between these extreme positions regarding this matter is that the extreme indeterminist maintains that we are always in control of our acts and decisions, i.e., we are "absolutely free," never "unfree," and so always responsible. As Sartre says, "Absolute responsibility . . . is simply the logical requirement of the consequences of our freedom." He concludes that man is totally "without excuse."

It would seem then that if Matson is correct, free will is not a necessary condition for the assignment of responsibility, but if either extreme determinism or extreme indeterminism are correct, then the absence of free will is a necessary condition for excusability (i.e., non-responsibility). But these positions are logically incompatible. In effect one asserts that free will is relevant to assignments or non-assignments of responsibility and the other position asserts that it is not.

But let us examine this disagreement a little further. When the extreme determinist argues that you cannot hold a person responsible because his acts are wholly determined, it is not at all clear why this must be so. It does seem to make sense to ask, Why not? If a man has committed an injury, even though he may not be *solely* the cause of it, why should he not be penalized for it, at least to the extent that he is in part the cause? Similarly, when the extreme indeterminist asserts that you can always hold a man responsible because his acts are absolutely free, it does nonetheless make sense to ask, Why so? After all, are there not some circumstances which at least limit the scope of our actions? (Even Sartre admits that "brute things . . . [like a rocky crag] can from the start limit our freedom of action.") But insofar as the extreme determinist and the extreme indeterminist reject both questions, or ignore them, as is more usually the case, it becomes apparent that they mean to assert not simply the position that free will or freedom is a *necessary* condition of responsibility (or the lack of freedom is a necessary condition of excusability) but rather that freedom (or the lack of it) is both a *necessary and a sufficient* condition of responsibility (or excusability).

The common sense position, the position of most philosophers, and certainly that of the law courts, is that besides freedom (in some sense) several other conditions must be met in order to hold a person responsible for his acts. These include, for example, a consideration of whether what was done was wrong, whether the person charged actually did it, and whether the agent was capable of reasonable behavior. If, in opposition to this view, both extreme determinists and extreme indeterminists hold that freedom is both a necessary and a sufficient condition of moral responsibility, then none of these other conditions is relevant to assignments of responsibility. If that seems implausible, then it is clear that both views must be rejected, and interestingly enough, they can be rejected for the very same reason.

We are left with two possible positions regarding free will as a condition of responsibility:

1. Freedom is a necessary but not a sufficient condition of responsibility.

2. Freedom is not even a necessary condition, i.e., it is totally irrelevant to moral responsibility.

Matson argues for the second view. His arguments must be evaluated by the reader on their merits. Both modified determinism (McTaggart's view) and libertarianism (Campbell's view) accept the first position, but with a difference. Both agree that freedom in some sense is a necessary but not sufficient condition of responsibility, but each defines freedom differently. Insofar as "freedom" is defined as "free will" by the libertarian, the modified determinist rejects this kind of freedom as a necessary condition of responsibility, and the lack of it as grounds for excuse.

In order to uphold the view that freedom is a necessary condition of moral responsibility, but at the same time to sidestep the controversy between libertarians and determinists as to whether freedom means "free will," some philosophers have attempted a linguistic solution of the problem. According to this view, it is a necessary condition for holding someone responsible that he "could have acted otherwise." But by this all we need to mean is that "he could or would have . . . *if* he had chosen otherwise; or *if* circumstances were different; or *if* he had a different character or set of abilities." Both Campbell and Matson find reasons for rejecting this approach, and the reader should examine them.

In any case, and regardless of how one resolves the specific question of whether freedom in some sense (as "free will," as "freedom of action," as "freedom from constraint," or hypothetically as "would have or could have . . . if") is a necessary condition of moral responsibility, it is clear that so long as we do not regard it as the *sole* (i.e., necessary and sufficient) condition, the following question will remain to be answered by libertarians, modified determinists, and linguistic philosophers alike: "Why are some sets of circumstances or situations grounds of excuse, whereas other situations in which persons 'could have done otherwise' are not grounds of excuse?" Or as Nowell-Smith puts it: "Why [do] some 'would . . . ifs' excuse while others do not?" For example, ignorance sometimes excuses and at other times does not. Why?

It is not enough for the determinist to say that in the case in which ignorance is an excuse, the agent was prevented from knowing what he should have known or needed to know in order to avoid the injury, and in the case of no excuse, no such constraint was present. To be sure, if absence of freedom (in the determinist sense) is a necessary condition of excusability, then we understand his reasoning regarding the case in which the excuse is granted. But what of the case in which an excuse is not granted? To say that not being under constraint is the reason for not excusing him would be to treat freedom as a sufficient as well as a necessary condition for holding him responsible. And this the modified determinist does not claim to do. It is precisely this difference of opinion which, in part at least, distinguishes him from the fatalist. So he must come up with another and different reason which justifies not excusing him besides the absence of constraint.

So it is with the libertarian. It is understandable that he too would treat ignorance as an excuse if it could be shown that in the circumstances his will was not free (e.g., if the person was mentally incapable of learning). But again, what of the case where we do not excuse ignorance? The mere fact that he could have freely willed to learn what he needed to know is insufficient to account for holding him responsible. Other reasons need to be given, unless, again to repeat the predicament the determinist is also confronted with, we treat freedom as both a necessary and a sufficient condition of responsibility. The libertarian, however, no more subscribes to this principle than the modified determinist does.

Nowell-Smith's comments on this matter of excusability are expressed in term of the linguistic approach to the problem, but they nonetheless present relevant considerations even for the libertarian and determinist. He discusses the various sorts of reasons that can be given for excusing and not excusing, and does so in relation to the particular sorts of situations in which the question of excusability arises. Each of the pleas for exemption from responsibility deserves careful study.

A Defense of Determinism

J. M. E. McTaggart

Free Will—Does It Exist?

. . . A man is free in any action, if his choice of that action is not completely determined. The supporters of this view do not, I conceive, maintain that a man can ever act without a motive, nor do they consider that the existence of a motive is incompatible with freedom. But if the motive completely determined the act — either because there was no other motive, or because it was determined to be more effective than any other — then the act would not be freely done. It is essential for freedom that there should be motives prompting to different courses, between

From J. M. E. McTaggart, *Some Dogmas of Religion* (London: Edward Arnold Ltd., 1906), chapter V, by permission of the publisher.

which the agent chooses. And it is essential that this choice should not be determined. We may call this freedom of indetermination. My object in this chapter is to consider whether it exists.

Freedom of indetermination is commonly spoken of as Free Will. This seems to be justified. If freedom were defined otherwise, the proper question might be 'Am I free to act?' not 'Am I free to will?' But, if freedom is to imply the absence of complete determination, it can only be the will that is free. The voluntary act is completely determined — in so far as it is not determined by outside circumstances it is determined by the volition on which it follows. No indeterminist would deny this. It is only the volition which is undetermined, and only the volition which is free. When an indeterminist says, for example, that a man has freely committed a murder, he means that he was free in willing to do it. Indeed, in so far as the will did not completely determine the act, as when a bullet meant for a tiger kills a man, the indeterminist would deny that the shooter had acted freely in killing the man.

The law of Causality asserts that every event is determined by previous events in such a way that, if the previous events are as they are, it is impossible that the subsequent event should not be as it is. If this was the only general principle valid as to causality, however, we should not be able to accept as valid any of the laws of science which deal with causation. For these are all general laws, which assert that whatever has a particular quality produces an effect with a particular quality. Thus it is said that all alcohol, taken in large quantities, produces intoxication. But claret differs from whisky, and the effects produced by drinking them are not completely alike, nor are the effects exactly the same with all men. In order to have any warrant for such generalizations we need the additional principle that for any quality, B, in an effect, there is always a quality A in the cause, of such a nature that every other cause which has the quality A produces an effect having the quality B. In other words, the knowledge that exactly similar causes will produce exactly similiar effects has no practical utility, since we could never know two causes to be exactly similar, even if it were possible that they should be so. What is required is the knowledge that partially similar causes will produce partially similar effects.

I do not propose to consider whether Causality and the Uniformity of Nature are valid of events other than volitions. To deny that they had any validity at all would involve almost complete scepticism, since no expectation of any future event would have the least justification, and all arguments for the existence of anything not perceived at the moment would be absolutely baseless. The indeterminist does not, as a rule, deny that all events except volitions must be completely determined by previous events. Indeed, all his arguments as to the goodness or badness of particular volitions imply that such volitions will result in consequences which will inevitably follow from them, unless interfered with by fresh volitions. He only maintains that volitions are not subject to the law of Causality in so far as to be themselves completely determined. . . .

Determinists, on the other hand, maintain that our volitions are as completely determined as all other events. From this it is generally, and I think correctly, held to follow that it would be ideally possible to deduce the whole of the future course of events from the present state of reality—though, of course, a mind enormously more powerful than ours would be required to do it.

We have now to consider the arguments advanced by indeterminists in favour of their contention that volitions are not completely determined. . . .

The argument from the judgement of obligation is perhaps the most usual argument for free will. It seems to me that it is also the strongest, though I cannot regard it as satisfactory. 'If the will is completely determined, judgements of obligation cannot be valid.' The first question which this suggests is the question whether judgements of obligation *are* valid.

I do not think that we need trouble to inquire how, if at all, the validity of judgements of obligation could be proved to any one who denied it — should such a person be found. Determinism has always, as a matter of fact, been defended, and, as I believe, can be successfully defended, on the basis that judgements of obligation are valid.

Let us, then, admit their validity. This does not, of course, mean that no such judgement is ever mistaken, but that there are possible judgements of obligation which would be valid when made, even if we have not as yet succeeded in our efforts to find them. Is this compatible with the truth of complete determination?

If the truth of complete determination were incompatible with the truth of any proposition logically presupposed in judgements of obligation, it is clear that it would be incompatible with the validity of those judgements, since they cannot be valid unless their presuppositions are true. Every judgement of obligation seems to me to have two such presuppositions. (*a*) Something is such that its existence would be good or bad.[1] (*b*) The person as to whom the judgement of obligation is passed

---

[1]When I use good and bad without any qualification, I do not mean only moral good and bad, but good and bad in the widest sense—that in which it may be said that happiness and beauty are good. I use virtuous and wicked as synonyms of moral good and bad, when the objects spoken of are volitions.

can exercise, by his will, some effect in determining the existence or non-existence of that thing. No one would say that a man ought to will the existence of anything unless the thing willed was judged to be such that its existence would be good. And, again, no man can will anything (though he may desire it) if he knows that he cannot possibly have any influence on the matter. I should not will that an eruption of Vesuvius should cease, though under certain circumstances I might desire it most passionately. And no sane man would say that I ought to will it, or blame me for not doing so. But if I were a magician, with powers so great that they might possibly stop an eruption, I might then will to stop it, and might possibly be morally bound to will it.

Would either of these presuppositions be necessarily false if complete determination were true? I cannot see that either of them would. Would the existence of anything cease to be good or bad because it was completely determined whether I should will its existence or not? Would my own possession of knowledge, or the satisfaction of my own hunger, or the relief of the distress of others, cease to be good because it was absolutely certain that I should will to bring them about, or because it was absolutely certain that I should not will to bring them about? Surely this cannot be maintained.

As to the second presupposition, it is clear that the complete determination of my will can make no difference to the question of the effect of my will on the result contemplated. Whether my will is completely determined or not, it is clear that I shall not learn classical Greek or satisfy my hunger unless I will to do so, while it is not improbable that I shall do both if I will to do them. Again, if I will to relieve the distress of others, it is at least possible that some distress will be relieved which would not have been relieved otherwise, and this is not in the least affected by the question whether my will is inevitably determined to take the course which it does take.

We pass from the presuppositions of the judgement to the judgement itself. Is a volition to produce a good result, or the man who makes it, to be less approved, is the volition to produce a bad result, or the man who makes it, to be less condemned, because the volition is completely determined? It does not seem to me that this should make any difference to the approval or condemnation. We approve or condemn whatever tends to produce good or evil results, without further consideration.

If I do not save a man's life because he died before I was born, I do not condemn myself for not saving him, since it is not my individual nature but the general nature of reality which prevents me from altering the past. If I do not save him, because I am tied with a chain I cannot break, do I condemn myself? If I had a stronger body, I could break the chain, and this would be a good thing to do. I shall therefore condemn the nature of my body for being unable to do it. If I regard the body as a part of myself, I shall condemn myself for this bodily imperfection. If I only regard it as an external reality with which I am in close connexion, I shall condemn the body and not myself.[2]

If I fail to save a man's life because I mistake the nature of his illness, and so treat him in the wrong manner, this is a purely intellectual mistake on my part, unless my ignorance is due to past or present misconduct. Postponing this latter possibility, I shall certainly condemn myself for the failure. For the failure is due to my want of knowledge, or of acuteness. These are qualities in my mind which tend to produce evil, and as my mind is certainly myself, whatever my body is, I shall condemn myself. I shall pronounce myself a worse person than I might have been. But I shall not condemn myself morally.

But now suppose that I do not will to save him, because I should be enriched by his death. Or suppose that I do will to save him, but that my efforts are frustrated by ignorance due to past indolence, or to confusion caused by intoxication. In these cases I shall again condemn myself. And in these cases the condemnation will be — as it was not before — moral condemnation. For the result does in these cases — as it did not before — depend upon my will.[3] If I had willed differently in the past, I should not now be ignorant or a drunkard. If I had willed differently at the moment, I should not have preferred my own wealth to the life of another.

I do not think that it would be denied by indeterminists that, even if the will were completely determined, moral condemnation of this sort would be possible. The will would still be, as the body and intellect had been in the previous cases, something which tended to produce a bad result. And there could be no reason why it should not be condemned, as they, although regarded as completely determined, were condemned in the previous cases.

The indeterminist, I conceive, would say that while the complete determination of the will would not destroy the validity of *all* approval or condemnation of volitions, yet it would destroy the validity of the

---

[2]The intensity of the condemnation will, of course, vary according to the standard attained by similar bodies. We should think very badly of a man's body which was so weak that it could not break sewing-cotton. But if the chain that defied my efforts were the cable of a battle-ship, my condemnation would be no more than the recognition that I shoud have approved of a strength which is absent from my body, and from the bodies of all other men.

[3]I do not say that all moral qualities are qualities of volition, but that all volitions have moral qualities.

particular variety of approval or condemnation which is found in judgements of obligation.

Judgements of obligation are, of course, different from other judgements of approval or condemnation, or else they could not be distinguished as a class. But they are distinguished as a class by the fact that they are judgements which approve or condemn volitions. And we have seen that the complete determination of volitions could not destroy the validity of all approval or condemnation of them. It must be some other characteristic of judgements of obligation, and not their reference to volitions, which is incompatible with the complete determination of the volitions to which they refer.

Two such characteristics have been suggested. The first is the supreme value of right volition, which, as it is said, is affirmed by our judgements of obligation. The second is the sense of responsibility which follows on those judgements.

It is said that we approve right volition more than any other excellence, and that we condemn wrong volition more than any other defect. Some reason, it is said, is required for this fact, and the reason is found in the incomplete determination of the will. There was nothing which made it certain beforehand that we should will rightly or wrongly. And this makes right volition more precious and wrong volition more detestable.

I can see no reason whatever why the moral quality of an act should be regarded as intensified because it happened without complete determination. It seems to me that the moral quality of the act would be just the same, while that of the agent would vanish. The latter point will be dealt with later.[4] But however this may be, it would be impossible to prove Free Will in this way, for two reasons. Firstly, if the alleged fact were true, it would admit of another explanation. Secondly, there is reason to believe that the alleged fact is not true.

Our judgement of the value of excellences which are not excellences of volition is different in different cases. We regard the intellectual excellence of Shakespeare with more approval than the excellence shown by the most brilliant punster. Each of them has excelled all other men in a particular direction, but we admire Shakespeare most, because we regard excellence in his direction as more important, in the general scale of values, than excellence in punning. Yet it would be universally admitted that Shakespeare's genius, on the one hand, and the absence of equal genius in myself, on the other hand, were facts completely determined. They do not depend on volition, and it is only in volition that the indeterminist denies complete determination.

---

[4]Cf. below, pp. 329-32.—Ed.

If excellences which are admitted to be completely determined can be judged to have different values, so that one is placed above another, then the fact that one excellence is placed above all others is quite compatible with its determination. It would be quite adequately explained by our judgement that the presence of this excellence, however certainly determined, was better, and its absence, however certainly determined, was worse, than the presence or absence of any other excellence.

And, again, is it the fact that right volition is always placed above all other excellences? I think that few people would be prepared to assert this. A man who gives water to a thirsty dog has willed rightly. If that man were Shakespeare, or Newton, or Kant, should we be prepared to say that that volition had more value than anything in his nature except some other volition? Surely most people would regard the intellect which was capable of producing Hamlet, or the Principia, or the three Critiques, as of greater value.

Can we even say that the most important right volitions are approved more than any other excellence, and the most important wrong volitions are condemned more than any other defect? I doubt if we can say even this. It might be possible to maintain another proposition which is sometimes confused with the former — namely that the greatest moral excellence is approved more than any other excellence, and that the greatest moral defects are condemned more than any other defects. But the two propositions are very different.

The argument, it will be remembered, rests on the assertion that we can place nothing higher than right volitions, from which it is argued that they must be undetermined. Now, if we must place the greatest moral excellence highest, it is clear that the argument breaks down unless the greatest moral excellence consists in right volition.

The simplest way of proving this would be to show that all moral excellence was right volition. But what, in this case, are we to say of a loving disposition, a fervent patriotism, or a passion for humanity? They are not volitions, or tendencies to volitions, or habits of volition. Nor can they be obtained by willing. (They must, of course, be distinguished from resolutions to act in particular ways. A man's will can cause him to act as he would act if he loved his wife, or his country, or mankind. But it cannot make him love them.)

Love and patriotism, then, are qualities which, by the indeterminists' own position, are as completely determined as artistic or literary excellence. Will indeterminists be prepared to say that, while justice and beneficence are moral excellences, love and patriotism are mere gifts of fortune, and have no moral import at all? I think that few of them would do so, in spite of the inconsistency in which their refusal plunges them.

Kant, indeed, accepted the paradox rather than the inconsistency, but he had few precursors, and he has few successors. His attempt to prove that the teaching of Jesus is on his side can only be described as astounding.[5]

The indeterminist might save his position if he were prepared to maintain that, although certain completely determined qualities are to be called moral excellences, yet they are not to be ranked as the highest moral excellences, a position which is to be reserved exclusively for excellences of the will. But if he maintained this he would have against him the authority of most of the churches — certainly of the Christian church — and of most of the philosophers.

We have now to consider the second ground on which judgements of obligation are considered incompatible with the complete determination of volition. A man who is condemned by a judgement of obligation — who is condemned, that is, as having done wrong in what he has willed or omitted to will — is held responsible for his conduct. And people are not held responsible for anything else except an error of volition. In ordinary language we say that a man may be responsible for his ignorance, unskillfulness, or some other defect which is not a defect of volition. But what we really hold him responsible for is his will not to remove the defect, or his abstention from willing to remove it. If his circumstances were such, for example, that he could not have ceased to be ignorant, however much he had tried, we should not call him responsible for his ignorance. Even if the cause is not external, but internal, we do not call him responsible unless it is a volition or abstention from one. If I write a play, I am responsible for writing it, for I should not have done so if I willed not to do it. But, if I write it, I am not responsible for its inferiority to Hamlet, for the cause of that inferiority, though it is to be found in my nature, is not in anyway dependent on my will.

It is asserted that this responsibility would be incompatible with complete determination, and that any one who is not prepared to reject responsibility must be prepared to deny complete determination of volitions. . . .

I suppose that every determinist who need be reckoned with would admit that we are responsible to our fellow creatures for defects of will, and that this responsibility is only for defects of will and for their results.

But is this inconsistent with determinism? I cannot see that it is. For although the determinist does not hold that volitions are distinguished from all other events by not being completely determined, he admits, like every one else, that they are marked off from other events by being

---

[5]*Critique of Practical Reason,* Part I, Book I, chap. iii.

determinable by expectation of pleasure and pain. Expectations of pleasure and pain are not the only motives to will, but every one knows that they are motives. On the other hand, nothing but volitions can be directly determined by those expectations, though other things may be determined by them through volitions. The fear of pain may make a boy will to learn his lesson, or it may make him will it more earnestly. And if the only obstacle in the way was the absence or weakness of will, he will now learn it. But if it is entirely beyond his powers, the fear of pain may make him unhappy, but will not make him successful.

Society, therefore, is quite justified in giving rewards for right volitions and in inflicting punishments for wrong volitions, whether those rewards and punishments are deliberately bestowed by the state, or whether they are the less deliberate, but scarcely less powerful rewards and punishments of social praise and blame. For the expectation of such rewards and punishments may encourage right volitions and discourage wrong volitions. But to carry out a system of this sort with regard to good and evil qualities not dependent on volitions would be foolish, and (in so far as it was a system of punishments) brutal, since in these cases the expectation would produce no effect on the results.

Now I submit that my responsibility to my fellow men for my volitions consists in the fact that it is reasonable for them to reward and punish me for my volitions, and in that fact only. And, in support of this, we may notice that it is universally agreed that a man is not responsible in cases where his action cannot be affected by considerations of pleasure and pain. A lunatic who suffers from acute homicidal mania is not hanged for murder, because the expectation of such punishment would not deter a man in such a condition. (It cannot, I imagine, be said that he is not punished because he has not willed the action. He has willed it as much as a sane murderer has.) But when the same murderer is in the asylum it is not thought wrong that he should be punished for infraction of rules by exclusion from an entertainment, because experience shows that the expectation of this may affect his conduct for the future. The homicidal maniac, then, is not held responsible for murder, but is held responsible for untidiness, because punishment will not prevent him from murdering, but may keep him tidy. On the other hand, the cases of certain of the more tyrannical despots, such as Nero, support the contention from the other side. Psychologically their states may have been quite as abnormal as those of the ordinary homicidal maniac. From a medical point of view they might perhaps be called mad. But no court would hold them to have been legally mad. It would have declared them responsible for their actions. And this, I think, would have been right. It is in the highest degree improbable that Nero would have committed any of his crimes if he had known that he would certainly have been executed for them within a month or two. And since the volitions of such men can be affected by the expectation of punishment, it is right to punish them — unless, of course, the punishment required to affect them is so severe as to be a greater evil than the crime.

It is clear from all this that the determinist is not in the least inconsistent in advocating that crimes should be punished. A preventive punishment is obviously defensible in exactly the same way for determinists and for indeterminists. Whether the will is free or not, it is clear that while a man is in prison he cannot be robbing on the highway or breaking into houses. Deterrent punishment is justified for the determinist by the fact that experience shows that the expectation of punishment will deter men from committing crimes which they would otherwise have committed. And other sorts of punishment are justified for him by the fact that experience also shows that a man's moral nature may in some cases be improved by influences brought to bear on him during the period of his punishment, or perhaps even by the punishment itself.[6]

There remains vindictive punishment. With regard to this it need only be said here that the justification of it is at least as easy for the determinist as for the indeterminist — or, rather, not more impossible. So far as punishment is vindictive, it makes a wicked man miserable, without making him less wicked, and without making any one else either less wicked or less miserable. It can only be justified on one of two grounds. Either something else can be ultimately good, besides the condition of conscious beings, or the condition of a person who is wicked and miserable is better, intrinsically and without regard to the chance of future amendment, than the condition of a person who is wicked without being miserable. If either of these statements is true — to me they both seem patently false — then vindictive punishment may be justifiable both for determinists and indeterminists. If neither of them is true, it is no more justifiable for indeterminists than it is for determinists. . . .

There remains the question of responsibility to self. I think that this must be admitted to exist — that a man does feel a responsibility to himself for defects of volition, or for defects caused by defects of volition, which he does not feel in cases of a defect with which volition has nothing to do. The analogy between this and responsibility to others seems to be that in the latter I recognize that the others do well to punish me, and in the former I recognize that I do well to feel shame and remorse. Now why should I recognize that it is well to feel shame and remorse for defects which are — directly or indirectly — defects of volition, and not

---

[6]Cp. my *Studies in Hegelian Cosmology,* chap. v.

for other defects? The indeterminist would suggest that it is because the defects of volition are not completely determined. But why should I judge it less good to feel shame or remorse for a defect because it is an essential part of my character? Surely, the more closely a defect is bound up with me, the more it is essential to my nature, the more reason I have to feel ashamed of it.

It seems to me that the real reason why it is good that I should feel shame and remorse in one case and not in the other is the same as the reason why it is good that other people should punish me in one case and not in the other — namely, that in the one case it may improve matters, and in the other case it cannot. The only part of our nature which is influenced by the expectation of pleasure and pain is the will. If, therefore, a defect is not a defect of volition, or dependent on one, it will not be in any way affected by the fact that I am miserable about it. And the misery, being useless and painful, will be evil, and it will be well to avoid it.

It is well that I should recognize my defects of all sorts, since ignorance of one's limitations often produces evil. But when I have once recognized that I cannot write a play as good as Hamlet, it is profitless self-torture if I am miserable about it, since my misery will certainly not remove this particular limitation.

With defects of volition, the matter is different. My will can be affected by expectations of pleasure and pain, and so, if the contemplation of a defect of volition, or its consequence, gives me pain, I may be led to cure the defect to escape from the pain. Or if the defect is in the past, and irrevocable, the dread of experiencing similar pain may keep me from similar faults. In such cases shame and remorse may bring advantages outweighing the evil of their painfulness, and, since they will be profitable, it will be good to feel them.

We now pass from the considerations drawn from the validity of judgements of obligation to the . . . [argument] that the will must be free because, if it were not free, all choice would be absurd. It may be conceded that scarcely any determinist would admit that all choice was absurd, and therefore, if it can be shown that this would be a result of determinism, they are logically bound to give up determinism.

It is said that it is inconsistent for a determinist to take duty as a motive for action. For he believes, it is argued, that it is already completely determined whether he will act according to his conception of duty, or whether he will act otherwise. And this, it is said, will render it unreasonable to choose to do his duty.

The absurdity of this particular choice is the one which is most often emphasized. But similar considerations would prove that any other choice is as absurd as the choice to do one's duty. For in each case the determinist would believe his action to be already completely determined, and if this made choice absurd in one case it would do so in all others.

I cannot, however, see the least ground for the conclusion that the belief in determinism makes choice unreasonable. Of course, if the belief of the determinist was that the end at which he was aiming was completely determined to occur or not to occur, irrespective of what he chose, then choice would be unreasonable.[7] I should be very unreasonable to choose that the sun should rise to-morrow, or that it should not rise. But the ordinary determinist, like everybody else, believes when he chooses any course that his choice may have some effect on the event. And he is quite consistent in this belief. He is a determinist because he believes that, while the event may well be determined by his choice, his choice is in its turn completely determined.

Why should the belief that, if I choose to shut the door, my choice to shut it was completely determined beforehand, make it unreasonable of me to choose to shut it? (This is all the information my determinism can give me on the question. For, so long as I am not omniscient, I can never be absolutely certain beforehand what I shall choose. My certainty may be very great but it can never be quite complete.) I cannot see that it should have any such paralysing effect. The contention that it ought to do so is, I think, due to a confusion of this belief with the other belief, mentioned above, which treats the choice as impotent to affect the result, and which asserts that the result is determined irrespective of it.

But suppose that I was omniscient, so that I could not choose anything without knowing beforehand that it was certain that I should choose it, would that render choice unreasonable? I find it rather difficult to conceive what would happen in circumstances so unlike those of which I have any experience. But I can see no absurdity in a choice which is preceded by a perfect knowledge that it would be made. It is to be observed that most theists would hold that God could predict with absolute certainty how he would will in any circumstances, and that they would not hold that this made it absurd in him to will. . . .

---

[7]Such a belief has been held. Napoleon, for example, seems to have believed that the time of each man's death was fixed, independently of all other events. If I go here, I may be drowned, if I go there, I may be shot, but wherever I go, I shall die somehow at that hour. Such a belief *does* render absurd all choice directed to the preservation of my life. Why should I protect my life? I shall either lose it to-day, even if I protect it, or keep it till another time, even if I do not protect it.

But this is not identical with determinism. It does not even involve it, for a man could hold this who held that my choice to protect life or not to protect it was not completely determined. It is compatible, no doubt, with determinism, but in this case the absurdity of choice would not be due to the determinism, but to this quite separate belief.

I have now considered the principal arguments brought forward by indeterminists in favour of their position. It remains to consider some arguments which may be brought forward against that position. The main argument against it is that which proceeds by establishing the universal validity of the law of Causality, and so showing that volitions, like all other events, must be completely determined. This argument, as I said at the beginning of the chapter, I do not propose to consider here. I shall only point out two inconsistencies in the position of the average indeterminist. The average indeterminist, like other men, admits the validity of morality; and he attaches some value to expectations that men will, under certain circumstances, act in certain ways. I maintain that indeterminism is inconsistent with both these positions.

In the first place indeterminism is inconsistent with the validity of morality. Determinism, as we have seen, was reproached with its inconsistency with the validity of judgements of obligation, and reproached wrongly. The accusation can be retorted with greater truth.[8] Judgements of obligation are judgements which approve or condemn the person who wills a certain thing. I say that I myself, or some one else, is better or worse on account of a particular volition than would have been the case if the volition had not occurred. The approval or condemnation of the agent is essential to morality. If we are not entitled to say that a man is virtuous or wicked, what is left?

But how are we justified in passing from the volition to the person who makes it? There is, perhaps, no difficulty on any theory in saying that a man is good or bad at the moment when he is willing well or badly. But this is not all that we do say. Half an hour after ordering a murder, Nero may be eating his dinner, and thinking about nothing else. In the intervals of his labours, St. Francis, too, must eat, and may be too fatigued even to plan fresh labours. Yet we should call the one wicked, on account of his past crimes, and the other good, on account of his past services. The whole fabric of morality would be upset, if our approval or condemnation of a man for his volition had no right to last longer than the volition itself. Nor would any indeterminist, I imagine, be prepared to deny its right to last longer.

The determinist can explain this consistently with his position. According to him the volitions of each man spring from his character, and are the inevitable result of that character when it finds itself in a certain situation. The approval or condemnation of the agent is based on the

---

[8] It is interesting to note in passing that this view is maintained by thinkers so different from one another as Hume and Green. Compare *Treatise of Human Nature,* Book II, Part III, Section 2; and *Prolegomena to Ethics,* Section 110.

belief that the character, indicated by the past acts, survives in the present, and is ready, on appropriate occasions, to manifest itself in similar acts. Nero is condemned in the present, because he still has the character which will probably cause him, when he is tired of eating, to amuse himself with another murder. St. Francis is approved in the present, because he still has the character which will probably cause him, when he has satisfied his hunger, to perform fresh works of benevolence.

But how can the indeterminist defend his judgement? According to him the volition in each case is a perfectly undetermined choice between two motives. When the volition is over, it has ceased to exist, and it has not, on the indeterminist theory, left a permanent cause behind it. For, according to that theory, it has no permanent cause at all. Directly Nero has ceased to think of a murder, nothing at all connected with it remains in his moral nature, except the mere abstract power of undetermined choice, which is just as likely to be exercised on the next occasion in an utterly different way. How then can the indeterminist venture to call Nero a wicked man between his crimes? And yet he certainly would call him so.

Are we to say that it is, after all, the same person who committed the murder and who is now being condemned, and that this forms a sufficient justification of the condemnation? I cannot see that this should justify it. For the judgement passed on Nero at dinner is not only that he was wicked when willing the murders before dinner, but that he is wicked now. But what is wicked in him now? Not his volition, for he is now willing to gratify his palate, which is not wicked. Not his character, for his previous volition consisted in an undetermined choice of the wrong alternative, and this has no root in his character—or anywhere else.

Moreover, if the indeterminist adopts this defence, he involves himself in fresh inconsistencies. If a man is to be approved or condemned now, simply because he is the same man who willed well or badly in the past, then all past volitions are equally grounds for such an approval or condemnation. But there are cases in which every one, including indeterminists, would admit that past volitions are not equally grounds of approval or condemnation in the present.

We often will in our dreams to commit evil actions. And men often will, in a state of intoxication, to commit evil actions which they would not will to commit when sober. Now we never consider a man to be wicked, after he has awaked, on account of his evil volitions in dreams. And we do not consider him wicked, when sober, on account of the wickedness which he willed when drunk. In ordinary cases, indeed, we should blame him for getting drunk. But when this is not his fault—as in the case of a savage who tastes alcohol for the first time—then no blame whatever is attributed to him after he has got sober for the volitions he formed when drunk.

Such judgements are quite inconsistent with the theory in which the indeterminist has now taken refuge—the theory that a man may be approved or condemned in the present for any volition which he has made in the past. For the man who dreamed or was drunk is certainly the same man who is now awake and sober.

But the determinist avoids all inconsistency. Experience shows us that the conditions of dreaming or of intoxication so affect the moral character that no inference can be drawn from volitions made in one of these states as to the probable volitions of the same man when he is not in that state. I have no reason to think that the brutal murder, which I planned in a dream on Monday night, gives even the least indication that I should be likely to yield, when awake on Tuesday morning, to any temptation to commit murder. And therefore, when awake on Tuesday morning, I do not condemn myself for it.

Again, in so far as we believe a man to have really altered his character, we no longer blame him for what happened before it was altered. If, since he willed a certain crime, his conduct has shown that he can resist temptations similar to those to which he yielded before, we no longer condemn him. Even without this experience, if we have reason to believe that he has repented his crime so sincerely and effectually that he would not in future yield to a similar temptation, we condemn him no longer. It may be necessary to punish such men, either as an example to others, or because the law cannot safely take account of such delicate and doubtful matters. But from the point of view of morality, he is not condemned.

For determinists this is completely consistent. They pronounce a man to be wicked in the present, who has committed a crime in the past, because they regard it as evidence of a still-existing character of the kind which tends to produce crimes. But if they have reason to believe—such as amendment or repentance can give them — that his character has changed since the crime, and is no longer such as tends to produce similar crimes, they have no longer any reason to condemn him.

The indeterminist recognizes that amendment and repentance may remove wickedness as much as the determinist recognizes it. To deny this would be to break with every religion in the world's history, and with the moral judgement of all mankind. But his recognition of this is quite inconsistent with his indeterminism. We have seen that he can only condemn a man for a past crime at all, on the basis that it is sufficient ground for condemnation that he is the same man who committed the crime.

And if this is a sufficient ground, then it is clearly unjustifiable to condemn him the less on account of his amendment or repentance.

We pass to the second inconsistency involved in the position of the indeterminist. The indeterminist, like every one else, assumes that it is possible to predict, with some probability, though not with absolute certainty, how men will act under particular circumstances. To reject this would render impossible all trade, all government, and all intercourse with our fellow men.

We continually act on the faith of such predictions. We assume that a postmaster will sell a penny stamp for a penny, that he will not sell two for a penny, that a policeman will not try to kill us for walking along the Strand, that a soldier in battle will try to kill the enemy, and the like. There is, of course, no certainty. The postmaster may be drunk, the policeman a homicidal maniac, the soldier a disciple of Tolstoi. But we are confident of the probabilities. I am more likely to get one penny stamp for a penny than to get two. My life is more likely to be attempted in a fight at close quarters than in a walk through London.

The indeterminist admits that on his theory there can be no certainty of prediction. For all practical purposes the determinist must admit the same, since only an omniscient person could be quite certain what causes were at work, and with what strength. The indeterminist, however, thinks that his theory admits of statements of probability as to volitions.

If, however, indeterminism is true, there is no justification whatever for making any statement as to the probability of future volitions. The indeterminist theory assumes that in every case the choice between motives is undetermined. There cannot then be the slightest probability that this choice will be of one motive rather than another. Our only ground for supposing that a particular man will choose in a particular way, under particular circumstances, is that experience has shown us that he has previously acted in a similar way under similar circumstances, or else that most men, or most men who resemble him in certain ways, have previously acted in a similar way under similar circumstances. Now why should we suppose that similar circumstances will be followed by similar results? There is no reason to do so unless the circumstances determine the results, or the circumstances and the results are both determined by the same cause. Otherwise the expectation that the similar results would follow would be as foolish as the expectation that I should win at cards on one Lord Mayor's day because I had won at cards on the previous one.

According to the indeterminist theory our choice between motives is not determined by anything at all. And thus it follows that all ground for predicting the action of any man, so far as it depends on his volition, vanishes altogether.

One result of this is that the indeterminist is quite inconsistent in expecting one line of conduct from one man and another from another. It is just as probable that an English general to-day should eat his prisoners, as it was that a Maori chief should do so a hundred years ago. It is just as probable that the drunken man in the street should be Johnson as that it should be Boswell.

But this is a trifle. If the indeterminist is right we have no reason to expect any line of conduct from any one, rather than any other line of conduct which is physically possible. It is just as likely that the majority of Londoners will burn themselves alive to-morrow, as it is that they will partake of food to-morrow. I am just as likely to be hanged for brushing my hair as for committing a murder. When men commit suicide, or eat, or hang other men, their action depends on their volition, and their volition cannot be anticipated.

A Special Problem for Determinists

Richard Taylor

Deliberation and Foreknowledge

Deliberation is often confused, particularly in discussions of free will, with speculation and reasoning concerning one's future behavior. It has even been suggested that unless one could infer from certain things—e.g., from his intentions or whatnot—what he was going to do and unless, accordingly, determinism were true, then one would have no way of

From "Deliberation and Foreknowledge," *American Philosophical Quarterly* I (January 1964): 73-80, by permission of the author and the *American Philosophical Quarterly*. This paper (revised) was initially presented at the meetings of the Eastern Division of the American Philosophical Association, New York City, December 28, 1962.

knowing what he was going to do—as if statements of the form "I am going to do A" were all just predictions.[1]

I want to make clear the great difference between deliberation, on the one hand, and speculation and inference, on the other, by eliciting some of the things that are involved in the former but not in the latter. Some of these appear to have important consequences for the "free will" controversy. It is not, however, my purpose to defend any theory of free will.

I shall go about this by listing some of the things that appear to be involved in deliberation and which distinguish it from everything else, illustrating these with examples as I go along. I shall begin with the more obvious things and conclude with the more controversial.

I

One cannot deliberate about anything except his own possible future actions, though one can speculate or make inferences about almost anything he likes.

With respect to acts of other people, for instance, one can speculate about them, try to predict them, or to infer what they are going to be; but, one cannot deliberate about them. A statement such as "I am deliberating whether Jones will do E" cannot be true, unless it means "I am deliberating whether I shall have Jones do E," in which case it expresses deliberation about one's own possible future act. The reason for this is that one can deliberate only about what he believes to be within his own power. Thus, "I am deliberating whether Smith shall be reprieved" entails "I believe it to be within my power alone to reprieve Smith." If I believe this to be within the power of another—the governor, for example—then I can speculate about what he will do, or I can deliberate about what I would do if I were the governor; but I cannot deliberate about what will be done.

Even in case of my own acts, moreover, I cannot deliberate about what I have already done or am already doing. I can deliberate only about my possible *future* acts. With respect to things I have already

---

[1]See e.g., J. M. E. McTaggart, *Some Dogmas of Religion* (London, Edward Arnold and Co., 1930) pp. 182-184 [cf. pp. 332-33 of this volume], and R. E. Hobart, "Free-will as Involving Determinism and Inconceivable Without It," *Mind,* vol. 43 (1924), pp. 1-27.

done, I can regret them, take satisfaction in them, and so on. If I have forgotten what those acts were, I can try to find out, infer, or guess; but I cannot deliberate about them. Though I may not know, for example, whether I took my vitamin pill yesterday, I can no longer deliberate about whether or not to take it *then*. There is simply nothing there to decide and, besides, past and present things, even if they are my own acts, are not within my power to do or to forego, and I can deliberate only about things which are. Similarly, if I am sitting, I cannot deliberate about whether to be sitting. I can only deliberate about whether to remain sitting; and this has to do with the future.

Now it would not, to be sure, be outrageously incongruous for one to say that he is deliberating or (synonymously) trying to decide whether he ought to have done something which he has in fact done, which might seem to render doubtful the claim that deliberation is concerned only with the future. Deliberation in this sense, however, is both logically and psychologically different from what I am here concerned with. It is essentially no different from what a meteorologist would be doing if, studying his data and charts, he truly said that he was trying to *decide* what tomorrow's weather is going to be, or what a moralist would be doing if he truly said he was deliberating or trying to decide whether, say, Socrates should have taken the hemlock. In such cases one is, obviously, doing nothing more than trying to resolve a question or doubt of one kind or another. The meteorologist, unless he happens also to be a rainmaker, is not trying to decide whether to have it rain tomorrow, since this is not within his power, nor is the moralist trying to decide whether to have Socrates drink the hemlock. Similarly, in deliberating or trying to decide whether I ought to have done what I in fact did, I am not trying to decide whether to do it or not, it being no longer within my power to alter the fact. I am trying only to resolve a doubt, which in this case happens to be a moral one, and what I am doing is essentially no different from what the moralist, pondering Socrates' behavior, is doing. Thoughts and reflections which are aimed merely at the resolution of doubt, however, are essentially speculative rather than deliberative. When, unlike such cases, I am deliberating whether I ought *to do* something, which it is within my power to do or to forego, I am *not* merely trying to resolve a doubt or settle my opinion about something. Unlike the meteorologist who reflects about the weather, or the moralist who reflects upon the moral implications of Socrates' behavior, I *am* trying to decide whether to do something, or whether to leave it undone. I am trying, not merely to settle upon certain opinions, moral or otherwise, concerning what I do, but to decide just what it is that I shall do.

Whatever may be the permissiveness of "ordinary usage," it is *this* which I prefer to call deliberation, in the strict sense, just to distinguish it from all those thoughts and reflections which are essentially intellectual and speculative.

Again, one cannot deliberate about such things as the future behavior of some heavenly body, even though this may be unknown to him, though he may make inferences or speculations concerning such things. One reason for this is that such things occur by necessity, as Aristotle pointed out, and are not within anyone's power to control. But that is not the only reason. One could no more deliberate about, say, the outcome of the spin of a roulette wheel, even if he assumed this to be causally undetermined. He could only guess, make bets on it, and so on— unless, of course, he thought he could influence this outcome. But then he would be deliberating on his own future activity—namely, whether or not to try influencing this outcome.

Finally, I have said that deliberation is concerned with one's *possible* future actions, and this is a qualification that is dictated by the preconditions of deliberation as well as by logic. As we shall see shortly, an action which is believed to be inevitable can be no subject of deliberation nor, by the same token, can one which is believed to be impossible. Beyond that, however, if one is deliberating concerning certain *alternative* actions, then not all of them can be, simply, his future actions. Each can be no more than a *possible* action. If, for example, I am deliberating whether to leave the room or to stay, then not both of these can be my future actions, for on the supposition that either of them is my future action, it logically follows that the other is not.

II

One cannot deliberate about his own future act, in case he believes the act in question is already inevitable.

This is, again, a consequence of the fact that one can deliberate only about what he believes to be within his power to do and to forego, and the very point in calling anything inevitable is to deny that this condition exists. Thus, one cannot deliberate about whether to (eventually) die; he can only deliberate on how to make the best of it, with insurance and so on. The husband of a pregnant woman cannot deliberate on whether to become a father, unless this is a question of whether to terminate the pregnancy. A passenger in an airplane cannot deliberate about whether or not to return to earth; he well knows that he will, in one way or another. He cannot even deliberate about when or where to come down, unless he is the pilot—i.e., unless this is up to him, or within his power. In case such things are thought not to be "acts," we can add that a soldier cannot deliberate about whether or not to arm himself, in case he knows that there is a regulation requiring him to do so, and that the regulation will be enforced. What to do is, in this case, not up to him.

Now of course one can deliberate whether to do this or that *if* a certain condition is fulfilled, not knowing whether that condition will be fulfilled but believing that it has already been rendered inevitable that it will be, or that it will not. One might, for example, deliberate whether to study in France or in Italy in case he gets a certain award, knowing that the awards have already been finally decided but not yet announced. In that case he can only guess, speculate, or even try by secret intelligence to find out whether he has won an award. But without doing any of this he can still deliberate about whether to go to France or to Italy, in case he does get it. In that case, however, he must believe that neither of these two alternatives is likewise already rendered inevitable, in case he has won the award. He cannot, for example, believe that the award, in case he has won it, will turn out to be one permitting him to study only in Italy, or only in France, and still deliberate about where to study on the award. At most he can then only deliberate about whether or not to accept the award, in case he turns out to have won it.

III

One cannot deliberate about what he is going to do, even though this may be something that is up to him, at the same time knowing what he is going to do.[2]

This is one thing that deliberation has in common with speculation, inference, and guesswork; namely, that all presuppose ignorance, in the absence of which they can only be shammed. Inference about things future, however, has for its purpose the *discovery* of what is *going* to happen, whereas deliberation, which is necessarily about things future, has for its purpose a *decision* or "making up one's mind" about what to *make* happen, and in this respect the two are utterly different.

There seem, in fact, to be only these two ways in which one could know what he is going to do; namely, by *inferring* what he is going to do,

---

[2]This point is derived from Carl Ginet's paper, "Can the Will be Caused?" *Philosophical Review,* vol. 71 (1962), pp. 49-55. See also Stuart Hampshire and H.L.A. Hart, "Decision, Intention and Certainty," *Mind,* vol. 67 (1958), pp. 1-12, referred to by Ginet.

or by *deciding* what he is going to do. In neither case can one deliberate about what he is going to do.

Thus, if a governor said "I am, as a result of my forthcoming deliberations, going to reprieve Smith," he would indicate that his mind was already made up, and hence, that he was not going to deliberate about it—unless, of course, with a view to possibly changing his mind. But in that case he could not know that his statement was true. He could, of course, pretend to deliberate about it, discuss the matter with his assistants, perhaps publicly review the pros and cons once again, but if he did so he would be shamming deliberation. His purpose would not be to arrive at a decision, this having been already arrived at, but something else — perhaps that of conveying a desirable public image of himself.

Similarly, if anyone said "I see, by reliable signs and portents, that I am about to do E, so I shall deliberate about it," he could not possibly be expressing himself accurately. If he does already know what he is going to do, there is nothing there for him to decide, and hence nothing to deliberate about.

For example, it might be possible for a group of observers to infer reliably from certain signs that a certain man is about to be married. They see the flowers, witnesses assembled, preacher waiting, music playing, groom suitably attired, and so on. From the same evidence, which is apparent to the groom himself, he too can gather that he is about to be married, though for him, unless he doesn't realize what he has gotten himself into, such signs and portents are superfluous. If, however, he regards these signs as reliable evidence of what he is about to do, he cannot deliberate about what to do—he is past deliberation, and the die is cast. If, on the other hand, he still does deliberate about whether to get married—if he has last minute misgivings and second thoughts—then he obviously does not regard the signs as reliable evidence of what he is going to do. He is, in fact, contemplating confuting the very thing those signs point to, by walking right out of the church.

Of course deliberation is seldom if ever so pure as this. More commonly one finds himself partly trying to decide what to do, partly trying to predict what he is going to do, partly deliberating about what to do if the predictions turn out right and, perhaps in addition, partly deliberating about whether to hold to a decision that has been at least tentatively made, and so on. Mixed with our governor's deliberations, for instance, might be all sorts of attempts at predicting what his opponents will do, what he will be forced to do in response, and what, in light of these, he ought to do about this reprieve, and so on. Still, deliberation about what *to* do is essentially different, but logically and psychologically, from prediction about what one is *going* to do, or what other people or things are going to do. One can deliberate, but not predict, about what to *make* happen, and one can predict, but not really deliberate, about what *is going* to happen. The fact that both can occur together and have significant connections with each other, and are for this and other reasons often confused in the minds of philosophers and others, does not obliterate the essential differences at all.

IV

If one's act is caused, in the usual sense—i.e., is the inevitable consequence of certain conditions existing antecedently—then he can, simply by his awareness of those causes, know by inference what his act is going to be.[3]

Under such circumstances—i.e., the awareness of such causes and knowledge of their consequences—one cannot, of course, deliberate whether to do the thing in question, for he already knows that he will. Examples are supplied by compulsions, addictions, solemn agreements, and the like. Or consider some such act as sneezing, which is ordinarily performed involuntarily but which can be done deliberately. If one feels a sneeze coming on, in the sense that he is forewarned of this impending convulsion by a certain familiar nasal tickle, then he cannot deliberate whether to sneeze or not; he can only prepare for it. The only exception would be in case he thought he might be able to repress the sneeze; but in that case he would not, obviously, consider the felt irritation to be causally sufficient to make him sneeze. One might, on the other hand, have some occasion to deliberate whether to sneeze, if he were considering ways of attracting someone's attention, for example, or perhaps of feigning illness in order to avoid some irksome chore. His deliberation would have to cease, however, the moment he became aware of any condition sufficient either for his sneezing, or for his not sneezing, for he would then know what he was going to do.

From this it of course follows that one's deliberate acts cannot be caused, in the usual sense, or, if they are, then he cannot know that those causes exist at the time he deliberates. Like speculation about what is going to happen, then, deliberation about what is going to happen, or, more precisely, about what one is going to make happen, rests upon ignorance.

---

[3]Ginet, *op. cit.*, p. 50.

But now the question arises whether deliberation rests upon anything more; that is, whether it presupposes only an *ignorance* of the causes of one's deliberate act, or the actual *absence* of such causes. We shall return to this important question shortly, but here we can note that it is quite possible for one to deliberate about whether to do a certain thing even in the presence of conditions causally sufficient for his doing what he contemplates doing, provided, of course, that he is ignorant of the existence of such conditions. One might, for instance, be deliberating whether to sneeze, thinking that this might be an effective way of feigning illness, not knowing that a sneezing powder has been liberated into the room, the inevitable effect of which will soon be to cause everyone in the room to begin sneezing. Or one might be deliberating whether to leave a certain house, wholly unaware that the house is on fire and he will shortly be forced to leave. One can hardly help noting, however, that in such cases one's deliberation is otiose and pointless, since what one then does is not the *result* of his deliberation at all. There was really nothing for him to decide; he only thought there was.

V

If one does not know what he is going to do, but knows that conditions already exist sufficient for his doing whatever he is going to do, then he cannot deliberate about what to do, even though he may not know what those conditions are.

One can, in such a case, only guess or speculate about what he will do, or try to find out what it is that he will be forced to do. This is a consequence of the fact that one can deliberate whether to do a certain act only if he believes it is up to him whether to do it or not, or, that it is within his power equally to do it, and to forego it.

For example, consider a soldier who knows that daily orders regarding the bearing of arms are enforced, and that he has no choice but to obey them. Suppose he does not know whether or not he shall be required to arm himself today, though he knows that the order has been posted. He cannot deliberate about whether to arm himself today. He can only check to see what order has been posted and, until then, perhaps try to guess. Of course he might deliberate whether to comply with his order; but if he did he would not be assuming that such orders are really *enforced*. He would be assuming only that there are strong, but perhaps insufficient, inducements for obedience.

Or consider a man—we'll call him Adam—who has spent the evening at the distant home of a friend and is then invited by his host to spend the night. This might call for careful consideration of the pros and cons on Adam's part, for weighing in his mind the pleasures of staying over as against considerations of his responsibilities at home, and so on. Suppose further, however, that another guest—we'll call him Brown— knows that there exist conditions which render it causally impossible for Adam to go home. He knows, for instance, that the last train has left, and that there is no other way for Adam to get home. Now clearly, Adam can still deliberate about whether to remain or not, in ignorance of what Brown knows. But now suppose Brown announces that he knows what Adam is going to do, without giving any hint as to what this is, and that he knows it on the basis of certain unnamed conditions which are causally sufficient for Adam's doing what Brown knows he will do. If Adam *believes* this, he cannot any longer deliberate about what to do, even though he does not know what he is going to do and is not himself aware of any conditions sufficient for his doing either the one thing or the other. All he can do is speculate, guess, and wait to see what he will have to do, meanwhile exhorting Brown to tell him. He can no longer deliberate about the matter because, if he believes Brown, then he believes it is not up to him what he does; the matter has already been "decided," one way or the other, and there is no decision for Adam to make.

It is no good here, incidentally, to introduce such vague and familiar slogans as "Deliberation might, after all, be a natural process," or "Deliberation is only the way some, perhaps psychological, causes work themselves out," and so on. If such remarks are unpacked, and "natural processes" are found to be nothing but causal chains, and "causes" are understood to be causes of the usual kind—namely, antecedent conditions, psychological or other, which are sufficient for, and thus render inevitable, whatever it is that they cause—then far from being rejoinders to what has been said they only illustrate something that is painfully well known; namely, that philosophers, no less than the vulgar, are perfectly capable of holding speculative opinions that are inconsistent with some of their own beliefs of common sense.[4]

---

[4] A well-known philosopher is alleged to have announced to an audience that he was a solipsist, and that he could not understand why they were not all solipsists too, and I once heard a philosopher claim that he knew nothing at all, not even that he was enunciating that opinion to me. These are extreme examples of the kind of muddle some philosophers have appeared to me to be involved in when they have said that they are determinists who deliberate — as if this were some sort of challenge or rejoinder to something. Merely pointing out that certain views are held, even by philosophers, or even by oneself, does not prove that the views are consistent and is sometimes a *prima facie* reason for suspecting they are not.

Now I believe the principle involved here can be generalized, such that if a man believes that there are, or ever will be, conditions, not themselves within his control, sufficient for his doing whatever it is that he is going to do, then he cannot deliberate about what to do, even though he may not have the slightest idea what this is, or the slightest idea what those conditions are, or will be, or what they will be sufficient for.

Consider a man at a cocktail party, for instance, who knows, in a cognitive sense of "knows" which entails that what he knows is true, that he will accept any standard cocktail that is offered provided it is made with gin, but that he will drink nothing alcoholic otherwise, having a nausea for any other type of spiritous beverage. Now this man cannot deliberate about whether to drink gin, for he already knows that he will, *if* it is offered. There is, then, nothing there for him to decide. Nor can he deliberate about whether to drink at all, for he already knows that he will not, *unless* gin is offered, so there is nothing there to be decided. All he can do is try to speculate, or guess, whether gin will be served, this being, we are supposing, something that is not up to him. And it should be noted that under the conditions assumed it is impossible for him to deliberate, even though he may not know what he is going to do, and may even doubt that conditions already exist which are sufficient for his doing whatever he is going to do.

This example is imperfect, however, for one can justly wonder how anyone could have such knowledge. One can "know" what he is going to do under certain and as yet undecided alternative circumstances, in the sense of having firmly made up his mind — and still, for instance, fall dead before having a chance to do it, showing that his "knowledge" was not of the kind that entails that what was thus "known" was true. This observation does not really affect the argument, but since the doubt raised about the illustration can easily transfer itself to the argument we should perhaps supply a better example. Consider, then, a man who is watching the spinning of a roulette wheel, and who knows (and has not merely resolved) that he will take the purse in case it stops on an even number, but that he will have to surrender his own stake in case it stops on an odd number. Now he cannot deliberate about whether to take the purse or surrender his own, even though this has not been at all determined. And, it should be noted, this is still true, even if he believes the behavior of the wheel to be causally undetermined with respect to where it stops, and hence believes that his own act will have been causally undetermined as well, such that there are not yet any conditions sufficient either for his doing the one thing, or for his doing the other. The reason for this is obvious; namely, that having got this far into the game it is no longer up to him what he does. It is entirely up to the roulette wheel, and there is nothing for him to decide. All he can do is guess, and hope.

Now we can, I believe, extend this principle still farther, and say that if a man knows that there will at any future time be some condition sufficient for his having done a certain act in the meantime, then he cannot deliberate whether to do that act, even though he does not know what his act will be or what that condition will be.

This is, of course, plainly false on one natural interpretation, for one sometimes knows that, whichever of two alternative things he does, there will then be traces from which it can be certainly inferred what he has done, and he can, nevertheless, deliberate about which thing to do.

Nevertheless, if one were to learn that there was going to be a certain condition, as yet unspecified, for his doing a certain act in the meantime, then he could not deliberate about that act, even though he did not yet know which act it is. He knows, or can infer, that he can act only in whatever way is necessary for the occurrence of that condition, whatever it is.

For example, suppose a man knows that if he is found in a certain place at some given future time, this will be sufficient for his having gone there in the meantime, whereas if he is found in another place at that time, this will be sufficient for his having gone to that other place. He does not know where he will be found, and hence, where he will have gone in the meantime. There is nothing so far, then, that prevents his deliberating, with a view to making up his mind, where to go, and where, accordingly, to be found. But now suppose he learns that some other person does somehow already know where he will be found — not that this other person has a fair idea or can make a more or less educated guess, but that, somehow or other, he actually knows. Now I believe the first man cannot, if he knows that another man is in possession of such knowledge, any longer deliberate about where to go; he can only wait and see where he is going. It is not within the power of any man to render false what another man knows to be true.[5] To the extent that he *can* deliberate about where to go, to that extent he must consider it doubtful that anyone could already know where he will subsequently be found. One deliberates, not about what *will* happen, but about what to *make*

---

[5]There is room for endless misunderstanding in this statement, but one must try to resist the temptation to say that while it is within a man's *power* to render false what another knows to be true—meaning by that only that what is known to be true could be false—no man ever *does* render false what another knows to be true. That familiar modal fallacy, taught to all philosophy students early in the game, is not involved here.

happen; and if it is up to him what he shall make happen, then it is also up to him what shall eventually be true about what has happened.

VI

No one can know what another is going to do as a result of forthcoming deliberation, nor could God have such foreknowledge.

One can, of course, know what another is going to do as a result of deliberation that is already concluded, for that person can then simply announce what he is going to do. But one can make no such announcement while still deliberating, for he could not himself know that it was true. There is no way that he could possibly know, before he has decided, nor is there any way that anyone else could know.

If someone knew what another was going to do as a result of forthcoming deliberation, then he would know on the basis of some kind of evidence; that is, on the basis of his knowledge of certain conditions that were sufficient for the agent's doing the thing in question, and from which it could be inferred that he would do that. But if there were such conditions, then they could also be known by, or made known to, the agent himself, such that he too could infer what he was going to do. This, however, is impossible, so long as the agent has not yet himself decided what to do. Indeed, the agent cannot even believe that any such conditions, known or unknown, exist, and at the same time believe that it is within his power both to do, and to forego doing, the thing in question. This, as we have seen, appears to be a necessary condition of deliberation.

The foregoing is not to be confused with a familiar type of fallacy, whereby one truly asserts what cannot happen in case something else happens, and then, ignoring this qualification, draws some categorical conclusion about what cannot happen. The point is rather, that no one can know by inference that a certain event is going to happen, except on the basis of his knowledge of certain conditions sufficient to produce that event. If no such conditions exist, then it obviously cannot be known by inference that the event in question is going to happen, and if it is so known, then there must be such conditions. If the event in question is the act of some agent, however, then that agent cannot deliberate about whether to do it, believing that any such conditions already exist, even though he may not know what they are; for the fact that *any* such conditions already exist would entail that it is no longer up to him what he is going to do. And moreover, if another person knows by inference what his act will be, then he cannot know that this act will be the result of deliberation still forthcoming. He will, on the contrary, know that it will be the result of conditions, known by him, sufficient to produce it.

Suppose, for example, that I feel confident that a certain man, now deliberating whether to go to Boston or to New York, is going to decide to go to New York. Now if I am really confident of this, and my confidence rests upon something more than a mere feeling or hunch, then I cannot believe that he is really deliberating with a view to deciding where to go. I must instead believe that the matter is already fairly settled in his own mind, and that he is, at best, only reviewing the pros and cons of what he has already fairly decided. If, on the other hand, I believe that he is really deliberating about where to go, in the sense which presupposes that it is up to him where he goes, then I cannot feel confident that he will go to either place rather than the other. What he finally decides is something that is up to him, if his decision is really the result of his deliberation.

Now I might, to be sure, know a person and his habits well enough to know that, whenever he is confronted with a certain choice — say, that of going to New York or to Boston — then he invariably decides the same way — say, by going to New York. And it is possible to suppose that, before deciding, he always or often deliberates about the matter. In that case I could predict with confidence what he was going to do, and this would be consistent with his always deliberating first. But then I would know what he was going to do, *not* as a result of his deliberation, but as a result of something else — of habit, for example. If, as a result of sheer habit, or as a result of some other condition that is always present when such a decision is made, the man invariably decides in the same way, then his decision is not the result of his deliberation, and not something that is really up to him. It is the result, or causal consequence, of something else; of habit, for example, or of whatever other condition we are supposing determines the matter.[6]

If, moreover, I know that another person is deliberating about a certain choice that is before him, and know what his decision is going to be, on the basis of some consideration that is known to me and which must sooner or later also come to his attention and certainly decide the matter, then I know what he is going to do, not as a result of his deliberation, but as a result of this further consideration, which will terminate his deliberation. If, for instance, I know that someone is deliberating whether to remain in the room or leave, and I know, further, that the room is on fire, and that he will shortly notice this himself, and leave as a conse-

---

[6]See John Canfield, "Knowing about Future Decisions," *Analysis,* vol. 22 (1962), pp. 127-129.

quence of this, then I know what he is going to do. But I know this only because I know that what he is going to do will *not* be the result of his deliberation, but of his knowledge of the circumstances. What he does is not up to him at all, assuming the fire to be of such a nature as leaves him no real alternative.

From the foregoing it becomes apparent that the inability of anyone to know what someone is going to do, as a result of deliberation, does not result from any limitations of human sagacity, but from the very nature of a deliberately chosen act. God, accordingly, can have no more such foreknowledge than any man; and it is no rejoinder to this simply to *define* God as an omniscient being.

If God had foreknowledge of the deliberate act of some man, then that knowledge could be shared with that man himself. At least, there is no reason why it could not. But that is impossible, for no man can continue to deliberate about whether to do something, if he already knows or can know what he is going to do. There is an absurdity in the conception of a man learning (as contrasted with merely hearing) from God that he is going to deliberate about whether to do or forego doing a certain act, and then, as a result of his deliberation, that he is going to forego it. Nor is this just a consequence of the fact that, if a man is deliberating about what to do, then it would be a contradiction to say that he already knows what he is going to do. The fact that a man is deliberating is no *obstacle* to his knowing, or learning, anything whatever, any more than a man's being a bachelor is an obstacle to his marrying someone. The fact that a man knows or can find out by inquiry what he is going to do, on the other hand, is an obstacle to his deliberating about it and then doing it as a result of such deliberation, just as the fact that a man has a wife is an obstacle to his having still another.[7]

Even if such supposed divine knowledge could not, for some reason, be shared with men, it still could not exist, even for God. For to the extent that a man can deliberate whether to do one act or another, to that extent he believes that each act is equally within his power. Hence, on the supposition that God believes the man will do the first of these acts and not the second, or that he will do the second and not the first — whichever of these suppositions one chooses — the man must also *believe* it to be within his power to confute God's belief, which is absurd. This is not, it should be noted, to say that foreknowledge, whether human or divine, is ever any cause by itself, or that it exerts any compulsion on anything whatever.

---

[7]Any reader to whom the point of this analogy is unclear may ignore it.

VII

There can be no truth or falsity in any assertion about what any man's future deliberate act will be.

This, combined with the supposition of God's omniscience, is a consequence of what has already been said. For if God is omniscient, then he knows everything that can be known, which is for God exactly coextensive with everything that is true. Hence, if as between the assertion and the denial that a man will, as a result of deliberation still forthcoming, do a certain act, God cannot know which is true, it follows that neither is true, and accordingly, that neither is false.

A Defense of Free Will

C. A. Campbell

Has the Self "Free Will"?

1. . . . . It is something of a truism that in philosophic enquiry the exact formulation of a problem often takes one a long way on the road to its solution. In the case of the Free Will problem I think there is a rather special need of careful formulation. For there are many sorts of human freedom; and it can easily happen that one wastes a great deal of labour in proving or disproving a freedom which has almost nothing to do with the freedom which is at issue in the traditional problem of Free Will. The abortiveness of so much of the argument for and against Free Will

From C. A. Campbell, *On Selfhood and Godhood* (London: George Allen & Unwin, Ltd., 1957), Lecture IX, by permission of the publisher.

in contemporary philosophical literature seems to me due in the main to insufficient pains being taken over the preliminary definition of the problem. There is, indeed, one outstanding exception, Professor Broad's brilliant inaugural lecture entitled, 'Determinism, Indeterminism, and Libertarianism,'[1] in which forty-three pages are devoted to setting out the problem as against seven to its solution! I confess that the solution does not seem to myself to follow upon the formulation quite as easily as all that:[2] but Professor Broad's eminent example fortifies me in my decision to give here what may seem at first sight a disproportionate amount of time to the business of determining the essential characteristics of the kind of freedom with which the traditional problem is concerned.

Fortunately we can at least make a beginning with a certain amount of confidence. It is not seriously disputable that the kind of freedom in question is the freedom which is commonly recognized to be in some sense a precondition of moral responsibility. Clearly, it is on account of this integral connection with moral responsibility that such exceptional importance has always been felt to attach to the Free Will problem. But in what precise sense is free will a precondition of moral responsibility, and thus a postulate of the moral life in general? This is an exceedingly troublesome question; but until we have satisfied ourselves about the answer to it, we are not in a position to state, let alone decide, the question whether 'Free Will' in its traditional, ethical, significance is a reality.

Our first business, then, is to ask, exactly what kind of freedom is it which is required for moral responsibility? And as to method of procedure in this inquiry, there seems to me to be no real choice. I know of only one method that carries with it any hope of success; viz. the critical comparison of those acts for which, on due reflection, we deem it proper to attribute moral praise or blame to the agents, with those acts for which, on due reflection, we deem such judgments to be improper. The ultimate touchstone, as I see it, can only be our moral consciousness as it manifests itself in our more critical and considered moral judgments. The 'linguistic' approach by way of the analysis of moral *sentences* seems to me, despite its present popularity, to be an almost infallible method for reaching wrong results in the moral field; but I must reserve what I have to say about this for the next lecture.

2. The first point to note is that the freedom at issue (as indeed the very name 'Free *Will* Problem' indicates) pertains primarily not to overt acts

---

[1] Reprinted in *Ethics and the History of Philosophy, Selected Essays.*

[2] I have explained the grounds for my dissent from Broad's final conclusions on pp. 27 ff. of *In Defense of Free Will* (Jackson Son & Co., 1938).

but to inner acts. The nature of things has decreed that, save in the case of one's self, it is only overt acts which one can directly observe. But a very little reflection serves to show that in our moral judgments upon others their overt acts are regarded as significant only in so far as they are the expression of inner acts. We do not consider the acts of a robot to be morally responsible acts; nor do we consider the acts of a man to be so save in so far as they are distinguishable from those of a robot by reflecting an inner life of choice. Similarly, from the other side, if we are satisfied (as we may on occasion be, at least in the case of ourselves) that a person has definitely elected to follow a course which he believes to be wrong, but has been prevented by external circumstances from translating his inner choice into an overt act, we still regard him as morally blameworthy. Moral freedom, then, pertains to *inner* acts.

The next point seems at first sight equally obvious and uncontroversial; but, as we shall see, it has awkward implications if we are in real earnest with it (as almost nobody is). It is the simple point that the act must be one of which the person judged can be regarded as the *sole* author. It seems plain enough that if there are any *other* determinants of the act, external to the self, to that extent the act is not an act which the *self* determines, and to that extent not an act for which the self can be held morally responsible. The self is only part-author of the act, and his moral responsibility can logically extend only to those elements within the act (assuming for the moment that these can be isolated) of which he is the *sole* author.

The awkward implications of this apparent truism will be readily appreciated. For, if we are mindful of the influences exerted by heredity and environment, we may well feel some doubt whether there is any act of will at all of which one can truly say that the self is sole author, sole determinant. No man has a voice in determining the raw material of impulses and capacities that constitute his hereditary endowment, and no man has more than a very partial control of the material and social environment in which he is destined to live his life. Yet it would be manifestly absurd to deny that these two factors do constantly and profoundly affect the nature of a man's choices. That this is so we all of us recognise in our moral judgments when we 'make allowances,' as we say, for a bad heredity or a vicious environment, and acknowledge in the victim of them a diminished moral responsibility for evil courses. Evidently we do *try*, in our moral judgments, however crudely, to praise or blame a man only in respect of that of which we can regard him as *wholly* the author. And evidently we do recognise that, for a man to be the author of an act in the full sense required for moral responsibility, it is not enough merely that he 'wills' or 'chooses' the act: since even the most unfortunate victim of heredity or environment does, as a rule, 'will' what he does. It is significant, however, that the ordinary man, though well enough aware of the influence upon choices of heredity and environment, does not feel obliged thereby to give up his assumption that moral predicates *are* somehow applicable. Plainly he still believes that there is *something* for which a man is morally responsible, something of which we can fairly say that he is the sole author. *What is this something?* To that question common-sense is not ready with an explicit answer — though an answer is, I think, implicit in the line which its moral judgments take. I shall do what I can to give an explicit answer later in this lecture. Meantime it must suffice to observe that, if we are to be true to the deliverances of our moral consciousness, it is very difficult to deny that *sole* authorship is a necessary condition of the morally responsible act.

Thirdly we come to a point over which much recent controversy has raged. We may approach it by raising the following question. Granted an act of which the agent is sole author, does this 'sole authorship' suffice to make the act a morally free act? We may be inclined to think that it does, until we contemplate the possibility that an act of which the agent is sole author might conceivably occur as a necessary expression of the agent's nature; the way in which, e.g. some philosophers have supposed the Divine act of creation to occur. This consideration excites a legitimate doubt; for it is far from easy to see how a person can be regarded as a proper subject for moral praise or blame in respect of an act which he *cannot help* performing — even if it be his own 'nature' which necessitates it. Must we not recognise it as a condition of the morally free act that the agent 'could have acted otherwise' than he in fact did? It is true, indeed, that we sometimes praise or blame a man for an act about which we are prepared to say, in the light of our knowledge of his established character, that he 'could no other.' But I think that a little reflection shows that in such cases we are not praising or blaming the man strictly for what he does *now* (or at any rate we ought not to be), but rather for those past acts of his which have generated the firm habit of mind from which his *present* act follows 'necsessarily.' In other words, our praise and blame, so far as justified, are really retrospective, being directed not to the agent *qua* performing *this* act, but to the agent *qua* performing those past acts which have built up his present character, and in respect to which we presume that he *could* have acted otherwise, that there really *were* open possibilities before him. These cases, therefore, seem to me to constitute no valid exception to what I must take to be the rule, viz. that a man can be morally praised or blamed for an act only if he could have acted otherwise.

Now philosophers today are fairly well agreed that it is a postulate of the morally responsible act that the agent 'could have acted otherwise' in *some* sense of that phrase. But sharp differences of opinion have arisen over the way in which the phrase ought to be interpreted. There is a strong disposition to water down its apparent meaning by insisting that it is not (as a postulate of moral responsibility) to be understood as a straightforward categorical proposition, but rather as a disguised hypothetical proposition. All that we really require to be assured of, in order to justify our holding X morally responsible for an act, is, we are told, that X could have acted otherwise *if* he had *chosen* otherwise (Moore, Stevenson); or perhaps that X could have acted otherwise *if* he had had a different character, or *if* he had been placed in different circumstances.

I think it is easy to understand, and even, in a measure, to sympathise with, the motives which induce philosophers to offer these counter-interpretations. It is not just the fact that 'X could have acted otherwise,' as a bald categorical statement, is incompatible with the universal sway of causal law — though this is, to some philosophers, a serious stone of stumbling. The more widespread objection is that it at least looks as though it were incompatible with that causal continuity of an agent's character with his conduct which is implied when we believe (surely with justice) that we can often tell the sort of thing a man will do from our knowledge of the sort of man he is.

We shall have to make our accounts with that particular difficulty later. At this stage I wish merely to show that neither of the hypothetical propositions suggested — and I think the same could be shown for *any* hypothetical alternative — is an acceptable substitute for the categorical proposition 'X could have acted otherwise' as the presupposition of moral responsibility.

Let us look first at the earlier suggestion — 'X could have acted otherwise *if* he had chosen otherwise.' Now clearly there are a great many acts with regard to which we are entirely satisfied that the agent is thus situated. We are often perfectly sure that — for this is all it amounts to — if X had chosen otherwise, the circumstances presented no external obstacle to the translation of that choice into action. For example, we often have no doubt at all that X, who in point of fact told a lie, could have told the truth *if* he had so chosen. But does our confidence on this score allay all legitimate doubts about whether X is really blameworthy? Does it entail that X is free in the sense required for moral responsibility? Surely not. The obvious question immediately arises: 'But *could* X have *chosen* otherwise than he did?' It is doubt about the true answer to *that* question which leads most people to doubt the reality of moral responsibility. Yet on this crucial question the hypothetical proposition which is offered as a sufficient statement of the condition justifying the ascription of moral responsibility gives us no information whatsoever.

Indeed this hypothetical substitute for the categorical 'X could have acted otherwise' seems to me to lack all plausibility unless one contrives to forget why it is, after all, that we ever come to feel fundamental doubts about man's moral responsibility. Such doubts are born, surely, when one becomes aware of certain reputable world-views in religion or philosophy, or of certain reputable scientific beliefs, which in their several ways imply that man's actions are necessitated, and thus could not be otherwise than they in fact are. But clearly a doubt so based is not even touched by the recognition that a man could very often act otherwise *if* he so chose. That proposition is entirely compatible with the necessitarian theories which generate our doubt: indeed it is this very compatibility that has recommended it to some philosophers, who are reluctant to give up either moral responsibility or Determinism. The proposition which we *must* be able to affirm if moral praise or blame of X is to be justified is the categorical proposition that X could have acted otherwise because — not if — he could have chosen otherwise; or, since it is essentially the inner side of the act that matters, the proposition simply that X could have chosen otherwise.

For the second of the alternative formulae suggested we cannot spare more than a few moments. But its inability to meet the demands it is required to meet is almost transparent. 'X could have acted otherwise,' as a statement of a precondition of X's moral responsibility, really means (we are told) 'X could have acted otherwise *if* he were differently constituted, or *if* he had been placed in different circumstances.' It seems a sufficient reply to this to point out that the person whose moral responsibility is at issue is X; a specific individual, in a specific set of circumstances. It is totally irrelevant to X's moral responsibility that we should be able to say that some person differently constituted from X, or X in a different set of circumstances, could have done something different from what X did.

3. Let me, then, briefly sum up the answer at which we have arrived to our question about the kind of freedom required to justify moral responsibility. It is that a man can be said to exercise free will in a morally significant sense only in so far as his chosen act is one of which he is the sole cause or author, and only if — in the straightforward, categorical sense of the phrase — he 'could have chosen otherwise.'

I confess that this answer is in some ways a disconcerting one, disconcerting, because most of us, however objective we are in the actual conduct of our thinking, would like to be able to believe that moral responsibility is real: whereas the freedom required for moral responsibility, on the analysis we have given, is certainly far more difficult to establish than the freedom required on the analyses we found ourselves obliged to reject. If, e.g. moral freedom entails only that I could have acted otherwise *if* I had chosen otherwise, there is no real 'problem' about it at all. I am 'free' in the normal case where there is no external obstacle to prevent my translating the alternative choice into action, and not free in other cases. Still less is there a problem if all that moral freedom entails is that I could have acted otherwise *if* I had been a differently constituted person, or been in different circumstances. Clearly I am *always* free in *this* sense of freedom. But, as I have argued, these so-called 'freedoms' fail to give us the pre-conditions of moral responsibility, and hence leave the freedom of the traditional free-will problem, the freedom that people are really concerned about, precisely where it was. . . .

5. That brings me to the second, and more constructive, part of this lecture. From now on I shall be considering whether it is reasonable to believe that man does in fact possess a free will of the kind specified in the first part of the lecture. If so, just how and where within the complex fabric of the volitional life are we to locate it? — for although free will must presumably belong (if anywhere) to the volitional side of human experience, it is pretty clear from the way in which we have been forced to define it that it does not pertain simply to volition as such; not even to all volitions that are commonly dignified with the name of 'choices.' It has been, I think, one of the more serious impediments to profitable discussion of the Free Will problem that Libertarians and Determinists alike have so often failed to appreciate the comparatively narrow area within which the free will that is necessary to 'save' morality is required to operate. It goes without saying that this failure has been gravely prejudicial to the case for Libertarianism. I attach a good deal of importance, therefore, to the problem of locating free will correctly within the volitional orbit. Its solution forestalls and annuls, I believe, some of the more tiresome clichés of Determinist criticism.

We saw earlier that Common Sense's practice of 'making allowances' in its moral judgments for the influence of heredity and environment indicates Common Sense's conviction, both that a just moral judgment must discount determinants of choice over which the agent has no control, and also (since it still accepts moral judgments as legitimate) that *something* of moral relevance survives which can be regarded as genuinely self-originated. We are now to try to discover what this 'something' is. And I think we may still usefully take Common Sense as our guide. Suppose one asks the ordinary intelligent citizen *why* he deems it proper to make allowances for X, whose heredity and/or environment are unfortunate. He will tend to reply, I think, in some such terms as these: that X has more and stronger temptations to deviate from what is right than Y or Z, who are normally circumstanced, so that he must put forth a *stronger moral effort* if he is to achieve the same level of external conduct. The intended implication seems to be that X is just as morally praiseworthy as Y or Z *if* he exerts an equivalent moral effort, even though he may not thereby achieve an equal success in conforming his will to the 'concrete' demands of duty. And this implies, again, Common Sense's belief that *in moral effort* we have something for which a man is responsible *without qualification*, something that is *not* affected by heredity and environment but depends *solely* upon the self itself.

Now in my opinion Common Sense has here, in principle, hit upon the one and only defensible answer. Here, and here alone, so far as I can see, in the act of deciding whether to put forth or withhold the moral effort required to resist temptation and rise to duty, is to be found an act which is free in the sense required for moral responsibility; an act of which the self is sole author, and of which it is true to say that 'it could be' (or, after the event, 'could have been') 'otherwise.' Such is the thesis which we shall now try to establish.

6. The species of argument appropriate to the establishment of a thesis of this sort should fall, I think, into two phases. First, there should be a consideration of the evidence of the moral agent's own inner experience. What *is* the act of moral decision, and what does it imply, from the standpoint of the actual participant? Since there is no way of knowing the act of moral decision — or for that matter any other form of activity — except by actual participation in it, the evidence of the subject, or agent, is on an issue of this kind of palmary importance. It can hardly, however, be taken as in itself conclusive. For even if that evidence should be overwhelmingly to the effect that moral decision does have the characteristics required by moral freedom, the question is bound to be raised — and in view of considerations from other quarters pointing in a contrary direction is *rightly* raised — Can we *trust* the evidence of inner experience? That brings us to what will be the second phase of the argument. We shall have to go on to show, if we are to make good our case, that the extraneous considerations so often supposed to be fatal to the belief in moral freedom are in fact innocuous to it.

In the light of what was said in the last lecture about the self's experience of moral decision as a *creative* activity, we may perhaps be absolved from developing the first phase of the argument at any great length. The appeal is throughout to one's own experience in the actual taking of the moral decision in the situation of moral temptation. 'Is it possible,' we must ask, 'for anyone so circumstanced to *dis*believe that he could be deciding otherwise?' The answer is surely not in doubt. When we decide to exert moral effort to resist a temptation, we feel quite certain that we *could* withhold the effort; just as, if we decide to withhold the effort and yield to our desires, we feel quite certain that we *could* exert it — otherwise we should not blame ourselves afterwards for having succumbed. It may be, indeed, that this conviction is mere self-delusion. But that is not at the moment our concern. It is enough at present to establish that the act of deciding to exert or to withhold moral effort, as we know it from the inside in actual moral living, belongs to the category of acts which 'could have been otherwise.'

Mutatis mutandis, the same reply is forthcoming if we ask, 'Is it possible for the moral agent in the taking of his decision to *dis*believe that he is the *sole* author of that decision?' Clearly he cannot disbelieve that it is *he* who takes the decision. That, however, is not in itself sufficient to enable him, on reflection, to regard himself as *solely* responsible for the act. For his 'character' as so far formed might conceivably be a factor in determining it, and no one can suppose that the constitution of his 'character' is uninfluenced by circumstances of heredity and environment with which *he* has nothing to do. But as we pointed out in the last lecture, the very essence of the moral decision as it is experienced is that it is a decision whether or not to *combat* our strongest desire, and our strongest desire *is* the expression in the situation of our character as so far formed. Now clearly our character cannot be a factor in determining the decision whether or not to *oppose* our character. I think we are entitled to say, therefore, that the act of moral decision is one in which the self is for itself not merely 'author' but 'sole author.'

7. We may pass on, then, to the second phase of our constructive argument; and this will demand more elaborate treatment. Even if a moral agent *qua* making a moral decision in the situation of 'temptation' cannot help believing that he has free will in the sense at issue — a moral freedom between real alternatives, between genuinely open possibilities — are there, nevertheless, objections to a freedom of this kind so cogent that we are bound to distrust the evidence of 'inner experience'?

I begin by drawing attention to a simple point whose significance tends, I think, to be under-estimated. If the phenomenological analysis we have offered is substantially correct, no one while functioning as a moral agent can help believing that he enjoys free will. Theoretically he may be completely convinced by Determinist arguments, but when actually confronted with a personal situation of conflict between duty and desire he is quite certain that it lies with him here and now whether or not he will rise to duty. It follows that if Determinists could produce convincing theoretical arguments against a free will of this kind, the awkward predicament would ensue that man has to deny as a theoretical being what he has to assert as a practical being. Now I think the Determinist ought to be a good deal more worried about this than he usually is. He seems to imagine that a strong case on general theoretical grounds is enough to prove that the 'practical' belief in free will, even if inescapable for us as practical beings, is mere illusion. But in fact it proves nothing of the sort. There is no reason whatever why a belief that we find ourselves obliged to hold *qua* practical beings should be required to give way before a belief which we find ourselves obliged to hold *qua* theoretical beings; or, for that matter, *vice versa*. All that the theoretical arguments of Determinism can prove, unless they are reinforced by a refutation of the phenomenological analysis that supports Libertarianism, is that there is a radical conflict between the theoretical and the practical sides of man's nature, an antinomy at the very heart of the self. And this is a state of affairs with which no one can easily rest satisfied. I think therefore that the Determinist ought to concern himself a great deal more than he does with the phenomenological analysis, in order to show, if he can, that the assurance of free will is not really an inexpugnable element in man's practical consciousness. There is just as much obligation upon him, convinced though he may be of the soundness of his theoretical arguments, to expose the errors of the Libertarian's phenomenological analysis, as there is upon us, convinced though we may be of the soundness of the Libertarian's phenomenological analysis, to expose the errors of the Determinist's theoretical arguments.

8. However, we must at once begin the discharge of our own obligation. The rest of this lecture will be devoted to trying to show that the arguments which seem to carry most weight with Determinists are, to say the least of it, very far from compulsive.

Fortunately a good many of the arguments which at an earlier time in the history of philosophy would have been strongly urged against us make almost no appeal to the bulk of philosophers today, and we may here pass them by. That applies to any criticism of 'open possibilities' based on a metaphysical theory about the nature of the universe as a whole. Nobody today *has* a metaphysical theory about the nature of the universe as a whole! It applies also, with almost equal force, to criticisms based upon the universality of causal law as a supposed postulate of science. There have always been, in my opinion, sound philosophic reasons for doubting the validity, as distinct from the convenience, of the causal postulate in its universal form, but at the present time, when scientists themselves are deeply divided about the need for postulating causality even within their own special field, we shall do better to concentrate our attention upon criticisms which are more confidently advanced. I propose to ignore also, on different grounds, the type of criticism of free will that is sometimes advanced from the side of religion, based upon religious postulates of Divine Omnipotence and Omniscience. So far as I can see, a postulate of human freedom is every bit as necessary to meet certain religious demands (e.g. to make sense of the 'conviction of sin'), as postulates of Divine Omniscience and Omnipotence are to meet certain other religious demands. If so, then it can hardly be argued that religious experience as such tells more strongly against than for the position we are defending; and we may be satisfied, in the present context, to leave the matter there. It will be more profitable to discuss certain arguments which contemporary philosophers do think important, and which recur with a somewhat monotonous regularity in the literature of anti-Libertarianism.

These arguments can, I think, be reduced in principle to no more than two: first, the argument from 'predictability'; second, the argument from the alleged meaninglessness of an act supposed to be the self's act and yet not an expression of the self's character. Contemporary criticism of free will seems to me to consist almost exclusively of variations on these two themes. I shall deal with each in turn.

9. On the first we touched in passing at an earlier stage. Surely it is beyond question (the critic urges) that when we know a person intimately we can foretell with a high degree of accuracy how he will respond to at least a large number of practical situations. One feels safe in predicting that one's dog-loving friend will not use his boot to repel the little mongrel that comes yapping at his heels; or again that one's wife will not pass with incurious eyes (or indeed pass at all) the new hat-shop in the city. So to behave would not be (as we say) 'in character.' But, so the criticism runs, you with your doctrine of 'genuinely open possibilities,' of a free will by which the self can diverge from its own character, remove all rational basis from such prediction. You require us to make the absurd supposition that the success of countless predictions of the sort in the past has been mere matter of chance. If you *really* believed in your theory, you

would not be surprised if tomorrow your friend with the notorious horror of strong drink should suddenly exhibit a passion for whisky and soda, or if your friend whose taste for reading has hitherto been satisfied with the sporting columns of the newspapers should be discovered on a fine Saturday afternoon poring over the works of Hegel. But of course you *would* be surprised. Social life would be sheer chaos if there were not well-grounded social expectations; and social life is not sheer chaos. Your theory is hopelessly wrecked upon obvious facts.

Now whether or not this criticism holds good against some versions of Libertarian theory I need not here discuss. It is sufficient if I can make it clear that against the version advanced in this lecture, according to which free will is localised in a relatively narrow field of operation, the criticism has no relevance whatsoever.

Let us remind ourselves briefly of the setting within which, on our view, free will functions. There is X, the course which we believe we ought to follow, and Y, the course towards which we feel our desire is strongest. The freedom which we ascribe to the agent is the freedom to put forth or refrain from putting forth the moral effort required to resist the pressure of desire and do what he thinks he ought to do.

But then there is surely an immense range of practical situations—covering by far the greater part of life—in which there is no question of a conflict within the self between what he most desires to do and what he thinks he ought to do? Indeed such conflict is a comparatively rare phenomenon for the majority of men. Yet over that whole vast range there is nothing whatever in our version of Libertarianism to prevent our agreeing that character determines conduct. In the absence, real or supposed, of any 'moral' issue, what a man chooses will be simply that course which, after such reflection as seems called for, he deems most likely to bring him what he most strongly desires; and that is the same as to say the course to which his present character inclines him.

Over by far the greater area of human choices, then, our theory offers no more barrier to successful prediction on the basis of character than any other theory. For where there is no clash of strongest desire with duty, the free will we are defending has no business. There is just nothing for it to do.

But what about the situations—rare enough though they may be—in which there *is* this clash and in which free will does therefore operate? Does our theory entail that there at any rate, as the critic seems to suppose, 'anything may happen'?

Not by any manner of means. In the first place, and by the very nature of the case, the range of the agent's possible choices is bounded by what he thinks he ought to do on the one hand, and what he most strongly desires on the other. The freedom claimed for him is a freedom of decision to make or withhold the effort required to do what he thinks he ought to do. There is no question of a freedom to act in some 'wild' fashion, out of all relation to his characteristic beliefs and desires. This so-called 'freedom of caprice,' so often charged against the Libertarian, is, to put it bluntly, a sheer figment of the critic's imagination, with no *habitat* in serious Libertarian theory. Even in situations where free will does come into play it is perfectly possible, on a view like ours, given the appropriate knowledge of a man's character, to predict within certain limits how he will respond.

But 'probable' prediction in such situations can, I think, go further than this. It is obvious that where desire and duty are at odds, the felt 'gap' (as it were) between the two may vary enormously in breadth in different cases. The moderate drinker and the chronic tippler may each want another glass, and each deem it his duty to abstain, but the felt gap between desire and duty in the case of the former is trivial beside the great gulf which is felt to separate them in the case of the latter. Hence it will take a far harder moral effort for the tippler than for the moderate drinker to achieve the same external result of abstention. So much is matter of common agreement. And we are entitled, I think, to take it into account in prediction, on the simple principle that the harder the moral effort required to resist desire the less likely it is to occur. Thus in the example taken, most people would predict that the tippler will very probably succumb to his desires, whereas there is a reasonable likelihood that the moderate drinker will make the comparatively slight effort needed to resist them. So long as the prediction does not pretend to more than a measure of probability, there is nothing in our theory which would disallow it.

I claim, therefore, that the view of free will I have been putting forward is consistent with predictability of conduct on the basis of character over a very wide field indeed. And I make the further claim that that field will cover all situations in life concerning which there is any empirical evidence that successful prediction is possible.

10. Let us pass on to consider the second main line of criticism. This is, I think, much the more illuminating of the two, if only because it compels the Libertarian to make explicit certain concepts which are indispensable to him, but which, being desperately hard to state clearly, are apt not to be stated at all. The critic's fundamental point might be stated somewhat as follows:

'Free will as you describe it is completely unintelligible. On your own showing no *reason* can be given, because there just *is* no reason, why a man decides to exert rather than to withhold moral effort, or *vice versa*. But such an act — or more properly, such an "occurrence" — it is nonsense to speak of as an act of a *self*. If there is nothing in the self's character to which it is, even in principle, in any way traceable, the self has nothing to do with it. Your so-called "freedom," therefore, so far from supporting the self's moral responsibility, destroys it as surely as the crudest Determinism could do.'

If we are to discuss this criticism usefully, it is important, I think, to begin by getting clear about two different senses of the word 'intelligible.'

If, in the first place, we mean by an 'intelligible' act one whose occurrence is in principle capable of being inferred, since it follows necessarily from something (though we may not know in fact from what), then it is certainly true that the Libertarian's free will is unintelligible. But that is only saying, is it not, that the Libertarian's 'free' act is not an act which follows necessarily from something! This can hardly rank as a *criticism* of Libertarianism. It is just a description of it. That there can be nothing unintelligible in *this* sense is precisely what the Determinist has got to *prove*.

Yet it is surprising how often the critic of Libertarianism involves himself in this circular mode of argument. Repeatedly it is urged against the Libertarian, with a great air of triumph, that on his view he can't say *why* I now decide to rise to duty, or now decide to follow my strongest desire in defiance of duty. Of course he can't. If he could he wouldn't *be* a Libertarian. To 'account for' a 'free' act is a contradiction in terms. A free will is *ex hypothesi* the sort of thing of which the request for an *explanation* is absurd. The assumption that an explanation must be in principle possible for the act of moral decision deserves to rank as a classic example of the ancient fallacy of 'begging the question.'

But the critic usually has in mind another sense of the word 'unintelligible.' He is apt to take it for granted that an act which is unintelligible in the *above* sense (as the morally free act of the Libertarian undoubtedly is) is unintelligible in the *further* sense that we can attach no meaning to it. And this is an altogether more serious matter. If it could really be shown that the Libertarian's 'free will' were unintelligible in this sense of being meaningless, that, for myself at any rate, would be the end of the affair. Libertarianism would have been conclusively refuted.

But it seems to me manifest that this can *not* be shown. The critic has allowed himself, I submit, to become the victim of a widely accepted but fundamentally vicious assumption. He has assumed that whatever is meaningful must exhibit its meaningfulness to those who view it from the standpoint of external observation. Now if one chooses thus to limit one's self to the rôle of external observer, it is, I think, perfectly true that one can attach no meaning to an act which is the act of something we call a 'self' and yet follows from nothing in that self's character. But then *why should we* so limit ourselves, when what is under consideration is a subjective activity? For the apprehension of subjective acts there is *another* standpoint available, that of *inner experience*, of the practical consciousness in its actual functioning. If our free will should turn out to be something to which we can attach a meaning from *this* standpoint, no more is required. And no more ought to be expected. For I must repeat that only from the inner standpoint of living experience *could* anything of the nature of 'activity' be directly grasped. Observation from without is in the nature of the case impotent to apprehend the active *qua* active. We can from without observe sequences of states. If into these we read activity (as we sometimes do), this can only be on the basis of what we discern in ourselves from the inner standpoint. It follows that if anyone insists upon taking his criterion of the meaningful simply from the standpoint of external observation, he is really deciding in advance of the evidence that the notion of activity, and *a fortiori* the notion of a free will, is 'meaningless.' He looks for the free act through a medium which is in the nature of the case incapable of revealing it, and then, because inevitably he doesn't find it, he declares that it doesn't exist!

But if, as we surely ought in this context, we adopt the inner standpoint, then (I am suggesting) things appear in a totally different light. From the inner standpoint, it seems to me plain, there is no difficulty whatever in attaching meaning to an act which is the self's act and which nevertheless does not follow from the self's character. So much I claim has been established by the phenomenological analysis, in this and the previous lecture, of the act of moral decision in face of moral temptation. It is thrown into particularly clear relief where the moral decision is to make the moral effort required to rise to duty. For the very function of moral effort, as it appears to the agent engaged in the act, is to enable the self to act against the line of least resistance, against the line to which his character as so far formed most strongly inclines him. But if the self is thus conscious here of *combating* his formed character, he surely cannot possibly suppose that the act, although his own act, *issues from* his formed character? I submit, therefore, that the self knows very well indeed — from the inner standpoint — what is meant by an act which is the *self's* act and which nevertheless does not follow from the self's *character*.

What this implies — and it seems to me to be an implication of cardinal importance for any theory of the self that aims at being more than superficial — is that the nature of the self is for itself something more than just its character as so far formed. The 'nature' of the self and what we commonly call the 'character' of the self are by no means the same thing, and it is utterly vital that they should not be confused. The 'nature' of the self comprehends, but is not without remainder reducible to, its 'character'; it must, if we are to be true to the testimony of our experience of it, be taken as including *also* the authentic creative power of fashioning and re-fashioning 'character.'

The misguided, and as a rule quite uncritical, belittlement, of the evidence offered by inner experience has, I am convinced, been responsible for more bad argument by the opponents of Free Will than has any other single factor. How often, for example, do we find the Determinist critic saying, in effect, '*Either* the act follows necessarily upon precedent states, *or* it is a mere matter of chance and accordingly of no moral significance.' The disjunction is invalid, for it does not exhaust the possible alternatives. It seems to the critic to do so only because he *will* limit himself to the standpoint which is proper, and indeed alone possible, in dealing with the physical world, the standpoint of the external observer. If only he would allow himself to assume the standpoint which is not merely proper for, but necessary to, the apprehension of subjective activity, the inner standpoint of the practical consciousness in its actual functioning, he would find himself obliged to recognise the falsity of his disjunction. Reflection upon the act of moral decision as apprehended from the inner standpoint would force him to recognise a *third* possibility, as remote from chance as from necessity, that, namely, of *creative activity*, in which (as I have ventured to express it) nothing determines the act save the agent's doing of it.

A Special Problem for Libertarians

W. I. Matson

On the Irrelevance of Free-Will to Moral Responsibility

It is futile for any party to the free-will controversy to attempt to vanquish the others by a frontal assault. Metaphysical or inductive proofs of universal causal connexions will always be pronounced fallacious or inconclusive; intuitions of freedom will go on eluding the introspective researches of sceptics; and conjuring the problem away by making distinctions will only call forth contrary incantations.

In the two millennia of controversy the most notable — almost the *only* — advance toward agreement among all disputants, with respect

From "On the Irrelevance of Free-Will to Moral Responsibility," *Mind* LXV (October 1956), by permission of the author and the editor of *Mind*.

to some of the issues involved, was made by Hume. He annihilated naïve or Epicurean free-will, not by showing it to be false (though he attempted this also), but by proving it to have consequences in morals exactly opposite to those claimed by its partisans. I am emboldened to follow up Hume's success in a similarly indirect manner, by drawing the more or less unnoticed consequences of his polemic (*Treatise*, Book III, Pt. III, § IV) against the distinction between moral and natural virtues.

The free-will problem differs from some other traditional philosophical puzzles in that it has, *prima facie*, immediate practical consequences, to wit: what stand we take here determines our solution of the problem of moral responsibility and its sub-problem, the justification of punishment. (For the sake of brevity, no distinction between problem and sub-problem will be made in this paper.) Thus in so far as we are rational, our notions of justice and penology seem to depend on whether we are necessitarians or libertarians or perhaps somewhere in between. I shall attempt to show that on the contrary no conceivable physical or metaphysical doctrine of causality entails consequences in the field of moral responsibility that differ from those of any other view; further, that the concept of "moral responsibility" is vacuous, at any rate when taken in its usual sense. The irenic aim of this reasoning is to reduce the controversy about free-will by showing that it has no practical bearing.

1. *The Problem*

"I did the deed," says the villain, "I did it with malice aforethought, and nobody forced me to do it. Yet it is unjust to punish me. The deed was unavoidable, given the malicious intent working in a foul character such as mine; and as for *that*, it was the equally inevitable resultant of hereditary and environmental factors over which I had no control. So you see, I am the victim of circumstances."

The problem of moral responsibility is the problem of composing a suitable rejoinder to the above argument. Everybody agrees that there is something wrong with it; the question is whether it is empty sophistry from beginning to end, or whether it should be allowed *some* force.

The necessitarian admits the premises, but rejects the conclusion on the ground that it is nevertheless just to administer punishment to some kinds of wrongdoers, as a therapeutic measure. The libertarian denies that the deed was inevitable, given the motive, or that the motive was inevitable, given the life history of the agent. The positivist pronounces the premises irrelevant: it is sufficient for the justification of punishment that the tort feasor acted freely, which he did, since he admits he was not constrained. Let us scrutinize these replies.

2. Necessitarianism

The contented resident of a block universe regards the infliction of punishment as at best a deplorable necessity, needing justification in terms of a showing of compensatory good to be brought into being by it. If there is reason to believe that the good effects of the punishment will outweigh the ill — either by causing the wrongdoer to desist from such practices in the future, or by deterring others from their commission, or by protecting the innocent from further depredations — then the infliction of evil is ethically warranted. This warrant is not only compatible with necessitation but requires it.

It is important to note, however, that this way of justifying punishment stands in need of a number of qualifications:

1. It is not allowable to assume that punishment, in general or in particular, *will* be efficacious for the purposes envisaged. This is an empirical question; such evidence as we possess seems to indicate that ordinary judicial punishments are very inefficient, and may, on the whole, even do more harm than good.

2. At best, punishment hardly ever accomplishes what we really want it to do: *reform* the wrongdoer. It may terrorize him and others into outward conformity; but that is far from the same thing as making him a moral agent in the desired sense of one who does right without constraint. That is why Plato was guilty not just of paradox but of fallacy when in the *Gorgias* he argued that the criminal would best serve his own interest by turning himself in to the police. Granted that it is in his interest to rid himself of his beastly desires, it does not follow that undergoing punishment will aid him in his worthy enterprise. He would do better — or at least no worse — to put himself into the hands of a psychiatrist, or hypnotist, or clergyman, or even moral philosopher.

3. Unless calling a man morally responsible is the same as saying that probably punishing him will have a good effect (and surely these are *not* the same: see § 3), the necessitarian theory cannot ascribe 'moral responsibility' to anyone. There are good reasons for abstraining from punishing the innocent, the insane, the constrained; but these reasons consist of empirical generalizations. The prohibition on punishing the

innocent is absolute, since to do so would in *every* case be subversive of the purposes of punishment. The others admit of exceptions, real as well as imaginary.

4. The plea "I am a victim of circumstances" cannot be dismissed as nothing but an *ad misericordiam* fallacy. It is of course an abuse of language to fail to distinguish between being a victim of one's heredity and upbringing, and being an unwilling tool of superior brute force; and the distinction may often be the basis of a justification for punishment, in that there is much more chance that punishment will have good effects in the former case. Yet the plea is a legitimate counter to the reproach: "You are a wicked person; your crimes are *your* doing *entirely*; hence it is right in itself to make you suffer, whether or not any further good is realised."

Not all philosophers will agree with this last contention. It is said that we intuit a relation of fittingness between crime and punishment; in support it is observed that necessitarian philosophers exult just like ordinary men when the perpetrator of atrocities is brought before the bar of justice; yet in theory their feelings should be like those they have when they hear of some virtuous person having to undergo a painful but necessary operation.

The objection may be countered in part by pointing out that we need no intuition to know that wickedness should be frustrated since that is a tautology; but it is false that it is desirable, in itself, for the frustration to be painful. If we are not always mindful of this — if we all hanker after vengeance when our blood is up — this is just one fact about human nature to be condemned by philosophy, which in this lax age needs desperately to relearn and resume her proper office of *censor morum*.

Such, at any rate as I see it, is the logical consequence for 'moral responsibility' of the necessitarian position: the conception of moral responsibility is supererogatory and misleading, a dignified mask to disguise the hideous face of Vengeance when she goes to and fro among moral philosophers.

3. *Positivism*

The position of the positivists is a disingenuous verbal variant of necessitarianism. This will be clear from a glance at its genesis in § VIII, "Of Liberty and Necessity," of Hume's *Enquiry Concerning Human Understanding*. The section of the same title in the *Treatise* is a straightforward necessitarian tract, containing dozens of arguments to show that human actions are no exception to the universal reign of causal necessity, interlarded with derision of the "fantastical system of liberty." Liberty and chance are proved to be "synonimous"; any adversary who "chuses, that this question shou'd be decided by fair arguments before philosophers, than by declamations before the people" is challenged to attack this proof. "I dare be positive," Hume concludes, "no one will ever endeavour to refute these reasonings otherwise than by altering my definitions, and assigning a different meaning to the terms of *cause, and effect, and necessity, and liberty, and chance.*"

In the *Enquiry*, after a sermon on the vanity of verbal disputes, Hume proceeds to repeat the arguments of the *Treatise*, even inserting, as a footnote, an immaterially altered version of the *Treatise* passage accounting for "the prevalence of the [erroneous] doctrine of liberty" by "a false sensation or seeming experience . . . of liberty. . . ." In the very next paragraph we are astounded to learn that "by liberty . . . we can only mean *a power of acting or not acting, according to the determinations of the will*; that is, if we choose to remain at rest, we may; if we choose to move, we also may. Now this hypothetical liberty is universally allowed to belong to every one who is not a prisoner and in chains. Here, then, is no subject of dispute."

Is a more flabbergasting instance of the fallacy of changing the subject to be encountered anywhere in the complete history of sophistry? That the spectre of the Treatise haunted Hume at this point (*"Now* who is 'altering my definitions'? *Now* who is 'declaiming before the people'?"*) is evidenced by the lame defence of his definition: "Whatever definition we may give of liberty, we should be careful to observe two requisite circumstances; *first*, that it be consistent with plain matter of fact." That is, with usage? In the context of the problem his *Treatise* meaning was the customary one. Or does he mean that a proper definition must be such that there are known instances of its denotation? O *petitio*! O St. Anselm! "*Secondly*, that it be consistent with itself." If liberty, as "synonimous with chance," is a self-contradictory notion, that is not alleged anywhere in Hume's writings.

Nobody ever doubted that men have "a power of acting or not acting, according to the determinations of the will." But it is equally evident that this is irrelevant to the traditional problem of the freedom of the will, which is *not* formulated in the trivial question "Can I ever do what I want to do?" but (in Humean terms) "Are there any exceptions to the rule that my wants are subsequent, constantly conjoined, and necessarily connected to events which are not my wants?"

Thus while positivism asks a trivial question and replies with a trivial answer, as a solution to the free-will problem it is, in G. E. Moore's words, "plainly a mere abuse of language" (*Ethics*, p. 203). It is an abuse of language because whatever, if anything, we *do* mean by "the will is free" we certainly do *not* mean "one can sometimes do what one wants to do."

Is this unfair to Hume? Perhaps. The motivation for his stratagem was the "love of literary fame," an innocent or even praiseworthy passion. The doctrine of liberty is respectable; the refutation of it in the *Treatise* must have given offence. Very well, said Hume to himself, I shall, by taking 'liberty' in another of its senses, make myself out a libertarian; thus I may even win some persons to the doctrine of the *Treatise*, for I shall not *really* alter *that*. A more solid defence of Hume can be made by noting that in the following pages he pondered whether, if necessity is universal, we must not impute all human sin ultimately to God — which is an alternative mode of discussing the problem of moral responsibility. He concluded that this is a "mystery" which reason cannot fathom (for which, read, in accordance with canons of Humean exegesis, that we must indeed impute sin to God).

Hume's ploy was intended to take in the vulgar, but it has beguiled the learned in our time. One might say that Hume's changed subject has become the stock textbook solution for the problem. Indeed, real discussion was silenced until C. A. Campbell's devastating article "Is 'Freewill' a Pseudo-Problem?" (*Mind*, 1951) cleared away the smog.

Some modern Humeans are not entitled to what I have called the "more solid defence," for they go further than — even against — their master, in claiming that the pseudo-solution vindicates the "plain man's' view of moral responsibility, according to which the whole and absolute guilt for a wrong action lies with the agent, just so long as he was not constrained. But this is surely a non-sequitur, unless there is some mistake in my reasoning concerning the moral consequences of necessitarianism; for the arguments for pseudo-libertarianism in the *Enquiry* are not different from those for necessitarianism in the *Treatise*, and no post-Humean has added anything to them. Thus the positivists, like Hume, differ from the necessitarians only in a misleading verbal way; or else they go beyond the franchise of their arguments.

It may be of some moment to add, in concluding this section, that the fashionable equation of moral responsibility with absence of constraint is absurd, because the latter admits of degree (a fact always overlooked by the positivists) while the former does not.

4. *Libertarianism*

Having seen that pseudo-libertarianism offers no real alternative to the doctrine of necessity, we pass to consideration of the genuine article.

Since Hume's destruction of the Epicurean position, libertarians have been obliged to seek a middle way beween randomness and necessity. They require for their theory a kind of causality which shall satisfy the following conditions: If A is a free act, then (1) at the time when A is performed, the performance of an act non-A is not incompatible with the total state of the universe, including the psychic state of the agent, at that time; (2) there is a reason for A, in some sense that rules out randomness; (3) the 'reason for A' shall not in every case be derivable from the agent's 'character as so far formed.'

The first requirement, the doctrine of Real Possibilities, is made in order to assure the satisfaction of the condition for moral responsibility that 'ought implies can,' which libertarians interpret as entailing the legitimacy of interpreting "he did it, but he could have done otherwise" in a categorical sense. The third requirement is needed to allow for the important cases in which an agent of bad character may, and sometimes does, 'reform himself' by an act of free will; also, to turn the edge of the criticism that character is almost always *obviously* the resultant of heredity and conditioning.

It is not plausible that these requirements can be met; nor does the libertarian recourse to a non-empirical Self allay our suspicions. Nevertheless, I for one do not perceive that the position is *contradictory*, nor even that it is *known* to be incompatible with physicalism reinterpreted in the light of quantum theory. Moreover, the libertarian will turn a deaf ear to accusations of oddness, an unscientific temper, vagueness, and metaphysics so long as he remains convinced that his theory is a necessary presupposition of important moral principles. The way to deal with him, therefore, is to criticize *this* conviction. To this task I now turn.

I wish to be completely fair to the libertarian, to concede him everything that can possibly be conceded. Fortunately, in pursuance of this desire, no superhuman feats of the logical imagination are requisite. For in order to grant the libertarian everything he could wish for, we need only . . . grant it!

Let us assume, then, that there *are* real possibilities. Let us assume a *via media*, whether we can conceive it or not, between chance and necessity; and let this kind of causality be independent, to just the right degree, of the agent's character as so far formed.

All right, we have endowed our villain with these extraordinary *modi operandi. Must* he now admit that the fault lies altogether in him, and not in *any* sense or degree in his stars?

Why *should* he admit it? He need only ask whether these powers are innate or acquired, and the libertarian is at once overthrown.

If this is not evident, a few words should make it so. Suppose the powers are declared innate; then the villain may sensibly ask whether he is responsible for what he was born with? A negative reply is inevitable. Are they then acquired? Then the ability to acquire them — was *that* innate? or acquired? It is innate? Very well, then . . . ?

There seems to be no stopping the vicious regress thus generated — not even with God, for it is not clear that we are precluded from asking these questions about Him. (I mean, of course, about His Goodness. A Necessary Being *may* be exempt; I can excuse myself from investigating this sublime question, since no one would claim that *men* are necessary beings.)

There is no escaping this elenchus by claiming that we are all born with equal (even absolute) potential for making moral choices; that it is our duty and responsibility to develop this capacity; and that merit and blameworthiness consist in our developing or failing to develop it. For — leaving aside the odd consequence that we would thus be more morally responsible in infancy than ever afterward — we would in that case again be forced to embark on our tedious quest for the reasons, innate or acquired, for differences in development of the capacity.

If it is objected that the ostensibly banished notion of determining cause has been smuggled in again as an element of the "innate or acquired powers," I reply that my language is intended to be neutral, but that, in accordance with the necessary concession of the libertarian to Hume, a so-called free act *must* be one which stands in *some* relation to *something else* — and something *abiding* — about the agent, such that the something else makes *some* difference to the free act. I confess inability to conceive how any property (again, this word is to be understood neutrally) of an agent can stand in a relation of "making some difference" to an act, without being a determining cause of the act, perhaps more or less diluted by randomness; nor does the libertarian literature come to my aid. However, the requirement that there be a difference-making property (power, influence, contra-causal potentiality — call it what you will) in (about, connected with, qualifying, characterizing) the agent necessarily makes the question, whether this property be innate or acquired, a sensible one; and the argument needs no more than this admission.

Let it be well noted that, if this argument is sound, the libertarian is *not* merely obliged to temper, in some degree, his claim of superiority to the necessitarian with respect to the validation of moral responsibility; rather, he lands *in the very same position*; the consequences of necessitarianism and libertarianism for moral responsibility are *precisely the same*; there cannot be any philosophical justification whatsoever for the *lex talionis*, unless we are prepared to give up the principle that wanton production of evil is wrong.

5. *Conclusion*

I do not wish to emulate those philosophers, denounced by Hume, who strive to clinch their arguments by claiming that their conclusions accord with 'sound morality.' Much less do I desire to pose as the champion of the plain man. I shall therefore abstain from abusing 'moral responsibility' as a fiction concocted in the schools. On the contrary, the concept refers to a very prevalent mode of moral thinking which I consider pernicious. To lend prestige to these conclusions I point to Marcus Aurelius, to Spinoza, and to that paradigm of kindly humanity, Uncle Toby, who opined that the best thing to do was to "wipe it up, and say no more about it."

Excusability

P. H. Nowell-Smith

Freedom and Responsibility

. . . I [have] tried to show that 'could have' sentences in non-moral contexts can be analysed in terms of 'would have . . . if . . .'; and we must now
see whether the application of this analysis to moral cases is consistent
with our ordinary use of moral language.

The first question to be considered is the question what sorts of if-
clauses are in fact allowed to excuse a man from blame. Clearly 'I could

From P. H. Nowell-Smith, *Ethics,* pp. 291-300. Copyright © P. H. Nowell-Smith,
1954. By permission of the author and Penguin Books Ltd., Harmondsworth,
Middlesex.

not have kept my promise because I was kidnapped' will exculpate me while 'I could not have kept my promise because I am by nature a person who takes promises very lightly' will not. Translated into the hypothetical form, these become respectively 'I would have kept my promise if I had not been kidnapped' and 'I would have kept my promise if I had been a more conscientious person.' Again it is clear that the first exculpates while the second does not. The philosophical difficulties, however, are to decide just why some 'would . . . ifs' excuse while others do not and to provide a criterion for distinguishing the exculpating from the non-exculpating cases. Forcible seizure exculpates; but do threats or psychological compulsion? And if, as some suggest, desires are internal forces which operate on the will, do they exculpate in the way in which external forces do? The problem of free will is puzzling just because it seems impossible, without indulging in sheer dogmatism, to know just where to stop treating desires as 'compelling forces.'

Now before tackling this difficulty it will be prudent to examine what goes on in a place where questions of responsibility are settled every day and have been settled daily for hundreds of years, namely a court of law. Lawyers have evolved a terminology of remarkable flexibility, refinement, and precision and, although there may be a difference between moral and legal verdicts, it would be strange if the logic of lawyers' talk about responsibility were very different from our ordinary moral talk.

To establish a verdict of 'guilty' in a criminal case it is necessary to establish that the accused did that which is forbidden by the law or, in technical language, committed the *actus reus*, and also that he had what is called *mens rea*. This last phrase is sometimes translated 'guilty mind' and in many modern textbooks of jurisprudence it is supposed to consist of two elements, (a) foresight of the consequences and (b) voluntariness. But, whatever the textbooks may say, in actual practice lawyers never look for a positive ingredient called volition or voluntariness. A man is held to have *mens rea*, and therefore to be guilty, if the *actus reus* is proved, *unless* there are certain specific conditions which preclude a verdict of guilty. "What is meant by the mental element in criminal liability (*mens rea*) is only to be understood by considering certain defences or exceptions, such as Mistake of Fact, Accident, Coercion, Duress, Provocation, Insanity, Infancy."[1] The list of pleas that can be

---

[1]Professor H. L. A. Hart: *Proceedings of the Aristotelian Society,* 1948-9. Aristotle in effect defines 'the voluntary' in the same negative way as what is done not under compulsion and not through ignorance.

put up to rebut criminal liability is different in different cases; but in the case of any given offence there is a restricted list of definite pleas which will preclude a verdict of guilty.

This is not to say that the burden of proof passes to the defence. In some cases, such as murder, it is necessary for the prosecution to show that certain circumstances were not present which would, if present, defeat the accusation. The essential point is that the concept of a 'voluntary action' is a negative, not a positive one. To say that a man acted voluntarily is in effect to say that he did something when he was not in one of the conditions specified in the list of conditions which preclude responsibility. The list of pleas is not exhaustive; we could, if we wished, add to it; and in making moral judgments we do so. For example we sometimes allow the fact that a man acted impulsively to exonerate him morally or at least to mitigate his offence in a case in which the law would not allow this. But it remains true that, in deciding whether an action was voluntary or not, we do not look for a positive ingredient but rather for considerations that would preclude its being voluntary and thereby exonerate the agent. In moral cases the most important types of plea that a man can put forward are (a) that he was the victim of certain sorts of ignorance, and (b) that he was the victim of certain sorts of compulsion.

Ignorance. A man may be ignorant of many elements in the situation in which he acts. For example he may not know that it was a policeman who told him to stop, that the stuff he put in the soup was arsenic, that the money he took was not his own. In such cases he would be blamed only if it was thought that he ought to have known or taken the trouble to find out. And his vicious trait of character was not contumacy or callousness or greed or disregard for any moral principle, but carelessness; and carelessness can amount to a vice. Fire-arms are so notoriously dangerous that the excuse 'I didn't know it was loaded' will not do. The reason why he is blamed for carelessness and not for the specific vice for which he would have been blamed if he had done any of these things intentionally is that, although he intended to do what he did, he did not intend to break a moral rule. He intended to take the money, but not to steal. His action was not, therefore, a manifestation of the particular vice that the actions of thieves manifest. Ignorance of fact excuses or reduces the seriousness of an offence; but there is one type of ignorance that never excuses; and that is, in legal contexts, ignorance of the law and, in moral contexts, ignorance of right and wrong.

Now why should ignorance of fact excuse while ignorance of rules does not? Why should a man who takes someone else's money, thinking it to be his own, be guiltless of anything (except possibly carelessness), while a man who takes it, knowing it not to be his own but because he sees nothing wrong in taking other people's money, be held guilty and therefore blameworthy? We are not here concerned with the question why some types of action should be stigmatized as 'wrong,' but solely with the question why ignorance of what is wrong should not be held to exculpate.

The reason is that while the man who thought the money was his own did not intend to act on the maxim 'It is permitted to take other people's money,' the thief does act on this maxim. If a man does something because he does not think it wrong he cannot plead that he did not choose to do it, and it is for choosing to do what is *in fact* wrong, whether he knows it or not, that a man is blamed. The situation is exactly analogous to that in which some non-moral capacity is concerned. 'I would have solved the problem, if I had known all the data' would, if substantiated, allow me to get full marks. But 'I would have solved the problem if I had known more mathematics' would not. Since competence at mathematics is not a moral trait of character, men are not blamed for lack of it; but they are given low marks and denied prizes.

Compulsion. So long as 'compulsion' is used in the literal sense it is not difficult to see why it should be held to exonerate. If a man is compelled to do something, he does not choose to do it and his action is not a manifestation of his moral character or principles. Now, since the purpose of blame and punishment is to change a man's character and principles, neither blame nor punishment is called for in such a case. It would be unjust to punish him since the rules for punishing lay down that a man who acts under compulsion is not to be punished; and the rules lay this down because, with due allowance for superstition and stupidity, we do not have pointless rules. Once more we must be careful to avoid the mistake of saying that the justice of a sentence turns on the question whether the accused is likely to be reformed by it. What is at issue here is not our reason for exonerating this accused, but our reason for making a *general* exception in the case of men whose actions are not expressions of their moral character. Physical compulsion is an obvious case where this is so.

But what if the source of compulsion is within the man himself? It is not an accident that we use 'compulsion' in a psychological way and exonerate compulsives. There are two questions that are relevant here. In the first place we ask whether the man could have resisted the 'compulsion'; and we decide this in the way that we decide all 'could have' questions. We look for evidence of his past behaviour in this, and also in related matters; for the behaviour of the compulsive is usually odd in matters unconnected with his special compulsion; and we compare his case with other known cases. Once the capacity to resist the compulsion is established beyond reasonable doubt we do not allow unsupported sceptical doubts about his capacity to resist it in a particular case to rebut the conclusion that he could have helped it. And we do not allow this because there is no way of establishing or refuting the existence of a capacity except by appeal to general evidence. If the capacity has been established and all the necessary conditions were present, we would not say that, in this case, he was the victim of a compulsion. Indeed a 'compulsion' is not something that could be said to operate in a particular case only; for to say that a man has a psychological compulsion is to say something about his behaviour over a long period. A compulsion is more like a chronic disorder than like a cold; and it is still less like a sneeze.

It is also relevant to raise the question whether he had any motive for doing what he did. Part of the difference between a kleptomaniac and a thief lies in the fact that the former has no motive for what he does; and he escapes blame because the point of blame is to strengthen some motives and weaken others. We are sometimes inclined to take the psychologists' talk about compulsions too seriously. We think that a man is excused because he has a 'compulsion,' as if the compulsion could be pointed to in the way that an external object which pushed him could be pointed to. But compulsions are not objects inside us; and we use the word 'compulsion,' not because we have isolated and identified the object which caused him to do what he did, but because we want to excuse him in the same sort of way that we excuse someone who is literally pushed; and we want to excuse him for the same sort of reason. We know that it will do no good to punish him.

Desires. A man might plead that he would have acted otherwise if he had not had a strong desire to do what he did; but the desire was so strong that, as things were, he could not have acted otherwise. Would this plea be allowed to exonerate him? In some cases it would; for there are, as we have seen, cases of addiction in which we allow that a man is not to blame since his craving was too strong for him. But in most cases it would be considered frivolous to say 'I would have done the right thing if I hadn't wanted to do the wrong thing'; for it is just for this that men are blamed.

To distinguish an overwhelming desire from one that the agent could have resisted is not always easy; but the criterion that we in fact use for making the distinction is not difficult to understand. We know from experience that most men can be trained to curb some desires, but not others; and we assume that what is true in most cases is true in a given case unless special reasons are given for doubting this. Now it might seem that, although this evidence enables us to predict that we shall be able to train the man to curb his desire in future, it sheds no light on the question whether he could have curbed it on the occasion in question. I shall say more about this question of moral training later; here I only wish to point out that we have no criterion for deciding whether a man could have resisted a desire on a given occasion other than general evidence of his capacity and the capacity of others like him. We do not, because we cannot, try to answer this question as if it referred solely to the given occasion; we treat it as a question about a capacity.

Character. Finally a man might plead that he could not help doing what he did because that's the sort of man he is. He would not have done it if he had been more honest or less cowardly or less mean and so on. This sort of plea is paradoxical in the same sort of way that the plea of ignorance of moral rules and the plea that he did it because he wanted to are paradoxical. And all three paradoxes stem from the same source, the uncritical extension of 'ought implies can' and of the exculpatory force of 'he could not have acted otherwise' to cases which they will not cover. We know that these pleas are not in fact accepted; the puzzle is to see why.

The plea 'I could not help it because I am that sort of person' might be backed up by an explanation of how I came to be that sort of person. Just as the discovery of a compelling cause exonerates, so, it might be argued, to reveal the causes of my character being what it is is to show that I could not help being what I am and thus to exonerate me. But this argument is fallacious. In the first place to discover the cause of something is not to prove that it is inevitable. On the contrary the discovery of the cause of a disease is often the first step towards preventing it.

Now it is logically impossible to prevent something happening if we know the cause of it, since it could not have a cause unless it occurred and therefore it was not prevented. So when we talk of preventing diseases or accidents we are not talking about preventing cases which have occurred but about ensuring that there are no future cases. Similarly, if I know how Jones came to be a dishonest man I cannot prevent him from being dishonest now; but it may be possible to prevent others from becoming dishonest and to cure Jones of his dishonesty.

Secondly, the discovery of a cause of something has no necessary bearing on a verdict about that thing. We know that a man has come to be what he is because of three main types of cause, heredity, education, and his own past actions. These three factors are not independent of each other and it is not the business of a philosopher to say exactly what is the effect of each or which is the most important for moral training. The question 'Granted that we want people to be better and that we have fairly clear ideas about what "being better" means, should we try to breed a superior race or pay more attention to education?' is not a philosophical question. But it is the business of a philosopher to show in what ways these 'causes' are related to responsibility.

Now these three factors also play a part in situations in which non-moral verdicts are given. Leopold Mozart was a competent musician; his son Wolfgang was given a good musical education and practised his art assiduously. Each of these facts helps to explain how he was able to compose and play so well. There is plenty of evidence that musical ability runs in families and still more of the effects of teaching and practice. But, having learnt these facts, we do not have the slightest tendency to say that, because Mozart's abilities were 'due' to heredity, teaching, and practice, his compositions were not 'really' his own, or to abate one jot of our admiration. In the same way, however a man came by his moral principles, they are still *his* moral principles and he is praised or blamed for them. The plea that, being what he is he cannot help doing what he does, will no more save the wicked man than it will save the bad pianist or actor who has the rashness to expose his incompetence in public. Nor is he saved by being able to explain how he has come to be what he is.

Hereditary tendencies are not causes and do not compel, although a man may inherit a tendency to some form of psychological compulsion. In general to say that a man has a tendency to do something is to say that he usually does it; and to add that the tendency is hereditary is to say that his father also used to do the same sort of thing; and neither of these facts has any tendency to exculpate.

The belief that heredity or a bad upbringing excuse a man's present character is partly due to the false belief that to explain something is to assign an antecedent cause to it and that, to be voluntary, an action must be uncaused. But there is also a good reason for this belief. In fact we do sometimes allow these factors to exculpate; and if the question of explanation was as irrelevant to the question of responsibility as I have suggested it would be hard to understand why we do this. Why do we tend to deal less harshly with juvenile delinquents who come from bad homes than with those who have had every chance? The question is not one of justice, since it is not a question whether Jones ought to be punished, but whether the law should lay down that people whose bad characters are due to certain causes should be punished. We must therefore ask what is our reason for differentiating between two boys whose characters and actions are the same but who come respectively from bad and good homes. And the reason is that in the first case we have not had a chance to see what kindness and a good education could do, while in the second we know that they have failed. Since punishment involves the infliction of pain and since it is a moral rule that unnecessary pain should not be inflicted, there is a general presumption that people should not be punished if the same end could be achieved without the infliction of pain. This consideration is, of course, irrelevant to the question whether Jones should be punished; but it is highly relevant to the question whether a distinction should be made between those whose characters have come to be what they are because of a bad education and those whose characters are bad in spite of a good one.

· But suppose a man should plead that he cannot now help doing what he does because his character was formed by his own earlier actions? This also will not excuse him. The logic of this plea is that he did X because he was, at the time, the sort of man to do X and that he became this sort of man because he did Y and Z in the past. But if he cannot be blamed for doing X now, can he be blamed for having done Y and Z in the past? It would seem that he cannot, for he will exculpate himself in exactly the same way.

Once again the argument presupposes that if his present character can be explained in terms of what happened in the past he necessarily escapes blame. The assumption is that a man's actions form a causal chain in which each necessitates the next. Now, if we suppose that, to be free, an action must be uncaused, either we shall find a genuinely uncaused action at the beginning of the chain or we shall not. If we do not, then no action is culpable; and if we do, then we must suppose that, while most of our actions are caused and therefore blameless, there was in the past some one uncaused action for which alone a man can be held responsible. This theory has in fact been held, although even in the history of philosophy it would be hard to find another so bizarre. The objections to it are clear. In the first place we praise and blame people for what they do now, not for what they might have done as babies; and secondly this hypothetical infantile action could hardly be said to be an action of the agent at all, since it is *ex hypothesi* inexplicable in terms of his character.

The conclusion of the foregoing argument is that 'He could not have acted otherwise' does not always exculpate and, in particular, that it does not exculpate if the reason which is adduced to explain just why he could not have acted otherwise is that he was a man of a certain moral character. We have seen that 'He could have acted otherwise' is to be construed as 'He would have acted otherwise, if . . .' and we have seen which types of 'if' are not allowed to exculpate.

V

MORAL ACTION

Introduction

Voluntary Acts

In response to the question, "What is time?" Saint Augustine replied: "If no one asks me, I know; if I wish to explain it to one that asks, I know not." Much the same reply has been given to the question, "What is an act?" by those who have seriously considered the subject. We commonly assume that we understand what "doing" something involves. We frequently make moral judgments about acts, and though we may at times have qualms about assigning responsibility or granting excuses for certain acts, the problem rarely appears to us to be connected with determining whether a person's behavior constitutes an act, but only with whether what he has done is wrongful or not.

Of course, we realize that moral judgments, rules, and principles do not apply to some things, e.g., the flow of blood through our veins, reflex actions such as a knee jerk caused by a physician's hammer, the movements of animals, or the crying of very small children. But aside from these "obvious" cases, we generally think we know which forms of behavior are subject to moral approval or disapproval.

Yet, if we pointedly ask ourselves, "What is, after all, the difference between, say, a knee jerk and a kick?" the answer does not come very readily. Perhaps most persons would explain the difference by saying that the kick is voluntary whereas the knee jerk is involuntary and would explain that in the case of the kick, it "could have been avoided." It is then said that only voluntary acts are capable of being moral or immoral because it does not make sense to ascribe morality to types of behavior which could not be helped.

So far we have a plausible account, but unless considerably amplified, an overly simple one. For what does "voluntary" really mean? Consider the troublesome cases which Aristotle mentions. A man is ordered by a tyrant to do something dishonorable under threat of death to his family; a ship's captain jettisons cargo during a storm. Are these acts voluntary or involuntary? If we say that they are voluntary, then we must explain the difference between these acts and other voluntary acts such as a simple act of kicking someone. If we say that they are involuntary acts, then we must explain the difference between them and human phenomena such as knee jerks. That there is a substantial difference is obvious. Furthermore, if "voluntariness" is what differentiates an act from a non-act, the concept of an "involuntary act" is self-contradictory, and the expression "voluntary act" at best redundant. Yet, as a matter of fact we often use both these expressions.

While admitting genuine doubt about the so-called mixed cases mentioned above, Aristotle proceeds to distinguish between voluntary and involuntary acts in a somewhat negative way. If an act is done neither under compulsion nor as a result of ignorance, it is voluntary; otherwise, it is involuntary. He admits, however, that we ought not to commit some acts, such as slaying one's mother, even though faced with death and torture, and that some kinds of ignorance, such as not knowing whether a weapon is loaded, will not excuse. These admissions raise the question of whether Aristotle can maintain both (1) that only voluntary acts are subject to praise or blame and (2) that acts done under compulsion or in ignorance are involuntary. Siegler briefly discusses this problem. The reader should discover for himself how Aristotle attempts to resolve the dilemma and evaluate his success or failure.

In addition to this negative characterization of a voluntary act, Aristotle also has a positive definition which may be restated as follows: "A voluntary act is one that is initiated by the agent himself when he is aware of the particular circumstances in which the act occurs." A slightly different definition, which has often been criticized but which continues to find supporters, is that of the nineteenth-century legal philosopher, John Austin: "An act is a voluntary bodily movement." The point of this definition is to restrict the term "act" to those bodily movements over which we have control, for it is only those things within our control for which we can be held responsible. It turns out that in Austin's theory only those muscular movements which are the immediate effects of our will are "acts." "I tensed the muscles in my forefinger" describes an act; "He fired a gun and killed someone" describes only a further consequence of that act. The curious implication of this view, as far as the problem of assigning responsibility is concerned, is that although we do often hold persons responsible for the consequences of their acts as well as for their acts, we rarely if ever hold them responsible for "muscular contractions." This theory proposes that the only *acts* for which we should ever hold persons responsible are just such muscular contractions. Of course, Austin would say that we can, and in certain circumstances should hold a person responsible for killing someone, but he would also have to say that killing, strictly speaking, is not an act but a consequence of an act. The selection by D'Arcy discusses further the implications and difficulties which confront this theory.

Negative Acts: Omissions and Forbearances

Perhaps equally as puzzling as the problem of defining an act is the problem of omissions. It might be thought that if once we could settle upon a definition of an act, then an omission would simply be a "not-doing" of such an act. Unfortunately, there are several difficulties here. One is that there does not seem to be a one-to-one correlation between acts and omissions. For example, it makes sense to say that I omitted to keep my promise, but not to say that I omitted to commit murder. Another difficulty is that not every not-doing is an omission. For example, I did not buy a Cadillac today, but that does not necessarily mean that I omitted to buy a Cadillac. Still another difficulty is that in conceiving of an omission as a not-doing, we are likely to think that it does not involve doing anything positive. Yet if I fail to keep my promise, this is as positive and effective in damaging human relationships as my actually keeping my promise is effective in maintaining a certain relationship of trust. To emphasize this positive feature of an essentially negative act, we often speak of "breaking" a promise. Also, it is common to speak of "acts of omission" as contrasted with "acts of commission."

Bentham expresses what he takes to be the difference between acts and omissions as follows:

> By positive [acts] are meant such as consist in motion or exertion: by negative, such as consist in keeping at rest; that is, in forbearing to move or exert oneself in such and such circumstances. Thus, to strike is a positive act: not to strike on a certain occasion, a negative one.

D'Arcy finds that this analysis fails to provide an adequate criterion of an omission. Simply "relaxing in an arm chair," he says, is not necessarily an omission. He does agree, however, that "keeping at rest," or as he interprets the phrase, "physical non-movement," is a *necessary* condition for an omission. Siegler questions D'Arcy's interpretation of Bentham's phrase "keeping at rest." In addition he questions whether physical non-movement is a necessary condition and uses the counterexample of a person who fidgets before a photographer when he should be standing still. By fidgeting, which is a physical movement, he has omitted to stand still.

There is also a question whether, as the passage from Bentham suggests, omissions are the same as forbearances. Siegler thinks not. An omission, he says, may be either intentional or unintentional, but there are no unintentional forbearances. Nor, he says, are all intentional omissions forbearances, or all forbearances intentional omissions. I might intentionally omit a dividend check from my income tax report, but that would hardly be called a forbearance. On the other hand, he says, I might forbear from punching a man who angered me, and that would hardly be called an omission. Just how important it is to make this distinction between the kinds of negative acts is left for the reader to decide. In any case, he should carefully examine Siegler's criticism of von Wright's conception of a forbearance, and also Siegler's criticism of D'Arcy's definition of an omission, which goes as follows: "A person is said to have omitted X if, and only if, (1) he did not do X, and (2) X was in some way expected of him."

The legal case of *Rex* v. *Russell* illustrates the problem of assigning responsibility in cases of omitted acts. A husband stands by while his wife drowns herself along with their two infant children. At least three problems are connected with this case: (1) Did the defendant do anything at all? (2) If he acted, how many acts did he perform? (3) What, if anything, did he do that was wrong?

It is obvious that unless the defendant did something, the question about the legal or moral wrongness of his act is simply irrelevant. But does just "standing by" constitute an act in any sense at all? Is it an omission? Was he obligated, legally or morally, to intervene? If so, on what basis would that obligation rest? Must we always prevent others from harming themselves? Is there a special duty in the case of a husband and father? The jury, with the help of the trial judge, answers the last question affirmatively, and on this basis finds that he omitted to perform a legal and moral duty to his wife and children.

The problem of assigning responsibility in this case is further complicated by the fact that there were three deaths. Should we say that by "standing by" he committed three acts of omission or only one? Perhaps it would not matter if his obligations were the same to both his wife and to his children, but are they? Apparently the wife took the children into the water. Is the husband as responsible for her positive act as he is for the helpless condition of the children? If the wife in fact committed suicide, could it be said that the husband killed her? His omission to prevent her death would then be different, and perhaps less serious than his omission to save the children. If, because the obligation to both the children is the same, we consider the latter omission as a single one, then there are only two omissions.

Such questions are of considerable moment if we are to intelligently assess exactly what the man did wrong. Aside from the failure to perform his moral obligations to his family—the factor which enabled the jury to decide that he did in fact do something—the court was confronted by a variety of possible characterizations of the man's actions. Among the possibilities considered are the following:

1. He murdered his wife and his two children.
2. He committed manslaughter of all three.
3. He murdered his wife and manslaughtered his children.
4. He was a participator in the murder of his children by his wife.
5. He aided and abetted his wife in the deaths of his children.
6. He aided and abetted his wife's suicide.
7. He killed no one.

The jury finally decides upon the second description of the act, although, in his review of the case, Justice Mann (the judge who presided at the original trial) thinks that the appropriate label with respect to the wife's death should have been murder. Justice McArthur believes that the wife committed suicide, and that therefore the manslaughter conviction with respect to her case should not be allowed to stand. Despite these differences of opinion with respect to the proper characterization of the wrong, or wrongs, committed, the case does illustrate the close connection there often is between determining *that* an act (or omission) has been committed and *what kind* of act it is.

Acts and Consequences

The problem of correctly describing an act is often associated with the problem of drawing a line between the act and its consequences. One of D'Arcy's illustrations is the following: "A tells a lie and B is deceived; A is thus able to rob B." Is A's *act* "telling a lie," the consequences being deceiving B and robbing him? Or is the act "deceiving B" (by means of a lie), the consequence being the robbery? Or, we might add, is the act simply one of "robbing B" with no further consequences taken into account?

It is tempting to say that perhaps there may be several different but equally correct descriptions of the same act, depending on how we distinguish act from consequences. D'Arcy presents this view as a thesis. Yet there are difficulties with it and only a few can be mentioned here. One is that often it does make a difference, as far as our evaluation of the act is concerned, whether a person's act is described in one way rather than another. To lie is one thing but to rob is quite another. To pull a trigger on a gun may be quite innocent but to shoot a man is something else. Also, if it makes no difference how many consequences we include in the description of the act, the task of describing any act completely may be literally and actually impossible. We may find ourselves in the position of never really being sure what a given agent did. Third, there is some question whether it makes sense to include certain consequences in the description of an act. Some may be the effects of other causes and other agents and so not really a part of "my" act at all. Even being deceived by a lie presupposes that the one deceived was himself in a condition to be deceived, and this condition (e.g. stupidity) may not have been the effect of the lie itself in any way whatever. There is a final qualm about the propriety of incorporating consequences into acts. If we give two different descriptions of the "same" act by incorporating different consequences, we may end up with morally incompatible judgments of the act. For example, many philosophers have claimed that most, if not all, acts produce both good and bad consequences. If we describe an act, involving a lie for instance, as one of "achieving a benefit for oneself" and also as an act of "taking advantage of others," and if both are "equally correct," then we may be in a position of having to say that the act is both morally right and wrong.

Unfortunately, if we try to deny the statement that an act may have (perhaps infinitely) many different but equally correct descriptions and assert that it may have only *one* correct description, there are difficulties that must also be faced. Suppose we attempt to exclude all consequences from the description and consider only "the act" itself. What kernel of human behavior are we left with? A simple muscular contraction? But if so, how do we distinguish such a contraction from other purely physical movements, such as the blood's flow, which we would ordinarily not describe as a human act at all? Do we then say that the act is nothing but a "willing" or an "act of will"? How is this to be described apart from all overt physical movement? How are we to distinguish it from other mental processes such as imagining or thinking, which do not obviously resemble what we ordinarily call acts?

D'Arcy does qualify his thesis that "there is not necessarily one, and only one, correct description of a given act" in the following way. There are certain kinds of acts, he says, of such significance that they may not be redescribed in terms of consequences which conceal that significance or fail to reveal the nature of the act itself. For example, he says, it is legitimate to redescribe "Macbeth's stabbing of Duncan" as "Macbeth's killing of Duncan," but it is illegitimate to redescribe "Macbeth's killing of Duncan" as "Macbeth's succeeding Duncan," i.e., in terms of the consequences that Macbeth succeeded him as king.

When D'Arcy speaks of the "significance" of actions, he is of course referring to acts such as killing, maiming, slandering, torturing, deceiving, betraying, and promise breaking. His insight is no doubt correct, but one may perhaps wonder whether he has begged the whole question by this limitation. After all, one of the purposes in describing acts is to put us in a better position to evaluate them. But if we must first evaluate them and are only then in a position to describe the acts, we have presumably defeated the point of our analysis.

Despite this objection, which the reader should assess for himself, D'Arcy's discussion of the problem should be useful in further understanding the disparate claims of such classical moral philosophers as Kant and Mill. Mill emphasizes consequences as the sole basis for evaluating acts. Kant emphasizes the necessity for excluding them. Of course neither of these philosophers denies that there is a distinction between acts and consequences, but still, neither of them provides a criterion for making it. The considerations of this chapter should suggest a new way of looking at their dispute and the merits of relying or not relying on consequences as a basis for judging the morality of acts.

Voluntary Behavior

Aristotle

Nicomachean Ethics

Book III

1. Since virtue is concerned with passions and actions, and on voluntary passions and actions praise and blame are bestowed, on those that are involuntary pardon, and sometimes also pity, to distinguish the voluntary and the involuntary is presumably necessary for those who are studying the nature of virtue, and useful also for legislators with a view to the assigning both of honours and of punishments.

From *Ethica Nicomachea,* trans. W. D. Ross, in *The Oxford Translation of Aristotle,* ed. W. D. Ross, vol. IX (1925), by permission of The Clarendon Press, Oxford.

Those things, then, are thought involuntary, which take place under compulsion or owing to ignorance; and that is compulsory of which the moving principle is outside, being a principle in which nothing is contributed by the person who is acting or is feeling the passion, e.g., if he were to be carried somewhere by a wind, or by men who had him in their power.

But with regard to the things that are done from fear of greater evils or for some noble object (e.g. if a tyrant were to order one to do something base, having one's parents and children in his power, and if one did the action they were to be saved, but otherwise would be put to death), it may be debated whether such actions are involuntary or voluntary. Something of the sort happens also with regard to the throwing of goods overboard in a storm; for in the abstract no one throws goods away voluntarily, but on condition of its securing the safety of himself and his crew any sensible man does so. Such actions, then, are mixed, but are more like voluntary actions; for they are worthy of choice at the time when they are done, and the end of an action is relative to the occasion. Both the terms, then, 'voluntary' and 'involuntary,' must be used with reference to the moment of action. Now the man acts voluntarily; for the principle that moves the instrumental parts of the body in such actions is in him, and the things of which the moving principle is in a man himself are in his power to do or not to do. Such actions, therefore, are voluntary, but in the abstract perhaps involuntary; for no one would choose any such act in itself.

For such actions men are sometimes even praised, when they endure something base or painful in return for great and noble objects gained; in the opposite case they are blamed, since to endure the greatest indignities for no noble end or for a trifling end is the mark of an inferior person. On some actions praise indeed is not bestowed, but pardon is, when one does what he ought not under pressure which overstrains human nature and which no one could withstand. But some acts, perhaps, we cannot be forced to do, but ought rather to face death after the most fearful sufferings; for the things that 'forced' Euripides' Alcmaeon to slay his mother seem absurd. It is difficult sometimes to determine what should be chosen at what cost, and what should be endured in return for what gain, and yet more difficult to abide by our decisions; for as a rule what is expected is painful, and what we are forced to do is base, whence praise and blame are bestowed on those who have been compelled or have not.

What sort of acts, then, should be called compulsory? We answer that without qualification actions are so when the cause is in the external circumstances and the agent contributes nothing. But the things that in themselves are involuntary, but now and in return for these gains are worthy of choice, and whose moving principle is in the agent, are in themselves involuntary, but now and in return for these gains voluntary. They are more like voluntary acts; for actions are in the class of particulars, and the particular acts here are voluntary. What sort of things are to be chosen, and in return for what, it is not easy to state; for there are many differences in the particular cases.

But if some one were to say that pleasant and noble objects have a compelling power, forcing us from without, all acts would be for him compulsory; for it is for these objects that all men do everything they do. And those who act under compulsion and unwillingly act with pain, but those who do acts for their pleasantness and nobility do them with pleasure; it is absurd to make external circumstances responsible, and not oneself, as being easily caught by such attractions, and to make oneself responsible for noble acts but the pleasant objects responsible for base acts. The compulsory, then, seems to be that whose moving principle is outside, the person compelled contributing nothing.

Everything that is done by reason of ignorance is *not* voluntary; it is only what produces pain and repentance that is *in*voluntary. For the man who has done something owing to ignorance, and feels not the least vexation at his action, has not acted voluntarily, since he did not know what he was doing, nor yet involuntarily, since he is not pained. Of people, then, who act by reason of ignorance he who repents is thought an involuntary agent, and the man who does not repent may, since he is different, be called a not voluntary agent; for, since he differs from the other, it is better that he should have a name of his own.

Acting by reason of ignorance seems also to be different from acting *in* ignorance; for the man who is drunk or in a rage is thought to act as a result not of ignorance but of one of the causes mentioned, yet not knowingly but in ignorance.

Now every wicked man is ignorant of what he ought to do and what he ought to abstain from, and it is by reason of error of this kind that men become unjust and in general bad; but the term 'involuntary' tends to be used not if a man is ignorant of what is to his advantage—for it is not mistaken purpose that causes involuntary action (it leads rather to wickedness), nor ignorance of the universal (for *that* men are *blamed*,) but ignorance of particulars, i.e., of the circumtances of the action and the objects with which it is concerned. For it is on these that both pity and pardon depend, since the person who is ignorant of any of these acts involuntarily.

Perhaps it is just as well, therefore, to determine their nature and number. A man may be ignorant, then, of who he is, what he is doing, what or whom he is acting on, and sometimes also what (e.g. what instrument) he is doing it with, and to what end (e.g. he may think his act will conduce to some one's safety), and how he is doing it (e.g. whether gently or violently). Now of all of these no one could be ignorant unless he were mad, and evidently also he could not be ignorant of the agent; for how could he not know himself? But of what he is doing a man might be ignorant, as for instance people say 'it slipped out their mouths as they were speaking,' or 'they did not know it was a secret,' as Aeschylus said of the mysteries, or a man might say he 'let it go off when he merely wanted to show its working,' as the man did with the catapult. Again, one might think one's son was an enemy, as Merope did, or that a pointed spear had a button on it, or that a stone was pumice-stone; or one might give man a draught to save him, and really kill him; or one might want to touch a man, as people do in sparring, and really wound him. The ignorance may relate, then, to any of these things, i.e. of the circumstances of the action, and the man who was ignorant of any of these is thought to have acted involuntarily, and especially if he was ignorant on the most important points; and these are thought to be the circumstances of the action and its end. Further, the doing of an act that is called involuntary in virtue of ignorance of this sort must be painful and involve repentance.

Since that which is done under compulsion or by reason of ignorance is involuntary, the voluntary would seem to be that of which the moving principle is in the agent himself, he being aware of the particular circumstances of the action. Presumably acts done by reason of anger or appetite are not rightly called involuntary. For in the first place, on that showing none of the other animals will act voluntarily, nor will children; and secondly, is it meant that we do not do voluntarily *any* of the acts that are due to appetite or anger, or that we do the noble acts voluntarily and the base acts involuntarily? Is not this absurd, when one and the same thing is the cause? But it would surely be odd to describe as involuntary the things one ought to desire; and we ought both to be angry at certain things and to have an appetite for certain things, e.g. for health and for learning. Also what is involuntary is thought to be painful, but what is in accordance with appetite is thought to be pleasant. Again, what is the difference in respect of involuntariness between errors committed upon calculation and those committed in anger? Both are to be avoided, but the irrational passions are thought not less human than reason is, and therefore also the actions which proceed from anger or appetite are the man's actions. It would be odd, then, to treat them as involuntary. . . .

5. . . . Now the exercise of the virtues is concerned with means. Therefore virtue also is in our own power, and so too vice. For where

it is in our power to act it is also in our power not to act, and *vice versa*; so that, if to act, where this is noble, is in our power, not to act, which will be base, will also be in our power, and if not to act, where this is noble, is in our power, to act, which will be base, will also be in our power. . . .

The saying that 'no one is voluntarily wicked nor involuntarily happy' seems to be partly false and partly true; for no one is involuntarily happy, but wickedness *is* voluntary. Or else we shall have to dispute what has just been said, at any rate, and deny that man is a moving principle or begetter of his actions as of children. But if these facts are evident and we cannot refer actions to moving principles other than those in ourselves, the acts whose moving principles are in us must themselves also be in our power and voluntary.

Witness seems to be borne to this both by individuals in their private capacity and by legislators themselves; for these punish and take vengeance on those who do wicked acts (unless they have acted under compulsion or as a result of ignorance for which they are not themselves responsible), while they honour those who do noble acts, as though they meant to encourage the latter and deter the former. But no one is encouraged to do the things that are neither in our power nor voluntary; it is assumed that there is no gain in being persuaded not to be hot or in pain or hungry or the like, since we shall experience these feelings none the less. Indeed, we punish a man for his very ignorance, if he is thought responsible for the ignorance, as when penalties are doubled in the case of drunkenness; for the moving principle is in the man himself, since he had the power of not getting drunk and his getting drunk was the cause of his ignorance. And we punish those who are ignorant of anything in the laws that they ought to know and that is not difficult, and so too in the case of anything else that they are thought to be ignorant of through carelessness; we assume that it is in their power not to be ignorant, since they have the power of taking care.

But perhaps a man is the kind of man not to take care. Still they are themselves by their slack lives responsible for becoming men of that kind, and men make themselves responsible for being unjust or self-indulgent, in the one case by cheating and in the other by spending their time in drinking bouts and the like; for it is activities exercised on particular objects that make the corresponding character. This is plain from the case of people training for any contest or action; they practise the activity the whole time. Now not to know that it is from the exercise of activities on particular objects that states of character are produced is the mark of a thoroughly senseless person. Again, it is irrational to suppose that a man who acts unjustly does not wish to be unjust or a man who acts self-indulgently to be self-indulgent. But if *without* being ignorant a man does the things which will make him unjust, he will be unjust voluntarily. Yet it does not follow that if he wishes he will cease to be unjust and will be just. For neither does the man who is ill become well on those terms. We may suppose a case in which he is ill voluntarily, through living incontinently and disobeying his doctors. In that case it was *then* open to him not to be ill, but not now, when he has thrown away his chance, just as when you have let a stone go it is too late to recover it; but yet it was in your power to throw it, since the moving principle was in you. So, too, to the unjust and to the self-indulgent man it was open at the beginning not to become men of this kind, and so they are unjust and self-indulgent voluntarily; but now that they have become so it is not possible for them not to be so.

But not only are the vices of the soul voluntary, but those of the body also for some men, whom we accordingly blame; while no one blames those who are ugly by nature, we blame those who are so owing to want of exercise and care. So it is, too, with respect to weakness and infirmity; no one would reproach a man blind from birth or by disease or from a blow, but rather pity him, while every one would blame a man who was blind from drunkenness or some other form of self-indulgence. Of vices of the body, then, those in our own power are blamed, those not in our power are not. And if this be so, in the other cases also the vices that are blamed must be in our own power.

Now some one may say that all men desire the apparent good, but have no control over the appearance, but the end appears to each man in a form answering to his character. We reply that if each man is somehow responsible for his state of mind, he will also be himself somehow responsible for the appearance; but if not, no one is responsible for his own evildoing, but every one does evil acts through ignorance of the end, thinking that by these he will get what is best, and the aiming at the end is not self-chosen but one must be born with an eye, as it were, by which to judge rightly and choose what is truly good, and he is well endowed by nature who is well endowed with this. For it is what is greatest and most noble, and what we cannot get or learn from another, but must have just such as it was when given us at birth, and to be well and nobly endowed with this will be perfect and true excellence of natural endowmen. If this is true, then, how will virtue be more voluntary than vice? To both men alike, the good and the bad, the end appears and is fixed by nature or however it may be, and it is by referring everything else to this that men do whatever they do.

Whether, then, it is not by nature that the end appears to each man such as it does appear, but something also depends on him, or the end is natural but because the good man adopts the means voluntarily virtue is voluntary, vice also will be none the less voluntary; for in the case of the bad man there is equally present that which depends on himself in his actions even if not in his end. If, then, as is asserted, the virtues are voluntary (for we are ourselves somehow partly responsible for our states of character, and it is by being persons of a certain kind that we assume the end to be so and so), the vices also will be voluntary; for the same is true of them.

Negative Acts

Frederick A. Siegler

Omissions

According to Aristotle, in order reasonably to blame a man for his act, he must have acted voluntarily. This necessary condition for blame is characterized in two ways. Negatively, it is characterized as the absence of ignorance of what one is doing and the absence of force; positively, it is characterized as knowledge of what one is doing and the agent's own initiation of the act. If either of the conjuncts (negative or positive) is not satisfied the act is not voluntary and cannot be blamed (or praised). Both conjuncts (negative or positive) must be satisfied for the act to be voluntary and thereby to allow reasonably for blame.

From "Omissions," *Analysis* 28 (January 1968), by permission of the author and Basil Blackwell & Mott Ltd., Oxford.

According to Aristotle, acts done in ignorance of an important particular are involuntary. And he holds that involuntary acts cannot reasonably be blamed. But these two theses conflict with the fact that there are some acts done in ignorance which we do blame and, it seems, reasonably. Thus either Aristotle is wrong in saying that acts done in ignorance are involuntary or he is wrong in saying that involuntary acts cannot reasonably be blamed or we are wrong (contrary to what *seems* reasonable) in blaming acts done in ignorance.

There are two sorts of case which reveal this problem. First, careless and reckless acts, done in ignorance, and second, negligent omissions which are done (which occur) in ignorance. Aristotle's own solution is that we can be blamed if we are responsible for our ignorance (1113b 24-1114a3). This leaves it unclear whether in being blamed for forgetting to lock the gate (when one had a duty to) one is being blamed for a prior failure to take precautions against forgetting which itself was not voluntary in Aristotle's sense or whether one is being blamed for the forgetting to lock the gate in virtue of a prior failure to take precautions against forgetting. In either case, one is being blamed for something done in ignorance.

A similar problem arises in legal thought. Graham Hughes ('Criminal Omissions,' *Yale Law Journal*, 1958, reprinted in Morris, *Freedom and Responsibility*, Stanford, 1961), for example, says that the notion of a *mens rea* or guilty mind, particularly when interpreted in terms of intention and advertent recklessness 'work(s) very nicely with regard to "offenses of commission".' But 'with omissions, the great difficulty is that the mind of the offender may not be addressed at all to the enjoined conduct, if he is unaware of the duty to act.'

In the paper I shall not defend my interpretation of Aristotle or discuss the problems that arise from what he says. Rather, I shall discuss some recent attempts in philosophical literature to clarify the notion of an omission. First I shall discuss some remarks of von Wright which bear on 'ignorance for which one is responsible' and 'omission' and then I shall discuss Bentham's and D'Arcy's analyses of 'omission.' My discussion is almost entirely critical. I shall leave the difficult task of a positive account of omissions for another occasion.

Von Wright (*The Varieties of Goodness,* Routledge and Kegan Paul, 1963) discusses mixed action in a strikingly similar way to Aristotle. But his discussion suffers from a failure to account for 'ignorance for which one is responsible' (p. 124). He says that 'If the agent, at the time when he is acting, does not foresee the consequences (or at least realize the "serious possibility" that it will happen), then he can, in a sense, not even be rightly said to have *done* the consequent thing.' But surely a man can *do* something inadvertently, without realizing it, by accident, by mistake, *etc.,* where it is perfectly clear that he did it; and it is not at all clear what could be meant by saying that, in a sense, he did not *do* it at all, unless that 'sense' were to mean that he did not do it intentionally. But that is *not* a sense of 'do.' Von Wright notes later that an aspect of the analysis of goodness 'to which moralists in a Kantian spirit . . . have habitually paid but little attention,' is that of 'blame for ignorance.' He rightly notes that 'Because of ignorance, much bad is done for good motives.' Although these issues are not essential to von Wright's immediate concern with the goodness or badness of intention, it is surprising that he fails to see how important it is that much bad is done without any motive at all but from carelessness, recklessness, negligence, *etc.*

This omission leads von Wright to underestimate the 'asymmetry between moral goodness and moral badness' for he claims that 'the first presupposes that some good should be *intended* and, moreover, intended for its own sake' whereas 'moral badness . . . requires that some bad should be *foreseen* to follow from the act' (p. 130, my italics). Moral badness does not, however, require that some bad should be foreseen to follow from the act. For the cases which I have mentioned — those of carelessness, recklessness and negligence — are cases where the agent failed to foresee bad consequences, and where his act is nevertheless morally bad precisely because of his lack of foresight.

Von Wright contrasts 'foreseeing harm' as a necessary condition for moral badness with 'harm which follows, but which could not have been foreseen at the time of acting,' which 'is not relevant to the question of the morality of the act' (p. 130). I have argued that this classification is incomplete because it omits mention of harm which the agent could have foreseen but failed to foresee. The proper contrast is, therefore, between (a) 'could not have been foreseen' and (b) 'did foresee' or 'did not foresee but should have foreseen.'

A good deal has been written recently on actions in terms of intentions, reasons or motives for acting (Melden, Anscombe, Kenny, Peters), and this work has helped to clarify some of the grounds for praising and blaming people for what they do. It is perhaps because most of this recent work was written from the point of view of psychological rather than moral concepts, and because we do not praise actions done unwittingly, inadvertently, or, generally speaking, done when the agent is not aware of what he is doing, that very little light has been shed on the conceptual connections between blame or criticism and omissions.

Perhaps another reason is that some forms of omissions are describable as acts, *viz.* intentional omissions. Von Wright (in *Norm and Action,* Routledge and Kegan Paul, 1963) does discuss the neglected topic of 'forbearances,' a variety of acts which is open to praise and blame; but his discussion is unsatisfactory. He gives the following definition: 'An agent, on a given occasion, forbears the doing of a certain thing if, and only if, he *can do* this thing, but *does* in fact *not do* it' (p. 45). In English, however, 'forbearance' does require awareness of the opportunity; in order to say that I have forborne doing something, it is not sufficient to say that I did not do something which I could have done. (Contrary to von Wright's beliefs, each of the five definitions in the OED use 'abstain' or 'refrain.') It would follow from von Wright's definition that, if A knows how to open windows and if the windows in his house are closed, he is forbearing from opening them. Indeed, he is forbearing from opening all closed windows, since von Wright characterizes 'can do' in terms of ability (know-how) and opportunity; and the only way that he suggests the opportunity can be lost is when somebody else actually opens the windows. Furthermore, von Wright, as he recognizes, is committed by his definition to the view that 'unsuccessful trying to do something which it is within the agent's *ability* to accomplish, counts as forbearing' (p. 52).

Now clearly what von Wright claims is simply false as an analysis of the use of the English word 'forbearance' and its cognates. However, though he purports to be analyzing the notion of forbearance, he also thinks that he is 'moulding' the notion. This notion of 'moulding' a notion or concept (both here and in *Varieties of Goodness*) is unclear, both as to what it means and as to what justification there could be for it. If he has a specific purpose in drawing a new distinction with old words, then there should be a clear statement of that purpose. But as it is, he presents neither an analysis of the notion of forbearance that we do have nor, in fact, a coherent account of some new notion that he wishes to introduce.

It would not be adequate to say that von Wright can do what he pleases with the word 'forbearance.' First, he offers no justification for his distortion of the language. And secondly, he contradicts himself precisely because he in fact continues on occasion to give the word its ordinary meaning even when he is supposedly discussing his new concept. He argues that 'the notion of forbearing we have thus defined (lacuna in the text? — implies?) that ability to do and ability to forbear doing the same thing are *reciprocal* abilities' (p. 53). No explicit account of 'reciprocal abilities' is offered; but from von Wright's comments the claim seems to be that (1) if someone has the ability to forbear ϕ-ing then he has the ability to ϕ, and (2) if someone has the ability to ϕ then he has the ability to forbear from ϕ-ing. Thus he remarks: 'It may appear more plausible to say that what an agent can do he can also forbear doing than to say that what an agent can forbear doing he can also do' (p. 53). This appearance, von Wright argues, is largely due to confusions.

So, according to von Wright, the ability to ϕ entails and is entailed by the ability to forbear ϕ-ing. But according to his own definition the two abilities would not be merely reciprocal, but, rather, identical. For forbearing ϕ-ing is defined as (1) having the ability to ϕ, (2) having the opportunity to ϕ, and (3) not ϕ-ing. But to speak of the ability to forbear ϕ-ing must be to ignore (2) and (3), and then the ability to forbear ϕ-ing would be defined in terms of (1) the ability to ϕ. Again, according to von Wright, the only ability necessary to forbear ϕ-ing is the ability to ϕ, and therefore, on his account, the ability to ϕ is the ability to forbear ϕ-ing.

This, then, gives a sense of the notion of reciprocal abilities, though it is perhaps odd to argue that two abilities are reciprocal because they are in fact identical; nevertheless, this appears to follow, as von Wright claims, from his definition of forbearance. He goes on immediately, however, to consider whether 'it is somehow "easier" to forbear than to do' (p. 53), and his conclusion is the following: 'In a sense, therefore, forbearing is precisely as "difficult" as doing. But in another sense, forbearing can rightly be said to be, normally, *easier* than doing' (p. 53). But if, as von Wright's definition implies, the ability to forbear ϕ-ing and the ability to ϕ are logically identical, then his argument here is that, in one sense, the ability to ϕ is precisely as difficult as itself, and in another sense, it is, normally, easier, than itself. And this is straightforwardly contradictory.

Von Wright is led into asserting this self-contradiction, because although he has arbitrarily re-defined a term in our language, he has failed to emancipate himself from its ordinary use. We sometimes find it very difficult to forbear from ϕ-ing when there is no question about one's ability to ϕ, for example, taking a drink, treating rudeness with rudeness. Thus, because it does normally make sense to speak of the *difficulty* of forbearing from ϕ-ing as compared to ϕ-ing von Wright is induced to consider such comparison even where by his own explicit definition, he is committed to denying the appropriateness of such a comparison. But even on the ordinary use of 'forbearance' von Wright would be wrong.

Normally, and perhaps always, when A forbears from ϕ-ing he has some inclination to ϕ from desire or provocation and the ease or difficulty with which A forbears would depend on what act ϕ stands for. One might think that *similarly* the ease or difficulty A has in ϕ-ing would depend on what ϕ stands for. Some acts are more difficult to perform than others. But the difficulty in swimming across a lake is not at all commensurable with the difficulty in forbearing from doing it. Forbearing sometimes takes great effort but not physical skill or physical effort. If there is to be comparison it would have to be between forbearing from ϕ-ing and deciding to ϕ. But although such a comparison might make sense with regard to particular cases it seems that nothing sensible could be said about the two in general.

Von Wright is confused perhaps, in part, because thinking wrongly that omissions are either identical with, or a species of forbearances, and realizing that norms apply not only to intentional omissions, he discusses forbearances and gives an analysis which attempts to encompass unintentional omissions.

A similar confusion is found in Bentham's definitions: 'By positive (acts) are meant such as consist in motion or exertion: by negative, such as consist in keeping at rest; that is, in forbearing to move or exert oneself in such and such circumstances. Thus to strike is a positive act: not to strike on a certain occasion, a negative one. Positive acts are styled also acts of commission; negative, acts of omission or forbearance' (p. 72, *Introduction to the Principles of Morals and Legislation*, Oxford, 1907). This is criticized by D'Arcy on the grounds that 'To the question, "What were you doing at two o'clock this afternoon?" any of the following could be appropriate replies: "Taking a siesta," "Relaxing in an arm chair," "Sunbathing" . . . Each of these replies would satisfy Bentham's definition of an omission as physical non-movement, "keeping at rest," yet we should not call any of them an omission' (*Human Acts*, p. 41). But this will not do as a criticism of Bentham for (1) though sitting in an arm chair may be, in some sense, 'physical non-movement' (*D'Arcy's* phrase), it is not necessarily 'keeping at rest' (*Bentham's* phrase). To say that I was keeping at rest implies that I considered moving and decided not to. (2) Bentham specifies or elaborates what he means by 'keeping at rest' in saying 'that is, in forbearing to move or exert oneself in such and such circumstances,' so D'Arcy's examples of 'physical non-movement' are not cases of 'keeping at rest' and therefore do not fall under Bentham's definition of negative acts. Bentham simply does not mean by 'keeping at rest' or 'forbearance to move" what D'Arcy says, namely 'physical non-movement.'

Nevertheless, Bentham's analysis does not illuminate the notion of an omission or forbearance. For one thing, as I have said, omissions and forbearances are different. There are both intentional and unintentional omissions, but there are no unintentional forbearances, and so the phrase 'intentional forbearance' is pleonastic and likely to be misleading. Neither is it the case that all intentional omissions are forbearances or that all forbearances are intentional omissions. On the one hand, I might intentionally omit a dividend check from my income tax report, but that would hardly be called a forbearance. On the other hand, I might forbear from punching a man who angered me, which would hardly be called an omission. But more important, to define 'forbearance' in terms of 'forbearing' is of no value. Furthermore, it is possible to forbear from punching somebody without forbearing to move or exert oneself. I might punch a wall in forbearing from punching a man. Forbearance is not connected with not moving or not exerting oneself, and it is useless to say that it is forbearing from *doing* something. Again, omission does not require forbearance from moving or exerting oneself. It can be unintentional or unwitting, and when deliberate it might involve movement and exertion. Nor is it any explanation to say that omission involves an omission of something.

Now D'Arcy's account is also deficient; however, his intentions are clear. He wishes to tell, or remind, us what is meant by 'omission.' This is evident both from his criticism of Bentham's examples ('we should not call any of them an omission') and from his own definition: 'A person *is said* to have omitted X if, and only if, (1) he did not do X, and (2) X was in some way expected of him' (p. 41, my italics).

D'Arcy also says that ' "physical non-movement" is no doubt a necessary condition for an omission' (p. 41). But, as Sachs points out ('A Few Morals About Acts,' *Philosophical Review*, 1966), 'if his statement of the sufficient and necessary conditions is correct, then his further claim about physical non-movement cannot be maintained. For instance, if my family expects me to stand still when the wedding photographs are being taken, and I fidget, then by D'Arcy's statement of sufficient and necessary conditions, I shall have omitted X; however, D'Arcy's physical non-movement condition will not be satisfied' (p. 95).

Even if we eliminate the condition of physical non-movement there are serious difficulties in D'Arcy's account. He argues:

A's not-having-done-X is said to be an omission only if X was in some way expected of A; and that may be verified in two ways. First, it may be expected because X is something that A usually does, or people usually do, in the situation in question. If it is a man's custom to walk down to the Post Office every day to inquire for mail, . . . we come to expect that he will do it *this* time; hence we often say that he "omits" the action when he does not fulfill the expectation: as we commonly do of any person who, say, does not . . . collect mail delivered to his letter box. However, we are inclined to say that A 'failed' to do X only when his omission has occasioned us either disappointment on our account: *e.g.* 'The Queen failed to appear on the Palace balcony as she usually does';

. . . or worry on A's account: *e.g.* 'It was my neighbour's failure to take in his milk bottles two days running that first made me fear that he might be ill.'

Second, we also speak of A's not-doing-X as an omission when X is required of him by some rule with which he is expected to comply (pp. 42-43).

First of all, since D'Arcy says that X 'may be expected because X is something that A usually does or people usually do,' it would follow that, if A does not do what people usually do, then he omits to do it, but surely it is absurd to say, because A has odd habits, *e.g.* he sleeps during the day and reads at night, that he omits to sleep at night or that his not sleeping at night is an omission. Second, it is not clear what D'Arcy means when he speaks of *verifying* that something is expected of A. B might expect that A will come to visit him, not because A usually does, or because people usually do, but because C told him that A would come. If B believes C then, even if C was lying, and even if A knew nothing about the matter, it might still be true that B expects that A will come, but it is ridiculous to say that because A did not in fact come he omitted to come or that his staying at home was an omission. Further, A might be expected to come, say even because he usually does, and he does not because he is *prevented* by force, or because he is dead, and in neither case should we say he omitted to come or that his not coming was an omission. And, incidentally, none of these reasons for expecting are *verifications* that something is expected.

Next, it is false that 'we are inclined to say that A "failed" to do X only when his omission has occasioned us either disappointment . . . or worry on A's account.' A man who failed to stop for a traffic light need occasion neither our disappointment nor our worry on his account. (Indeed, there are some people whom we *expect* to do this.) And clearly, we might be *pleased* that Napoleon failed to take into account the Russian temperatures and temperament.

As for D'Arcy's other way of 'verifying' that X is expected of A, namely 'when S is required of him by some rule,' this is not necessary even when the other supposed mode of verification fails. For if I omit Jones' name from a guest list it might be simply because I forgot, or it might be a deliberate omission. In neither case is it an omission only if I usually put his name on a guest list, or if I am required by some rule to put his name on the list.

D'Arcy seems to be seriously confused on two major points. First, he speaks of 'omissions' and 'omitting' as though there were no differences. Sachs remarks that if a man 'omits to check (his mail box one morning) *that* may or may not constitute an omission' (p. 96). He gives no explanation of this alleged difference, nor does he say *why* this is a criticism of D'Arcy. But D'Arcy does rest all of his points about omissions on 'what we say,' and consequently it is perfectly in order to criticise him on his own grounds. To say that A omitted to check the mail box is not enough to say that his not checking the box was an omission, at least partly because to say 'it was an omission' is to imply that it was something both unintentional and in some way untoward. There can be intentional omissions but the adjective does not simply modify 'omission,' it also cancels the *implication* that it was unintentional. While omissions can be both intentional and unintentional, and omitting *something* (*e.g.* a name on a list) can be both as well, we do not speak normally of intentionally omitting *to do* something (*e.g.* to lock the safe). And if such locution were used, one would in using it cancel the very strong implication that the omitting to do something was unintentional. Second, D'Arcy speaks of 'expecting something *of* a person' and 'expecting *that* a person will do something' as though there were no differences. To expect something *of* a person (sometimes 'expect something *from* a person') is often to hold him responsible or required to do it, even when there is little expectation *that* he will do it. Among the many evidential reasons for expecting that A will do X is that 'A usually does, or people usually do,' and among the reasons for expecting X of A is that 'X is required of him by some rule.' But as I have argued, expecting that A would do X when in fact he didn't is not sufficient for saying that he omitted to do X or that his not doing X was an omission; and when X is expected of A, the expectation is not verified by reference to a rule, but is supported or at least explained by reference to a rule.

The study of omissions is only a small part of the study of what can be praised and blamed, but it should be clear that a great deal of work has yet to be done and that the study of omissions should not be relegated to the appendix of a study of other objects of praise and blame.

It is interesting to note that while we sometimes contrast acts with omissions and forbearances, we also sometimes speak of acts of omission and forbearance, to be contrasted with acts of commission. But there is less sense in the notion of an action of omission or forbearance. This oddity might be accounted for by the view that motion is essential to actions (human and non-human) but not to acts. The view finds grammatical support in the fact that (1) there are omissions *e.g.* forgetting to lock the gate, which do not involve motion; (2) we speak of acts of love, mercy, gratitude, vengeance, courage, but not actions of love, mercy, gratitude, *etc.* And where we speak of these acts it is not necessary that there is motion. All of these acts when they are acts of forbearance can be performed without moving, *e.g.* not criticizing a child for a wrong (love), not killing an enemy (mercy), letting a foe drown (vengeance), not telling the secrets (courage). Even philosophers speak of mental acts, not of mental actions. And mental acts, whatever they are, surely do not require motion.

A Case of Omission to Save Life

Supreme Court of Victoria

Rex Versus Russell

The prisoner, Harold James Russell, was charged on three counts of murder, and was convicted of manslaughter on each count in the following circumstances: The accused was a married man living with his wife at Sunshine. He had three children, of whom only the two youngest were living with him at any material time. Those two were aged about three and a half years and eighteen months respectively. On the 19th May, 1932, the accused bigamously married one Alma Davey, telling her that he was a widower, and after visiting her at the home of her

From *Rex* v. *Russell*, Supreme Court of Victoria [Australia], 1932. [1933] *Vict. L. R.* 59, 39 *Arg. L. R.* 76.

relatives for some time, engaged rooms which they were to occupy on the 11th June as their future home, and arranged to furnish those rooms with the furniture from his then residence, which he had received notice to quit. The position on the 11th June was thus that he had one house with furniture and a wife in it, and another with a lady who supposed herself to be his wife in it, and by that night he had to move the furniture from one house to the other without arousing the suspicions of either woman. During that evening the accused and his wife and two children were in a park at Sunshine, in which there was a swimming pool, and the wife and the children there met their deaths by drowning.

The Crown case, based on the circumstances already summarised, and on certain alleged admissions of the prisoner, was that he had solved his problem by murdering them. The accused gave evidence to the following effect: He proposed to solve his problem by telling his wife that he would have to break up the home, and sending her back to her parents, and if that failed he proposed to confess his bigamy to her and induce her to pass herself off to his second "wife" as his married sister. He told her the home would have to be broken up, but did not tell her of his matrimonial entanglements. About half-past 9 at night he met his wife in the street in Sunshine. She was wheeling the two children in a perambulator, and he walked with her and the children to the pool in question. On other occasions she had threatened to kill herself, and that day, upset by the home being broken up and her parents' unsympathetic attitude when she had applied for assistance on an earlier occasion, she said that she might drown herself in the pool. When the prisoner met her that night he asked her what she was doing. She said — "I am going to do what I promised to do." He endeavoured to dissuade her, and then said, "Well, give me the kiddies, and you can go where you like." She replied — "Where I go they go." Finally they continued on until the pool was reached, the prisoner attempting to dissuade his wife. Finally she appeared to yield, and said — "Go on and I will follow you." He turned to walk away from the pool, did not hear his wife following, and turned just in time to see his wife and the perambulator, with the two children in it, hit the water. He tried to reach her, but she struggled away from him. He then stripped off his clothes, and first attempted to rescue them, but failed, then attempted to commit suicide also, but found he could not as he could swim, and finally dressed and went back to his new home. He did not seek help or report the occurrence because he was frightened.

The indictment contained three counts, the first relating to the wife and the others to the two children.

At the trial the jury asked the question — "Assuming that the woman took the children into the water without the assistance of putting them in the water by the man, but that he stood by conniving to the act, what would be the position from the standpoint of the law?" The presiding judge, after discussing with the jury the implications of these questions, and hearing argument, directed the jury that in those circumstances the prisoner would be guilty of manslaughter. . . .

The jury found the prisoner guilty of manslaughter on all three counts. He thereupon applied to the Full Court for leave to appeal against his conviction. . . .

MANN, J. . . . It was with some doubt as the principles of law applicable to the case that I answered the question propounded by the jury, and I therefore postponed judgment, and intimated my intention of reserving a case for the Full Court. This became unnecessary when the prisoner decided to appeal against the verdict. The appeal attacks the verdict on all three counts, while a case reserved by me would have dealt with the second and third counts only.

The question of the jury was: "Assuming that the woman took the children into the water without the assistance of putting them in the water by the man, but that he stood by conniving to the act, what is the position from the standpoint of the law?" This question, heard with knowledge of the course of the trial, including the addresses of Counsel and my own charge to the jury, was clearly directed, as I thought and still think, to the second and third counts only, which charged the accused with murder of his two children. Upon the further consideration given to the matter on this appeal, I am of opinion that the proper answer for me to have given to the question was that, in the case supposed, the accused would be guilty of murder.

But, apart altogether from the question of murder or manslaughter, it is important that a decision as to the criminal liability of the accused in given circumstances should be referred to the right legal principles. I rested my answer to the jury in effect upon the principle of such cases as *Reg. v. Instan, R. v. Gibbins, Reg. v. Bubb* [Citations omitted]. These cases may be regarded as defining the legal sanctions which the law attaches to the moral duty of a parent to protect his child of tender years from physical harm. If applicable to the present case those authorities would point to the accused being guilty of what I may call an independent crime of murder. The outstanding difference between the facts of such cases as I have cited and the facts of the present case is the interposition in the latter of a criminal act of a third person, which is the immediate cause of death, and the difficulty in such a case is in saying, in the absence of express authority, that the inaction of the accused has caused the death of the children within the meaning of the criminal law.

I think the more correct view in the present case is that the prisoner, on the facts supposed, while perhaps guilty of an independent crime was certainly guilty as participator in the murder committed by his wife. The moral duty of the accused to save his children, the control which by law he has over his wife, and his moral duty to exercise that control, do not in this view cease to be elements in his crime. On the contrary, it is these elements which, as a matter of law, give to the acquiescence of the father in the acts of the mother committed in his presence the quality of participation. The control which the law recognizes as exerciseable by a husband over his wife is well illustrated in the doctrine that the mere presence of the husband at the commission by his wife of a felony other than murder is generally enough to exempt the wife altogether from criminal liability. The physical presence and the "connivance" of a parent in the position of the accused has in law, in my opinion, a criminal significance not attaching to the presence and connivance of the mere "passerby" referred to in some of the cases.

It follows that the case put by me to the jury by way of contrast, though based upon a sound theoretical distinction, was not applicable to the special facts. The facts necessary to constitute aiding and abetting were too narrowly conceived, since no legal distinction can be made between tacit and oral concurrence, and a correct direction would be that not only was the accused morally bound to take active steps to save his children from destruction, but by his deliberate abstention from so doing, and by giving the encouragement and authority of his presence and approval to his wife's act, he became an aider and abettor, and liable as a principal offender in the second degree. . . .

With regard to the first count, my brother Cussen's view is that the verdict shows a belief in the mind of the jury that in answering the question submitted to me I was also directing them as to the law applicable to the first count, and he thinks that with regard to this count also the prisoner was criminally liable as aiding and abetting in the suicide of his wife. I do not take this view of the matter. I can find no reason, having regard to the various hypotheses put forward at the trial, for saying with certainty that the jury thought the wife committed suicide at all. I think that this verdict upon the first count being one which was legally open to the jury upon the evidence and no misdirection being established with regard to it, it is unnecessary and unwise to enter upon what seems to me a speculative inquiry as to the process, or perhaps the different processes of thought by which the jury arrived at that verdict.

I think the appeal fails as to all three counts.

McARTHUR, J. . . . The distinction between "assenting to," "concurring in," or the "countenancing or encouraging" by one person of the commission of a crime by another, so as to make the one a participator with the other in the commission of the crime, and the mere inaction of the one person, who is present while the other is committing a crime, may in some circumstances be a fine one, but it is nevertheless, in my opinion, a real one.

In the present case, for instance, the distinction, though a fine one, is (or might have been) of vital importance, because if the jury had found that the prisoner had "assented to, concurred in, countenanced, or encouraged" his wife to commit the crime of drowning herself and the children, as distinguished from merely standing by and not interfering with her, he would have been a participator in those crimes, and would in law have been guilty of murder. Whether he was a participator or was merely an inactive onlooker was a question of fact for the jury, and the difficulty I have in basing my judgment on the ground that he was a participator is that, though this question of fact was not in express terms left to the jury, and was not in express terms pronounced upon by them, it seems to me that the effect of their verdict (having regard to the learned Judge's charge) is either that they have found him not to be a participator or at least that they have not found that he was a participator. I use the word "participator" as meaning a principal in the second degree — a person present at the time of the commission of the felony "aiding and abetting" (as it is technically called) the actual perpetrator of the crime. . . .

The question put to the learned trial Judge by the jury was: What would the position be from the standpoint of the law if he "stood by, conniving to the act"? Whereupon His Honour said — "Are you supposing a case where he is offering no encouragement or persuasion to her to do it, but simply standing by and watching his wife drown the children?" And the Foreman replied — "That is the position." His Honour then told the jury that, that being the position, "the accused man being under a duty, by reason of his parenthood, of caring for the safety of children in his charge and his power, would come under a duty to take steps to prevent the commission of that crime by his wife, and his failure to discharge that duty — standing by, as you put it, and doing nothing — would make him guilty of the crime of manslaughter." He then put the other position — "By way of contrast, suppose the man was not merely a silent observer, but supposing that he was encouraging and persuading his wife to commit suicide and to do away with the children at the same time, he would then be guilty of the crime of murder."

The two positions which were contrasted were made quite plain: standing by and doing nothing, having it in his power to interfere and not interfering — manslaughter; encouraging and persuading her to do the act — murder. The jury found manslaughter, and thereby negatived the "encouraging and persuading," and affirmed the "standing by, doing nothing," thus in effect finding that the prisoner was not a participator. Or if they did not find that he was not a participator they at least, in my opinion, did not find that he was, for the following reasons. "Consenting to, concurring in, or countenancing" the crime would admittedly make him a participator. The learned Judge did not, however, use these words in describing to the jury what would constitute participating, but used only the words "encourage and persuade." The jury have, therefore, not found one way or the other whether the prisoner "consented to, concurred in, or countenanced" the crime — assuming, as I think we must, that those words have a different meaning from "encouraged and persuaded." And therefore in this view they have not found one way or the other whether the prisoner was a participator in the crime.

But it is said that we should hold that "standing by conniving to the act" (to use the expression at first used by the jury), or even "standing by doing nothing" (to use the Judge's expression when interpreting the jury's question, which interpretation was assented to by the jury), is "assenting to, concurring in, or countenancing" the act, so as to make the prisoner a participator. I do not agree with this. I think the question whether the prisoner "consented to, concurred in, or countenanced" the act is a question of fact for the jury to determine, and not a question for us. To begin with, what is the precise view which we are to presume the jury ultimately took? Was it "standing by conniving to the act," or "standing by doing nothing"? I would think the latter, because that is the interpretation which was placed by the Judge upon the jury's question and which was accepted by the jury as correct. If there is any difference in meaning between the two expressions it was for the jury, and is not for us, to say which is to be taken as correct. If there is no difference in meaning between the two expressions, then it was for the jury, and is not for us, to say whether in their opinion "standing by doing nothing" really amounted to "assenting to, concurring in, or countenancing." The expression "conniving to the act" comes nearer, I think, to "assenting to, concurring in, or encouraging" than "simply . . . standing by doing nothing"; but I can see no justification for our first picking out the word "conniving" as the word intended by the jury to express the precise meaning which they ultimately wished to convey, and then saying that that word means the same as "assenting to, concurring in, or countenancing."

For these reasons I am of opinion that the jury have either found (in effect) that the prisoner was not a participator, or that at least they have not found that he was. And so they found him not guilty of murder.

The question whether the verdict of manslaughter can stand depends, in my opinion, upon whether the learned Judge's charge to the jury on that subject was correct in law, and whether, having regard to His Honour's charge, the jury were justified in finding that the death of the prisoner's wife and children or any of them was caused by the prisoner's gross and culpable neglect.

Leaving over for the moment the question of the prisoner's responsibility for the death of his wife, I am of opinion that the learned Judge's charge with regard to the prisoner's responsibility for the death of the children was correct, and that the conviction on the second and third counts should stand. The learned Judge bases the responsibility primarily upon the duty of the father, by reason of his parenthood, of caring for the safety of his children, who were in his charge and power. So far that is quite correct, and his direction that neglect of that duty would constitute manslaughter, and not murder, is also, in my opinion, correct.

The authorities which establish the principle of criminal responsibility for the death of one person caused by the neglect of another are mostly cases where young and helpless children, or helpless adults, were placed under the care and control of the prisoner, and death was caused by the prisoner starving or otherwise neglecting to properly attend to the wants of such child or helpless adult — as, for instance, by omitting to provide necessary medical attention. And these authorities make it clear that if the omission to properly feed or otherwise attend to such child or helpless adult was deliberate — done with the intention of causing death — then it would be murder. But if it were not deliberate and intentional, but was due merely to gross and culpable neglect on the part of the prisoner, then it would be manslaughter. And so in the present case a similar distinction was drawn by the learned Judge, the distinction being, as already pointed out, between encouraging and persuading, on the one hand, and merely standing by and doing nothing on the other.

In describing the duty of the prisoner, it would, perhaps, have been more accurate to have said that he came under a duty to take all reasonable steps to prevent the commission of the crime. A man is not bound to take steps which in the circumstances no reasonable man would take in an attempt to save the life of his child. But it is clear that the learned

Judge's charge would convey nothing more than that to the jury, because he almost immediately pointed out that it was only where he had "power to interfere," and "could have saved them" and "refrained from interfering," that he was criminally responsible; and moreover, on the facts and in the circumstances of the case, and having regard to the view which the jury were taking (as indicated by the question they asked), it was obvious that the steps which the prisoner might have taken in order to have prevented his wife from drowning the children were such as any reasonable man would have taken, and could have taken, without risk or serious trouble to himself.

The learned Judge did not expressly tell the jury that, in order to convict the prisoner of manslaughter, they must be satisfied that the neglect was gross and culpable, but I think this omission is of no substantial importance in the present case, because, on the facts and in the circumstances of the case, and having regard to the view the jury were taking, as indicated by the question they asked, it is obvious that the neglect of the prisoner to make any effort whatever to save the life of his children was gross and culpable neglect.

Neither of these two points was raised in argument before us; but, assuming them to have been technically misdirection or non-direction, I am clearly of opinion that no miscarriage of justice has been caused thereby. Dr. Brennan, for the prisoner, however, contended that the principle laid down in the authorities to which I have referred does not apply to a case like the present, where the immediate cause of death was the criminal act of a third party — in this case the wife. This question resolves itself into two. First, does the duty extend to protecting children or other helpless persons against the wrongful or criminal acts of a third party? Secondly, assuming that the performance of the duty would have saved the child or other helpless person, can it be said that the child's or other person's death was caused by the neglect of duty, when the immediate cause of death was the criminal act of a third party?

In my opinion, both these questions should be answered in the affirmative. If a little child in charge of and in the presence of its father was seen by the father to leave the pavement as if to toddle across the street, and the father saw a bolting horse and vehicle coming towards the child in circumstances which obviously placed the child's life in jeopardy, would it not be the duty of the father to step off the pavement and pull the child back to safety? And would it make any difference if, instead of a bolting horse and vehicle, it were a negligently driven horse and vehicle or motor car? . . . And if the child were killed by the negligently driven horse or motor car, . . . could it not be said that the death of the child . . . was caused by the gross and culpable neglect of the father? . . .

The true position is that it is sufficient if the negligence complained of is a direct cause of the death or injury, it is not necessary that it should be *the* (*i.e.*, the sole) direct cause. Whether or not a suggested cause is too remote, so that it cannot be said to be a "direct" cause, is a question of law. And I have no hesitation in saying in the present case that the neglect of the prisoner to make any effort to save his children is not too remote a cause, but may, as a matter of law, be relied upon as a direct cause of the children's death.

I think the conviction on the first count — manslaughter of the wife — cannot stand. Having regard to the questions asked by the jury and to the whole conduct of the case, we must assume, I think, that the jury were of opinion that the wife committed suicide. For the reasons already given, I am of opinion that the jury have either found that the prisoner was not a participator in that crime committed by the wife, or they have at least not found that he was. And I am not prepared to say that the rules applicable to persons having the care and control of young and helpless children, or of helpless adults, can be applied to persons having the care of, or having under their protection, adults who are not helpless, but are quite capable mentally and physically of looking after themselves. I am therefore of opinion that the prisoner cannot be convicted of the manslaughter of his wife merely because he stood by and did nothing while she committed suicide.

For these reasons I am of opinion that the conviction on the first count should be quashed, and that the convictions on the second and third counts should stand.

[The opinion of Acting Chief Justice Cussen is omitted.]

The application [for leave to appeal] is refused, and the accused is remanded in custody for sentence.

The Line Between Acts and Consequences

Eric D'Arcy

Human Acts

The question with which our inquiry begins is this: In analysing the elements which constitute a given human performance, how are we to decide which of them belong to the act and which of them belong to the consequences of the act? We may illustrate the point at issue with two examples. First, A tells a lie and B is deceived; A is thus able to rob B. Where are we to draw the line between 'act' and 'consequences'? Are we to say that A's *act* is simply 'deceiving B,' with the *consequence* of being in a position to rob him? Or is A's act 'telling a lie,' with the two conse-

From Eric D'Arcy, *Human Acts* (Oxford: The Clarendon Press, 1963), pp. 2-21, by permission of The Clarendon Press, Oxford.

quences (1) B is deceived, and (2) A is thus in a position to rob him? Second, Macbeth killed Duncan, and as a consequence of that act became King. But could one not also say that Macbeth stabbed Duncan, and as a consequence of this act the King died? Was his *act* 'stabbing,' which produced the *consequence* of the King's death; the further consequence of Macbeth's becoming King following from the circumstances of Duncan's being King and Macbeth's standing in (some sort of) line to the throne? Or was his act 'killing the King,' with the consequence of succeeding to the throne? The examples indicate one possible answer to our question. Perhaps the line to be drawn between 'act' and 'consequences' is not a fixed line: perhaps it is possible to make several different but equally correct statements as to what is the act and what the consequences. Let us first consider two other answers that stand at opposite extremes.

(i) Two extremes

During the racial troubles in Arkansas in 1956, Professor J. J. C. Smart read a paper in defence of Extreme Utilitarianism. In the discussion which followed, he considered a hypothetical case in which white people believed that some crime had been committed by a negro. Since the criminal's identity was not established they proposed to lynch five negroes chosen at random. The local sheriff knew this, and after investigation felt that the only alternative was to arrest some negro, 'frame' a case against him, 'pack' the jury, and have him found guilty, sentenced to death, and shot. From premises of Extreme Utilitarianism Smart argued that, if this were indeed the only alternative to the lynching of the five, he would be a wicked man if he did not carry out the plan; and that the correct description of what he did would be, not 'judicial murder,' but 'saving four lives.'[1] There are, of course, two separate problems here: one, Was the sheriff justified, or even obliged, so to act? the other, What would be the correct characterization of such an act? It is only with the latter that we are concerned.

Now suppose that the sheriff himself acted as executioner; consider the following possible descriptions of his last act in the drama:

1. He tensed his forefinger.
2. He pressed a piece of metal.

---

[1]This was put forward purely for the sake of discussion, to see where such a suggestion might lead. I do not wish to imply, here or elsewhere, that Professor Smart personally holds this view.

3. He released a spring.
4. He pulled the trigger of a gun.
5. He fired a gun.
6. He fired a bullet.
7. He shot a bullet at a man.
8. He shot a bullet towards a man.
9. He shot a man.
10. He killed a man.
11. He committed judicial murder.
12. He saved four lives.

One possibility would be to say that the sheriff's act was to tense his finger, with the consequence that he pressed a piece of metal; another, that his act was to press a piece of metal, with the consequence that he released a spring; another, that his act was to kill a man, with the consequence that he saved five others; or simply, that his act was to save four lives. At one extreme, then is Smart's suggestion that the last is the correct characterization.

At the opposite extreme is the theory of the nineteenth-century jurist Austin, which has passed into a good deal of modern legal theory, and with some modification into more purely philosophic writing: for instance, in Prichard. The following remarks are taken from the eighteenth of Austin's Lectures in Jurisprudence:

> Certain movements of our bodies follow invariably and *immediately* our wishes and desires for these *same* movements. . . . If my arm be free from disease, and from chains and other hindrances, my arm rises, so soon as I wish that it should. . . . These antecedent wishes and these consequent movements are human *volitions* and *acts* (strictly and properly so called). They are the only objects to which those terms properly apply. . . . The wishes which are immediately followed by the bodily movements wished, are the only wishes *immediately followed by their objects* . . . the only wishes which attain their *ends* without the intervention of *means*. In every other instance of wish or desire, the object of the will is attained (in case it be attained) through a *series* of means: each of the means being (in its turn) the object of a distinct wish; and each of them being wished (in its turn) as a step to that object which is the end at which we aim. . . . And as our desires of those bodily movements which immediately follow our desires for them are the only *volitions;* so are the bodily movements, by which they are immediately followed, the only *acts* or *actions* (properly so called). . . . As the bodily movements which immediately follow volitions are the only *ends* of volition, it follows that those bodily movements are the only objects to which the term 'acts' can be applied

with perfect precision and propriety. . . . Most of the names which seem to be names of acts are names of acts *coupled with certain of their consequences*. For example, if I kill you with a pistol or gun I *shoot* you. And the long train of incidents which are denoted by that brief expression are considered (or spoken of) as if they constituted an act perpetrated by me. In truth the only parts of the train which are my act or acts are the muscular motions by which I raise the weapon, point it at your head or body, and pull the trigger. These I *will*. The contact of the flint and steel; the ignition of the powder, the flight of the ball towards your body, the wound and the subsequent death, with the numberless incidents included in these are *consequences* of the act which I *will*. I *will* not those consequences, though I may intend them.[2]

This offers a clear answer to our question; for Austin, the line between 'act' and 'consequences' is to be drawn at the point where muscular control ends. The term 'act' applies only to voluntary movements of the limbs, organs, or muscles; the term 'circumstances' to any relevant facts prior to or concomitant with the act; and the term 'consequences' to the events subsequent to, and caused by, that act in those circumstances. For Austin, then, the sheriff's *act* would be tensing his forefinger; the *circumstances* of the act, that his finger was on the trigger of a cocked and loaded gun which was pointing at a man whom he had framed; the *consequences* of his act, the movement of the trigger, the release of the hammer, the explosion of the cartridge, the expulsion of the bullet, its flight towards the victim, its entry into his body, his wound and death; plus, of course, whatever followed from that. In the litany, suggested above, of twelve possible answers to the question, 'What was his act?', Austin would say that only the first is correct. Notice that it is not the fourth, 'He pulled the trigger,' but 'the muscular motions by which' he pulled the trigger; hence, 'He tensed his forefinger.'

The argument that leads to this conclusion seems to take four steps. First, only a voluntary act is an act; second, only that which is immediately produced by the will is voluntary; third, only the movements of certain muscles, organs, and limbs can be immediately produced by the will; therefore, fourth, only those movements can be acts. Each of these steps presents difficulties. For instance, the first suggests that the phrase 'voluntary act' is pleonastic, and the phrase 'involuntary act' self-contradictory. But this is to deal rather high-handedly with English usage. If the act X is ascribed to A, it makes perfectly good sense to accept the ascription as correct, but to inquire whether or not the act

---

[2]*Lectures in Jurisprudence* (London, 1885), vol. i, pp. 411-15.

was voluntary; whereas if murder is ascribed to him, it does not make sense to accept the ascription as correct and to inquire whether or not his victim died. If A is accused of having done X, and one pleads on his behalf that X was 'not a voluntary act,' it is the adjective that one is stressing, not the noun: one is saying that, though admittedly A did in some sense do X, he did not do it in the relevant sense, viz. 'voluntarily.' If it were the noun which one meant to stress, one would not say, 'X was not a voluntary act,' but something quite different: for instance, 'A did not do X; B did.'

It is curious that Austin is apparently satisfied to treat *act* and *action* as synonymous. He is right, of course, in suggesting that there are many bodily movements which are not 'acts.' We may think of the beating of the heart, the circulation of the blood, the functioning of the liver, motions within the brain, the expansion and contraction of the pupil of the eye, the imperceptible growth of the finger-nails and hair, the working of the salivary glands; it is quite true that these phenomena are not called 'acts'; but on Austin's theory they would also lose the name of 'action.' That would be odd; for we often speak of the action of the heart, the action of the salivary glands, the action of the liver, and so on; and these actions are not called acts. When may we substitute 'act' for 'action'? As a general rule, an action is called an act only when it can be described in a proposition with a personal subject; the actions of signing a cheque or killing a rival are acts, for one can say, 'I signed the cheque,' or 'He killed his rival'; but the beating of the heart and the working of the liver are not acts: one cannot say, 'I beat my heart,' or 'I worked my liver.' The fact that one may say, 'I am bleeding,' does not tell against this test, for the test applies only to *actions* which may be called acts; and one does not naturally call bleeding an action. Wittgenstein contrasts things that simply *happen* to us, such as the subsidence of a violent thudding of the heart, with things that we *do*, such as raising an arm. If one were asked, 'What were you doing at noon yesterday?', the answer, 'Bleeding from the nose,' would be taken for a slightly grim form of humour; and the humour arises from the fact that bleeding is not something that one 'does': it is not an action, let alone an act. A slightly different version of the test is to say that one may substitute 'act' for 'action' only when the action may be spoken of as 'my action': for example, the action of signing a cheque, or killing a man, may be called 'my action,' and is an act; the beating of the heart cannot be called 'my action,' and is not an act. It is true that a doctor discussing a patient may speak of 'his heart-action': but this is probably medical shorthand for 'his heart's action,' and, as Wittgenstein would say, the heart-action is not something that one does.

Every act, then (whether voluntary or involuntary), is an action; but not every action is an act. The sense of the term 'action' which applies to bodily movements which are not acts is rather akin to the sense of the term 'action' in which it is used in the language of processes: of the language, for instance, of chemical processes, as 'the action of sulphuric acid on iron filings,' 'the action of light on a photographic plate,' 'the action of the gastric juices on the food in the stomach'; or the language of physical processes, as 'the action of the sea on the rocks'; or the language of mechanical processes, as 'the action of the cylinders in a V8-type engine,' 'the action of the wheels in a pulley.' In none of these cases does one naturally substitute 'act' for 'action'; and the word 'process' provides a rough criterion for distinguishing between those events taking place in or proceeding from us which are involuntary acts, and those which are not. The term 'involuntary acts' does not apply to those events which either simply are, or are closely analogous to, chemical, physical, or mechanical processes which could take place in a non-human system or apparatus; it does often apply to those events which are similar to actions which I perform voluntarily. The action of the heart is not an act, either voluntary or involuntary: in neither sense is it something one 'does'; the action of overturning a bottle of ink on one's desk is an act, which may be voluntary or involuntary: one may 'do' it in either sense. Other types of involuntary act, or action, may be voluntarily inhibited or imitated; but process-type actions cannot. One may delay a sneeze; a trained actor may mimic a nervous twitch, or sneeze at will; but one cannot at will, unfortunately, affect the functioning of the liver. One may imitate the action of the tiger; but one cannot have one's heart imitate the action of the tiger's heart.

Austin's theory carries the further implication that only a physiologist could tell us the names of our acts. When I speak, for instance, my *act*, what I *do*, is not 'to speak,' but to tighten certain muscles in and around and behind my mouth; the sounds produced are simply *consequences* of my act. I could not name or identify the muscles involved, and am not aware of the existence of most of them; yet on this theory it is my desire for their movement which causes them to move. There is irony in this. One defect of a theory such as Austin's is its inability to account for the fact that people are often held responsible for actions which were not preceded by conscious choice or 'act of the will,' e.g. omissions through negligent inadvertence; yet the theory involves the conclusion that one is hardly ever conscious of the main elements of one's voluntary act, viz. the muscles which one moves by one's desire for their movement, though usually not knowing of their existence. To find out what I 'really do' I should have to consult a trained physiologist. Only he could tell me, too, with a precision and a certainty that the most skilful psychoanalyst might well envy, what I 'really desire' — when I speak, or open a door, or press the self-starter button of my car: for he alone knows the muscular contractions which on Austin's theory are caused by my desire for them, and constitute my act.

The theory therefore offers answers to two questions: (1) To what does the term 'act' apply? (2) What is it for an act to be voluntary? The answer to the second has much in common with the theories of Hume and Thomas Brown, as well as of Prichard. This kind of answer has been attacked, successfully as it seems to me, by Wittgenstein, Ryle, and Hart. But even were one to grant Austin his answer to the second question, his answer to the first would not be thereby established. It involves dealing high-handedly with other phrases in ordinary language than 'involuntary acts.' For moral discourse it carries the implication that no act can be morally good or bad, right or wrong; no act-term can be the subject of a proposition expressing a moral evaluation; murder, treason, and rape are not bad or wicked acts, because they are not acts: they are acts followed by many, complex, consequences. But Austin's doctrine goes wider even than that. It boldly proclaims that most of the names which we speak of as denoting acts do not do so at all: to kick or punch, to lift or carry, to speak, or strike a match, or sign a contract — none of these is an act. But surely a particular theory about the will warrants no such conclusions about the language of acts. There is no parallel here with a scientist who, after careful experimental research, announces that, contrary to prevailing opinion, X is not really A: say, that smallpox is not a virus-disease, or that a certain metal is not an element. There is a standard definition of A — of what a virus-disease is, or an element — and he reports his finding that, in the case of X, some element of the definition is not verified. But Austin is not taking the standard definition of 'act' and showing that some element of it is lacking in the things which we usually call acts; he is, in effect, telling us that the standard definition is wrong: that what the word is thought to mean, both in ordinary and philosophical usage, is not what it *really* means.

(ii) Three theses

As answers to our question, then, Smart's suggestion and Austin's theory stand at opposite extremes. In suggesting that the truth lies somewhere between them, I shall put forward three theses. The first is of rather general application; the second and third apply specifically to the problem of distinguishing between 'act' and 'consequence.'

Thesis One: There is not necessarily one, and only one, correct description of a given act. This tells against the implication of a theory such as Austin's, that it is only a trained physiologist who can give the correct description of an act; and it helps to reassure us about the connotation and denotation of the term 'act' in ordinary language. Three points may be made.

1. The description of an act appropriate to a given occasion may vary with the specialized interest of the inquirer or narrator. In the list, given above, of twelve contemplated alternative descriptions of a given episode, there is none that can be rejected as simply false, but the first eight would in most contexts, and certainly in contexts where a moral evaluation or a legal trial of the act was being made, be misleading in various degrees. Justice would not be done if, in a subsequent trial, the sheriff were exonerated because 'All he did was to release a spring.'

But there are contexts in which the first of those twelve descriptions ('He tensed his forefinger'), or the third ('He released a spring'), could be the most appropriate answer to the question 'What did he do?' because of the special sort of answer required by the questioner, the particular aspect of the incident in which he was interested. For instance, a person who is being introduced to fire-arms for the first time, and learning to shoot, may have got as far as loading and cocking the gun, holding and aiming it, and crooking his right forefinger on the trigger. Later he happens to be watching a newsreel film of the execution, and sees the sheriff carry out the movements which he himself has learnt; then there is a report, and the negro falls; and he asks, 'What did the sheriff do after he got his hands and fingers right?' The answer, 'He tensed, or suddenly squeezed, his forefinger,' would then be perfectly in place. Again, a student of elementary ballistics may know that the bullet is driven out of the barrel by the gases which are suddenly released when the cartridge explodes, and that the cartridge is exploded by the sudden impact of the hammer upon it; but why did the hammer make such an impact when the sheriff pulled the trigger? The answer will begin with an explanation of the way that trigger and hammer are connected by a spring-mechanism, and conclude with some such words as, 'So you see, when he pulled the trigger he released the spring.'

The same is true of some interests of an observer or inquirer a little less highly specialized. For instance, a spectator of a game of poker might say, 'A is relaxing while waiting his turn to bid'; but a player who has made a close study of the mannerisms of each member of his school may say (to himself), 'A is closing his eyes and leaning sideways in his chair; that means that he's going to bluff.' Or to take a different sort of case, think of a clerk still at his desk two hours after the time that the office usually closes. To the question, 'What are you doing?', he may give different answers to different inquirers. For instance, to his wife on the telephone he may say, 'I'm working late'; to the manager of the firm, 'I'm finishing the Blair contract at the request of the Department Head'; to the Department Head, 'I'm just beginning the last clause'; to a policeman who has noticed a light burning unusually late, 'It's quite all right, Officer, I work here'; to a trade union official, 'It's all right, I'm getting double rates for working overtime.' Each of these answers may be perfectly true and, according to the particular concern of each questioner, perfectly appropriate.

2. A different factor is the presence of specialized efforts, interests, or intentions of the agent. Hart has pointed out that there are occasions when my act, what I intend to do, is precisely to produce a particular muscular contraction: as, for example, when, in a gymnasium, the instructor says, 'Lift your right hand and contract the muscles of the upper arm.' Hampshire has remarked that, although at a given moment there may be a set of possible true answers to the question 'What are you doing now?', there is generally one that seems to the agent peculiarly appropriate to his present intentions. We might think of a test-pilot who could truthfully answer, 'Holding the joy-stick'; 'Looking through the windscreen'; 'Listening to the control-tower'; 'Smoking a cigarette'; or 'Flying over the North Sea.' But the answer that seemed most appropriate to him might be, 'Testing the new Vickers jet.' Probably it was in these last terms that he would look forward to 'what he would be doing' on this day, or apologize for being unable to accept some other commitment; and if he were later trying to 'date' some other event, he might say, 'It must have been Tuesday, because I remember it was the day before I was to test the new Vickers jet.'

The agent's intention may have a very different effect. Instead of rendering one of several possible true descriptions of a given overt act more or less *appropriate* than another description, it may make the difference between a particular description's being *true or false*. Several people, A, B, and C, may be performing the same overt act; yet because of their different intentions, it may be true to say that A is doing X, B is doing Y, and C is doing Z: though false to say that A is doing Y or Z, B doing X or Z, or C doing X or Y. For instance, in the Deep South of the United States there are some 'All White' restaurants, and coloured people have sometimes recently made a point of entering them and eating there.

A white man who sat and ate beside them might describe his action as joining their protest; or, perhaps making a slightly different point, as showing his solidarity with all citizens of the U.S.A.; or, quite differently, as simply having his lunch, 'not being interested in politics'; or, quite differently again, as reporting the incident for his newspaper. The point holds for acts of omission as well as for positive acts. For example, think of four people who, over a significant period of time, are abstaining from food. It may be that four quite different descriptions characterize their action, or omission: one of them is dieting, or slimming; another, hunger-striking; the third, keeping a religious fast; the other, conducting experiments on the nutritional needs of the human body. Within each of these descriptions, other descriptions, more precise and mutually exclusive, are possible: the third person, for instance, may be fasting to observe the Mohammedan Ramadan or the Christian Lent; and if the latter, it may be an act of impetration on behalf of a friend, or an act of atonement on behalf of a friend, or an act of atonement for his own sins, or a step in a deliberately plotted ascetic programme, say, in the 'Purgative Way.' It may then be that, according to the person's intentions, several of these descriptions would be not only inappropriate, but false. This is so because some of these act-descriptions are verbs which are defined in terms of intention; one may intend, or not intend, to do them; but one cannot do them unintentionally. The definitions of these verbs include, as a common element, the same physical movement or non-movement, but the specifying element is the particular intention; hence according to the different intentions, different verbs will be required. If the verbs X, Y, and Z are defined respectively as *pr*, *ps*, and *pt*, where *p* is the overt action common to all three, and *r*, *s*, and *t* the several proper intentions: then according to the presence of *r*, *s*, or *t*, the act will be described as X, Y, or Z. There will commonly be a general term for *p*, which will therefore be truly applicable to each of the three people who are performing the different acts X, Y, and Z; though of course it will be less informative. Thus the description, 'keeping Ramadan,' applies only to the Moslem: it conveys the fact that he is fasting, and a number of other facts as well; but the general description, 'fasting,' could be applied either to the Moslem or the Christian: and to the Christian bent on impetration, personal or vicarious atonement, or personal spiritual progress.

3. A third point draws attention to the fact that makes the other two possible. One's description of a person's act may vary according to the special interest of the inquirer or the specialized intention of the agent because, as Hampshire says, at any moment of a man's waking life there is always a set of possible true answers to the question, 'What is he doing

now?' All the following answers to that question might be true at the very same time of, say, an actor who is in his dressing-room in a theatre: 'Sitting in a chair'; 'Warming himself in front of the fire'; 'Breathing quickly'; 'Resting his sore ankle'; 'Holding a book in his left hand'; 'Tapping his right hand on the arm of his chair'; 'Moving his eyes backwards and forwards'; 'Reading'; 'Reading *The Cherry Orchard*'; 'Memorizing his part'; 'Waiting to be called on stage for rehearsal'; 'Fulfilling a contract.' Clearly the possibilities of multiple alternative descriptions are very numerous; it would be difficult even to summarize the main headings of cases in which one may equally well say of a person either that he is doing X, or that he is doing Y. For instance, (1) X may be a species of the genus Y: as one may say of a surgeon that he is amputating a limb, or performing an operation; or of a woman, that she is making the beds, or doing housework. (2) X may be a tactic in the strategy Y: as one may say of a general that he is bringing up a unit into a new position, or strengthening his left flank; or of a politician, that he is advocating more liberal terms for marriage-loans, or building up support among the younger voters. (3) X may be one of several possible ways of doing Y: as one may say of a mother, that she is reading to the children, or putting them to sleep; or of a golfer, that he is exploding out of a bunker, or playing out of it. (4) X may be a step in the process Y, or a part of the operation Y: as one may say of a surgeon that he is making an incision, or performing an operation; or of a chef, that he is turning a joint, or cooking a meal. (5) X may be a particular duty or function of the station in life or official position Y: as one may say of a judge, that he is hearing a case, or administering justice; or of a viceroy, that he is opening Parliament, or governing a colony. (6) Y may be a consequence, and especially an intended consequence, of the act X. This is the case with which we are concerned, and it brings us to our second thesis. Our first thesis has been concerned with act-descriptions in general; our second applies specifically to 'act' and 'consequences.'

Thesis Two: The term which denotes the act, in the description of a given incident, may often be elided into the term which denotes a consequence of the act: 'doing X with the consequence Y,' may often be re-described simply as 'doing Y.' For instance, if A stabbed B, and thus killed him, we may say simply that A killed B. The act of flicking a switch may produce the consequences that (1) contact is made between two points, so that (2) current flows from outside the room, through these points and the wire in the room, into the globe and through its filament, and thus (3) the globe is illuminated; but this may also be described simply as, 'putting on the light,' or 'lighting the lamp.' If a person sings a song, and thus entertains a group of people, we may say either that he is singing a song, or entertaining them; and if as a result of the latter he raises money for the Red Cross, we may say that he is raising money for the Red Cross; and if as a result of that he boosts morale, or helps the war effort, we may also say that he is boosting morale, or helping the war effort. We may therefore often *elide* one possible description, the term X, into another term Y, where (1) Y is the result or consequence of the agent A's doing X; (2) A is nevertheless said to be doing Y, e.g. entertaining people; (3) the elision is so complete that Y gives no hint of the specific nature of X.

As a rule, then, the line between 'act' and 'consequence' may be drawn at different points when the elements of a given episode are being analysed. If a is the number of relevant elements comprised in the term which is used to denote the act, c the number of relevant elements comprised in the term used to denote the consequences, and t the number of relevant elements comprised in the description of the whole episode, so that

$$a = t - c:$$

then while t is of course a constant for a given episode, a and c are variables. But now, is this true for all values of a and c, or is their range of possible values restricted? In answer to this question I shall make three suggestions, of which the first two simply state in different form conclusions already reached.

First, apart from special contexts of the sort we have noticed, there are values *below which a* does not extend. For instance, we saw that Austin would give a minimal value to a; where the t elements were connoted by a single verb, a would usually be only a small fraction of t. We argued that this account was unsound. Doing X may involve producing the muscular contractions p, q, and r, and so in some sense 'doing' p, q, and r; but for most contexts, p, q, r, and X are not four concurrent or consecutive discrete 'acts,' nor one act followed by three consequences. In most contexts it is not appropriate to say, as Austin would, that 'doing X' is a misnomer for 'doing p, q, and r, with the consequence X'; one is doing X. X is the act-term, and p, q, and r would be at most elements in the act-definition.

Second, there is a wide range of values *within which a* may vary. The line between 'act' and 'consequences' may often be drawn at several different places; 'doing X with the consequence Y' may often be redescribed, or alternatively described, as 'doing Y'; the act-term may often be elided without trace into the term which denotes the consequence of the act; we may say that Macbeth stabbed Duncan and, as a consequence, killed him: but we may also simply say that he killed him.

Third, there are values *above which a* does not extend; that is, there are some act-terms which can *not* be elided into the corresponding consequence-description. In making this suggestion, I broach my third thesis concerning the distinction between 'act' and 'consequences.'

The trend of suggestions such as those of Professor Smart, quoted above, would rather lead to denying this contention. They would give a maximal value to a; indeed, if the saving of the four negroes' lives were looked on as the final consequence, we should have

$$t-a=o;$$

there would be no point at which a line could be drawn between 'act' and 'consequence.' Since the sheriff encompassed the one man's death in order to save the lives of four others, Smart suggested that it would be quite proper to re-describe his act as 'saving four lives.' Just as the description, 'singing a song,' may be elided into the description, 'entertaining people,' and the latter description shows no trace of the former, because the latter was a consequence of the former: so the description of the sheriff's act, 'committing judicial murder,' would be elided without trace into the description, 'saving four lives,' since that was the consequence of the murder.

In discussions of the moral evaluation of an act, the importance of such re-descriptions is considerable. An apologist for killing people who are suffering from incurable diseases may say that such an act is 'really just putting an end to the unfortunate people's suffering'; Dr. Verwoerd said that he would 'really describe *apartheid* as good neighbourliness.' St. Paul said that one must not lie, even in order to promote the glory of God; but if an act may always be re-described in terms of its consequences, then the act of the person who told lies so highmindedly could be re-described simply as 'promoting the glory of God.' Such suggestions have macabre possibilities. Imperious Caesar, dead and turned to clay, might stop a hole to keep the wind away; but if our formula holds for all values of a, killing him with that end in view might be re-described simply as 'blocking a draught.'

Hence the importance of the contention that there are values *above which a* does not extend. Our third thesis takes up that contention.

Thesis Three: Certain kinds of act are of such significance that the terms which denote them may not, special contexts apart, be elided into terms which (a) *denote their consequences, and* (b) *conceal, or even fail to reveal, the nature of the act itself.* Typical examples are the acts of killing, maiming, slandering, torturing, deceiving, or seriously offending another person; betraying or deserting a friend or an ally; breaking a contract or a promise or a confidence; stealing or destroying or spoiling something which the owner, or the community, looks on as precious; sacrificing or endangering one's own life, happiness, good name, health, or property. For instance, 'Macbeth stabbed Duncan and, as a consequence, killed him,' may be re-described simply as, 'Macbeth killed Duncan'; but, 'Macbeth killed Duncan and, as a consequence, succeeded him,' may not be re-described simply as, 'Macbeth succeeded Duncan.' To quote a more recent example, it was alleged during the Eichmann trial that a Nazi research institute asked a concentration-camp commandant to supply it with a number of infant bodies for use in some experiments, and that in order to comply with this request the commandant had the required number of babies of Jewish women prisoners gassed. Now to describe his act as 'assisting medical research,' or 'promoting the advancement of science,' simply would not do, even though research may have been assisted or scientific knowledge advanced as a result of his act. Taking human life, we feel, is an act of such significance that one cannot elide its description into a term which denotes its consequence, or an end to which it was a means, unless that term makes clear that this was the means used. Had the commandant gassed the children in order to comply with Hitler's decree that the Jewish people were to be destroyed, it might not be altogether inaccurate to subsume his act under some such description as 'genocide'; though perhaps the relation of particular murders to a policy of genocide is not that of act to consequence, or of means to end, but of part to whole.

This thesis, then, is supplementary to the theses that several alternative descriptions of a given act are possible, and that one may often, in analysing a given incident, draw the line between 'act' and 'consequences' now at one point, now at another. It beholds that in certain cases there is one point at least at which an 'act'/'consequences' line *must* be drawn. The previous thesis is exemplified by the fact that 'A told B an untruth with the consequence that B was deceived' may be re-described as simply, 'A deceived B'; the present thesis is exemplified by the fact that 'A deceived B with the consequence that he won his vote' may not be re-described simply as 'A won B's vote.' In the terms of the twelve contemplated descriptions of the sheriff's act, Number 1 ('He tensed his finger') usually *should* be elided into one of the latter descriptions, e.g. Number 9 ('He shot a man'); similarly, Number 9 may be elided into Number 10 ('He killed a man'). But Number 10 may not be elided into

Number 12 ('He saved four lives'); an 'act'/'consequences' line must be drawn between Numbers 10 and 12. Tensing one's finger is simply part of thè act of shooting, or shooting a man; but killing a man is not simply part of the act of saving four lives. It might be objected that each is a means to an end: tensing the forefinger a means, firing the gun the end; killing one man a means, saving four others the end. But for one thing, this overlooks the fact that a means is often an act, and that an act is often a means. Furthermore, even if killing a man is intended by the agent, and characterized by an observer, simply as a means to an end, it is a means whose nature must be clearly revealed in any normal account of what was done. It is true that there are many cases in which the particular way of obtaining a certain result is of no particular interest or significance at all; in those cases, to which our previous thesis applied, the description of the act by which the result was achieved may quite properly be absorbed into the description of the result itself. We may even hesitate in such cases to make any 'act'/'consequence' distinction, and feel that this was simply one of several possible ways of doing the same thing. Perhaps my gas-fire's being alight is, as it happens, a consequence of my putting a match to it; but the same result would have been achieved by using a cigarette-lighter, or a built-in spring-and-flint device; and it is usually sufficient to say, 'I lit the gas-fire.' There is no need to specify the nature of the act by which I did so, unless it was *either* of peculiar interest in a *special* context: as might be the case, for instance, when an experiment was being made for commercial purposes with some new gadget for flameless, sparkless, lighting; *or* unless the act was of such a nature as to be of great significance in *any* normal context; for instance, because I used a rare and precious manuscript with which to light the fire.

Some elements of an incident, then, may figure merely as part of an act-description, not themselves demanding specific mention or characterization or manifestation when the incident is described, the term which denotes them being elided into the act-description, or into a consequence-description. But some elements, or combinations of elements, are such that, whenever they are present, they verify an autonomous act-definition. They constitute an instance of some kind of act whose description, special contexts apart, cannot be absorbed into some other: that 'other' remains a consequence of the act, not a part of it: extrinsic, not intrinsic, to it. They constitute a 'case' of morally significant action.

VI

MORAL REASONING

Introduction

The Questions of Moral Philosophy

It has become almost a habit among many contemporary philosophers, particularly those who write textbooks on the subject, to dichotomize the problems of moral philosophy. There are, it is said, two main types of problems, namely, problems of *normative ethics* and problems of *critical ethics* (or *meta-ethics*). The first are described as issues involved in the formulation of defensible judgments, principles, and theories about what things are good, what acts are right, and what things we may be held responsible for. The second main classification concerns issues about the types of answers given to the first set of questions. Specifically these concern the meaning of ethical terms and the kinds and validity of the evidence which can be given in support of moral judgments. It is a very useful distinction in one sense. It draws to our attention the fact that there are many different types of moral issues. There are, however, difficulties with the distinction. One is that it does not fairly represent the way most traditional philosophers have dealt with the problems of moral philosophy. In itself perhaps this is not too serious an objection. Maybe they were confused, and we, after centuries of philosophical discussion, are now in a better position to avoid their confusions. But another difficulty is more serious. Can the distinction really be maintained? Can we really separate a question about the rightness of a given type of action, e.g., promise-breaking, from a consideration of what "right" means, or the kind of evidence needed to establish whether promise-breaking is right or not?

Consider once again Socrates' discussion with Euthyphro (Part I) regarding Euthyphro's decision to indict his own father for murder. There is, of course, the "normative" question whether his decision is defensible or not. Is it a pious act? What principle can be formulated which would convincingly show that it is? There are also "critical" questions involved: "What is to be meant by 'pious'?" "What kind of evidence can there be to support Euthyphro's interpretation (i.e. his principle) that 'piety is what the gods approve'?" The latter questions are intimately involved in Socrates' attempt to find an answer to the normative question. In fact, one wonders how the discussion could have proceeded unless Socrates raised just such questions. Furthermore, Socrates seems not to have confused any issues. It might be contended that Euthyphro at least was confused, and that he was confused because he didn't understand the difference between the normative issue, on the one hand, and Socrates' critical questions, on the other. It might also be contended that the discussion is really concerned, not with the substantive normative question at all, but basically with questions in critical ethics. That Euthyphro was confused there can be no doubt, but what good reason is there to suppose that Socrates was not just as interested in the formulation of a defensible moral principle and with the success or failure of Euthyphro's defense as he was in defining the term "piety"? It's difficult to see how this can be maintained. Socrates consistently, and it can be argued, properly, resists the dualistic approach to all moral problems. His approach, and that of other traditional philosophers, appears to have been to regard the different philosophical problems of ethics as essentially intertwined and related, to be separated out and distinguished only insofar as the inquiry requires it.

There is no doubt that the traditional method, while avoiding the apparent arbitrariness of what we have called the dualistic approach, has tended to overlook the importance of certain kinds of ethical issues. This is the claim, at least, of G. E. Moore. In particular he says that philosophers and non-philosophers alike have tended to confuse the following two questions: "What kinds of things are good in themselves, or ought to exist for their own sakes?" and "What kinds of actions ought we to perform?" In other words, Moore believes that there has been a confusion of questions about what things are *good* with questions about *right* actions.

Especially with respect to the question, "What is good?" philosophers have not been sufficiently analytical, according to Moore. Some have interpreted the question to mean, "What is good or bad in human conduct?" and have thought it an adequate definition of ethics to state that it deals with questions of good and bad conduct. Besides neglecting a distinction he thinks should be made between "right" and "good," Moore objects to limiting the subject of ethics to human conduct, because, he says, other things besides conduct are good, and so if we restrict our attention only to good conduct, we may "be in danger of mistaking for this property [i.e. good] some property which is not shared by those other things." It is not that Moore thinks that moral philosophers ought not to be concerned with the question of what good conduct is, it is just that the question, "What is the meaning of 'good'," has a higher logical priority. We must first know what it means and whether it can be defined before we can understand what it means to say that conduct is good (or bad). A similar kind of claim might be made about the concept of "conduct" or "moral action," namely, that until we know what moral judgments involving the words "good" or "right" are about, or to which such moral terms apply, then it is at least premature to inquire what the term "good" means. Even Moore himself admits that actions are "the most frequent objects of ethical judgments," but he dismisses any proposed inquiry into the nature of moral action with the comment, "We all know pretty well what 'conduct' is." After studying the selections in the previous chapter on moral action, the reader may well wonder whether Moore himself hasn't overlooked the importance and complexities of this particular philosophical problem.

Nevertheless, Moore's view is that the most *fundamental* question in ethics is "How is 'good' to be defined?" He does not think that it is the *only* question which philosophers should consider. He thinks that philosophers should also investigate the questions of "practical philosophy," e.g., What acts are right? What particular things are good? What is "the good," or ultimate goal of human action? He simply thinks that all of

437

these other questions are dependent for their answers on the answer to the central question regarding the meaning of "good." Once this question is decided, all the conceptual distinctions needed to answer the other questions will be provided, and all the questions regarding the kinds of evidence which we may legitimately use to support our moral judgments will also be answered.

Moore's views have had a tremendous influence on twentieth-century moral philosophers. One of the by-products of Moore's approach to ethics has been the development of a theory that ethics is properly concerned only with the analysis of the language of morals. As A. J. Ayer puts it, "The question for moral philosophy is not whether a certain action is right or wrong, but what is implied by saying that it is right or saying that it is wrong." R. M. Hare similarly speaks of ethics as "the study of the logical properties of . . . moral words." Both agree that questions about the logic of moral discourse constitute the *sole* subject matter of ethics. Moore himself does not go so far. He is concerned that method-ological questions have been unduly neglected, but he defines "ethics" as "the general inquiry into what is good," not so that it will cover *less* than an inquiry into "good conduct," but *more* than that topic. In short, he means to include methodological and logical questions along with all the rest. He gives logical issues a higher priority, but he does not espouse the view that they totally exhaust the subject matter.

Regarding Ayer and Hare's conception of ethics, it is fair to ask, "What guidance can ethics provide to the person who occasionally has to make up his mind whether a certain act is right or wrong?" Both answer in the same way: It is a mistake to look to moral philosophers for such guidance. "To analyse moral judgements is not itself to moralize," says Ayer. Analysis is all that can reasonably be expected of the philos-opher. He has no special insight into particular moral problems, and so he is in no better position to give advice than anyone else.

Two possible misunderstandings of this view of the subject matter, nature, and task of the moral philosopher should be avoided. It should not be thought that what Ayer, Hare, and other contemporary authors are attempting to do is totally useless, or that they themselves are un-sympathetic to the ordinary person who has to make practical moral decisions. Moore thinks that if one comes to realize that good is an indefinable property of things, then this logically leads to a definition of a "right action" as one that is productive of the most good, and therefore if anyone has a moral problem, he can solve it by asking himself which of all the alternatives he could choose would probably bring about the most good. Ayer and Hare do not share Moore's conviction that there is a logical connection between one's ethical theory and any particular kinds of moral judgments, but this does not mean that ethical inquiry is useless. It does serve a very important function. It provides us, or should if it is a correct theory, with clarity in our thinking about what we are saying when we use moral language, and the achievement of clarity ought to be quite enough.

Another way of expressing the point is to say that ethics (understood as the study of moral language) is "morally neutral." Both Ayer and Hare express themselves in this way. As Ayer puts it, his ethical theory is "neutral as regards all moral principles. And here I may repeat that in saying that it is neutral as regards all moral principles I am not saying that it recommends them all alike, nor that it condemns them all alike. It is not that sort of thing." Hare is more expansive on the point. He draws a parallel with the role of mathematics in scientific inquiry. Mathematics is neutral in the sense that it does not by itself determine matters of fact, but that is not to say that it is scientifically useless. Hare draws another parallel with the rules of a game. The rules are neutral as between the players in the sense that they do not determine which player is going to win, but that does not mean that they don't have a very important function. In a similar way, ethical theory is neutral with respect to which moral judgments on which occasions are to be made.

Does this mean that it is of no consequence which judgments I make? Doesn't it matter whether I judge murder wrong or not? Of course it matters, but, according to Ayer and Hare, this is a concern of morals, not philosophy. The point here is that Ayer and Hare make a distinction between morals (i.e., the actual moral conduct and moral decisions of individual persons or groups) and moral philosophy or ethics (the logical study of moral language). There is no intermediate "ethical science" (normative ethics, if you will) which bridges the gap between the two, as many other philosophers have imagined. What I decide to do is important and non-trivial. How I go about making judgments is also very important. And it is up to the moral philosopher to analyze how I express myself in moral language and arrive at moral conclusions, but it is expecting too much of the philosopher to solve my problems for me. Of course, it should be noted that even among philosophers who hold this view there are great differences in their analyses. Ayer, for instance, as we shall see, regards ethical judgments as emotive expressions which are neither true nor false and denies that there is such a thing as genuine disagreement or reasoning concerning matters of morality. Hare does not share quite the same views, but they both share the view that morals is one thing, moral philosophy quite another.

The Meaning of Ethical Terms

Let us turn now to an examination of the specific question, "Can ethical terms be defined?" The answer might seem obvious. Ethical terms can be defined because they have been. "Good" means pleasure; "good" means utility; "good" means self-realization, or self-interest, and so on. Classical moral philosophers have apparently had no difficulty at all in defining terms like "good." It was just this multitude of different and incompatible definitions, however, which led Moore to have some doubts about whether philosophers knew what they were doing when they attempted to define "good." Is it really possible to define "good" as one might define "triangle" or "horse"? Are there not some important differences? Moore is convinced that there are. In the first place, when we define "triangle" or "horse" we know what we're defining in the sense that we can see, or at least formulate an empirical representation of, what we're talking about. We aren't able to see goodness, or point to it, at least in the same way. Furthermore, when we define "triangle" as "an enclosed three-sided plane figure," it makes no sense to ask, "But is an enclosed three-sided plane figure a triangle?" — not at least if we know what we're talking about, i.e., a triangle. But if we define "good" as pleasure, for instance, it does seem to make sense to ask, "But is pleasure (really or always) good?" Moore is convinced that it makes sense to ask this question, not merely because we may happen to be ignorant of what goodness is, and have thus made a mistake such as would be the case if we defined a triangle as a four-sided figure; rather, the error occurs because we have confused two quite different *kinds* of things with one another. We have confused a natural property (pleasure) with a non-natural property (good). He calls this kind of error a "naturalistic fallacy." Since it is bound to occur whenever we attempt to identify good with something that it isn't, all purported definitions of "good" commit the fallacy. "Good," he concludes, is indefinable.

This does not mean, however, that the term "good" is meaningless. On the contrary, it is no more meaningless than the term "yellow" which is also indefinable in the requisite sense. Still the question remains, "What does 'good' then refer to?" Certainly not to any sensed property like yellow. It refers, according to Moore, to an *intuited* and unanalyzable property of goodness which some things have and others do not have.

In *Principia Ethica* Moore does not adopt the same approach to the term "right" as he does to the term "good." "Right" is there defined as "productive of the greatest possible good." While agreeing with Moore's position with respect to "good," Ross argues, in effect, that Moore himself commits the naturalistic fallacy with respect to "right." The same argument by which Moore shows that good is indefinable is used by Ross to show that "right" is also indefinable and that it refers to an unanalyzable property which some things are known to have, not through the senses to be sure, but by intuition.

Thus both Moore and Ross, insofar as their positions on the meanings of ethical terms are concerned, are "intuitionists," or as they are sometimes called, "non-naturalists." *Ethical naturalism,* in contrast to *ethical intuitionism,* may be defined as the view that moral terms are definable in naturalistic terms and are capable of being understood by empirical means. In contrast to both intuitionism and naturalism is another view known as *emotivism.* A. J. Ayer is a proponent of this position regarding the meaning of ethical terms. He basically agrees with both Ross and Moore that such terms are unanalyzable but for a quite different reason. They are not unanalyzable notions because they refer to simple properties of things, but because they are totally non-descriptive of anything whatsoever. They are, in other words, cognitively meaningless. Instead he proposes the theory that words such as "good," "bad," "right," and "wrong" are used to express one's feelings, attitudes, and emotions.

It follows from Ayer's view that judgments which include ethical expressions are also non-descriptive utterances. If I say "Theft is wrong," I am not describing anything in the sense that what I have said is either true or false. I am rather using words to express a certain feeling or attitude of disapproval, and the expression of attitudes is neither true nor false. In the selection in this chapter Ayer modifies a view which he held in an earlier work, *Language Truth and Logic.* There he asserted that moral judgments are *merely* expressions of feeling. He now thinks that is an oversimplification. Instead, he says, we should think of moral attitudes as "certain patterns of behaviour, and that the expression of a moral judgement is an element in the pattern." In no way, however, does this modification of his view affect his fundamental belief that moral judgments are non-cognitive, i.e., not such as to be claims to knowledge.

In contrast to this view of moral judgments, Moore, Ross, and the ethical naturalists are "cognitivists." That is to say, both intuitionists and naturalists believe that moral judgments make assertions which are either true or false, and therefore are, if true, contributions to knowledge. They differ, insofar as the cognitive status of moral judgments is concerned, only in that the intuitionists believe that moral judgments are descriptive of non-natural properties whereas naturalists think that such judgments are descriptive of natural properties and are thus empirically verifiable.

R. M. Hare holds the view that two features distinguish moral judgments from other kinds of judgments. The features are prescriptivity and universalizability. By saying that moral judgments are prescriptive he means that they primarily serve to "commend" or "recommend" rather than to "describe" certain kinds of behavior. By saying that moral judgments are universalizable he means that they can be applied to all relevantly similar persons in relevantly similar circumstances. (A relevant similarity is a feature of the original situation which the person making the judgment thought entitled him to make it in the first place). Thus a moral judgment such as "Don't lie" or "It is wrong to lie" is different from an ordinary imperative statement such as "Close the door" because the latter is not universalizable (i.e., we don't mean to say "Let everyone close the door."). A moral judgment is different from an ordinary descriptive statement such as "The door is closed" because the latter serves no commendatory or prescriptive function. His general view differs from cognitivism (or as he calls it, "descriptivism") in both its natural and non-natural forms. He believes that the cognitivist's claim that the descriptive component in moral terms exhausts their meaning is misleading for it suggests that moral judgments are merely statements of fact. He does not believe that that is an accurate account of them. On the other hand, his view differs from emotivism in that he believes that moral judgments do more than merely express our feelings and attitudes or evoke responses. Since he holds that there are logical relations between moral prescriptions (even imperatives can contradict one another) and that they can serve as reasons for drawing moral conclusions, he believes that they are in that sense "rational." Hare calls his own view "universal prescriptivism."

It is clear that the issue whether moral judgments are true or false cannot be settled short of an examination of many other disputes. Since a judgment cannot be said to be true or false unless it makes an assertion, it is important to consider the conflicting claims of cognitivists versus the non-cognitivists. Even if we should find the cognitivist's arguments convincing, it will still be necessary to evaluate the differences among them. Are the intuitionists right in their contention that moral terms denote objective but non-natural properties of things, or are the naturalistic philosophers correct? To establish the latter it will be necessary to show that Moore's "naturalistic fallacy" is either not committed by the naturalists, as he claims, or that it is not in fact a fallacy. If we should agree with the contention of Hare and others, including Kant, that moral judgments are essentially prescriptive in character, then we shall have to explain in what sense it can be said that a prescription such as "Don't kill" or "Thou shalt not kill" is cognitively meaningful. Normally a statement in imperative form such as "Close the door" is not regarded as having "truth value." Why should "Don't kill" or "Don't lie" be regarded any differently? In this regard the reader will want to review Baier's argument in Part II that moral convictions can be true or false, even insofar as they are imperatival in character. It should be instructive to compare his view on this topic with the views of Ayer and Hare.

Moral Reasons

Another question which deserves special discussion is the following: "What reasons do we have for making one particular moral judgment rather than another? That is to say, if I judge that X is good or Y is wrong, how can I be sure that I have made an appropriate or correct judgment? What evidence or kinds of evidence are there for supporting particular applications of moral predicates?

According to Moore, the kind of moral evidence we can give depends on the kind of judgment we make. If I judge that something is good, i.e., if I intuit something as good, then my judgment (or intuition) is "self-evident." Another way of putting it is to say, as Moore does, that for answers to what things are good in themselves or ought to exist for their own sakes, "no relevant evidence whatever can be adduced: from no other truth, except themselves alone, can it be inferred that they are either true or false."

Two points need to be noted in connection with this aspect of Moore's view. By "intuition" he means to refer to certain types of propositions or judgments which are self-evidently true (i.e., are incapable of any other kind of proof); he does not mean to imply anything about the manner or origin of our cognitions of such judgments. Second, he is aware of the possibility of error in the sense that we may be confused with regard to exactly which question we are asking ourselves. If we confuse a question about goodness with a question about rightness, for instance, there is bound to be uncertainty with respect to whether a judgment that something is good (or right?) is self-evidently true. But if we clear away such confusions, as he tries to do, and address ourselves simply to the question whether a certain thing ought to exist for its own sake, then either we intuit that it should or we do not. No further appeals to any other kind of evidence will help us decide such a question.

On the other hand, questions regarding the rightness of certain acts are subject to proof or disproof. Since in Moore's view, as expressed in *Principia Ethica*, "right" is defined as that which is productive of the greatest possible good, another kind of evidence is relevant to establishing the truth of such a judgment. "It must consist," he says, "of truths with regard to the results of the action in question — of *causal* truths — but it must also contain ethical truths of our first or self-evident class." According to Moore, it follows that there may be considerable disagreement and argument with respect to what one ought to do; that the settlement of such disputes involves empirical investigation; and that the best we can hope for is some degree of probability in our judgments that certain acts will produce the greatest sum of good.

In a later book, *Ethics*, Moore appears to shift his position regarding the definition of "right." Instead of claiming that "right" *means* "productive of the greatest possible good," Moore says that the *reason* we say that something is right is that it is productive of the greatest good. Ross interprets this as an abandonment of the claim that "right" is any more definable than "good." He then goes on to challenge Moore's suggestion that the sole reason for calling something right is that it is productive of good and offers instead his own account of such reasons. This entails his theory of "prima facie duties."

By a "prima facie duty" or "conditional duty" Ross means to refer to a kind of act which we ought to perform simply for the reason that it is the kind of act it is, unless there is another act which in the same circumstances is more binding on us. Thus if I have made a promise, the act of keeping it is my prima facie duty, and I should keep it simply because I made the promise unless some other prima facie duty is seen to be more binding. Ross distinguishes many kinds of prima facie duties. All are to be contrasted with what he calls our "duty proper." The fact that we have made a promise does not necessarily mean that our primary obligation (what we really ought to do) in a given situation is to keep the promise, although it is *a reason* for doing so. There may be other prima facie duties binding on us at the same time in the same situation which provide other reasons for not keeping the promise. For example, I may have promised to meet a friend at a certain time to return a book, but on my way to do so I encounter an accident victim who needs my assistance. I may find that I am at least as bound to relieve distress as I am to keep my promise. How do I decide what to do? What reason should I allow to determine my action? In such a situation, Ross suggests that we should take many different factors into account — not only the fact that we have in the past made a promise, but also, though by no means exclusively, the future good which I will cause by helping the accident victim. Unlike Moore, Ross does not believe that the right thing to do will always be the "optimific" thing to do (i.e., the act that will produce the greatest possible good). In other words, there is no self-evident relationship between "right" and "optimific." The only things that are self-evident are our prima facie duties. That I ought to keep my promises is self-evidently true, but my particular judgment that I ought to keep my promise in a given situation is not self-evident, either in the same sense that my prima facie duty is self-evident or in the sense that it follows from self-evident premises. We cannot "deduce" what we ought to do in a given situation. We must make the best judgment we can with respect to which prima facie duty is more binding or "stringent." There are no general rules to which we can appeal to decide this question. After taking all the relevant facts into consideration, we must ultimately appeal to simple inspection or intuition. We must *see* what is our duty proper. No further reason can be given.

Ayer thinks of "moral reasons" in a quite different way. Since moral judgments are non-cognitive, the only "reasons" there can be for such judgments are reasons in the sense of causal influences on our attitudes. Thus if I wish to persuade a person to keep his promises, I may point out that he has made a promise or that certain unhappy consequences will follow if he doesn't. In this respect Ayer's procedure differs little from that of Ross. The difference consists in the fact that Ross believes that by such a procedure we can come to an accurate perception of what our duty truly is, whereas Ayer feels that it will, if successful, only provoke a desired response, which can be described as neither correct nor incorrect.

Another way of bringing out this difference between Ayer and Ross (and other cognitivists) is to indicate that, for Ayer, moral judgments do not and cannot contradict one another. If you say "Theft is wrong" and I say "Theft is right," I am not contradicting what you assert. I am only expressing a conflicting attitude, one that you don't happen to share. According to Ayer, there can be no cognitive argument regarding morality. I cannot provide reasons which will convince you of the *falsity* of what you assert. The most I can do is to provide a causal explanation of your attitude and point out some of the consequences of the acts which you are motivated to do in the hope of changing those attitudes and motives. It is only in this sense that Ayer admits that there are "moral reasons."

In addition to the intuitionist and emotivist theories of moral reasoning, there is also what we may call the "rationalist" theory. It is, in general, the view that there are logical relations between certain kinds of statements such that moral conclusions can be drawn from them; in short, that there is genuine moral argument which does not depend ultimately on the evidence of intuition nor appeal to purely motivational considerations. There are many rationalist theories of moral reasoning. They differ tremendously regarding the kinds of statements which can constitute the premises of moral arguments and also with regard to the kinds of logical relation which are involved. They nonetheless agree that there are definite rules of moral reasoning and definite tests by which "good" moral reasons may be distinguished from "bad" ones.

Naturalistic philosophers have long thought that from certain factual premises moral conclusions can be deduced; that given certain definitions of "good" and "right," reasoning in morals is not essentially different from reasoning regarding anything else. Moore's critique of naturalism has cast doubt in the minds of many philosophers on that view. But instead of siding with the intuitionists like Ross and Moore, whose final appeal is not to reason but to intuition, or with emotivists like Ayer, who discounts moral reasoning altogether except insofar as it involves changing attitudes, these philosophers have chosen different approaches. Kurt Baier (Part II) argues that a valid moral reason is a relevant consideration-making belief which can be shown to be consistent with that set of formal and material conditions which define the moral point of view. Marcus Singer (Part III) argues that all moral reasons are justified by means of the generalization argument. The reader will want to review their positions.

R. M. Hare and John Searle offer still different "rationalist" approaches to moral reasoning. It is Hare's view that given a set of premises at least one of which is a moral prescription, it is possible validly to derive a moral judgment as a conclusion. In order for the conclusion to be valid, however, it must not only be prescriptive in character but also universalizable. He illustrates his theory of moral reasoning by means of an example adapted from a biblical parable. The parable (see Matthew 18:23-35) concerns a king who, out of pity, remits a very large debt that a servant owes him. The servant then goes out and tries to ring from his own debtor a pittance owed to him. The debtor pleads for patience and promises to pay. He is refused and callously thrown into debtor's prison.

The king learns of his servant's behavior and inquires why he has not treated others as he himself has been treated. In his anger the king then condemns the man to be tortured until he should pay his debt in full.

Hare formalizes the argument by letting A stand for the servant's debtor, B for the servant, and C for the king. Assuming the facts that A owes money to B, and B owes money to C, and that it is the law that creditors may exact their debts by putting debtors into prison, the moral question for B is "Can I say that I ought to take this measure against A in order to make him pay?" He cannot conclude that he ought to for if he attempts to universalize the ought statement, then he would also be committed to the principle that "Anyone who is in my position ought to put his debtor into prison if he does not pay." This would entail that C, the king, ought to put B into prison. This latter consequence B is not ready to accept. He must then reject the moral judgment that he ought to put A into prison for his debt.

Hare goes on to examine the various "ways of escape" from the conclusion of this type of "golden-rule argument," as he calls it. In each case, the way of escape is seen to fail either because the "ought" involved is not used prescriptively or not universalizably. If any of the ways of escape succeed, i.e., if the conclusion of the argument is not accepted, then it is at the price of abandoning the moral discussion altogether. The reader is advised to examine the argument and each of the proposed ways of escape carefully. He should pay particular attention to Hare's claim that the argument only leads to the *rejection* of the moral judgment "I ought to imprison A for debt," and that it does not force B to assent to any particular moral judgment.

Throughout Hare's discussion, he is careful not to commit what he calls a "breach of Hume's Law (No 'ought' from an 'is')." He is not in effect saying to B "You are as a matter of fact averse to this being done to you in a hypothetical case and from this it follows logically that you ought not to do it to another." This would be equivalent to deriving an "ought" from an "is," and Hare rejects all such attempts. Incidentally, it should be pointed out here that many philosophers have understood Moore's "naturalistic fallacy" as being in effect just another way of warning us of the same sort of thing, namely, of not attempting to derive a normative claim such as "This is good" from a purely descriptive one such as "This is pleasure."

But just as some philosophers have questioned Moore's claim that "good" is indefinable, so others have questioned whether "Hume's Law" is altogether justified. John Searle undertakes to provide a counter-example in which he attempts to show that from the statement "Jones uttered the words, 'I hereby promise to pay you, Smith, five dollars'," he can derive the statement, "Jones ought to pay Smith five dollars." Each step of the argument deserves careful attention, since it is important to notice whether Searle has incorporated any normative or evaluative statements in his premises. He claims not to have done so. If he has, the argument fails as a derivation of an "ought" from an "is," though many a rationalist moral philosopher would not necessarily regard this as implying that there is no such thing as moral reasoning, but simply as a reinforcement of the principle that every moral argument must contain at least one value statement as a premise.

A second but nonetheless important objective of Searle's article is to cast suspicion on the usual dichotomy between "descriptive" and "evaluative" statements. Such a distinction, he thinks, fails to account for statements descriptive of what he calls "institutional facts." For example, statements such as "Jones got married," "Smith made a promise," "Jackson has five dollars," and "Brown hit a home run" are as factual and descriptive as "Jones is six feet tall" or "Smith has brown hair." The former, however, differ from the latter in that they presuppose the existence of certain institutions. The statement "Jones got married" has a descriptive meaning only if there is an institution of marriage. Such institutions are systems of what he calls constitutive rules, i.e. rules which constitute as well as regulate the forms of activity whose existence is logically dependent on the rules. Some of these systems involve obligations, commitments, and responsibilities, and it is within such systems, he says, that we can derive "oughts" from "is's".

Some may still regard the introduction of the notion of an "institutional fact" the basis for begging the entire question of whether an ought can be derived from an is. The reader must judge that for himself. The distinction between "brute facts" and "institutional facts" is an interesting notion which may have other important applications, as we shall see in our final section on justice.

Kinds of Moral Evidence

G. E. Moore

Principia Ethica

Preface

It appears to me that in Ethics, as in all other philosophical studies, the difficulties and disagreements, of which its history is full, are mainly due to a very simple cause: namely to the attempt to answer questions, without first discovering precisely *what* question it is which you desire to answer. I do not know how far this source of error would be done away, if philosophers would *try* to discover what question they were asking,

From *Principia Ethica* (New York: Cambridge University Press, 1903), by permission of the publisher.

before they set about to answer it; for the work of analysis and distinction is often very difficult: we may often fail to make the necessary discovery, even though we make a definite attempt to do so. But I am inclined to think in many cases a resolute attempt would be sufficient to ensure success; so that, if only this attempt were made, many of the most glaring difficulties and disagreements in philosophy would disappear. At all events, philosophers seem, in general, not to make the attempt; and, whether in consequence of this omission or not, they are constantly endeavouring to prove that 'Yes' or 'No' will answer questions, to which *neither* answer is correct, owing to the fact that what they have before their minds is not one question, but several, to some of which the true answer is 'No,' to others 'Yes.'

I have tried in this book to distinguish clearly two kinds of question, which moral philosophers have always professed to answer, but which, as I have tried to shew, they have almost always confused both with one another and with other questions. These two questions may be expressed, the first in the form: What kinds of things ought to exist for their own sakes? the second in the form: What kind of actions ought we to perform? I have tried to shew exactly what it is that we ask about a thing, when we ask whether it ought to exist for its own sake, is good in itself or has intrinsic value; and exactly what it is that we ask about an action, when we ask whether we ought to do it, whether it is a right action or a duty.

But from a clear insight into the nature of these two questions, there appears to me to follow a second most important result: namely, what is the nature of the evidence, by which alone any ethical proposition can be proved or disproved, confirmed or rendered doubtful. Once we recognise the exact meaning of the two questions, I think it also becomes plain exactly what kind of reasons are relevant as arguments for or against any particular answer to them. It becomes plain that, for answers to the *first* question, no relevant evidence whatever can be adduced: from no other truth, except themselves alone, can it be inferred that they are either true or false. We can guard against error only by taking care, that, when we try to answer a question of this kind, we have before our minds that question only, and not some other or others; but that there is great danger of such errors of confusion I have tried to shew, and also what are the chief precautions by the use of which we may guard against them. As for the *second* question, it becomes equally plain, that any answer to it *is* capable of proof or disproof—that, indeed, so many different considerations are relevant to its truth or falsehood, as to make the attainment of probability very difficult, and the attainment of certainty impossible. Nevertheless the *kind* of evidence, which is both necessary and alone relevant to such proof and disproof, is capable of exact definition. Such evidence must contain propositions of two kinds and of two kinds only: it must consist, in the first place, of truths with regard to the results of the action in question—of *causal* truths— but it must *also* contain ethical truths of our first or self-evident class. Many truths of both kinds are necessary to the proof that any action ought to be done; and any other kind of evidence is wholly irrelevant. It follows that, if any ethical philosopher offers for propositions of the first kind any evidence whatever, or if, for propositions of the second kind, he either fails to adduce both causal and ethical truths, or adduces truths that are neither, his reasoning has not the least tendency to establish his conclusions. But not only are his conclusions totally devoid of weight: we have, moreover, reason to suspect him of the error of confusion; since the offering of irrelevant evidence generally indicates that the philosopher who offers it has had before his mind, not the question which he professes to answer, but some other entirely different one. Ethical discussion, hitherto, has perhaps consisted chiefly in reasoning of this totally irrelevant kind. . . .

In order to express the fact that ethical propositions of my *first* class are incapable of proof or disproof, I have sometimes followed Sidgwick's usage in calling them 'Intuitions.' But I beg it may be noticed that I am not an 'Intuitionist,' in the ordinary sense of the term. Sidgwick himself seems never to have been clearly aware of the immense importance of the difference which distinguishes his Intuitionism from the common doctrine, which has generally been called by that name. The Intuitionist proper is distinguished by maintaining that propositions of my *second* class—propositions which assert that a certain action is *right* or a *duty*— are incapable of proof or disproof by any enquiry into the results of such actions. I, on the contrary, am no less anxious to maintain that propositions of this kind are *not* 'Intuitions,' than to maintain that propositions of my *first* class *are* Intuitions.

Again, I would wish it observed that, when I call such propositions 'Intuitions,' I mean *merely* to assert that they are incapable of proof; I imply nothing whatever as to the manner or origin of our cognition of them. Still less do I imply (as most Intuitionists have done) that any proposition whatever is true, *because* we cognise it in a particular way or by the exercise of any particular faculty: I hold, on the contrary, that in every way in which it is possible to cognise a true proposition, it is also possible to cognise a false one. . . .

Chapter I

2. . . . Many ethical philosophers are disposed to accept as an adequate definition of 'Ethics' the statement that it deals with the question what is

good or bad in human conduct. They hold that its enquiries are properly confined to 'conduct' or to 'practice'; they hold that the name 'practical philosophy' covers all the matter with which it has to do. Now, without discussing the proper meaning of the word (for verbal questions are properly left to the writers of dictionaries and other persons interested in literature; philosophy, as we shall see, has no concern with them), I may say that I intend to use 'Ethics' to cover more than this—a usage, for which there is, I think, quite sufficient authority. I am using it to cover an enquiry for which, at all events, there is no other word: the general enquiry into what is good.

Ethics is undoubtedly concerned with the question what good conduct is; but, being concerned with this, it obviously does not start at the beginning, unless it is prepared to tell us what is good as well as what is conduct. For 'good conduct' is a complex notion: all conduct is not good; for some is certainly bad and some may be indifferent. And on the other hand, other things, beside conduct, may be good; and if they are so, then, 'good' denotes some property, that is common to them and conduct; and if we examine good conduct alone of all good things, then we shall be in danger of mistaking for this property, some property which is not shared by those other things: and thus we shall have made a mistake about Ethics even in this limited sense; for we shall not know what good conduct really is. This is a mistake which many writers have actually made, from limiting their enquiry to conduct. And hence I shall try to avoid it by considering first what is good in general; hoping, that if we can arrive at any certainty about this, it will be much easier to settle the question of good conduct: for we all know pretty well what 'conduct' is. This, then, is our first question: What is good? and What is bad? and to the discussion of this question (or these questions) I give the name of Ethics, since that science must, at all events, include it. . . .

5. But [by] our question 'What is good?' . . . we may . . . mean to ask, not what thing or things are good, but how 'good' is to be defined. This is an enquiry which belongs only to Ethics, not to Casuistry; and this is the enquiry which will occupy us first.

It is an enquiry to which most special attention should be directed; since this question, how 'good' is to be defined, is the most fundamental question in all Ethics. That which is meant by 'good' is, in fact, except its converse 'bad,' the *only* simple object of thought which is peculiar to Ethics. Its definition is, therefore, the most essential point in the definition of Ethics; and moreover a mistake with regard to it entails a far larger number of erroneous ethical judgments than any other. Unless this first question be fully understood, and its true answer clearly recognised, the rest of Ethics is as good as useless from the point of view of systematic knowledge. . . .

6. What, then, is good? How is good to be defined? Now, it may be thought that this is a verbal question. A definition does indeed often mean the expressing of one word's meaning in other words. But this is not the sort of definition I am asking for. Such a definition can never be of ultimate importance in any study except lexicography. If I wanted that kind of definition I should have to consider in the first place how people generally used the word 'good'; but my business is not with its proper usage, as established by custom. I should, indeed, be foolish, if I tried to use it for something which it did not usually denote: if, for instance, I were to announce that, whenever I used the word 'good,' I must be understood to be thinking of that object which is usually denoted by the word 'table.' I shall, therefore, use the word in the sense in which I think it is ordinarily used; but at the same time I am not anxious to discuss whether I am right in thinking that it is so used. My business is solely with that object or idea, which I hold, rightly or wrongly, that the word is generally used to stand for. What I want to discover is the nature of that object or idea, and about this I am extremely anxious to arrive at an agreement.

But, if we understand the question in this sense, my answer to it may seem a very disappointing one. If I am asked 'What is good?' my answer is that good is good, and that is the end of the matter. Or if I am asked 'How is good to be defined?' my answer is that it cannot be defined, and that is all I have to say about it. But disappointing as these answers may appear, they are of the very last importance. To readers who are familiar with philosophic terminology, I can express their importance by saying that they amount to this: That propositions about the good are all of them synthetic and never analytic; and that is plainly no trivial matter. And the same thing may be expressed more popularly, by saying that, if I am right, then nobody can foist upon us such an axiom as that 'Pleasure is the only good' or that 'The good is the desired' on the pretense that this is 'the very meaning of the word.'

7. Let us, then, consider this position. My point is that 'good' is a simple notion, just as 'yellow' is a simple notion; that, just as you cannot, by any manner of means, explain to any one who does not already know it, what yellow is, so you cannot explain what good is. Definitions of the kind that I was asking for, definitions which describe the real nature of the object or notion denoted by a word, and which do not merely tell us what the word is used to mean, are only possible when the object or notion in question is something complex. You can give a definition of a horse, because a horse has many different properties and qualities, all of which

you can enumerate. But when you have enumerated them all, when you have reduced a horse to his simplest terms, then you can no longer define those terms. They are simply something which you think of or perceive, and to any one who cannot think of or perceive them, you can never, by any definition, make their nature known. It may perhaps be objected to this that we are able to describe to others, objects which they have never seen or thought of. We can, for instance, make a man understand what a chimaera is, although he has never heard of one or seen one. You can tell him that it is an animal with a lioness's head and body, with a goat's head growing from the middle of its back, and with a snake in place of a tail. But here the object which you are describing is a complex object; it is entirely composed of parts, with which we are all perfectly familiar— a snake, a goat, a lioness; and we know, too, the manner in which those parts are to be put together, because we know what is meant by the middle of a lioness's back, and where her tail is wont to grow. And so it is with all objects, not previously known, which we are able to define: they are all complex; all composed of parts, which may themselves, in the first instance, be capable of similar definition, but which must in the end be reducible to simplest parts, which can no longer be defined. But yellow and good, we say, are not complex: they are notions of that simple kind, out of which definitions are composed and with which the power of further defining ceases.

8. When we say, as Webster says, 'The definition of horse is "A hoofed quadruped of the genus Equus," ' we may, in fact, mean three different things. (1) We may mean merely: 'When I say "horse," you are to understand that I am talking about a hoofed quadruped of the genus Equus.' This might be called the arbitrary verbal definition: and I do not mean that good is indefinable in that sense. (2) We may mean, as Webster ought to mean: 'When most English people say "horse," they mean a hoofed quadruped of the genus Equus.' This may be called the verbal definition proper, and I do not say that good is indefinable in this sense either; for it is certainly possible to discover how people use a word: otherwise, we could never have known that 'good' may be translated by 'gut' in German and by 'bon' in French. But (3) we may, when we define horse, mean something much more important. We may mean that a certain object, which we all of us know, is composed in a certain manner: that it has four legs, a head, a heart, a liver, etc., etc., all of them arranged in definite relations to one another. It is in this sense that I deny good to be definable. I say that it is not composed of any parts, which we can substitute for it in our minds when we are thinking of it. We might think just as clearly and correctly about a horse, if we thought of all its parts

and their arrangement instead of thinking of the whole: we could, I say, think how a horse differed from a donkey just as well, just as truly, in this way, as now we do, only not so easily; but there is nothing whatsoever which we could so substitute for good; and that is what I mean, when I say that good is indefinable.

9. But I am afraid I have still not removed the chief difficulty which may prevent acceptance of the proposition that good is indefinable. I do not mean to say that *the* good, that which is good, is thus indefinable; if I did think so, I should not be writing on Ethics, for my main object is to help towards discovering that definition. It is just because I think there will be less risk of error in our search for a definition of "the good," that I am now insisting that *good* is indefinable. I must try to explain the difference between these two. I suppose it may be granted that 'good' is an adjective. Well 'the good,' 'that which is good,' must therefore be the substantive to which the adjective 'good' will apply; it must be the whole of that to which the adjective will apply, and the adjective must *always* truly apply to it. But if it is that to which the adjective will apply, it must be something different from that adjective itself; and the whole of that something different, whatever it is, will be our definition of *the* good. Now it may be that this something will have other adjectives, beside 'good,' that will apply to it. It may be full of pleasure, for example; it may be intelligent: and if these two adjectives are really part of its definition, then it will certainly be true, that pleasure and intelligence are good. And many people appear to think that, if we say 'Pleasure and intelligence are good,' or if we say 'Only pleasure and intelligence are good,' we are defining 'good.' Well, I cannot deny that propositions of this nature may sometimes be called definitions; I do not know well enough how the word is generally used to decide upon this point. I only wish it to be understood that that is not what I mean when I say there is no possible definition of good, and that I shall not mean this if I use the word again. I do most fully believe that some true proposition of the form 'Intelligence is good and intelligence alone is good' can be found; if none could be found, our definition of *the* good would be impossible. As it is, I believe *the* good to be definable; and yet I still say that good itself is indefinable.

10. 'Good,' then, if we mean by it that quality which we assert to belong to a thing, when we say that the thing is good, is incapable of any definition, in the most important sense of that word. The most important sense of 'definition' is that in which a definition states what are the parts which invariably compose a certain whole; and in this sense 'good' has no definition because it is simple and has no parts. It is one of those innumerable objects of thought which are themselves incapable of defini-

tion, because they are the ultimate terms by reference to which whatever *is* capable of definition must be defined. That there must be an indefinite number of such terms is obvious, on reflection; since we cannot define anything except by an analysis, which, when carried as far as it will go, refers us to something, which is simply different from anything else, and which by that ultimate difference explains the peculiarity of the whole which we are defining: for every whole contains some parts which are common to other wholes also. There is, therefore, no intrinsic difficulty in the contention that "good" denotes a simple and indefinable quality. There are many other instances of such qualities.

Consider yellow, for example. We may try to define it, by describing its physical equivalent; we may state what kind of light-vibrations must stimulate the normal eye, in order that we may perceive it. But a moment's reflection is sufficient to shew that those light-vibrations are not themselves what we mean by yellow. *They* are not what we perceive. Indeed we should never have been able to discover their existence, unless we had first been struck by the patent difference of quality between the different colours. The most we can be entitled to say of those vibrations is that they are what corresponds in space to the yellow which we actually perceive.

Yet a mistake of this simple kind has commonly been made about 'good.' It may be true that all things which are good are *also* something else, just as it is true that all things which are yellow produce a certain kind of vibration in the light. And it is a fact, that Ethics aims at discovering what are those other properties belonging to all things which are good. But far too many philosophers have thought that when they named those other properties they were actually defining good; that these properties, in fact, were simply not 'other,' but absolutely and entirely the same with goodness. This view I propose to call the 'naturalistic fallacy' and of it I shall now endeavour to dispose.

11. Let us consider what it is such philosophers say. And first it is to be noticed that they do not agree among themselves. They not only say that they are right as to what good is, but they endeavour to prove that other people who say that it is something else, are wrong. One, for instance, will affirm that good is pleasure, another, perhaps, that good is that which is desired; and each of these will argue eagerly to prove that the other is wrong. But how is that possible? One of them says that good is nothing but the object of desire, and at the same time tries to prove that it is not pleasure. But from his first assertion, that good just means the object of desire, one of two things must follow as regards his proof:

(1) He may be trying to prove that the object of desire is not pleasure. But if this be all, where is his Ethics? The position he is main-

taining is merely a psychological one. Desire is something which occurs in our minds, and pleasure is something else which so occurs; and our would-be ethical philosopher is merely holding that the latter is not the object of the former. But what has that to do with the question in dispute? His opponent held the ethical proposition that pleasure was the good, and although he should prove a million times over the psychological proposition that pleasure is not the object of desire, he is no nearer proving his opponent to be wrong. The position is like this. One man says a triangle is a circle: another replies 'A triangle is a straight line, and I will prove to you that I am right: *for* (this is the only argument) 'a straight line is not a circle.' 'That is quite true,' the other may reply; 'but nevertheless a triangle is a circle, and you have said nothing whatever to prove the contrary. What is proved is that one of us is wrong, for we agree that a triangle cannot be both a straight line and a circle: but which is wrong, there can be no earthly means of proving, since you define triangle as straight line and I define it as circle.' — Well, that is one alternative which any naturalistic Ethics has to face; if good is *defined* as something else, it is then impossible either to prove that any other definition is wrong or even to deny such definition.

(2) The other alternative will scarcely be more welcome. It is that the discussion is after all a verbal one. When A says 'Good means pleasant' and B says 'Good means desired,' they may merely wish to assert that most people have used the word for what is pleasant and for what is desired respectively. And this is quite an interesting subject for discussion: only it is not a whit more an ethical discussion than the last was. Nor do I think that any exponent of naturalistic Ethics would be willing to allow that this was all he meant. They are all so anxious to persuade us that what they call the good is what we really ought to do. 'Do, pray, act so, because the word "good" is generally used to denote actions of this nature': such, on this view, would be the substance of their teaching. And in so far as they tell us how we ought to act, their teaching is truly ethical, as they mean it to be. But how perfectly absurd is the reason they would give for it! 'You are to do this, because most people use a certain word to denote conduct such as this.' 'You are to say the thing which is not, because most people call it lying.' That is an argument just as good!— My dear sirs, what we want to know from you as ethical teachers, is not how people use a word; it is not even, what kind of actions they approve, which the use of this word 'good' may certainly imply: what we want to know is simply what *is* good. We may indeed agree that what most people do think good, is actually so; we shall at all events be glad to know their opinions: but when we say their opinions about what *is* good, we do

mean what we say; we do not care whether they call that thing which they mean 'horse' or 'table' or 'chair,' 'gut' or 'bon' or 'ἀγαθός'; we want to know what it is that they so call. When they say 'Pleasure is good,' we cannot believe that they merely mean 'Pleasure is pleasure' and nothing more than that.

12. Suppose a man says 'I am pleased'; and suppose that is not a lie or a mistake but the truth. Well, if it is true, what does that mean? It means that his mind, a certain definite mind, distinguished by certain definite marks from all others, has at this moment a certain definite feeling called pleasure. 'Pleased' *means* nothing but having pleasure, and though we may be more pleased or less pleased, and even, we may admit for the present, have one or another kind of pleasure; yet in so far as it is pleasure we have, whether there be more or less of it, and whether it be of one kind or another, what we have is one definite thing, absolutely indefinable, some one thing that is the same in all the various degrees and in all the various kinds of it that there may be. We may be able to say how it is related to other things: that, for example, it is in the mind, that it causes desire, that we are conscious of it, etc., etc. We can, I say, describe its relations to other things, but define it we can *not*. And if anybody tried to define pleasure for us as being any other natural object; if anybody were to say, for instance, that pleasure *means* the sensation of red, and were to proceed to deduce from that that pleasure is a colour, we should be entitled to laugh at him and to distrust his future statements about pleasure. Well, that would be the same fallacy which I have called the naturalistic fallacy. That 'pleased' does not mean 'having the sensation of red,' or anything else whatever, does not prevent us from understanding what it does mean. It is enough for us to know that 'pleased' does mean 'having the sensation of pleasure,' and though pleasure is absolutely indefinable, though pleasure is pleasure and nothing else whatever, yet we feel no difficulty in saying that we are pleased. The reason is, of course, that when I say 'I am pleased,' I do *not* mean that 'I' am the same thing as 'having pleasure.' And similarly no difficulty need be found in my saying that 'pleasure is good' and yet not meaning that 'pleasure' is the same thing as 'good,' that pleasure *means* good, and that good *means* pleasure. If I were to imagine that when I said 'I am pleased,' I meant that I was exactly the same thing as 'pleased,' I should not indeed call that a naturalistic fallacy, although it would be the same fallacy as I have called naturalistic with reference to Ethics. The reason of this is obvious enough. When a man confuses two natural objects with one another, defining the one by the other, if for instance, he confuses himself, who is one natural object, with 'pleased' or with 'pleasure' which

are others, then there is no reason to call the fallacy naturalistic. But if he confuses 'good,' which is not in the same sense a natural object, with any natural object whatever, then there is a reason for calling that a naturalistic fallacy; its being made with regard to 'good' marks it as something quite specific, and this specific mistake deserves a name because it is so common. As for the reasons why good is not to be considered a natural object, they may be reserved for discussion in another place. But, for the present, it is sufficient to notice this: Even if it were a natural object, that would not alter the nature of the fallacy nor diminish its importance one whit. All that I have said about it would remain quite equally true: only the name which I have called it would not be so appropriate as I think it is. And I do not care about the name: what I do care about is the fallacy. It does not matter what we call it, provided we recognise it when we meet with it. It is to be met with in almost every book on Ethics; and yet it is not recognised: and that is why it is necessary to multiply illustrations of it, and convenient to give it a name. It is a very simple fallacy indeed. When we say that an orange is yellow, we do not think our statement binds us to hold that 'orange' means nothing else than 'yellow,' or that nothing can be yellow but an orange. Supposing the orange is also sweet! Does that bind us to say that 'sweet' is exactly the same thing as 'yellow,' that 'sweet' must be defined as 'yellow'? And supposing it be recognised that 'yellow' just means 'yellow' and nothing else whatever, does that make it any more difficult to hold that oranges are yellow? Most certainly it does not: on the contrary, it would be absolutely meaningless to say that oranges were yellow, unless yellow did in the end mean just 'yellow' and nothing else whatever — unless it was absolutely indefinable. We should not get any very clear notion about things, which are yellow — we should not get very far with our science, if we were bound to hold that everything which was yellow, *meant* exactly the same thing as yellow. We should find we had to hold that an orange was exactly the same thing as a stool, a piece of paper, a lemon, anything you like. We could prove any number of absurdities; but should we be the nearer to the truth? Why, then, should it be different with 'good'? Why, if good is good and indefinable, should I be held to deny that pleasure is good? Is there any difficulty in holding both to be true at once? On the contrary, there is no meaning in saying that pleasure is good, unless good is something different from pleasure. It is absolutely useless, so far as Ethics is concerned, to prove, as Mr. Spencer tries to do, that increase of pleasure coincides with increase of life, unless good *means* something different from either life or pleasure. He might just as well try to prove that an orange is yellow by shewing that it always is wrapped up in paper.

13. In fact, if it is not the case that 'good' denotes something simple and indefinable, only two alternatives are possible: either it is a complex, a given whole, about the correct analysis of which there may be disagreement; or else it means nothing at all, and there is no such subject as Ethics. In general, however, ethical philosophers have attempted to define good, without recognising what such an attempt must mean. They actually use arguments which involve one or both of the absurdities considered in § 11. We are, therefore, justified in concluding that the attempt to define good is chiefly due to want of clearness as to the possible nature of definition. There are, in fact, only two serious alternatives to be considered, in order to establish the conclusion that "good" does denote a simple and indefinable notion. It might possibly denote a complex, as 'horse' does; or it might have no meaning at all. Neither of these possibilities has, however, been clearly conceived and seriously maintained, as such, by those who presume to define good; and both may be dismissed by a simple appeal to facts.

(1) The hypothesis that disagreement about the meaning of good is disagreement with regard to the correct analysis of a given whole, may be most plainly seen to be incorrect by consideration of the fact that, whatever definition be offered, it may be always asked, with significance, of the complex so defined, whether it is itself good. To take, for instance, one of the more plausible, because one of the more complicated, of such proposed definitions, it may easily be thought, at first sight, that to be good may mean to be that which we desire to desire. Thus if we apply this definition to a particular instance and say 'When we think that A is good, we are thinking that A is one of the things which we desire to desire,' our proposition may seem quite plausible. But, if we carry the investigation further, and ask ourselves 'Is it good to desire to desire A?' it is apparent, on a little reflection, that this question is itself as intelligible, as the original question 'Is A good?' — that we are, in fact, now asking for exactly the same information about the desire to desire A, for which we formerly asked with regard to A itself. But it is also apparent that the meaning of this second question cannot be correctly analysed into 'Is the desire to desire A one of the things which we desire to desire?': we have not before our minds anything so complicated as the question 'Do we desire to desire to desire to desire A?' Moreover any one can easily convince himself by inspection that the predicate of this proposition — 'good' — is positively different from the notion of 'desiring to desire' which enters into its subject: 'That we should desire to desire A is good' is *not* merely equivalent to 'That A should be good is good.' It may indeed be true that what we desire to desire is always also good; perhaps,

even the converse may be true: but it is very doubtful whether this is the case, and the mere fact that we understand very well what is meant by doubting it, shews clearly that we have two different notions before our minds.

(2) And the same consideration is sufficient to dismiss the hypothesis that 'good' has no meaning whatsoever. It is very natural to make the mistake of supposing that what is universally true is of such a nature that its negation would be self-contradictory: the importance which has been assigned to analytic propositions in the history of philosophy shews how easy such a mistake is. And thus it is very easy to conclude that what seems to be a universal ethical principle is in fact an identical proposition; that, if, for example, whatever is called 'good' seems to be pleasant, the proposition 'Pleasure is the good' does not assert a connection between two different notions, but involves only one, that of pleasure, which is easily recognised as a distinct entity. But whoever will attentively consider with himself what is actually before his mind when he asks the question 'Is pleasure (or whatever it may be) after all good?' can easily satisfy himself that he is not merely wondering whether pleasure is pleasant. And if he will try this experiment with each suggested definition in succession, he may become expert enough to recognise that in every case he has before his mind a unique object, with regard to the connection of which with any other object, a distinct question may be asked. Every one does in fact understand the question 'Is this good?' When he thinks of it, his state of mind is different from what it would be, were he asked 'Is this pleasant, or desired, or approved?' It has a distinct meaning for him, even though he may not recognise in what respect it is distinct. Whenever he thinks of 'intrinsic value,' or 'intrinsic worth,' or says that a thing 'ought to exist,' he has before his mind the unique object — the unique property of things — which I mean by 'good.' Everybody is constantly aware of this notion, although he may never become aware at all that it is different from other notions of which he is also aware. But, for correct ethical reasoning, it is extremely important that he should become aware of this fact; and, as soon as the nature of the problem is clearly understood, there should be little difficulty in advancing so far in analysis. . . .

15. Our first conclusion as to the subject matter of Ethics is, then, that there is a simple, indefinable, unanalysable object of thought by reference to which it must be defined. By what name we call this unique object is a matter of indifference, so long as we clearly recognise what it is and that it does differ from other objects. The words which are commonly taken as the signs of ethical judgments all do refer to it; and they are expressions of ethical judgments solely because they do so refer. But

they may refer to it in two different ways, which it is very important to distinguish, if we are to have a complete definition of the range of ethical judgments. Before I proceeded to argue that there was such an indefinable notion involved in ethical notions, I stated that it was necessary for Ethics to enumerate all true universal judgments, asserting that such and such a thing was good, whenever it occurred. But although all such judgments do refer to that unique notion which I have called 'good,' they do not all refer to it in the same way. They may either assert that this unique property does always attach to the thing in question, or else they may assert only that the thing in question is *a cause or necessary condition* for the existence of other things to which this unique property does attach. The nature of these two species of universal ethical judgments is extremely different; and a great part of the difficulties, which are met with in ordinary ethical speculation, are due to the failure to distinguish them clearly. Their difference has, indeed, received expression in ordinary language by the contrast between the terms 'good as means' and 'good in itself,' 'value as a means' and 'intrinsic value.' But these terms are apt to be applied correctly only in the more obvious instances; and this seems to be due to the fact that the distinction between the conceptions which they denote has not been made a separate object of investigation. This distinction may be briefly pointed out as follows.

16. Whenever we judge that a thing is 'good as a means,' we are making a judgment with regard to its causal relations: we judge *both* that it will have a particular kind of effect, *and* that that effect will be good in itself. But to find causal judgments that are universally true is notoriously a matter of extreme difficulty. The late date at which most of the physical sciences became exact, and the comparative fewness of the laws which they have succeeded in establishing even now, are sufficient proofs of this difficulty. With regard, then, to what are the most frequent objects of ethical judgments, namely actions, it is obvious that we cannot be satisfied that any of our universal causal judgments are true, even in the sense in which scientific laws are so. We cannot even discover hypothetical laws of the form 'Exactly this action will always, under these conditions, produce exactly that effect.' But for a correct ethical judgment with regard to the effects of certain actions we require more than this in two respects. (1) We require to know that a given action will produce a certain effect, *under whatever circumstances it occurs*. But this is certainly impossible. It is certain that in different circumstances the same action may produce effects which are utterly different in all respects upon which the value of the effects depends. Hence we can never be entitled to more than a generalisation — to a proposition of the form

'This result *generally* follows this kind of action'; and even this general-isation will only be true, if the circumstances under which the action occurs are generally the same. This is in fact the case, to a great extent, within any one particular age and state of society. But, when we take other ages into account, in many most important cases the normal cir-cumstances of a given kind of action will be so different, that the general-isation which is true for one will not be true for another. With regard then to ethical judgments which assert that a certain kind of action is good as a means to a certain kind of effect, none will be *universally* true; and many, though generally true at one period, will be generally false at others. But (2) we require to know not only that *one* good effect will be produced, but that, among all subsequent events affected by the action in question, the balance of good will be greater than if any other possible action had been performed. In other words, to judge that an action is generally a means to good is to judge not only that it generally does *some* good, but that it generally does the greatest good of which the circum-stances admit. In this respect ethical judgments about the effects of action involve a difficulty and a complication far greater than that involved in the establishment of scientific laws. For the latter we need only consider a single effect; for the former it is essential to consider not only this, but the effects of that effect, and so on as far as our view into the future can reach. It is, indeed, obvious that our view can never reach far enough for us to be certain that any action will produce the best possible effects. We must be content, if the greatest possible balance of good seems to be produced within a limited period. But it is important to notice that the whole series of effects within a period of considerable length is actually taken account of in our common judgments that an action is good as a means; and that hence this additional complication, which makes ethical generalisations so far more difficult to establish than scientific laws, is one which is involved in actual ethical discussions, and is of practical importance. The commonest rules of conduct involve such considerations as the balancing of future bad health against immediate gains; and even if we can never settle with any certainty how we shall secure the greatest possible total of good, we try at least to assure ourselves that probable future evils will not be greater than the immediate good.

17. There are, then, judgments which state that certain kinds of things have good effects; and such judgments, for the reasons just given, have the important characteristics (1) that they are unlikely to be true, if they state that the kind of thing in question *always* has good effects, and (2) that, even if they only state that it *generally* has good effects, many of them will only be true of certain periods in the world's history.

On the other hand there are judgments which state that certain kinds of things are themselves good; and these differ from the last in that, if true at all, they are all of them universally true. It is, therefore, extremely important to distinguish these two kinds of possible judgments. Both may be expressed in the same language: in both cases we commonly say 'Such and such a thing is good.' But in the one case 'good' will mean 'good as means,' *i.e.* merely that the thing is a means to good — will have good effects: in the other case it will mean 'good as end' — we shall be judging that the thing itself has the property which, in the first case, we asserted only to belong to its effects. It is plain that these are very different assertions to make about a thing; it is plain that either or both of them may be made, both truly and falsely, about all manner of things; and it is certain that unless we are clear as to which of the two we mean to assert, we shall have a very poor chance of deciding rightly whether our assertion is true or false. It is precisely this clearness as to the meaning of the question asked which has hitherto been almost entirely lacking in ethical speculation. Ethics has always been predominantly concerned with the investigation of a limited class of actions. With regard to these we may ask *both* how far they are good in themselves *and* how far they have a general tendency to produce good results. And the arguments brought forward in ethical discussion have always been of both classes — both such as would prove the conduct in question to be good in itself and such as would prove it to be good as a means. But that these are the only questions which any ethical discussion can have to settle, and that to settle the one is *not* the same thing as to settle the other — these two fundamental facts have in general escaped the notice of ethical philosophers. Ethical questions are commonly asked in an ambiguous form. It is asked 'What is a man's duty under these circumstances?' or 'Is it right to act in this way?' or 'What ought we to aim at securing?' But all these questions are capable of further analysis; a correct answer to any of them involves both judgments of what is good in itself and causal judgments. This is implied even by those who maintain that we have a direct and immediate judgment of absolute rights and duties. Such a judgment can only mean that the course of action in question is *the* best thing to do; that, by acting so, every good that *can* be secured will have been secured. Now we are not concerned with the question whether such a judgment will ever be true. The question is: What does it imply, if it is true? And the only possible answer is that, whether true or false, it implies both a proposition as to the degree of goodness of the action in question, as compared with other things, and a number of causal propositions. For it cannot be denied that the action will have consequences:

and to deny that the consequences matter is to make a judgment of their intrinsic value, as compared with the action itself. In asserting that the action is *the* best thing to do, we assert that it together with its consequences presents a greater sum of intrinsic value than any possible alternative. And this condition may be realised by any of the three cases: — (*a*) If the action itself has greater intrinsic value than any alternative, whereas both its consequences and those of the alternatives are absolutely devoid either of intrinsic merit or intrinsic demerit; or (*b*) if, though its consequences are intrinsically bad, the balance of intrinsic value is greater than would be produced by any alternative; or (*c*) if, its consequences being intrinsically good, the degree of value belonging to them and it conjointly is greater than that of any alternative series. In short, to assert that a certain line of conduct is, at a given time, absolutely right or obligatory, is obviously to assert that more good or less evil will exist in the world, if it be adopted than if anything else be done instead. But this implies a judgment as to the value both of its own consequences and of those of any possible alternative. And that an action will have such and such consequences involves a number of causal judgments. . . .

Chapter V

88. . . . What ought we to do? . . . This question . . . and its nature was briefly explained in Chap. I (§§ 15-17). It introduces into Ethics, as was there pointed out, an entirely new question — the question what things are related as *causes* to that which is good in itself; and this question can only be answered by an entirely new method — the method of empirical investigation; by means of which causes are discovered in the other sciences. To ask what kind of actions we ought to perform, or what kind of conduct is right, is to ask what kind of effects such action and conduct will produce. Not a single question in practical Ethics can be answered except by a causal generalisation. All such questions do, indeed, *also* involve an ethical judgment proper — the judgment that certain effects are better, in themselves, than others. But they *do* assert that these better things are effects — are causally connected with the actions in question. Every judgment in practical Ethics may be reduced to the form: This is a cause of that good thing.

89. That this is the case, that the questions, What is right? What is my duty? What ought I to do? belong exclusively to this . . . branch of ethical enquiry, is the first point to which I wish to call attention. All moral laws, I wish to shew, are merely statements that certain kinds of

actions will have good effects. The very opposite of this view has been generally prevalent in Ethics. 'The right' and 'the useful' have been supposed to be at least *capable* of conflicting with one another, and, at all events, to be essentially distinct. It has been characteristic of a certain school of moralists, as of moral common sense, to declare that the end will never justify the means. What I wish first to point out is that 'right' does and can mean nothing but 'cause of a good result,' and is thus identical with 'useful'; whence it follows that the end always will justify the means, and that no action which is not justified by its results can be right. That there may be a true proposition, meant to be conveyed by the assertion 'The end will not justify the means,' I fully admit: but that, in another sense, and a sense far more fundamental for ethical theory, it is utterly false, must first be shewn.

That the assertion 'I am morally bound to perform this action' is identical with the assertion 'This action will produce the greatest possible amount of good in the Universe' has already been briefly shewn in Chap. I. (§ 17); but it is important to insist that this fundamental point is demonstrably certain. This may, perhaps, be best made evident in the following way. It is plain that when we assert that a certain action is our absolute duty, we are asserting that the performance of that action at that time is unique in respect of value. But no dutiful action can possibly have unique value in the sense that it is the sole thing of value in the world; since, in that case, *every* such action would be the *sole* good thing, which is a manifest contradiction. And for the same reason its value cannot be unique in the sense that it has more intrinsic value than anything else in the world; since *every* act of duty would then be the *best* thing in the world, which is also a contradiction. It can, therefore, be unique only in the sense that the whole world will be better, if it be performed, than if any possible alternative were taken. And the question whether this is so cannot possibly depend solely on the question of its own intrinsic value. For any action will also have effects different from those of any other action; and if any of these have intrinsic value, their value is exactly as relevant to the total goodness of the Universe as that of their cause. It is, in fact, evident that, however valuable an action may be in itself, yet, owing to its existence, the sum of good in the Universe may conceivably be made less than if some other action, less valuable in itself, had been performed. But to say that this is the case is to say that it would have been better that the action should not have been done; and this again is obviously equivalent to the statement that it ought not to have been done — that it was not what duty required. 'Fiat iustitia, ruat caelum' can only be justified on the ground that by the doing of justice the Universe gains more than it loses by the falling of the heavens. It is, of course, possible that this is the case: but, at all events, to assert that justice *is* a duty, in spite of such consequences, is to assert that it is the case.

Our 'duty,' therefore, can only be defined as that action, which will cause more good to exist in the Universe than any possible alternative. And what is 'right' or 'morally permissible' only differs from this, as what will *not* cause *less* good than any possible alternative. When, therefore, Ethics presumes to assert that certain ways of acting are 'duties' it presumes to assert that to act in those ways will always produce the greatest possible sum of good. If we are told that to 'do no murder' is a duty, we are told that the action, whatever it may be, which is called murder, will under no circumstances cause so much good to exist in the Universe as its avoidance.

90. But, if this be recognised, several most important consequences follow, with regard to the relation of Ethics to conduct.

(1) It is plain that no moral law is self-evident, as has commonly been held by the Intuitional school of moralists. The Intuitional view of Ethics consists in the supposition that certain rules, stating that certain actions are always to be done or to be omitted, may be taken as self-evident premises. I have shewn with regard to judgments of what is *good in itself*, that this is the case; no reason can be given for them. But it is the essence of Intuitionism to suppose that rules of action — statements not of what ought to *be*, but of what we ought to do — are in the same sense intuitively certain. Plausibility has been lent to this view by the fact that we do undoubtedly make immediate judgments that certain actions are obligatory or wrong: we are thus often intuitively certain of our duty, *in a psychological sense*. But, nevertheless, these judgments are not self-evident and cannot be taken as ethical premises, since, as has now been shewn, they are capable of being confirmed or refuted by an investigation of causes and effects. It is, indeed, possible that some of our immediate intuitions are true; but since *what* we intuit, *what* conscience tells us, is that certain actions will always produce the greatest sum of good possible under the circumstances, it is plain that reasons can be given, which will shew the deliverances of conscience to be true or false.

91. (2) In order to shew that any action is a duty, it is necessary to know both what are the other conditions, which will, conjointly with it, determine its effects; to know exactly what will be the effects of these conditions; and to know all the events which will be in any way affected by our action throughout an infinite future. We must have all this causal knowledge, and further we must know accurately the degree of value both

of the action itself and of all these effects; and must be able to determine how, in conjunction with the other things in the Universe, they will affect its value as an organic whole. And not only this: we must also possess all this knowledge with regard to the effects of every possible alternative; and must then be able to see by comparison that the total value due to the existence of the action in question will be greater than that which would be produced by any of these alternatives. But it is obvious that our causal knowledge alone is far too incomplete for us ever to assure ourselves of this result. Accordingly it follows that we never have any reason to suppose that an action is our duty: we can never be sure that any action will produce the greatest value possible.

Ethics, therefore, is quite unable to give us a list of duties: but there still remains a humbler task which may be possible for Practical Ethics. Although we cannot hope to discover which, in a given situation, is the best of all possible alternative actions, there may be some possibility of shewing which among the alternatives, *likely to occur to any one*, will produce the greatest sum of good. This second task is certainly all that Ethics can ever have accomplished: and it is certainly all that it has ever collected materials for proving; since no one has ever attempted to exhaust the possible alternative actions in any particular case.

Prima Facie Evidence

W. D. Ross

What Makes Right Acts Right?

I

The most deliberate claim that 'right' is definable as 'productive of so and so' is made by Prof. G. E. Moore, who claims in *Principia Ethica* that 'right' means 'productive of the greatest possible good.' Now it has often been pointed out against hedonism, and by no one more clearly than by Professor Moore, that the claim that 'good' just means 'pleasant'

From W. D. Ross, *The Right and the Good* (Oxford: The Clarendon Press, 1930), pp. 8-11, 16-20, 20-22, 28-30, 30-31, 32-41, by permission of The Clarendon Press, Oxford.

cannot seriously be maintained; that while it may or may not be true that the only things that are good are pleasant, the statement that the good is just the pleasant is a synthetic, not an analytic proposition; that the words 'good' and 'pleasant' stand for distinct qualities, even if the things that possess the one are precisely the things that possess the other. If this were not so, it would not be intelligible that the proposition 'the good is just the pleasant' should have been maintained on the one hand, and denied on the other, with so much fervour; for we do not fight for or against analytic propositions; we take them for granted. Must not the same claim be made about the statement 'being right means being an act productive of the greatest good producible in the circumstances'? Is it not plain on reflection that this is not what me *mean* by right, even if it be a true statement about what *is* right? It seems clear for instance that when an ordinary man says it is right to fulfil promises he is not in the least thinking of the total consequences of such an act, about which he knows and cares little or nothing. 'Ideal utilitarianism'[1] is, it would appear, plausible only when it is understood not as an analysis or definition of the notion of 'right' but as a statement that all acts that are right, and only these, possess the further characteristic of being productive of the best possible consequences, and are right because they possess this other characteristic.

If I am not mistaken, Professor Moore has moved to this position, from the position that 'right' is *analysable* into 'productive of the greatest possible good.' In *Principia Ethica* the latter position is adopted: e.g. 'This use of "right," as denoting what is good as a means, whether or not it is also good as an end, is indeed the use to which I shall confine the word.'[2] 'To assert that a certain line of conduct is, at a given time, absolutely right or obligatory, is obviously to assert that more good or less evil will exist in the world, if it be adopted, than if anything else be done instead.'[3] 'To ask what kind of actions one ought to perform, or what kind of conduct is right, is to ask what kind of effects such action and conduct will produce . . . What I wish first to point out is that "right" does and can mean nothing but "cause of a good result," and is thus always identical with "useful" . . . That the assertion "I am morally bound to perform this action" is identical with the assertion "this action will produce the greatest possible amount of good in the Universe" has already been briefly shewn . . . ; but it is important to insist that this fundamental

---

[1] I use this as a well-known way of referring to Professor Moore's view. 'Agathistic utilitarianism' would indicate more distinctly the difference between it and hedonistic utilitarianism.

[2] p. 18.

[3] p. 25.

point is demonstrably certain. . . . Our "duty," therefore, can only be defined as that action, which will cause more good to exist in the Universe than any possible alternative. And what is "right" or "morally permissible" only differs from this, as what will *not* cause *less* good than any possible alternative.'[4]

In his later book, *Ethics*, Professor Moore seems to have come to adopt the other position, though perhaps not quite unequivocally. On page 8 he names as one of the 'more fundamental questions' of ethics the question 'what, after all, is it that we mean to say of an action when we say that it is right or ought to be done?' Here it is still suggested that 'right' is perhaps analysable or definable. But to this question *Ethics* nowhere distinctly offers an answer, and on page 9 we find, 'Can we discover any single reason, applicable to all right actions equally, which is, in every case, *the* reason why an action is right, when it is right?' This is the question which Professor Moore in fact sets himself to answer. But the *reason* for an action's being right is evidently not the same as its *rightness*, and Professor Moore seems already to have passed to the view that productivity of maximum good is not the definition of 'right' but another characteristic which underlies and accounts for the rightness of right acts. Again, he describes hedonistic utilitarianism as asking, 'can we discover any characteristic, over and above the mere fact that they *are* right, which belongs to absolutely *all* voluntary actions which are right, and which at the same time does not belong to any except those which are right?'[5] This is the question which he describes hedonism as essentially answering, and since his own view differs from hedonism not in logical form but just by the substitution of 'good' for 'pleasure,' his theory also seems to be essentially an answer to this question, i.e. not to the question what is rightness but to the question what is the universal accompaniment and, as he is careful to add,[6] the necessitating ground of rightness. Again, he describes hedonistic utilitarianism as giving us 'a criterion, or test, or standard by which we could discern with regard to any action whether it is right or wrong.'[7] And similarly, I suppose, he regards his own theory as offering a different criterion of rightness. But obviously a criterion of rightness is not rightness itself. And, most plainly of all, he says, 'It is indeed quite plain, I think, that the meaning of the two words' ('duty' and 'expediency,' the latter being equivalent to 'tendency to produce the maximum good') 'is *not* the same;

---

[4]pp. 146-8. Cf. also pp. 167, 169, 180-1.

[5]p. 17.

[6]pp. 44, 54.

[7]p. 43.

for, if it were, then it would be a mere tautology to say that it is always our duty to do what will have the best possible consequences.'[8] If we contrast this with *Principia Ethica*, page 169, 'if I ask whether an action is *really* my duty or *really* expedient, the predicate of which I question the applicability to the action in question is precisely the same,' we see how much Professor Moore has changed his position, and changed it in the direction in which, as I have been urging, it must be changed if it is to be made plausible. And if it is clear that 'right' does not mean 'productive of the greatest possible good,' it is *a fortiori* clear that it does not *mean* 'productive of the greatest possible pleasure, for the agent or for mankind,' but that productivity of the greatest possible pleasure for the agent or for mankind is at most the ground of the rightness of acts, rightness itself being admitted to be a distinct characteristic, and one which utilitarianism does not claim to define. . . .

II

The real point at issue between hedonism and utilitarianism on the one hand and their opponents on the other is not whether 'right' means 'productive of so and so'; for it cannot with any plausibility be maintained that it does. The point at issue is that to which we now pass, viz. whether there is any general character which makes right acts right, and if so, what it is. Among the main historical attempts to state a single characteristic of all right actions which is the foundation of their rightness are those made by egoism and utilitarianism. But I do not propose to discuss these, not because the subject is unimportant, but because it has been dealt with so often and so well already, and because there has come to be so much agreement among moral philosophers that neither of these theories is satisfactory. A much more attractive theory has been put forward by Professor Moore: that what makes actions right is that they are productive of more *good* than could have been produced by any other action open to the agent.[9]

This theory is in fact the culmination of all the attempts to base rightness on productivity of some sort of result. The first form this attempt takes is the attempt to base rightness on conduciveness to the advantage or pleasure of the agent. This theory comes to grief over the fact, which stares us in the face, that a great part of duty consists in an

---

[8]p. 173.

[9]I take the theory which, as I have tried to show, seems to be put forward in *Ethics* rather than the earlier and less plausible theory put forward in *Principia Ethica*. For the difference, cf. [pp. 469-72 of this volume].

observance of the rights and a furtherance of the interests of others, whatever the cost to ourselves may be. Plato and others may be right in holding that a regard for the rights of others never in the long run involves a loss of happiness for the agent, that 'the just life profits a man.' But this, even if true, is irrelevant to the rightness of the act. As soon as a man does an action *because* he thinks he will promote his own interests thereby, he is acting not from a sense of its rightness but from self-interest.

To the egoistic theory hedonistic utilitarianism supplies a much-needed amendment. It points out correctly that the fact that a certain pleasure will be enjoyed by the agent is no reason why he *ought* to bring it into being rather than an equal or greater pleasure to be enjoyed by another, though, human nature being what it is, it makes it not unlikely that he *will* try to bring it into being. But hedonistic utilitarianism in its turn needs a correction. On reflection it seems clear that pleasure is not the only thing in life that we think good in itself, that for instance we think the possession of a good character, or an intelligent understanding of the world, as good or better. A great advance is made by the substitution of 'productive of the greatest good' for 'productive of the greatest pleasure.'

Not only is this theory more attractive than hedonistic utilitarianism, but its logical relation to that theory is such that the latter could not be true unless *it* were true, while it might be true though hedonistic utilitarianism were not. It is in fact one of the logical bases of hedonistic utilitarianism. For the view that what produces the maximum pleasure is right has for its bases the views (1) that what produces the maximum good is right, and (2) that pleasure is the only thing good in itself. If they were not assuming that what produces the maximum *good* is right, the utilitarians' attempt to show that pleasure is the only thing good in itself, which is in fact the point they take most pains to establish, would have been quite irrelevant to their attempt to prove that only what produces the maximum *pleasure* is right. If, therefore, it can be shown that productivity of the maximum good is not what makes all right actions right, we shall *a fortiori* have refuted hedonistic utilitarianism.

When a plain man fulfils a promise because he thinks he ought to do so, it seems clear that he does so with no thought of its total consequences, still less with any opinion that these are likely to be the best possible. He thinks in fact much more of the past than of the future. What makes him think it right to act in a certain way is the fact that he has promised to do so — that and, usually, nothing more. That his act will produce the best possible consequences is not his reason for calling it right. What lends colour to the theory we are examining, then, is not the actions (which form probably a great majority of our actions) in which some such reflection as 'I have promised' is the only reason we give ourselves for thinking a certain action right, but the exceptional cases in which the consequences of fulfilling a promise (for instance) would be so disastrous to others that we judge it right not to do so. It must of course be admitted that such cases exist. If I have promised to meet a friend at a particular time for some trivial purpose, I should certainly think myself justified in breaking by engagement if by doing so I could prevent a serious accident or bring relief to the victims of one. And the supporters of the view we are examining hold that my thinking so is due to my thinking that I shall bring more good into existence by the one action than by the other. A different account may, however, be given of the matter, an account which will, I believe, show itself to be the true one. It may be said that besides the duty of fulfilling promises I have and recognize a duty of relieving distress,[10] and that when I think it right to do the latter at the cost of not doing the former, it is not because I think I shall produce more good thereby but because I think it the duty which is in the circumstances more of a duty. This account surely corresponds much more closely with what we really think in such a situation. If, so far as I can see, I could bring equal amounts of good into being by fulfilling my promise and by helping some one to whom I had made no promise, I should not hesitate to regard the former as my duty. Yet on the view that what is right is right because it is productive of the most good I should not so regard it.

There are two theories, each in its way simple, that offer a solution of such cases of conscience. One is the view of Kant, that there are certain duties of perfect obligation, such as those of fulfilling promises, of paying debts, of telling the truth, which admit of no exception whatever in favour of duties of imperfect obligation, such as that of relieving distress. The other is the view of, for instance, Professor Moore and Dr. Rashdall, that there is only the duty of producing good, and that all 'conflicts of duties' should be resolved by asking 'by which action will most good be produced?' But it is more important that our theory fit the facts than that it be simple, and the account we have given above corresponds (it seems to me) better than either of the simpler theories with what we really think, viz. that normally promise-keeping, for example, should come before benevolence, but that when and only when the good to be produced by the benevolent act is very great and the promise comparatively trivial, the act of benevolence becomes our duty.

---

[10]These are not strictly speaking duties, but things that tend to be our duty, or *prima facie* duties. [Cf. pp. 475-76 of this volume].

In fact the theory of 'ideal utilitarianism,' if I may for brevity refer so to the theory of Professor Moore, seems to simplify unduly our relations to our fellows. It says, in effect, that the only morally significant relation in which my neighbours stand to me is that of being possible beneficiaries by my action.[11] They do stand in this relation to me, and this relation is morally significant. But they may also stand to me in the relation of promisee to promiser, of creditor to debtor, of wife to husband, of child to parent, of friend to friend, of fellow countryman to fellow countryman, and the like; and each of these relations is the foundation of a *prima facie* duty, which is more or less incumbent on me according to the circumstances of the case. When I am in a situation, as perhaps I always am, in which more than one of these *prima facie* duties is incumbent on me, what I have to do is to study the situation as fully as I can until I form the considered opinion (it is never more) that in the circumstances one of them is more incumbent than any other; then I am bound to think that to do this *prima facie* duty is my duty *sans phrase* in the situation.

I suggest '*prima facie* duty' or 'conditional duty' as a brief way of referring to the characteristic (quite distinct from that of being a duty proper) which an act has, in virtue of being of a certain kind (e.g. the keeping of a promise), of being an act which would be a duty proper if it were not at the same time of another kind which is morally significant. Whether an act is a duty proper or actual duty depends on *all* the morally significant kinds it is an instance of. . . .

There is nothing arbitrary about these *prima facie* duties. Each rests on a definite circumstance which cannot seriously be held to be without moral significance. Of *prima facie* duties I suggest, without claiming completeness or finality for it, the following division.[12]

---

[11]Some will think it, apart from other considerations, a sufficient refutation of this view to point out that I also stand in that relation to myself, so that for this view the distinction of oneself from others is morally insignificant.

[12]I should make it plain at this stage that I am *assuming* the correctness of some of our main convictions as to *prima facie* duties, or, more strictly, am claiming that we *know* them to be true. To me it seems as self-evident as anything could be, that to make a promise, for instance, is to create a moral claim on us in someone else. Many readers will perhaps say that they do *not* know this to be true. If so, I certainly cannot prove it to them; I can only ask them to reflect again, in the hope that they will ultimately agree that they also know it to be true. The main moral convictions of the plain man seem to me to be, not opinions which it is for philosophy to prove or disprove, but knowledge from the start; and in my own case I seem to find little difficulty in distinguishing these essential convictions from other moral convictions which I also have, which are merely fallible opinions based on an imperfect study of the working for good or evil of certain institutions or types of action.

(1) Some duties rest on previous acts of my own. These duties seem to include two kinds, (*a*) those resting on a promise or what may fairly be called an implicit promise, such as the implicit undertaking not to tell lies which seems to be implied in the act of entering into conversation (at any rate by civilized men), or of writing books that purport to be history and not fiction. These may be called the duties of fidelity. (*b*) Those resting on a previous wrongful act. These may be called the duties of reparation. (2) Some rest on previous acts of other men, i.e. services done by them to me. These may be loosely described as the duties of gratitude. (3) Some rest on the fact or possibility of a distribution of pleasure or happiness (or of the means thereto) which is not in accordance with the merit of the persons concerned; in such cases there arises a duty to upset or prevent such a distribution. These are the duties of justice. (4) Some rest on the mere fact that there are other beings in the world whose condition we can make better in respect of virtue, or of intelligence, or of pleasure. These are the duties of beneficence. (5) Some rest on the fact that we can improve our own condition in respect of virtue or of intelligence. These are the duties of self-improvement. (6) I think that we should distinguish from (4) the duties that may be summed up under the title of 'not injuring others.' No doubt to injure others is incidentally to fail to do them good; but it seems to me clear that non-maleficence is apprehended as a duty distinct from that of beneficence, and as a duty of a more stringent character. It will be noticed that this alone among the types of duty has been stated in a negative way. An attempt might no doubt be made to state this duty, like the others, in a positive way. It might be said that it is really the duty to prevent ourselves from acting either from an inclination to harm others or from an inclination to seek our own pleasure, in doing which we should incidentally harm them. But on reflection it seems clear that the primary duty here is the duty not to harm others, this being a duty whether or not we have an inclination that if followed would lead to harming them; and that when we have such an inclination the primary duty not to harm others gives rise to a consequential duty to resist the inclination. The recognition of this duty of non-maleficence is the first step on the way to the recognition of the duty of beneficence; and that accounts for the prominence of the commands 'thou shalt not kill,' 'thou shalt not commit adultery,' 'thou shalt not steal,' 'thou shalt not bear false witness,' in so early a code as the Decalogue. But even when we have come to recognize the duty of beneficence, it appears to me that the duty of non-maleficence is recognized as a distinct one, and as *prima facie* more binding. We

should not in general consider it justifiable to kill one person in order to keep another alive, or to steal from one in order to give alms to another.

The essential defect of the 'ideal utilitarian' theory is that it ignores, or at least does not do full justice to, the highly personal character of duty. If the only duty is to produce the maximum of good, the question who is to have the good — whether it is myself, or my benefactor, or a person to whom I have made a promise to confer that good on him, or a mere fellow man to whom I stand in no such special relation — should make no difference to my having a duty to produce that good. But we are all in fact sure that it makes a vast difference. . . .

It is necessary to say something by way of clearing up the relation between *prima facie* duties and the actual or absolute duty to do one particular act in particular circumstances. If, as almost all moralists except Kant are agreed, and as most plain men think, it is sometimes right to tell a lie or break a promise, it must be maintained that there is a difference between *prima facie* duty and actual or absolute duty. When we think ourselves justified in breaking, and indeed morally obliged to break, a promise in order to relieve some one's distress, we do not for a moment cease to recognize a *prima facie* duty to keep our promise, and this leads us to feel, not indeed shame or repentance, but certainly compunction, for behaving as we do; we recognize, further, that it is our duty to make up somehow to the promisee for the breaking of the promise. We have to distinguish from the characteristic of being our duty that of tending to be our duty. Any act that we do contains various elements in virtue of which it falls under various categories. In virtue of being the breaking of a promise, for instance, it tends to be wrong; in virtue of being an instance of relieving distress it tends to be right. Tendency to be one's duty may be called a parti-resultant attribute, i.e. one which belongs to an act in virtue of some one component in its nature. *Being* one's duty is a toti-resultant attribute, one which belongs to an act in virtue of its whole nature and of nothing less than this. . . .

Another instance of the same distinction may be found in the operation of natural laws. *Qua* subject to the force of gravitation towards some other body, each body tends to move in a particular direction with a particular velocity; but its actual movement depends on *all* the forces to which it is subject. It is only by recognizing this distinction that we can preserve the absoluteness of laws of nature, and only by recognizing a corresponding distinction that we can preserve the absoluteness of the general principles of morality. But an important difference between the two cases must be pointed out. When we say that in virtue of gravitation a body tends to move in a certain way, we are referring to a causal influence actually exercised on it by another body or other bodies. When we say that in virtue of being deliberately untrue a certain remark tends to be wrong, we are referring to no causal relation, to no relation that involves succession in time, but to such a relation as connects the various attributes of a mathematical figure. And if the word 'tendency' is thought to suggest too much a causal relation, it is better to talk of certain types of act as being *prima facie* right or wrong (or of different persons as having different and possibly conflicting claims upon us), than of their tending to be right or wrong.

Something should be said of the relation between our apprehension of the *prima facie* rightness of certain types of act and our mental attitude towards particular acts. It is proper to use the word 'apprehension' in the former case and not in the latter. That an act, *qua* fulfilling a promise, or *qua* effecting a just distribution of good, or *qua* returning services rendered, or *qua* promoting the good of others, or *qua* promoting the virtue or insight of the agent, is *prima facie* right, is self-evident; not in the sense that it is evident from the beginning of our lives, or as soon as we attend to the proposition for the first time, but in the sense that when we have reached sufficient mental maturity and have given sufficient attention to the proposition it is evident without any need of proof, or of evidence beyond itself. It is self-evident just as a mathematical axiom, or the validity of a form of inference, is evident. The moral order expressed in these propositions is just as much part of the fundamental nature of the universe (and, we may add, of any possible universe in which there were moral agents at all) as is the spatial or numerical structure expressed in the axioms of geometry or arithmetic. In our confidence that these propositions are true there is involved the same trust in our reason that is involved in our confidence in mathematics; and we should have no justification for trusting it in the latter sphere and distrusting it in the former. In both cases we are dealing with propositions that cannot be proved, but that just as certainly need no proof. . . .

Our judgements about our actual duty in concrete situations have none of the certainty that attaches to our recognition of the general principles of duty. A statement is certain, i.e. is an expression of knowledge, only in one or other of two cases: when it is either self-evident, or a valid conclusion from self-evident premises. And our judgements about our particular duties have neither of these characters. (1) They are not self-evident. Where a possible act is seen to have two characteristics, in virtue of one of which it is *prima facie* right, and in virtue of the other *prima facie* wrong, we are (I think) well aware that we are not certain whether we ought or ought not to do it; that whether we do it or not, we are taking a moral risk. We come in the long run, after consideration, to think one duty more pressing than the other, but we do not feel certain that it is so. And though we do not always recognize that a possible act has two such characteristics, and though there *may* be cases in which it has not, we are never certain that any particular possible act has not, and therefore never certain that it is right, nor certain that it is wrong. For, to go no further in the analysis, it is enough to point out that any particular act will in all probability in the course of time contribute to the bringing about of good or of evil for many human beings, and thus have a *prima facie* rightness or wrongness of which we know nothing. (2) Again, our judgements about our particular duties are not logical conclusions from self-evident premises. The only possible premises would be the general principles stating their *prima facie* rightness or wrongness *qua* having the different characteristics they do have; and even if we could (as we cannot) apprehend the extent to which an act will tend on the one hand, for example, to bring about advantages for our benefactors, and on the other hand to bring about disadvantages for fellow men who are not our benefactors, there is no principle by which we can draw the conclusion that it is on the whole right or on the whole wrong. In this respect the judgement as to the rightness of a particular act is just like the judgement as to the beauty of a particular natural object or work of art. A poem is, for instance, in respect of certain qualities beautiful and in respect of certain others not beautiful; and our judgement as to the degree of beauty it possesses on the whole is never reached by logical reasoning from the apprehension of its particular beauties or particular defects. Both in this and in the moral case we have more or less probable opinions which are not logically justified conclusions from the general principles that are recognized as self-evident. . . .

The general principles of duty are obviously not self-evident from the beginning of our lives. How do they come to be so? The answer is, that they come to be self-evident to us just as mathematical axioms do. We find by experience that this couple of matches and that couple make four matches, that this couple of balls on a wire and that couple make four balls: and by reflection on these and similar discoveries we come to see that it is of the nature of two and two to make four. In a precisely similar way, we see the *prima facie* rightness of an act which would be the fulfilment of a particular promise, and of another which would be the fulfilment of another promise, and when we have reached sufficient maturity to think in general terms, we apprehend *prima facie* rightness to belong to the nature of any fulfilment of promise. What comes first in time is the apprehension of the self-evident *prima facie* rightness of an individual act of a particular type. From this we come by reflection to apprehend the self-evident general principle of *prima facie* duty. From this, too, perhaps along with the apprehension of the self-evident *prima facie* rightness of the same act in virtue of its having another characteristic as well, and perhaps in spite of the apprehension of its *prima facie* wrongness in virtue of its having some third characteristic, we come to believe something not self-evident at all, but an object of probable opinion, viz. that this particular act is (not *prima facie* but) actually right. . . .

Supposing it to be agreed, as I think on reflection it must, that no one *means* by 'right' just 'productive of the best possible consequences,' or 'optimific,' the attributes 'right' and 'optimific' might stand in either of two kinds of relation to each other. (1) They might be so related that we could apprehend *a priori*, either immediately or deductively, that any act that is optimific is right and any act that is right is optimific, as we can apprehend that any triangle that is equilateral is equiangular and *vice versa*. Professor Moore's view is, I think, that the coextensiveness of 'right' and 'optimific' is apprehended immediately.[13] He rejects the possibility of any proof of it. Or (2) the two attributes might be such that the question whether they are invariably connected had to be answered by means of an inductive inquiry. Now at first sight it might seem as if the constant connexion of the two attributes could be immediately apprehended. It might seem absurd to suggest that it could be right for any one to do an act which would produce consequences less good than those which would be produced by some other act in his power. Yet a little thought will convince us that this is not absurd. The type of case in which it is easiest to see that this is so is, perhaps, that in which one has made a promise. In such a case we all think that *prima facie* it is our duty to fulfill the promise irrespective of the precise goodness of the total consequences. And though we do not think it is necessarily our actual or absolute duty to do so, we are far from thinking that any, even the slightest, gain in the value of the total consequences will necessarily justify us in doing something else instead. Suppose, to simplify the case by abstraction, that the fulfilment of a promise to A would produce 1,000 units of good for him, but that by doing some other act I could produce 1,001 units of good for B, to whom I have made no promise, the other consequences of the two acts being of equal value; should we really think it self-evident that it was our duty to do the second act and not the first? I think not. We should, I fancy, hold that only a much greater disparity of value between the total consequences would justify us in failing to dis-

---

[13]*Ethics*, 181.

charge our *prima facie* to A. After all, a promise is a promise, and is not to be treated so lightly as the theory we are examining would imply. What, exactly, a promise is, is not so easy to determine, but we are surely agreed that it constitutes a serious moral limitation to our freedom of action. To produce the 1,001 units of good for B rather than fulfil our promise to A would be to take, not perhaps our duty as philanthropists too seriously, but certainly our duty as makers of promises too lightly.

Or consider another phase of the same problem. If I have promised to confer on A a particular benefit containing 1,000 units of good, is it self-evident that if by doing some different act I could produce 1,001 units of good for A himself (the other consequences of the two acts being supposed equal in value), it would be right for me to do so? Again, I think not. Apart from my general *prima facie* duty to do A what good I can, I have another *prima facie* duty to do him the particular service I have promised to do him, and this is not to be set aside in consequence of a disparity of good of the order of 1,001 to 1,000, though a much greater disparity might justify me in so doing.

Or again, suppose that A is a very good and B a very bad man, should I then, even when I have made no promise, think it self-evidently right to produce 1,001 units of good for B rather than 1,000 for A? Surely not. I should be sensible of a *prima facie* duty of justice, i.e. of producing a distribution of goods in proportion to merit, which is not outweighed by such a slight disparity in the total goods to be produced.

Such instances—and they might easily be added to—make it clear that there is no self-evident connexion between the attributes 'right' and 'optimific.' The theory we are examining has a certain attractiveness when applied to our decision that a particular act is our duty (though I have tried to show that it does not agree with our actual moral judgements even here). But it is not even plausible when applied to our recognition of *prima facie* duty. For if it were self-evident that the right coincides with the optimific, it should be self-evident that what is *prima facie* right is *prima facie* optimific. But whereas we are certain that keeping a promise is *prima facie* right, we are not certain that it is *prima facie* optimific (though we are perhaps certain that it is *prima facie* bonific). Our certainty that it is *prima facie* right depends not on its consequences but on its being the fulfilment of a promise. The theory we are examining involves too much difference between the evident ground of our conviction about *prima facie* duty and the alleged ground of our conviction about actual duty.

The coextensiveness of the right and the optimific is, then, not self-evident. And I can see no way of proving it deductively; nor, so far as I know, has any one tried to do so. There remains the question whether it can be established inductively. Such an inquiry, to be conclusive, would have to be very thorough and extensive. We should have to take a large variety of the acts which we, to the best of our ability, judge to be right. We should have to trace as far as possible their consequences, not only for the persons directly affected but also for those indirectly affected, and to these no limit can be set. To make our inquiry thoroughly conclusive, we should have to do what we cannot do, viz. trace these consequences into an unending future. And even to make it reasonably conclusive, we should have to trace them far into the future. It is clear that the most we could possibly say is that a large variety of typical acts that are judged right appear, so far as we can trace their consequences, to produce more good than any other acts possible to the agents in the circumstances. And such a result falls far short of proving the constant connexion of the two attributes. But it is surely clear that no inductive inquiry justifying even this result has ever been carried through. The advocates of utilitarian systems have been so much persuaded either of the identity or of the self-evident connexion of the attributes 'right' and 'optimific' (or 'felicific') that they have not attempted even such an inductive inquiry as is possible. And in view of the enormous complexity of the task and the inevitable inconclusiveness of the result, it is worth no one's while to make the attempt. What, after all, would be gained by it? If, as I have tried to show, for an act to be right and to be optimific are not the same thing, and an act's being optimific is not even the ground of its being right, then if we could ask ourselves (though the question is really unmeaning) which we ought to do, right acts because they are right or optimific acts because they are optimific, our answer must be 'the former.' If they are optimific as well as right, that is interesting but not morally important; if not, we still ought to do them (which is only another way of saying that they *are* the right acts), and the question whether they are optimific has no importance for moral theory.

There is one direction in which a fairly serious attempt has been made to show the connexion of the attributes 'right' and 'optimific.' One of the most evident facts of our moral consciousness is the sense which we have of the sanctity of promises, a sense which does not, on the face of it, involve the thought that one will be bringing more good into existence by fulfilling the promise than by breaking it. It is plain, I think, that in our normal thought we consider that the fact that we have made a promise is in itself sufficient to create a duty of keeping it, the sense of duty resting on remembrance of the past promise and not on thoughts of the future consequences of its fulfilment. Utilitarianism tries to show that this is not so, that the sanctity of promises rests on the good consequences of the fulfilment of them and the bad consequences of their non-fulfilment. It does so in this way: it points out that when you break a promise you not only fail to confer a certain advantage on your promisee but you diminish his confidence, and indirectly the confidence of others, in the fulfilment of promises. You thus strike a blow at one of the devices that have been found most useful in the relations between man and man—the device on which, for example, the whole system of commercial credit rests—and you tend to bring about a state of things wherein each man, being entirely unable to rely on the keeping of promises by others, will have to do everything for himself, to the enormous impoverishment of human well-being.

To put the matter otherwise, utilitarians say that when a promise ought to be kept it is because the total good to be produced by keeping it is greater than the total good to be produced by breaking it, the former including as its main element the maintenance and strengthening of general mutual confidence, and the latter being greatly diminished by a weakening of this confidence. They say, in fact, that the case I put some pages back never arises—the case in which by fulfilling a promise I shall bring into being 1,000 units of good for my promisee, and by breaking it 1,001 units of good for some one else, the other effects of the two acts being of equal value. The other effects, they say, never are of equal value. By keeping my promise I am helping to strengthen the system of mutual confidence; by breaking it I am helping to weaken this; so that really the first act produces $1,000 + x$ units of good, and the second $1,001 - y$ units, and the difference between $+x$ and $-y$ is enough to outweigh the slight superiority in the *immediate* effects of the second act. In answer to this it may be pointed out that there must be *some* amount of good that exceeds the difference between $+x$ and $-y$ (i.e. exceeds $x+y$); say, $x+y+z$. Let us suppose the *immediate* good effects of the second act to be assessed not at 1,001 but at $1,000 + x + y + z$. Then its *net* good effects are $1,000 + x + z$, i.e. greater than those of the fulfilment of the promise; and the utilitarian is bound to say forthwith that the promise should be broken. Now, we may ask whether that is really the way we think about promises? Do we really think that the production of the slightest balance of good, no matter who will enjoy it, by the breach of a promise frees us from the obligation to keep our promise? We need not doubt that a system by which promises are made and kept is one that has great advantages for the general well-being. But that is not the whole truth. To make a promise is not merely to adapt an ingenious device for promoting the general well-being; it is to put oneself in a new relation to one person in particular, a relation which creates a specifically new *prima facie* duty to him, not reducible to the duty of promoting the general well-being of society. By all means let us try to foresee the net good effects of keeping one's promise and the net good effects of breaking it, but even if we assess the first at 1000 + x and the second at 1,000 + x + z, the question still remains whether it is not our duty to fulfil the promise. It may be suspected, too, that the effect of a single keeping or breaking of a promise in strengthening or weakening the fabric of mutual confidence is greatly exaggerated by the theory we are examining. And if we suppose two men dying together alone, do we think that the duty of one to fulfil before he dies a promise he has made to the other would be extinguished by the fact that neither act would have any effect on the general confidence? Any one who holds this may be suspected of not having reflected on what a promise is.

I conclude that the attributes 'right' and 'optimific' are not identical, and that we do not know either by intuition, by deduction, or by induction that they coincide in their application, still less that the latter is the foundation of the former. It must be added, however, that if we are ever under no special obligation such as that of fidelity to a promisee or of gratitude to a benefactor, we ought to do what will produce most good; and that even when we are under a special obligation the tendency of acts to promote general good is one of the main factors in determining whether they are right.

In what has preceded, a good deal of use has been made of 'what we really think' about moral questions; a certain theory has been rejected bcause it does not agree with what we really think. It might be said that this is in principle wrong; that we should not be content to expound what our present moral consciousness tells us but should aim at a criticism of our existing moral consciousness in the light of theory. Now I do not doubt that the moral consciousness of men has in detail undergone a good deal of modifications as regards the things we think right, at the hands of moral theory. But if we are told, for instance, that we should give up our view that there is a special obligatoriness attaching to the keeping of promises because it is self-evident that the only duty is to produce as much good as possible, we have to ask ourselves whether we really, when we reflect, *are* convinced that this is self-evident, and whether we really *can* get rid of our view that promise-keeping has a bindingness independent of productiveness of maximum good. In my own experience I find that I cannot, in spite of a very genuine attempt to do so; and I venture to think that most people will find the same, and that just because they cannot lose the sense of special obligation, they cannot accept as self-evident, or even as true, the theory which would require them to do so. In fact it seems, on reflection, self-evident that a promise, simply as such, is something that *prima facie* ought to be kept, and it does *not*, on reflection, seem self-evident that production of maximum good is the only thing that makes an act obligatory. And to ask us to give up at the bidding of a theory our actual apprehension of what is right and what is wrong seems like asking people to repudiate their actual experience of beauty, at the bidding of a theory which says 'only that which satisfies such and such conditions can be beautiful.' If what I have called our actual apprehension is (as I would maintain that it is) truly an apprehension, i.e. an instance of knowledge, the request is nothing less than absurd.

I would maintain, in fact, that what we are apt to describe as 'what we think' about moral questions contains a considerable amount that we do not think but know, and that this forms the standard by reference to which the truth of any moral theory has to be tested, instead of having itself to be tested by reference to any theory. I hope that I have in what precedes indicated what in my view these elements of knowledge are that are involved in our ordinary moral consciousness.

It would be a mistake to found a natural science on 'what we really think,' i.e. on what reasonably thoughtful and well-educated people think about the subjects of the science before they have studied them scientifically. For such opinions are interpretations, and often misinterpretations, of sense-experience; and the man of science must appeal from these to sense-experience itself, which furnishes his real data. In ethics no such appeal is possible. We have no more direct way of access to the facts about rightness and goodness and about what things are right or good, than by thinking about them; the moral convictions of thoughtful and well-educated people are the data of ethics just as sense-perceptions are the data of a natural science. Just as some of the latter have to be rejected as illusory, so have some of the former; but as the latter are rejected only when they are in conflict with other more accurate sense-perceptions, the former are rejected only when they are in conflict with other convictions which stand better the test of reflection. The existing body of moral convictions of the best people is the cumulative product of the moral reflection of many generations, which has developed an extremely delicate power of appreciation of moral distinctions; and this the theorist cannot afford to treat with anything other than the greatest respect. The verdicts of the moral consciousness of the best people are the foundation on which he must build; though he must first compare them with one another and eliminate any contradictions they may contain.

Non-Cognitivism

A. J. Ayer

On the Analysis of Moral Judgements

'Most of us would agree,' said F. P. Ramsey, addressing a society in Cambridge in 1925, 'that the objectivity of good was a thing we had settled and dismissed with the existence of God. Theology and Absolute Ethics are two famous subjects which we have realized to have no real objects.' There are many, however, who still think that these questions have not been settled; and in the meantime philosophers of Ramsey's persuasion

From "On the Analysis of Moral Judgements" in *Philosophical Essays* by A. J. Ayer (London and Basingstoke: Macmillan & Co., 1954), pp. 231-49, originally published in *Horizon* XX (1949), by permission of the author, St. Martin's Press, Inc., Macmillan & Co., Ltd., London and Basingstoke, and The Macmillan Company of Canada, Ltd.

have grown more circumspect. Theological and ethical statements are no longer stigmatized as false or meaningless. They are merely said to be different from scientific statements. They are differently related to their evidence; or rather, a different meaning is attached to 'evidence' in their case. 'Every kind of statement,' we are told, 'has its own kind of logic.'

What this comes to, so far as moral philosophy is concerned, is that ethical statements are *sui generis*; and this may very well be true. Certainly, the view, which I still wish to hold, that what are called ethical statements are not really statements at all, that they are not descriptive of anything, that they cannot be either true or false, is in an obvious sense incorrect. For, as the English language is currently used—and what else, it may be asked, is here in question?—it is by no means improper to refer to ethical utterances as statements; when someone characterizes an action by the use of an ethical predicate, it is quite good usage to say that he is thereby describing it; when someone wishes to assent to an ethical verdict, it is perfectly legitimate for him to say that it is true, or that it is a fact, just as, if he wished to dissent from it, it would be perfectly legitimate for him to say that it was false. We should know what he meant and we should not consider that he was using words in an unconventional way. What is unconventional, rather, is the usage of the philosopher who tells us that ethical statements are not really statements at all but something else, ejaculations perhaps or commands, and that they cannot be either true or false.

Now when a philosopher asserts that something 'really' is not what it really is, or 'really' is what it really is not, that we do not, for example, 'really' see chairs or tables, whereas there is a perfectly good and familiar sense in which we really do, or that we cannot 'really' step into the same river twice, whereas in fact we really can, it should not always be assumed that he is merely making a mistake. Very often what he is doing, although he may not know it, is to recommend a new way of speaking, not just for amusement, but because he thinks that the old, the socially correct, way of speaking is logically misleading, or that his own proposal brings out certain points more clearly. Thus, in the present instance, it is no doubt correct to say that the moralist does make statements, and, what is more, statements of fact, statements of ethical fact. It is correct in the sense that if a vote were taken on the point, those who objected to this way of speaking would probably be in the minority. But when one considers how these ethical statements are actually used, it may be found that they function so very differently from other types of statement that it is advisable to put them into a separate category altogether either to say that they are not to be counted as statements at all, or, if this proves inconvenient, at least to say that they do not express propositions, and consequently that there are no ethical facts. This does not mean that all ethical statements are held to be false. It is merely a matter of laying down a usage of the words 'proposition' and 'fact,' according to which only propositions express facts and ethical statements fall outside the class of propositions. This may seem to be an arbitrary procedure, but I hope to show that there are good reasons for adopting it. And once these reasons are admitted the purely verbal point is not of any great importance. If someone still wishes to say that ethical statements are statements of fact, only it is a queer sort of fact, he is welcome to do so. So long as he accepts our grounds for saying that they are not statements of fact, it is simply a question of how widely or loosely we want to use the word 'fact.' My own view is that it is preferable so to use it as to exclude ethical judgements, but it must not be inferred from this that I am treating them with disrespect. The only relevant consideration is that of clarity.

The distinctions that I wish to make can best be brought out by an example. Suppose that someone has committed a murder. Then part of the story consists of what we may call the police-court details; where and when and how the killing was effected; the identity of the murderer and of his victim; the relationship in which they stood to one another. Next there are the questions of motive: the murderer may have been suffering from jealousy, or he may have been anxious to obtain money; he may have been avenging a private injury, or pursuing some political end. These questions of motive are, on one level, a matter of the agent's reflections before the act; and these may very well take the form of moral judgements. Thus he may tell himself that his victim is a bad man and that the world would be better for his removal, or, in a different case, that it is his duty to rid his country of a tyrant, or, like Raskolnikov in *Crime and Punishment*, that he is a superior being who has in these circumstances the right to kill. A psycho-analyst who examines the case may, however, tell a different story. He may say that the political assassin is really revenging himself upon his father, or that the man who persuades himself that he is a social benefactor is really exhibiting a lust for power, or, in a case like that of Raskolnikov, that the murderer does not really believe that he has the right to kill.

All these are statements of fact; not indeed that the man has, or has not, the right to kill, but that this is what he tells himself. They are verified or confuted, as the case may be, by observation. It is a matter of fact, in my usage of the term, that the victim was killed at such and such a place and at such and such a time and in such and such a manner. It is also a matter of fact that the murderer had certain conscious motives. To himself they are known primarily by introspection; to others by various features of his overt behaviour,, including what he says. As regards his unconscious motives the only criterion is his overt behaviour. It can indeed plausibly be argued that to talk about the unconscious is always equivalent to talking about overt behaviour, though often in a very complicated way. Now there seems to me to be a very good sense in which to tell a story of this kind, that this is what the man did and that these were his reasons for doing it, is to give a complete description of the facts. Or rather, since one can never be in a position to say that any such description is complete, what will be missing from it will be further information of the same type; what we obtain when this information is added is a more elaborate account of the circumstances of the action, and of its antecedents and consequences. But now suppose that instead of developing the story in this circumstantial way, one applies an ethical predicate to it. Suppose that instead of asking what it was that really happened, or what the agent's motives really were, we ask whether he was justified in acting as he did. Did he have the right to kill? Is it true that he had the right? Is it a fact that he acted rightly? It does not matter in this connection what answer we give. The question for moral philosophy is not whether a certain action is right or wrong, but what is implied by saying that it is right, or saying that it is wrong. Suppose then that we say that the man acted rightly. The point that I wish to make is that in saying this we are not elaborating or modifying our description of the situation in the way that we should be elaborating it if we gave further police-court details, or in the way that we should be modifying it if we showed that the agent's motives were different from what they had been thought to be. To say that his motives were good, or that they were bad, is not to say what they were. To say that the man acted rightly, or that he acted wrongly, is not to say what he did. And when one has said what he did, when one has described the situation in the way that I have outlined, then to add that he was justified, or alternatively that he was not, is not to say any more about what he did; it does not add a further detail to the story. It is for this reason that these ethical predicates are not factual; they do not describe any features of the situation to which they are applied. But they do, someone may object, they describe its ethical features. But what are these ethical features? And how are they related to the other features of the situation, to what we may provisionally call its natural features? Let us consider this.

To begin with, it is, or should be, clear that the connection is not logical. Let us assume that two observers agree about all the circumstances of the case, including the agent's motives, but that they disagree in their evaluation of it. Then neither of them is contradicting himself. Otherwise the use of the ethical term would add nothing to the circumstantial description; it would serve merely as a repetition, or partial repetition, of it. But neither, as I hope to show, is the connection factual. There is nothing that counts as observing the *designata* of the ethical predicates, apart from observing the natural features of the situation. But what alternative is left? Certainly it can be said that the ethical features in some way depend upon the natural. We can and do give reasons for our moral judgements, just as we do for our aesthetic judgements, where the same argument applies. We fasten on motives, point to consequences, ask what would happen if everyone were to behave in such a way, and so forth. But the question is: In what way do these reasons support the judgements? Not in a logical sense. Ethical argument is not formal demonstration. And not in a scientific sense either. For then the goodness or badness of the situation, the rightness or wrongness of the action, would have to be something apart from the situation, something independently verifiable, for which the facts adduced as the reasons for the moral judgment were evidence. But in these moral cases the two coincide. There is no procedure of examining the value of the facts, as distinct from examining the facts themselves. We may say that we have evidence for our moral judgments, but we cannot distinguish between pointing to the evidence itself and pointing to that for which it is supposed to be evidence. Which means that in the scientific sense it is not evidence at all.

My own answer to this question is that what are accounted reasons for our moral judgments are reasons only in the sense that they determine attitudes. One attempts to influence another person morally by calling his attention to certain natural features of the situation, which are such as will be likely to evoke from him the desired response. Or again one may give reasons to oneself as a means of settling on an attitude or, more importantly, as a means of coming to some practical decision. Of course there are many cases in which one applies an ethical term without there being any question of one's having to act oneself, or even to persuade others to act, in any present situation. Moral judgements passed upon the behaviour of historical or fictitious characters provide obvious examples. But an action or a situation is morally evaluated always as an action or a situation of a certain kind. What is approved or disapproved is something repeatable. In saying that Brutus or Raskolnikov acted rightly, I

am giving myself and others leave to imitate them should similar circumstances arise. I show myself to be favourably disposed in either case
towards actions of that type. Similarly, in saying that they acted wrongly,
I express a resolution not to imitate them, and endeavour also to discourage others. It may be thought that the mere use of the dyslogistic
word 'wrongly' is not much of a discouragement, although it does have
some emotive force. But that is where the reasons come in. I discourage
others, or at any rate hope to discourage them, by telling them why
I think the action wrong; and here the argument may take various forms.
One method is to appeal to some moral principle, as, for example, that
human life is sacred, and show that it applies to the given case. It is
assumed that the principle is one that already has some influence upon
those to whom the argument is addressed. Alternatively, one may try to
establish certain facts, as, for example, that the act in question caused, or
was such as would be likely to cause, a great deal of unhappiness; and here
it is assumed that the consideration of these facts will modify the hearer's
attitude. It is assumed that he regards the increase of human misery as
something undesirable, something if possible to be avoided. As for the
moral judgement itself, it may be regarded as expressing the attitude which
the reasons given for it are calculated to evoke. To say, as I once did, that
these moral judgements are merely expressive of certain feelings, feelings of approval or disapproval, is an oversimplification. The fact is
rather that what may be described as moral attitudes consist in certain
patterns of behaviour, and that the expression of a moral judgement is
an element in the pattern. The moral judgement expresses the attitude
in the sense that it contributes to defining it. Why people respond favourably to certain facts and unfavourably to others is a question for the
sociologist, into which I do not here propose to enter. I should imagine
that the utilitarians had gone some way towards answering this question,
although theirs is almost certainly not the whole answer. But my concern
at present is only to analyse the use of ethical terms, not scientifically to
explain it.

At this point it may be objected that I have been excessively dogmatic. What about the people who claim that they do observe ethical
properties, non-natural properties, as G. E. Moore once put it,[1] not
indeed through their senses, but by means of intellectual intuition? What
of those who claim that they have a moral sense, and mean by this not
merely that they have feelings of approval and disapproval, or whatever
else may go to define a moral attitude, but that they experience such

---

[1]Vide his *Principia Ethica*, chap I.

things as goodness or beauty in a way somehow analogous to that in which they experience sounds or colours? What are we to say to them? I may not have any experiences of this sort myself, but that, it may be said, is just my shortcoming. I am surely not entitled to assume that all these honest and intelligent persons do not have the experiences that they say they do. It may be, indeed, that the differences between us lie not so much in the nature of our respective experiences as in our fashion of describing them. I do in fact suspect that the experiences which some philosophers want to describe as intuitions, or as quasi-sensory apprehensions, of good are not significantly different from those that I want to describe as feelings of approval. But whether this be so or not, it does not in any way affect my argument. For let it be granted that someone who contemplates some natural situation detects in it something which he describes as 'goodness' or 'beauty' or 'fittingness' or 'worthiness to be approved.' How this experience of goodness, or whatever it may be, is supposed to be related to the experiences which reveal the natural features of the situation has not yet been made clear, but I take it that it is not regarded merely as their effect. Rather, the situation is supposed to look good, or fitting, in much the same way as a face may be said to look friendly. But then to say that this experience is an experience of good will be to say no more than that it is this type of experience. The word 'good,' or whatever other value term may be used, simply comes to be descriptive of experiences of this type, and here it makes no difference whether they are regarded as intuitions or as moral sensations. In neither case does anything whatsoever follow as regards conduct. That a situation has this peculiar property, the property whose presence is established by people's having such experiences, does not entail that it is preferable to other situations, or that it is anyone's duty to bring it into existence. To say that such a situation ought to be created, or that it deserves to exist, will be to say something different from merely saying that it has this property. This point is obscured by the use of an ethical term to describe the property, just because the ethical term is tacitly understood to be normative. It continues to fulfil its function of prescribing the attitude that people are to take. But if the ethical term is understood to be normative, then it does not merely describe the alleged non-natural property, and if it does merely describe this property, then it is not normative and so no longer does the work that ethical terms are supposed to do.

This argument may become clearer if, instead of designating the supposed property from the outset as 'good,' we refer to it simply as 'X.' The question then arises whether X is identical with good. How is this question to be interpreted? If it is interpreted as merely asking whether

X is of a certain quality, whether it exhibits the character for which the word 'good' is being made to stand, then the answer may very well be that the two are identical; but all that this amounts to is that we have decided to use the word 'good' to designate what is also designated by 'X.' And from this no normative conclusion follows. It does not follow that the situation characterized by X has any value, if its having value is understood as implying not merely that it answers to a certain description but that it has some claim upon us, that it is something that we ought to foster or desire. Having appropriated the word 'good' to do duty for X, to serve as a mere description of a special tone or colouring of the situation, we shall need some other word to do the normative work that the word 'good' did before. But if 'good' is allowed to keep its normative sense, then goodness may indeed be attributed to X, but the two cannot be identified. For then to say that X is good is not just to say that 'X' stands for a certain property. It is to say that whatever has this property is to be valued, sought, approved of, brought into existence in preference to other things, and so on. Those who talk of non-natural qualities, moral intuitions, and all the rest of it, may be giving peculiar descriptions of commonplace experiences, or they may be giving suggestive descriptions of peculiar experiences; it does not matter which view we take. In either case we are left with the further question whether what is so described is to be valued; and this is not simply equivalent to asking what character it has, whether natural, or non-natural, whatever that may mean. Thus even if an intuitionist does have experiences that others do not have, it makes no difference to the argument. We are still entitled to say that it is misleading for him to use a value-term to designate the content of such experiences; for in this way he contrives to smuggle a normative judgement into what purports to be a statement of fact. A valuation is not a description of something very peculiar; it is not a description at all. Consequently, the familiar subjective-objective antithesis is out of place in moral philosophy. The problem is not that the subjectivist denies that certain wild, or domesticated, animals, 'objective values,' exist and the objectivist triumphantly produces them; or that the objectivist returns like an explorer with tales from the kingdom of values and the subjectivist says he is a liar. It does not matter what the explorer finds or does not find. For talking about values is not a matter of describing what may or may not be there, the problem being whether it really is there. There is no such problem. The moral problem is: What am I to do? What attitude am I to take? And moral judgements are directives in this sense.

We can now see that the whole dispute about the objectivity of values, as it is ordinarily conducted, is pointless and idle. I suppose that what underlies it is the question: Are the things that I value really valuable, and how can I know that they are? Then one party gives the answer: They are really valuable if they reflect, or participate in, or are in some other mysterious way related to an objective world of values; and you can know that they are by inspecting this world. To which their opponents reply that there is no such world, and can therefore be no such inspection. But this sort of argument, setting aside the question whether it is even intelligible, is nothing to the purpose. For suppose that someone did succeed in carrying out such an inspection. Suppose that he had an experience which we allowed him to describe in these terms. He can still raise the questions: Are these values the real ones? Are the objects that I am inspecting themselves really valuable, and how can I know that they are? And how are these questions to be answered? They do not arise, it may be said. These objective values carry the stamp of authenticity upon their faces. You have only to look at them to know that they are genuine. But, in this sense, any natural situation to which we attach value can carry the stamp of authenticity upon its face. That is to say, the value which is attached to it may be something that it does not occur to us to question. But in neither case is it inconceivable that the value should be questioned. Thus, these alleged objective values perform no function. The hypothesis of their existence does no work; or rather, it does no work that is not equally well done without it. Its effect is to answer the question: Are the things that I value really valuable? by Yes, if you have a certain sort of experience in connection with them. Let us assume that these experiences can be identified and even that there is some method for deciding between them when they appear to yield contradictory results. Even so, that someone does or does not have them is itself a "natural" fact. Moreover, this answer merely lays down one of many possible standards. It is on a par with saying: 'The things that you value are really valuable if they increase human happiness, or they are really valuable if certain persons, your pastors and masters, approve of them.' Then either one accepts the standard, or one raises the question again. Why should I value human happiness? Why should I be swayed by my pastors and masters? Why should I attach such great importance just to these experiences? In the end there must come a point where one gets no further answer, but only a repetition of the injunction: Value this because it is valuable.

In conducting this argument, I have put the most favourable interpretation upon my opponents' claims; for I have assumed that what is described as the apprehension of objective values may be a different experience from the everyday experience of attaching value to some natural situation; but, in fact, I am fairly confident that what we have here are two different ways of describing the same experience. And in that case the answer that the 'objectivists' give to the question: Are the things that I value really valuable? is the 'subjective' answer that they are really valuable if you value them, or perhaps that they are really valuable if certain other people value them. What we are given is an injunction not to worry, which may or may not satisfy us. If it does not, perhaps something else will. But in any case there is nothing to be done about it, except look at the facts, look at them harder, look at more of them, and then come to a moral decision. Then, asking whether the attitude that one has adopted is the right attitude comes down to asking whether one is prepared to stand by it. There can be no guarantee of its correctness, because nothing counts as a guarantee. Or rather, something may count for someone as a guarantee, but counting something as a guarantee is itself taking up a moral standpoint.

All this applies equally to 'naturalistic' theories of ethics, like Utilitarianism. By defining 'right,' in the way that Bentham does, as 'conducive to the greatest happiness of the greatest number,' one does give it a descriptive meaning; but just for that reason one takes it out of the list of ethical terms. So long as the word 'right' keeps its current emotive force, the implication remains that what is right ought to be done, but this by no means follows from Bentham's definition. Nevertheless, it is clearly intended that the definition should somehow carry this implication; otherwise it would not fulfil its purpose. For the point of such a definition, as Professor Stevenson has well brought out in his *Ethics and Language*, is not that it gives precision to the use of a word, but that it covertly lays down a standard of conduct. The moral judgement is that happiness is to be maximized, and that actions are to be evaluated, praised or blamed, imitated or avoided, in proportion as they militate for or against this end. Now this is not a statement of act, but a recommendation; and in the ordinary way the sense of such a recommendation is contained in some ethical term. These ethical terms can also be given a descriptive meaning, but it is not *qua* descriptive that they are ethical. If, for example, the word 'wrong' is simply equated with 'not conducive to human happiness,' some other term will be needed to carry the normative implication that conduct of this sort is to be avoided; and it is terms of this kind, which are not descriptive, that I am treating as distinctively ethical.

I hope that I have gone some way towards making clear what the theory which I am advocating is. Let me now say what it is not. In the first place, I am not saying that morals are trivial or unimportant, or that people ought not to bother with them. For this would itself be a judgement of value, which I have not made and do not wish to make. And even if I did wish to make it it would have no logical connection with my theory. For the theory is entirely on the level of analysis; it is an attempt to show what people are doing when they make moral judgements; it is not a set of suggestions as to what moral judgements they are to make. And this is true of all moral philosophy, as I understand it. All moral theories, intuitionist, naturalistic, objectivist, emotive, and the rest, in so far as they are philosophical theories, are neutral as regards actual conduct. To speak technically, they belong to the field of meta-ethics, not ethics proper. That is why it is silly, as well as presumptuous, for any one type of philosopher to pose as the champion of virtue. And it is also one reason why many people find moral philosophy an unsatisfying subject. For they mistakenly look to the moral philosopher for guidance.

Again, when I say that moral judgements are emotive rather than descriptive, that they are persuasive expressions of attitudes and not statements of fact, and consequently that they cannot be either true or false, or at least that it would make for clarity if the categories of truth and falsehood were not applied to them, I am not saying that nothing is good or bad, right or wrong, or that it does not matter what we do. For once more such a statement would itself be the expression of a moral attitude. This attitude is not entailed by the theory, nor do I in fact adopt it. It would indeed be a difficult position to maintain. It would exclude even egotism as a policy, for the decision to consult nothing but one's own pleasure is itself a value judgement. What it requires is that one should live without any policy at all. This may or may not be feasible. My point is simply that I am not recommending it. Neither, in expounding my meta-ethical theory, am I recommending the opposite. It is indeed to be expected that a moral philosopher, even in my sense of the term, will have his moral standards and that he will sometimes make moral judgements; but these moral judgements cannot be a logical consequence of his philosophy. To analyse moral judgements is not itself to moralize.

Finally, I am not saying that anything that anybody thinks right is right; that putting people into concentration camps is preferable to allowing them free speech if somebody happens to think so, and that the contrary is also preferable if somebody thinks that it is. If my theory did entail this, it would be contradictory; for two different courses of action cannot each be preferable to the other. But it does not entail anything of the sort. On my analysis, to say that something which somebody thinks right really is right is to range oneself on his side, to adhere to that particular standpoint, and certainly I do not adhere to every standpoint whatsoever. I adhere to some, and not to others, like everybody else who has any moral views at all. It is, indeed, true that in a case where one person A approves of X, and another person B approves of not-X, A may correctly express his attitude towards X by saying that it is good, or right, and that B may correctly use the same term to express his attitude towards not-X. But there is no contradiction here. There would be a contradiction if from the fact that A was using words honestly and correctly when he said that X was good, and that B was using words honestly and correctly when he said that not-X was good, it followed that both X and not-X were good, or that X was both good and bad. But this does not follow, inasmuch as the conclusion that X is good, or that not-X is good, itself expresses the attitude of a third party, the speaker, who is by no means bound to agree with both A and B. In this example, indeed, he cannot consistently agree with both, though he may disagree with both if he regards both X and not-X as ethically neutral, or as contraries rather than contradictories in respect of value. It is easy to miss this point, which is essential for the understanding of our position. To say that anything is right if someone thinks so is unobjectionable if it means no more than that anyone is entitled to use the word 'right' to refer to something of which he morally approves. But this is not the way in which it is ordinarily taken. It is ordinarily taken as the enunciation of a moral principle. As a moral principle it does appear contradictory; it is at least doubtful whether to say of a man that he commits himself morally both to X and not-X is to describe a possible attitude. But it may perhaps be construed as a principle of universal moral tolerance. As such, it may appeal to some; it does not, in fact, to me. But the important point is that it is not entailed by the theory, which is neutral as regards all moral principles. And here I may repeat that in saying that it is neutral as regards all moral principles I am not saying that it recommends them all alike, nor that it condemns them all alike. It is not that sort of theory. No philosophical theory is.

But even if there is no logical connection between this meta-ethical theory and any particular type of conduct, may there not be a psychological connection? Does not the promulgation of such a theory encourage moral laxity? Has not its effect been to destroy people's confidence in accepted moral standards? And will not the result of this be that something mischievous will take their place? Such charges have, indeed, been made, but I do not know upon what evidence. The question how people's conduct is actually affected by their acceptance of a meta-ethical theory is one for empirical investigation; and in this case, so far as I know, no serious investigation has yet been carried out. My own observations, for what they are worth, do not suggest that those who accept the 'positivist' analysis of moral judgements conduct themselves very differently as a class from those who reject it; and, indeed, I doubt if the study of moral philosophy does, in general, have any very marked effect upon people's conduct. The way to test the point would be to convert a sufficiently large number of people from one meta-ethical view to another and make careful observations of their behaviour before and after their conversions. Assuming that their behaviour changed in some significant way, it would then have to be decided by further experiment whether this was due to the change in their philosophical beliefs or to some other factor. If it could be shown, as I believe it could not, that the general acceptance of the sort of analysis of moral judgements that I have been putting forward would have unhappy social consequences, the conclusion drawn by illiberal persons might be that the doctrine ought to be kept secret. For my part I think that I should dispute this conclusion on moral grounds, but this is a question which I am not now concerned to argue. What I have tried to show is not that the theory I am defending is expedient, but that it is true.

A Golden-Rule Argument

R. M. Hare

A Moral Argument

6.1. Historically, one of the chief incentives to the study of ethics has been the hope that its findings might be of help to those faced with difficult moral problems. That this is still a principal incentive for many people is shown by the fact that modern philosophers are often reproached for failing to make ethics relevant to morals.[1] This is because

From R. M. Hare, *Freedom and Reason* (Oxford: The Clarendon Press, 1963), pp. 86-90, 90-102, 106-9, by permission of The Clarendon Press, Oxford. For a full understanding of Prof. Hare's argument, the reader is advised to consult the complete work.

[1] I have tried to fill in some of the historical background of these reproaches, and to assess the justification for them, in my article in *The Philosophy of C. D. Broad*, ed. P. Schilpp.

one of the main tenets of many recent moral philosophers has been that the most popular method by which it was sought to bring ethics to bear on moral problems was not feasible — namely the method followed by the group of theories loosely known as 'naturalist'.

The method of naturalism is so to characterize the *meanings* of the key moral terms that, given certain factual premisses, not themselves moral judgements, moral conclusions can be deduced from them. If this could be done, it was thought that it would be of great assistance to us in making moral decisions; we should only have to find out the non-moral facts, and the moral conclusion as to what we ought to do would follow. Those who say that it cannot be done leave themselves the task of giving an alternative account of moral reasoning.

Naturalism seeks to make the findings of ethics *relevant* to moral decisions by making the former not morally *neutral*. It is a very natural assumption that if a statement of ethics is relevant to morals, then it cannot be neutral as between different moral judgements; and naturalism is a tempting view for those who make this assumption. Naturalistic definitions are not morally neutral, because with their aid we could show that statements of non-moral facts *entailed* moral conclusions. And some have thought that unless such an entailment can be shown to hold, the moral philosopher has not made moral reasoning possible.

One way of escaping this conclusion is to say that the relation between the non-moral premisses and the non-moral conclusion is not one of entailment, but that some other logical relation, peculiar to morals, justifies the inference. This is the view put forward, for example, by Mr. Toulmin.[2] Since I have argued elsewhere against this approach, I shall not discuss it here. Its advocates have, however, hit upon an important insight: that moral reasoning does not necessarily proceed by way of *deduction* of moral conclusions from non-moral premisses. Their further suggestion, that therefore it makes this transition by means of some other, peculiar, non-deductive kind of inference, is not the only possibility. It may be that moral reasoning is not, typically, any kind of 'straight-line' or 'linear' reasoning from premisses to conclusion.

6.2. A parallel from the philosophy of science will perhaps make this point clear. It is natural to suppose that what the scientist does is to reason from premisses, which are the data of observation, to conclusions, which are his 'scientific laws', by means of a special sort of inference called 'inductive'. Against this view, Professor Popper has forcibly argued

---

[2] S. E. Toulmin, *The Place of Reason in Ethics,* esp. 38-60. See my review in *Philosophical Quarterly,* i (1950/I), 372, and *LM* 3.4.

that in science there are no inferences other than deductive; the typical procedure of scientists is to propound hypotheses, and then look for ways of testing them — i.e. experiments which, if they are false, will show them to be so. A hypothesis which, try as we may, we fail to falsify, we accept provisionally, though ready to abandon it if, after all, further experiment refutes it; and of those that are so accepted we rate highest the ones which say most, and which would, therefore, be most likely to have been falsified if they were false. The only inferences which occur in this process are deductive ones, from the truth of certain observations to the falsity of a hypothesis. There is no reasoning which proceeds from the data of observation to the *truth* of a hypothesis. Scientific inquiry is rather a kind of *exploration*, or looking for hypotheses which will stand up to the test of experiment.[3]

We must ask whether moral reasoning exhibits any similar features. I want to suggest that it too is a kind of exploration, and not a kind of linear inference, and that the only inferences which take place in it are deductive. What we are doing in moral reasoning is to look for moral judgements and moral principles which, when we have considered their logical consequences and the facts of the case, we can still accept. As we shall see, this approach to the problem enables us to reject the assumption, which seemed so natural, that ethics cannot be relevant to moral decisions without ceasing to be neutral. This is because we are not going to demand any inferences in our reasoning other than deductive ones, and because none of these deductive inferences rely for their validity upon naturalistic definitions of moral terms.

Two further parallels may help to make clear the sense in which ethics is morally neutral. In the kind of scientific reasoning just described, mathematics plays a major part, for many of the deductive inferences that occur are mathematical in character. So we are bound to admit that mathematics is relevant to scientific inquiry. Nevertheless, it is also neutral, in the sense that no discoveries about matters of physical fact can be made with the aid of mathematics alone, and that no mathematical inference can have a conclusion which says more, in the way of prediction of observations, than its premises implicitly do.

An even simpler parallel is provided by the rules of games. The rules of a game are neutral as between the players, in the sense that they do not, by themselves, determine which player is going to win. In order to decide who wins, the players have to play the game in accordance with

---

[3]K. R. Popper, *The Logic of Scientific Discovery* (esp. pp. 32 f.). See also his article in C. A. Mace (ed.), *British Philosophy in the Mid-Century*, p. 155.

the rules, which involves their making, themselves, a great many individual decisions. On the other hand, the 'neutrality' of the rules of a game does not turn it into a game of chance, in which the bad player is as likely to win as the good.

Ethical theory, which determines the meanings and functions of the moral words, and thus the 'rules' of the moral 'game', provides only a clarification of the conceptual framework within which moral reasoning takes place; it is therefore, in the required sense, neutral as between different moral opinions. But it is highly relevant to moral reasoning because, as with the rules of a game, there could be no such thing as moral reasoning without this framework, and the framework dictates the form of the reasoning. It follows that naturalism is not the only way of providing for the possibility of moral reasoning; and this may, perhaps, induce those who have espoused naturalism as a way of making moral thought a rational activity to consider other possibilities.

The rules of moral reasoning are, basically, two, corresponding to the two features of moral judgements which I argued for in the first half of this book, prescriptivity and universalizability. When we are trying, in a concrete case, to decide what we ought to do, what we are looking for (as I have already said) is an action to which we can commit ourselves (prescriptivity) but which we are at the same time prepared to accept as exemplifying a principle of action to be prescribed for others in like circumstances (universalizability). If, when we consider some proposed action, we find that, when universalized, it yields prescriptions which we cannot accept, we reject this action as a solution to our moral problem — if we cannot universalize the prescription, it cannot become an 'ought'. . . .

6.3. I will now try to exhibit the bare bones of the theory of moral reasoning that I wish to advocate by considering a very simple (indeed over-simplified) example. As we shall see, even this very simple case generates the most baffling complexities; and so we may be pardoned for not attempting anything more difficult to start with.

The example is adapted from a well-known parable.[4] A owes money to B, and B owes money to C, and it is the law that creditors may exact their debts by putting their debtors into prison. B asks himself, 'Can I say that I ought to take this measure against A in order to make him pay?' He is no doubt *inclined* to do this, or *wants* to do it. Therefore, if there were no question of universalizing his prescriptions, he would assent readily to the singular prescription 'Let me put A into prison' (4.3). But when he seeks to turn this prescription into a moral judge-

---

[4]Matthew xviii. 23.

ment, and say, 'I *ought* to put A into prison because he will not pay me what he owes', he reflects that this would involve accepting the principle 'Anyone who is in my position ought to put his debtor into prison if he does not pay'. But then he reflects that C is in the same position of unpaid creditor with regard to himself (B), and that the cases are otherwise identical; and that if anyone in this position ought to put his debtors into prison, then so ought C to put him (B) into prison. And to accept the moral prescription 'C ought to put me into prison' would commit him (since, as we have seen, he must be using the word 'ought' prescriptively) to accepting the singular prescription 'Let C put me into prison'; and this he is not ready to accept. But if he is not, then neither can he accept the original judgement that he (B) ought to put A into prison for debt. Notice that the whole of this argument would break down if 'ought' were not being used both universalizably *and prescriptively*; for if it were not being used prescriptively, the step from 'C ought to put me into prison' to 'Let C put me into prison' would not be valid.

The structure and ingredients of this argument must now be examined. We must first notice an analogy between it and the Popperian theory of scientific method. What has happened is that a provisional or suggested moral principle has been rejected because one of its particular consequences proved unacceptable. But an important difference between the two kinds of reasoning must also be noted; it is what we should expect, given that the data of scientific observation are recorded in descriptive statements, whereas we are here dealing with prescriptions. What knocks out a suggested hypothesis, on Popper's theory, is a singular statement of fact: the hypothesis has the consequence that p; but not-p. Here the logic is just the same, except that in place of the observation-statements 'p' and 'not-p' we have the singular *prescriptions* 'Let C put B into prison for debt' and its contradictory. Nevertheless, given that B is disposed to reject the first of these prescriptions, the argument against him is just as cogent as in the scientific case.

We may carry the parallel further. Just as science, seriously pursued, is the search for hypotheses and the testing of them by the attempt to falsify their particular consequences, so morals, as a serious endeavour, consists in the search for principles and the testing of them against particular cases. Any rational activity has its discipline, and this is the discipline of moral thought: to test the moral principles that suggest themselves to us by following out their consequences and seeing whether we can accept *them*.

No argument, however, starts from nothing. We must therefore ask what we have to have before moral arguments of the sort of which I have given a simple example can proceed. The first requisite is that the facts of the case should be given; for all moral discussion is about some particular set of facts, whether actual or supposed. Secondly we have the logical framework provided by the meaning of the word 'ought' (i.e. prescriptivity and universalizability, both of which we saw to be necessary). Because moral judgements have to be universalizable, B cannot say that he ought to put A into prison for debt without committing himself to the view that C, who is *ex hypothesi* in the same position *vis-à-vis* himself, ought to put *him* into prison; and because moral judgements are prescriptive, this would be, in effect, prescribing to C to put him into prison; and this he is unwilling to do, since he has a strong inclination not to go to prison. This inclination gives us the third necessary ingredient in the argument: if B were a completely apathetic person, who literally did not mind what happened to himself or to anybody else, the argument would not touch him. The three necessary ingredients which we have noticed, then, are (1) facts; (2) logic; (3) inclinations. These ingredients enable us, not indeed to arrive at an evaluative conclusion, but to *reject* an evaluative proposition. We shall see later that these are not, in all cases, the only necessary ingredients.

6.4. In the example which we have been using, the position was deliberately made simpler by supposing that B actually stood to some other person in exactly the same relation as A does to him. Such cases are unlikely to arise in practice. But it is not necessary for the force of the argument that B should *in fact* stand in this relation to anyone; it is sufficient that he should consider hypothetically such a case, and see what would be the consequences in it of those moral principles between whose acceptance and rejection he has to decide. Here we have an important point of difference from the parallel scientific argument, in that the crucial case which leads to rejection of the principle can itself be a supposed, not an observed, one. That hypothetical cases will do as well as actual ones is important, since it enables us to guard against a possible misinterpretation of the argument which I have outlined. It might be thought that what moves B is the *fear* that C will actually do to him as he does to A — as happens in the gospel parable. But this fear is not only irrelevant to the moral argument; it does not even provide a particularly strong non-moral motive unless the circumstances are somewhat exceptional. C may, after all, not find out what B has done to A; or C's moral principles may be different from B's, and independent of them, so that what moral principle B accepts makes no difference to the moral principles on which C acts.

Even, therefore, if C did not exist, it would be no answer to the argument for B to say 'But in my case there is no fear that anybody will ever be in a position to do to me what I am proposing to do to A'. For the argument does not rest on any such fear. All that is essential to it is that B should disregard the fact that he plays the particular role in the situation which he does, without disregarding the inclinations which people have in situations of this sort. In other words, he must be prepared to give weight to A's inclinations and interests as if they were his own. This is what turns selfish prudential reasoning into moral reasoning. It is much easier, psychologically, for B to do this if he is actually placed in a situatioin like A's *vis-à-vis* somebody else; but this is not necessary, provided that he has sufficient imagination to envisage what it is like to be A. For our first example, a case was deliberately chosen in which little imagination was necessary; but in most normal cases a certain power of imagination and readiness to use it is a fourth necessary ingredient in moral arguments, alongside those already mentioned, viz. logic (in the shape of universalizability and prescriptivity), the facts, and the inclinations or interests of the people concerned.

It must be pointed out that the absence of even one of these ingredients may render the rest ineffective. For example, impartiality by itself is not enough. If, in becoming impartial, B becomes also completely dispassionate and apathetic, and moved as little by other people's interests as by his own, then, as we have seen, there would be nothing to make him accept or reject one moral principle rather than another. That is why those who, like Adam Smith and Professor Kneale, advocate what have been called 'Ideal Observer Theories' of ethics, sometimes postulate as their imaginary ideal observer not merely an impartial spectator, but an impartially *sympathetic* spectator.[5] To take another example, if the person who faces the moral decision has no imagination, then even the fact that someone can do the very same thing to him may pass him by. If, again, he lacks the readiness to universalize, then the vivid imagination of the sufferings which he is inflicting on others may only spur him on to intensify them, to increase his own vindictive enjoyment. And if he is ignorant of the material facts (for example about what is likely to happen

---

[5]It will be plain that there are affinities, though there are also differences between this type of theory and my own. For such theories see W. C. Kneale, *Philosophy,* xxv (1950), 162; R. Firth and R. B. Brandt, *Philosophy and Phenomenological Research,* xii (1951/2), 317, and xv (1954/5), 407, 414, 422; and J. Harrison, *Aristotelian Society,* supp. vol. xxviii (1954), 132. Firth, unlike Kneale, says that the observer must be 'dispassionate', but see Brandt, op. cit., p. 411 n. For a shorter discussion see Brandt, *Ethical Theory,* p. 173. Since for many Christians God occupies the role of 'ideal observer', the moral judgements which they make may be expected to coincide with those arrived at by the method of reasoning which I am advocating.

to a person if one takes out a writ against him), then there is nothing to tie the moral argument to particular choices.

6.5. The best way of testing the argument which we have outlined will be to consider various ways in which somebody in B's position might seek to escape from it. There are indeed a number of such ways; and all of them may be successful, at a price. It is important to understand what the price is in each case. We may classify these manœuvres which are open to B into two kinds. There are first of all the moves which depend on his using the moral words in a different way from that on which the argument relied. We saw that for the success of the argument it was necessary that 'ought' should be used universalizably and prescriptively. If B uses it in a way that is either not prescriptive or not universalizable, then he can escape the force of the argument, at the cost of resigning from the kind of discussion that we thought we were having with him. We shall discuss these two possibilities separately. Secondly, there are moves which can still be made by B, even though he is using the moral words in the same way as we are. We shall examine three different sub-classes of these.

Before dealing with what I shall call the *verbal* manœuvres in detail, it may be helpful to make a general remark. Suppose that we are having a simple mathematical argument with somebody, and he admits, for example, that there are five eggs in this basket, and six in the other, but maintains that there are a dozen eggs in the two baskets taken together; and suppose that this is because he is using the expression 'a dozen' to mean 'eleven'. It is obvious that we cannot compel him logically to admit that there are not a dozen eggs, in his sense of 'dozen'. But it is equally obvious that this should not disturb us. For such a man only appears to be dissenting from us. His dissent is only apparent, because the proposition which his words express is actually consistent with the conclusion which we wish to draw; he *says* 'There are a dozen eggs'; but he *means* what we should express by saying 'There are eleven eggs'; and this we are not disputing. It is important to remember that in the moral case also the dissent may be only apparent, if the words are being used in different ways, and that it is no defect in a method of argument if it does not make it possible to prove a conclusion to a person when he is using words in such a way that the conclusion does not follow.

It must be pointed out, further (since this is a common source of confusion), that in this argument nothing whatever hangs upon our *actual* use of the words in common speech, any more than it does in the arithmetical case. That we use the sound 'dozen' to express the meaning that we customarily do use it to express is of no consequence for the argument about the eggs; and the same may be said of the sound 'ought'. There is, however, something which I, at any rate, customarily express by the sound 'ought', whose character is correctly described by saying that it is a universal or universalizable prescription. I hope that what I customarily express by the sound 'ought' is the same as what most people customarily express by it; but if I am mistaken in this assumption, I shall still have given a correct account, so far as I am able, of that which I express by this sound.[6] Nevertheless, this account will interest other people mainly in so far as my hope that they understand the same thing as I do by 'ought' is fulfilled; and since I am moderately sure that this is indeed the case with many people, I hope that I may be of use to them in elucidating the logical properties of the concept which they thus express.

At this point, however, it is of the utmost importance to stress that the fact that two people express the same thing by 'ought' does not entail that they share the same moral opinions. For the formal, logical properties of the word 'ought' (those which are determined by its *meaning*) are only one of the four factors (listed earlier) whose combination governs a man's moral opinion on a given matter. Thus ethics, the study of the logical properties of the moral words, remains morally neutral (its conclusions neither are substantial moral judgements, nor entail them, even in conjunction with factual premisses); its bearing upon moral questions lies in this, that it makes logically impossible certain combinations of moral and other prescriptions. Two people who are using the word 'ought' in the same way may yet disagree about what ought to be done in a certain situation, either because they differ about the facts, or because one or other of them lacks imagination, or because their different inclinations make one reject some singular prescription which the other can accept. For all that, ethics (i.e. the logic of moral language) is an immensely powerful engine for producing moral agreement; for if two people are willing to use the moral word 'ought', and to use it in the same way (viz. the way that I have been describing), the other possible sources of moral disagreement are all eliminable. People's inclinations about most of the important matters in life tend to be the same (very few people, for example, like being starved or run over by motor-cars); and, even when they are not, there is a way of generalizing the argument, to be described in the next chapter, which enables us to make allowance for differences in inclinations. The facts are often, given sufficient patience, ascertainable. Imagination can be cultivated. If these three factors are looked after, as they can be, agreement on the use of 'ought' is the only other necessary

---

[6]Cf, Moore, *Principia Ethica*, p. 6.

condition for producing moral agreement, at any rate in typical cases. And, if I am not mistaken, this agreement in use is already there in the discourse of anybody with whom we are at all likely to find ourselves arguing; all that is needed is to think clearly, and so make it evident.

After this methodological digression, let us consider what is to be done with the man who professes to be using 'ought' in some different way from that which I have described—because he is not using it prescriptively, or not universalizably. For the reasons that I have given, if he takes either of these courses, he is no longer in substantial moral disagreement with us. Our apparent moral disagreement is really only verbal; for although, as we shall see shortly, there may be a residuum of substantial disagreement, this cannot be moral. It cannot even be an evaluative disagreement, in the sense of 'evaluative' above defined (2.8).

Let us take first the man who is using the word 'ought' prescriptively, but not universalizably. He can say that he ought to put his debtor into prison, although he is not prepared to agree that his creditor ought to put *him* into prison. We, on the other hand, since we are not prepared to admit that our creditors in these circumstances ought to put us into prison, cannot say that we ought to put our debtors into prison. So there is an appearance of substantial moral disagreement, which is intensified by the fact that, since we are both using the word 'ought' prescriptively, our respective views will lead to different particular actions. Different *singular* prescriptions about what to do are (since both our judgements are prescriptive) derivable from what we are respectively saying. But this is not enough to constitute a moral disagreement. For there to be a moral disagreement, or even an evaluative one of any kind, we must differ, not only about what *is* to be done in some particular case, but about some universal principle concerning what *ought* to be done in cases of a certain sort; and since B is (on the hypothesis considered) advocating no such universal principle, he is saying nothing with which we can be in moral or evaluative disagreement. Considered purely as prescriptions, indeed, our two views are in substantial disagreement; but the moral, evaluative (i.e. the *universal* prescriptive) disagreement is only verbal, because, when the expression of B's view is understood as he means it, the view turns out not to be a view about the morality of the action at all. So B, by this manœuvre, can go on prescribing to himself to put A into prison, but has to abandon the claim that he is justifying the action morally, as we understand the word 'morally'. One may, of course, use any word as one pleases, at a price. But he can no longer claim to be giving that sort of justification of his action for which, as I think, the common expression is 'moral justification' (10.7).

I need not deal at length with the second way in which B might be differing from us in his use of 'ought', viz. by not using it prescriptively. If he were not using it prescriptively, it will be remembered, he could assent to the singular prescription 'Let not C put me into prison for debt', and yet assent also to the non-prescriptive moral judgement 'C ought to put me into prison for debt'. And so his disinclination to be put into prison for debt by C would furnish no obstacle to his saying that he (B) ought to put A into prison for debt. And thus he could carry out his own inclination to put A into prison with apparent moral justification. The justification would be, however, only apparent. For if B is using the word 'ought' non-prescriptively, then 'I ought to put A into prison for debt' does not entail the singular prescription 'Let me put A into prison for debt'; the 'moral' judgement becomes quite irrelevant to the choice of what to do. There would also be the same lack of substantial moral disagreement as we noticed in the preceding case. B would not be disagreeing with us other than verbally, so far as the moral question is concerned (though there might be points of *factual* disagreement between us, arising from the *descriptive* meaning of our judgements). The 'moral' disagreement could be only verbal, because whereas we should be dissenting from the universalizable prescription 'B ought to put A into prison for debt', *this* would not be what B was expressing, though the words he would be using would be the same. For B would not, by these words, be expressing a prescription at all.

6.6. So much for the ways (of which my list may well be incomplete) in which B can escape from our argument by using the word 'ought' in a different way from us. The remaining ways of escape are open to him even if he is using 'ought' in the same way as we are, viz. to express a universalizable prescription.

We must first consider that class of escape-routes whose distinguishing feature is that B, while using the moral words in the same way as we are, refuses to make positive moral judgements at all in certain cases. There are two main variations of this manœuvre. B may either say that it is indifferent, morally, whether he imprisons A or not; or he may refuse to make any moral judgement at all, even one of indifference, about the case. It will be obvious that if he adopts either of these moves, he can evade the argument as so far set out. For that argument only forced him to *reject* the moral judgement 'I ought to imprison A for debt'. It did not force him to assent to any moral judgement; in particular, he remained free to assent, either to the judgement that he ought not to imprison A for debt (which is the one that we want him to accept) or to the judgement that it is neither the case that he ought, not the case that he ought not (that it is, in short, indifferent); and he remained free, also, to say 'I am just not making any moral judgements at all about this case'.

We have not yet, however, exhausted the arguments generated by the demand for universalizability, provided that the moral words are being used in a way which allows this demand. For it is evident that these manœuvres could, in principle, be practised in any case whatever in which the morality of an act is in question. And this enables us to place B in a dilemma. Either he practises this manœuvre in *every* situation in which he is faced with a moral decision; or else he practises it only *sometimes*. The first alternative, however, has to be sub-divided; for 'every situation' might mean 'every situation in which he himself has to face a moral decision regarding one of his own actions', or it might mean 'every situation in which a moral question arises for him, whether about his own actions or about somebody else's'. So there are three courses that he can adopt: (1) He either refrains altogether from making moral judgements, or makes none except judgements of indifference (that is to say, he either observes a complete moral silence, or says 'Nothing matters morally'; either of these two positions might be called a sort of amoralism); (2) He makes moral judgements in the normal way about other people's actions, but adopts one or other of the kinds of amoralism, just mentioned, with regard to his own; (3) He expresses moral indifference, or will make no moral judgement at all, with regard to *some* of his own actions and those of other people, but makes moral judgements in the normal way about others.

Now it will be obvious that in the first case there is nothing that we can do, and that this should not disturb us. Just as one cannot win a game of chess against an opponent who will not make any moves—and just as one cannot argue mathematically with a person who will not commit himself to any mathematical statements—so moral argument is impossible with a man who will make no moral judgements at all, or—which for practical purposes comes to the same thing—makes only judgements of indifference. Such a person is not entering the arena of moral dispute, and therefore it is impossible to contest with him. He is compelled also— and this is important—to abjure the protection of morality for his own interests.

In the other two cases, however, we have an argument left. If a man is prepared to make positive moral judgements about other people's actions, but not about his own, or if he is prepared to make them about some of his own decisions, but not about others, then we can ask him on what principle he makes the distinction between these various cases. This is a particular application of the demand for universalizability. He will still have left to him the ways of escape from this demand which are available in all its applications, and which we shall consider later. But there is no way of escape which is available in this application, but not in others. He must either produce (or at least admit the existence of) some principle which makes him hold different moral opinions about apparently similar cases, or else admit that the judgements he is making are not moral ones. But in the latter case, he is in the same position, in the present dispute, as the man who will not make any moral judgements at all; he has resigned from the contest.

In the particular example which we have been considering, we supposed that the cases of B and of C, his own creditor, were identical. The demand for universalization therefore compels B to make the same moral judgement, whatever it is, about both cases. He has therefore, unless he is going to give up the claim to be arguing morally, either to say that neither he nor C ought to exercise their legal rights to imprison their debtors; or that both ought (a possibility to which we shall recur in the next section); or that it is indifferent whether they do. But the last alternative leaves it open to B and C to do what they like in the matter; and we may suppose that, though B himself would like to have this freedom, he will be unwilling to allow it to C. It is as unlikely that he will *permit* C to put him (B) into prison as that he will *prescribe* it (10.5). We may say, therefore, that while move (1), described above, constitutes an abandonment of the dispute, moves (2) and (3) really add nothing new to it. . . .[7]

6.8 The remaining manœuvre that B might seek to practise is probably the commonest. It is certainly the one which is most frequently brought up in philosophical controversies on this topic. This consists in a fresh appeal to the facts—i.e. in asserting that there are in fact morally relevant differences between his case and that of others. In the example which we have been considering, we have artificially ruled out this way of escape by assuming that the case of B and C is exactly similar to that of A and B; from this it follows *a fortiori* that there are no morally relevant differences. Since the B/C case may be a hypothetical one, this condition of exact similarity can always be fulfilled, and therefore this manœuvre is based on a misconception of the type of argument against which it is directed. Nevertheless it may be useful, since this objection is so commonly raised, to deal with it at this point, although nothing further will be added thereby to what has been said already.

It may be claimed that no two actual cases would ever be exactly similar; there would always be some differences, and B might allege that

---

[7][In the next section (6.7), which is here omitted, a further "way of escape" is mentioned by Professor Hare to be dealt with later in *Freedom and Reason*.]—ED.

some of these were morally relevant. He might allege, for example, that, whereas his family would starve if C put him into prison, this would not be the case if he put A into prison, because A's family would be looked after by A's relatives. If such a difference existed, there might be nothing logically disreputable in calling it morally relevant, and such arguments are in fact often put forward and accepted.

The difficulty, however, lies in drawing the line between those arguments of this sort which are legitimate, and those which are not. Suppose that B alleges that the fact that A has a hooked nose or a black skin entitles him, B, to put him in prison, but that C ought not to do the same thing to him, B, because his nose is straight and his skin white. Is this an argument of equal logical respectability? Can I say that the fact that I have a mole in a particular place on my chin entitles me to further my own interests at others' expense, but that they are forbidden to do this by the fact that they lack this mark of natural pre-eminence?

The answer to this manœuvre is implicit in what has been said already about the relevance, in moral arguments, of hypothetical as well as of actual cases. The fact that no two actual cases are ever identical has no bearing on the problem. For all we have to do is to imagine an identical case in which the roles are reversed. Suppose that my mole disappears, and that my neighbour grows one in the very same spot on his chin. Or, to use our other example, what does B say about a hypothetical case in which he has a black skin or a hooked nose, and A and C are both straight-nosed and white-skinned (9.4; 11.7)? Since this is the same argument, in essentials, as we used at the very beginning, it need not be repeated here. B is in fact faced with a dilemma. Either the property of his own case, which he claims to be morally relevant, is a properly universal property (i.e. one describable without reference to individuals), or it is not. If it is a universal property, then, because of the meaning of the word 'universal', it is a property which might be possessed by another case in which he played a different role (though in fact it may not be); and we can therefore ask him to ignore the fact that it is he himself who plays the role which he does in this case. This will force him to count as morally relevant only those properties which he is prepared to allow to be relevant even when other people have them. And this rules out all the attractive kinds of special pleading. On the other hand, if the property in question is not a properly universal one, then he has not met the demand for universalizability, and cannot claim to be putting forward a moral argument at all.

6.9. It is necessary, in order to avoid misunderstanding, to add two notes to the foregoing discussion. The misunderstanding arises through a too literal interpretation of the common forms of expression—which constantly recur in arguments of this type—'How would you like it if . . .?' and 'Do as you would be done by'. Though I shall later, for convenience, refer to the type of arguments here discussed as 'golden-rule' arguments, we must not be misled by these forms of expression.

First of all, we shall make the nature of the argument clearer if, when we are asking B to imagine himself in the position of his victim, we phrase our question, never in the form 'What *would* you say, or feel, or think, or how *would* you like it, if you were he?', but always in the form 'What *do* you say (*in propria persona*) about a hypothetical case in which you are in your victim's position?' The importance of this way of phrasing the question is that, if the question were put in the first way, B might reply 'Well, of course, if anybody did this to me I should resent it very much and make all sorts of adverse moral judgements about the act; but this has absolutely no bearing on the validity of the moral opinion which I am *now* expressing'. To involve him in contradiction, we have to show that he *now* holds an opinion about the hypothetical case which is inconsistent with his opinion about the actual case.

The second thing which has to be noticed is that the argument, as set out, does not involve any sort of deduction of a moral judgment, or even of the negation of a moral judgement, from a factual statement about people's inclinations, interests, &c. We are not saying to B 'You are as a matter of fact averse to this being done to you in a hypothethical case; and from this it follows logically that you ought not to do it to another'. Such a deduction would be a breach of Hume's Law ('No "ought" from an "is" '), to which I have repeatedly declared my adherence (*LM* 2.5). The point is, rather, that because of his aversion to its being done to him in the hypothetical case, he cannot accept the singular *prescription* that in the hypothetical case it should be done to him; and this, because of the logic of 'ought', precludes him from accepting the moral judgement that he ought to do likewise to another in the actual case. It is not a question of a factual statement about a person's inclinations being inconsistent with a moral judgement; rather, his inclinations being what they are, he cannot assent sincerely to a certain singular prescription, and if he cannot do this, he cannot assent to a certain universal prescription which entails it, when conjoined with factual statements about the circumstances whose truth he admits. Because of this entailment, if he assented to the factual statements and to the universal prescription, but refused (as he must, his inclinations being what they are) to assent to the singular prescription, he would be guilty of a logical inconsistency.

An Alleged Moral Fallacy

John R. Searle

How to Derive "Ought" from "Is"

I

It is often said that one cannot derive an "ought" from an "is." This thesis, which comes from a famous passage in Hume's *Treatise*, while not as clear as it might be, is at least clear in broad outline: there is a

From "How to Derive 'Ought' from 'Is'," *The Philosophical Review* 73 (January 1964), by permission of the author and *The Philosophical Review*. Earlier versions of this paper were read before the Stanford Philosophy Colloquim and the Pacific Division of the American Philosophical Association. I [Searle] am indebted to many people for helpful comments and criticisms, especially Hans Herzberger, Arnold Kaufmann, Benson Mates, A. I. Melden, and Dagmar Searle.

class of statements of fact which is logically distinct from a class of statements of value. No set of statements of fact by themselves entails any statement of value. Put in more contemporary terminology, no set of *descriptive* statements can entail an *evaluative* statement without the addition of at least one evaluative premise. To believe otherwise is to commit what has been called the naturalistic fallacy.

I shall attempt to demonstrate a counterexample to this thesis.[1] It is not of course to be supposed that a single counterexample can refute a philosophical thesis, but in the present instance if we can present a plausible counterexample and can in addition give some account or explanation of how and why it is a counterexample, and if we can further offer a theory to back up our counterexample— a theory which will generate an indefinite number of counterexamples—we may at the very least cast considerable light on the original thesis; and possibly if we can do all these things, we may even incline ourselves to the view that the scope of that thesis was more restricted than we had originally supposed. A counterexample must proceed by taking a statement or statements which any proponent of the thesis would grant were purely factual or "descriptive" (they need not actually contain the word "is") and show how they are logically related to a statement which a proponent of the thesis would regard as clearly "evaluative." (In the present instance it will contain an "ought.")[2]

Consider the following series of statements:

(1) Jones uttered the words "I hereby promise to pay you, Smith, five dollars."

(2) Jones promised to pay Smith five dollars.

(3) Jones placed himself under (undertook) an obligation to pay Smith five dollars.

(4) Jones is under an obligation to pay Smith five dollars.

(5) Jones ought to pay Smith five dollars.

I shall argue concerning this list that the relation between any statement and its successor, while not in every case one of "entailment," is nonetheless not just a contingent relation; and the additional statements necessary to make the relationship one of entailment do not need to involve any evaluative statements, moral principles, or anything of the sort.

---

[1] In its modern version. I shall not be concerned with Hume's treatment of the problem.

[2] If this enterprise succeeds, we shall have bridged the gap between "evaluative" and "descriptive" and consequently have demonstrated a weakness in this very terminology. At present, however, my strategy is to play along with the terminology, pretending that the notions of evaluative and descriptive are fairly clear. At the end of the paper I shall state in what respects I think they embody a muddle.

Let us begin. How is (1) related to (2)? In certain circumstances, uttering the words in quotation marks in (1) is the act of making a promise. And it is a part of or a consequence of the meaning of the words in (1) that in those circumstances uttering them is promising. "I hereby promise" is a paradigm device in English for performing the act described in (2), promising.

Let us state this fact about English usage in the form of an extra premise:

(1a) Under certain conditions C anyone who utters the words (sentence) "I hereby promise to pay you, Smith, five dollars" promises to pay Smith five dollars.

What sorts of things are involved under the rubric "conditions C"? What is involved will be all those conditions, those states of affairs, which are necessary and sufficient conditions for the utterance of the words (sentence) to constitute the successful performance of the act of promising. The conditions will include such things as that the speaker is in the presence of the hearer Smith, they are both conscious, both speakers of English, speaking seriously. The speaker knows what he is doing, is not under the influence of drugs, not hypnotized or acting in a play, not telling a joke or reporting an event, and so forth. This list will no doubt be somewhat indefinite because the boundaries of the concept of a promise, like the boundaries of most concepts in a natural language, are a bit loose.[3] But one thing is clear; however loose the boundaries may be, and however difficult it may be to decide marginal cases, the conditions under which a man who utters "I hereby promise" can correctly be said to have made a promise are straightforward empirical conditions.

So let us add as an extra premise the empirical assumption that these conditions obtain.

(1b) Conditions C obtain.

From (1), (1a), and (1b) we derive (2). The argument is of the form: If C then (if U then P): C for conditions, U for utterance, P for promise. Adding the premises U and C to this hypothetical we derive (2). And as far as I can see, no moral premises are lurking in the logical woodpile. More needs to be said about the relation of (1) to (2), but I reserve that for later.

---

[3]In addition the concept of a promise is a member of a class of concepts which suffer from looseness of a peculiar kind, viz. defeasibility. Cf. H. L. A. Hart, "The Ascription of Responsibility and Rights," *Logic and Language,* First Series, ed. by A. Flew (Oxford, 1951).

What is the relation between (2) and (3)? I take it that promising is, by definition, an act of placing oneself under an obligation. No analysis of the concept of promising will be complete which does not include the feature of the promiser placing himself under or undertaking or accepting or recognizing an obligation to the promisee, to perform some future course of action, normally for the benefit of the promisee. One may be tempted to think that promising can be analyzed in terms of creating expectations in one's hearers, or some such, but a little reflection will show that the crucial distinction between statements of intention on the one hand and promises on the other lies in the nature and degree of commitment or obligation undertaken in promising.

I am therefore inclined to say that (2) entails (3) straight off, but I can have no objection if anyone wishes to add — for the purpose of formal neatness — the tautological premise:

(2a) All promises are acts of placing oneself under (undertaking) an obligation to do the thing promised.

How is (3) related to (4)? If one has placed oneself under an obligation, then, other things being equal, one is under an obligation. That I take it also is a tautology. Of course it is possible for all sorts of things to happen which will release one from obligations one has undertaken and hence the need for the *ceteris paribus* rider. To get an entailment between (3) and (4) we therefore need a qualifying statement to the effect that:

(3a) Other things are equal.

Formalists, as in the move from (2) to (3), may wish to add the tautological premise:

(3b) All those who place themselves under an obligation are, other things being equal, under an obligation.

The move from (3) to (4) is thus of the same form as the move from (1) to (2): If E then (if PUO then UO): E for other things are equal, PUO for place under obligation and UO for under obligation. Adding the two premises E and PUO we derive UO.

Is (3a), the *ceteris paribus* clause, a concealed evaluative premise? It certainly looks as if it might be, especially in the formulation I have given it, but I think we can show that, though questions about whether other things are equal frequently involve evaluative considerations, it is not logically necessary that they should in every case. I shall postpone discussion of this until after the next step.

What is the relation between (4) and (5)? Analogous to the tautology which explicates the relation of (3) and (4) there is here the tautology that, other things being equal, one ought to do what one is under an obligation to do. And here, just as in the previous case, we need some premise of the form:

(4a) Other things are equal.

We need the *ceteris paribus* clause to eliminate the possibility that something extraneous to the relation of "obligation" to "ought" might interfere.[4] Here, as in the previous two steps, we eliminate the appearance of enthymeme by pointing out that the apparently suppressed premise is tautological and hence, though formally neat, it is redundant. If, however, we wish to state it formally, this argument is of the same form as the move from (3) to (4): If E then (if UO then O); E for other things are equal, UO for under obligation, O for ought. Adding the premises E and UO we derive O.

Now a word about the phrase "other things being equal" and how it functions in my attempted derivation. This topic and the closely related topic of defeasibility are extremely difficult and I shall not try to do more than justify my claim that the satisfaction of the condition does not necessarily involve anything evaluative. The force of the expression "other things being equal" in the present instance is roughly this. Unless we have some reason (that is, unless we are actually prepared to give some reason) for supposing the obligation is void (step 4) or the agent ought not to keep the promise (step 5), then the obligation holds and he ought to keep the promise. It is not part of the force of the phrase "other things being equal" that in order to satisfy it we need to establish a universal negative proposition to the effect that no reason could ever be given by anyone for supposing the agent is not under an obligation or ought not to keep the promise. That would be impossible and would render the phrase useless. It is sufficient to satisfy the condition that no reason to the contrary can in fact be given.

If a reason is given for supposing the obligation is void or that the promiser ought not to keep a promise, then characteristically a situation calling for an evaluation arises. Suppose, for example, we consider a promised act wrong, but we grant that the promiser did undertake an obligation. Ought he to keep the promise? There is no established procedure

---

[4]The *ceteris paribus* clause in this step excludes somewhat different sorts of cases from those excluded in the previous step. In general we say, "He undertook an obligation, but nonetheless he is not (now) under an obligation" when the obligation has been *removed,* e.g., if the promisee says, "I release you from your obligation." But we say, "He is under an obligation, but nonetheless ought not to fulfill it" in cases where the obligation is *overridden* by some other considerations, e.g. a prior obligation.

for objectively deciding such cases in advance, and an evaluation (if that is really the right word) is in order. But unless we have some reason to the contrary, the *ceteris paribus* condition is satisfied, no evaluation is necessary, and the question whether he ought to do it is settled by saying "he promised." It is always an open possibility that we may have to make an evaluation in order to derive "he ought" from "he promised," for we may have to evaluate a counterargument. But an evaluation is not logically necessary in every case, for there may as a matter of fact be no counterarguments. I am therefore inclined to think that there is nothing necessarily evaluative about the *ceteris paribus* condition, even though deciding whether it is satisfied will frequently involve evaluations.

But suppose I am wrong about this: would that salvage the belief in an unbridgeable logical gulf between "is" and "ought"? I think not, for we can always rewrite my steps (4) and (5) so that they include the *ceteris paribus* clause as part of the conclusion. Thus from our premises we would then have derived "Other things being equal Jones ought to pay Smith five dollars," and that would still be sufficient to refute the tradition, for we would still have shown a relation of entailment between descriptive and evaluative statements. It was not the fact that extenuating circumstances can void obligations that drove philosophers to the naturalistic fallacy; it was rather a theory of language, as we shall see later on.

We have thus derived (in as strict a sense of "derive" as natural languages will admit of) an "ought" from an "is." And the extra premises which were needed to make the derivation work were in no case moral or evaluative in nature. They consisted of empirical assumptions, tautologies, and descriptions of word usage. It must be pointed out also that the "ought" is a "categorical" not "hypothetical" ought. (5) does not say that Jones ought to pay up if he wants such and such. It says he ought to pay up, period. Note also that the steps of the derivation are carried on in the third person. We are not concluding "I ought" from "I said 'I promise,'" but "he ought" from "he said 'I promise.'"

The proof unfolds the connection between the utterance of certain words and the speech act of promising and then in turn unfolds promising into obligation and moves from obligation to "ought." The step from (1) to (2) is radically different from the others and requires special comment. In (1) we construe "I hereby promise . . ." as an English phrase having a certain meaning. It is a consequence of that meaning that the utterance of that phrase under certain conditions is the act of promising. Thus by presenting the quoted expressions in (1) and by describing their use in (1a) we have as it were already invoked the institution of promising. We might have started with an even more ground-floor premise than (1) by saying:

(1b) Jones uttered the phonetic sequence: /ai⁺hirbai⁺pramis⁺təpei⁺ yu⁺smiθ⁺faiv⁺dalərz/

We would then have needed extra empirical premises stating that this phonetic sequence was associated in certain ways with certain meaningful units relative to certain dialects.

The moves from (2) to (5) are relatively easy. We rely on definitional connections between "promise," "obligate," and "ought," and the only problem which arises is that obligations can be overridden or removed in a variety of ways and we need to take account of that fact. We solve our difficulty by adding further premises to the effect that there are no contrary considerations, that other things are equal.

II

In this section I intend to discuss three possible objections to the derivation.

First Objection

Since the first premise is descriptive and the conclusion evaluative, there must be a concealed evaluative premise in the description of the conditions in (1b).

So far, this argument merely begs the question by assuming the logical gulf between descriptive and evaluative which the derivation is designed to challenge. To make the objection stick, the defender of the distinction would have to show how exactly (1b) must contain an evaluative premise and what sort of premise it might be. Uttering certain words in certain conditions just *is* promising and the description of these conditions needs no evaluative element. The essential thing is that in the transition from (1) to (2) we move from the specification of a certain utterance of words to the specification of a certain speech act. The move is achieved because the speech act is a conventional act; and the utterance of the words, according to the conventions, constitutes the performance of just that speech act.

A variant of this first objection is to say: all you have shown is that "promise" is an evaluative, not a descriptive, concept. But this objection again begs the question and in the end will prove disastrous to the original distinction between descriptive and evaluative. For that a man uttered certain words and that these words have the meaning they do are surely objective facts. And if the statement of these two objective facts plus a description of the conditions of the utterance is sufficient to entail the statement (2) which the objector alleges to be an evaluative statement (Jones promised to pay Smith five dollars), then an evaluative conclusion is derived from descriptive premises without even going through steps (3), (4), and (5).

Second Objection

Ultimately the derivation rests on the principle that one ought to keep one's promises and that is a moral principle, hence evaluative.

I don't know whether "one ought to keep one's promises" is a "moral" principle, but whether or not it is, it is also tautological; for it is nothing more than a derivation from the two tautologies:

All promises are (create, are undertakings of, are acceptances of) obligations,

and

One ought to keep (fulfill) one's obligations.

What needs to be explained is why so many philosophers have failed to see the tautological character of this principle. Three things I think have concealed its character from them.

The first is a failure to distinguish external questions about the institution of promising from internal questions asked within the framework of the institution. The questions "Why do we have such an institution as promising?" and "Ought we to have institutionalized forms of obligation as promising?" are external questions asked about and not within the institution of promising. And the question "Ought one to keep one's promises?" can be confused with or can be taken as (and I think has often been taken as) an external question roughly expressible as "Ought one to accept the institution of promising?" But taken literally, as an internal question, as a question about promises and not about the institution of promising, the question "Ought one to keep one's promises?" is as empty as the question "Are triangles three-sided?" To recognize something as a promise is to grant that, other things being equal, it ought to be kept.

A second fact which has clouded the issue is this. There are many situations, both real and imaginable, where one ought not to keep a promise, where the obligation to keep a promise is overridden by some further considerations, and it was for this reason that we needed those clumsy *ceteris paribus* clauses in our derivation. But the fact that obligations can be overridden does not show that there were no obligations in the first place. On the contrary. And these original obligations are all that is needed to make the proof work.

Yet a third factor is the following. Many philosophers still fail to realize the full force of saying that "I hereby promise" is a performative expression. In uttering it one performs but does not describe the act of promising. Once promising is seen as a speech act of a kind different from describing, then it is easier to see that one of the features of the act is the undertaking of an obligation. But if one thinks the utterance of "I promise" or "I hereby promise" is a peculiar kind of description—for example, of one's mental state—then the relation between promising and obligation is going to seem very mysterious.

Third Objection

The derivation uses only a factual or inverted-commas sense of the evaluative terms employed. For example, an anthropologist observing the behavior and attitudes of the Anglo-Saxons might well go through these derivations, but nothing evaluative would be included. Thus step (2) is equivalent to "He did what they call promising" and step (5) to "According to them he ought to pay Smith five dollars." But since all of the steps (2) to (5) are in *oratio obliqua* and hence disguised statements of fact, the fact-value distinction remains unaffected.

This objection fails to damage the derivation, for what it says is only that the steps *can* be reconstrued as in *oratio obliqua,* that we can construe them as a series of external statements, that we can construct a parallel (or at any rate related) proof about reported speech. But what I am arguing is that, taken quite literally, without any *oratio obliqua* additions or interpretations, the derivation is valid. That one can construct a similar argument which would fail to refute the fact-value distinction does not show that this proof fails to refute it. Indeed it is irrelevant.

III

So far I have presented a counterexample to the thesis that one cannot derive an "ought" from an "is" and considered three possible objections to it. Even supposing what I have said so far is true, still one feels a certain uneasiness. One feels there must be some trick involved somewhere. We might state our uneasiness thus: How can my granting a mere fact about a man, such as the fact that he uttered certain words or that he made a promise, commit *me* to the view that *he* ought to do something? I now want briefly to discuss what broader philosophic significance my attempted derivation may have, in such a way as to give us the outline of an answer to this question.

I shall begin by discussing the grounds for supposing that it cannot be answered at all.

The inclination to accept a rigid distinction between "is" and "ought," between descriptive and evaluative, rests on a certain picture of the way words relate to the world. It is a very attractive picture, so attractive (to me at least) that it is not entirely clear to what extent the mere presentation of counterexamples can challenge it. What is needed is an explanation of how and why this classical empiricist picture fails to deal with such counterexamples. Briefly, the picture is constructed something like this: first we present examples of so-called descriptive statements ("my car goes eighty miles an hour," "Jones is six feet tall," "Smith has brown hair"), and we contrast them with so-called evaluative statements ("my car is a good car," "Jones ought to pay Smith five dollars," "Smith is a nasty man"). Anyone can see that they are different. We articulate the difference by pointing out that for the descriptive statements the question of truth or falsity is objectively decidable, because to know the meaning of the descriptive expressions is to know under what objectively ascertainable conditions the statements which contain them are true or false. But in the case of evaluative statements the situation is quite different. To know the meaning of the evaluative expressions is not by itself sufficient for knowing under what conditions the statements containing them are true or false, because the meaning of the expressions is such that the statements are not capable of objective or factual truth or falsity at all. Any justification a speaker can give of one of his evaluative statements essentially involves some appeal to attitudes he holds, to criteria of assessment he has adopted, or to moral principles by which he has chosen to live and judge other people. Descriptive statements are thus objective, evaluative statements subjective, and the difference is a consequence of the different sorts of terms employed.

The underlying reason for these differences is that evaluative statements perform a completely different job from descriptive statements. Their job is not to describe any features of the world but to express the speaker's emotions, to express his attitudes, to praise or condemn, to laud or insult, to commend, to recommend, to advise, and so forth. Once we see the different jobs the two perform, we see that there must be a logical gulf between them. Evaluative statements must be different from descriptive statements in order to do their job, for if they were objective they could no longer function to evaluate. Put metaphysically, values cannot lie in the world, for if they did they would cease to be values and would just be another part of the world. Put in the formal mode, one cannot define an evaluative word in terms of descriptive words, for if one did, one would no longer be able to use the evaluative word to commend, but only to describe. Put yet another way, any effort to derive an "ought" from an "is" must be a waste of time, for all it could show even if it succeeded would be that the "is" was not a real "is" but only a disguised "ought" or, alternatively, that the "ought" was not a real "ought" but only a disguised "is."

This summary of the traditional empirical view has been very brief, but I hope it conveys something of the power of this picture. In the hands of certain modern authors, especially Hare and Nowell-Smith, the picture attains considerable subtlety and sophistication.

What is wrong with this picture? No doubt many things are wrong with it. In the end I am going to say that one of the things wrong with it is that it fails to give us any coherent account of such notions as commitment, responsibility, and obligation.

In order to work toward this conclusion I can begin by saying that the picture fails to account for the *different types* of "descriptive" statements. Its paradigms of descriptive statements are such utterances as "my car goes eighty miles an hour," "Jones is six feet tall," "Smith has brown hair," and the like. But it is forced by its own rigidity to construe "Jones got married," "Smith made a promise," "Jackson has five dollars," and "Brown hit a home run" as descriptive statements as well. It is so forced, because whether or not someone got married, made a promise, has five dollars, or hit a home run is as much a matter of objective fact as whether he has red hair or brown eyes. Yet the former statement (statements containing "married," "promise," and so forth) seem to be quite different from the simple empirical paradigms of descriptive statements. How are they different? Though both kinds of statements state matters of objective fact, the statements containing words such as "married," "promise," "home run," and "five dollars" state facts whose existence presupposes certain institutions: a man has five dollars, given the institution of money. Take away the institution and all he has is a rectangular bit of paper with green ink on it. A man hits a home run only given the institution of baseball; without the institution he only hits a sphere with a stick. Similarly, a man gets married or makes a promise only within the institutions of marriage and promising. Without them, all he does is utter words or make gestures. We might characterize such facts as institutional facts, and contrast them with noninstitutional, or brute, facts: that a man has a bit of paper with green ink on it is a brute fact, that he has five dollars is an institutional fact.[5] The classical picture fails to account for the differences between statements of brute facts and statements of institutional fact.

The word "institution" sounds artificial here, so let us ask: what sorts of institutions are these? In order to answer that question I need to distinguish between two different kinds of rules or conventions. Some rules regulate antecedently existing forms of behavior. For example, the rules of polite table behavior regulate eating, but eating exists independently of these rules. Some rules, on the other hand, do not merely regulate but create or define new forms of behavior: the rules of chess, for example, do not merely regulate an antecedently existing activity called playing chess; they, as it were, create the possibility of or define that activity. The activity of playing chess is constituted by action in accordance with these rules. Chess has no existence apart from these rules. The distinction I am trying to make was foreshadowed by Kant's distinction between regulative and constitutive principles, so let us adopt his terminology and describe our distinction as a distinction between regulative and constitutive rules. Regulative rules regulate activities whose existence is independent of the rules; constitutive rules constitute (and also regulate) form of activity whose existence is logically dependent on the rules.[6]

Now the institutions that I have been talking about are systems of constitutive rules. The institutions of marriage, money, and promising are like the institutions of baseball or chess in that they are systems of such constitutive rules or conventions. What I have called institutional facts are facts which presuppose such institutions.

Once we recognize the existence of and begin to grasp the nature of such institutional facts, it is but a short step to see that many forms of obligations, commitments, rights, and responsibilities are similarly institutionalized. It is often a matter of fact that one has certain obligations, commitments, rights, and responsibilities, but it is a matter of institutional, not brute fact. It is one such institutionalized form of obligation, promising, which I invoked above to derive an "ought" from an "is." I started with a brute fact, that a man uttered certain words, and then invoked the

---

[5] For a discussion of this distinction see G. E. M. Anscombe, "Brute Facts," *Analysis* (1958).

[6] For a discussion of a related distinction see J. Rawls, "Two Concepts of Rules," *Philosophical Review*, LXIV (1955).

institution in such a way as to generate institutional facts by which we arrived at the institutional fact that the man ought to pay another man five dollars. The whole proof rests on an appeal to the constitutive rule that to make a promise is to undertake an obligation.

We are now in a position to see how we can generate an indefinite number of such proofs. Consider the following vastly different example. We are in our half of the seventh inning and I have a big lead off second base. The pitcher whirls, fires to the shortstop covering, and I am tagged out a good ten feet down the line. The umpire shouts, "Out!" I, however, being a positivist, hold my ground. The umpire tells me to return to the dugout. I point out to him that you can't derive an "ought" from an "is." No set of descriptive statements describing matters of fact, I say, will entail any evaluative statements to the effect that I should or ought to leave the field. "You just can't get orders or recommendations from facts alone." What is needed is an evaluative major premise. I therefore return to and stay on second base (until I am carried off the field). I think everyone feels my claim here to be preposterous, and preposterous in the sense of logically absurd. Of course you can derive an "ought" from an "is," and though to actually set out the derivation in this case would be vastly more complicated than in the case of promising, it is in principle no different. By undertaking to play baseball I have committed myself to the observation of certain constitutive rules.

We are now also in a position to see that the tautology that one ought to keep one's promise is only one of a class of similar tautologies concerning institutionalized forms of obligation. For example, "one ought not to steal" can be taken as saying that to recognize something as someone else's property necessarily involves recognizing his right to dispose of it. This is a constitutive rule of the institution of private property.[7] "One ought not to tell lies" can be taken as saying that to make an assertion necessarily involves undertaking an obligation to speak truthfully. Another constitutive rule. "One ought to pay one's debts" can be construed

---

[7]Proudhon said: "Property is theft." If one tries to take this as an internal remark it makes no sense. It was intended as an external remark attacking and rejecting the institution of private property. It gets its air of paradox and its force by using terms which are internal to the institution in order to attack the institution.

Standing on the deck of some institutions one can tinker with constitutive rules and even throw some other institutions overboard. But could one throw all institutions overboard (in order perhaps to avoid ever having to derive an "ought" from an "is")? One could not and still engage in those forms of behavior we consider characteristically human. Suppose Proudhon had added (and tried to live by): "Truth is a lie, marriage is infidelity, language is uncommunicative, law is a crime," and so on with every possible institution.

as saying that to recognize something as a debt is necessarily to recognize an obligation to pay it. It is easy to see how all these principles will generate counterexamples to the thesis that you cannot derive an "ought" from an "is."

My tentative conclusions, then, are as follows:

1. The classical picture fails to account for institutional facts.

2. Institutional facts exist within systems of constitutive rules.

3. Some systems of constitutive rules involve obligations, commitments, and responsibilities.

4. Within those systems we can derive "ought's" from "is's" on the model of the first derivation.

With these conclusions we now return to the question with which I began this section: How can my stating a fact about a man, such as the fact that he made a promise, commit me to a view about what he ought to do? One can begin to answer this question by saying that for me to state such an institutional fact is already to invoke the constitutive rules of the institution. It is those rules that give the word "promise" its meaning. But those rules are such that to commit myself to the view that Jones made a promise involves committing myself to what he ought to do (other things being equal).

If you like, then, we have shown that "promise" is an evaluative word, but since it is also purely descriptive, we have really shown that the whole distinction needs to be re-examined. The alleged distinction between descriptive and evaluative statements is really a conflation of at least two distinctions. On the one hand there is a distinction between different kinds of speech acts, one family of speech acts including evaluations, another family including descriptions. This is a distinction between different kinds of illocutionary force.[8] On the other hand there is a distinction between utterances which involve claims objectively decidable as true or false and those which involve claims not objectively decidable, but which are "matters of personal decision" or "matters of opinion." It has been assumed that the former distinction is (must be) a special case of the latter, that if something has the illocutionary force of an evaluation, it cannot be entailed by factual premises. Part of the point of my argument is to show that this contention is false, that factual premises can entail evaluative conclusions. If I am right, then the alleged distinction between descriptive and evaluative utterances is useful only as a distinction between two kinds of illocutionary force, describing and evaluating,

---

[8]See J. L. Austin, *How to Do Things with Words* (Cambridge, Mass., 1962), for an explanation of this notion.

and it is not even very useful there, since if we are to use these terms strictly, they are only two among hundreds of kinds of illocutionary force; and utterances of sentences of the form (5) — "Jones ought to pay Smith five dollars" — would not characteristically fall in either class.

VII

MORALITY AND JUSTICE

Introduction

Institutional Facts and Values

It will be recalled that William James (see Part II) asked us to imagine "an absolutely material world containing only physical and chemical facts, and existing from eternity without a God, without even an interested spectator." It is difficult not to agree with him that in such a universe there would be no place for moral values. It takes people (or at least sentient beings) to introduce the notion of moral relationships and moral values. However much one might disagree with James' subsequent analysis of those relationships and values, he seems nonetheless correct in his claim that a world of "brute facts" is an amoral one.

This is not to say that facts have no relation to values. Even those philosophers who argue that "ought" statements cannot be derived from "is" statements would not deny that factual circumstances do affect, and ought to affect, the moral judgments we make. Killing is wrong, we say, except in certain kinds of circumstances, such as those of self-defense. The question arises, however, whether we do not ourselves create at least some of the circumstances which affect our moral judgments. It would seem that we often do. We make a promise and thereby create a situation in which it is appropriate for someone to criticize us if we fail to keep it. Or we condemn a person because he has stolen something, but at some point in our social evolution someone, if not ourselves, invented the institution of property, without which the whole notion of theft would be meaningless. What is "yours" and what is "mine" becomes a fact which complicates our lives, our actions, and our moral judgments. Searle and others have aptly referred to these kinds of things as "institutional facts."

Some philosophers have been more impressed than others with the relationship between social institutions and the "facts" they create and our notions of morality. Philosophers who speak of "moralities," in contrast to the more traditional notion of a single "morality," are usually those who tend to attribute differences in moral judgments to differences in social institutions. Thus the judgment that "polygamy is morally wrong" is defended in terms of the general acceptance by a given society of the contrary institution of monogamy. Other philosophers view the matter differently. Utilitarians, for instance, evaluate judgments about polygamy, property, political organization — in fact all social institutions — from the standpoint of their principle of utility. Which institutions in those circumstances tend to promote the greatest happiness? Kant evaluates them on the basis of their agreement with certain rational principles of freedom and equality, not merely on the fact that differences in social institutions exist. Thus he says, "Justice must never be accommodated to the political system, but always the political system to justice." (See his essay, p. 258 above). Morality should dictate institutions, not institutions morality.

The claims of both groups may be correct in certain respects. Those who stress the institutional basis of (at least some) moral judgments may be correct regarding their *origin* but wrong with respect to their *validity*. Certainly many of the judgments we make, such as those regarding the forms of marriage, presuppose the existence of certain kinds of institutions. But those who ignore the institutional origins of our moral judgments may nonetheless be correct with respect to the tests by which we must evaluate them. Institutions are themselves surely as subject to moral criticism as are individual acts.

But is this all there is to the relationship between specific social institutions and judgments of morality? Do institutions merely provide the necessary conditions for such judgments, such that without the institution of promising there could be no judgments regarding promise breaking, and without the institution of monogamous marriage there could be no condemnation of polygamy? The relationship can be made even more tenuous. Some philosophers who grant that the existence of various institutions conditions moral judgments do not agree that *all* of our judgments are so conditioned. For example, Baier (Part II) distinguishes two kinds of moral judgments. There are moral judgments (or "convictions" as he calls them) which are dependent for their truth on different social institutions, but others are not. "Lending money for interest is wrong" and "A man ought not to marry his brother's widow," he says, "may be true moral convictions in one set of social conditions," but "Killing is wrong," Harming others is wrong," and "Lying is wrong" are true "irrespective of the particular set up of given societies." The latter are based, he claims, on human nature and as such are "independent of particular variations of the social pattern."

Hobbes (Part I) appears to be of a quite different opinion. Outside of the institutions of society (i.e., in a "state of nature") "the notions of right or wrong, justice and injustice, have there no place." Without a common sovereign and a set of laws promulgated by him and binding on all his subjects, even a judgment that "killing is wrong" cannot be maintained. Hobbes does speak of equity, justice, gratitude, and other "moral virtues" as "dictates of reason" even in a state of nature, but he quickly qualifies this by denying that they are properly called laws or that they have any obligatory character in the "mere condition of nature." They are simply "dispositions" which incline persons to accept the social contract. Once men have consented to that social arrangement, genuine obligations follow, but not before.

It is clear that, for Hobbes, the institution of society (and its various subinstitutions) is not merely a necessary condition of morality but is a sufficient condition as well. Two types of criticism have been made of Hobbes' view which require mention here. One is that he fails to appreciate the fact that institutions themselves are subject to moral criticism. The other is that he confuses justice with other aspects or branches of morality. Regarding the first, it does seem to follow from Hobbes' theory that no law can be unjust. Whatever the sovereign commands is right. Implicitly, however, and perhaps inconsistently, Hobbes suggests that although particular laws and social institutions may not be unjust, they may nonetheless fail to achieve the goal for which the social contract was entered into, namely, everyone's survival and well-being, in short, the "good of the people." In effect, then, he adopts a utilitarian criterion for judging acts of the sovereign "bad," even though, strictly speaking, they cannot be "unjust" or "wrong."

This admission raises doubt whether it can be maintained as a general proposition that all our bases for moral evaluation are the products of social conventions. It also makes it plausible to suppose that Hobbes confuses justice with the notion of morality generally. From his third law of nature, "that men perform their covenants," he derives his concept of justice. He says, "For when no covenant hath preceded, there hath no right been transferred, and every man has a right to everything; and consequently, no action can be unjust. But when a covenant is made, then to break it is unjust: and the definition of *injustice* is no other than the *not performance of covenant*. And whatsoever is not unjust is just." If in a state of nature every man has a right to everything, then it follows, not only that no action is unjust but also that no action can be wrong. Right is thus as dependent on keeping one's covenant as justice, and, for Hobbes, right and justice are in fact synonymous terms.

But does this represent a confusion on Hobbes' part? Certainly other philosophers have identified justice with right action. Plato often uses the term "justice" to mean what we would now generally mean by the term "morality." Furthermore, as many subsequent philosophers, including Mill, have pointed out, we hesitate to speak of something as unjust if we cannot also speak of it as wrong, or of anything as just which is not right. Yet to use Mill's own example (see Frankena, p. 580), "In order to save a life it may not only be allowable, but a duty," to do something which is contrary to the principles of justice, for example, "to steal or take by force the necessary food or medicine, or to kidnap and compel to officiate the only qualified medical practitioner." Or take another example. Suppose a parcel of land has been inherited by three persons who are equally entitled to a share of it, and the land must be divided. But suppose also that an absolutely equal division of the land would make each part worthless. An unequal division would give two of the three heirs very valuable property, but the third only a useable but not very profitable share. Would it not be wrong to divide the land equally although that would be the just thing to do, and wouldn't it therefore be right to divide it unequally although this would be unjust? Add to these considerations the claim that there are some acts of benevolence or truth telling to which the terms "just" and "unjust" simply don't apply (although the terms "right" and "wrong" do), and Hobbes' thesis, and that of others, is seen to be at the very least disputable.

534

But regarding justice, considered by itself, Hobbes may have been on the right track. There does seem to be something about justice which is intimately connected with social institutions of one kind or another. Many writers have observed that the Latin word "jus," from which "justitia" (justice) is derived, means the same as "law." We speak of "courts of justice," and even use "Justice" as a title for various legal officers. We do, of course, use the term justice outside the purely legal context, but when someone has committed an act which we regard as unjust but which is not legally forbidden, we often hear it said, "There ought to be a law against that sort of thing." Perhaps we cannot and should not press this connection too strongly. Many philosophers have cautioned against doing so. They say, for example, that acts of incest or suicide may be "wrong," but that it makes no sense to speak of them as "unjust." These examples do not seem to be well chosen, however, for insofar as these acts are violations of specific laws forbidding them, it does not seem any more unusual to speak of them as unjust or as "acts of injustice" than it would be to speak of theft, or any other legal violation, as unjust. Of course, if they are considered apart from any law (laws prohibiting suicide, for example, have for the most part been repealed), and simply as individual acts of private persons, then it is true that the terms do not seem to fit.

What this line of thinking seems to lead to, however, is a definition of justice as simply "conformity to law," and this is clearly not an adequate conception. For the fact remains that we often think of laws and of acts of conformity with certain laws as themselves "unjust," and this is inconsistent with the definition. This has led many philosophers to abandon the initial thought that law is a necessary condition of justice and to suggest that it has no important or essential relationship to it. Yet perhaps all that needs to be granted is that specific laws, or even whole bodies of law, do not set the limits as to what is just and what is unjust, but that the "idea of law" is nonetheless a component of justice. What needs to be shown, however, if "justice" is to be distinguished from other kinds of moral expressions such as "right," is that the idea of law, or some component element thereof, is connected with justice in a way which is not the case with respect to other moral notions.

The Principle of Equality

Some authors have felt that the essential ingredient in the idea of justice is the idea of equality, or equal treatment, and that this notion is derived from the traditional association of justice with law. Certainly it is not difficult to see that the notion of "law" implies the notion of a rule which is intended to apply equally to all members of the class covered by it. A rule or law which applied one way to some members of a class and differently to others of the same class would hardly be recognized as a law. The so-called principle of justice that "similar persons in similar circumstances be treated similarly" is incorporated into the very notion of law. It has been debated, however, whether the idea of equal treatment is essential to the idea of justice. Basically two questions have been raised. One is whether it is not simply a requirement of any moral action, namely, that the action be based on rules that are universalizable, and so not at all peculiar to just actions. The other question is whether the principle of equal treatment or equality exhausts what we mean by justice, or whether there are not other principles which qualify and restrict it.

Philosophers have taken definite sides with respect to the first question. Some, like Kant and Marcus Singer, assert that the principle of equality (Singer calls it the "generalization principle") is a requirement of all moral actions. Those like Aristotle who hold that rules may not be properly applied to all members of the same class (i.e., who hold that there may be *individual* exceptions) suggest that it is sometimes *right* not to treat persons equally. Yet as far as justice itself is concerned, Aristotle tends to identify it with equal treatment. He says (see *Nicomachean Ethics*, 1131a): "In any kind of action in which there is a more and a less there is also what is equal. If, then, the unjust is unequal, the just is equal, as all men suppose it to be, even apart from argument."

This disagreement, however, may not be what it at first appears to be, for there is surely a difference between saying that the rules upon which we act should apply equally and saying that the rules themselves must specify equal treatment. For example, the rule "Wrongdoers should be punished" may very well be universalized, i.e., be made to apply to all wrongdoers, without specifying that all wrongdoers are to be punished equally or in the same way. It would, of course, be unjust to treat one person who had committed theft differently from another similar individual who had committed the same or similar crime, and so far the principle of generalization applies in matters of justice as in all other moral cases, but given differences in the persons or in the circumstances or in the crimes committed, differences in treatment might not be unjust. Nor would such difference in treatment defeat the universality of the rule, "Wrongdoers should be punished."

Along this same line, consider the cases mentioned above in which "just" and "right" did not appear to mean the same thing. If Mill is correct, then it would be right on occasion to steal, i.e., to commit an unjust act. Given a sufficient description of the circumstances we could perhaps universalize a rule which would justify the act. But some philosophers, including Mill, would not wish to call it a just rule, for it would allow a preferential treatment of persons, i.e., some but not all are allowed to steal. Or consider the case involving the division of land. Let us suppose that it would be wrong in that case to divide the property equally. A rule could be formulated which took account of all such cases; yet, we might still have reservations about whether it was just. Frankena's suggestion that "right-making" considerations are not necessarily the same as "just-making" or "justicizing" considerations is a succinct way of expressing this same idea.

There is much room for debate regarding such attempts to distinguish "right" from "just" in terms of the principle of equal treatment, and the reader is advised to reflect upon both sets of arguments. But let us now turn to the second major difficulty in maintaining that the principle of equality constitutes the essence of justice, or if you will, whether it is a necessary condition of justice. Is there nothing more to justice than equal treatment? Isn't there such a thing as a "just inequality" or conversely, an "unjust equality" of treatment? Frankena argues that "Justice does not call for similar treatment of every similarity or for dissimilar treatment of every dissimilarity." We do think it just to deal similarly, for example, with people of different colors, and dissimilarly with people of the same color. Furthermore, we need not think that just treatment means identical treatment. Consider Frankena's illustration: If C prefers a banjo and D a guitar, and if each is given the instrument he prefers, it is clear that they have been treated *differently* yet *justly*. Certainly no one is likely to question that it would be unjust to give both C and D banjos, even though D prefers a guitar. One way to accommodate these apparent counterexamples to the principle of equality is to redefine equality to mean "proportionate" or "comparative" equality, as contrasted with equality in the sense of simple identity. There is merit in doing so, and both Aristotle and Frankena affirm the notion that justice is in this way "comparative." Both also recognize that other criteria are needed to determine which differences allow such comparatively equal treatment and which differences do not.

Egalitarianism and Meritarianism

Among the principles or criteria which have been advanced to enable us to justify treating similar persons dissimiliarly or dissimilar persons similarly have been the following: merit, ability, need, desert, rank, wealth, status, or position. In the above example about the allotment of musical instruments, what makes it seem particularly appropriate to give C a banjo and D a guitar is perhaps our assumption that C knows how to play the banjo and D a guitar. This difference in their personal abilities and interests is what justifies our not giving to each of them exactly the same kind of instrument. In other cases, we might find that desert based on past performance might justify our treating two otherwise similar persons differently. In other cases the fact that a person holds a government post might allow him privileges not granted to other citizens.

Sometimes, as we are all aware, these factors compete with one another. One applicant for a scholarship pleads financial need and another academic merit. If there is but one scholarship, how are we to decide who ought to get it? Stated more generally, how are all these different criteria of justice to be related and ordered with respect to one another? Two kinds of theory have been advanced which attempt to settle this problem. One is known as the *egalitarian* theory of justice; the other the *meritarian* theory of justice. The egalitarian theory maintains the belief that all persons are equal at least with respect to their humanity or human dignity, and therefore in those difficult situations in which the allotment of goods is to be made among dissimilar claimants, the controlling consideration is the benefit (happiness or well-being) which the respective individuals will receive. What does the prospective recipient require, and how much, to promote his dignity as a human being? Has he been treated fairly in the sense that he has at least been given an equal opportunity to compete for benefits that, for one reason or another, cannot be equally distributed? The meritarian bases his decisions in such situations on desert: What has a person done? What special qualifications does he possess? What other meritorious characteristics does he exhibit? These are the basic considerations which would justify unequal allotments to otherwise similar claimants.

By far the more popular of these theories today is the egalitarian one. The generally favorable attitude towards welfare programs stems largely from the conviction that everyone, regardless of his special talents and circumstances, counts for something and that the aim of social institutions ought to be the improvement of the lot of everybody. There is, however, even today one set of problems involving justice with respect to which the meritarian position is still quite persuasive. These are the problems connected with punishment, or what has sometimes been called "corrective justice." Just as justice is involved in awarding rewards and alloting various goods ("distributive justice" as it is called), so it is also involved in meting out punishment for wrongs. According to many persons, especially those known as "retributivists," punishment is justly imposed only insofar as a person "merits" or "deserves" it.

According to retributivists, the trouble with the classical utilitarian position, which justifies punishment not on the basis of the wrong done but on the good to be achieved by punishing the wrongdoer, is that it allows for the punishment of innocent persons. Rawls correctly points out that no utilitarian ever *intended* his theory to justify any such thing. In fact, utilitarians generally assume that the concept of punishment itself presupposes a violation of law. The problem for the utilitarians is whether on their view they have not proved too much; that is to say, have they not in fact also given grounds for what Rawls calls "telishment," a system of rules in terms of which innocent persons are punished for the benefit of society?

Neither a meritarian nor an egalitarian would of course regard such a consequence as consistent with justice. Classical utilitarianism has perhaps given rise to such a criticism because, although egalitarian in spirit and tradition, it does not explicitly include the notion of equality as a first principle of their philosophy. Bentham did maintain the view that "everyone is to count for one, and nobody for more than one," but for some strange reason omitted to include this idea in his statement of his moral principle. The greatest happiness principle leaves unsaid whether *everyone's* happiness is to count equally with that of everyone else's. Nonetheless, Bentham and Mill were both staunch democrats and in practice, if not explicitly in theory, were egalitarians. Perhaps their theory does appear to subordinate the individual to community needs, but clearly this was not their design.

Can traditional utilitarianism then be revised so as to avoid the criticism that it provides no acceptable justification of punishment? Rawls believes that it can be. Punishment must be looked upon as a system of rules, i.e., as an institution, not as a particular kind of act. Insofar as we apply the principle of utility to punishment conceived as an institution, we shall find, he says, that the consequences with respect to innocent persons cannot be sustained. For we shall find that "telishment" as an institution would involve "enormous risks" and "serve no useful purpose." On this basis, he says, "a utilitarian justification for this institution is most unlikely."

Aside from noting that Rawls' solution of the utilitarian's problem involves the adoption of a form of "rule-utilitarianism" as opposed to "act-utilitarianism," there are two other aspects of his account to which attention should be directed. The first is his view that whether telishment is justifiable depends on the actual consequences of adopting such a system of rules. His belief is that such a justification is "unlikely." Yet, "scape-goat" techniques are ever recurrent. Can we be sure that they haven't been successful? The point here is that to base one's philosophy on such empirical considerations may not in fact provide the kind of justification for punishment that we need and want. Consider the empirical arguments based on deterrence that have been advanced against capital punishment. How persuasive have they been? In any case, it seems fair to ask, Do we really wish to base our opposition to telishment or to capital punishment (if in fact we do object to the latter) merely on the fact that such practices "don't work"? Non-utilitarian critics, of course, would deny that that is what we mean by condemning them as morally wrong.

The second point about Rawls' solution is that only by relating "corrective justice" to the notion of an "institution" or to institutional "practices" does he find what he takes to be a defensible utilitarian account. If Rawls is correct, it would seem that we are again presented with the view that justice is inextricably related to the existence of institutions, not to be sure in exactly the same way that Hobbes would have us regard that relation, but certainly in a way that incorporates the concept of institution into the very idea of corrective justice.

Almost without exception the ancient Greek philosophers were meritarians. This view is clearly and classically expressed in the formula that "Justice is rendering (giving) to others what is due (owed) them." As Frankena points out, and as Socrates in the Plato selection dramatically illustrates, the chief problem with this view is that it fails to tell us what is due others. Presumably it is whatever they deserve, but what exactly does that tell us? And who is the "they" we mean to speak of anyway?

Socrates quickly disposes of Cephalus' simplistic notion that what is due others is "honest dealings," by which he means speaking the truth and paying one's debts. Socrates points out that (in the case of the homicidal maniac) it might be just to lie or to refuse to return a deposit (of a weapon). He also rejects Polemarchus' emendation of the formula to the effect that "Justice is helping one's friends and harming one's enemies." Aside from the difficulty there is in knowing who are our real friends and enemies, Socrates convinces him that it can never be just to harm anyone.

It must not be concluded from these criticisms, however, that Socrates or Plato mean to reject the meritarian theory of justice altogether. On the contrary, Plato goes on in *The Republic* to develop a detailed set of answers to the questions, What is due others? and Which persons are entitled by meritorious considerations to awards or punishments, rights or privileges? As Plato sees it, the problem of justice is complex and nothing short of an entire book is required to deal with it adequately. Although his analysis cannot be capsulated here, one point is prominent enough in all his discussions so that it ought not to be overlooked, and in fact can be surmised even from the few selections in this section. That point is that justice is a function of an ordered society. Although we may speak of "individual justice" as well as "social justice" (or "justice in the State," as Plato calls it) still each entails the other. A just society cannot exist without just individuals, but similarly he believes that there cannot be just individuals in a wholly unjust society. Thus it is more than a literary technique when Plato leads the discussion quickly from a discussion of the "honest dealings" which Cephalus has in mind to the consideration of justice from the standpoint of the ruler, i.e., to justice in society, justice "writ large" as he says. The reader should look for this transition in Plato's thought and hopefully follow it up by reading the whole of *The Republic*.

Power and Justice

Like Thrasymachus, in Plato's dialogue, the reader may feel slightly overwhelmed and a bit annoyed by all the distinctions we have been discussing. Are they all truly relevant to an understanding of justice? Take the distinction between equality and merit—what have these really to do with justice? Looked at from a coldly practical and slightly cynical point of view, isn't what really counts for justice in the courts simply what the judge says it is? Or in economic systems, what moneyed interests determine it to be? Or in educational systems, what the chief administrator dictates? Or in the family, what the dominant parent decides? Many, like Thrasymachus, have thought that justice is nothing but "the interest of the stronger."

At first glance, it seems astounding that anyone should confuse power with justice (or for that matter, might with right), yet this view is as ancient as any of them. Furthermore, it is a view which has reappeared in many different guises. Elements of it, as we have seen, are to be found in Hobbes' view that whatever the sovereign legislates is just. Laissez faire economics expresses it in another way. Paternalism in government and in the family are other forms. Old fashioned authoritarianism in education expresses the idea in still another context.

Perhaps the only effective antidote to this way of thinking about justice is the one Plato supplies. And that is to inquire (1) whether those holding power are fallible, and (2) whether it is to the interest of the stronger party to do that which injures those who are within his control. The admission of fallibility, i.e., that we can all make mistakes, is a first and vital step, for it is only then possible to take a more informed view of the limits and purposes of power and authority. Regarding the second inquiry, it should be clear from Plato's argument that even from a purely self-interested point of view, the debilitation of those under our control is no benefit to ourselves. What rational person, unless he had a hope of changing things, would choose to live in a society which permitted a certain segment of the population to starve, or because of their miserable condition to become of necessity law-breakers and criminals? Since we have to live with them as neighbors, our true interest lies in benefiting, not injuring, those less able to regulate their own destinies.

An example of the kind of injustice that can result from a commitment to the philosophy of power is the treatment which the American Indians have systematically received from the U. S. government for over a century. In a Supreme Court case, *Johnson* v. *M'Intosh*, decided in 1823, involving a suit by certain Indian Chiefs to give title to land originally occupied and possessed by their people, Chief Justice John Marshall denied that they had such a right. He upheld the principle that discovery followed by conquest (or purchase) gives the conqueror exclusive title to the land. The Indians' lands had been acquired in this way, and thus the original possessors had no title which they were free to convey. That legal principle was defended by Marshall as one which the court could not challenge since it was part of the political policy of this country and has been ever since its beginning. In short, the white man's claims, though supported and enforced only "by the sword," as he says, were nonetheless valid as against those of the Indians.

A more blatant expression of Thrasymachus' theory of justice is difficult to imagine. However, it must be added that since Marshall's decision Congress has made numerous attempts to deal fairly with Indian claims by authorizing suits against the government, waiving statutes of limitations for this purpose, and by setting up a special Indian Claims Commission to hear such cases. Even in Marshall's day Congress had authorized suits based on original Indian title, but as he himself notes, "no recovery has as yet been obtained on that ground." By "Indian title" or "aboriginal title" the courts mean an Indian claim to lands based on an officially *unrecognized* "right of occupancy." It is, in effect, a kind of euphemism for "We realize you were here first, but . . ."

Unfortunately for the Indians, this conception of Indian title and the principle of discovery have become part of our legal tradition and our body of federal law. So far the precedent set by Marshall's decision has not been overturned, and though many Indian claims have been filed in the courts of this country, comparatively few settlements in their favor have in fact been made.

The case of the *Northwestern Shoshone Indians* v. *United States* was decided in 1944. The basis of the suit is not that the Indians originally occupied the land and were subsequently dispossessed of it, but rather, the legally stronger one that their title to the land had been officially recognized by a treaty with the U. S. Government and ratified by Congress in 1863. The Indians bringing suit seek only to have the title reaffirmed and damages paid (at $1.00 an acre) for the lands confiscated. The case report includes a majority opinion which denies the Indians' petition, a concurring opinion in which Justices Jackson and Black agree with the judgment but express sympathy with the Indians' grievance, and several dissenting opinions of which Justice Douglas' is reprinted here. The reader should find it interesting to examine the problems discussed earlier in this section in terms of the reasoning offered in these opinions.

The Justification of Punishment

John Rawls

Two Concepts of Rules

In this paper I want to show the importance of the distinction between justifying a practice[1] and justifying a particular action falling under it, and I want to explain the logical basis of this distinction and how it is possible to miss its significance. While the distinction has frequently been

From "Two Concepts of Rules," *The Philosophical Review* LXIV (1955): 3-13, by permission of the author and *The Philosophical Review*. This is a revision of a paper given at the Harvard Philosophy Club on April 30, 1954.

[1]I use the word "practice" throughout as a sort of technical term meaning any form of activity specified by a system of rules which defines offices, roles, moves, penalties, defenses, and so on, and which gives the activity its structure. As examples one may think of games and rituals, trials and parliaments.

made,[2] and is now becoming commonplace, there remains the task of explaining the tendency either to overlook it altogether, or to fail to appreciate its importance.

To show the importance of the distinction I am going to defend utilitarianism against those objections which have traditionally been made against it in connection with punishment and the obligation to keep promises. I hope to show that if one uses the distinction in question then one can state utilitarianism in a way which makes it a much better explication of our considered moral judgments than these traditional objections would seem to admit.[3] Thus the importance of the distinction is shown by the way it strengthens the utilitarian view regardless of whether that view is completely defensible or not.

To explain how the significance of the distinction may be overlooked, I am going to discuss two conceptions of rules. One of these conceptions conceals the importance of distinguishing between the justification of a rule or practice and the justification of a particular action falling under it. The other conception makes it clear why this distinction must be made and what is its logical basis.

I

The subject of punishment, in the sense of attaching legal penalties to the violation of legal rules, has always been a troubling moral question.[4]

---

[2] The distinction is central to Hume's discussion of justice in *A Treatise of Human Nature,* bk. III, pt. II, esp. secs. 2-4. It is clearly stated by John Austin in the second lecture of *Lectures on Jurisprudence* (4th ed.; London, 1873), I, 116ff. (1st ed., 1832). Also it may be argued that J. S. Mill took it for granted in *Utilitarianism;* on this point cf. J. O. Urmson, "The Interpretation of the Moral Philosophy of J. S. Mill," *Philosophical Quarterly,* vol. III (1953). In addition to the arguments given by Urmson there are several clear statements of the distinction in *A System of Logic* (8th ed.; London, 1872), bk VI, ch. xii pars. 2, 3, 7. The distinction is fundamental to J. D. Mabbott's important paper, "Punishment," *Mind,* n.s., vol. XLVIII (April, 1939). More recently the distinction has been stated with particular emphasis by S. E. Toulmin in *The Place of Reason in Ethics* (Cambridge, 1950), see esp. ch. xi, where it plays a major part in his account of moral reasoning. Toulmin doesn't explain the basis of the distinction, nor how one might overlook its importance, as I try to in this paper, and in my review of his book (*Philosophical Review,* vol. LX [October, 1951]), as some of my criticisms show, I failed to understand the force of it. See also H. D. Aiken, "The Levels of Moral Discourse," *Ethics,* vol. LXII (1952), A. M. Quinton, "Punishment," *Analysis,* vol. XIV (June, 1954), and P. H. Nowell-Smith, *Ethics* (London, 1954), pp. 236-239, 271-273.

[3] On the concept of explication see the author's paper, *Philosophical Review,* vol. LX (April, 1951).

[4] While this paper was being revised, Quinton's appeared; footnote 2 supra. There are several respects in which my remarks are similar to his. Yet as I consider some further questions and rely on somewhat different arguments, I have retained the discussion of punishment and promises together as two test cases for utilitarianism.

The trouble about it has not been that people disagree as to whether or not punishment is justifiable. Most people have held that, freed from certain abuses, it is an acceptable institution. Only a few have rejected punishment entirely, which is rather surprising when one considers all that can be said against it. The difficulty is with the justification of punishment: various arguments for it have been given by moral philosophers, but so far none of them has won any sort of general acceptance; no justification is without those who detest it. I hope to show that the use of the aforementioned distinction enables one to state the utilitarian view in a way which allows for the sound points of its critics.

For our purposes we may say that there are two justifications of punishment. What we may call the retributive view is that punishment is justified on the grounds that wrongdoing merits punishment. It is morally fitting that a person who does wrong should suffer in proportion to his wrongdoing. That a criminal should be punished follows from his guilt, and the severity of the appropriate punishment depends on the depravity of his act. The state of affairs where a wrongdoer suffers punishment is morally better than the state of affairs where he does not; and it is better irrespective of any of the consequences of punishing him.

What we may call the utilitarian view holds that on the principle that bygones are bygones and that only future consequences are material to present decisions, punishment is justifiable only by reference to the probable consequences of maintaining it as one of the devices of the social order. Wrongs committed in the past are, as such, not relevant considerations for deciding what to do. If punishment can be shown to promote effectively the interest of society it is justifiable, otherwise it is not.

I have stated these two competing views very roughly to make one feel the conflict between them: one feels the force of *both* arguments and one wonders how they can be reconciled. From my introductory remarks it is obvious that the resolution which I am going to propose is that in this case one must distinguish between justifying a practice as a system of rules to be applied and enforced, and justifying a particular action which falls under these rules; utilitarian arguments are appropriate with regard to questions about practices, while retributive arguments fit the application of particular rules to particular cases.

We might try to get clear about this distinction by imagining how a father might answer the question of his son. Suppose the son asks, "Why was *J* put in jail yesterday?" The father answers, "Because he robbed the bank at *B*. He was duly tried and found guilty. That's why he was put in jail yesterday." But suppose the son had asked a different question, namely, "Why do people put other people in jail?" Then the father might answer, "To protect good people from bad people" or "To stop people from doing things that would make it uneasy for all of us; for otherwise we wouldn't be able to go to bed at night and sleep in peace." There are two very different questions here. One question emphasizes the proper name: it asks why *J* was punished rather than someone else, or it asks what he was punished for. The other question asks why we have the institution of punishment: why do people punish one another rather than, say, always forgiving one another?

Thus the father says in effect that a particular man is punished, rather than some other man, because he is guilty, and he is guilty because he broke the law (past tense). In this case the law looks back, the judge looks back, the jury looks back, and a penalty is visited upon him for something he did. That a man is to be punished, and what his punishment is to be, is settled by its being shown that he broke the law and that the law assigns that penalty for the violation of it.

On the other hand we have the institution of punishment itself, and recommend and accept various changes in it, because it is thought by the (ideal) legislator and by those to whom the law applies that, as a part of a system of law impartially applied from case to case arising under it, it will have the consequence, in the long run, of furthering the interests of society.

One can say, then, that the judge and the legislator stand in different positions and look in different directions: one to the past, the other to the future. The justification of what the judge does, *qua* judge, sounds like the retributive view; the justification of what the (ideal) legislator does, *qua* legislator, sounds like the utilitarian view. Thus both views have a point (this is as it should be since intelligent and sensitive persons have been on both sides of the argument); and one's initial confusion disappears once one sees that these views apply to persons holding different offices with different duties, and situated differently with respect to the system of rules that make up the criminal law.[5]

One might say, however, that the utilitarian view is more fundamental since it applies to a more fundamental office, for the judge carries out the legislator's will so far as he can determine it. Once the legislator decides to have laws and to assign penalties for their violation (as things are there must be both the law and the penalty) an institution is set up

---

[5]Note the fact that different sorts of arguments are suited to different offices. One way of taking the differences between ethical theories is to regard them as accounts of the reasons expected in different offices.

which involves a retributive conception of particular cases. It is part of the concept of the criminal law as a system of rules that the application and enforcement of these rules in particular cases should be justifiable by arguments of a retributive character. The decision whether or not to use law rather than some other mechanism of social control, and the decision as to what laws to have and what penalties to assign, may be settled by utilitarian arguments; but if one decides to have laws then one has decided on something whose working in particular cases is retributive in form.[6]

The answer, then, to the confusion engendered by the two views of punishment is quite simple: one distinguishes two offices, that of the judge and that of the legislator, and one distinguishes their different stations with respect to the system of rules which make up the law; and then one notes that the different sorts of considerations which would usually be offered as reasons for what is done under the cover of these offices can be paired off with the competing justifications of punishment. One reconciles the two views by the time-honored device of making them apply to different situations.

But can it really be this simple? Well, this answer allows for the apparent intent of each side. Does a person who advocates the retributive view necessarily advocate, as an *institution*, legal machinery whose essential purpose is to set up and preserve a correspondence between moral turpitude and suffering? Surely not.[7] What retributionists have rightly insisted upon is that no man can be punished unless he is guilty, that is, unless he has broken the law. Their fundamental criticism of the utilitarian account is that, as they interpret it, it sanctions an innocent person's being punished (if one may call it that) for the benefit of society.

On the other hand, utilitarians agree that punishment is to be inflicted only for the violation of law. They regard this much as understood from the concept of punishment itself.[8] The point of the utilitarian account concerns the institution as a system of rules: utilitarianism seeks

---

[6]In this connection see Mabbott, *op. cit.*, pp. 163-164.

[7]On this point see Sir David Ross, *The Right and the Good* (Oxford, 1930), pp. 57-60.

[8]See Hobbes's definition of punishment in *Leviathan*, ch. xxviii; and Bentham's definition in *The Principles of Morals and Legislation,* ch. xii, par. 36, ch. xv, par. 28, and in *The Rationale of Punishment,* (London, 1830), bk. I, ch. i. They could agree with Bradley that: "Punishment is punishment only when it is deserved. We pay the penalty, because we owe it, and for no other reason; and if punishment is inflicted for any other reason whatever than because it is merited by wrong, it is a gross immorality, a crying injustice, an abominable crime, and not what it pretends to be." *Ethical Studies* (2nd ed.; Oxford, 1927), pp. 26-27. Certainly by definition it isn't what it pretends to be. The innocent can only be punished by mistake; deliberate "punishment" of the innocent necessarily involves fraud.

to limit its use by declaring it justifiable only if it can be shown to foster effectively the good of society. Historically it is a protest against the indiscriminate and ineffective use of the criminal law.[9] It seeks to dissuade us from assigning to penal institutions the improper, if not sacrilegious, task of matching suffering with moral turpitude. Like others, utilitarians want penal institutions designed so that, as far as humanly possible, only those who break the law run afoul of it. They hold that no official should have discretionary power to inflict penalties whenever he thinks it for the benefit of society; for on utilitarian grounds an institution granting such power could not be justified.[10]

The suggested way of reconciling the retributive and the utilitarian justifications of punishment seems to account for what both sides have wanted to say. There are, however, two further questions which arise, and I shall devote the remainder of this section to them.

First, will not a difference of opinion as to the proper criterion of just law make the proposed reconciliation unacceptable to retributionists? Will they not question whether, if the utilitarian principle is used as the criterion, it follows that those who have broken the law are guilty in a way which satisfies their demand that those punished deserve to be punished? To answer this difficulty, suppose that the rules of the criminal law are justified on utilitarian grounds (it is only for laws that meet his criterion that the utilitarian can be held responsible). Then it follows that the actions which the criminal law specifies as offenses are such that, if they were tolerated, terror and alarm would spread in society. Consequently, retributionists can only deny that those who are punished deserve to be punished if they deny that such actions are wrong. This they will not want to do.

The second question is whether utilitarianism doesn't justify too much. One pictures it as an engine of justification which, if consistently adopted, could be used to justify cruel and arbitrary institutions. Retribu-

---

[9]Cf. Leon Radzinowicz, *A History of English Criminal Law: The Movement for Reform 1750-1833* (London, 1948), esp. ch. xi on Bentham.

[10]Bentham discusses how corresponding to a punitory provision of a criminal law there is another provision which stands to it as an antagonist and which needs a name as much as the punitory. He calls it, as one might expect, the *anaetiosostic,* and of it he says: "The punishment of guilt is the object of the former one: the preservation of innocence that of the latter." In the same connection he asserts that it is never thought fit to give the judge the option of deciding whether a thief (that is, a person whom he believes to be a thief, for the judge's belief is what the question must always turn upon) should hang or not, and so the law writes the provision: "The judge shall not cause a thief to be hanged unless he have been duly convicted and sentenced in course of law" (*The Limits of Jurisprudence Defined,* ed. C. W. Everett [New York, 1945], pp. 238-239.

tionists may be supposed to concede that utilitarians *intend* to reform the law and to make it more humane; that utilitarians do not *wish* to justify any such thing as punishment of the innocent; and that utilitarians may appeal to the fact that punishment presupposes guilt in the sense that by punishment one understands an institution attaching penalties to the infraction of legal rules, and therefore that it is logically absurd to suppose that utilitarians in justifying *punishment* might also have justified punishment (if we may call it that) of the innocent. The real question, however, is whether the utilitarian, in justifying punishment, hasn't used arguments which commit him to accepting the infliction of suffering on innocent persons if it is for the good of society (whether or not one calls this punishment). More generally, isn't the utilitarian committed in principle to accepting many practices which he, as a morally sensitive person, wouldn't want to accept? Retributionists are inclined to hold that there is no way to stop the utilitarian principle from justifying too much except by adding to it a principle which distributes certain rights to individuals. Then the amended criterion is not the greatest benefit of society *simpliciter*, but the greatest benefit of society subject to the constraint that no one's rights may be violated. Now while I think that the classical utilitarians proposed a criterion of this more complicated sort, I do not want to argue that point here.[11] What I want to show is that there is *another* way of preventing the utilitarian principle from justifying too much, or at least of making it much less likely to do so: namely, by stating utilitarianism in a way which accounts for the distinction between the justification of an institution and the justification of a particular action falling under it.

I begin by defining the institution of punishment as follows: a person is said to suffer punishment whenever he is legally deprived of some of the normal rights of a citizen on the ground that he has violated a rule of law, the violation having been established by trial according to the due process of law, provided that the deprivation is carried out by the recognized legal authorities of the state, that the rule of law clearly specifies both the offense and the attached penalty, that the courts construe statutes strictly, and that the statute was on the books prior to the time of the offense.[12] This definition specifies what I shall understand by punishment. The question is whether utilitarian arguments may be found to justify

---

[11]By the classical utilitarians I understand Hobbes, Hume, Bentham, J. S. Mill, and Sidgwick.

[12]All these features of punishment are mentioned by Hobbes; cf. *Leviathan,* ch. xxviii.

institutions widely different from this and such as one would find cruel and arbitrary.

This question is best answered, I think, by taking up a particular accusation. Consider the following from Carritt:

> . . . the utilitarian must hold that we are justified in inflicting pain always and only to prevent worse pain or bring about greater happiness. This, then, is all we need to consider in so-called punishment, which must be purely preventive. But if some kind of very cruel crime becomes common, and none of the criminals can be caught, it might be highly expedient, as an example, to hang an innocent man, if a charge against him could be so framed that he were universally thought guilty; indeed this would only fail to be an ideal instance of utilitarian "punishment" because the victim himself would not have been so likely as a real felon to commit such a crime in the future; in all other respects it would be perfectly deterrent and therefore felicific.[13]

Carritt is trying to show that there are occasions when a utilitarian argument would justify taking an action which would be generally condemned; and thus that utilitarianism justifies too much. But the failure of Carritt's argument lies in the fact that he makes no distinction between the justification of the general system of rules which constitutes penal institutions and the justification of particular applications of these rules to particular cases by the various officials whose job it is to administer them. This becomes perfectly clear when one asks who the "we" are of whom Carritt speaks. Who is this who has a sort of absolute authority on particular occasions to decide that an innocent man shall be "punished" if everyone can be convinced that he is guilty? Is this person the legislator, or the judge, or the body of private citizens, or what? It is utterly crucial to know who is to decide such matters, and by what authority, for all of this must be written into the rules of the institution. Until one knows these things one doesn't know what the institution is whose justification is being challenged; and as the utilitarian principle applies to the institution one doesn't know whether it is justifiable on utilitarian grounds or not.

Once this is understood it is clear what the countermove to Carritt's argument is. One must describe more carefully what the *institution* is which his example suggests, and then ask oneself whether or not it is likely that having this institution would be for the benefit of society in the long run. One must not content oneself with the vague thought that, when

[13]*Ethical and Political Thinking* (Oxford, 1947), p. 65.

it's a question of *this* case, it would be a good thing if *somebody* did something even if an innocent person were to suffer.

Try to imagine, then, an institution (which we may call "telishment") which is such that the officials set up by it have authority to arrange a trial for the condemnation of an innocent man whenever they are of the opinion that doing so would be in the best interests of society. The discretion of officials is limited, however, by the rule that they may not condemn an innocent man to undergo such an ordeal unless there is, at the time, a wave of offenses similar to that with which they charge him and telish him for. We may imagine that the officials having the discretionary authority are the judges of the higher courts in consultation with the chief of police, the minister of justice, and a committee of the legislature.

Once one realizes that one is involved in setting up an *institution*, one sees that the hazards are very great. For example, what check is there on the officials? How is one to tell whether or not their actions are authorized? How is one to limit the risks involved in allowing such systematic deception? How is one to avoid giving anything short of complete discretion to the authorities to telish anyone they like? In addition to these considerations, it is obvious that people will come to have a very different attitude towards their penal system when telishment is adjoined to it. They will be uncertain as to whether a convicted man has been punished or telished. They will wonder whether or not they should feel sorry for him. They will wonder whether the same fate won't at any time fall on them. If one pictures how such an institution would actually work, and the enormous risks involved in it, it seems clear that it would serve no useful purpose. A utilitarian justification for this institution is most unlikely.

It happens in general that as one drops off the defining features of punishment one ends up with an institution whose utilitarian justification is highly doubtful. One reason for this is that punishment works like a kind of price system: by altering the prices one has to pay for the performance of actions it supplies a motive for avoiding some actions and doing others. The defining features are essential if punishment is to work in this way; so that an institution which lacks these features, e.g., an institution which is set up to "punish" the innocent, is likely to have about as much point as a price system (if one may call it that) where the prices of things change at random from day to day and one learns the price of something after one has agreed to buy it.[14]

---

[14]The analogy with the price system suggests an answer to the question how utilitarian considerations insure that punishment is proportional to the offense. It

If one is careful to apply the utilitarian principle to the institution which is to authorize particular actions, then there is *less* danger of its justifying too much. Carritt's example gains plausibility by its indefiniteness and by its concentration on the particular case. His argument will only hold if it can be shown that there are utilitarian arguments which justify an institution whose publicly ascertainable offices and powers are such as to permit officials to exercise that kind of discretion in particular cases. But the requirement of having to build the arbitrary features of the particular decision into the institutional practice makes the justification much less likely to go through.

---

is interesting to note that Sir David Ross, after making the distinction between justifying a penal law and justifying a particular application of it, and after stating that utilitarian considerations have a large place in determining the former, still holds back from accepting the utilitarian justification of punishment on the grounds that justice requires that punishment be proportional to the offense, and that utilitarianism is unable to account for this. Cf. *The Right and the Good,* pp. 61-62. I do not claim that utilitarianism can account for this requirement as Sir David might wish, but it happens, nevertheless, that if utilitarian considerations are followed penalties will be proportional to offenses in this sense: the order of offenses according to seriousness can be paired off with the order of penalties according to severity. Also the absolute level of penalties will be as low as possible. This follows from the assumption that people are rational (i.e., that they are able to take into account the "prices" the state puts on actions), the utilitarian rule that a penal system should provide a motive for preferring the less serious offense, and the principle that punishment as such is an evil. All this was carefully worked out by Bentham in *The Principles of Morals and Legislation,* chs. xiii-xv.

Classical Definitions of Justice

Plato

The Republic

THE SCENE *is laid in the house of Cephalus at the Piraeus; and the whole dialogue is narrated by Socrates the day after it actually took place . . .*

[*Justice is Giving to Others What is Due Them*]

I went down yesterday to the Piraeus with Glaucon the son of Ariston, that I might offer up my prayers to the goddess [Bendis]; and also because

From Plato's dialogue, *The Republic,* Book I, 327-347e, trans. B. Jowett, 3rd ed. (1892).

I wanted to see in what manner they would celebrate the festival, which was a new thing. I was delighted with the procession of the inhabitants; but that of the Thracians was equally, if not more, beautiful. When we had finished our prayers and viewed the spectacle, we turned in the direction of the city; and at that instant Polemarchus the son of Cephalus chanced to catch sight of us from a distance as we were starting on our way home, and told his servant to run and bid us wait for him. The servant took hold of me by the cloak behind, and said: Polemarchus desires you to wait.

I turned round, and asked him where his master was.

There he is, said the youth, coming after you, if you will only wait.

Certainly we will, said Glaucon; and in a few minutes Polemarchus appeared, and with him Adeimantus, Glaucon's brother, Niceratus the son of Nicias, and several others who had been at the procession.

Polemarchus said to me: I perceive, Socrates, that you and your companion are already on your way to the city.

You are not far wrong, I said.

But do you see, he rejoined, how many we are?

Of course.

And are you stronger than all these? for if not, you will have to remain where you are.

May there not be the alternative, I said, that we may persuade you to let us go?

But can you persuade us, if we refuse to listen to you? he said.

Certainly not, replied Glaucon.

Then we are not going to listen; of that you may be assured.

Adeimantus added: Has no one told you of the torch-race on horseback in honour of the goddess which will take place in the evening?

With horses! I replied: That is a novelty. Will horsemen carry torches and pass them one to another during the race?

Yes, said Polemarchus, and not only so, but a festival will be celebrated at night, which you certainly ought to see. Let us rise soon after supper and see this festival; there will be a gathering of young men, and we will have a good talk. Stay then, and do not be perverse.

Glaucon said: I suppose, since you insist, that we must.

Very good, I replied.

Accordingly we went with Polemarchus to his house; and there we found his brothers Lysias and Euthydemus, and with them Thrasymachus the Chalcedonian, Charmantides the Paeanian, and Cleitophon the son of Aristonymus. There too was Cephalus the father of Polemarchus, whom I had not seen for a long time, and I thought him very much aged. He was seated on a cushioned chair, and had a garland on his head, for he had been sacrificing in the court; and there were some other chairs in the room arranged in a semicircle, upon which we sat down by him. He saluted me eagerly, and then he said: —

You don't come to see me, Socrates, as often as you ought: If I were still able to go and see you I would not ask you to come to me. But at my age I can hardly get to the city, and therefore you should come oftener to the Piraeus. For let me tell you, that the more the pleasures of the body fade away, the greater to me is the pleasure and charm of conversation. Do not then deny my request, but make our house your resort and keep company with these young men; we are old friends, and you will be quite at home with us.

I replied: There is nothing which for my part I like better, Cephalus, than conversing with aged men; for I regard them as travellers who have gone a journey which I too may have to go, and of whom I ought to enquire, whether the way is smooth and easy, or rugged and difficult. And this is a question which I should like to ask of you who have arrived at that time which the poets call the 'threshold of old age' — Is life harder towards the end, or what report do you give of it?

I will tell you, Socrates, he said, what my own feeling is. Men of my age flock together; we are birds of a feather, as the old proverb says; and at our meetings the tale of my acquaintance commonly is — I cannot eat, I cannot drink; the pleasures of youth and love are fled away: there was a good time once, but now that is gone, and life is no longer life. Some complain of the slights which are put upon them by relations, and they will tell you sadly of how many evils their old age is the cause. But to me, Socrates, these complainers seem to blame that which is not really in fault. For if old age were the cause, I too being old, and every other old man, would have felt as they do. But this is not my own experience, nor that of others whom I have known. How well I remember the aged poet Sophocles, when in answer to the question, How does love suit with age, Sophocles, — are you still the man you were? Peace, he replied; most gladly have I escaped the thing of which you speak; I feel as if I had escaped from a mad and furious master. His words have often occurred to my mind since, and they seem as good to me now as at the time when he uttered them. For certainly old age has a great sense of calm and freedom; when the passions relax their hold, then, as Sophocles says, we are freed from the grasp not of one mad master only, but of many. The truth is, Socrates, that these regrets, and also the complaints about relations, are to be attributed to the same cause, which is not old age, but men's characters and tempers; for he who is of a calm and happy nature will hardly feel the pressure of age, but to him who is of an opposite disposition youth and age are equally a burden.

I listened in admiration, and wanting to draw him out, that he might go on — Yes, Cephalus, I said; but I rather suspect that people in general are not convinced by you when you speak thus; they think that old age sits lightly upon you, not because of your happy disposition, but because you are rich, and wealth is well known to be a great comforter.

You are right, he replied; they are not convinced: and there is something in what they say; not, however, so much as they imagine. I might answer them as Themistocles answered the Seriphian who was abusing him and saying that he was famous, not for his own merits but because he was an Athenian: 'If you had been a native of my country or I of yours, neither of us would have been famous.' And to those who are not rich and are impatient of old age, the same reply may be made; for to the good poor man old age cannot be a light burden, nor can a bad rich man ever have peace with himself.

May I ask, Cephalus, whether your fortune was for the most part inherited or acquired by you?

Acquired! Socrates; do you want to know how much I acquired? In the art of making money I have been midway between my father and grandfather: for my grandfather, whose name I bear, doubled and trebled the value of his patrimony, that which he inherited being much what I possess now; but my father Lysanias reduced the property below what it is at present: and I shall be satisfied if I leave to these my sons not less but a little more than I received.

That was why I asked you the question, I replied, because I see you are indifferent about money, which is a characteristic rather of those who have inherited their fortunes than of those who have acquired them; the makers of fortunes have a second love of money as a creation of their own, resembling the affection of authors for their own poems, or of parents for their children, besides that natural love of it for the sake of use and profit which is common to them and all men. And hence they are very bad company, for they can talk about nothing but the praises of wealth.

That is true, he said.

Yes, that is very true, but may I ask another question? — What do you consider to be the greatest blessing which you have reaped from your wealth?

One, he said, of which I could not expect easily to convince others. For let me tell you, Socrates, that when a man thinks himself to be near death, fears and cares enter into his mind which he never had before; the tales of a world below and the punishment which is exacted there of deeds done here were once a laughing matter to him, but now he is tormented with the thought that they may be true: either from the weakness of age, or because he is now drawing nearer to that other place, he has a clearer view of these things; suspicions and alarms crowd thickly upon him, and he begins to reflect and consider what wrongs he has done to others. And when he finds that the sum of his transgressions is great he will many a time like a child start up in his sleep for fear, and he is filled with dark forebodings. But to him who is conscious of no sin, sweet hope, as Pindar charmingly says, is the kind nurse of his age:

'Hope,' he says, 'cherishes the soul of him who lives in justice and holiness, and is the nurse of his age and the companion of his journey; — hope which is mightiest to sway the restless soul of man.'

How admirable are his words! And the great blessing of riches, I do not say to every man, but to a good man, is, that he has had no occasion to deceive or to defraud others, either intentionally or unintentionally; and when he departs to the world below he is not in any apprehension about offerings due to the gods or debts which he owes to men. Now to this peace of mind the possession of wealth greatly contributes; and therefore I say, that, setting one thing against another, of the many advantages which wealth has to give, to a man of sense this is in my opinion the greatest.

Well said, Cephalus, I replied; but as concerning justice, what is it? — to speak the truth and to pay your debts — no more than this? And even to this are there not exceptions? Suppose that a friend when in his right mind has deposited arms with me and he asks for them when he is not in his right mind, ought I to give them back to him? No one would say that I ought or that I should be right in doing so, any more than they would say that I ought always to speak the truth to one who is in his condition.

You are quite right, he replied.

But then, I said, speaking the truth and paying your debts is not a correct definition of justice.

Quite correct, Socrates, if Simonides is to be believed, said Polemarchus interposing.

I fear, said Cephalus, that I must go now, for I have to look after the sacrifices, and I hand over the argument to Polemarchus and the company.

Is not Polemarchus your heir? I said.

To be sure, he answered, and went away laughing to the sacrifices.

[Justice is Benefiting One's Friends and Harming One's Enemies]

Tell me then, O thou heir of the argument, what did Simonides say, and according to you truly say, about justice?

He said that the re-payment of a debt is just, and in saying so he appears to me to be right.

I should be sorry to doubt the word of such a wise and inspired man, but his meaning, though probably clear to you, is the reverse of clear to me. For he certainly does not mean, as we were just now saying, that I ought to return a deposit of arms or of anything else to one who asks for it when he is not in his right senses; and yet a deposit cannot be denied to be a debt.

True.

Then when the person who asks me is not in his right mind I am by no means to make the return?

Certainly not.

When Simonides said that the repayment of a debt was justice, he did not mean to include that case?

Certainly not; for he thinks that a friend ought always to do good to a friend and never evil.

You mean that the return of a deposit of gold which is to the injury of the receiver, if the two parties are friends, is not the repayment of a debt, — that is what you would imagine him to say?

Yes.

And are enemies also to receive what we owe to them?

To be sure, he said, they are to receive what we owe them, and an enemy, as I take it, owes to an enemy that which is due or proper to him—that is to say, evil.

Simonides, then, after the manner of poets, would seem to have spoken darkly of the nature of justice; for he really meant to say that justice is the giving to each man what is proper to him, and this he termed a debt.

That must have been his meaning, he said.

By heaven! I replied; and if we asked him what due or proper thing is given by medicine, and to whom, what answer do you think that he would make to us?

He would surely reply that medicine gives drugs and meat and drink to human bodies.

And what due or proper thing is given by cookery, and to what?

Seasoning to food.

And what is that which justice gives, and to whom?

If, Socrates, we are to be guided at all by the analogy of the preceding instances, then justice is the art which gives good to friends and evil to enemies.

That is his meaning then?

I think so.

And who is best able to do good to his friends and evil to his enemies in time of sickness?

The physician.

Or when they are on a voyage, amid the perils of the sea?

The pilot.

And in what sort of actions or with a view to what result is the just man most able to do harm to his enemy and good to his friend?

In going to war against the one and in making alliances with the other.

But when a man is well, my dear Polemarchus, there is no need of a physician?

No.

And he who is not on a voyage has no need of a pilot?

No.

Then in time of peace justice will be of no use?

I am very far from thinking so.

You think that justice may be of use in peace as well as in war?

Yes.

Like husbandry for the acquisition of corn?

Yes.

Or like shoemaking for the acquisition of shoes, — that is what you mean?

Yes.

And what similar use or power of acquisition has justice in time of peace?

In contracts, Socrates, justice is of use.

And by contracts you mean partnerships?

Exactly.

But is the just man or the skilful player a more useful and better partner at a game of draughts?

The skilful player.

And in the laying of bricks and stones is the just man a more useful or better partner than the builder?

Quite the reverse.

Then in what sort of partnership is the just man a better partner than the harp-player, as in playing the harp the harp-player is certainly a better partner than the just man?

In a money partnership.

Yes, Polemarchus, but surely not in the use of money; for you do not want a just man to be your counsellor in the purchase or sale of a horse; a man who is knowing about horses would be better for that, would he not?

Certainly.

And when you want to buy a ship, the shipwright or the pilot would be better?

True.

Then what is that joint use of silver or gold in which the just man is to be preferred?

When you want a deposit to be kept safely.

You mean when money is not wanted, but allowed to lie?

Precisely.

That is to say, justice is useful when money is useless?

That is the inference.

And when you want to keep a pruning-hook safe, then justice is useful to the individual and to the state; but when you want to use it, then the art of the vine-dresser?

Clearly.

And when you want to keep a shield or a lyre, and not to use them, you would say that justice is useful; but when you want to use them, then the art of the soldier or of the musician?

Certainly.

And so of all the other things; — justice is useful when they are useless, and useless when they are useful?

That is the inference.

Then justice is not good for much. But let us consider this further point: Is not he who can best strike a blow in a boxing match or in any kind of fighting best able to ward off a blow?

Certainly.

And he who is most skilful in preventing or escaping from a disease is best able to create one?

True.

And he is the best guard of a camp who is best able to steal a march upon the enemy?

Certainly.

Then he who is a good keeper of anything is also a good thief?

That, I suppose, is to be inferred.

Then if the just man is good at keeping money, he is good at stealing it.

That is implied in the argument.

Then after all the just man has turned out to be a thief. And this is a lesson which I suspect you must have learnt out of Homer; for he, speaking of Autolycus, the maternal grandfather of Odysseus, who is a favourite of his, affirms that

He was excellent above all men in theft and perjury.

And so, you and Homer and Simonides are agreed that justice is an art of theft; to be practised however 'for the good of friends and for the harm of enemies,'—that was what you were saying?

No, certainly not that, though I do not now know what I did say; but I still stand by the latter words.

Well, there is another question: By friends and enemies do we mean those who are so really, or only in seeming?

Surely, he said, a man may be expected to love those whom he thinks good, and to hate those whom he thinks evil.

Yes, but do not persons often err about good and evil: many who are not good seem to be so, and conversely?

That is true.

Then to them the good will be enemies and the evil will be their friends?

True.

And in that case they will be right in doing good to the evil and evil to the good?

Clearly.

But the good are just and would not do an injustice?

True.

Then according to your argument it is just to injure those who do no wrong?

Nay, Socrates; the doctrine is immoral.

Then I suppose that we ought to do good to the just and harm to the unjust?

I like that better.

But see the consequence: — Many a man who is ignorant of human nature has friends who are bad friends, and in that case he ought to do harm to them; and he has good enemies whom he ought to benefit; but, if so, we shall be saying the very opposite of that which we affirmed to be the meaning of Simonides.

Very true, he said; and I think that we had better correct an error into which we seem to have fallen in the use of the words 'friend' and 'enemy.'

What was the error, Polemarchus? I asked.

We assumed that he is a friend who seems to be or who is thought good.

And how is the error to be corrected?

We should rather say that he is a friend who is, as well as seems, good; and that he who seems only, and is not good, only seems to be and is not a friend; and of an enemy the same may be said.

You would argue that the good are our friends and the bad our enemies?

Yes.

And instead of saying simply as we did at first, that it is just to do good to our friends and harm to our enemies, we should further say: It is just to do good to our friends when they are good and harm to our enemies when they are evil.

Yes, that appears to me to be the truth.

But ought the just to injure any one at all?

Undoubtedly he ought to injure those who are both wicked and his enemies.

When horses are injured, are they improved or deteriorated?

The latter.

Deteriorated, that is to say, in the good qualities of horses, not of dogs?

Yes, of horses.

And dogs are deteriorated in the good qualities of dogs, and not of horses?

Of course.

And will not men who are injured be deteriorated in that which is the proper virtue of man?

Certainly.

And that human virtue is justice?

To be sure.

Then men who are injured are of necessity made unjust?

That is the result.

But can the musician by his art make men unmusical?

Certainly not.

Or the horseman by his art make them bad horsemen?

Impossible.

And can the just by justice make men unjust, or speaking generally, can the good by virtue make them bad?

Assuredly not.

Any more than heat can produce cold?

It cannot.

Or drought moisture?

Clearly not.

Nor can the good harm any one?

Impossible.

And the just is the good?

Certainly.

Then to injure a friend or any one else is not the act of a just man, but of the opposite, who is the unjust?

I think that what you say is quite true, Socrates.

Then if a man says that justice consists in the repayment of debts, and that good is the debt which a man owes to his friends, and evil the debt which he owes to his enemies,—to say this is not wise; for it is not true, if, as has been clearly shown, the injuring of another can be in no case just.

I agree with you, said Polemarchus.

Then you and I are prepared to take up arms against any one who attributes such a saying to Simonides or Bias or Pittacus, or any other wise man or seer?

I am quite ready to do battle at your side, he said.

Shall I tell you whose I believe the saying to be?

Whose?

I believe that Periander or Perdiccas or Xerxes or Ismenias the Theban, or some other rich and mighty man, who had a great opinion of his own power, was the first to say that justice is "doing good to your friends and harm to your enemies."

Most true, he said.

Yes, I said; but if this definition of justice also breaks down, what other can be offered?

[*Justice is the Interest of the Stronger*]

Several times in the course of the discussion Thrasymachus had made an attempt to get the argument into his own hands, and had been put down by the rest of the company, who wanted to hear the end. But when Polemarchus and I had done speaking and there was a pause, he could no longer hold his peace; and, gathering himself up, he came at us like a wild beast, seeking to devour us. We were quite panic-stricken at the sight of him.

He roared out to the whole company: What folly, Socrates, has taken possession of you all? And why, sillybillies, do you knock under to one another? I say that if you want really to know what justice is, you should not only ask but answer, and you should not seek honour to yourself from the refutation of an opponent, but have your own answer; for there is many a one who can ask and cannot answer. And now I will not have you say that justice is duty or advantage or profit or gain or interest, for this sort of nonsense will not do for me; I must have clearness and accuracy.

I was panic-stricken at his words, and could not look at him without trembling. Indeed I believe that if I had not fixed my eye upon him, I should have been struck dumb: but when I saw his fury rising, I looked at him first, and was therefore able to reply to him.

Thrasymachus, I said, with a quiver, don't be hard upon us. Polemarchus and I may have been guilty of a little mistake in the argument, but I can assure you that the error was not intentional. If we were seeking for a piece of gold, you would not imagine that we were 'knocking under to one another,' and so losing our chance of finding it. And why, when we are seeking for justice, a thing more precious than many pieces of gold, do you say that we are weakly yielding to one another and not doing our utmost to get at the truth? Nay, my good friend, we are most willing and anxious to do so, but the fact is that we cannot. And if so, you people who know all things should pity us and not be angry with us.

How characteristic of Socrates! he replied, with a bitter laugh;—that's your ironical style! Did I not foresee—have I not already told you, that whatever he was asked he would refuse to answer, and try irony or any other shuffle, in order that he might avoid answering?

You are a philosopher, Thrasymachus, I replied, and well know that if you ask a person what numbers make up twelve, taking care to prohibit him whom you ask from answering twice six, or three times four, or six times two, or four times three, 'for this sort of nonsense will not do for me,'—then obviously, if that is your way of putting the question, no one can answer you. But suppose that he were to retort, 'Thrasymachus, what do you mean? If one of these numbers which you interdict be the true answer to the question, am I falsely to say some other number which is not the right one?—is that your meaning?'—How would you answer him?

Just as if the two cases were at all alike! he said.

Why should they not be? I replied; and even if they are not, but only appear to be so to the person who is asked, ought he not to say what he thinks, whether you and I forbid him or not?

I presume then that you are going to make one of the interdicted answers?

I dare say that I may, notwithstanding the danger, if upon reflection I approve of any of them.

But what if I give you an answer about justice other and better, he said, than any of these? What do you deserve to have done to you?

Done to me!—as becomes the ignorant, I must learn from the wise —that is what I deserve to have done to me.

What, and no payment! a pleasant notion!

I will pay when I have the money, I replied.

But you have, Socrates, said Glaucon: and you, Thrasymachus, need be under no anxiety about money, for we will all make a contribution for Socrates.

Yes, he replied, and then Socrates will do as he always does—refuse to answer himself, but take and pull to pieces the answer of some one else.

Why, my good friend, I said, how can any one answer who knows, and says that he knows, just nothing; and who, even if he has some faint notions of his own, is told by a man of authority not to utter them? The natural thing is, that the speaker should be some one like yourself who professes to know and can tell what he knows. Will you then kindly answer, for the edification of the company and of myself?

Glaucon and the rest of the company joined in my request and Thrasymachus, as any one might see, was in reality eager to speak; for he thought that he had an excellent answer, and would distinguish himself. But at first he affected to insist on my answering; at length he consented to begin. Behold, he said, the wisdom of Socrates; he refuses to teach himself, and goes about learning of others, to whom he never even says Thank you.

That I learn of others, I replied, is quite true; but that I am ungrateful I wholly deny. Money I have none, and therefore I pay in praise, which is all I have; and how ready I am to praise any one who appears to me to speak well you will very soon find out when you answer; for I expect that you will answer well.

Listen, then, he said; I proclaim that justice is nothing else than the interest of the stronger. And now why do you not praise me? But of course you won't.

Let me first understand you, I replied. Justice, as you say, is the interest of the stronger. What, Thrasymachus, is the meaning of this? You cannot mean to say that because Polydamas, the pancratiast, is stronger than we are, and finds the eating of beef conducive to his bodily strength, that to eat beef is therefore equally for our good who are weaker than he is, and right and just for us?

That's abominable of you, Socrates; you take the words in the sense which is most damaging to the argument.

Not at all, my good sir, I said; I am trying to understand them; and I wish that you would be a little clearer.

Well, he said, have you never heard that forms of government differ; there are tyrannies, and there are democracies, and there are aristocracies?

Yes, I know.

And the government is the ruling power in each state?

Certainly.

And the different forms of government make laws democratical, aristocratical, tyrannical, with a view to their several interests; and these laws, which are made by them for their own interests, are the justice which they deliver to their subjects, and him who transgresses them they punish as a breaker of the law, and unjust. And that is what I mean when I say that in all states there is the same principle of justice, which is the interest of the government; and as the government must be supposed to have power, the only reasonable conclusion is, that everywhere there is one principle of justice, which is the interest of the stronger.

Now I understand you, I said; and whether you are right or not I will try to discover. But let me remark, that in defining justice you have yourself used the word 'interest' which you forbade me to use. It is true, however, that in your definition the words 'of the stronger' are used.

A small addition, you must allow, he said.

Great or small, never mind about that: we must first enquire whether what you are saying is the truth. Now we are both agreed that justice is interest of some sort, but you go on to say 'of the stronger'; about this addition I am not so sure, and must therefore consider further.

Proceed.

I will; and first tell me, Do you admit that it is just for subjects to obey their rulers?

I do.

But are the rulers of states absolutely infallible, or are they sometimes liable to err?

To be sure, he replied, they are liable to err.

Then in making their laws they may sometimes make them rightly, and sometimes not?

True.

When they make them rightly, they make them agreeably to their interest; when they are mistaken, contrary to their interest; you admit that?

Yes.

And the laws which they make must be obeyed by their subjects,— and that is what you call justice?

Doubtless.

Then justice, according to your argument, is not only obedience to the interest of the stronger but the reverse?

What is that you are saying? he asked.

I am only repeating what you are saying, I believe. But let us consider: Have we not admitted that the rulers may be mistaken about their own interest in what they command, and also that to obey them is justice? Has not that been admitted?

Yes.

Then you must also have acknowledged justice not to be for the interest of the stronger, when the rulers unintentionally command things to be done which are to their own injury. For if, as you say, justice is the obedience which the subject renders to their commands, in that case, O wisest of men, is there any escape from the conclusion that the weaker are commanded to do, not what is for the interest, but what is for the injury of the stronger?

Nothing can be clearer, Socrates, said Polemarchus.

Yes, said Cleitophon, interposing, if you are allowed to be his witness.

But there is no need of any witness, said Polemarchus, for Thrasymachus himself acknowledges that rulers may sometimes command what is not for their own interest, and that for subjects to obey him is justice.

Yes, Polemarchus,—Thrasymachus said that for subjects to do what was commanded by their rulers is just.

Yes, Cleitophon, but he also said that justice is the interest of the stronger, and, while admitting both these propositions, he further acknowledged that the stronger may command the weaker who are his subjects to do what is not for his own interest; whence follows that justice is the injury quite as much as the interest of the stronger.

But, said Cleitophon, he meant by the interest of the stronger what the stronger thought to be his interest,—this was what the weaker had to do; and this was affirmed by him to be justice.

Those were not his words, rejoined Polemarchus.

Never mind, I replied, if he now says that they are, let us accept his statement. Tell me, Thrasymachus, I said, did you mean by justice what the stronger thought to be in his interest, whether really so or not?

Certainly not, he said. Do you suppose that I call him who is mistaken the stronger at the time when he is mistaken?

Yes, I said, my impression was that you did so, when you admitted that the ruler was not infallible but might be sometimes mistaken.

You argue like an informer, Socrates. Do you mean, for example, that he who is mistaken about the sick is a physician in that he is mistaken? or that he who errs in arithmetic or grammar is an arithmetician or grammarian at the time when he is making the mistake, in respect of the mistake? True, we say that the physician or arithmetician or grammarian has made a mistake, but this is only a way of speaking; for the fact is that neither the grammarian nor any other person of skill ever makes a mistake in so far as he is what his name implies; they none of them err unless their skill fails them, and then they cease to be skilled artists. No artist or sage or ruler errs at the time when he is what his name implies; though he is commonly said to err, and I adopted the common mode of speaking. But to be perfectly accurate, since you are such a lover of accuracy, we should say that the ruler, in so far as he is a ruler, is unerring, and being unerring, always commands that which is for his own interest; and the subject is required to execute his commands; and therefore, as I said at first and now repeat, justice is the interest of the stronger.

Indeed, Thrasymachus, and do I really appear to you to argue like an informer?

Certainly, he replied.

And do you suppose that I ask these questions with any design of injuring you in the argument?

Nay, he replied, 'suppose' is not the word—I know it; but you will be found out, and by sheer force of argument you will never prevail.

I shall not make the attempt, my dear man; but to avoid any misunderstanding occurring between us in future, let me ask, in what sense do you speak of a ruler or stronger whose interest, as you were saying, he being the superior, it is just that the inferior should execute—is he a ruler in the popular or in the strict sense of the term?

In the strictest of all senses, he said. And now cheat and play the informer if you can; I ask no quarter at your hands. But you never will be able, never.

And do you imagine, I said, that I am such a madman as to try and cheat Thrasymachus? I might as well shave a lion.

Why, he said, you made the attempt a minute ago, and you failed.

Enough, I said, of these civilities. It will be better that I should ask you a question: Is the physician, taken in that strict sense of which you are speaking, a healer of the sick or a maker of money? And remember that I am now speaking of the true physician.

A healer of the sick, he replied.

And the pilot—that is to say, the true pilot—is he a captain of sailors or a mere sailor?

A captain of sailors.

The circumstance that he sails in the ship is not to be taken into account; neither is he to be called a sailor; the name pilot by which he is distinguished has nothing to do with sailing, but is significant of his skill and of his authority over the sailors.

Very true, he said.

Now, I said, every art has an interest?

Certainly.

For which the art has to consider and provide?

Yes, that is the aim of art.

And the interest of any art is the perfection of it—this and nothing else?

What do you mean?

I mean what I may illustrate negatively by the example of the body. Suppose you were to ask me whether the body is self-sufficing or has wants, I should reply: Certainly the body has wants; for the body may be ill and require to be cured, and has therefore interests to which the art of medicine ministers; and this is the origin and intention of medicine, as you will acknowledge. Am I not right?

Quite right, he replied.

But is the art of medicine or any other art faulty or deficient in any quality in the same way that the eye may be deficient in sight or the ear fail of hearing, and therefore requires another art to provide for the interests of seeing and hearing—has art in itself, I say, any similar liability to fault or defect, and does every art require another supplementary art to provide for its interests, and that another and another without end? Or have the arts to look only after their own interests? Or have they no need either of themselves or of another?—having no faults or defects, they have no need to correct them, either by the exercise of their own art or of their subject-matter. For every art remains pure and faultless while remaining true—that is to say, while perfect and unimpaired. Take the words in your precise sense, and tell me whether I am not right.

Yes, clearly.

Then medicine does not consider the interest of medicine, but the interest of the body?

True, he said.

Nor does the art of horsemanship consider the interests of the art of horsemanship, but the interests of the horse; neither do any other arts care for themselves, for they have no needs; they care only for that which is the subject of their art?

True, he said.

But surely, Thrasymachus, the arts are the superiors and rulers of their own subjects.

To this he assented with a good deal of reluctance.

Then, I said, no science or art considers or enjoins the interest of the stronger or superior, but only the interest of the subject and weaker.

He made an attempt to contest this proposition also, but finally acquiesced.

Then, I continued, no physician, in so far as he is a physician, considers his own good in what he prescribes, but the good of his patient; for the true physician is also a ruler having the human body as a subject, and is not a mere moneymaker; that has been admitted?

Yes.

And the pilot likewise, in the strict sense of the term, is a ruler of sailors and not a mere sailor?

That has been admitted.

And such a pilot and ruler will provide and prescribe for the interest of the sailor who is under him, and not for his own or the ruler's interest?

He gave a reluctant 'Yes.'

Then, I said, Thrasymachus, there is no one in any rule who, in so far as he is a ruler, considers or enjoins what is for his own interest, but always what is for the interest of his subject or suitable to his art; to that he looks, and that alone he considers in everything which he says and does.

When we had got to this point in the argument, and every one saw that the definition of justice had been completely upset, Thrasymachus, instead of replying to me, said: Tell me, Socrates, have you got a nurse?

Why do you ask such a question, I said, when you ought rather to be answering?

Because she leaves you to snivel, and never wipes your nose: she has not even taught you to know the shepherd from the sheep.

What makes you say that? I replied.

Because you fancy that the shepherd or neatherd fattens or tends the sheep or oxen with a view to their own good and not to the good of himself or his master; and you further imagine that the rulers of states, if they are true rulers, never think of their subjects as sheep, and that they are not studying their own advantage day and night. Oh, no; and so entirely astray are you in your ideas about the just and unjust as not even to know that justice and the just are in reality another's good; that is to say, the interest of the ruler and stronger, and the loss of the subject and servant; and injustice the opposite; for the unjust is lord over the truly simple and just: he is the stronger, and his subjects do what is for his interest, and minister to his happiness, which is very far from being their own. Consider further, most foolish Socrates, that the just is always a loser in comparison with the unjust. First of all, in private contracts: wherever the unjust is the partner of the just you will find that, when the partnership is dissolved, the unjust man has always more and the just less. Secondly, in their dealings with the State: when there is an income-tax, the just man will pay more and the unjust less on the same amount of income; and when there is anything to be received the one gains nothing and the other much. Observe also what happens when they take an office; there is the just man neglecting his affairs and perhaps suffering other losses, and getting nothing out of the public, because he is just; moreover he is hated by his friends and acquaintances for refusing to serve them in unlawful ways. But all this is reversed in the case of the unjust man. I am speaking, as before, of injustice on a large scale in which the advantage of the unjust is more apparent; and my meaning will be most clearly seen if we turn to that highest form of injustice in which the criminal is the happiest of men, and the sufferers or those who refuse to do injustice are the most miserable — that is to say tyranny, which by fraud and force takes away the property of others, not little by little but wholesale; comprehending in one, things sacred as well as profane, private and public; for which acts of wrong, if he were detected perpetrating any one of them singly, he would be punished and incur great disgrace — they who do such wrong in particular cases are called robbers of temples, and man-stealers and burglars and swindlers and thieves. But when a man besides taking away the money of the citizens has made slaves of them, then, instead of these names of reproach, he is termed happy and blessed, not only by the citizens but by all who hear of his having achieved the consummation of injustice. For mankind censure injustice, fearing that they may be the victims of it and not because they shrink from committing it. And thus, as I have shown, Socrates, injustice, when on a sufficient scale, has more strength and freedom and mastery than justice; and, as I said at first, justice is the interest of the stronger, whereas injustice is a man's own profit and interest.

Thrasymachus, when he had thus spoken, having, like a bathman, deluged our ears with his words, had a mind to go away. But the company would not let him; they insisted that he should remain and defend his position; and I myself added my own humble request that he would not leave us. Thrasymachus, I said to him, excellent man, how suggestive are your remarks! And are you going to run away before you have fairly taught or learned whether they are true or not? Is the attempt to determine the way of man's life so small a matter in your eyes — to determine how life may be passed by each one of us to the greatest advantage?

And do I differ from you, he said, as to the importance of the enquiry?

You appear rather, I replied, to have no care or thought about us, Thrasymachus — whether we live better or worse from not knowing what you say you know, is to you a matter of indifference. Prithee, friend, do not keep your knowledge to yourself; we are a large party; and any benefit which you confer upon us will be amply rewarded. For my own part I openly declare that I am not convinced, and that I do not believe injustice to be more gainful than justice, even if uncontrolled and allowed to have free play. For, granting that there may be an unjust man who is able to commit injustice either by fraud or force, still this does not convince me of the superior advantage of injustice, and there may be others who are in the same predicament with myself. Perhaps we may be wrong; if so, you in your wisdom should convince us that we are mistaken in preferring justice to injustice.

And how am I to convince you, he said, if you are not already convinced by what I have just said; what more can I do for you? Would you have me put the proof bodily into your souls?

Heaven forbid! I said; I would only ask you to be consistent; or, if you change, change openly and let there be no deception. For I must remark, Thrasymachus, if you will recall what was previously said, that although you began by defining the true physician in an exact sense, you did not observe a like exactness when speaking of the shepherd; you thought that the shepherd as a shepherd tends the sheep not with a view to their own good, but like a mere diner or banquetter with a view to the pleasures of the table; or, again, as a trader for sale in the market, and not as a shepherd. Yet surely the art of the shepherd is concerned only with the good of his subjects; he has only to provide the best for them, since the perfection of the art is already ensured whenever all the requirements of it are satisfied. And that was what I was saying just now about the ruler. I conceived that the art of the ruler, considered as ruler, whether in a state or in private life, could only regard the good of his flock or subjects; whereas you seem to think that the rulers in states, that is to say, the true rulers, like being in authority.

Think! Nay, I am sure of it.

Then why in the case of lesser offices do men never take them willingly without payment, unless under the idea that they govern for the advantage not of themselves but of others? Let me ask you a question: Are not the several arts different, by reason of their each having a separate function? And, my dear illustrious friend, do say what you think, that we may make a little progress.

Yes, that is the difference, he replied.

And each art gives us a particular good and not merely a general one — medicine, for example, gives us health; navigation, safety at sea, and so on?

Yes, he said.

And the art of payment has the special function of giving pay: but we do not confuse this with other arts, any more than the art of the pilot is to be confused with the art of medicine, because the health of the pilot may be improved by a sea voyage. You would not be inclined to say, would you, that navigation is the art of medicine, at least if we are to adopt your exact use of language?

Certainly not.

Or because a man is in good health when he receives pay you would not say that the art of payment is medicine?

I should say not.

Nor would you say that medicine is the art of receiving pay because a man takes fees when he is engaged in healing?

Certainly not.

And we have admitted, I said, that the good of each art is specially confined to the art?

Yes.

Then, if there be any good which all artists have in common, that is to be attributed to something of which they all have the common use?

True, he replied.

And when the artist is benefited by receiving pay the advantage is gained by an additional use of the art of pay, which is not the art professed by him?

He gave a reluctant assent to this.

Then the pay is not derived by the several artists from their respective arts. But the truth is, that while the art of medicine gives health, and the art of the builder builds a house, another art attends them which is the art of pay. The various arts may be doing their own business and benefiting that over which they preside, but would the artist receive any benefit from his art unless he were paid as well?

I suppose not.

But does he therefore confer no benefit when he works for nothing?

Certainly he confers a benefit.

Then now, Thrasymachus, there is no longer any doubt that neither arts nor governments provide for their own interests; but, as we were before saying, they rule and provide for the interests of their subjects who are the weaker and not the stronger — to their good they attend and not to the good of the superior. And this is the reason, my dear Thrasymachus, why, as I was just now saying, no one is willing to govern; because no one likes to take in hand the reformation of evils which are not his concern without remuneration. For, in the execution of his work, and in giving his orders to another, the true artist does not regard his own interest, but always that of his subjects; and therefore in order that rulers may be willing to rule, they must be paid in one of three modes of payment, money, or honour, or a penalty for refusing.

What do you mean, Socrates? said Glaucon. The first two modes of payment are intelligible enough, but what the penalty is I do not understand, or how a penalty can be a payment.

You mean that you do not understand the nature of this payment which to the best men is the great inducement to rule? Of course you know that ambition and avarice are held to be, as indeed they are, a disgrace?

Very true.

And for this reason, I said, money and honour have no attraction for them; good men do not wish to be openly demanding payment for governing and so to get the name of hirelings, nor by secretly helping themselves out of the public revenues to get the name of thieves. And not being ambitious they do not care about honour. Wherefore necessity must be laid upon them, and they must be induced to serve from the fear of punishment. And this, as I imagine, is the reason why the forwardness to take office, instead of waiting to be compelled, has been deemed dishonourable. Now the worst part of the punishment is that he who refuses to rule is liable to be ruled by one who is worse than himself. And the fear of this, as I conceive, induces the good to take office, not because they would, but because they cannot help — not under the idea that they are going to have any benefit or enjoyment themselves, but as a necessity, and because they are not able to commit the task of ruling to any one who is better than themselves, or indeed as good. For there is reason to think that if a city were composed entirely of good men, then to avoid office would be as much an object of contention as to obtain office is at present; then we should have plain proof that the true ruler is not meant by nature to regard his own interest, but that of his subjects; and every one who knew this would choose rather to receive a benefit from another than to have the trouble of conferring one. So far am I from agreeing with Thrasymachus that justice is the interest of the stronger.

Social Justice

William K. Frankena

The Concept of Social Justice

I. *Preliminaries*

I propose to take social justice, not as a property of individuals and their actions, but as a predicate of societies — particularly such societies as are called nations — and of their acts and institutions. The terms "justice" and "injustice" may also refer to the actions of individuals, but our concern is with their social application — with justice and injustice writ large, to use Plato's phrase — that is, with their manifestation by a society in its dealings with its individual members and subsocieties.

Although social justice will be considered as a property or virtue of national societies, it is not simply a property or virtue of such a society in its *formal*, or legal aspect — what is called the state. That is political justice, a part of social justice. But society does not consist merely of the law or the state: it has also a more *informal* aspect, comprised of its cultural institutions, conventions, moral rules, and moral sanctions. In order for a society to be fully just, it must be just in its informal as well as in its formal aspect.

Niebuhr and many other theologians usually associate justice with love. They assert, on the one hand, that justice is a function or political application of the law of love, and, on the other, that love is the fulfilment of justice. Now, it is true that in a society of love all of the demands of justice would be fulfilled. But, to use medieval terminology, they would be fulfilled *eminently*, not *formally* — that is, they would be over-fulfilled rather than literally fulfilled. Such a society would not be called unjust, of course, but it would hardly be correct to describe it as just. It seems more accurate to contrast love and justice than to link them; even the theologians referred to like to say there is a "tension" between them. I shall, therefore, here adopt the view that social justice cannot be defined in terms of love. This view is represented by Emil Brunner.[1]

> The sphere in which there are just claims, rights, debits and credits, and in which justice is therefore the supreme principle, and the sphere in which the gift of love is supreme, where there are no deserts, where love, without acknowledging any claim, gives all—these two spheres lie as far apart as heaven from hell. . . . If ever we are to get a clear conception of the nature of justice, we must also get a clear idea of it as differentiated from and contrasted with love.

That is a bit strong, as theological pronouncements sometimes are, but it is on the right track. Also it implies what is the last of my preliminary points: that social justice is not the only feature of an ideal society. Societies can be loving, efficient, prosperous, or good, as well as just, but they may well be just without being notably benevolent, efficient, prosperous, or good. Our problem is to define the concept of a just society, not that of an ideal society.

---

[1]*Justice and the Social Order* (London: Lutterworth Press, 1945), pp. 104, 114.

II. *An Ancient Formula for Justice*

To define the concept of social justice we must answer two questions which it is important to distinguish from one another. First, what are the criteria or principles of social justice? In other words, what features make or render a society just or unjust? Second, what are we doing or saying when we say of a society that it is just or unjust? Let us begin with the former. As is stated in an ancient formula, a society is just if it renders to its various members what is due them. But what is it that is due them? To reply that that is due them which is justly theirs or to which they have a right, is to add nothing. For we must still determine what it is that is their due or their right. To specify that their due or their right is what is accorded to them by the laws of the state may, speaking legally, suffice. The laws of the state, however, may be themselves unjust, and if so, it follows that social justice cannot consist wholly in their observance. Since social justice includes moral as well as legal justice, one might say that a society is just if its laws and actions conform to its moral standards. But even the prevailing moral principles of a society may be unjust or oppressive.

It may be said that a man's due or right is that which is his by virtue not merely of the law or of prevailing moral rules, but of valid moral principles, and that a society is just if it accords its members what it is required to accord them by valid moral principles. According to this view, social justice consists in the apportionment of goods and evils, rewards and punishments, jobs and privileges, in accordance with moral standards which can be shown to be valid. In other words, social justice is any system of distribution and retribution which is governed by valid moral principles. This view, if true, still leaves unsolved the very difficult question of which moral principles are valid, but at least simplifies matters by telling us that the answer to this question will provide the definition of justice. The concept of justice, it says, involves no special problems; all we have to do is to find out what is right.

This view is indeed plausible, for what could be more obvious than that a society is just if it treats its members as it ought to? And yet can justice be so simply equated with acting rightly? It does not seem to me that it can. Not all right acts — for example, acts of benevolence, mercy, or returning good for evil — can be properly described as just. Nor are all wrong acts unjust. As R. B. Brandt points out, incest may be wrong but the terms "just" and "unjust" simply do not apply.[2] Not all moral

---

[2]*Ethical Theory* (Englewood Cliffs, N.J.: Prentice-Hall, Inc., 1959), p. 409. Cf. also J. Hospers, *Human Conduct* (New York: Harcourt, Brace and World, Inc., 1961), pp. 416f.

principles are "principles of justice" even if they are valid — for example, the principles J. S. Mill calls generosity and beneficence are not. Justice, then, is acting in accordance with the principles of justice; it is not simply acting in accordance with valid moral principles.

This point may be emphasized in another way. Whether justice can be defined as a process of distributing and retributing in accordance with valid moral principles seems to depend on which moral principles turn out to be valid. Suppose the so-called principle of utility is understood, as some utilitarians seem to understand it, to mean that the right course of action is simply that which produces the greatest quantitative balance of something good (say, pleasure) over something evil (say, pain) regardless of how this quantity is distributed. Suppose, furthermore, that this principle of utility turns out to be the only valid principle of morality. Then distributing and retributing in accordance with valid moral principles will not coincide with what is called justice, though it may yield what is called beneficence. Justice is not simply the greatest possible balance of pleasure over pain or of good over evil. Justice has to do, not so much with the quantity of good or evil, as with the manner in which it is distributed. Two courses of action may produce the same relative quantities of good and evil, yet one course may be just and the other unjust because of the ways in which they apportion these quantities.

Therefore, unless we depart from our ordinary understanding of the term "justice," social justice cannot be defined merely by saying that a society is just which acts, distributes, and so on, in accordance with valid moral principles. If this is correct, however, then right-making characteristics or justifying considerations must be distinguished from just-making or justicizing considerations. Just-making considerations are only one species of right-making considerations. And, theoretically at least, a consideration of one kind may overrule a consideration of the other. In particular, a just-making consideration may be overruled by a right-making one which is not included under justice. As Portia says to Shylock,

> . . . earthly power doth then show likest God's
> When mercy seasons justice.

Furthermore, an inequality may sometimes be justified by its utility; the action or policy that promotes the inequality would then be right — but it might not be, strictly speaking, just.

It is true, as Brandt has pointed out,[3] that in such a case we should not call the action or policy unjust — that we hesitate to speak of some-

---

[3]*Op. cit.*, pp. 409f. But cf. Hospers, *op. cit.*, pp. 417, 421f; G. Vlastos, "Justice," *Revue internationale de philosophie*, 41 (1957), p. 17.

thing as unjust if we cannot also correctly speak of it as wrong. And this seems to imply that justice can be defined in terms of right-dealing after all. The answer may perhaps lie in an interesting passage in Mill. He writes that in order to save a life, "it may not only be allowable, but a duty" to do something which is contrary to the principles of justice — for example, "to steal or take by force the necessary food or medicine, or to kidnap and compel to officiate the only qualified medical practitioner." He continues:[4]

> In such cases, as we do not call anything justice which is not a virtue, we usually say, not that justice must give way to some other moral principle, but that what is just in ordinary cases is, by reason of that other principle, not just in the particular case. By this useful accommodation of language, the character of indefeasibility attributed to justice is kept up, and we are saved from the necessity of maintaining that there can be laudable injustice.

The point is that "just" and "unjust" seem to play a double role. On the one hand, they refer to certain sorts of right-making considerations as against others; on the other hand, they have much the same force as do the more general terms "right" and "wrong," so much so that one can hardly conjoin "just" and "wrong," or "right" and "unjust." It is the first of these roles which is especially important in defining the criteria of social justice, and which is neglected by the view we have been discussing. . . .

V. *Equality and Justice*

Justice, whether social or not, seems to have at its center the notion of an allotment of something to persons — duties, goods, offices, opportunities, penalties, punishments, privileges, roles, status, and so on. Moreover, at least in the case of distributive justice, it seems centrally to involve the notion of *comparative* allotment. In the paradigm case, two things, A and B, are being allotted to two individuals, C and D, A to C and B to D. Whether justice is done depends on how A's being given to C compares with B's being given to D. In this sense Aristotle was right in saying

---

[4]All references to Mill are to *Utilitarianism*. Ch. V. Here see, e.g., O. Piest's ed. (New York: Liberal Arts Press, 1949), pp. 68f.

that justice involves a proportion in which A is to B as C is to D. It is a requirement both of reason and of common thinking about justice that similar cases be treated similarly. This means that if C and D are similar, then A and B must be similar. But, if this is so, then it would appear that justice also demands that if C and D are dissimilar, then A and B must be dissimilar. That is to say, justice is comparative.

Actually, of course, justice does not require that all similarities and dissimiliarities be respected in this way. We do not regard it as unjust to treat similar blocks of wood dissimilarly or dissimilar ones similarly: we are concerned only about human beings (and possibly animals). Even in the case of human beings, however, justice does not call for similar treatment of every similarity or for dissimilar treatment of every dissimilarity. We do not think it is necessarily unjust, even if other things are equal, to deal similarly with people of different colors or dissimilarly with people of the same color. In fact, the historical quest for social justice has consisted largely of attempts to eliminate certain dissimilarities as bases for difference of treatment and certain similarities as bases for sameness of treatment. That is, it seems to be part of the concept of justice that not all similarities justify (or justicize) similar treatment or all differences different treatment. The point of the quest for social justice has not been merely that similarities and differences in people have too often been arbitrarily ignored; it has been mainly that the wrong similarities and differences have been taken as a basis for action. Similarities and differences should form the basis for action if it is to be just, but not all of them are relevant. The question is "Which of them are just- or unjust-making? Which of them are relevant? And is there a relation between them?"

It is important to remember that not all morally justifying considerations are just-making or justicizing. "Relevant" considerations in matters of justice cannot therefore be identified with "moral" ones, as D. D. Raphael does.[5] And it will not do to say, as Brandt does, that justice consists in treating people equally except as unequal treatment is justified by *moral* considerations of substantial weight in the circumstances.[6] If I am right, this description should be revised: justice is treating persons equally, except as unequal treatment is required by *just-making* considerations (i.e., by principles of *justice*, not merely *moral* principles) of substantial weight in the circumstances. With this emendation, the description seems to me to be correct, both in theory and as a reflection of the ordi-

[5]"Equality and Equity," *Philosophy*, XXI (1946), p. 5.
[6]*Op. cit.*, p. 410.

nary notion of justice. The only question then is whether there are any principles of *justice* which overrule the principle of equality, what they are, and whether they are such as to render the principle of equality otiose or not.

So far treating people equally has been equated with treating them similarly or in the same way. But suppose that society is alloting musical instruments to C and D, and that C prefers a banjo and D a guitar. If society gives C a banjo and D a guitar it is treating them *differently* yet *equally*. If justice is equal treatment of all men, then it is treatment which is equal in this sense and not simply identical. Surely neither morality nor justice, however stuffy and universalizing they may be in the eyes of Nietzsche and the existentialists, can require such monotony as identical treatment would involve. It is hard to believe that even the most egalitarian theory of justice calls for complete uniformity and not merely for substantial equality. I shall, therefore, speak in terms of equality, except when it does not matter or when it is necessary to speak in terms of similarity of treatment.

What considerations, and especially what similarities and dissimilarities in people, are just- (or unjust-) making? It is agreed that justice prescribes equals to equals and unequals to unequals, but what are the relevant respects in which people must be equal or unequal for treatment of them to be just or unjust? I have anticipated an at least partially egalitarian answer to this question, but the classical reply of Plato, Aristotle, and their many followers was different. According to them, social justice does not involve any kind of equal allotment to all men. Justice is not linked with any quality in which men are all necessarily similar or which they all share by virtue of being men. It is tied to some property which men may or may not have, and which, in fact, they have in varying amounts or degrees or not at all. Justice simply is the apportionment of what is to be apportioned in accordance with the amount or degree in which the recipients possess some required feature — personal ability, desert, merit, rank, or wealth.

This position has lately been maintained by Sir David Ross and, inconsistently, I think, by Brunner.[7] According to W. B. Gallie, it is characteristic of "liberal" as against "socialist" morality.[8] It is, however, not necessarily inegalitarian in substance; how inegalitarian it turns out to

---

[7]W. D. Ross, *The Right and the Good* (Oxford: The Clarendon Press, 1930), pp. 26f.; Brunner, *op. cit.*, pp. 29ff.

[8]"Liberal Morality and Socialist Morality," *Philosophy, Politics and Society,* ed. Peter Laslett (Oxford: Basil Blackwell, 1956), p. 123.

be depends on how unequal it finds men to be in the respect which it takes as basic. If it found them to be equal in this respect it would in practice have to be egalitarian, but, of course, it would not be taking equality of treatment for all men, or indeed any pair of men, as a basic requirement of justice. In this respect it may represent the classical concept of social justice, but, as Gallie and Vlastos have pointed out,[9] it hardly does justice to the modern concept in which, as Mill's list[10] shows, equality of treatment (not merely the equal treatment of equals, but the equal treatment of all human beings as such) is one of the basic principles of justice. It is, however, true, as Gallie, Vlastos, and Mill recognize, that the modern concept of social justice is complex and includes a meritarian as well as an egalitarian element. It recognizes the demand to respect differences between persons as well as the demand to respect personality as such.[11]

Views which accept the principle of equality as a basic and at least *prima facie* requirement of justice may, of course, take less complex forms. It might be held, for example, that justice calls for a strict equality in the treatment of C and D, no matter who C and D are, and that no inequality is ever justified. Or it might be maintained that, although inequalities are sometimes justified and right, they are never just. Every departure from complete equality would then be regarded as beyond the pale of justice, though not beyond that of the morally right or obligatory. Such theories are possible and have an apparent simplicity, but they limit the usual scope of justice. Not every departure from equality is ordinarily regarded as a departure from justice, let alone from morality. For one thing, such departures are allowed on the ground of differences in ability, merit, or desert. Certain other departures from a direct or simple equality, called for by differences in need, or involved in carrying out agreements, covenants, contracts, and promises, are also recognized as just, and not merely as justified or right.

Much more reasonable, as well as closer to ordinary thinking, is the conception of social justice as the equal treatment of all persons, except as inequality is required by relevant — that is, just-making —

---

[9]Gallie, *op. cit.*, pp. 122, 129; Vastos, *op. cit.*, p. 9.

[10]I.e. his list of what he calls "the various modes of action and arrangements of human affairs which are classed, by universal or widely spread opinion, as just or as unjust." Cf. *Utilitarianism*, Ch. V, pp. 47ff.—ED.

[11]This complexity may, perhaps have the following justification. The formal rule of reason which we took to be central to justice, insofar as it is comparative, has two parts: to treat similars similarly and to treat dissimilars dissimilarly. The egalitarian principle may be regarded as a way of specifying the first part, and the meritarian as a way of specifying the second.

considerations or principles. This is the view which I accepted as an emendation of Brandt's. It takes equality of treatment to be a basic *prima facie* requirement of justice, but allows that it may on occasion be overruled by other principles of justice (or by some other kind of moral principle). This view, however, is not necessarily very egalitarian. It does hold that all men are to be treated equally and that inequalities must be justified. But it also allows that inequalities may be justified, and everything depends on the ease and the kinds of considerations by which they may be justified. In fact, it tells us very little until it gives us answers to the following questions: What is meant by equal or similar treatment? What considerations are relevant to the justification of inequalities or dissimilarities? Are there are any respects in which men are actually to be treated equally or similarly, or is this requirement always overruled by other considerations? Are there not always differences in personality, need, desert, merit, which completely nullify the *prima facie* rule of equality?

VI. *Other Principles of Justice and Their Relation to Equality*

The concept of social justice which prevails in our culture has now been partly defined. According to this concept, a society is without justice insofar as it is without rules (statutes or precedents, written or unwritten rules, legal and moral rules); it must, in both its formal and informal aspects, treat similar cases similarly. It must also treat human beings equally, or it must show why—a requirement which governs its rules as well as its acts and institutions. That is, the primary similarity to be respected is that which all men, as such, have. But a just society must also respect some though not all differences. In particular it must respect differences in capacities and needs, and in contribution, desert, or merit. Such differences may often make it just to treat people unequally in certain respects, thus at least qualifying the *prima facie* requirements of equality. But many other differences—for example, differences in blood and color—are not just-making. The recognition of capacity and need and the recognition of contribution and desert are not, however, the only principles of justice which may qualify the principle of equality. There is also the principle that agreements should be kept.

Are there any other principles of social justice besides the principle of equality, that of recognizing capacity and need, and that of keeping agreements? I have argued that the principle of beneficence or utility is not a principle of justice, though it is a moral principle. That is, a society is not unjust if it is not by its own direct action bringing about the greatest possible balance of good over evil. It is still, however, an old and familiar view (which I accept) that it is unjust for society or the state to injure a citizen, to withhold a good from him, or to interfere with his liberty (except to prevent him from committing a crime, to punish him for committing one, or to procure the money and other means of carrying out its just functions), and that this is unjust even if society or the state deals similarly with all of its citizens. It seems to me also that a society is unjust if, by its actions, laws, and mores, it unnecessarily impoverishes the lives of its members materially, aesthetically, or otherwise, by holding them to a level below that which some members at least might well attain by their own efforts. If such views are correct, we must add to the principles of social justice those of non-injury, non-interference, and non-impoverishment.

These additions make it harder to discover what it is, if anything, that relates these principles of justice. It has sometimes been argued, however, that they are linked in that they all involve and ultimately depend on a recognition of the equality or equal intrinsic value of every human personality—or at least that they do so insofar as they are principles of justice. If this could be established, the area of justice could then be described as the area of moral reasoning in which the final appeal is to the ideal of the equality of all men. There is much to be said for this suggestion. Raphael, for instance, has very plausibly contended that differences in treatment on grounds of special need may be construed as attempts to restore inequalities due to natural or extraneous causes.[12] This would account for the justice of giving special attention to people — for example, those who are disabled or mentally backward—who are, for no fault of their own, at a disadvantage with respect to others.

More generally, it seems as if much, if not all, of the justice of recognizing differences in capacity, need, and so on, might be accounted for in terms of the ideal of equality, as follows. One of the chief considerations which not only justifies but also establishes as *just* differences in the treatment of human bengs is the fact that the good life (not in the sense of the morally good life but in the sense, roughly, of the happy life) and its conditions are not the same for all, due to their differences in needs and potentialities. I am inclined to think that it is this fact, rather than

---

[12]*Op. cit.,* p. 9.

that of differences in ability, merit, and the like, which primarily justifies differences in the handling of individuals. It is what justifies, for example, giving *C* a banjo, *D* a guitar, and *E* a skindiving outfit. Although *C, D,* and *E* are treated differently, they are not dealt with unequally, since their differing needs and capacities so far as these relate to the good life are equally considered and equally well cared for. The ideal of equality itself may require certain differences of treatment, including for example, differences in education and training. The principle involved in this claim is independent of the principle of recognizing differences in merit, but also of the principle of utility. For the differences in treatment involved are not justified simply by arguing that they are conducive to the general good life (though they may also be justified in this way), but by arguing that they are required for the good lives of the individuals concerned. It is not as if one must first look to see how the general good is best subserved and only then can tell what treatment of individuals is just. Justice entails the presence of equal *prima facie* rights prior to any consideration of *general* utility.

Yet inequalities and differences in treatment are often said to be justified by their general utility. I do not deny this, but I do doubt that they can be shown to be *just* merely by an appeal to general utility. They can, however, often be shown to be just by an argument which is easily confused with that from the principle of utility: that initial inequalities in the distribution of offices, rewards, and so on, are required for the promotion of equality in the long run. In fact, much of what still needs to be done consists not so much of building up the biggest possible balance of welfare over illfare as in promoting the conditions for its equal distribution. It therefore seems plausible that much, if not all, of the justification of differences of function, as well as the recognition of ability, contribution, merit, and need—at least insofar as these may be denominated "just"—is based on such an indirect appeal to the ideal of equality. It also seems plausible that the introduction of incentives into economic and social systems, the redistribution of wealth through progressive taxation, and the reformation of the law may be *justicized*, if at all, only by such a line of argument, even if they may also be *justified* on other grounds.

If the duty to keep faith is assumed to be a requirement of justice, can it be justified in terms of the principle of equality? It does seem as if the practice of keeping promises and fulfilling contracts may be at least partly justified—and justicized—by such an indirect appeal to the promotion of equality. But perhaps the breaking of a promise can also be called unjust on the ground that it entails a direct violation of equality.

The man who makes a promise and then breaks it, presumably for his own interest, is not only violating a useful practice but also favoring his good life over that of the others involved in the practice—in short, he is not treating persons as equals.

Retributive justice—for example, punishment—must also be considered. Aristotle and others have brought it under the principle of equality between the offender and the injured which had been disturbed. It might also be contended that, having violated the principle of equality, the criminal may justly be regarded as having forfeited his claim to a good life on equal terms with others, and even his claim not to be pained. Critics of the retributive theory of punishment might prefer to argue that punishment is made just, and perhaps also obligatory, by the fact that it tends to promote the most equality in the long run by preventing people from infringing on the claims of others. This is a non-utilitarian line of reasoning which looks not to the past, but to the future—not to future welfare, but to future equality.

There is, then, a good deal to be said for the suggestion that the principles of justice are distinguished from other principles of morality by being governed by the ideal of equality. Certainly the *prima facie* duty of treating people as equals is not rendered otiose because it so often permits inequalities of one sort of another. Nevertheless, G. F. Hourani may not be wholly right when he says that justice is equality "evident or disguised."[13] The claims of special desert may remain at least partially recalcitrant to such an interpretation. But even if Raphael's conclusion that the unequal treatment called for by special desert is a "real deviation from equality,"[14] is false, there still remain the principles of non-injury, non-interference, and non-punishment. Although the rule that a just society must provide a certain minimum level of welfare for everyone may be construed as an offshoot of the rule of equality, violations of these negative principles are unjust but do not necessarily entail any inequality of treatment, direct or indirect. If a ruler were to boil his subjects in oil, jumping in afterward himself, it would be an injustice, but there would be no inequality of treatment.

It might be argued that the injustice involved depends on an inequality after all because the ruler did not permit his subjects to participate in the decision to commit national suicide. And perhaps it might be further argued that whenever society or the state injures, interferes, or impoverishes unjustly, the injustice consists in the fact that it does not

---

[13]*Ethical Value* (Ann Arbor: University of Michigan Press, 1955), p. 86.
[14]*Op. cit.,* p. 10.

provide the individuals victimized an equal share in the process of deci-sion-making. Then, excepting possibly the principle of recognizing desert, the principles of justice might all be claimed to rest, directly or indirectly, on the ideal of equality. I should myself welcome this conclusion, but it seems that a so-called primitive society might be so bound by tradition that although all its members had a substantially equal voice in all deci-sions its rules might nevertheless be unnecessarily restrictive or injurious, and therefore unjust.

If not all of these principles can be subsumed under equality, it might be argued that the recalcitrant ones should not be regarded as principles of justice, however valid they may be as moral principles. This strikes me as a rather drastic bit of conceptual legislation. Though such a departure from our ordinary understanding of social justice may be desirable in the interests of neatness, and not objectionable in principle, I am inclined to think that there is a less radical alternative.

VII. *Basic Theory of Justice*

What we need at this point is a plausible line of thought that will explain both the role of equality in the concept of justice and those principles of justice which are not derivable from the ideal of equality. With the rule of non-interference with liberty particularly in mind, H. L. A. Hart has maintained that the sphere of justice and rights coincides not with that of equality, but with that in which the final appeal is to the claim of equal liberty for all.[15] Using a more positive conception of liberty, Raphael contends similarly that the essential points of justice and liberty are the same. The claims of desert and equality are both subsumed under the one concept of justice, he thinks, because both are concerned with protecting the interests of the individual, and so their concern is basically that of liberty.[16] Following a somewhat different line of thought, S. M. Brown argues that justice requires of society only that it provide institutions protecting the moral interests, persons, and estates of its members.[17] By restating what I take to be a familiar position, I shall not so much question as supplement these conclusions. In doing so I propose to argue that the principles of the family of justice, insofar as they go beyond the require-ments of equality, direct or indirect, go beyond them only because they

---

[15]"Are There Any Natural Rights?" *Philosophical Review,* LXIV (1955), pp. 177ff.

[16]*Moral Judgment* (London: Allen & Unwin Ltd., 1955), pp. 67, 94.

[17]"Inalienable Rights," *Philosophical Review,* LXIV (1955) pp. 192-211.

express a certain limited concern for the good lives of individual persons as such.

In opposition to the classical meritarian view of social justice, I accepted as part of my own view the principle that all men are to be treated as equals, not because they are equal in any respect but simply because they are human. They are human because they have emotions and desires, and are able to think, and hence are capable of enjoying a good life in a sense in which other animals are not. They are human because their lives may be "significant" in the manner which William James made so graphic in his essays "On a Certain Blindness in Human Beings" and "What Makes a Life Significant?":

> Whenever a process of life communicates an eagerness to him who lives it, there the life becomes genuinely significant. Sometimes the eagerness is more knit up with the motor activities, sometimes with the perceptions, sometimes with the imagination, sometimes with reflective thought. But, wherever it is found . . . there *is* importance in the only real and positive sense in which importance ever anywhere can be.[18]

By the good life is meant not so much the morally good life as the happy or satisfactory life. As I see it, it is the fact that all men are similarly capable of enjoying a good life in this sense that justifies the *prima facie* requirement that they be treated as equals. To quote James again, "The practical consequence of such a philosophy [as is expressed in the passage just cited] is the well-known democratic respect for the sacredness of individuality. . . ."[19] It seems plausible to claim, however, that this insight (which Royce calls "moral" and James "religious") into the "sacredness" of human beings justifies not only their equal treatment but also a real, even if limited, concern for the goodness of their lives. It justifies treating them not only as equals but also, at least in certain ways, as ends.

A just society, then, is one which respects the good lives of its members and respects them equally. A just society must therefore promote equality; it may ignore certain differences and similarities but must consider others; and it must avoid unnecessary injury, interference, or impoverishment — all without reference to beneficence or general utility. The demand for equality is built into the very concept of justice. The just society, then, must consider and protect the good life of each man equally with that of any other, no matter how different these men may be,

---

[18]*Talks to Teachers on Psychology, and to Students on Some of Life's Ideals* (New York: Holt, Rinehart, and Winston, Inc., 1899), pp. 264f.

[19]*Ibid.,* pp. vf.

and so it must allow them equal consideration, equal opportunity, and equality before the law. The equal concern for the good lives of its members also requires society to treat them differently, for no matter how much one believes in a common human nature, individual needs and capacities differ, and what constitutes the good life for one individual may not do so for another. It is the society's very concern for the good lives of its members that determines which differences and which similarities it must respect (and which are relevant to justice). A society need not respect those differences which have only an *ad hoc* bearing or none at all, on the good lives of their possessors — for example, color of skin. But it must respect differences like preferring one religion to another, which do have a bearing on the individual good life.

None of this implies that society may impose or presuppose any fixed conception of the good life. As James says, "The pretension to dogmatize about [this] is the root of most human injustices and cruelties. . . ."[20] Nor does it mean that society must seek to make the life of one man as good as that of any other, for men may well be so different that the best life of which one is capable is not as good as that of which another is capable. The good lives open to men may not be equally good— even if they are called incommensurable they may still not be equally good. Nevertheless, they must be equally respected and protected. That is why I reject Rashdall's formula for justice, that "every man's good [is] to count as equal to the *like good* of every other man,"[21] for this suggests that two people are to be treated as equals only if they are capable of equally good lives. It is more accurate, in my opinion, to say that the just society must insofar as possible make *the same relative contribution* to the good life of every individual — except, of course, in cases of reward and punishment, and provided that a certain minimum standard has been achieved by all. This is what I understand as the recognition of equal intrinsic value of individual human beings.

But the regard which the just society must have for the good lives of its members involves more than equal treatment. If I am right, it does not involve direct action on the part of society to promote the good life of its members, whether this be conceived of as pleasure, happiness, self-realization, or some indefinable quality. Such direct action is beneficence, not justice. Nevertheless, a just society must be concerned for the goodness of its members' lives, and not merely for their equality, though in a more limited way than beneficence implies. A just society must protect each member from being injured or interfered with by

---

[20]*Ibid.*, p. 265.

[21]H. Rashdall, *The Theory of Good and Evil* (London: Oxford University Press, 1907), I, p. 240.

others, and it must not, by omission or commission, itself inflict evil upon any of them, deprive them of goods which they might otherwise gain by their own efforts, or restrict their liberty — except so far as is necessary for their protection or the achievement of equality. Although we are speaking of the *just* society, and not of the *good* society, its concern with the goodness of the lives of its members need not be considered merely negative and protective. It seems reasonable to assign to the just society a more positive interest (though one which falls short of beneficence) by saying that it must, so far as possible, provide equally the conditions under which its members can by their own efforts (alone or in voluntary associations) achieve the best lives of which they are capable. This means that the society must at least maintain some minimum standard of living, education, and security for all its members.

Social justice then does not, as Ross thinks, consist *simply* in the apportionment of happiness or good life in accordance with the recipient's degree of moral goodness. In fact, society must for the most part allow virtue to be its own reward, else it is not virtue.[22] In the poem, "Easter," Arthur Clough complains that the world

> . . . visits still
> With equalest apportionment of ill
> Both good and bad alike, and brings to one same dust
> The just and the unjust.

Society, however, must be wary of taking on the whole enterprise of cosmic or poetic justice.[23] It must honor first of all the so-called intrinsic dignity of man, which is not the same as his moral worth. Still, it is difficult to deny that the recognition of differences in desert, merit, and service, in the form of reward and punishment and unequal apportionment, is one of the principles of social justice. It remains, therefore, to see how this principle — insofar as it is a requirement of justice and not merely of utility — can be provided for by our basic theory. It has already been suggested that recognition of this principle is required for the promotion of equality in the long run. It seems to be required also for protection, one of the duties of a just society. Punishments have often been plausibly justicized on this ground, but so may rewards and privileges of various kinds. The good life of one member of society is not independent of what other members do not do. Certain forms of reward may in themselves show respect for individual freedom and goodness of life, by protecting one member against the acts or failures to act on the

---

[22]Cf. Rashdall, *op. cit.*, pp. 256ff.
[23]Cf. Hospers, *op. cit.*, pp. 462ff.

part of others, or by guaranteeing that individual talents shall not be lost or squandered.

More might be said on this point, but it is clear that a recognition of desert, contribution, or merit can be justicized without appealing either to an ultimate principle of retribution or to the principle of beneficence. This theory of social justice lies between those of the classical liberals and those of the more extreme welfare theorists. The one group includes too little under justice, the other too much. Both tend to equate just-making or justicizing considerations with right-making or justifying ones, but classical liberals greatly restrict the range of *justified* social action while the welfare theorists unduly extend that of *justicized* social action. I hold that justice includes a more positive concern for equality and goodness of life than the classical liberals allow, and that the area of right social action may extend even further in a welfare direction. I am not so much concerned to deny the conclusions the welfare theorists draw about what society and the state may or should do — I mean to leave this an open question — as to argue that they cannot plausibly defend them all as requirements of justice.

A just society is, strictly speaking, not simply a loving one. It must in its actions and institutions fulfil certain formal requirements dictated by reason rather than love; it must be rule-governed in the sense that similars are treated similarly and dissimilars dissimilarly. But only certain similarities and differences are relevant: those relating to the good life, merit, and so on. To a considerable extent, the recognition of these differences and similarities is required by the very ideal of equality, which is part of the concept of justice. But there are other principles of justice as well. Social justice is the equal (though not always similar) treatment of all persons, at least in the long run. This equal treatment must be qualified in the light of certain principles: the recognition of contribution and desert, the keeping of agreements, non-injury, non-interference, non-impoverishment, protection, and perhaps the provision and improvement of opportunity. These principles seem to go beyond the requirements of equality, even in the long run — but, insofar as they are principles of justice, they may be roughly unified under a conception of social justice as involving a somewhat vaguely defined but still limited concern for the goodness of people's lives, as well as for their equality. This double concern is often referred to as respect for the intrinsic dignity or value of the human individual. This is not the position of the extreme egalitarian but it is essentially egalitarian in spirit; in any case it is not the position of the meritarian, although it does seek to accommodate his principles.

A Case of Injustice

Supreme Court of the United States

Northwestern Shoshone Indians Versus United States

Mr. Justice REED delivered the opinion of the Court:

The Northwestern Bands of Shoshone Indians, petitioners here, seek to recover from the United States damages estimated at fifteen million dollars for the taking of some fifteen million acres of the lands held by these Indians by aboriginal or immemorial title. This title was alleged by the Indians to have been recognized by the United States by the treaty between the petitioners and the United States at Box Elder, Utah Territory, July 30, 1863.

From *Northwestern Bands of Shoshone Indians v. United States,* Supreme Court of the United States (1944). 324 U.S. 335, 89 L.Ed. 985, 65 Sup. Ct. 690. Footnotes by the Court and most case and statutory citations are omitted.

The suit was begun in the Court of Claims against the United States by the bands pursuant to a special jurisdictional act of Congress of February 28, 1929, 45 Stat. 1407, c 377. The Act consented to suit and recovery against the United States upon the following conditions:

"That jurisdiction be, and hereby is, conferred upon the Court of Claims, notwithstanding lapse of time or statutes of limitations, to hear, adjudicate, and render judgment in any and all claims which the northwestern bands of Shoshone Indians may have against the United States arising under or growing out of the treaty of July 2, 1863 . . . and any subsequent treaty, Act of Congress, or Executive order, which claims have not heretofore been determined and adjudicated on their merits by the Court of Claims or the Supreme Court of the United States." . . .

The suit is based upon the unlawful taking after the alleged recognition of the Indian title by the Box Elder treaty. We do not read the petition as claiming any right to compensation for the extinguishment of an Indian aboriginal title, which was unrecongized or unacknowledged by the Box Elder treaty. Under the words of the jurisdictional act, "arising under or growing out of the treaty," suit is authorized only for rights acknowledged by the treaty. The act does not authorize a suit for loss of Indian tribal rights arising from any other acts of the United States. If the treaty recognized the aboriginal or Indian title, the authority to sue for the taking under the jurisdictional act is not questioned. . . .

The Court of Claims determined that the claim for the taking of land sued upon by petitioners did not grow out of the Box Elder treaty. Certiorari was sought and granted to determine whether there was "recognition" or "acknowledgment" of the Indian title by this treaty through the language employed or by the act of entering into a treaty with the Indians as to the use by the United States of lands which were claimed by the petitioners.

Even where a reservation is created for the maintenance of Indians, their right amounts to nothing more than a treaty right of occupancy. . . . Prior to the creation of any such area, formally acknowledged by the United States as subject to such right of Indian occupancy, a certain nation, tribe or band of Indians may have claimed the right because of immemorial occupancy to roam certain territory to the exclusion of any other Indians and in contradistinction to the custom of the early nomads to wander at will in the search for food. . . . This claim has come to be known as Indian title and is likewise often spoken of as the right of occupancy. To distinguish from a recognized right of occupancy, we shall refer to the aboriginal usage without definite recognition of the right by the United States as Indian title.

Since Johnson v. M'Intosh, 8 Wheat. (US) 543, 5 L.ed 681, decided in 1823, gave rationalization to the appropriation of Indian lands by the white man's government,[1] the extinguishment of Indian title by that sovereignty has proceeded, as a political matter, without any admitted legal responsibility in the sovereign to compensate the Indian for his loss. Exclusive title to the lands passed to the white discoverers, subject to the Indian title with power in the white sovereign alone to extinguish that right by "purchase or conquest." 8 Wheat. at 574, 585-588, 5 L. ed 688, 691, 692. The whites enforced their claims by the sword and occupied the lands as the Indians abondoned them. Congress has authorized suits

---

[1]The issue in Johnson v. M'Intosh was whether the Courts of the United States could recognize the right of certain Indian Chiefs to give title to land, originally occupied and possessed by their people, to private individuals. In denying the Indians' right, Chief Justice John Marshall upheld the principle that discovery followed by conquest gives the conqueror exclusive title. This had been the universally acknowledged principle of the various Europeans who first acquired territory in America, and by the adoption of the principle, the government of this country, following the American Revolution, acquired exclusive title to all Indian lands. As he put it:

"The power now possessed by the government of the United States to grant lands, resided, while we were colonies, in the crown, or its grantees. The validity of the titles given by either has never been questioned in our courts. It has been exercised uniformly over territory in possession of Indians. The existence of this power must negative the existence of any right which may conflict with, and control it. An absolute title to lands cannot exist, at the same time, in different persons, or in different governments." (587-88)

"Conquest gives a title which the courts of the conqueror cannot deny, whatever the private and speculative opinions of individuals may be, respecting the original justice of the claim which has been successfully asserted. The British government, which was then our government, and whose rights have passed to the United States, asserted a title to all the lands occupied by Indians within the chartered limits of the British colonies. It asserted also a limited sovereignty over them, and the exclusive right of extinguishing the title which occupany gave to them. These claims have been maintained and established as far west as the river Mississippi, by the sword. The title to a vast portion of the lands we now hold, originates in them. It is not for the courts of this country to question the validity of this title, or to sustain one which is incompatible with it." (588-89)

Marshall prefaces his opinion with the revealing comment: "It will be necessary, in pursuing this inquiry, to examine, not singly those principles of abstract justice, which the Creator of all things has impressed on the mind of his creature man, and which are admitted to regulate, in a great degree, the rights of civilized nations, whose perfect independence is acknowledged; but those principles also which our own government has adopted in the particular case, and given us as the rule for our decision." (572)

The specific rule derived from this case, and repeatedly cited in subsequent cases, is the following: "Indian occupation of land without government recognition of ownership creates no rights against the taking of lands or extinction of Indian title by the United States." Such taking is therefore not compensable under the Fifth Amendment which states that no private property "shall be taken for public use, without just compensation."—ED.

on the original Indian title but no recovery has as yet been obtained on that ground. . . .

The decisive question in this case is whether it was intended by the Northwestern Shoshone or Box Elder Treaty of July 30, 1863, to recognize or acknowledge by implication the Indian title to the lands mentioned in that treaty. . . . From such recognition or acknowledgement by this treaty would flow a right of occupancy which would be compensable under the jurisdictional act.

Full findings of fact appear with the opinion below in Northwestern Bands of Shoshone Indians v. United States, 95 Ct Cl(F) 642. These findings show that petitioners here, the Northwestern bands, were at the time of the treaty a part of the Shoshone tribe, a nomadic Indian nation of less than ten thousand people which roamed over eighty million acres of prairie, forest and mountain in the present states of Wyoming, Colorado, Utah, Idaho and Nevada. The group with which we are concerned was comprised of some fifteen or eighteen hundred persons and claimed, by the treaty, Indian title to some ten million acres and now claim compensation for over six million additional acres.

After the discovery of gold in California, white travelers and settlers began to traverse and people the Shoshone domain with the result that the Indians' game disappeared from their hunting grounds. Racial relations degenerated to the point that Indian depredations interfered with travel and settlement, the overland mails and the new telegraph lines. By the time of the outbreak of the Civil War the Commissioner of Indian Affairs, the agents and superintendents of the Shoshone territory were aware of the misery of the Shoshones, the dangers to the emigrant trains and need for peace to enable travel and settlement in the area. Word had reached the Commissioner from his superintendent in Utah that the Shoshones were inclined toward accepting support on limited reservations and were willing in return to cede their other lands to the United States.

On July 5, 1862, . . . Congress appropriated $20,000 for defraying the expenses of negotiating a treaty with the Shoshones. The appropriation followed a letter from the Secretary of the Interior to the chairman of the House Committee on Indian Affairs expressing the view that the lands owned by the Indians of Utah were largely unfit for cultivation and that it was "not probable that any considerable portion of them will be required for settlement for many years." A special commission was promptly appointed and instructed that it was not expected that the proposed treaty would extinguish Indian title to the lands but only secure freedom from molestation for the routes of travel and "also a definite acknowledgement as well of the boundaries of the entire country they claim as of the limits within which they will confine themselves, which limits it is hardly necessary to state should be as remote from said routes as practicable."

As the distances made it impracticable to gather the Shoshone Nation into one council for treaty purposes, the commissioners made five treaties in an endeavor to clear up the difficulties in the Shoshone country. . . . It is sufficient here to say that by the treaties the Indians agreed not to molest travelers, stage coaches, telegraph lines or projected railroads. . . .

Petitioners' treaty, the Northwestern Shoshone Treaty, needs to be set out in full for ready examination. It reads as follows:

"Articles of agreement made at Box Elder, in Utah Territory, this thirtieth day of July, A. D., eighteen hundred and sixty-three, by and between the United States of America, represented by Brigadier-General P. Edward Connor, commanding the military district of Utah, and James Duane Doty, commissioner, and the northwestern bands of the Shoshonee Indians, represented by their chiefs and warriors:

"ARTICLE I. It is agreed that friendly and amicable relations shall be reestablished between the bands of the Shoshonee Nation, parties hereto, and the United States, and it is declared that a firm and perpetual peace shall be henceforth maintained between the said bands and the United States.

"ARTICLE II. The treaty concluded at Fort Bridger on the 2nd day of July, 1863, between the United States and the Shoshonee Nation, being read and fully interpreted and explained to the said chiefs and warriors, they do hereby give their full and free assent to all of the provisions of said treaty, and the same are hereby adopted as a part of this agreement, and the same shall be binding upon the parties hereto.

"ARTICLE III. In consideration of the stipulations in the preceding articles, the United States agree to increase the annuity to the Shoshonee nation five thousand dollars, to be paid in the manner provided in said treaty. And the said northwestern bands hereby acknowledge to have received of the United States, at the signing of these articles, provisions and goods to the amount of two thousand dollars, to relieve their immediate necessities, the said bands having been reduced by the war to a state of utter destitution.

"ARTICLE IV. The country claimed by Pokatello, for himself and his people, is bounded on the west by Raft River and on the east by the Porteneuf Mountains." 13 Stat. 663.

Before it or the other treaties were ratified by the Senate an additional article was added to each and, except for one treaty not further involved here, accepted by the Indians. The addition reads as follows:

"Nothing herein contained shall be construed or taken to admit any other or greater title or interest in the lands embraced within the territories described in said treaty in said tribes or bands of Indians than existed in them upon the acquisition of said territories from Mexico by the laws thereof." . . .

Without seeking any cession or relinquishment of claim from the Shoshone, except the Eastern Shoshone relinquishment of July 3, 1868, . . . the United States has treated the rest of the Shoshone territory as a part of the public domain. School lands were granted. . . . National forests were freely created. . . . The lands were opened to public settlement under the homestead laws. . . . Thus we have administration of this territory by the United States proceeding as though no Indian land titles were involved.

The Court of Claims examined the evidence adduced before it and reached the conclusion as a finding of fact that the United States "did not intend that it [the treaty] should be a stipulation of recognition and acknowledgment of any exclusive use and occupancy right or title of the Indians, parties thereto. . . . The treaty was intended to be, and was, a treaty of peace and amity with stipulated annuities for the purposes of accomplishing those objects and achieving that end." . . . This finding molded the opinion and judgment below.

Whether the issue as to acknowledgment by a treaty of Indian title to land is treated as a question of fact, like Indian right to occupancy itself, . . . or as a matter of inference to be drawn by the trier of fact from the treaty and surrounding circumstances or as a conclusion of law to be reviewed by this Court upon the record, this finding places the burden on petitioners to overthrow the judgment of the Court of Claims. In reaching its conclusion, the lower court pointed out in its opinion that nothing in the legislation or official documents, communications or instructions which brought about the treaty indicated any purpose to recognize Indian title to the territory over which the Shoshone roamed and hunted. The commissioners were instructed specifically on July 22, 1862, that they were not expected to negotiate for the extinction of the Indian title but for the security of routes over the lands and "a definite acknowledgment as well of the boundaries of the entire country they [the Indians] claim." . . .

An examination of the text of the Northwestern Shoshone Treaty and the others which were entered into with the other Shoshone tribes . . . shows the commissioners carefully followed their instructions. In the Eastern Shoshone Treaty, the boundaries are spoken of "as defined and described by said nation," . . . In the Northwestern Shoshone Treaty the land is described as "The country claimed by Pokatello, for himself and his people." In the Western Shoshone Treaty permission was given for mineral prospecting and extracting and the boundaries are said to define "the country claimed and occupied." The same language is used as to the boundaries in the Shoshonee-Goship Treaty. This treaty also permitted prospecting for and the working of mines. The Mixed Bands treaty described a country "claimed by the said bands" and "as described by them." Nowhere in any of the series of treaties is there a specific acknowledgment of Indian title or right of occupancy. It seems to us a reasonable inference that had either the Indians or the United States understood that the treaties recognized the Indian title to these domains, such purpose would have been clearly and definitely expressed by instruction, by treaty text or by the reports of the treaty commissioners, to their superiors or in the transmission of the treaties to the Senate for ratification.

Petitioners argue that the permission from the Indians for travel or mining and for the maintenance of communication and transportation facilities by the United States for its citizens imply a recognition by the United States of the Indian title. They quote, as persuasive, these words from an early Indian case: "The acceptance of these cessions is an acknowledgment of the right of the Cherokees to make or withhold them." Worcester v. Georgia. . . . And examination of the circumstances under which this Court made the just-quoted statement illustrates how inapposite its use by petitioners is to the present question. The quotation was written in explanation of rights of passage which were granted by the Cherokees through lands which by other articles of the treaty had been specifically set apart and solemnly guaranteed to the Cherokees. . . . No such specific recognition is in the Box Elder treaty. But we see nothing inconsistent with non-recognition of the Indian title and the insertion of these provisions against molestation of structures, travelers or exploiters of mineral deposits within the territories. The United States undoubtedly might have asserted, at the time of the treaty, its purpose to extinguish Indian title or it might have recognized Indian title or it might, as the Court of Claims held, have sought only freedom from hostile acts from roving bands by the commitments for supplies. The treaties were made in the midst of civil war and before the outcome of that conflict was clear.

Petitioners urge that recognition of the Indian title was inferred from the language of the Fort Laramie treaty of September 17, 1851, . . . and that a different inference in the present case is inconsistent with those holdings. Apart from the fact that different treaties are involved, the circumstances surrounding the execution of the Fort Laramie treaty

indicate a purpose to recognize the Indian title to the lands described in
the Fort Laramie treaty which may well have induced the Court of Claims
to reach one conclusion in those cases and another in this. . . .

Petitioners point out that the word "claim" or the phrase "country
claimed" was often used on the frontier to indicate title or right. We know
this meaning in mining law and in entries for land patents. The meaning
of the word or phrase depends upon its use. In these treaties it seems
clearly to designate the boundaries over which the Indians asserted Indian
title but that falls short of acknowledgment of such right by the United
States. . . .

Petitioners suggest that in the construction of Indian treaties we, as
a self-respecting nation, hesitate to construe language, which is selected
by us as guardian of the Indians, to our ward's prejudice. "All doubts,"
say petitioners, "must be resolved in their [the Indians'] favor." Mr.
Justice M'Lean, concurring in Worcester v. Georgia, . . . said, "The
language used in treaties with the Indians should never be construed to
their prejudice." But the context shows that the Justice meant no more
than that the language should be construed in accordance with the tenor
of the treaty. That, we think, is the rule which this Court has applied
consistently to Indian treaties. We attempt to determine what the parties
meant by the treaty. We stop short of varying its terms to meet alleged
injustices. Such generosity, if any may be called for in the relations
between the United States and the Indians, is for the Congress.

It seems to us clear from the circumstances leading up to and following the execution of the Box Elder Treaty that the parties did not intend
to recognize or acknowledge by that treaty the Indian title to the lands in
question. Whether the lands were in fact held by the Shoshones by Indian
title from occupancy or otherwise or what rights flow to the Indians from
such title is not involved. Since the rights, if any the Shoshones have,
did not arise under or grow out of the Box Elder Treaty, no recovery
may be had under the jurisdictional act.

Affirmed.

Mr. Justice ROBERTS is of the view that the judgment should be
reversed.

Mr. Justice JACKSON, concurring: Mr. Justice BLACK and I
think it may be desirable to state some of the difficulties which underlie
efforts to leave such an Indian grievance as this to settlement by a law-suit.

It is hard to see how any judicial decision under such a jurisdictional act can much advance solution of the problem of the Shoshones.
Any judgment that we may render gives to these Indians neither their
lands nor money. The jurisdictional act provides that the proceeds above

attorneys' fees shall "be deposited in the Treasury of the United States to the credit of the Indians" at 4 per cent interest and "shall be subject to appropriation by Congress only for the health, education, and industrial advancement of said Indians." The only cash payment is attorneys' fees. Section 7 provides that the Court of Claims shall determine a reasonable fee, not to exceed 10 per cent of the recovery, together with expenses, to be paid to the attorneys for the Northwestern Bands out of the sums found due. After counsel are thus paid, not a cent is put into the reach of the Indians; all that is done for them by a judgment is to earmark some funds in the Treasury from which Congress may as it sees fit from time to time make appropriations "for the health, education, and industrial advancement of said Indians." Congress could do this, of course, without any judgment or earmarking of funds, as it often has done. Congress, even after judgment, still must decide the amount and times of payment to the Indians according to their needs.

We would not be second to any other in recognizing that — judgment or no judgment — a moral obligation of a high order rests upon this country to provide for decent shelter, clothing, education, and industrial advancement of the Indian. Nothing is gained by dwelling upon the unhappy conflicts that have prevailed between the Shoshones and the whites — conflicts which sometimes leave one in doubt which side could make the better claim to be civilized. The generation of Indians who suffered the privations, indignities, and brutalities of the westward march of the whites have gone to the Happy Hunting Ground, and nothing that we can do can square the account with them. Whatever survives is a moral obligation resting on the descendants of the whites to do for the descendants of the Indians what in the conditions of this twentieth century is the decent thing.

It is most unfortunate to try to measure this moral duty in terms of legal obligations and ask the Court to spell out Indian legal rights from written instruments made and probably broken long ago and to put our moral duty in figures as legal damages. The Indian problem is essentially a sociological problem, not a legal one. We can make only a pretense of adjudication of such claims, and that only by indulging the most unrealistic and fictional assumptions.

Here we are asked to go back over three quarters of a century to spell out the meaning of a most ambiguous writing made in 1863. One of the parties did not keep, or know how to keep, written records of negotiations. Written evidence bearing on intention is only that which the whites chose to make. It does not take a particularly discerning eye to see that these records, written usually by Indian agents, are quite apt to speak well of the writer's virtue and good intention. Evidence from the memory of man is no longer available. Even if both parties to these agreements were of our own stock, we being a record-keeping people, a court would still have the gravest difficulty determining what their motives and intentions and meanings were. Statutes of limitation cut off most such inquiries, not because a claim becomes less just the longer it is denied, but because another policy intervenes — the policy to leave in repose matters which can no longer be the subject of intelligent adjudication.

Even if the handicap of time could be overcome, we could not satisfactorily apply legal techniques to interpretation of this treaty. The Indian parties to the treaty were a band of simple, relatively peaceful, and extremely primitive men. The population of the band was only about 1500, and the territories claimed to have been occupied as their home consisted of over 15,000,000 acres of land in Idaho, Utah, and Nevada — about 10,000 acres for every individual in the band. Of course so few could not patrol and defend so vast a territory against the more aggressive and efficient whites. The white was a better killer. The game disappeared, the lands were not productive, and in peace the Indians became destitute. Desperation stimulated or perhaps produced predatory tendencies and they began to fall upon the overland caravans and to steal and rob. The whites brought forth their armies and reduced the Indians to submission. Then the whites "negotiated" a treaty.

We realize that for over a century it has been a judicial practice to construe these "agreements" with Indians, as if they were contracts between white men. In some cases, where the provisions are simple and definite and deal with concrete lands or matters, this may be practicable. But despite antiquity of the custom, to apply the litigation process to such a problem as we have here seems farfetched. The most elemental condition of a bargain was not present, for there was nothing like equality of bargaining power. On one side were dominant, powerful, shrewd, and educated whites, who knew exactly what they wanted. On the other side were destitute, illiterate Indians who primarily wanted to be let alone and who wanted by some means to continue to live their own accustomed lives. Here we are asked to decide whether their intent was to relinquish titles or make reservations of titles or recognition of titles. The Indian parties did not know what titles were, had no such concept as that of individual land title, and had no sense of property in land. Here we are asked to attribute legal meanings to subscribers of a written instrument who had no written language of their own in which to express any meaning. We doubt if any interpreter could intelligently translate the contents of a writing that deals with the property concept, for the Indians did not have a word for it. People do not have words to fit ideas that have never occurred to them. Ownership meant no more to them than to roam the land as a great common, and to possess and enjoy it in the same way that they possessed and enjoyed sunlight and the west wind and the feel of spring in the air. Acquisitiveness, which develops a law of real property, is an accomplishment only of the "civilized."

Of course the Indians may have had some vague idea that thereafter they were to stay off certain lands and the white men in return were to stay off certain other land. But we do not think it is possible now to reduce such a nebulous accord to terms of common-law contract and conveyancing. The treaty was a political document. It was intended to pacify the Indians and to let the whites travel in peace a route they somehow were going to travel anyway.

How should we turn into money's worth the rights, if any, of which the Indians have been deprived? Should we measure it in terms of what was lost to a people who needed 10,000 acres apiece to sustain themselves through hunting and nomadic living, who had no system or standard of exchange, and whose representatives in making the treaty appear to have been softened for the job by gifts of blankets and trinkets? Should we measure it in terms of what was gained to our people, who sustain themselves in large numbers on few acres by greater efficiency and utilization? Of course amends can be made only to progeny in terms of their present needs as the jurisdictional Act recognizes will ultimately be done. The Indians' grievance calls for sympathetic, intelligent, and generous help in developing the latent talents and aspirations of the living generation, and there is little enlightenment for that task from endless and pointless lawsuits over the negotiation of generations long gone to their rest.

We agree with Mr. Justice REED that no legal rights are today to be recognized in the Shoshones by reason of this treaty. We agree with Mr. Justice DOUGLAS and Mr. Justice MURPHY as to their moral deserts. We do not mean to leave the impression that the two have any relation to each other. The finding that the treaty creates no legal obligations does not restrict Congress from such appropriations as its judgment dictates "for the health, education, and industrial advancement of said Indians" which is the position in which Congress would find itself if we found that it did create legal obligations and tried to put a value on them.

Mr. Justice DOUGLAS dissenting: I think the claims which these Indians assert are claims "arising under or growing out of the treaty of July 30, 1863."

He who comes to my abode and bargains for free transit or a right of way across the land on which I live and which I proclaim to be my own certainly recognizes that I have a claim to it. That and more was done here. Routes of travel through this Shoshone country, the establishment of military agricultural settlements and military posts, the maintenance of ferries over the rivers, the erection of houses and settlements, the location, construction, and operation of a railroad, the maintenance of telegraph and overland stage lines were all negotiated. These provisions alone constitute plain recognition by the United States that it was dealing with people who had the power to grant these rights of travel and settlement. The United States, of course, did not need to follow that course. It could have invaded this Indian country and extinguished Indian title by the sword or by appropriation. . . . But it did not choose that course. It chose to negotiate a treaty. And through the medium of the treaty it obtained from these Indians rights of way, rights to settle, rights of transit. It was stated in Worcester v. Georgia . . . that "The acceptance of these cessions is an acknowledgment of the right of the Cherokees to make or withhold them." That is good law. It is as applicable here as it was in that early case, there, to be sure, lands had been specifically set apart for the Cherokees. But that is not a material difference. Indian title is the right of occupancy based on aboriginal possession. . . . It has been the policy of the United States from the beginning to respect that right of occupancy. . . . As stated in Mitchel v. United States . . . the Indian "right of occupancy is considered as sacred as the fee simple of the whites." Thus we may not say that because these Indians had only Indian title this case can be distinguished from Worcester v. Georgia. . . . When the United States obtained these cessions it acknowledged whatever claim to the land these Indians had. The Indians ask no more now.

Moreover, the Senate in ratifying the treaty made clear that it construed the treaty as recognizing the title or claim of these Indians to this land. The amendment added in the Senate provided: "Nothing herein contained shall be construed or taken to admit any other or greater title or interest in the lands embraced within the territories described in said treaty in said tribes or bands of Indians than existed in them upon the acquisition of said territories from Mexico by the laws thereof." That should put beyond dispute that the Senate understood the treaty to accord recognition of the title which the Indians had under Mexican law. To say it gives no recognition to any claim is to erase this provision from the treaty.

But if there is still any doubt as to the meaning of the treaty it should be wholly removed by another of its provisions. The treaty stated that "The country claimed by Pokatello for himself and his people is bounded on the west by Raft River and on the east by the Porteneuf Mountains."

That is now brushed aside as irrelevant. But we should remember that no counsel sat at the elbow of Pokatello when the treaty was drafted. It was written in a language foreign to him. He was not a conveyancer. He was not cognizant of distinctions in title. He neither had nor gave deeds to his lands. There was no recording office. But he knew the land where he lived and for which he would fight. If the standards of the frontier are to govern, his assertion of ownership and its recognition by the United States could hardly have been plainer.

We should remember the admonition in Jones v. Meehan . . . that in construing a treaty between the United States and an Indian tribe it must always be borne in mind "that the negotiations for the treaty are conducted, on the part of the United States, an enlightened and powerful nation, by representatives skilled in diplomacy, masters of a written language, understanding the modes and forms of creating the various technical estates known to their law, and assisted by an interpreter employed by themselves; that the treaty is drawn up by them and in their own language; that the Indians, on the other hand, are a weak and dependent people, who have no written language and are wholly unfamiliar with all the forms of legal expression, and whose only knowledge of the terms in which the treaty is framed is that imparted to them by the interpreter employed by the United States; and that the treaty must therefore be construed, not according to the technical meaning of its words to learned lawyers, but in the sense in which they would naturally be understood by the Indians."

When the standard is not observed, what these Indians did not lose to the railroads and to the land companies they lose to the fine web of legal niceties.

As stated by the Attorneys General of Idaho and Utah who appear here as amici curiae: "The result is that a peaceful and friendly people, lulled into a sense of security by the proffers of the United States of peace and amity, have been reduced from a nation able to wrest their living from their primitive ancestral home to a nondescript, homeless, and poverty-stricken aggregation of bands of Indians, without the means to compete in modern civilization which had disseised them. Until the treaty with petitioners, petitioners were so strong and formidable that the trouble and expense of taking their lands by war — leaving out of account the dishonor that would have been involved in proceeding against a nation which had given no cause for war — would have far outweighed the expense of settling with them for their lands at whatever the cost in money. But the United States did neither. Congress felt it could not at that time afford to extinguish petitioners' title by purchase. Consequently, for a meager consideration, the petitioners granted respondent certain valuable rights in those lands. For respondent, under these circumstances, to attempt to deny petitioners' title is unworthy of our country. The faith of this nation having been pledged in the treaties, the honor of the nation demands, and the jurisdictional act requires, that these long-unsettled grievances be settled by this court in simple justice to a downtrodden people."

The story has been told before. Chester Fee, Chief Joseph (1936); Howard Fast, The Last Frontier (1944).

Mr. Justice FRANKFURTER and Mr. Justice MURPHY join in this dissent.

[The separate dissenting opinion of Mr. Justice MURPHY, in which both Mr. Justice FRANKFURTER and Mr. Justice DOUGLAS concur, is omitted.]

RECOMMENDED READING

I. Moral Principles

Bayles, Michael D., ed. *Contemporary Utilitarianism.* Garden City, N. Y.: Anchor Books, 1968.

Harrison, Jonathan. "Kant's Examples of the First Formulation of the Categorical Imperative." *Philosophical Quarterly* 7 (January 1957): 50-62. Reprinted together with a critical article by J. Kemp and a response by Harrison in *Foundations of the Metaphysics of Morals with Critical Essays,* edited by Robert Paul Wolff. Indianapolis: Bobbs-Merrill, 1969.

Kretzmann, Norman. "Desire as Proof of Desirability." *Philosophical Quarterly* 8 (1958): 246-58. A defense of Mill's proof. Reprinted in Smith and Sosa (see below).

Liddell, Brendan E. A. *Kant on the Foundation of Morality.* Bloomington and London: Indiana University Press, 1970. A very useful passage-by-passage commentary and translation of Kant's *Grundlegung (Fundamental Principles of the Metaphysic of Morals).*

Moore, G. E. *Principia Ethica.* Cambridge: Cambridge University Press, 1903, chap. III. A critique of hedonism and classical utilitarianism, particularly of Mill's proof of his principle.

Mortimer, R. C. *Christian Ethics.* London: Hutchinson University Library, 1950, chaps. 1 & 2. A modern exposition and defense of the divine will theory.

Smith, James M., and Sosa, Ernest. *Mill's Utilitarianism: Text and Criticism.* Belmont, Calif.: Wadsworth, 1969. Also contains Mill's "Remarks on Bentham's Moral Philosophy."

Tussman, Joseph. *Obligation and the Body Politic.* New York: Oxford University Press, 1960, Appendix: "Nature and Politics." A modern discussion of the relation between morality and politics from the Hobbesian point of view.

Urmson, J. O. "The Interpretation of the Moral Philosophy of J. S. Mill." *Philosophical Quarterly* 3 (1953): 33-39. Reprinted along with other restatements of utilitarianism in Bayles (see above).

Walsh, James J., and Shapiro, Henry L. *Aristotle's Ethics: Issues and Interpretations*. Belmont, Calif.: Wadsworth, 1967.

II. Moral Points of View

Baier, Kurt. *The Moral Point of View: A Rational Basis of Ethics*. New York: Random House, 1965. An abridged edition.

Brandt, Richard B. *Ethical Theory: The Problems of Normative and Critical Ethics*. Englewood Cliffs, N.J.: Prentice-Hall, 1959, chaps. 11 & 14.

Danto, Arthur C. *Nietzsche as Philosopher*. New York: Macmillan, 1965.

De Beauvoir, Simone. *The Ethics of Ambiguity*. New York: Philosophical Library, 1949. An existentialist point of view.

Fletcher, Joseph. *Moral Responsibility: Situation Ethics at Work*. Philadelphia: Westminster Press, 1967.

Fotion, N. *Moral Situations*. Yellow Springs, Ohio: Antioch Press, 1968.

Gauthier, David P., ed. *Morality and Rational Self-Interest*. Englewood Cliffs, N.J.: Prentice-Hall, 1970.

Medlin, Brian. "Ultimate Principles and Ethical Egoism." *Australasian Journal of Philosophy* 35 (1957): 111-18. Reprinted in Gauthier (see above).

Nietzsche, Friedrich. *The Complete Works of Friedrich Nietzsche*. New York: Russell & Russell, reissued 1964.

Pound, Roscoe. "A Theory of Social Interests." *Papers and Proceedings of the American Sociological Society* 15 (May 1921). Revised and republished as "A Survey of Social Interests." *Harvard Law Review* 57 (1943): 1-39, and reprinted in *Law and Philosophy*, edited by Edward A. Kent. New York: Appleton-Century-Crofts, 1970. A development and application by a legal philosopher of William James' view that a claim is a source of obligation.

Sartre, Jean-Paul. *Existentialism and Humanism*. London: Methuen, 1948.

Wellman, Carl. "The Ethical Implications of Cultural Relativity." *Journal of Philosophy* 60 (1963): 169-84. Reprinted in *Philosophy For a New Generation*, edited by A. K. Bierman and James A. Gould. New York: Macmillan, 1970.

III. Moral Rules and Exceptions

Brandt, Richard B. "Toward a Credible Form of Utilitarianism." In *Morality and the Language of Conduct,* edited by Hector-Neri Casteñeda and George Naknikian. Detroit: Wayne State University Press, 1963. Reprinted in Bayles (see I above).

Brody, Baruch A., ed. *Moral Rules and Particular Circumstances*. Englewood Cliffs, N.J.: Prentice-Hall, 1970.

Diggs, B. J. "Rules and Utilitarianism." *American Philosophical Quarterly* 1 (1964): 32-44. Reprinted in Bayles (see I above).

Harrison, Jonathan. "Utilitarianism, Universalisation, and Our Duty to be Just." *Proceedings of the Aristotelian Society* 53 (1952-53): 105-34. Reprinted in Bayles (see I above) and in Brody (see above).

Kant, Immanuel. *The Metaphysical Principles of Virtue.* Translated by James Ellington. Indianapolis and New York: Bobbs-Merrill, 1964. Also contains an excellent introduction by Warner Wick on Kant's entire moral philosophy.

Paton, H. J. "An Alleged Right to Lie: A Problem in Kantian Ethics." *Kant-Studien,* Band 45 (1953-54): 190-203.

Patterson, Edwin W., *Jurisprudence: Men and Ideas of the Law.* Brooklyn: Foundation Press, 1953, chap. 19, sec. 5.05. A discussion of legal exceptions involving hardship. Some of the cases discussed are included in Davis (see IV below).

Smart, J. J. C. "Extreme and Restricted Utilitarianism." *Philosophical Quarterly* 6 (1956): 344-54. Reprinted in Bayles (see I above) and in Brody (see III above). A defense of act-utilitarianism.

Sobel, J. Howard. "Generalization Arguments." *Theoria* 31 (1965): 32-60. Reprinted in *Readings in Ethical Theory,* edited by Wilfrid Sellars and John Hospers, 2d ed. New York: Appleton-Century-Crofts, 1970. A critique of Singer's theory.

Strang, Colin. "What if Everyone Did That?" *Durham University Journal* 53 (1960): 5-10. Reprinted in Brody (see III above).

IV. Moral Responsibility and Excuses

Austin, J. L. "A Plea for Excuses." *Proceedings of the Aristotelian Society* 57 (1956-57): 1-30. Reprinted in White (see below).

Baier, Kurt. "Responsibility and Freedom," in *Ethics and Society,* edited by Richard T. De George. Garden City: Anchor Books, 1966. Discusses various concepts of responsibility and their relationships to punishment.

Campbell, C. A. "Is 'Free Will' a Pseudo-Problem?" *Mind* 60 (1951): 441-65. Reprinted in *Free Will and Determinism,* edited by Bernard Berofsky. New York and London: Harper and Row, 1966.

Davis, Philip E., ed. *Moral Duty and Legal Responsibility.* New York: Appleton-Century-Crofts, 1966, chaps. 2 and 3. Legal cases which illustrate moral problems of assigning responsibility.

Hart, H. L. A. *Punishment and Responsibility.* New York and Oxford: Oxford University Press, 1968.

Hospers, John. "What Means This Freedom?" in *Determinism and Freedom in the Age of Modern Science,* edited by Sidney Hook. New York: Collier Books, 1961. The problem of human freedom from the psycho-analytical point of view.

Jones, David H. "Deliberation and Determinism." *Southern Journal of Philosophy* 6 (Winter 1968): 255-64. A critique of Taylor's thesis. Taylor responds in the same volume.

Raab, Francis V. "The Relevance of Morals to our Denials of Responsibility." in *Morality and the Language of Conduct,* edited by Hector-Neri Casteñeda and George Naknikian. Detroit: Wayne State University Press, 1963.

Taylor, Richard. "Fatalism." *The Philosophical Review* 71 (1962): 56-66.

V. Moral Action

Brand, Myles, ed. *The Nature of Human Action.* Glenview, Ill.: Scott, Foresman, 1970.

Care, Norman S., and Landesman, Charles. *Readings in the Theory of Action.* Bloomington and London: Indiana University Press, 1968.

Cody, Arthur B. "Can a Single Action Have Many Different Descriptions?" *Inquiry* 10 (1967): 164-80.
Davis, Philip E., ed. *Moral Duty and Legal Responsibility*. New York: Appleton-Century-Crofts, 1966, chap. 4. Legal cases illustrating various kinds of legal and moral acts.
Feinberg, Joel. "Action and Responsibility," in *Philosophy in America*, edited by M. Black. London: George Allen and Unwin, 1965. Reprinted in White (see below).
Fitzgerald, P. J. "Voluntary and Involuntary Acts," in *Oxford Essays in Jurisprudence*, edited by A. G. Guest. Oxford: Clarendon Press, 1961. Reprinted in White (see below).
Louch, A. R. *Explanation and Human Action*. Berkeley and Los Angeles: University of California Press, 1966. The author argues that the explanation of human action is only possible by means of moral categories.
Melden, A. I. "Action." *The Philosophical Review* 65 (1956): 523-41. Reprinted in Care and Landesman (see above) and partially in Brand (see above). A discussion of many different theories of action as well as that of the author.
Sachs, David. "A Few Morals About Acts." *The Philosophical Review* 75 (1966): 91-98. A critique of D'Arcy's theory of human acts and omissions.
Von Wright, G. H. *Norm and Action*. London: Routledge and Kegan Paul, 1963. Discusses the logic of action.
White, Alan R., ed. *The Philosophy of Action*. Oxford: Oxford University Press, 1968.

VI. Moral Reasoning

Anscombe, G. E. M. "On Brute Facts." *Analysis* 18 (1958): 69-72. Reprinted in Judith J. Thomson and Gerald Dworkin, *Ethics*. New York: Harper and Row, 1968.
Ayer, A. J. *Language Truth and Logic*. 2d ed. London: Victor Gollancz, 1946.
Edwards, Paul. *The Logic of Moral Discourse*. New York: Free Press, 1955.
Foot, Phillipa. "Moral Arguments." *Mind* 67 (1958): 502-13. Reprinted in Thomson and Dworkin (see Anscombe entry above).
Frankena, W. K. "The Naturalistic Fallacy" *Mind* 48 (1939): 464-77. Reprinted in Philippa Foot, *Theories of Ethics*. Oxford: Oxford University Press, 1967. A critique of Moore's view.
Gauthier, David P. "Hare's Debtors" *Mind* 77 (1968): 400-5.
Hampshire, Stuart. "Fallacies in Moral Philosophy." *Mind* 58 (1949): 466-82. Reprinted in Joseph Margolis, *Contemporary Ethical Theory*. New York: Random House, 1966.
Hare, R. M. *The Language of Morals*. Oxford: Clarendon Press, 1952.
Kerner, George C. *The Revolution in Ethical Theory*. New York and Oxford: Oxford University Press, 1966. A discussion of Moore, Stevenson, Toulmin, and Hare.
Stevenson, Charles L. *Ethics and Language*. New Haven: Yale University Press, 1944.
Strawson, P. F. "Ethical Intuitionism." *Philosophy* 24 (1949): 347-57. Reprinted in Margolis (see Hampshire entry above).
Taylor, Paul W. *Normative Discourse*. Englewood Cliffs, N.J.: Prentice-Hall, 1961.
Thomson, James, and Thomson, Judith. "How Not to Derive 'Ought' from 'Is'." *The Philosophical Review* 73 (1964): 512-16. Reprinted in Sellars and Hospers (see Sobel entry, III, above). A critique of Searle's article.

Toulmin, Stephen. *An Examination of the Place of Reason in Ethics*. Cambridge: Cambridge University Press, 1950.

VII. Morality and Justice

Bedau, Hugo A., ed. *Justice and Equality*. Englewood Cliffs, N.J.: Prentice-Hall, 1971. Classical and contemporary discussions of the subjects.

Brandt, Richard B., ed. *Social Justice*. Englewood Cliffs, N.J.: Prentice-Hall, 1962. Essays on the philosophical, economic, political, and legal aspects of justice.

Cahn, Edmond. *The Sense of Injustice*. Bloomington: Indiana University Press, 1964.

Deloria, Vine, Jr. *Custer Died For Your Sins: An Indian Manifesto*. New York: Avon Books, 1969.

_____. *Of Utmost Good Faith*. New York: Bantam Books, 1972. Documents supporting the case of the American Indian against the federal government of the United States.

Hart, H. L. A. *The Concept of Law*. Oxford: Clarendon Press, 1961, chap. VIII.

Honoré, A. M. "Social Justice." 8 *McGill Law Journal* 78 (1962). Revised and included in *Essays in Legal Philosophy*, edited by Robert S. Summers. Oxford: Basil Blackwell, 1968.

Melden, A. I., ed. *Human Rights*. Belmont, Calif.: Wadsworth, 1970.

Morris, Herbert. "Punishment for Thoughts." *Monist* 49 (1965): 342-76. Reprinted in Summers (see Honoré entry above).

Perelman, Chaim. *Justice*. New York: Random House, 1957.

Rawls, John. *A Theory of Justice*. Cambridge: Harvard University Press, 1971.

Rescher, Nicholas. *Distributive Justice*. Indianapolis: Bobbs-Merrill, 1966.

Index

Absolutism, ethical, 135, 140, 143, 192-93

Act: of commission and omission, 388; and consequences, 390-91, 418-32; free, 311; negative, 387-90, 399-408; optimific, 223-24, 481-82; overt or inner, 350-51; of a self, 311, 359; voluntary, 318, 385-87, 392-98, 421-22. *See also* Action

Action: distinguished from "act," 422-23; freedom of, 309, 318; maxim of, 68-69, 231; subject of moral valuation, 161-62; voluntary, 376, 392-98. *See also* Act

Act-utilitarianism, 7, 285, 292-93, 419. *See also* Rule-utilitarianism; Utilitarianism

Altruism, 164

Anscombe, G. E. M., 525 n

Antinomianism, 8, 182-85

Aristotle, 4, 8, 12-13, 43-61, 188, 239-40, 294-302, 386, 392-400, 536, 582, 587

Austin, John, 387, 420-24

Autonomy of the will, 85, 87-89

Ayer, A. J., 438-39, 441, 445-46, 486-98

Baier, Kurt, 142-44, 205-24, 229, 232, 235-37, 446, 533

Bentham, Jeremy, 5, 9-10, 95-102, 106-7, 146, 285, 388, 404, 495, 539, 549 n

Black, Hugo L., judicial opinion of, 600-603

Blame, and praise, 311, 392, 399-400

Bonhoeffer, Dietrich, 186

Brandt, Richard B., 237 n, 578-81, 584

Broad, C. D., 350

Brunner, Emil, 185, 577, 582

Buddha, 165

Campbell, C. A., 310, 315, 349-64, 370

Carritt, E. F., 551

Casuistry, 153, 181, 185-89
Categorical imperative, 11, 70-71,
    143, 213, 221, 232, 233, 242,
    277-81, 283; distinguished from
    hypothetical imperatives, 75; first
    formulation of, 77; sample
    applications of, 77-79, 82-83;
    second formulation of, 80-82; third
    formulation of, 83-87
Choice, 328; absolutely free, 137; of a
    mean, 54-55; of oneself, 176
Christianity: and antinomianism,
    182-85; legalism in, 179-82; as a
    moral guide, 119; Nietzsche's
    critique of, 165-67
Clough, Arthur, 591
Cognitivism, 441. *See also* Non-
    cognitivism
Cohen, Morris R., 266 n
Compulsion, 377-78, 393-94
Consequences: and acts, 390-91,
    418-32; obverse principle of, 237;
    principle of, 233, 262
Constant, Benjamin, 232, 254-57

D'Arcy, Eric, 387-88, 390-91, 404-7,
    418-32
De Beauvoir, Simone, 184
Deliberation, 334-48
Deontological ethics, 6-7, 215, 223
Descartes, René, 172
Determinism, 310-13, 317-48, 358,
    367-68
Divine will principle, 4, 13-30
Douglas, William O., judicial opinion
    of, 603-6
Duty: acting from, 66; conflicts of,
    230, 474; imperfect or broad,
    229-30; perfect or strict, 229-30;
    to secure happiness, 67. *See also*
    Obligation, Prima facie duties

Egalitarianism, 537-41, 582-84, 592

Egoism: enlightened, 142, 213;
    ethical, 141-44; psychological,
    141-42; shortsighted, 142, 213
Epicureanism, 108
Epicurus, 108
Equality: and justice, 580-88; before
    the law, 302; of all men, 31, 39;
    principle of, 258, 535-37
Equity, 39, 294-302
Ethics: aim of, 145-46; fundamental
    question of, 437; ideal observer
    theories of, 505; legalistic, 139,
    179-82; linguistic conception of,
    438, 495-98, 499-502; and morals,
    499; neutrality of, 439, 500-502;
    normative or critical, 435-36;
    questions of, 435-39, 449-50;
    situation, 178-89; theistic or
    humanistic basis, 152. *See also*
    Meta-ethics
Evaluative statements, 448, 493, 504,
    515, 524
Evidence: kinds of moral, 449-68;
    prima facie, 469-85
Evil, and good, 41, 136, 157, 161,
    327
Ewing, A. C., 271
Exceptions: Aristotle's theory of,
    239-40, 294-302; classes of, 277;
    compared to violations, 235;
    deserving cases, 216-17, 235;
    justified by the generalization
    argument, 270-74, 289-91; Kant
    on, 229-32, 254-58, 289; Mill on,
    119; in one's favor, 77 n, 80, 142,
    144, 215-18, 237; problem of,
    227-29; singular, 153, 235; as
    threats to the moral enterprise, 227;
    "to" rules and "of" rules, 215,
    232-36, 290; and uncertainty,
    241-53. *See also* Duty, conflicts of
Excusability, 313-16, 374-82
Excuse: bad character as an, 379-80;
    compulsion, 377-78, 393-94;

Excuse (*continued*)
ignorance, 376-77, 394, 400-401;
kinds of legal, 375-76; mankind
without any, 138, 175, 177; strong
desires as an, 378-79

Facts: institutional or brute, 172,
448, 488, 525, 531; related to
ethical values, 157, 531-35
Fairness, principle of, 261
Fatalism, 310-11, 328
Firth, Roderick, 505 n
Fletcher, Joseph, 7, 137, 139-40,
178-89, 228
Forbearance, 387-90, 402-4
Foreknowledge, 334-48. *See also*
Predictability of human actions
Formalism, ethical, 7
Frank, Jerome, 295 n
Frankena, William K., 537, 540,
576-92
Freedom, 258, 309-16; absolute, 137,
171-77; of action, 309; negative
and positive concepts of, 88-89; as
a presupposition, 89-90; "to be
free," meaning of, 173-74. *See also*
Free will
Free will, 88-90, 171-77, 309-33, 335,
349-73. *See also* Freedom

Gallie, W. B., 582
Generalization Argument, 233,
259-81; invertibility of, 233;
reiterability of, 234
Generalization Principle, 233, 261
God: existence of, 152, 486;
foreknowledge of, 312, 328,
347-48; as ideal observer, 505 n;
love of, 139; point of view of, 222;
and responsibility for human sin,
370; as ultimate claimant, 149;
universe without a, 147; and
utilitarianism, 118; will of, 13-14,
118

Golden mean, 53-54
Golden rule, 36, 115, 223; argument,
447; negative version of, 40, 82n,
222
Good: and bad, 161; definitions of
word, 6, 147, 153-54, 437-38; and
evil, 41, 136, 157, 161; highest
or greatest, 8; indefinability of
word, 440, 452-65
Good will, 62-71
Greatest happiness principle, 96,
106-7, 111

Hampshire, Stuart, 338 n
Happiness: Aristotle's conception of,
56-61; Aristotle's definition of, 48;
and good will, 62; as highest good,
45; Mill's conception, 112-13;
as pleasure and absence of pain,
107; as sole object of desire, 125
Hare, R. M., 438-39, 442-43, 446-47,
499-513, 524
Hart, H. L. A., 338 n, 375 n, 424,
516 n, 588
Hedonic calculus, 99-102
Hedonism, psychological, 10, 95-96
Heidegger, Martin, 172
Heschel, Abraham, 187
Hobbes, Thomas, 4, 6, 8, 12-13, 142,
533-34, 540-41
Hospers, John, 237-38, 282-93
Hourani, G. F., 587
Hughes, Graham, 400
Hume, David, 368-70, 424
Hume's Law, 447, 513, 514-15. *See
also* Ought-Is derivation
Hypothetical imperatives, 75-77

Ideal utilitarianism, 470, 475, 477
Ignorance, 316, 327, 376-77, 394-95,
400-401
Imperatives: the Decalogue, 476;
defined, 74; kinds of, 75-77. *See
also* Categorical imperative

Indefinability of ethical terms, 452-61, 469-72. *See also* Good; Right
Indeterminism, 171-77, 310-13, 317-33, 349-64, 370-73
Indians, 542-43, 593-606
Injustice: act of, 535; a case of, 593-606; Hobbes' definition, 38, 534; of laws, 533. *See also* Justice
Institution: moral, 525, 532; of punishment, 548; of society, 210, 533; as a system of constitutive rules, 448, 525
Institutional facts, 448, 488, 525, 531-35. *See also* Facts
Intuition, 213, 215, 239, 443, 451
Intuitionism, ethical, 6, 147, 441, 451

Jackson, Robert H., judicial opinion of, 600-603
James, William, 6, 10, 134-35, 139, 145-58, 227, 531, 589
Jesus, 73, 178, 196-98, 202, 324
Johnson v. *M'Intosh,* 542
Judaism: legalism in, 179-80; situationism in, 187
Judgment: analysis of moral, 486-98; features of moral, 502, 533; of obligation, 319-20
Justice: classical definitions, 38, 554-75, 578-80; corrective, 540; distributive, 39, 538; duty of, 255 n; and the fall of heavens, 181, 466-67; Hobbes's definition of, 38, 534; kinds of, 298; of legal decisions, 294; and love, 577; and morality, 531-43; and the political system, 258, 577; and power, 541-43, 564-75; principle of, 261; social, 576-92; Thrasymachus's view of, 221-22, 564-75. *See also* Equality; Injustice
Justicizing considerations, 581

Justification: of exceptions, 233-36, 270-74, 289-91; of moral rules, 274-77; of a practice, 544-45; of punishment, 544-53
Kant, Immanuel, 4, 7, 8, 11-12, 62-94, 106, 134, 139, 187, 215-17, 221, 228-232, 254-58, 277-81, 285, 289, 323, 391, 474, 477, 525, 532, 536
Kingdom of ends, 85-86
Kneale, W. C., 505

Law: conformity to, 535; contrasted with morality, 207; as a dictate of reason, 42; divine, 42, 188; and justice, 535, 547, 577; and love, 188; natural, 35-42, 185; respect for, 69; scriptural, 185, 188; universality or generality of, 239
Legalism, ethical, 7, 140, 179-82
Libertarianism, 310-13, 349-64, 370-73
Liberty, concept of, 35. *See also* Freedom
Love: commandment of, 188; of enemies, 165-66; of God and neighbor, 139, 166; and justice, 577, 592; as a moral quality, 323; of neighbor, 165-66; versus principles, 188-89
Lying, 88, 119, 254-58, 275-77, 430. *See also* Truth telling

McArthur, Justice, judicial opinion of, 413-17
McTaggart, J. M. E., 311, 317-33
Mann, Justice, judicial opinion of, 411-13
Marcel, Gabriel, 183
Marshall, John, 542, 595 n
Matson, Wallace I., 312-15, 365-73
Maxims, moral, 68-69, 221, 230-31
Meaning of ethical terms, 440-43, 495, 500

Meritarianism, 537-41, 583-84, 592
Meta-ethics, 435, 496-98
Mill, John Stuart, 5, 7, 10-11,
    103-27, 139, 146, 244, 246, 276 n,
    285, 391, 534, 536-37, 539, 580
Miller, Alexander, 186
Miller, Leonard G., 229, 241-53
Monism: methodological, 134, 137;
    value, 134
Moore, G. E., 246, 253, 285, 369,
    437-38, 440, 443-45, 449-68,
    469-72, 474, 480, 491
Moral fallacies, 440, 447, 449, 456,
    470, 506-28
Moralities: contrasted with absolute
    morality, 143, 208-10; contrasted
    with Morality, 134; master or
    slave, 136, 161-63; and social
    institutions, 532; true, 206-10
Morality: absolute, 143, 208-10;
    meaning of "a," 206; Nietzsche's
    conception of, 159
Moral judgments. *See* Judgment
Moral laws, 465-66, 533. *See also*
    Law
Moral philosopher: Ayer's view of,
    438-39, 486, 496; Hare's view of,
    438-39, 499-502; James' view
    of, 145-58; Moore's criticism, 437,
    449-52
Moral philosophy. *See* Ethics
Moral point of view, 93-94, 131-44,
    146, 160, 210-24
Moral reasons, 252, 263, 275, 280,
    443-48. *See also* Reasoning, moral
Moral solitude, 148
Motive, 62-64, 66-71, 95-96, 116, 317

Naturalism, ethical, 6, 441, 446, 495,
    500
Naturalistic fallacy, 440, 447, 456,
    515
Natural law, 35-45, 185

Natural rights, 35
Newman, J. H., 181
Niebuhr, H. R., 186
Nietzsche, Friedrich, 134-37, 139,
    159-70, 582
Nihilism, ethical, 132, 140
Non-cognitivism, 6, 132, 441, 486-98
Norm scepticism, 133, 137-40
Northwestern Shoshone Indians v.
    U. S., 593-606
Nowell-Smith, P. H., 315-16, 374-82,
    524

Obligation: absolute, 186; Hobbes'
    view, 35; James' conception,
    147-51; judgments of, 319-20;
    Kant's definition, 74. *See also*
    Duty; Prima facie duties
Omission, 387-90, 399-408, 409-17
Ought, different uses of word, 507-8
Ought-Is derivation, 447-48, 514-28,
    532

Pain, and pleasure as motives, 95-96
Peace: articles of, 35; makers, 40;
    and obedience to rules, 276 n; time
    of, 33; as ultimate goal, 36
Perspectivism, moral, 133-37
Plato, 15-30, 104, 227, 309, 367,
    540-42, 554-75, 582
Pleasure: associated with human
    ideals, 146; attempt to define, 458;
    as intrinsic good, 246; and pain as
    motives, 95-96; quality of, 109-11.
    See also Hedonic calculus
Pluralism: ethical, 5; methodological,
    134, 140; value, 134, 140
Pound, Roscoe, 229, 295
Power: and justice, 541-43, 564-75;
    Nietzsche's use of term, 135
Practice, defined, 544
Praise, and blame, 311, 392, 399

Predictability of human actions:
contrasted with deliberation,
334-48; and free will, 332-33,
359-61. *See also* Foreknowledge
Prescriptives, moral, 446, 503, 508
Prescriptivity, 502
Prima facie duties, 444-45, 475-76
Prima facie rightness, 478-80
Principles, moral: acting on, 215-18;
compared with rules, 215, 233,
274; contrasted with principles of
justice, 581; inadequacies of
traditional, 153-54; nature of, 4, 20
Promise keeping and breaking, 38,
78, 82, 279-80, 483, 534
Promising, 515-528
Proof: *a priori*, 87; of Categorical
Imperative, 88-94; of moral
principles generally, 8-14; of
principle of utility, 97-99, 122-27.
See also Justification; Reasoning,
moral
Proudhon, P. J., 526 n
Psychological egoism, 141-42
Psychological hedonism, 10, 95-96
Punishment, 305, 308-9, 326, 367-68,
544-53

Raphael, D. D., 581, 585
Rashdall, Hastings, 474, 590
Rationalism, ethical, 446
Rawls, John, 308, 539-40, 544-53
Reasoning, moral: compared to legal,
235-36, 443-48; naturalist theory,
500; rationalist theory, 446-48;
rules of, 502. *See also*
Generalization Argument;
Justification; Proof
Reed, Stanley F., judicial opinion of,
593-600
Relativism, 190-204; ethical, 140-41;
cultural or anthropological, 141,
193-94
Relativity, ethical. *See* Relativism

Remorse, 177, 327
Responsibility, moral: and freedom,
309-13; irrelevance of free will,
365-73; and love, 186; meanings
of term, 138, 174; problems of,
305-16; retributivist theory, 307;
to self, 326-27; theories of, 309;
and wrongdoing, 306-09
Retributivist theory: of punishment,
546-49, 587; of responsibility, 307
Revelation, 13
Rex v. *Russell*, 388-90, 409-17
Right: definitions of, 5, 440, 466,
469-72; as distinguished from law,
35; indefinability of term, 441,
444; and "just" as moral terms,
536-37; to truth, 255
Ross, W. D., 7, 8, 229, 441, 444-45,
469-85, 533 n, 582, 591
Rules: compared to Kantian maxims,
221; conflicts of, 291-92;
contrasted with principles, 215,
233, 242, 274; effects of adopting,
283; exceptionless, 215, 244-48,
289; exceptively stated, 231;
fundamental, 276; for the good
of all, 221-24; versus intuition,
295; kinds of moral, 209-10; made
for man, 156; of moral game, 502;
morally impossible, 219-21;
provisional character of, 142,156,
186-87; self-defeating, 219-21;
self-frustrating, 218; universal,
218-21; universality or generality
of, 262, 265, 300. *See also*
Exceptions; Principles, moral
Rule-utilitarianism, 7, 236-40,
282-93, 539
Russell, Bertrand, 181

Sachs, David, 405
St. Augustine, 385
St. Paul, 178, 183, 188, 430

Sartre, Jean-Paul, 137-39, 171-77, 184, 228, 306, 310, 314
Scepticism, ethical, 5, 131-33, 140, 145-46; metaphysical, 133, 310-11, 328; norm, 133, 137-40, 171-89; semantic, 132, 486-98
Searle, John R., 446-48, 514-28, 532
Self-defense, 232, 236, 238, 532
Self-evidence, 443, 482
Self-interest: as moral point of view, 212-14; principle of, 31-42, 141-44, 215
Self-preservation: instinct of, 164; and law, 35, 165; natural right of, 35
Self-realization, principle of, 4, 43-61, 188
Self-sacrifice, 114-15
Shame, 327
Sidgwick, Henry, 142, 213-14, 229, 246, 248-49, 253, 451
Siegler, Frederick A., 388, 399-408
Singer, Marcus G., 232-37, 259-81, 446, 536
Situationism, 7, 137-40,157,171,178-79, 185-88
Smart, J. J. C., 419, 424
Social justice, 576-92
Socrates, 4, 15-30, 104, 110, 228, 436, 540, 554-75
Stace, W. T., 140-41, 190-204
Standards, moral: different senses of term, 191-92; nature of, 20; single, 190, 199; subjective, 192
State of nature, 33-34, 214, 533
Stevenson, Charles L., 495
Stoicism, 117
Subjectivism, 192, 493
Suicide, 78, 82, 137, 176

Taylor, Richard, 312, 334-48
Teachability of moral rules, 218-21
Teleological ethics, 6
Temple, William, 186

Thrasymachus, 221, 541-42, 564-75
Transvaluation of values, 168-70
Truth: and falsity of moral convictions, 205-10; right to, 255; test of moral convictions, 210-12
Truth telling, 119, 254-58, 277-81. *See also* Lying
Twain, Mark, 181

Universality: of laws, 239; of rules, 262
Universalizability: criterion in Kant, 62-94; criterion in rule-utilitarianism, 236-37, 283, 285; as defining feature of moral judgments, 502; of moral rules, 218-21. *See also* Generalization Argument
Utilitarianism, 95-127, 223, 284-85, 472-73, 482-83, 495; and exceptions, 241-53; and punishment, 308, 539, 545-53. *See also* Act-utilitarianism; Ideal utilitarianism
Utility: defined, 96; principle of, 96, 106-7, 242; public or private, 116

Values: created or discovered, 135, 162; life denying, 136; objective or subjective, 493
Veracity. *See* Truth telling
Virtue: and choice of mean, 54-55; desire of, 123, 392; excellences not dependent on right volitions, 322-24; and happiness, 57-58, 125; moral and intellectual, 50-53; as a state of character, 53
Vlastos, Gregory, 583
Volition. *See* Will
Voluntary acts. *See* Act, voluntary
Von Wright, G. H., 388, 400-404

War: and human choice, 175; time of, 33-34

Wasserstrom, Richard A., 239-40
Webb v. *McGowin*, 299-301
Will: defects of, 324; to denial of life,
168; Divine, 75, 185; to power,
168; value of right volitions,
322-24. *See also* Free will

Wrongdoing: and punishment, 546;
and responsibility, 306-9
Wrongness: contrasted with harm,
257-58; and disapproval, 275-76;
and responsibility, 306-7